VOLUME 2

BENNETT CERF'S BUMPER CROP

*of Anecdotes and Stories,
Mostly Humorous,
About the Famous and Near Famous*

His 5 Biggest Best Sellers—
The Life of the Party, Try and
Stop Me, Good for a Laugh,
Laughter Incorporated, Shake
Well Before Using—Complete
and Unabridged, in Two Volumes

GARDEN CITY BOOKS
Garden City, New York

Good for a Laugh

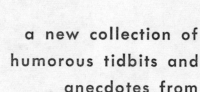

by BENNETT CERF

a new collection of
humorous tidbits and
anecdotes from
AARDVARK to ZYTHUM

with illustrations by
DOUG ANDERSON

printed in the United States of America

Foreword

Motion picture producers have discovered that Somerset Maugham's shrewd, crisp, and superbly told short stories are stuff from which sure-fire screen fare can be fashioned. To introduce the last sheaf they even persuaded him to face the camera personally and say a few words. He contented himself by pointing out that although his stories were founded on fact, they emerged as fiction. "Like every other author," he added, "I have looked upon it as my right to arrange my facts to suit my purpose, which was to entertain."

Mr. Maugham put the words right into my mouth. The stories in this collection—like the five others that preceded it—are, for the most part, not new, but I have retold them in my own fashion, adding a detail here and there to heighten an effect, changing the setting, props, or even the cast of characters when occasion seemed to warrant. *Good for a Laugh* is not history. It is meant for amusement. If in some cases I failed to credit the actual source of a story, I at least did my best to note who told it to *me*. Arthur Brisbane once quoted his rival editor, Herbert Bayard Swope, in a Sunday article. Swope phoned promptly to say, "I remember telling you that story, Arthur, but I believe it was first attributed to Count Metternich." "Swope," said Brisbane, "I always pin a story to the last man who told it to me, and you're the first man I've credited with a good one who ever objected!"

Many of the stories in this book are reprinted, with permission, from my "Cerf Board" column in *This Week Magazine*, "Trade Winds" in the *Saturday Review*, and my daily stint, "Try and Stop Me" for the King Features Syndicate. Because many after-dinner speakers, club officers, and members of the clergy and bar have complained that they experienced difficulty in my previous collection in finding just the story that would fill some need of their own, I've made an effort to arrange this volume for easier reference. I hope you will like it that way. I'd appreciate your letting me know. It's always pleasant to hear from readers—even if all they have to say is that their great-grandfather told the story on page 67 a heck of a lot better than I did.

There is nothing like a good, hearty laugh to relieve a tense situation, or soothe nerves that have been stretched too tight. I've always preferred hearing a funny story to being told just why it made me chuckle. I remember with a shudder the learned party who covered over three hundred pages some years ago explaining what caused people to laugh. Wolcott Gibbs inspected the result with dismay that topped mine. His exact comment—and heaven grant that he never says it about me!—was, "Mr. So-and-so has got humor down—and is breaking its arm."

BENNETT CERF

Mount Kisco, New York
September, 1952

Contents

Good for a Laugh

A is for our ARMED FORCES

It stood to reason that the current remobilization program would cause a revival of all the time-honored military gags that served so well in the two World Wars—and were already fully matured, in many cases, even earlier than that. Back into circulation have come the stories of the tough sergeant who caught a rookie with a single button of his blouse unfastened, and roared, "Sun-bathing, eh?"; the billy-goat who chewed up a congressional report and enthused, "Best darn propaganda I ever ate"; and the mermaid who bobbed up alongside a destroyer with an infant in her arms and asked a gob on deck, "Do you happen to know whether there's an Ensign Floyd attached to this ship?" And the day before this volume went to press, a TV comic revived the old favorite about the dear lass who cabled her sweetheart in Korea, "Couldn't wait another day for you, darling, so married your father. Love, Mother."

A detachment of Marines, sent to the rear after valiant service in the front lines, was engaged in the usual evening bull session, and the subject, as usual, got around to the girls who had been left behind. Were they faithful, or were they not?

The one who had the least doubt was a blond-haired young

corporal from Hoboken. "My girl's not doing any playing around," he announced with absolute conviction. "How can you be so sure?" asked a friend.

"Well, for one thing," said the corporal, "she's got three more years to serve in reform school."

A veteran of the Korean fighting, now in officer-candidate school, likes to tell about the day he was inducted into the Army. His physical over, he was taken in hand by a sergeant and asked, "Did you go to grammar school?"

"Yes, sir," said the draftee. "I also went through high school, graduated cum laude from college, completed three years of graduate studies at Cornell, and then acquired two more degrees at Columbia."

The sergeant nodded, reached for a rubber stamp, and slapped it on the questionnaire. It consisted of a single word: "Literate."

In the early days of World War II, wild rumors about invading Jap planes being sighted within range of the California coast swept the panicky denizens of Hollywood. One of the highest moguls of MGM took them so seriously that he summoned the most famous camouflage expert in the United States and told him, "I want the entire MGM studio camouflaged immediately, regardless of cost." "I'm sorry," said the expert, "but I can't take the job." The mogul, who hadn't heard the word "no" in twenty years, was aghast. "What do you mean you can't?" he sputtered. "This is rank discrimination against the motion-picture industry! I'll have you run out of the state." "Calm yourself," advised the expert. "If you will stop shouting long enough I'll explain why I can't take the job. The Army has ordered that for every essential plant we camouflage an alternate target has to be set up. And you might as well know that MGM has been designated the alternate target for Douglas Aircraft." The mogul was revived an hour or so later.

During the Nazi occupation of Paris, a burly, mean-looking storm trooper strode into a subway car and tripped headlong over the umbrella of a meek little old lady who sat near the door. He picked himself up, bruised and besmirched, and launched into a tirade of abuse against the terrified old lady. Then, suddenly conscious of the hostile glares of the other occupants of the car, he lurched out at the next station. The passengers waited until he was gone, then burst into spontaneous applause for the little woman with the umbrella. She hung her head modestly and said, "I know it isn't much—but he's the fifth one I bagged today."

Quentin Reynolds tells about the Englishman, Arabian and Yank who were conversing on a street corner in Casablanca when a spectacular Oriental beauty ankled by. The Englishman exclaimed, "By Jove!" The Arabian murmured a reverent, "By Allah!" The Yank breathed softly, "By tomorrow night!"

When Cecil Brown was reporting the early days of World War II in Mussolini's Rome, he became convinced that his regular waiter was spying on him, and demanded that he be fired forthwith. "But I cannot do that," expostulated the hotel manager. "How do I know whether the next spy will be such an efficient waiter?"

John Straley met a veteran pilot of World War II who was afraid that he couldn't begin to handle the 1952 model, because of all the new gadgets and refinements that had been installed. "I took one test," he confessed. "The elementary stuff was a cinch, but then the fellow who was asking questions demanded, 'Suppose you were at an altitude of 20,000 feet, going 650 miles an hour. Suddenly your oxygen tank breaks loose, one motor catches fire, and a wing crumples. You have no parachute. What do you do?' " Mr. Straley asked, "What did you answer?" "I didn't answer," confessed the former pilot. "From the question alone, I blacked out."

In Seattle, they've revived the story about the destroyer on a trial run whose captain suddenly noticed that the ship was zigzagging all over the Pacific. Charging to the bridge, he found a white-faced ensign at the helm, and roared, "Man alive, do you realize we're fully forty degrees off our course?" "Sorry, sir," mumbled the ensign (just graduated from a quickie course at a Midwestern naval station), "but you see, I never drove one of these things before!"

All the way back to Civil War days can be traced the yarn
about a captain who was offered a bribe to carry some contra-
band through the Northern blockade. "It's worth $250 to me,"
whispered the smuggler. "No," said the captain firmly. "I'm a man
of honor." The smuggler raised his offer to $500, then $750, but
the captain still turned a deaf ear. Finally the smuggler said, "I'll
give you $1000." The captain drew a gun and shouted, "Off my
ship, you varmint! You're getting too close to my price."

Sign spotted by Harold Helfer on a bulletin board of an army
airport in Indiana: "Notice! Absolutely no flying permitted over
nudist camp exactly eight miles SSW on a true course of 190 degrees."

Two effeminate-looking young men appeared to be inseparable
for months, but suddenly one of them was drafted, and the other
mournfully turned up at one of their old haunts alone. "Where's
your pal?" asked the bartender. "Oh, my dear," was the excited
reply, "haven't you heard? He's fighting for Aunt Sam!"

A Kentucky doctor, testing a hill boy's mental capacities for the
local draft board, asked, "What would you say is the difference
between a little boy and a dwarf?" "Might be a heap of difference," allowed the hill boy. "Such as?" encouraged the doctor.
The prospective infantryman drawled, "That dwarf might be a
girl."

A gawky new draftee from Tennessee suddenly recognized a
fellow townsman across the parade field. The fact that the fellow

townsman was sporting a first lieutenant's uniform didn't bother
him for a second. He strolled over, whacked the officer on the
back, and drawled, "Good to see you again, Joe, old fellah. How
goes it?" The lieutenant flushed with anger (fully a hundred other
soldiers had enjoyed the incident) and told the draftee off in a
three-minute oration that left nothing to anybody's imagination.
When he finally ran out of breath, the draftee, utterly unabashed,
exclaimed, "Lawdy, Joe. If I'd a-knowed you was going to carry
on like that, I'd never a-spoke to you at all."

A young man in Tallahassee claimed exemption on the grounds
of defective eyesight. He brought his wife along as evidence.

A tight-lipped general, obviously a martinet, descended upon
a draftee camp in New England on an inspection tour, and a
regimental parade was arranged in his honor. As the band
marched by the reviewing stand, the general emitted a snort of
disgust and roared, "Halt!" Three battalions stopped in their

tracks. "Now back up," hollered the general, "and the next time that band marches past me I want to see the slides of those trombones going in and out together!"

When I was taken for a ride in a new jet plane at Eglin Field, Florida, recently, the pilot didn't make me any happier by explaining, "If we have to bail out, just press this red button. You and the seat will go sailing out together. Then count ten and pull this strap." Fortunately this program, which struck me as somewhat drastic, never had to be executed. Back on terra firma, the pilot explained that you couldn't parachute out of a jet plane in the old way because you were going too darn fast; the rush of air would do you in before the parachute could be opened. One pilot, he added, had to abandon his craft in Korea. He managed to wriggle free of the seat and other encumbrances and landed reasonably intact back of the U.N. lines where a rescue crew picked him up. "Feel O.K.?" he was asked. "Well," he answered, "I guess you guys have heard of flotsam and jetsam. I'm the jetsam."

Bob Hope was having a tight golf match in Los Angeles one morning with the kingpin of the U. S. Air Force, General Hoyt Vandenburg, when a formation of jet planes whooshed above the course. Hope loudly instructed his caddy, "Better tell those lads to feather their engines. Their boss is trying to sink a twelve-foot putt!"

In an airborne recruit squadron learning the technique of parachute jumping, there was one lad who stuttered very badly. When his group made its first jump the instructions were, "Count ten, then pull the handle that releases your parachute." The stutterer's companions were floating gently to the ground when he plummeted by, his parachute unopened. "The poor bastard," mourned his pal, "I knew he'd never have time to count to ten."

A big dance hall, located across the way from a National Guard encampment in New England, enticed trade from the men in uniform with this sign: "Come and dance with our 50 beautiful hostesses—50. Generals: $10.00. Colonels: $8.00. Captains and Lieutenants: $6.00. Enlisted men: $3.00. Veterans of World War I: 25 cents an hour."

A is for AUTOMOBILES

The officially stated reasons for most divorces in the United States are infidelity, incompatibility, or non-support, but the rock on which thousands of these marital craft first begin to founder is undoubtedly women's unerring ability to get lost on the shortest and simplest of automobile journeys. The Lord gave women any number of alluring curves and protuberances, but unfortunately, a good bump of direction was not included among them.

I began pursuing this line of thought when I heard my wife on the phone one day telling Nedda (Mrs. Josh) Logan how to negotiate the dozen odd miles between her home in Connecticut and ours in Mount Kisco. "You can't miss the way," said my Phyllis cheerfully. "Just take Route 104—or is it 105?—till you hit Number 22 at Bedford, then swing left—or right—and you'll find yourself at a junction with 172—or maybe it's 182. At any rate, just cross the railroad tracks and go up a steep hill and you'll see a sign marked 'Cerf.' That's us." These instructions seemed a trifle ambiguous to me but they evidently didn't bother Mrs. Logan, for the girls were discussing animatedly what they were going to wear by the time I had staggered to the telephone. Needless to say, our dinner party was held up indefinitely by the non-arrival of Mrs. Logan. Some two hours after she had been scheduled to appear, she phoned to announce, "What do I do now? I seem to be in Buffalo."

Mrs. Logan did get to Mount Kisco in time for a midnight snack, but when the hour came for her to return home, she loftily declined my offer to draw her a small map. "I'll just go back the way I came," she announced confidently. Next day, however, I learned inadvertently that she had driven fifteen miles past her own entrance way. "How did you know you had gone too far?" I asked. She looked at me pityingly and snapped, "I guess I know the Stamford railroad station when I see it."

The real marital imbroglios on the open road occurred before our highways were numbered and marked, and tourists had to depend for directions on detailed routes in automobile blue books. The husband would crank up the old Maxwell or Winton, the wife would spread open the blue book on her lap, and off they would tootle, "jogging left at 31.8 with trolley tracks," "turning sharp right at 46.7 at statue of Ebeneazer Twuffle," or "avoiding steep-graded macadam turn-off at 58.3." Unfortunately, friend wife almost invariably forgot to mention one imperative turn somewhere along the line, and the happy couple would suddenly find themselves at a dead end in Princeton, instead of Mrs. Wimpfheimer's country seat in Asbury Park. Then the recriminations started and continued far into the night, with the husband usually concluding, "Until you learn how to read a simple printed page, I suggest we make our future journeys by rail."

Aunt Emma grew somewhat eccentric in her declining years, but since the whole family hoped to inherit some of her considerable fortune, she was humored in every impulse. One afternoon, at the height of a furious storm, Aunt Emma decided she'd like a ride in the family convertible, with the top down. Uncle Herbert dutifully escorted her to the car, climbed behind the wheel, and without ever budging from the garage, went through the motions of taking her for a drive. At the end of a half hour Aunt Emma

pronounced herself satisfied, and the two of them re-entered the living room. "Herbert is a fair enough driver," admitted Aunt Emma, "but I think he's just a little bit off his rocker. Here we were driving through a raging downpour, with the top down, and the darn fool never put on his hat!"

Two silver-haired old ladies wobbled down the main street of a New England town in their moth-eaten coupé, made an illegal turn, and compounded their felony by ignoring the outraged traffic officer's endeavors to stop them. He finally caught up with them in front of Ye Olde Waffle Shoppe. "Didn't you hear my whistle?" he demanded angrily. The perky octogenarian at the wheel looked at him coyly and admitted, "Yes, I did, officer—but I never flirt when I'm driving." The cop looked astonished, then broke into a broad grin, and said, "You win, lady! Drive on!"

Driving through a blinding rainstorm, Mr. Wheedle was further harassed by the incessant nagging and criticism of his wife beside him. Suddenly, however, she ceased talking, and simply sat there shaking her head back and forth vigorously. Mr. Wheedle enjoyed the respite without question for about twenty miles, but then decided to investigate the phenomenon. He soon discovered what had happened. Mrs. Wheedle's nose was firmly caught in the windshield wiper!

"A pessimist," explained Grover Whalen at a recent dinner for traffic regulators, "is a female who's afraid she won't be able to squeeze her car into a very small parking space. An optimist is a male who thinks she won't try." Lee Gillespie, of Council Bluffs, writes, "I've discovered how to get rid of a noise in your car. Let *her* drive." Allan McMahon, the Fort Wayne capitalist, says you can always pick out the owner of a car in which six ladies are riding. She's the one who, after somebody pulls the door shut, always opens it and slams it harder.

A chap named Williams and his wife journeyed from their home in Jackson Heights to visit an author in Pennsylvania. Mrs. Williams had a map spread out on her lap and suddenly exclaimed, "Slow up! You turn right on this road here." Williams turned right, but grumbled, "I don't like the looks of this road." He liked it even less when it tailed off into a cowpath through a thick wood. Stopping the car, he cried, "Let me look at that map." Aggrieved, Mrs. Williams protested, "You never will trust me. Here's the road on the map, just as I said it was." Mr. Williams investigated, closed his eyes wearily, and explained, "Darling, that is not a road. That is the state border line."

John Kimberley, of Minneapolis, celebrated his birthday recently with a gay party at which Mrs. Kimberley made a slight error. She drank a full glass of gasoline, happily convinced that it was straight imported gin. When the party broke up, recalls the host, all the other revelers were hiccuping. Poor Mrs. Kimberley, however, was honking.

A railroad claim agent was teaching his wife to drive, when the brakes suddenly failed on a steep downhill grade. "I can't stop," she shrilled. "What'll I do?" "Brace yourself," advised her husband, "and try to hit something cheap."

Mr. Young checked his monthly garage bill with growing ire, and complained to his wife, "Why, the robber charged me $20 to tow you a mile to the service station that day you got stuck on Ninetieth Street." "That's not exorbitant," maintained Mrs. Young. "He earned every penny of it. I had the brakes jammed on all the way."

What Henry Mencken would call a typical female motorist came tootling merrily down the wrong side of a crowded thoroughfare and ran smack into Mr. Jordan's brand-new convertible. While they were trying to untangle bumpers, the lady driver said grudgingly, "I'm afraid this was largely my fault." "Nonsense," said Mr. Jordan with a gallant bow. "I assure you the blame rests entirely with me. I saw you fully three blocks away and had ample time to dart down a side street."

B is for
BROADWAY

Sir Laurence Olivier, who returned in triumph to Broadway to co-star with his beautiful wife, Vivien Leigh, in Shakespeare's *Antony and Cleopatra* and Shaw's *Caesar and Cleopatra* (the dual bill was referred to by the trade as *Two on the Nile*), is one of the most charming and versatile actors alive. He's equally at home in stark tragedy, drawing-room comedy, or knockabout clowning in a benefit performance with Danny Kaye.

He learned his profession the hard way, touring the hinterlands of Britain and Wales with an obscure troupe, playing in houses so ill-equipped that most changes had to be made in public washrooms. Olivier still refers to those days as his "tour with the lavatory theatre." His fame in America dates back to the time Samuel Goldwyn persuaded him to play the lead in the memorable screen version of *Wuthering Heights*.

The picture was released in 1939—a banner year for the Oliviers, because it also marked Miss Leigh's triumph in *Gone with the Wind*.

Gone with the Wind having been written in Atlanta by a native daughter, Margaret Mitchell, it was fitting that the world première of the picture be given there. The hysterical hoop-la that attended the event gave ample indication that this celluloid epic of the Civil War was destined to be the biggest grossing picture in the history of Hollywood. Receipts now top the thirty-million mark, with the end nowhere in sight. The sum is greater than the total assessed value of all the Atlanta real estate and property actually burned down by General Sherman's order on that disastrous November day in 1864. People go to see the picture again and again. One English visitor was astounded recently by the skyscrapers and welter of traffic around the Five Points in Downtown Atlanta. "I'd seen Atlanta burned down so often in *Gone with the Wind*," he confessed, "that I was rather bowled over to find any of it standing at all."

The Five Points on that opening night in December, 1939, was a sight to behold. Governor Rivers had proclaimed a stateside holiday, urged the womenfolk to don hoop skirts and pantalets, and appealed to the males to sprout sideburns and goatees and try to look as much like Clark Gable as possible. They complied with a will—and also practically tore off Gable's uniform when he appeared in person. Georgia's immortal athlete, golfer Bobby Jones, and baseball's one and only Tyrus Raymond Cobb, were invited, along with the governors of five neighboring states. Only the authoress, Miss Mitchell, failed to appear.

Miss Leigh, possibly due to the influence of a well-known soft-drink company located in Atlanta, acknowledged the wild plaudits of the multitude with, "Ah, this is the applause that refreshes!" And an eleven-year-old girl, given her choice of a Christmas bicycle or meeting Clark Gable, unhesitatingly chose Gable. When he kissed her, she closed her eyes in ecstasy and exclaimed, "Now I am a woman!"

Gertrude Lawrence was starring in a London play that was honored by a visit from the late King and his Queen. As Queen Elizabeth entered the Royal Box, the entire audience arose to acclaim her. Miss Lawrence, watching from the wings, murmured, "What an entrance!" Noel Coward, on tiptoe behind her, added, "What a part!"

Deems Taylor tells a story to show that even the greatest get twinges of jealousy. He attended an audition of young talent with Alfred Lunt and Lynn Fontanne. The participants—mostly female—quavered their way through the sleepwalking scene in *Macbeth.*

Afterward, Lynn whispered to Taylor, "Absolutely no talent in the whole group," and added, "thank God!"

Carl Sandburg was persuaded to attend the dress rehearsal of a very serious play by a very serious young dramatist, but unfortunately slept through a greater part of the performance. The outraged dramatist chided him later, "How could you sleep when you knew how much I wanted your opinion?" Sandburg reminded him, "Young man, sleep *is* an opinion."

Veteran stage producer Max Gordon warns all aspiring new playwrights, "The curtain goes up and two people are out on the stage, and somebody better say something pretty damn fast."

London society blinked at the frankness of a former musical comedy star who married an earl and, when asked by a sob sister, "How does it feel to marry into royalty?" exulted, "Ah, the peace and tranquillity of the double bed after the hurly-burly of the chaise longue!"

Somerset Maugham gravely informed the students in a drama course at London University: "A sure formula for success is to write first a tragedy in five acts. Put it away in a drawer for six months, then change it into a comedy in three acts. Forget it for

another year. Then reduce it to a curtain raiser. That done, rush
right out and marry a rich American."

High among the countless anecdotes about the stuttering
comedian, Joe Frisco, ranks the one about the time Joe was regal-
ing his friends with a yarn when a midget walked over unob-
served, propped his chin on the edge of the table, and regarded
Joe with a melancholy stare. Joe took one look, gulped convul-
sively, and screamed to the waiter, "W-w-what's the idea? I didn't
order J-j-john the Baptist!"

Howard Lindsay, now engaged with Russel Crouse on their
tenth collaboration—as happy and successful a relationship as the
theatre has ever known—is punctilious about his business engagements but on the forgetful side when it comes to social functions.
He has been known to wander off from one of his own dinner
parties for a brief nap and then forget to come downstairs again.
Names of friends and acquaintances frequently elude him. When
in doubt he calls everybody Herb, except his friend Herb Mayes,
whom he hails as Jerry. For years he engaged in a bitter feud

with an actor who had let him down and wouldn't even stay in
the same room with him when they accidentally met at a party.
Then one night Lindsay's wife, Dorothy Stickney, was amazed to
find him in close and harmonious conversation with the actor at
the other end of a Hollywood drawing room. The conference
ended in a burst of laughter, and Lindsay clapped the actor on
the back. "I wonder what caused Howard to forgive him?"
thought Mrs. Lindsay. At this moment, Lindsay whispered
hoarsely in her ear, "Who *was* that fellow I just was talking to,
anyhow?"

Mrs. Howard Lindsay remembers with some qualms the special
performance of *Life with Father* she and her distinguished spouse
staged for Franklin D. Roosevelt in Washington. She was so terrified before the curtain rose that she was heard to murmur, "I
wouldn't do this again for the President of the United States!"
Later at an after-theatre dinner in the White House a member of
the troupe was even more nervous than Miss Stickney. She
quavered to the President, "What an imposing building the
White House is! Do you happen to recall the name of the artichoke who designed it?"

Monty Woolley slipped on the stairs of the Times Square subway station one rainy night when there were no taxis to be had.
Halfway down, he bumped into a stout lady, who toppled against
him, and landed in his lap at the bottom of the stairs. Woolley
tapped her on the shoulder and pointed out, "Madam, I'm sorry,
but this is as far as I go."

An actress who had received a magnificent diamond necklace
as a gift from "Diamond Jim" Brady hit upon what she thought
was an excellent device for safeguarding it. She simply left it

openly on her dressing table when she went out, with a note nearby reading, "This is just an imitation. The original is in my safe-deposit box." One night, however, she returned to find the necklace gone. In its place was this penciled message, "Thanks, lady. The substitute is just what I wanted. I'm a substitute myself. The burglar who usually covers this hotel is away on vacation."

A persistent playwright forced the same manuscript on the late producing wizard, David Belasco, seven times, always claiming that important revisions had made it the stuff from which sure hits were fashioned. "It's awful," Belasco said finally. "All the great playwrights combined couldn't doctor it sufficiently." "Isn't there some way you can put it on the stage?" persisted the playwright. "Yes," snapped Belasco, his patience exhausted. "Give me the script." He tossed it to his assistant and ordered, "Chop this up and use it as the snowstorm tonight."

A luscious chorus girl sued a rich playboy for breach of promise and was awarded the round sum of $25,000 by a sympathetic jury. Emerging from the courthouse in an understandably happy daze, she was promptly run into by a truck and couldn't sit down for four weeks. For this mishap, however, she collected only two hundred dollars' damages in court. The moral of this sad story is clear: Never trifle with a fair maid's heart: kick her in the pants!

There's a strip-tease making the rounds who has trained a flock of doves to divest her of as many of her seven veils as local gendarmes will allow. One evening, one of the doves got bored with its job, fluttered across the footlights and settled on the shoulder of a surprised spectator. The house manager observed, "I've been in show business twenty years—and that's the first time I ever saw an actress give the audience the bird."

In their history of the past fifty years in the theatre, *Show Biz*, Abel Green and Joe Laurie, Jr., chronicle the first public appearance of Mae West. The now-famous interpreter of the lush role of "Diamond Lil" made her debut at the Model Theatre in Philadelphia in 1912. Her billing read, "Watch her do a muscle dance sitting down—and her movement is all her own." By the time Miss West reached New Haven, the Yale boys were trying to tear down the house—and not from rage. The local critic observed, "Miss West wore a trick dress with a catch that seemed to break very easily, thereby delivering the full value of her personality."

A young lady from the Bronx landed a job in a big Broadway night club and by way of celebration brought home a small bottle of champagne to share with her family. She had barely popped the cork when her mother ran to the telephone and called the doctor. "You should come quick," ordered mama. "Sadie's got us drinking shampoo!"

Eddie Foy, Jr., tells about the chorus girl's daughter who attended public school for the first time. The teacher asked her, "What does Y-E-S spell?" The little girl answered, "Mink."

There's a featured aerialist in this year's big circus troupe who always misses his big trick a couple of times on purpose to emphasize its difficulty. Then, while the drums roll and audiences gasp, he does it to perfection. One night, however, he told the manager, "If you don't mind, I'm going to do my climactic trick right the first time tonight. I'm tired."

News flashes from the circus: A trapeze artist married the India-rubber man, and is now twisting him around her little finger. The lion tamer is angry at his lady friend because, he says, she kisses him and gives him a brush-off at the same time. Seems she's the bearded lady. And the assistant manager has tried tonics of eleven different colors to cure his dandruff. He reports, "I finally got rid of the dandruff, all right, but now my head is full of confetti."

When the rodeo was packing them in at Madison Square Garden, an elderly lady paused after the show for a cup of java in a beanery down the block. The coffee was too hot for her and she put it down with a sigh, exclaiming, "Oh, dear, my bus leaves in three minutes." A polite cowboy promptly handed his cup to her, explaining, "Lady, I'll be obliged if you drink this coffee of mine. It's already saucered and blowed."

A magician seeking booking at Radio City Music Hall asserted, "I've got a new trick that will panic them." "What is it?" asked the manager. "I saw a woman in half," announced the magician. "Call that a new trick?" scoffed the manager. "They've been doing that around here for years." "Oh, yeah?" countered the magician. "Lengthwise?"

Another unique stage attraction is a lady who has trained her dog to curl itself around her neck and remain absolutely motionless there—a perfect imitation of a fur neckpiece. "I taught my dog the trick for a special reason," she explained. "Lots of hotels are silly enough to keep dogs out entirely. Now that my Fido can look so much like a fur piece, I can smuggle him into all the hotels on earth." "And how," asked Mr. George S. Kaufman acidly, "do you get in yourself?"

"When I was a kid living in a tenement," says Eddie Cantor, "we didn't know what an elevator was. It was a six-story climb to our little apartment. When I got the sniffles, Mama would yell out of the window to the doctor, 'What should I give Eddie?' and he'd yell back, 'Give him a dose of castor oil and throw down a dollar.'"

Comedian Joe E. Brown, famous for the generous proportions of his buccal cavity, was dining at the home of a Broadway producer. The hostess urged him to try the new recipe for strawberry short cake. "Gotta watch my figure, but I'll try just a mouthful," compromised Joe. "That's fine," said the hostess. "Maggie, fill up the gentleman's plate."

Mrs. Gabor and her three talented and beautiful daughters, Eva, Zsa Zsa and Magda, attract publicity and men with equal facility. Recently one gentleman caller expressed a need for food to help him cope with the girls.

"Raid the icebox," suggested Mama Gabor. "It's always full of good things to eat." The visitor found that the entire contents of the icebox consisted of two dozen orchids and a salami.

The first time Martha Raye ate at the famous Pump Room in Chicago, she was a member of a dinner party hosted by Jimmy Durante. When a waiter passed with a portion of shishkebab (lamb on a flaming sword—a specialty of the house), Miss Raye was startled and exclaimed, "What on earth was that?" Durante explained, "A customer who only left a ten-dollar tip."

Novelist Robert Sylvester has a young friend who is an ardent devotee of bebop music. The wilder and more discordant it waxes, the better he likes it. He was walking his best girl home very late one night when a garbage van pulled up ahead and the crew began banging and rattling cans of refuse about the sidewalk in that copyrighted manner best calculated to wake up everybody on the block. At the height of the racket the bebop devotee clasped his girl's hand and murmured reverently, "Listen, darling! Our song!"

B is for
BARBERS

The fixtures and equipment of a big barber shop in a metro-politan hotel are a lot flossier than those of a tonsorial parlor in a small town, but the atmosphere and conversation within are re-markably similar and unchanging. The same cut-ups perform both in the chairs and behind them; the same badinage, political soothsaying, and sporting data are exchanged; the same amorous, if doddering, patrons furtively squeeze the hands of the same coy manicurists. One of the latter, who found it particularly difficult to laugh off the ardent advances of her chair-bound Lothario, finally told him, "Okay, I'll go to see your etchings if my husband will give his consent." "Where is this confounded husband of yours?" demanded the customer. She answered softly, "He's shav-ing your throat this very instant."

A lot of color went out of the barbering profession when lady practitioners dropped out of the running. The rotund and jolly TV star, Kate Smith, actually was one of the last ladies to master the tonsorial art as a little shaver (joke) in school. When she made her New York debut in a minor role in a musical in 1926, her salary didn't measure up to her appetite, so she wangled the per-mission of the management to do a little barbering on the side. She set up a revolving pole outside her dressing room and was soon making more in hair cutting than she was on stage. She also gave Bert Lahr the opportunity to take one look at his shorn locks in the mirror and go screaming through the wings, "Take to the hills, men! The Indians are attacking again! I've just been scalped!"

The barber pole with the spiral red stripes, incidentally, is a throwback to the time of King Henry VIII in England, when barbers were allowed also to practice minor surgery and dentistry. The red stripe presumably symbolized blood and was designed as a guide post for a majority of the citizenry who didn't know how to read. Centuries later, American barbers added a dash of blue for patriotic reasons.

When Mr. Greco moved his tonsorial parlor to the Hotel Weylin, he picked up a new assistant who was polite as all get out, but just didn't happen to be a very good barber. To one of his first customers he asked in his best Harvard accent, "Will you have anything on your face when I finish shaving you?" The customer, a crusty fellow named Knopf, answered, "I hope to save my nose, but judging by the way you're going, the odds are four to one against me."

Mr. Greco himself was shaving another customer named Colonel Pass when he paused to ask, "Well, Colonel, how do you like this new lather?" "Fine," sputtered the Colonel. "You must have lunch with *me* some day!" Undaunted, Mr. Greco demanded, "Am I not rejuvenating you? Isn't the razor taking hold?" "It's taking hold all right," admitted Colonel Pass, "but it just isn't letting go again."

The company barber, a stropping fellow, in a detachment base in Japan, tottered back to work after an epic binge in Tokyo. His first customer, a lieutenant, submitted to a shave, then inspected himself ruefully in the mirror. "If anybody tells you the Yanks aren't losing face in the Orient," he suggested, "send him round to get a look at me."

C is for the CHILDREN'S HOUR

A dapper New Yorker—one of the ten best-dressed men in America—came to collect his six-year-old daughter at a birthday party. Taking hold of her hand to guide her across the street, he observed, "Goodness, Vicki, your hands seem mighty sticky today." "Yours would be, too," she informed him, "if you had a piece of lemon pie and a chocolate éclair inside your muff."

Film producer Eddie Knopf's son came home from college at the age of 18 with a set of marks so glittering that the whole family glowed with pride. His brother Jonathan, then five, finally felt it was time for him to get into the act, however, and declared, "I got an 'A' today in arithmetic."

His father indulgently replied, "I didn't know they taught arithmetic in kindergarten. What's one and one?" Jonathan pondered a moment, then reported, "We haven't gotten that far yet."

On the maid's day out, a prominent publisher volunteered to take the heat off his wife and tackle the Herculean task of putting their four-year-old to bed. The exhausted wife threw herself on the chaise longue and picked up the evening papers. An hour later the four-year-old stole into the room and whispered, "Daddy's asleep at last!"

Two intrepid explorers met in the heart of the Brazilian jungle. "I'm here," declared one, "to commune with nature in the raw, to contemplate the eternal verities and to widen my horizons. And you, sir?"

"I," sighed the second explorer, "came because my young daughter has begun piano lessons."

Mr. Jones' pretty, twelve-year-old daughter came screaming around the corner of the house, with the neighbor's boy in hot pursuit. Mr. Jones leaped out of his hammock and halted the two. "Why are you chasing my Gwendolyn?" he asked the boy. "She pinched me," he complained. Mr. Jones turned to Gwendolyn. "Why did you pinch him?" he demanded. Gwendolyn answered demurely, "So he'd chase me."

A Beacon Hill youngster was showing her family album to some Boston friends from the wrong side of Commonwealth Avenue. "Isn't this one a scream?" she asked. "It's my Aunt Dorothy. She's the fattest lady who ever lived on Pinckney Street." The friend, duly impressed, said, "And who is that standing behind her?" The youngster said, "Don't be silly. That's still Aunt Dorothy."

L. Bracken, of Lakeland, Florida, sends the delectable story of the small boy who stood gazing at a horse and wagon while the milkman delivered milk. When he came out the boy observed, "Mister, that horse will never get you home." "And pray, why not?" asked the milkman. The small boy explained, "He just lost all his gasoline."

When Frank Pace, Jr., was Secretary of the Army, his wife pointed out that her husband's close association with the President and other responsible men in Government provided an excellent opportunity to give their young daughters a first-hand lesson on current events. "It is important that even the children know as much as possible these days about the tensions and problems that beset the world," urged Mrs. Pace. Frank agreed that there was great merit in his wife's proposal, and forthwith summoned his two young daughters, Paula and Priscilla, for lesson number one. The two girls were completely absorbed in his discourse. At its conclusion he asked if they had understood everything he had told them. The older daughter nodded yes. The younger—about six—admitted that one thing was bothering her very much. "Out with it," said Pace. "What is it you don't understand?" "Tell me, Daddy," she begged, "is President Truman a boy or a girl?"

A five-year-old lad in Minnesota was watching his mother change the baby. When she overlooked sprinkling the tot's backside with talcum powder and hurried him into his diaper, the five-year-old reproved her sharply, "Hey, Mom, you forgot to salt him!"

A lady who lives in Irvington-on-the-Hudson has a small son who fell out of a rowboat on a pond near the family mansion and came back to the house soaked from head to foot. She told him he must stay in his room until she could dry out his suit and iron it for him. A little later she heard a commotion in the cellar. Exasperated, she left the ironing board, and called down from the top of the basement stairs, "Are you down there wetting your pants again?" There was dead silence for a moment. Then a deep masculine voice answered meekly, "No, ma'am, I'm just reading the meter."

Oscar Levant's eight-year-old daughter, Lorna, hears the names of famous movie personages used in casual conversation at all hours of the day. Small wonder that when she saw a pair of twin boys dressed exactly alike, in a carriage in front of the Hampshire House, she exclaimed brightly, "Look, Daddy! The Warner Brothers!"

A dear little old lady entered a suburban bungalow and found a lad of four in sole possession, playing with his toy train. "You don't know me," said the old lady, "but I'm your grandmother—on your father's side." Without looking up from his train, the lad replied, "I'll tell you right now: you're on the wrong side."

A farmer in Maryland collared his nine-year-old son and demanded, "Who chopped down that there cherry tree?" The lad hung his head and admitted, "I did, Father dear. I cannot tell a lie. I chopped it with this little hatchet." The father thereupon hoisted the lad across his knees and whaled the what-for out of him. "But, Father," cried the outraged son, "George Washington cut down a cherry tree when he was a boy, too, and when he was manly enough to admit it, his father didn't wallop him. In fact, he wrote the story down for other little boys to study." "That is quite correct," said the father grimly, "but when George Washington chopped down the tree, his poor old father wasn't in it."

The teacher of a class of six-year-old girls in a progressive school found a suspicious puddle in the coat closet and demanded that the culprit step forward and identify herself. When no confession was forthcoming, the teacher registered deep disappointment and said, "Now, we're all going to close our eyes for three minutes. When we open them I confidently expect that the little girl who is guilty will be standing up at her desk." The three minutes passed, but when the class opened its eyes, no guilty little girl, alas, was standing at her desk. What the teacher did discover, however, was a second puddle next to the first in the coat closet, with a crudely lettered sign reading, "The green phantom strikes again!"

"Who says there's nothing in heredity?" demands Allen Saunders, the Toledo artist. There was a baby born in a Toledo hospital whose parents were two of the most expert and incorrigible pickpockets in the annals of Ohio crime. When the baby was two hours old, the doctors were still unable to pry open its right fist, and the mother wailed, "He's going to be deformed!" The nurse made a supreme effort, however, and bent back the infant's tiny fingers. In the palm of its hand was the obstetrician's gold watch.

Parents whose children fail to appreciate their genius may take heart from this story of Songstress Dinah Shore's baby daughter. Every time Dinah tries to sing one of her ten-thousand-dollar songs for the child, the latter begins a dreadful caterwauling, exclaiming, "Don't you sing! I want Nursie to sing for me!"

A mother of eleven unruly kids was visited by a sympathetic social worker who marveled, "How on earth are you able to care for all eleven of these children?" The mother explained, "When I only had one, he occupied every second of my time. What more can eleven do?"

Columnist Bob Considine boasts that his sons are the best-mannered lads on Ninety-sixth Street. "I've never had to lay hands on one of them," he declares, "—except in self-defense."

Arthur Krock, ace Washington news hawk, rated an invitation to a shindig at Senator Harry Byrd's Virginia manse. What's more, the Senator sent his family chariot around to give Krock a lift. Krock reports that a ferocious-looking Great Dane was

sprawled across the front seat, while the rear seat was loaded with a bevy of the Senator's small grandchildren. After some hesitation, he decided it was safer to cast his lot with the kids in back. It was a grievous error. The car had just about gotten under way when one of the kids bit him.

The Sunday-school teacher was recounting the story of the death of Joseph. When she finished, an undertaker's son raised his hand and asked, "Do you happen to know who got the funeral?"

A clever mother gave her eight-year-old son a wrist watch so that he could time himself when he practiced on the piano. A few days later the son enthused, "Gee, Mom, this watch is great. If I wind it up tight enough it does an hour in fifty-two minutes."

A little boy had been pawing over a stationer's stock of greeting cards for some time when a clerk asked, "Just what is it you're looking for, sonny? Birthday greeting? Message to a sick friend? Anniversary congratulations to your ma and dad?" The boy shook his head "no" and answered wistfully, "Got anything in the line of blank report cards?"

The eight-year-old daughter of a wealthy Park Avenue family was obsessed with fine clothes. She learned to read from the expensive fashion magazines, cut out pictures of fur coats for her scrap-book, and preferred window shopping to romping in the park. One day her mother decided the time had come to acquaint her with the facts of life and told her about the bees and flowers, et cetera, et cetera. The eight-year-old listened carefully, nodded her head, then remarked, "One thing you didn't tell me, Mama. What kind of a dress does a girl wear for a thing like that?"

One of the nicest stories I've heard in a long time concerns a writer who, through no fault of his own, lost two fine jobs in the space of a single year.

First, the magazine on which he served as managing editor folded, and then the newspaper to which he transferred was bought by a syndicate, with the casualty list embracing the entire staff.

He came home to his wife and three small sons and told them ruefully, "I'm out of a job again. The paper stopped publishing with this evening's edition." The wife comforted him as best she could. The three boys stared at him round-eyed.

Next morning the writer arose after the boys had left for school and wandered into his study.

In the wastebasket were the remains of three china piggy banks. On the dining-room table was a pile of nickels, dimes and quarters. There was a crudely lettered sign under the coins. It read, "We believe in you, Pop."

C is for
CHRISTMAS

The trouble with most Yuletide stories is that you hear them after the holidays are over, when they can no longer provide you with the maximum mileage. I suggest that you memorize a few of the following along about September or October, so you can do your Christmas swapping early.

Despite the best efforts of child psychiatrists, there are still a lot of kids of four or five—even in sophisticated New York—who believe in Santa Claus.

One of them was taken by his mother to the toy department in Macy's on a December morning last year and was duly propped up on Santa's lap. "What do you want for Christmas, my lad?" asked Santa Claus dutifully. "Better write it down," said the lad, "or you'll forget." "Trust me," urged Santa. "My memory never fails." The lad was dubious, but catalogued his demands.

The same afternoon, mother and son arrived at Gimbel's and the lad found himself on Santa's lap for a second time. The Gimbel Santa asked the usual question. "What do you want for Christmas?"

The lad slipped off his lap, kicked him lustily in the shin, and yelled, "You numskull, I *knew* you'd forget!"

In Hollywood, of course, they are faced with a different set of problems. One winsome child star instructed her private secretary, "Miss Kennedy, kindly take a letter: 'Dear Santa Claus . . .'" Another took her first ride on a department-store escalator and raised such a fuss they had to order her one for Christmas.

A star accepted a fat part in a Chicago company of a hit play, though it meant closing up his Hollywood home and moving his family to Chicago.

On October first, eve of the family's departure for the East, the star's wife told friends, "We'll have our hands full getting settled in Chicago, so I bought all my friends' Christmas presents this week." A luscious starlet regarded her with wonder and demanded, "But, my dear, how do you know who your friends will *be* by Christmastime?"

Ah, the happy Yuletide spirit! One scout reports that Mrs. Lodadoe bought Mr. Lodadoe a sixty-eight-foot yacht for a Christmas surprise last season and instructed the salesman, "Be sure to wrap it so he can't guess what it is." Mrs. Bemish called to her husband, "Last year we sent Mother a chair. What do you think we ought to do for her this year?" Mr. Bemish called back, "Electrify it." At a busy Chicago intersection a little cherub gave Santa's whiskers a yank, allowed them to snap smartly back into place. Santa retaliated by taking a pass at the cherub with his bell. He missed and landed instead on the noggin of another lad. The latter's father promptly dropped Saint Nick for a count of nine with a roundhouse right, and was in turn conked by a sturdy representative of the Chicago police force. When peace on earth and good will to men had been restored, Santa was in jail and two of the others were in the hospital.

The morning after Christmas, a harassed mother called in to her husband while he was shaving, "Remember that unbreakable toy you gave Vicki yesterday?" "I certainly do," he replied. "Don't tell me she's succeeded in breaking it already?"

"Not at all," said the mother grimly. "She's just broken all her other toys with it."

A French countess arrived here on the *Liberté* last year just in time to spend the holidays on a New England farm loaned to her by a Wall Street banker. Her friends ordered a variety of Christmas trinkets to be delivered to her by the local merchants. Word soon went around that every time the countess answered the bell, her feet were bound up in long strips of sheeting. One merchant, more curious than most, finally asked her why.

"Maybe I no understand your language so good," explained the countess. "But on ze radio zey tell me veree plainly whenever countree ladee receive visitor, she should keep ze dogs tied up."

D is for DOCTORS

A buxom lady tripped on the stairs and broke her leg. The doctor put it in a cast and warned her that she wasn't to attempt going up or down stairs until it came off. Four months later he removed the cast and pronounced her well on the way to recovery.

"Goody, goody," gurgled the lady. "Is it all right for me to walk the stairs now?" "Yes," said the doctor, "if you will promise to be careful."

"I can't tell you what a relief it will be," confessed the lady. "It was such a nuisance crawling outside and shinnying up and down that drainpipe all the time!"

According to Sam Levenson, an irate mother marched her ten-year-old son into a doctor's office and demanded, "Is a boy of this age able to perform an appendix operation?" "Of course not," snapped the doctor. Mama turned angrily on the boy and shouted, "So who was right? Put it back!"

Mr. Malcolm's wife was dead for a full year, and still the bereaved widower showed no signs of recovering his spirits.

Alarmed friends persuaded him to consult an analyst. After a long talk, the analyst said, "No wonder you're melancholy! A man of your age needs some female companionship." Malcolm protested this would be unfaithful to the memory of his departed wife, but the analyst scoffed, "Nonsense! The living cannot exist on memories. Get yourself a girl. I prescribe this as your doctor." Half convinced, Malcolm announced sheepishly that he didn't even know a girl. "That's easily remedied," said the analyst, reaching for a pad and pencil. "Just take this slip to Mary McGuire at 932 East Sixty-first Street, and she'll be glad to go out with you."

Mr. Malcolm found Miss McGuire's company satisfactory in every respect. As he was bidding her an affectionate adieu, she reminded him, "Most of my boy friends leave a little gift. Shall we say twenty-five dollars?" Mr. Malcolm was rather taken aback, but rallied quickly. "Okay," he said, "here's the twenty-five, but I'd like a written receipt if you don't mind. I belong to the Blue Shield Health Plan, and they take care of all my medical expenses."

The fattest woman Throat Specialist Sulzberger ever had seen waddled into his office one afternoon and demanded an examination. The good doctor absent-mindedly said, "Okay, open your mouth, please, and say 'moo.'"

"Quick!" ordered Dr. Fitch. "My bag of pills and a stomach pump! A fellow just called up and told me he couldn't live without me." "Daddy," his daughter informed him demurely, "I believe that call was for me."

The greatest surgeon in town was performing a difficult operation before a gallery of fascinated internes. At the most crucial

moment another doctor tapped the surgeon on the shoulder and
asked, "May I cut in?"

Frank Brookhauser vows that the chairman of a meeting of
throat specialists in Philadelphia declared on the platform, "You
now have all heard the motion. All in favor say 'ah.'"

An accountant in Duluth swallowed his glass eye and rushed to
a stomach specialist. The latter peered down the unfortunate fellow's throat and exclaimed, "I've looked into a lot of stomachs in
my day, but I must say this is the first one that ever looked back
at me."

A fashionable Park Avenue doctor recently entertained Beatrice
Lillie at a soirée, and served lobster salad as the main course. "I
find this so hard to digest," said Miss Lillie to her host. "Do you
really like it?" The doctor assured her, "I not only like lobster
salad. I'm grateful to it."

Dr. Pullman, the society dentist, tried desperately to soothe his
richest but most difficult patient, a Mrs. Gruber. "Don't shake
your arms like a semaphore and make those faces at me," he
begged. "I haven't even started drilling yet." "I know you haven't,"
said Mrs. Gruber, "but you're standing on my corns."

Feeling old and discouraged? The snap of youth gone from
your stride? Look over these statistics compiled by an agency

pushing old-age annuity policies, and take heart: Between the ages of 75 and 83 Commodore Vanderbilt added 100 million dollars to his fortune. Kant wrote his philosophical masterpiece at 74. Tintoretto painted his biggest and most famous canvas when he was 75. Verdi was 85 when he wrote "Ave Maria." Cato decided to study Greek when he was 80. Goethe was also 80 when he finished *Faust*. And—listen to this!—Titian painted his historic "The Battle of Lepanto" when he was exactly 98!

Sun shining a bit brighter?

A hospital patient gazed fondly at his winsome, red-headed nurse and told the doctor, "Wonderful nurse you've got here. One touch of her hands cooled my fever miraculously." "We know," the doctor answered him. "We could hear her slap clear to the end of the corridor."

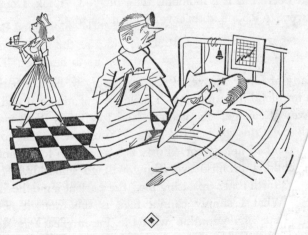

Bernard Gimbel, millionaire merchant and sportsman, tells about three octogenarians who were asked with whom they'd like to be buried. "John D. Rockefeller," said the first. "He not only made fortunes, but gave them away." "Franklin D. Roosevelt," said the second. "He was one of the greatest Presidents of all time." The third old man said, "My choice is Marillyn Monroe." "But Marillyn Monroe isn't dead yet," pointed out the questioner. "I know," was the answer. "Neither am I."

The Rorschach test is widely used by psychiatrists today to get an insight into the mentality and personality of new patients. The test consists of a series of cards, with different abstract designs thereon, which are shown to the patient one by one. The patient must report what each design suggests to him, and from his answers, sometimes short, sometimes wandering on for long stretches, the experienced analyst can draw a number of pertinent conclusions. The test is named after its Swiss inventor, Dr. Hermann Rorschach. There comes from the Bronx the story of one analyst who decided to use the Rorschach test on a troublesome new case. He flashed the first card on the bewildered patient and asked quietly, "Now what does this design suggest to you?" The patient peered at it a moment, then begged, "Look, Doctor, we both went to P.S. 46, didn't we? Give me a hint!"

A lady of forty discovered she was going to have a baby, and broke into loud lamentations. "I have sons of nineteen and eighteen away at college," she wailed, "and I certainly don't want another baby at this stage of the game." "You have nothing to worry about," soothed her doctor. "Forty is a good age for a mother to a child. I promise everything will go smoothly." "It's not my baby's birth that's upsetting me," the patient announced vehemently. "What I simply cannot face is the thought of going through that whole routine with the Parent-Teachers Association all over again!"

A friend, week-ending at a prominent psychoanalyst's home, noted a peculiar-looking butler in attendance who at least added spice to the activities by deliberately tripping up guests, fellow servants, and even his employer. As the analyst picked himself up from his third trip of the day, tenderly caressing a growing bump on his noggin, the friend burst out, "Why don't you do something about that crazy butler's tripping up everybody?" The analyst informed him coldly, "Why should I? That's *his* problem." (Later the friend predicted, "That doctor is riding for a fall. He's getting too big for his couch.")

A worried merchant sought the aid of a psychiatrist, explaining, "All day long I eat grapes." "So what?" scoffed the analyst. "Everybody eats grapes." The merchant gasped, "What? Off the *wallpaper?*"

Another patient's complaint was that he found himself slowly going mad over beautiful women. "Doc," he begged, "isn't there some way of speeding up the process?"

In California, a family of live-wire gypsies rented a store and attracted land-office business with a sign reading, "FORTUNES TOLD: $1; PSYCHOANALYSIS: 75 CENTS EXTRA."

Just before old Doc Lytton retired and turned the practice over to his son, he reminded the newly graduated young man, "One thing you got to bear in mind with patients in a small town, my boy. They find it hard sometimes to describe their symptoms accurately to you. Others hold back important details out of fear, bashfulness, or sheer orneriness. You gotta keep your eyes open and notice significant details for yourself.

"Take the case of fat Mrs. Jones, for example. Only thing wrong with her is that she stuffs herself full of candy all day. How do I know? You'll always see a dozen half empty boxes scattered all over the house. And Mr. Duncan. Liquor's at the bottom of that attack he had last night. I happened to notice an empty gin bottle in his trash basket. By observing details like that, you'll save yourself a heap of diagnosing!"

"I get it," said the son. The pair were about to enter the apartment of a luscious damsel who tossed fretfully about her bed. The new medico listened to her accentuated heartbeat, felt her fevered brow, then whipped out his thermometer. It slipped from his hands, but he recovered it quickly. Finally he told the damsel, "Nothing wrong with you that you can't cure by cutting down on your political activity. I think you're taking that part of your life a bit too seriously."

When they were back on the street, Doc Lytton asked his boy, "Where did you get the notion she was mixing too heavily in politics?"

"I just followed your tip about keeping my eyes open," said the son. "When I reached down to pick up that thermometer I'd dropped, *I saw the Governor under the bed.*"

E is for
EUROPE
And Other Continents

A bejeweled duchess waddled out of Claridge's Hotel in London where she had been cavorting—and eating—all evening at a big charity ball. As she stepped into her Rolls-Royce a beggar sidled up to her and whined, "Spare me a sixpence, m'lady, for charity. I ain't 'ad a bite for three days." The duchess recoiled. "You ungrateful fellow," she exclaimed. "Don't you realize I've been dancing for you all night?"

Lord Beaverbrook today is the all-powerful proprietor of a chain of great British newspapers. In his home town of Newcastle, New Brunswick, however, he is remembered as plain Max Aitken, inordinately ambitious son of a Presbyterian minister, and quite definitely outside the social swim. He engineered his first big "deal" when he was ten. A soap company offered prizes to lads who amassed the biggest collection of wrappers. Young Max took all of his savings out of the bank, bought soap by the case from the factory, and sold it by the cake at wholesale prices with the proviso that purchasers turn the wrappers over to him. Needless to say, he won first prize—a bicycle—by the proverbial mile.

There still lives in Newcastle an aged socialite who once kept Beaverbrook from membership in the local club. This summer he called Beaverbrook on the evening of his arrival and asked if he might have the pleasure of giving a dinner in his honor. "That's not possible, thank you," answered Beaverbrook, and could not resist adding, "You see, I'm expected to rejoin the King and Queen."

Jack Benny tells a good story on himself that came out of his first personal appearance in London's famous Palladium Theatre. The whole town turned out for the event, including London's No. 1 drama critic and his wife.

The critic liked Benny fine, but his wife watched him with a puzzled frown for a full twenty minutes and then whispered to her husband, "Tell me, dear, what does Mr. Benny do?"

J. B. Priestley tells about a dour-visaged, portly farmer from the Midland country in England who lumbered into the headquarters of the Tory Party in London and inquired, "How much does it cost to join?" "A half guinea," an official replied, "but surely you haven't waited until this stage of your life to become a member of the conservatives?" "That I haven't," the farmer exclaimed, "but it was only when the damn Labour Government came into power I was able to afford it!"

Socialized medicine is one of the accomplishments on which the British Labour Party prides itself most. Members of the American Medical Association, horrified that something of the same nature may be on its way over here, will like the story of what happened to one young married lady in London who believed that she was in the family way and went to the Public Health Station to make sure. The doctor there gave her a cursory examination, assured her that her suspicions were well founded, and then, to her astonishment, simply took a rubber stamp, printed something with it on her abdomen, and said "That's all."

She reported the strange goings-on to her husband that evening, and he, of course, asked, "What does it say?" "I can't read it," she admitted. He, too, found upon inspection that the print was too small for him, but a magnifying glass made everything clear. The inscription was, "When you can read this *without* a magnifying glass, rush your wife to the hospital."

An English gourmet ordered several baskets of succulent French snails, but found the customs tariff on "horned animals" exorbitant. So he crossed out "horned animals," classified them as "prefabricated houses" and brought them in duty free!

Colonel Effingham was walking to his club late one night in London when an ebony-hued hussy stepped out of the shadows, linked her arm in his, and said, "How would you like to take me home?" The startled colonel stared at her in horror and exclaimed, "Good heavens, girl, all the way to *Africa?*"

An American tourist in England asked the gardener at Kensington Gardens, "How do you ever get lawns as perfect as that?" The reply was, "Well, madam, the first thing you have to do is begin about 600 years ago."

When a Londoner wants an old-fashioned, pre-war meal these days, he flies over to Ireland to get it—if he can afford the trip, of course. One brought home the story of a stubborn old Dubliner who staggered into a dentist's office with a whopper of a toothache, but couldn't quite muster sufficient courage to have the infected molar extracted. The dentist poured him a stiff shot of whiskey to bolster his morale, then asked, "Ready now?" "Not quite yet," said the afflicted one with a smack of his lips. Two more slugs of whiskey found him still reluctant so the dentist let him polish off the bottle. "Now step into the chair," he begged. The Irishman, however, came out swinging to the middle of the room. "I'd like to see the confounded rascal," he bellowed, "who'd dare touch me teeth now."

Up in Scotland, a golfer stepped to the first tee, and sliced his ball so badly that it crashed through a window of the clubhouse way off to the right. He rushed to retrieve it, and found a half dozen fellow members in a dither of excitement. "Darnedest ricochet in the history of St. Albans," marveled one. "After that ball broke the window, it bounced off Mrs. McIntosh's head, knocked over MacTavish's whiskey and soda, bounced through another window, and broke the rector's windshield." "Never mind all the chatter," said the golfer severely. "Where's my ball now?"

One of the big manufacturers of plaids and tartans in Edinburgh received word that its traveling salesman had expired suddenly in a Liverpool hotel. The manager in Edinburgh wired—collect: "Return samples by freight and search his pants for orders."

Mrs. McDermott looked out of the window as the family was going on to dinner, and wailed, "Och, Sandy, here comes company. I bet they haven't eaten yet." Sandy, equal to the emergency, ordered, "Quick! Everybody out on the porch—with a toothpick."

The immigration authorities at Ellis Island were examining the credentials of a middle-aged Scotch couple that sought admission to our shores. The passport pictures caused trouble. "Mr. MacGregor," said the official, "this photograph of you is a perfect likeness, but I must say this other picture looks nothing like Mrs. MacGregor to me. Have you other substantiating evidence that this lady with you is indeed your wife?"

Mr. MacGregor sighed deeply and whispered to the official, "Laddie, if ya can prove she isn't, I'll gie ya twenty pounds."

King Christian of Denmark has been making a good-will tour through every hamlet in his little kingdom. In one village fully five hundred children waved flags and pelted him with flowers. "Where on earth do all these children come from?" laughed the King. "Your Majesty," the local mayor assured him gravely, "we have been making preparations for this day for ten years!"

En route by automobile to the Riviera in Southern France, movie tycoon Darryl Zanuck stayed overnight at a small inn south of Vichy. "You must fill out registration papers for the local gendarmes," the proprietor reminded him. "It is the law, you know." "I'm tired of these darn forms and regulations," said Zanuck. "Fill it out for me. My full name is on all the baggage." He went upstairs to refresh himself, and upon returning was presented with his filled-out registration form. The first line read, "Monsieur Warranted Genuine Leather."

A Western congressman who has been screaming continuously for expanded American financial accommodations to the Franco dictatorship in Spain went over to Madrid to inspect conditions for himself—and anybody who says he knew in advance he was going to find everything just hunky-dory is being deliberately unkind. When he returned to Washington an opponent challenged, "Well, how much do the Spaniards themselves respect their ruler?" "They're crazy about him," enthused the congressman. "I rode all over with him for three days in an open car and not a single shot was fired at either of us."

Seeking to steer clear of the Soviet orbit, Eliezer Kaplan, the finance minister of the very young state of Israel, journeyed to these shores recently to float a five-hundred-million-dollar bond issue.

The directors of a conservative Wall Street banking house listened courteously to his story, and then the chairman asked him, "Would it be possible, Mr. Kaplan, to let us see Israel's last three annual balance sheets?"

Kaplan answered, "The last two, Mr. Chairman, I can produce without difficulty. The one before that, I am afraid, disappeared when the Temple was destroyed in 586 B.C.!"

Two ancients in Israel were bemoaning the hardships of living in the new republic. "What we should do," proposed Semmish, "is declare war on the United States. They beat us, and like they do with all defeated enemies, immediately give us money, new roads, lots of food, houses and factories." "It's no good," sighed Lazarus. "With our luck, *we'd* win!"

Gregory Ratoff spotted this sign in an army barracks in Israel: "Privates will kindly refrain from giving advice to officers."

In Tel-Aviv, a citizen made a fortune selling prefabricated houses, but discovered he had to pay most of it in taxes. He signed his check with a deep sigh and remarked, "Over two thousand years we wait for a Jewish home state—and it has to happen to me!"

A raconteur in Haifa began a funny story at a dinner party with the standard introduction, "It seems there were two Jewish gentlemen . . ." A sensitive guest objected. "Why," he demanded, "do so many stories begin 'Once there were two Irishmen,' or 'Once there were two Jews'?" "Okay," soothed the raconteur, "I certainly intended no offense. Let's say there were two Chinese, named Ling Pu and Fo Wang. So, Pu and Wang were hustling over to the synagogue for a bar-mitzvah ceremony . . ."

A tourist in Algiers told his guide, "I'm tired of seeing all the places you show every American. I want to see the real Africa!" The guide said, "I will take you to the wildest, most exotic café this side of the Sahara. You will never forget it!" The two men walked to a dark and forbidding house on the edge of the town and, after a certain amount of hokus-pokus at the gate, were admitted.

Several nondescript characters were draped about the premises in various abandoned attitudes, but what immediately caught the tourist's eye was an English colonel, impeccably attired, swagger stick and all, who, believe it or not, was exactly *six inches tall!* As he stared in disbelief, the bartender threw a red silk cord over the edge of the bar, the colonel pulled himself up hand over hand, and perched on the top with a whiskey and soda in his hand.

The guide was delighted. "What luck," he told the tourist.

"You're going to meet Colonel Pringle, one of the most fascinating sights in all Africa!" Then he turned to the six-inch figure and boomed, "Be a good fellow, Colonel Pringle, and tell my tourist friend here about the night you told that witch doctor to go chase himself in the lake!"

The main course at Chief Zombongo's birthday dinner was a succulent missionary who had been caught wandering in the African bush three weeks previous and specially fattened for the occasion. Scarcely had the distinguished guests arisen from the festive board, however, when Chief Zombongo was seized with a violent stomach-ache, and disappeared hastily into his private hut. He was back a half hour later, seemingly none the worse for wear, explaining to his guests, "It's like I always told you. You can't keep a good man down."

Manners are on the upgrade among the cannibals in darkest Africa. One chief was heard reproving his son, "How often have I told you not to talk with someone in your mouth?" Another chief's wife became interested in a number of worthy charities. Her husband finally refused to bring home any more guests for dinner. He explained, "I'm tired of having my wife put the bite on them."

When Timothy McElligott was cast away on a desert island with two beautiful young ladies, he thought he was the luckiest man in the world. The island provided ample food and shelter, the climate was temperate—and there didn't seem to be another human within a thousand-mile radius. Soon, however, McElligott realized there was a fly in the ointment. The beautiful young ladies made constant demands: he had to set up a strict schedule: Mondays, Wednesdays and Fridays to make one happy; Tuesdays, Thursdays and Saturdays for the other. Sundays he reserved for general overhauling and resting his weary bones.

While fishing one day, McElligott was overjoyed to observe another shipwrecked sailor drifting ashore on a raft. "What luck— and just in time," he told himself. To the sailor he hallooed, "Welcome, mister. You'll love it here." The sailor answered, "For goodness sake, I should hope so. I'm in a perfect snit about the way that nasty sun has burned me. I hope you have some vanishing cream on this beastly island."

"Heaven help me," prayed McElligott, "here go my Sundays!"

A visitor from Australia walked into the Rolls-Royce showroom and paid cash on the line for the most expensive limousine model. "Ship it to my sheep ranch outside of Sydney," he instructed the sales manager. A year later he was back to order another car. "Best model I ever saw," he exclaimed, "and you can quote me on that. I particularly approve of the glass partition between the

front and rear seats. Most ingenious feature of the whole car."
"Why do you say that?" inquired the Rolls-Royce representative.
"It's like this," explained the Australian. "I roll that window up,
and I'd like to see the damn sheep that can lick the back of my
neck while I'm driving it to market!"

When Juan and Evita Perón were building a luxurious retreat
for themselves some miles outside of Buenos Aires they established a rigid guard around the project to prevent the stealth of
valuable materials. Every day at noon, the story goes, the same
workman began to appear at the exit gate with a wheelbarrow
loaded with straw. The guard, convinced that there was dirty
work afoot, searched the straw more carefully daily—even had it
analyzed to see if it possessed special chemical values—but could
find nothing to substantiate his suspicion, and had to let the
workman pass.

A year later, the guard met the workman, evidently enjoying
great prosperity. "Now that all is said and done," pleaded the
guard, "just what were you stealing every day on that Perón project?" The workman whispered, "Wheelbarrows."

Before China was engulfed by the Red tide, a family named
Lum—grandfather, father and twelve-year-old son—lived in pov-
erty in a tiny compound. The grandfather was crippled by arthritis and unable to continue his share of work in the rice paddy, so
the father decided to liquidate him. He trussed him up in a big
market basket and made for the shore of the Yangtze River. En
route he met his son who cried, "What are you doing to my poor
grandfather?" "Quiet," whispered the father. "By lowering him
into the stream we will end his suffering and at the same time
lighten our load." "I see," nodded the son, "but be sure to bring
back the basket. I'll need it for you one day."

F is for FARMERS

A New Hampshire farmer was so contented on his own little rocky plot of ground that he had ventured to the nearest city, Portsmouth, only five times in his life. On his last visit he suffered a painful experience. A fire siren sounded, and he hastily steered his horse and buggy over to the curbstone. When the engine had clanged by he proceeded on his way, only to be smacked squarely in the rear by the hook-and-ladder truck. When the doctors restored the poor man to consciousness they asked, "Why didn't you get out of the way? You must have heard the siren." "I heard it all right," he answered grimly, "but it wasn't the durn engine that hit me at all. It was that truckload of crazy house-painters careening along behind it!"

Farmer Jepson came storming out of the house brandishing his shotgun and shouting, "Dad bust it, Ezry Jones, I told you to quit courtin' my daughter. Now you git into that mangy old truck of yours, and git off my property once and for all." Ezry discreetly released Miss Jepson from his arms, and climbed into his truck— but as he drove off he had the last word. "You old skinflint," he jeered, "I'd run right over you if I wasn't scairt of puncturin' all my tires."

Nick Agropopolus, who did a mite of farming down Maryland way, received a notice from the town council that the license to maintain a cow on his premises had expired. Agropopolus took pen in hand and replied, "My cow she beat you to it. She expire two weeks ago. Much oblige: Your truly . . ."

In Washington, a government survey was ordered to study the migratory habits of birds. Thousands of all species were released with metal strips attached reading, "Notify Fish and Wild Life Division. Wash. Biol. Surv." Hugh Newton writes, "The abbreviation was changed abruptly following receipt of this penciled note from a vexed Alberta agriculturist: 'Gents: I shot one of your crows last week and followed instructions attached to it. I washed it, biled it, and surved it. It was awful. You should stop trying to fool the public with things like this.'"

Governor Luther Youngdahl, of Minnesota, says that the stingiest man in his bailiwick is the old Swedish-American who moseyed into a butcher shop and demanded ten cents worth of beefsteak. "But Mr. Olefson," protested the butcher, "you've got nine children. What are you going to do with the tiny scrap of meat I can give you for a dime?" "This ain't for eating purposes," explained Mr. Olefson. "I just like to have the smell in the house when company comes."

Old Pop Diggins had talked about a trip out West for twenty years, and now his dream was about to be realized. "One week from today," he exulted to his cronies at Green's General Store, "I'll be plumb in the middle of that there Yellowstone Park!" One of them cackled, "Don't you forget Old Faithful." "I won't," promised Pop Diggins. "I'm taking her with me."

An agricultural journal reports that a farmer in Wisconsin, who always complained that his wife didn't shoulder her share of the burden, agreed to run the household one day while his wife went to Madison for a medical examination. A methodical chap, he kept a minute record of his activities. It read as follows:

> Opened door for children: 106 times.
> Shouted, "Stop, Johnnie": 94
> Tied their shoes: 16
> Stopped quarrels: 19
> Provided glasses of water and cokes: 26
> Answered phone: 11
> Answered questions: 202
> Ran after children: about 4½ miles
> Lost temper: 45 times.

The next day the farmer himself journeyed to Madison—and bought his wife the washing machine she had long coveted.

Kenneth Roberts is a novelist of parts, the author of such best sellers as *Northwest Passage* and *Lydia Bailey*. When a man of his stature solemnly assures us that he believes in dowsing rods and the sensitive souls who manipulate same, it behooves us at least to examine his claims with an open mind.

A dowser is a man who can hold between his fingers any flexible Y-shaped tree branch and, by extending it straight in front of him, theoretically detect the presence of water. Through no effort of his own, the rod is supposed to turn downward with irresistible force the moment he passes above a spot where the subterranean sheets of water exist.

In his book, *Henry Gross and His Dowsing Rod*, Mr. Roberts details (with a host of corroborating witnesses) exploits of a Maine neighbor that certainly seem to tag him the real McCoy. However, scientific skeptics still hold to their story that it can't be done.

When Mr. Roberts first encountered Henry Gross, the nine springs on the writer's farm were wholly inadequate. Gross simply marched across the property with his forked stick and told Roberts exactly where to dig new wells. Now he has not only all the drinking water he needs, but a sizable pond besides.

By not sparing his rod, Mr. Gross even was able to tell the writer how far down in the earth the water would be found and how fast it flowed.

To cap the climax, and prove that Mr. Gross is the super-duper dowser of them all, he plunked himself down in a chair in Roberts' Kennebunkport, Me., library and waved his rod over a map of Bermuda. He located three sources of water on a tract of land where geologists and test drillers had sworn that not a drop of uncontaminated fresh water existed. And were their faces red when Mr. Gross's prediction held water!

Mr. Gross's rod, admits Kenneth Roberts, has its limitations as far as hard liquor is concerned. When touched to rye before being put to use, it works only on rye thereafter, ignoring any quantity of Scotch, blended whiskey, or Jack Daniel's Number Seven Sour Mash. This strikes me as a very minor defect. Any man who can't tell Number Seven without a dowsing rod doesn't deserve good liquor.

The dowsing rod behaved in exemplary fashion the day it was exhibited in a big Boston department store. Mr. Gross extended it before him and sallied forth. The rod led him unerringly to the ladies' washroom.

Farmer Thomas' barn had just gone up in smoke, and his insurance agent was trying to explain that he couldn't collect cash for it. "Read the policy," he insisted. "All our company engages to do is build you another barn exactly like the one that's been destroyed."

Farmer Thomas, apoplectic with rage, thundered, "If that's the way you varmints do business, cancel the policy on my wife before it's too late."

A fellow down in Pumpkin Creek bet a city slicker ten dollars he could ride the flywheel in a new sawmill. His widow, paying off the bet after the funeral, observed, "Cal was a right good husband, but he sure didn't know beans about flywheels."

Farmer Klopfcr sidled into the general store at Flemington with a look of acute melancholy on his face. "I kin tell by looking at you," said the knowing proprietor of the store, "that that danged old mule of yours has been acting up again." "You hit the nail right on the head," admitted Klopfer, reaching for a plug of chewing tobacco. "You'll never listen to me," said the proprietor. "Didn't I tell you that the next time that critter balked you should just build a fire under him and *make* him move?" "That's just what I done," complained Farmer Klopfer, "but that ornery beast moved just fur enough to pull the wagon over the fire and burn it up."

Art Noble dropped into our office the other day with a clipping from an Arkansas paper that read, "A roaring twister last Tuesday carried off John Squire's house and furniture. All four of his children are missing. Neighbors promptly donated a new bed to give John and his wife for a fresh start." . . . Art also told us that alert folks out his way have finally figured out why a farmer looks for a needle in a haystack. Seems that's where the farmer's daughter frequently does her fancy work.

My Uncle Herbert loves to rough it in the woods every summer, communing with nature in an outfit that sets him back about three hundred dollars at Abercrombie and Fitch. Last year we were gradually freezing to death in an overnight cabin in Maine when I suggested that Uncle Herbert blaze a trail to the kitchen and light the stove. A couple of moments later he was back with his impeccable costume strangely tattered and torn. "I thought you were going to light the stove?" I grumbled. "I did," maintained Uncle Herbert, "but it went out." "Well," I said impatiently, "light it again." "I can't," said Uncle Herbert. "It went out through the roof."

"My garden was such a success this year," boasted a gentleman farmer, "that my neighbor's chickens took first prize at the poultry show."

Reminded that Henry Ford had left an estate of over a hundred million dollars, an Iowa deacon shook his head slowly and observed, "Strikes me he must have had an awful savin' woman."

Barbara Anne, a freshman at Wellesley, came home to her tiny
home town for Christmas, and hastened to tell her father who was
waiting at the station to bundle her into the family station wagon,
"Paw, there's something you might as well know right off. I ain't a
good girl any more." Paw clapped one hand to his forehead and
cried out, "Twenty years your maw and I have made sacrifices so's
you could go to a smart Eastern college, and what happens? You
come home after three full months there—and you're still saying
'ain't'!"

Hoagy Carmichael is responsible for the story of the crack shot
of an Indiana community who was never over-modest in retailing
legends of his prowess. On one hunting trip, the marksman took
careful aim and fired, but the bird sailed on undisturbed into the
blue. The marksman watched it in dazed silence for a moment,

then dashed his gun to the ground, and cried out, "Fly on, you
blankety-blank fool bird! Fly on with your gol-durned heart shot
out!"

In the feuding country of the Blue Ridge Mountains, the Abernathys and the Spillanes shot at each other on sight for three generations. Townsfolk thought they might end the feud by appointing the heads of the two families joint mayors. The ancient enemies shook hands, then rushed forth to try to outdo each other in sartorial splendor at the inauguration ceremony. Old Tod Abernathy decided to wear the cutaway and striped trousers in which deceased males of his clan were laid out before burial. Thus adorned, he entered the kitchen to collect his womenfolk. His wife took one horrified look at him and cried, "Dawgone! Them Spillanes has got my Tod at last!"

An Ozark native, aged eighty or thereabouts, ambled into a doctor's office in Crane, Missouri, and announced, "Doc, I seem to have picked up a first-class case of insomnia somewhere. I keep wakin' up every few days."

Bob Uchitelle solemnly swears that this is an authentic excerpt from an Arkansas hillbilly's diary:

> March 15: Rainin', can't go huntin'!
> March 16: Still rainin', can't go huntin'!
> March 17: Still rainin'. Shot Gramma.

A native of the Ozarks was asked by a revenue agent, "Seen your grandpappy lately?" The native pointed with his corncob pipe to an indistinct object at the far end of his tomato patch and said, "See that figger over thar? It's either a tree stump or grandpappy. Keep your eyes on it. If it moves, it's a tree stump."

In George Heister's home town, Colonel Lemuel Witheringham, noble scion of an aristocratic but impoverished family, was known as its most silver-tongued and long-winded orator. When he died of old age, his obit in the *Gazette* read, "The late Colonel plunged into the unfathomable, soared into the infinite, and communed with the inscrutable—but he never paid cash."

A fine distinction between acquaintanceship and friendship has been established by such Southern tobacco auctioneers as haven't been exported to New York for radio appearances. Several were convening in a backwoods bar, when a newcomer approached. One of the group patted him on the back and said, "Russ, you know Joe Arbuckle, don't you?" Russ grudgingly extended a hand, and allowed, "We've howdied but we ain't shook."

As a result of a tip from a source considered reliable, the game warden of Shuckamockie County reluctantly donned his snow shoes and mushed halfway up a mountain to corner old Hermit Hawkins, a "character" in those hills for years. He dragged his weary bones back into his home some seven hours later. "Well," said his wife, "did you find that old Hawkins really was poaching?" "Yep," he reported with a sigh. "Deer or elk?" she asked. "Eggs," said the game warden.

A worried girl came down from the mountains to tell her doctor, "We gotta do somethin' 'bout grandmaw's smokin'. She inhales." "Nothing so terrible about that, Elviry," soothed the doctor. "Plenty of women inhale nowadays." "You don't understan'," persisted Elviry. "Grandmaw don't exhale!"

Stories about a succession of child marriages in the feudin'
country down South reminded Viola Swisher of the day a Blue
Ridge mountaineer fell ill. The doctor reassured the patient's worried husband, "That little wife of yours'll be perfectly all right in
a couple of days, son. She's just teething."

That traveling salesman you've always heard about ran out of
gas one evening on a lonely road and asked at the only farmhouse
in sight (where else?), "Can you put me up for the night?" The
farmer said, "I reckon I can—if you don't mind sharing a room
with my young son." "Good heavens," gasped the salesman, "I'm
in the wrong joke!"

G is for GAMING

A young bride's honeymoon in New York turned out disastrously because her husband, an inveterate bridge fiend, insisted upon spending every minute of his time watching the play at a Master Championship Tournament.

She picked expert Oswald Jacoby to be her confidant, complaining, "I stood it till the sixty-second hand. Then I lost my temper completely and walked out on him."

"The sixty-second hand?" mused Jacoby. "That was unforgivable, my dear. The sixty-second hand was by far the most interesting hand in the tournament."

In a Western gambling dive, a tenderfoot from New England lost his stake in suspiciously quick order. On the street he was voicing his suspicions about the dive, when a tough-looking gent, sporting extensive firearms, sidled up to him.

"Are you accusin' my associates inside of runnin' a crooked joint?" he demanded.

The tenderfoot paled and explained hastily:

"Nothing of the sort. I only said that I was watching the dealer in that twenty-one game—and the card on the top of the deck struck me as mighty dusty."

A lady who cannot resist the lure of roulette wheels and slot machines stopped off at Reno on her way home from the coast, and bumped into Walter Clark, author of *The Ox-Bow Incident*. "Fancy meeting you here," exclaimed Clark. "What hotel are you staying at?" "Hotel?" echoed the lady, as she bought a new stack of chips. "My dear boy, I've only been here four days!"

The going was even rougher than usual at the Guggenheims' weekly bridge joust with the Loebs. "Will you tell me," demanded the exasperated Mrs. G. of her spouse, "how you could make an original bid of three no-trumps when I was sitting there with all four aces and a king in my hand?" "If you must know," admitted the harassed Mr. Guggenheim, "I bid on three queens, two jacks and four highballs."

Latest "kibitzer" story tells of one of the most persistent of the breed, who hovered behind a card player for three solid hours giving advice. What's more, the player won consistently. Suddenly he found himself in a quandary. Turning to the kibitzer, he whispered, "Well, smart guy, what do I play now, the ten or the queen?" The kibitzer answered, "First you've got to tell me this: What game are you playing?"

Three ladies at a Saratoga hotel, desperately seeking a fourth for bridge, finally appealed to a little old lady in an alpaca dress who was crocheting and minding her own business in a sheltered corner of the porch. Flustered but obviously pleased by the invitation, she said, "I'll play, but I warn you, I'm not up on all those new conventions." "Don't worry," they assured her. "None of us are members of the Regency Club either." On the very first hand, three consecutive passes left the bidding strictly up to the little old lady. She studied her hand carefully, cocked her head to one side, and bid, "Two clovers."

Monte Carlo was the scene of a strange occurrence one night many years ago. An elderly gentleman took a seat in the casino and ventured fifty francs on Number 17. The number came up. The old man pointed at Number 17 again and made no move to rake in any of his winnings.

Again the little silver ball came to rest at Number 17! The croupier looked questioningly at the old man, who sat with his head down on one arm and his finger pointed at Number 17 on the board. Five more consecutive times the wheel hit Number 17. The old man's pile of chips was enormous. The crowd stood silent with admiration for his nerve. The croupier had a hurried consultation with the directors, and announced that the bank was broken and the roulette game was at an end.

But the winner of the fortune never stirred. He was dead. Furthermore, a doctor testified in court he had been dead ever since the second spin. A dead man broke the bank at Monte Carlo!

Elinor Maxwell heard a young Lothario confide to the custodian of the Whaling Bar, "If I only had enough money to marry her—I'd bet every cent of it on my favorite horse!"

Mr. John McNulty, who specializes in discovering—and writing about—slightly zany characters in Third Avenue saloons and joints adjacent, is himself a somewhat erratic bettor when the horses are running. One day he was observed leaving the press

box at Churchill Downs just after a long shot had come in to pay
$76 for every $2 ticket. By way of being pleasant, Joe Palmer
said, "I hope you had that one." Mr. McNulty answered indignantly, "At 38 to 1? Do you think I'm crazy?"

H is for HOLLYWOOD

Do you remember the old songs and lithographs that conveyed heartbreaking stories of little girls sneaking into the family entrance of a corner saloon trying to entice papa into laying off the lager beer and free lunch and coming home to his starving family? The present-day, Hollywood version of that sad situation has for its improbable setting a special table at the luxurious Hillcrest Golf Club, with a cast of characters consisting of eleven world-famous comedians. They love one another's company and jokes so much, their children can't even persuade them to come home to cash their salary checks.

The eleven members of this ultra-exclusive fraternity are Groucho, Harpo and Chico Marx, Danny Kaye, George Jessel, Lou Holtz, George Burns, Jack Benny, and the three zany Ritz Brothers. It's unlikely that the club will grow, since the rules state explicitly that any new candidate must get fifteen affirmative votes, which is rather difficult when only eleven men are eligible to cast ballots. Golf is the least of the members' worries. Groucho's son Arthur avers that eight years after the club had been established, Holtz and Jessel found themselves on the clubhouse veranda for the first time. Jessel spotted the eighteenth green and exclaimed, "When did they put in a golf course here?" Last year the most disliked member of the Hillcrest Club dropped dead on the first tee while practicing swings with a driver. When word of this percolated back to the comedians' table, George Burns turned to Danny Kaye triumphantly and said, "I *told* you this was a tough course."

One lady member of the Hillcrest Club sits for hours at the nearest table to the group's sacred meeting spot with a hearing aid pressed to her ear. "It's the only place," she explains, "you can hear all the latest jokes without one darn commercial."

Groucho Marx, explains his brother Harpo, is infatuated with words. "Groucho," he says, "doesn't regard words the way the rest of us do. He looks at them upside down, backwards, from the middle out to the end, and from the end back to the middle. Next he drops them in a mental Mixmaster, and studies them some more. Groucho doesn't look for double meanings. He looks for quadruple meanings. And usually finds them."

One day an officious lady at the Brown Derby in Hollywood pushed a waiter aside, leveled a finger at Groucho, and demanded, "Are you Harpo Marx?" Groucho raised an eyebrow and replied, "No. Are you?"

An elderly book clerk in Hollywood is still suffering from the shock sustained when Groucho entered her shop and inquired blandly, "Have you something obscene for a seven-year-old girl?"

Groucho is said to net over $4000 a week these days with his radio and television chores, but there was a time when all four Marx brothers together had a difficult job keeping the wolf away from the door. When traveling from one town to another their mother, Minnie Marx, dressed them up in short pants and Buster Brown collars so they could ride for half fare. Once, when a harassed conductor informed Mrs. Marx that her "little boys" were smoking cigars, chasing girls, and playing poker in the coach ahead, she beamed at him and confided, "They grow so fast."

Al Shean, famous as the partner of Mr. Gallagher, was also the man responsible for making Harpo Marx a silent comedian. Shean scripted the first vaudeville act for the then-unknown Marx Brothers, and inadvertently forgot to write in a part for Harpo.

When Harpo indignantly called the omission to his attention, Shean hastily explained, "I did it on purpose. I want you to play in pantomime. I've got a feeling you'll be terrific." Mr. Shean didn't know how right he was! Incidentally, one of the first towns to see the new Marx Brothers turn was Waukegan. In the orchestra pit, a kid named Kubelsky played the fiddle, and doubled up with laughter every time Groucho opened his mouth. Today, some thirty years later, Kubelsky is still laughing at Groucho. Now, however, he is known as Jack Benny.

Groucho owes it to his legion of admirers to revive some day the classic scene in which he played Napoleon bidding farewell to a slightly bleary-eyed Josephine. "Jo," he would declare, seizing her in his arms, "your eyes shine like the seat of my blue serge pants, and I know you are as true as a three-dollar cornet. But hark, they are playing the Mayonnaise! The army must be dressing." Josephine came out of her trance to aver, "Nappy, I am true to the French army." "Thank heaven," Groucho shouted, "France has no navy."

◆

A dashing young movie hero, delight of millions of bobby soxers, was told by his studio head, "It's time you played a different kind of role. We're casting you as a miner in your next picture." The hero announced firmly, "Nothing doing. I hate minors. The last one I met cost me fifty thousand dollars."

A near-sighted director was searching for locations for an impending farm epic when a gust of wind blew off his beret. He gave chase, but every time he apparently had it cornered, it was whisked from under his hand again. Finally a woman looked up from her gardening and called, "What are you trying to do over there, mister?" "I'm trying to recover my beret," he puffed. "Your beret is over there by the stone wall," said the woman. "That's our black hen you've been chasing."

Another near-sighted gentleman was heard moaning at a race-track bar, "I've got to get these glasses fixed fast. I've just walked into seven fellows I owe money to!"

S. Z. "Cuddles" Sakall, the rotund comedian, asked a pint-sized dancer how much she weighed. "A hundred and one," she told him. Sakall sighed and pointed out, "I ate more than that for lunch."

Cuts are so rampant in one Hollywood studio, chronicles Mike Connolly, they're signing all new contracts with styptic pencils. Mike also reports that Football Star Bob Waterfield, whose wife happens to be Jane Russell, told an interviewer, "Certainly I do the cooking. Do you think I want Jane to melt her career away over a hot stove?"

The late W. C. Fields, not noted for sobriety, was once asked if he ever had suffered delirium tremens in Hollywood. "That's impossible to answer," rasped the comedian. "It's impossible to tell where D.T.'s end and Hollywood begins." (It was Alexander Woollcott who described the whole Los Angeles area as "Seven suburbs in search of a city.")

A member of the census bureau, assigned to Hollywood, reports that the door of one sumptuous villa he visited was opened by a man in cerise pajamas. "How many people live in this house?" asked the census taker. "And what are their ages and occupations?" "How would I know?" answered the man in pajamas. "I've never been here before in my life."

Will Rogers, always down to earth and allergic to phony glamour, nevertheless had one "dream girl" whose doings he followed like any other star-struck citizen. Her name was Greta

Garbo. Will went six blocks out of his way every night on his way home from the studio just to get an occasional glimpse of Miss Garbo, and once in a while he'd get an extra dividend in the form of a wave of recognition from her. Those were red-letter days for Rogers! While Will was in New York one winter, however, Miss Garbo sold her hacienda and moved up into the more remote hills surrounding Hollywood. Thus it was that the next time Will sauntered by the old villa for a glimpse of Miss Garbo, the face on the porch belonged to his old, fat, and unglamorous friend, Irvin S. Cobb. Shocked and dismayed, Rogers made straight for a Western Union office and sent Cobb this wire: "Dearest Greta: Land sakes, gal, how you've changed."

Just last summer Miss Garbo came close to buying for herself a quaint and rambling old farmhouse on Long Ridge Road, Connecticut. At least she asked the aged owner to name a selling price. "But I don't want to sell it to you," said the owner bluntly. "I'm sure you do not understand," the actress protested. "I'm Greta Garbo." "Exactly," said the owner. "And that's why I don't want to sell my charming old house to you. You have the means to spoil it!"

A prominent and pulchritudinous starlet in Hollywood was discovered gazing blankly into space by Sid Skolsky. "Why the depression?" asked Sid. The starlet sighed deeply, then explained, "My analyst just told me I'm really in love with my father. What'll I do, Sid? He's a married man!"

A newly crowned Hollywood queen, very blonde, very sexy, told a reporter that her real love was a sixty-year-old banker in Wall Street. "Every time he phones me to the coast," she purred, "I get chinchillas up and down my spine."

Publicist Leo Guild solemnly swears that a new Warner Brothers contract player, intent upon making a big impression on her first visit to Hollywood, signed the Beverly Wilshire Hotel register, "Mary Blossom and made."

Two agents were seated at a table in Mike Romanoff's new Hollywood restaurant watching Clark Gable, Van Johnson, Dore Schary, Mervyn LeRoy and Spencer Tracy dine lengthily and well. "Look at them," sighed one of the agents. "How'd you like to have ten per cent of their salaries?" The other said, "The way things are in the film business today, I'd be satisfied with ten per cent of their dinner checks."

A fellow-producer persuaded Sam Goldwyn to attend a preview of a blood-and-thunder picture, and at its conclusion enthused, "Isn't that a real, old-fashioned swashbuckler for you?" Goldwyn wisely pointed out, "The trouble is, it buckles where it should swash!" And Moss Hart tells about the day Mr. Goldwyn asked how he was progressing with his script on the life of Hans Christian Andersen. "If you don't like the job I've done," proclaimed Moss earnestly, "I will emulate Van Gogh, cut off my ear, and present it to you." "My boy," said Goldwyn, "in my desk I've got a whole drawer full of ears. All I ask from you is a good box-office script."

One big Hollywood producer came home to find his wife sobbing uncontrollably. "That famous author of yours!" she wailed. "He came marching in this afternoon, seized me in his arms, and

despite my protests, made violent love to me for three hours."
"Hm-m-m," mused the producer, "I wonder what the so-and-so
wants?"

Things had gotten so tough for one independent producer in
Hollywood that he was filming an entire feature in four days flat.
In a final desperate gamble to recoup his fortune, he signed an
authentic star at five thousand dollars a day, and set frantically to
work. Toward the end of the second day, the cameraman reported, "Gotta stop a few moments, boss. Our star had to go to the
washroom." "Stop nothing," boomed the producer. "We'll shoot
around him!"

A Hollywood agent, usually very chipper, sat despondently at
the soda counter of Schwab's Pharmacy. "Whassamatter?" asked
a friend anxiously. "It's that new client I'm representing," groaned
the agent. "Sings like Lanza, fights like Flynn, and acts like Victor Mature." "So why do you worry," laughed the friend. "You'll
make a million out of this guy." "Guy nothing, you dope," cried
the agent. "It's a *girl!*"

I is for
INTOXICANTS

Colonel R. Juniper Bragg, asked why he always closed his eyes when he drank a mint julep, explained, "The sight of good lickah, suh, always makes my mouth watah, and I don't aim to have my drink diluted." The colonel, however, believes there is a time and place for everything. Observing his twenty-year-old son out on the veranda with a julep in one hand and the other hand around the waist of the belle of the county, he reflected, "That boy is squanderin' fifty per cent of his youth. He can drink when he gets old!"

A fugitive from Alcoholics Anonymous negotiated a job in a chinaware emporium, and succeeded in smashing an ornate vase before he had been there two hours. "Too bad," said the foreman, "but we'll have to deduct twenty per cent from your wages every week until the vase is paid for." "What did it cost?" asked the worker. "Five hundred bucks," said the foreman. The worker consoled himself, "My wife'll be pleased anyhow. This will be the first steady job I've had in ten years."

Hugh Ferry, of the Packard Motor Car Company, has a prescription for a hangover that he swears has never failed. "It's simplicity itself," says Ferry. "Just squeeze the juice from two quarts of Scotch."

A couple of vats at a beer brewery in Milwaukee were struck by lightning in a flash storm last summer. Not only were they undamaged, however, but experimentation proved that the beer within, instead of being spoiled, was actually improved in quality. The foreman smacked his lips over the unexpectedly fine flavor and wired the head of the outfit, "We believe this is the first case on record of a storm actually brewing."

An inquisitive guest asked Mrs. Cohalan: "What's in that bottle I saw in the kitchen?" Without looking up, Mrs. Cohalan replied, "Eight to one it's my husband Mike."

A long-suffering wife was about to berate her husband for staggering home at 3 A.M. "Before you begin," he warned her, "I want you to know I been sittin' up with a sick friend." "A likely story," mocked the wife. "What was his name?" The husband gave this problem deep thought, then announced triumphantly, "He was so sick he couldn't tell me."

I have it on the authority of expert William Feather that a Jeroboam of champagne contains 104 ounces of the bubbling vintage. A Split, furthermore, is a nip (6.4 ounces), a Fifth is a bottle (25.6 ounces), a Magnum is two bottles (52 ounces), a Rehoboam is six bottles (156 ounces), a Methuselah is eight bottles

(208 ounces), a Salmanazar is twelve bottles (312 ounces), a Balthazar is sixteen bottles (416 ounces), and a Nebuchadnezzar (wow!) is twenty bottles (520 ounces). Current quotation for a vintage Nebuchadnezzar is $375, plus $50 deposit for the bottle. First come, first served—and only two to a customer.

Old Colonel Archer, up from Kentucky, was describing his daily routine to a delighted group in Toots Shor's New York restaurant. "For breakfast," proclaimed the Colonel, "I ask only for a quart of bourbon, a pound of beefsteak, an' my ol' houn' dog." "What do you need the houn' dog for?" asked Toots. "The houn' dog," explained Colonel Archer, "eats the beefsteak."

J is for
JUDICIAL MATTERS

A couple of legal eagles in Reno, Nevada, write to say that while business never has been better, it does grow somewhat boring to be handling the same kind of cases all the time. Is divorce, they ask plaintively, the *only* subject engaging the attention of the Law in America today?

At any rate, while waiting for the Truckee River to unfreeze last winter, so they could resume fishing for the gold wedding rings divorcees impulsively throw in when their decrees are granted, the impatient attorneys composed these pertinent couplets:

Mrs. Camp's bereft today. She always knew a shorter way.

No longer wed is Mrs. Thorne. She hogged the bathroom every morn.

Each week poor Sue found some new diet. Worse still, she made her husband try it.

Marriage, thought Jones, was sure and stable. But then he fed the dog at table.

She left him flat and deserted the scene. He ended each sentence with "See what I mean?"

Their marital break was grim and gory. She never would let him finish a story.

The Campbells are no longer lovers. She always woke up with no bed covers.

In Reno, John Doe is slowly reviving. He couldn't stand the backseat driving.

There is a successful lawyer in Hollywood whose name has been romantically linked with at least a dozen top-flight actresses from time to time. Tendered a fiftieth birthday party by his friends, the lawyer had to stand for a great deal of good-natured kidding. Always-reliable Georgie Jessel earned the biggest laugh by remarking, "Our esteemed guest of honor is going to be the lead-off man on any ball team I manage. He gets to first base so often!"

Grover Whalen is asking friends if they heard about the street cleaner who was dropped from the force because he couldn't keep his mind in the gutter. And Commissioner Cullman discloses the name invented by the police for kids picked up in disorderly houses: brothel sprouts.

A dairy in Iowa sued a minister for non-payment of a bill, but the case was thrown out when the minister's lawyer produced an analysis of the milk, and assured the court, "My client wanted that milk for drinking, not christening."

Chauncey Depew, addressing a graduating class at the Harvard Law School, reminded his audience, "Everything you learned here will go for naught if you forget this fundamental rule: when it becomes apparent in a case that somebody on your side is headed for jail, be sure it is your client!"

A showgirl with Dagmar-like accessories shot her boy-friend
seven or eight times, and then cried her way through her trial—
incidentally giving the jury ample close-ups of her abundant
charms. The verdict was announced by the foreman in appropriately reverent tones: "We find the defendant breathtaking, en-
trancing, wholesome, lovable—and—oh, yes—not guilty."

A businessman was involved in a lawsuit that dragged on for
years. One afternoon he told his attorney, "Frankly, I'm getting
tired of all this litigation." "Nonsense," replied his lawyer. "I propose to fight this case down to your last nickel."

Judge Cohalan regarded the defendant at the bar severely and
asked, "Have you ever been in trouble before?" "Coitn'ly not,"
was the vehement reply, "and the only t'ing dey're tryin' to pin on
me dis time is robbin' me kid brudder's bank." "If I may be per-

mitted to interrupt," spoke up the district attorney, "the prisoner neglected to explain that his kid brother is cashier of the First National Trust."

A very dignified judge was married to an estimable creature, who, unfortunately, drank a bit too much. At a party one afternoon he reproved her, "My dear, that's the fifth time you've gone up to the bar and asked for another highball. Doesn't it embarrass you?"

"Why should it?" she answered happily. "I just explain I'm getting them for you."

George Allen, the White House jester, avers that he but carries on the tradition of his father, who practiced law, politics, and diplomacy in Booneville, Mississippi. One day a magistrate forgot his cue and had the gall to decide a case *against* Allen, Senior. The latter waved a volume of Blackstone under the justice's nose to emphasize his outrage. "Sit down, Mr. Allen," thundered the judge. "I know the law." "Of course you do," purred Mr. Allen. "I just wanted to read this paragraph to you to show you what a damn fool Blackstone was."

I like the story that's come down from Sing Sing—of the condemned man walking to the electric chair, oblivious to the attendants surrounding him, reading a copy of *Quick!*

The warden of a big Western penitentiary, reports the Phoenix *Flame,* is conducting a thorough investigation of his office. While looking for some documents recently, he found one of the files had a cake in it. And Bernie Hart had a solution to offer the warden of the Michigan jail whose prisoners rioted and barricaded themselves in a cell block. "Offer them," suggested Bernie, "time and a half."

The most sensational trial of the year was in progress in Iceland, country of the midnight sun. The prosecuting attorney shook a bony finger in the face of the accused and thundered, "I ask you again, sir: where were you on the night of November 8 to March 16?"

The House Un-American Activities Committee has become used to evasive witnesses maintaining "I refuse to answer on the grounds that it might incriminate me," but one radio writer on the stand came up with a new one. Abel Green, of *Variety*, reports that this witness pondered over a question momentarily, then had a long whispered consultation with his lawyer, and finally answered, "I refuse to answer because I don't understand one damn word of my counsel's advice."

There's a man in Hollywood who is a great picture producer, but a child when it comes to high finance. His safe deposit box is the repository for just about every worthless oil stock floated in California. One day an acquaintance tried to sell him a whole gold mine at a "bargain" price. The producer promised to think it over and said "I'll call you." He did, too—about three days later—and declared, "My lawyer says I'm crazy but I've decided to buy that gold mine." "You're too late," answered the acquaintance bitterly. "I'm already in jail!"

K is for
THE KREMLIN

It appears that the question, "Who is going to inherit the mantle of Joe Stalin?" has been settled at last. On Georgi Malenkov's last birthday, the Soviet press accorded him so many hooplas that every comrade must have comprehended the general idea. They'll soon be getting "Won't You Be My Malenkovy Baby" as mujik in their ears.

Malenkov, son of a Cossack in the Urals, first hit the big time as Stalin's personal secretary in 1925, and showed that he was there to stay when he personally maneuvered the dismissal of the mighty Molotov's wife from her cushy post as Commissar of the Fish Industry.

"There are many, many fish in the sea," she had proclaimed. "Why aren't they on our citizens' tables?" demanded Malenkov.

American diplomats who attended Kremlin banquets in what now seems like the dim and distant days of World War II remember that Georgi Malenkov was always among those present, but invariably maintained a surly silence. Probably he knew even less English than his boss did.

At the Teheran conference, according to *Time* magazine, Joe Stalin's mastery of the English language was confined to two graphic sentences: "The toilet is over there," and "What the hell goes on here?"

A year later at the meeting in Yalta, he had added, "You said it" and "So what?"

A fugitive from Moscow managed to elude the border guards and presented himself to the American authorities in West Berlin. On his person were found a great variety of pills—and an enormous portrait of Stalin, printed on rubber and folded inside his belt. "The red pills are for sinus trouble," explained the Russian. "The green ones are for arthritis, the orange ones for toothaches, and the purple ones for indigestion." "Yeah, yeah," scoffed the examining sergeant, "but what's that picture of Joe Stalin for?" "That," said the Russian with great dignity, "is for homesickness."

At a party celebration in Leningrad, a guest discovered a piece of rubber tire in his stew. About to protest, he noticed the eye of a secret-police official fixed upon him, and managed a cheerful, "Well, everything is going according to our most optimistic calculations. Here we've been in power only thirty-five years, and already the automobile is replacing the horse!"

A Polish journalist, back in Warsaw after a brief journey to Moscow, was asked, "Is the Soviet really in such wonderful shape? Does the subway now extend sixty miles? Is every worker living in a new house with radio and air-conditioning? Is there a pile of atom bombs in the Kremlin? Are the farmers all happy and prosperous?" "Yes, yes," agreed the journalist. "All these things I saw with my own eyes." An old graybeard then asked, "And where is your companion Ignace? Why did he not return with you from Moscow?" "Alas," sighed the journalist. "Ignace is in a slave labor camp in Siberia. Unfortunately he did not seem to see all these things!"

Stalin called in his top "yes-men" one morning and boomed, "Boys, I've got a great idea! Let's liberate the Pribilof Islands from the suffocating grasp of those money-mad Wall Street bankers." One "yes-man" was a little slow with his usual enthusiastic endorsement. "I must point out," he quavered, "that there isn't a single human being on the Pribilof Islands—nothing but seals." That didn't stop Stalin. "Seals? People?" he roared. "After we get finished liberating them, who'll be able to tell the difference?"

At the finish line of a big bicycle race from Prague to Warsaw, a Polish lad watched eagerly until the last contestant pedaled by, then burst into tears. "Why weren't there any Russians in the race?" he sobbed. "I was hoping to get my bike back."

Sneaked out of Budapest is the story of the secret police agent who was ordered by his chief to learn whether a skeleton in the museum really was, as alleged, that of Attila, fifth-century chieftain of the savage Huns. The agent marched off with the skeleton and returned forty-eight hours later with what was left of it—a few splinters of bone. "It's Attila, all right," averred the agent. "How did you confirm it?" asked the chief. The agent answered proudly, "He confessed."

Commissar Malipoofsky journeyed from Moscow to Budapest to see whether the Hungarian satellites were growing enough potatoes to meet their quota. "Ah, Comrade," sighed his Hungarian deputy, "under the inspiration of the incomparable Stalin our peasants are turning out a crop beyond our wildest dreams. When they are harvested, our spuds, if put into a single pile, will make a mighty mountain reaching to the feet of God." "Enough of your hammy dramatics," said Commissar Malipoofsky sharply. "Besides, you know perfectly well there isn't any God." The deflated deputy sighed, "There aren't any potatoes either."

John Cameron Swayze says that Stalin, Roosevelt, and Churchill were being driven in a staff car during their fateful Teheran conference, when a cow blocked the road and refused to budge. Neither Churchill's eloquence nor Roosevelt's charm was of any avail. Stalin, however, merely whispered one phrase in the cow's ear, and the animal bolted for the woods. When asked how he did it, Stalin explained, "I just told her I was going to put her in a collective farm."

The Soviet government recently hornswoggled a Swiss movie manager into showing a hot propaganda film in his string of theatres. It extolled Russian explorers in the frozen wastes of the Arctic, showing thrilling polar-bear hunts, seal killing, and the wonderful work of Russian ice-breaking ships and iceberg spotters. One of the trimmest vessels bore a Russian name prominently on the bow. Swiss audiences watched in respectful silence, bursting into laughter only once. That was during a split-second shot, when a sign on the "Soviet" boat read very clearly, "United States Coast Guard."

Near the close of the Spanish Civil War the Russians sent a brigade of "volunteers" to be in on the fighting. Arrived in Madrid, the commissar in charge delivered this note to Loyalist headquarters: "Herewith two hundred wildly enthusiastic volunteers for your army. Please return the ropes."

An Irishman spent some time in the local pub listening to a broadcast of the latest news. Returning home he remarked to his wife, "They're saying it's Stalin who really has Korea." "Well," said the wife. "Bless the girl what gave it to him."

L is for
LITERARY LIFE

Literary history is studded with stories of great best sellers that were snubbed by anywhere from one to a dozen publishers before a more perspicacious—or lucky—one decided to take a chance. Cases in point are *The Four Horsemen of the Apocalypse,* Viña Delmar's *Bad Girl,* Ludwig's *Napoleon,* Mika Waltari's *The Egyptian.* An English publisher actually turned down Pearl Buck's *The Good Earth* twice! After he rejected it the first time, several other English houses followed suit, and the agent brought it back, insisting it belonged on his list. Again he said "no." The book sold almost a half million copies in Britain when another publisher accepted it.

The late S. S. McClure, pioneer magazine and book publisher, was waylaid on the way to his inner office one morning by a determined lady who demanded, "Did you keep your promise and read the manuscript I gave you?" To be rid of her, he answered, "I did. We can't use it." She appeared crestfallen and murmured, "I suppose the little verses at the beginning of each chapter detracted from the story. Maybe they should come out." "No, no," said the publisher suavely. "Those little verses add to the interest. I'd leave them in by all means."

"Mr. McClure," the lady answered triumphantly, "there *are* no little verses at the head of each chapter. You simply haven't read the manuscript as you said you would and I'm going to sit right

here until you do." McClure realized he was trapped, and with a
sigh, sat down to skim through the manuscript as quickly as possible. He decided to accept it, however. The lady was Mrs. Ovid
Butler Jameson of Indianapolis, determined to set her brother
astride the high road to literary fame. Her brother's name was
Booth Tarkington. The manuscript was *Monsieur Beaucaire*.

In 1939, Author Chard Powers Smith finished a novel and submitted it to Scribner's. The publishers approved of the book but
were afraid his title would discourage customers. He consented
to change it, and the book appeared in 1939 under the title of *The
Artillery of Time*. Mr. Smith had occasion to doubt the wisdom of
his move within a matter of weeks, for by purest chance John
Steinbeck wrote a book with the very title Smith had been persuaded to discard—*The Grapes of Wrath*.

Publisher Richard Simon decided to include a half-dozen adhesives in a new juvenile called *Dr. Dan the Bandage Man*,
and wired to a friend at the Johnson and Johnson Company,
"Please ship two million band-aids immediately." Back came a
telegram reading, "Band-aids on the way. What the hell happened to you?"

An important author arrived unannounced to see his publisher
one Wednesday. "Sorry," said the receptionist, "but he's away for
the week end." The author asked sarcastically, "Last week end or
this week end?"

A man who had been a book salesman for twenty years decided
there was more money in selling vacuum cleaners, and secured

the local agency for a well-known brand. His very first prospect
was a skeptical housewife who asked, "Are you sure that contrap-
tion will gather up every single bit of dirt?" "Lady," said the salesman earnestly, "I ran this cleaner lightly over a copy of *Lady
Chatterley's Lover* yesterday, and when I was finished, it was
Louisa Alcott's *Little Women!*"

Ed Laycock defines an intellectual snob as a man who won't
speak to a beautiful girl on a train because he doesn't approve of
the book she's reading. . . . William Butler Yeats characterized
a literary movement as "two authors who live in the same city and
hate each other." . . . Rebecca West described a pretentious
society publisher as "every other inch a gentleman." . . . And
bookmen who continually complain about the bad breaks they're
getting might recall the words of Stephen Vincent Benét: "What
some people call hard luck—well, we made New England out of it
—that and codfish."

One of our most eloquent publishers, who will be disguised in
this story under the name of Jones, was panting to move to his
Westchester estate for the season, but found his plans stymied by
his wife's inability to persuade a suitable butler to expose his
precious carcass to the country air. "This servant problem is worse
than ever," she complained. "Really! You'd think it was the Sahara
we were asking them to come to, and not just twelve minutes
from the White Plains station." "Tommyrot," declared Mr. Jones
in his best *Life with Father* manner. "I will meet you at the
agency tomorrow morning and show you how quickly the whole
thing can be settled with the application of a modicum of common sense."

He was a few minutes late the next morning, and failing to
note that the agency sported two entrances, one marked "employers," the other "employees," strode imperiously into the latter.

"Yes?" said the man who blocked his path. "What are you looking for?" "I am looking for Mrs. Jones," he announced. "She wants a butler." "Indeed she does," agreed the man, and propelled him in the direction of his reasonably puzzled wife. "Here, Mrs. Jones," he said, "is a man I know you'll like. I've placed him with some of our best clients, and he has never failed to give complete satisfaction."

The Joneses are still in Manhattan. Mrs. Jones is rounding out the staff by herself.

The early twenties evidently was a propitious period for the launching of new magazines in America. The *Reader's Digest* got under way in 1922, *Time's* first issue appeared in 1923, Mencken and Nathan's *American Mercury* made its bow in 1924, and the *New Yorker* began operations in 1925.

Mencken's rejection slips certainly were different from any others. Authors would get their brain children back with a printed slip reading, "Mr. Mencken has just entered a Trappist monastery in Kentucky and left strict orders that no mail was to be forwarded. The enclosed is returned therefore for your archives."

Two attractive young employees of a dashing midtown magazine publisher were discussing his merits. "He's so good looking," enthused one, "and he dresses so well!" The other amended happily, "So quickly, too!"

One of the many celebrities who dwell in Stamford, Connecticut, is editor Herbert Mayes, but his sumptuous home is so far from the town that servants are hard to find—and harder to keep. Mrs. Mayes finally latched on to a couple who seemed ideal, however, and after all arrangements had been concluded satisfactorily, led them in to meet Mayes in his study. Seeing the crowded bookshelves and piles of manuscripts, the butler was moved to inquire, "What's your line, sir?" Mayes answered, "I'm the editor of *Good Housekeeping Magazine.*" "*Good Housekeeping!*" gasped the butler, heading for the door. "Come on, Hilda, this is no place for us!"

Gordon MacRae says that, what with all the science fiction stories flooding the market, editors will soon have to change their formula to "Man gets girl; man loses girl; man builds girl."

A near-sighted publisher, walking along the beach at Provincetown, Massachusetts, encountered a comely young lady who greeted him by name. Unable to recognize her without his glasses, the publisher stammered, "How nice to see you up here. How long are you staying?" "I've got to go home Sunday," she told him sadly. "What a pity," he remarked. "September is the best month on the Cape. Why don't you stay another week?" "I will if you'll let me," the girl said coyly.

The publisher examined her at close range and suddenly recognized her. It was his private secretary.

Editor Saxe Commins prevailed upon the beautiful new telephone operator to be his guest at luncheon, but when she returned she confided to a side-kick, "That's the last time I ever go to eat with an editor. He blue-penciled three fourths of my order!"

Charlie Marshall and Lew Miller, two of the most high powered and successful sales managers in publishing today, were, in their salad days, rival book peddlers covering the same insignificant territory. Marshall remembers catching Miller one morning dashing up and down a flight of stairs in their hotel as though his life depended on his activities. "What on earth are you up to now?" demanded Marshall. "Getting winded," explained Miller, "so the first account I call on will think I'm breathless with excitement over our spring list."

Publisher Virgil Gentillin attended a cocktail party during a recent librarians' convention. The discussion got around to the improvement of library service effected by more rigid requirements and better training for aspiring librarians. One bright young thing observed, "Do you know it takes five full years to make a librarian now?" One visiting salesman, new in the racket, was appalled. "I'm sorry, honey," he declared embarrassedly, "but I just haven't got that much time."

In Tulsa, an oil magnate, enamored of his secretary's chassis but appalled by her ignorance of literature, strove mightily to improve her I.Q. One morning she told him, "I took your advice. I borrowed a book from the library last night." "Great," enthused the magnate. "What was the name of it?" The secretary answered, "Dun and Bradstreet's."

Stripper Lily St. Cyr reports that she's having trouble with the books in her private library. "The minute I pick one up," she pouts, "the jacket slips off."

A small come-on ad in a Paris newspaper recently brought rich rewards to the bookseller who inserted it. "What every young girl should know best before she weds," promised the ad. "Profusely illustrated. Explicit instructions. Sent in a plain envelope." Every eager soul who clipped the coupon received a very good cook book.

Relaxing by the swimming pool at La Quinta, in the California desert, mining executive Carl Loeb, Jr., remarked to Jerry Devine, producer of the successful radio series, "This Is Your F.B.I.," that he had written a book in his spare time. "What's the name of it?" asked Devine. Loeb glibly reeled off the title: "The Isothermal Transformation of Austenite in Molybdenum Steels." "I don't think I'll read it," decided Devine. "I'll wait for the picture."

A Chicago bookseller called his clerks into a huddle one morning and cautioned them, "I've ordered 300 copies of *What an Expectant Mother Should Know* and I'm counting on you boys to create a demand for them."

A Rolls-Royce stopped in front of a Madison Avenue bookshop the other evening, and the chauffeur announced rather sheepishly, "My lady wants a couple of new murder stories committed by *nice people*."

A religious bookshop near the State Capitol in Boston put on a big Bible sale recently and quite a number of customers were lured by this bit of versification on a card in the window:

> Holy Scripture, Writ Divine
> At a dollar forty-nine;
> Satan trembles when he sees
> Bibles sold as cheap as these.

A little girl was having a hard time in Brentano's Bookstore selecting a book to be given to her mother as a birthday gift. "Does she like fiction?" asked the clerk. The little girl shook her head. "Biography? History? Books on art? Humor?" The little girl continued to register disapproval. Finally the exasperated clerk demanded, "Well, what on earth *does* she like?" The little girl said, "Men."

M is for

MARTS OF TRADE

There exists a whole army of executives who never have learned the vital secret for keeping their private secretaries contented. Hell hath no fury like a secretary who nurses a grievance—be it real or imaginary. Take heed, therefore, of the results of a survey conducted by the personnel manager of a big woolen company to determine what kind of bosses irritate their secretaries most.

Here are the "winners"—and very much disputed champions:

1. The boss who keeps his secretary overtime without previous notice.

2. The boss who dawdles around until five P.M. and then begins the day's dictation.

3. The boss who refers to his secretary as his "stenographer" and makes bad jokes about her in front of visitors. Samples:

(A) "Better make twelve copies of this, Miss Winter, so we may be able to find one if we need it."

(B) "We're all in rather a hurry today, Miss Lyon, so how about taking this note down in longhand?"

(C) "It's quite true that we have done business with Gimbel's for decades, but we still do not address the president as 'Dear Gimmie.'"

4. The boss who marks up work that could be corrected, and slashes a line through a four-page letter because one word is incorrectly spelled.

5. The boss who interrupts his secretary during her lunch hour, if she has stayed to eat in her office.

6. The boss who hovers over her while she is typing a letter, pointing out errors before she has had a chance to notice them herself.

7. The boss who has seen too many Grade-B movies and cheap cartoons, and believes in the motto, "Hands Across the Knee."

8. The boss who never voluntarily says, "Gosh, your letters have been immaculate lately—and done so quickly, too," or "By the way, Miss Jones, isn't this your birthday?"

9. The boss who only gives a raise after the secretary has gone through countless humiliating sessions to wangle one. This type boss is usually the one who is most apt to flash a hefty bankroll continuously before his secretary's eyes.

10. The boss who regards his secretary as general errand girl for his entire family. She is expected to devote her lunch hour—particularly when it is raining heavily—to exchanging nylon stockings for his wife, picking up theatre tickets for his mother-in-law, and going to a repair shop clear across the city to find out why his brother's 1939 Buick is still out of commission.

Have you heard about the stunning young stenographer who left her coat in the office and took her boss to the cleaners?

Joe Gilligan's contracting firm was famous for its ability to slap together a whole block front of snazzy-looking (from the outside) ranch houses in less time than it took a builder of the old school to erect a chicken coop. One morning, however, a foreman rushed up to Gilligan and shouted, "We just removed the scaffolding from the three new houses on 'K' Street and they collapsed in a heap." Gilligan investigated, and turned on his foreman in a rage. "How often do I have to tell you ninnies," he bellowed, "never to remove the scaffolding till you've put up the wallpaper?"

Dave Garroway is acquainted with a Chicago merchant who was summoned suddenly to a big business powwow in New York. It was scheduled to last four days, and he had to grab a plane at the Cicero airport within the hour. Problem: how to contact his wife, who was on a shopping spree in the Loop? The merchant thought hard and suddenly came up with a brilliant idea. He ordered his secretary to cancel all of his wife's charge accounts. She called up in a rage twelve minutes later.

New high in absent-minded bosses is the bemused paper manufacturer who put the typewriter on his lap and started to unfasten the ribbon.

The third vice president of a downtown bank is a notorious ladies' man, despite his seventy years, and the girls in the organization make wide detours to escape his pinching forays. One morning last month, however, he barely looked up when movie star Anne Baxter ankled by. "Get a load of old J.W.!" marveled a member of the staff. "I'm afraid his eyes are on their last legs."

"But I thought . . ." said the secretary meekly.

"Don't think," barked the industrialist. "That's not what I pay you for. Take down what I dictate and then type the letters. Is that quite clear? Now take this."

That afternoon, his secretary planked this letter on his desk for signature:

"Dear Smythe: The idiot spells it with an 'E'. Thinks it's aristocratic. His old man was a plumber. With regard to your letter of —look it up. Anybody who can read that handwriting deserves a medal. You ask the cost of replacing worn parts in the machinery at your plant. Our experts figure—hey, Joe, what was the estimate on that Smythe job? Two thousand? Okay—our experts figure that three thousand dollars is our rock-bottom price. The extra thousand is for that damn 'E' he sticks on his name. Trusting to receive your esteemed order, etc., etc., etc. There, that's done and you better get off my lap before my partner walks in on us."

Three old friends, all unemployed, set out together one morning to seek jobs. That evening, the wife of the eldest said, "Well, Joe, what luck today?" "Sam struck it rich anyhow," said Joe. "On his first call, a fellow took him up to a desk marked 'Treasurer' and told him he was now treasurer of the corporation." "What about Bill?" asked the wife. "Bill got a break, too," answered Joe. "A man showed him a room labeled 'Vice-president' and that's the job they gave him." "Wonderful," said the wife, "but what happened to you?" "Congratulate me, mama," said Joe quizzically. "At last, I'm a gentleman."

Stanley McMichael, author of *How to Make Money in Real Estate*, knows an operator who owned a loft building, a marble yard with dock privileges, a factory site and a summer garden, all of which he proposed to swap with another man who owned a row of tenements, a small subdivision, an abandoned lime kiln and a farm. "He assumes a $20,000 mortgage on the loft building," explained the first man to his wife, "and I take over a second mortgage on the subdivision. Get me?" "I guess so," responded the wife wearily, "but if you've got all the details so cleverly worked out, what's holding up the deal?" "I sign nothing," he declared firmly, "till he gives me four dollars in cash!"

The young man was obviously embarrassed. He explained haltingly, "I'm supposed to bring home either a casserole or camisole. I can't remember which." "That dilemma is easily resolved," chuckled the erudite storekeeper. "Is the chicken dead or alive?"

Drew Pearson recently wowed his audience at the Detroit Athletic Club with another story of a man who visited a Washington department store to buy a brassiere for his wife. "What kind do you want?" demanded the salesgirl. "We have the Stalin, the Salvation Army, and the Drew Pearson." Noting Pearson's utter mystification, she condescended to explain, "The Stalin model uplifts the masses. The Salvation Army supports the fallen. And the Drew Pearson make mountains out of molehills."

Andrew Carnegie once was showing a delegation through his plant when he stopped to talk to a stooped, gray-haired employee. "Let's see, Wilson," he said. "How many years exactly is it that you've been with me now?"

"Thirty-nine, sir," beamed Wilson. "And may I add that in that entire time I made only one trifling mistake?" "Good work," grunted Mr. Carnegie, "but from now on, please be more careful."

From Philadelphia comes the story of two suspender salesmen who were boasting of their products. "Five army mules pulled on either end of a pair of our braces," proclaimed one, "and they couldn't make them break."

"Paghh!" scoffed the other. "Yesterday I was rushing to catch a train at Penn Station in New York, and my suspenders got caught in a pillar on the platform. I made my train all right, but when the conductor opened the door in Philadelphia, those darn suspenders of ours snapped me right back to New York!"

A couple of furriers had had an unusually successful season and the senior partner flew down to Miami Beach for a well-earned vacation. He had been there two days when his partner in New York called him long distance to splutter, "Our safe has been robbed! $50,000 is missing!" The senior partner calmly replied, "Now, Joe, that's going entirely too far. You put $45,000 right back in the safe."

Landlord Vogel slid an overdue rent bill under the door of a dilatory Broadway character, who promptly slid it out again. Twice more Vogel pushed it back into the room—and twice more it came back. Vogel straightened up, sighed deeply, and reflected, "I guess I'll have to fix his window after all. There's certainly a powerful draught in here."

A wholesale outfit in New York has so many customers it's able to classify them according to their habits of speaking. To wit:

Musical buyer: I'll make a *note* of it.

Animal buyer: I'll *bear* your *lion* in mind.

Marine buyer: I'll be in to *sea* you when you have a *sail.*

Russian buyer: I'll take *one uv ich.*

Romantic buyer: I *love* everything you've shown me—but. . . .

Blanket buyer: I want you to *cover* me.

Barber buyer: Can't you *shave* your price a bit?

Ideal buyer (Imaginary): I'll take everything!

A young salesman in a dress manufacturer's office was assigned the task of entertaining a very important out-of-town buyer. The sky was the limit, and the boss gave him 200 smackeroos for an evening's fun and relaxation. The buyer, however, proved to be a very difficult hombre. He had seen *Guys and Dolls* eight times—"Everybody takes me to see *Guys and Dolls*"—and *Pal Joey* five times. He was bored with the show at the Copa and every other night club in town. Every suggestion the salesman made bounced back in his teeth. Finally, in desperation, he turned to the buyer and said, "I've got no more suggestions to make. Suppose *you* tell *me* what you'd like to do." Answered the buyer, "What I'd really like to do is visit a high-class sporting house."

The next day, the salesman reported for work and handed over to the boss $190 out of the $200 he had been given. His employer was flabbergasted and asked how come? "Well," said the salesman, "Mr. X wanted only one thing—to go to a high-class sporting house. So I took him to Abercrombie & Fitch, but it was closed."

Samson, notes Copywriting Genius Milton Biow, really had the right idea about advertising. He took two columns and brought down the house.

One of the kids at Deerfield Academy asked Washington correspondent Bert Andrews about his early days in the journalistic profession. Andrews knitted his brows, and pondered, "I believe I got my first scoop when I was four years old, and yes—it was vanilla."

At an alumni meeting of Public School 14, a member of the class of 1910, now balding and affluent, reminisced, "Do you fellows remember a skinny little shaver named Hughes from our class? His family was poor as church mice, but he had an instinctive business sense, and we all just knew he'd make the grade. I ran into Hughes the other day. When he got out of the Army in World War I, he bought himself an old push-cart and began buying and selling old bones, bottles, and rags. And what do you think Hughes is worth today?" Some guessed $100,000, some a million. "You're all wrong," chuckled the alumnus. "Hughes isn't worth a Confederate nickel. In fact, he never even paid for the push-cart."

One of the slickest operators in the garment district, relates Harry Hershfield, always dated his checks ahead. When he passed away, creditors erected a tombstone over his grave. It read, "Here lies Gabriel Gluntz. Died November 10, as of February first."

A tourist bought a bolt of beautiful British cloth in the Bahamas and presented it to his Fifth Avenue tailor, asking, "Is there enough material here for you to make me a suit?" "No," said the tailor. The disappointed tourist headed for home, and passed a tiny sidestreet tailoring shop en route. "No harm to try again," he thought, and sure enough, the second tailor was confident he could make him a very adequate suit from the material available.

He was true to his word, and a fortnight later turned out a garment that fitted the tourist like a glove. Just as the latter was reaching for his pocket book, however, the tailor's five-year-old son ran into the shop, garbed in a suit so obviously cut from the tourist's own material, the tailor didn't even attempt to alibi. "Yes, I made a suit for my boy from the goods left over," he said placatingly. "There wasn't enough to be of any use to you anyhow!" At that moment the tourist bethought himself of Tailor Number One. Angrily charging into that worthy's establishment he cried, "Remember telling me I didn't have enough material for a suit? A competitor down the block not only made me a very fine one, but had enough cloth left over to make a suit for his five-year-old son!" "So what?" scoffed Tailor Number One. "*My* son is eighteen!"

Delferd Clark, one of the directors of the Ford Foundation, describes the visit of a delegation to the home offices of one of the country's biggest manufacturers of business machinery. The head of the firm marched the visiting group from one mechanical marvel to another, and once the ground floor had been covered, led the way to the elevator. One of the other occupants of the elevator was a beautiful young blonde. Halfway to the second floor, the blonde suddenly jumped two feet in the air, and squealed, "Yipes!" The leader of the delegation nodded his head and said with great satisfaction, "I'm certainly glad to note that at least *one* thing in this building is still done by hand!"

N is for a
NEW PARLOR GAME

Bright young boys and girls in the literary set like radio tycoon Bill Paley, composer Harold Rome, Russell Austin, Gross-Vater Arthur Kober, and Quiz Kids originator Lou Cowan, have been knocking themselves out with a new parlor game called "In the Name Of." It demands the merest smattering of knowledge of great personalities in history and the arts plus a knack for making —and deciphering—atrocious puns. You can understand why *I* like it!

For example, a German plutocrat is showing his country estate to a friend. The friend declares "Most beautiful lawn and gardens I ever saw!" The German shrugs it off in the name of an English author (also, to make it easier, in the name of a popular brand of cigarettes) with "Ach, it's Chesterfield!" (Just a field). Another example: two Englishmen hail each other in the name of a famous French painter. Answer: Watteau (What, ho!). Everything clear? The solutions to all that follow will be found at the end of this section—but before you look there, try to solve them yourself.

1. The drama critic of a big New York daily fell ill on the eve of an important play's debut. His wife went to review it in his stead. The author of the play awaited her verdict in a fever of anxiety, finally called a friend on the paper.

"What did she say?" he implored. The friend answered in the name of an Indian lady who is much in the news.

2. A transcontinental express train was wrecked in the desert. The life of the engineer (a Frenchman) was spared, and he was speedily summoned by a board of inquiry. "In your opinion," he was asked, "what caused this catastrophe?"

"Eet is very seemple," he said, and explained in the name of a nineteenth-century painter, especially popular in America today.

3. Mrs. Jones thought the movers had taken everything out of her home but suddenly discovered they had overlooked a valuable vase. She told her Chinese houseboy, "The moving men must take this vase with them." "Lady too late," sighed the houseboy.

"Why?" asked the lady. The houseboy explained in the name of a Dutch painter who once cut off his ear.

4. Three fellows named Tom, Fred, and Ces decided to enact the famous jousting scene in *Don Quixote*. "I'll play the title role," proposed Tom, "Fred can portray Sancho Panza, and——."

5. A Montreal-bound lady woke up in her berth to find the temperature of the car down to 20°. Ringing for the attendant, she announced indignantly, "I'm ——."

6. A lady was playing Christmas songs at the piano, when a page of her songbook fluttered to the floor.

Her daughter pointed out what had happened in the name of the author of one of the world's best known children's classics.

7. A barker on a carnival midway beckoned a sweet young thing and enticed her with, "Wanna win a crisp new twenty-dollar bill, girlie? All ya gotta do is throw one of these rings over that cane in the back of the booth."

The sweet young thing sought further information in the name of another great Dutch painter.

8. A dairy farmer's whole livelihood was endangered when his prize cow suddenly went dry. Anxiously he summoned the most distinguished vet in the country—a foreigner whose skill had won him a dozen degrees.

The vet examined the ailing animal carefully, then rose and patted the worried farmer on the back, reassuring him in the name of a distinguished modern Russian composer.

ANSWERS: 1. Madame Pandit. 2. Toulouse-Lautrec (Too loose le track). 3. Van Gogh. 4. Cecil B. De Mille. 5. Cole Porter. 6. Lewis Carroll (Loose carol). 7. Vermeer (From here?). 8. Shostakovich ("Just a cow itch").

Let's see you do better!

O is for

OUR FOUR-LEGGED FRIENDS

Including Shaggy Dogs

A report from the jungle, difficult to track down but believed to emanate from horses considered reliable, has it that the animal world was anything but pleased when Mr. Aesop began composing his beastly fables. D. B. Wyndham, in fact, avers that one morning a grape-hating fox who felt that he had been libeled sneaked up behind Mr. Aesop and bit a substantial piece out of his hide. "Now go home and write that up," he sneered.

With unrest of this sort pervading the forest primeval, a proud and domineering lion decided it was time he checked the loyalty of his constituents. Collaring a stray antelope, he demanded, "Who is the king of the animal world?" The antelope, no fool he, hastily answered, "You, oh mighty lion." The lion roared his satisfaction and skulked along until he encountered a wise old chimpanzee. "Who is the king of the animal world?" snarled the lion who, as you can see, had something of a one-track mind. "You, of course," soothed the chimp. "What monk doesn't know a thing like that?" The lion was a happy beast until he ran into a ponderous and ill-tempered elephant. Again he demanded, "Who is the king of the elephant world?" By way of reply, the pachyderm promptly wrapped him up in his trunk, whirled him aloft four or five times, and deposited him in a bramble bush twenty feet away. Regaining his feet with difficulty, the bruised lion observed plaintively, "Just because you don't know the answer, you don't have to lose your temper!"

A persnickety mule on a Southern plantation, more obstreper-
ous even than his usual wont, kicked over an outhouse and considerable section of back fence, and was roundly beaten for his
pains. A poodle seized the occasion to point a moral to her pups.
"Children," she said, "let that jackass be a warning to you against
the habit of kicking. Just you notice how the better he does it the
more unpopular he gets." Play-agent Monica McCall's poodle, incidentally, recently started chewing up a college dictionary. Miss
McCall took the words right out of his mouth.

Blanche Rizzardi, of Minersville, Pa., writes about the frus-
trated glow-worm who tried to strike up a conversation with the
lighted end of a cigarette. Doris Warner, of the Hollywood
Solarium, knows a porcupine who got into even worse trouble.
He's so near-sighted that he made love to a cactus plant. Ray
Bowden, of Gloucester, Massachusetts, overheard a little germ on
the edge of a milking pail comment sadly to another little germ,
"Our relations seem to be getting strained."

A dog and a cat became embroiled in a street-corner fight, and
a big crowd gathered to watch. One unruly spectator suddenly
whipped a gun out of his pocket and shot the dog. A policeman
heard the report and came running on the double. The killer
threw his gun to the ground and appealed to the crowd, "Don't
say a word to the cop. He'll think the cat did it!" A lady in
Wichita loved goldfish so passionately that she kept her tub in the
bathroom filled to the brim with them. "But what happens when
you take a bath?" asked a friend. "What do you do with the goldfish?" The lady blushed modestly and explained, "I just blind-
fold them."

A hillbilly, notes Mrs. Arthur Magners, of Reading, Pennsylvania, spied a parrot atop a barn roof, and attracted by its plum-
age, decided to capture it for a pet. He climbed up to the rooftop
and made a grab, but the parrot moved out of his range, ruffled
his feathers, and snapped, "What do you think you're doing,
brother?" The hillbilly tipped his hat and apologized, "Beg pardon, sir. I thought you were a bird."

A health crank, partial to yogurt and such like, felt a sudden craving for a plate of clam chowder, and what with it being a Friday, decided to indulge himself. He took the precaution, however, of presenting the waiter with two huge vitamin pills, and instructed him to dissolve them in the chowder before serving. When a half hour went by without a sign of chowder, the health crank collared the waiter and hollered, "Why am I receiving no service around here?" "You'll get your chowder, sir," soothed the waiter, "the minute we can get the clams to lie down."

A city feller who doesn't know the front end of a goat from a magnolia bush was watching his week-end host's daughter milking her cow when a farm hand hollered, "Cheese it, here comes the bull!"

The city feller vaulted a fence for safety, but noted to his surprise that the girl never budged from her stool. Furthermore, the bull brought up abruptly, snorted almost apologetically and meekly retreated to his enclosure. "Weren't you petrified?" demanded the guest.

"Not me," said the daughter, "but I reckon the bull was. This here cow's his mother-in-law."

Some months ago, a collection of wealthy ornithologists in New Jersey triumphantly announced that they had tracked down the nesting grounds of a very elusive bird named the bristle-thighed curlew. This name, for some reason, caused numerous readers to begin inventing ridiculous species of non-existent birds, the craziest of which were duly listed in *Tide*, the advertisers' bible. Examples: the tufted dowager, red-eyed crosspatch, lesser stench, double-breasted seersucker, morning peewee, electric crane, week-end bat, vested interest, bleary-eyed hangover, and extra-marital lark.

A mother hen, experiencing difficulty in keeping a headstrong chick in line, finally declared, "If your pa could see you now, he'd turn over in his gravy."

A hunter with a big gun, goes a current legend, met up with a bear that had no gun at all. But the bear had claws—and wit—and refused to concede defeat. He asked the hunter, "What are you looking for?" "A fine fur coat," said the hunter. "Me, I'm looking for breakfast," declared the bear. "What do you say to coming round to my nice warm den and talking over our prospects?"

So they went to the den and worked out a satisfactory compromise. The bear, emerging solo from the den, had enjoyed a splendid breakfast, and the hunter was wrapped up in a fine fur coat.

Farmer Ekhamer owned a very tough ram, but discovered that music soothed its savage breast. Headed for town one day, Ekhamer reminded his son, "If that animal gets rambunctious just put a record on the Victrola." When he returned home he discovered that the ram had plunged against a stone wall and committed suicide. "Did you play music like I told you?" he demanded of the son. "I sure did," said the boy, "but the record I chose seemed to drive him crazy. It was Frank Sinatra singing, 'There'll Never be Another Ewe.'"

Patricia Richardson's dog, "Faun," had an aggravating habit of curling himself up in his mistress' favorite easy chair, and feigning sleep when she attempted to dislodge him. Next door there resided a cat whom Faun abhorred, however, and Miss R. learned that by going to the window and crying "Here comes that cat,"

Faun could be persuaded to vacate the chair and vanish from sight without further ado. She had worked this dodge effectively on several occasions when, one afternoon, she sat dozing in her chair. Faun walked in, studied her with his head on one side, suddenly bounded to the door and began barking furiously. The aroused Miss Richardson rushed to investigate. The street was absolutely empty. When she returned, Faun was curled up blissfully, his eyes closed, in the easy chair.

The cat is one reasonably domesticated animal that most people find impossible to take or leave casually. The reactions of my own friends, for instance, range from Authoress Leonora Hornblow, who verges on hysteria at mere sight of a cat to Authoress Bernardine Kielty, who considers a dinner incomplete unless her Siamese Suki drops at least once from some lofty perch into the ragout. John Beecroft, who picks books for the Literary Guild, has so many cats around the house that it's a lucky visitor who escapes without hurt felines. James Mason, the picture star, goes him about twenty better.

Fred Allen, bosom friend of the Masons, was dining one evening at the home of Mary and Jack Benny. "You're sitting at my usual place at the table," Mary informed him, "so will you please fish under your chair for the buzzer to summon the butler? Then tell me what the Masons do with all those cats around the house." "For one thing," answered Allen gravely, "they never have to hunt for a buzzer. They just step on one of the cats."

The old comedy team of Moran and Mack had a cat routine that always won a solid laugh. Moran claimed that he owned fifteen cats, and therefore drilled fifteen holes in his dining room door so he could get rid of them when he desired. "But one hole would be enough," Mack pointed out. "The cats could exit one by one." "Nothing doing," concluded Moran firmly. "When I say 'scat' I mean 'scat.'"

A pedigreed and very expensive cat was shipped from Philadelphia by overnight truck to a purchaser in New York. The

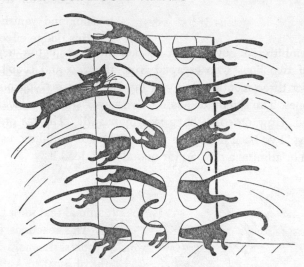

driver later confessed to Michael Gross, the poster artist, that while he was bumping along the cobblestones on Eleventh Avenue, the jarring loosened the cage in which the cat was confined. With one mighty leap he was off, high-tailing it up the avenue. Shouts of onlookers alerted the driver, who instituted an intensive cat-hunt, but to no avail.

All he found was a scurvy-looking scavenger in an alley. Figuring that all was lost anyhow, he collared the unsavory specimen, shoved him into the cage, and delivered him to the purchaser. Here's the pay-off. To this day the purchaser, evidently highly satisfied with his alley cat, has never registered a single word of protest!

The late Al Jolson had a cat which he told his friends was worth $5000. Came the day when he decided to sell the animal, and the skeptical friends waited eagerly for him to return from the pet shop and disclose the selling price. "Did you get the $5000?" they jeered. "Certainly," answered Al. "Did you think I was kidding you?" "Show us the dough," demanded the friends. "Well," admitted Al, "this pet shop fellow happened to be a little short of cash so he gave me these two $2500 dogs instead."

An embittered government worker in Washington tells the story of two lions who escaped from the zoo and didn't meet again for three months. One was fat, the other nothing but skin and bones. The skinny one said, "I've never seen you looking so well fed. How on earth have you managed?" The fat one said casually, "I've been holing up at the Pentagon Building, eating a general or admiral a day. So far nobody's noticed it."

From Montana comes a delectable new shaggy dog story. Seems an old prospector was reminiscing for some Eastern tenderfoots. "There I was," he asserted, "trapped in a narrow canyon, with a big grizzly twenty yards away behind a tree. Only way I could hit the critter was to ricochet a bullet off the high canyon wall on my right. Now I'm a champion shot, as you probably know. I just gauged my windage, calculated the lead of the barrel and the rate of twist, the hardness of the bullet and the angle of yaw it would have after being smacked out of shape against the canyon wall, and I judged my chances of nailing that bear were about 80–20. A one-rail bank shot. A controlled ricochet. So I took aim and fired."

The prospector paused. One of the tenderfeet asked softly, "Did you hit him?"

"Nope," answered the old man. "I missed the wall."

An outstanding social event of the Sewickley, Pennsylvania, season was the hunt tea given by Mr. and Mrs. Joseph Purslove, Jr., to fete "widows, widowers, and orphans of the hunt." The general idea, read the invitation, was to recognize the plight of unfortunates to whom "brush means Fuller, giving tongue is wife's noises, a good fencer parries thrusts with a rapier, a rising scent is inflation, a waving stern is a sinking ship, whip means prunes, and drawing a covert is caused by a sudden drop in the temperature at night."

Ted Weeks, editor of the *Atlantic Monthly*, brought home from England an essay by a ten-year-old that he swears is the genuine article, although I have a vague notion I read it somewhere before. Can any reader supply further details? The piece is called "A Bird and a Beast," and it reads as follows:

The bird that I am going to write about is the Owl. The Owl cannot see at all by day and at night is as blind as a bat.

I do not know much about the Owl, so I will go on to the beast which I am going to choose. It is the Cow. The Cow is a mammal. It has six sides—right, left, and upper and below. At the back it has a tail on which hangs a brush. With this it send the flies away so that they do not fall into the milk. The head is for the purpose of growing horns and so that the mouth can go somewhere. The horns are to butt with, and the mouth is to moo with. Under the cow hangs the milk. It is arranged for milking. When people milk, the milk comes and there is never an end to the supply. How the cow does it I have not yet realized, but it makes more and more.

The cow has a fine sense of smell; one can smell it far away. This is the reason for the fresh air in the country.

The man cow is called an ox. It is not a mammal. The cow does not eat much, but what it eats it eats twice, so that it gets enough. When it is hungry it moos, and when it says nothing it is because its inside is all full up with grass.

Ted Dealey, of the Dallas *News*, tells the story of the farmer whose plan to mate his mare and the prize stallion of the county was frustrated by the stallion's untimely demise. The farmer led up a zebra from the zoo as the likeliest substitute he could find, but the mare indicated plainly "No soap." "I went to a lot of trouble to get this zebra," the farmer complained to the mare, "and besides, he has an exceptional pedigree, so what are you getting so hoity-toity about?" The mare lowered her eyes bashfully and replied, "Who's getting hoity-toity? I'm just waiting for him to take off his pajamas."

P is for the
PUN-AMERICAN CONFERENCE

There are no two ways about puns. You either like them or you don't. If you don't, this section is not for you. If you do, gather round for some of the worst of the year. And to be successful, a pun really must be bad. It must make the listener groan dismally, shake his head disapprovingly, and stagger off to the next room where, no doubt, he promptly repeats it as his own.

Until the Pun-American Conference really got into the groove in my Cerf Board column in *This Week Magazine*, I never realized how many folks were in a punsive mood these days. Already three secretaries have been stricken with appundicitis merely from opening the mail.

One who may never recover at all drew a stunner that came all the way from Allan Bosworth, now a captain with the Atlantic fleet. It concerned a beauty-shop proprietor whose hired hands were out on strike. He didn't mind being picketed as long as the girls were pulchritudinous but rebelled when he discovered that the babe who was parading back and forth in front of his entrance had been a victim of smallpox.

He called union headquarters and roared, "This time you're going too far. My picket has been pocked!"

Gypsy Rose Lee was playing a sketch in an old musical revue that called for the property man to ring a deep gong off stage at a certain point in the proceedings. One day the property man misplaced his gong, and in desperation, shook a little dinner bell he found on the shelf. The unexpected, silvery tinkle caused Miss Lee to burst out laughing, and the punch line of the sketch was lost as a consequence.

When she returned to the wings, she demanded that the property man be fired forthwith. The stage manager, who had been out having a beer while the act was in progress, asked the cause of her ire. Gypsy explained, "He ain't done right by our knell."

Bob Campbell, of Westwood, hired three adjoining rooms at the Beverly Hills Hotel for a business powwow, and found a bottle of bitters in one of them. He tried to turn the bottle over to Manager Hernando Courtright, but the latter said, "Nay, nay. You've got to take the bitters with the suite." . . . Mrs. Charles Lederer avers that Ethel Barrymore, detected trimming her lawn with a nail scissors, explained her behavior with a well-modulated "That's all there is; there isn't any mower." . . . A final dispatch from our Hollywood chapter expresses regret that Abraham Lincoln never met Florenz Ziegfeld. Frank Larkin daydreams, "I can see the headline now: Abe and Flo."

At a dinner given by the Book-of-the-Month Club to honor Dorothy Canfield Fisher, she dropped a paper on the floor. Christopher Morley stooped to retrieve it for her, but a certain middle-age spread impeded his progress. Clifton Fadiman observed, "Chris is still as gallant as when Dorothy was a gal, but not as buoyant as when he was a boy."

Another double pun was perpetrated by a guest of a San Francisco hostelry. Several chess players had formed the habit of staging daily contests in the lobby, and a crowd of kibitzers gathered to watch them. The manager, noting that they produced no revenue for the hotel, ordered them cleared out one afternoon.

At the height of the resultant hullabaloo, a lady asked, "What's happened?" That's when the guest contributed his classic: "It's nothing, ma'am: just the manager pulling his chess nuts out of the foyer."

Irving Titsworth called on Judge Brown one evening during the dinner hour. "I'm sorry," the maid told him firmly, "but His Honor is at steak." . . . A hermit in an obsolete jalopy was apprehended driving in Pomona, California, at 70 miles an hour. The charge, of course, was recluse driving . . . Bess Vaughan says the trouble with her new nylons is that they're sheer today and torn tomorrow.

Near the conclusion of World War II, recalls John Pericola, a jeepload of Tito's soldiers was speeding along a sketchy, winding road in the Yugoslavian mountain country. Rounding a curve at high speed, the jeep plowed into an oxcart filled with natives. After the crash, they had the devil's own time separating the jeep from the Croats. . . . Mike Connolly knows why the population of Italy is soaring. Tony's Home Permanent.

America lost one of its first-rate humorists when Fred Taylor, known to millions as "Colonel Stoopnagle," died in Boston. Some of his screwball "inventions" were round dice for people who preferred marbles; red, white and blue starch to keep American flags waving when there was no wind; and the "tates," a compass that invariably pointed in the wrong direction. "In this manner," explained the Colonel, "he who has a tates is lost." Stoop also introduced an alarm clock with half a bell to wake only one person in a room, and a goldfish bowl surrounded by postcards so the fish would think they were going somewhere.

In the boundless ocean, notes Vera Lawrence, a father drop and a mother drop determined to teach their young offspring how to be a responsible part of the sea. After a month of intensive training the father drop observed his son's antics with satisfaction.

He then announced to the mother drop, "I do believe we've taught Junior everything he has to know. I hereby declare him fit to be tide."

In Paris, John Woodburn even negotiated a pun in French. He noticed that a lady's petticoat had slipped and was collecting dust as she promenaded down the Rue de la Paix.

Tapping her on the shoulder he pointed out, "Mademoiselle, your *quelque chose.*"

Richard Anderson's next-door neighbor has triplets, and since nobody can tell them apart, they're known simply as "A," "B" and "C." The three boys were having trouble learning to back up on their birthday tricycles. After many bumps and bruises, "A" finally mastered the reverse pedaling, and his mother exclaimed happily, "Ah, my 'A' can back!" . . . Mr. Anderson will kindly stand in the corner with Margaret Davis who writes from Monterey, California, about an elderly lady who hesitated at a busy intersection.

A gentleman, noting her confusion, inquired, "Have you vertigo, madam?" She replied, "Yes, a mile."

At one Puntagon session, first prize went by default—and de
fault was that of Major Al Furst, of Norfolk (that Furst family of
Virginia you've been hearing about).

Major Furst's atrocity concerns two German lads named Hans
and Fritz—who else?—who were proceeding gingerly along a narrow mountain ridge with their mother in tow. Below them was a
drop of five thousand feet.

Fritz, who was in the lead, suddenly discovered that his mother
had disappeared. So he called back to his brother, "Look, Hans:
no mom."

When *Guys and Dolls* was being organized, an aspirant for a
minor singing role failed to meet the requirements of composer
Frank Loesser (pronounced Lesser) and his wife, Lynn.

The aspirant skulked into the night, muttering angrily, "I owe
my predicament to the evil of two Loessers."

A poker-loving spiritualist wanted another player for a Satur-
day-night session and summoned the ghost of a departed companion. The ghost was delighted to sit in on the game, and on the
very first hand drew five beautiful hearts. He bet his stack.

Unfortunately, one of the flesh-and-blood players had a pat full
house and raked in the pot—just one more time when the spirit
was willing but the flush was weak.

Sigmund Spaeth insists that you hear about the Peruvian prince
who fished a beautiful maiden out of an enchanted lake and made
her his before the Inca was even dry. . . . In baseball-mad Chicago, Carl Kroch, endeavoring to teach his beautiful wife German, asked, "Was sagst du?" She answered, "They lost, 7 to 1."
. . . Matt Rae knows a dentist who was summoned by Poet Carl

Sandburg to alleviate a toothache. After some investigation he whispered to an assistant, "My reputation is made! I've discovered Carl's bad Caverns."

As Noah remarked while the animals were boarding the Ark, "Now I herd everything."

Q is for
QUALITY FOLK

Get Rich and Worry!

Life among the high and flighty is very luxurious and glittering, but with every million in the bank come new dilemmas and distractions that never bother ordinary folk at all. Even the children of the rich can't escape them—for all their silver spoons and golden high chairs.

The seven-year-old daughter of a Hollywood millionaire, for instance, was a guest at a birthday party where all the other kids were gobbling ice cream with gusto. She, however, sought out the birthday child's mother and asked severely, "May I feel quite sure that this is Harmon's Non-Allergic Ice Cream?"

Taxes, of course, are a perpetual thorn in the side of the wealthy. A member of the class of '19 at Princeton had a hard time persuading two of his wealthiest classmates to join him in promoting a new corporation that he hoped would earn a fortune. Both agreed the enterprise looked good, but pointed out that, because of taxes, it meant nothing more to them than additional headaches.

"I know," agreed the promoter, "but you two are my oldest friends, and I wouldn't feel right about going into this deal without you."

"All right," agreed the wealthier of the two reluctantly, "but one thing must be distinctly understood in advance. If we make the money you predict—you have to keep it."

As though a new house owner in the suburbs hasn't enough worries, with mortgages, furnishings, landscaping, and water supply to look after, he's also faced with the problem of finding a clever and appropriate name for the estate. Brilliant gems of wit like "Bankruptcy Court," "So-and-so's Folly," and "Tottering-on-the-Brink" usually are discarded in the nick of time, and when the shiny new station wagon makes its first trip to the village, a time-honored and safe stand-by like "The Willows," "River View," or "Gooseberry Hill" is painted on its side.

A few die-hards, however, have insisted on house names that are unique. Alexander Woollcott dubbed his place "Wit's End." A publisher selected "Galleys West." Thyra Samter Winslow, upon acquiring the smallest house in Greenwich Village, aptly named it "Writer's Cramp." Another author chose "The Palazzo Thickens."

The home of Westchester's most gracious and indefatigable hostess is known as "Sans Repos." An old geometry professor at Williams retired to a manse appropriately titled "After Math." A pillar of Alcoholics Anonymous selected "Chez When." A barrister converted a hayloft into a modernistic villa and christened it "Barn Yesterday." John Barrymore referred to his first country seat as "Barrymore's Bluff." The publisher of a successful line of 25-cent books named his hacienda "The Quarters." And they say that Paul Hoffman, appalled at the number of petitioners seeking largesse from the Ford Foundation he heads, is toying with re-naming his estate "Itching Palms."

The secretaries of mighty industrialists are not necessarily brilliant—but I've noticed they're always beautiful. A brand-new one was summoned by Banker Paul Warburg one morning and told, "My phone seems to be out of order. Please ask the phone company to get somebody over here to fix it." "Who shall I ask for?" inquired the secretary. "The president," suggested Warburg, sarcastically.

An hour later, a workman in overalls, toting a repair kit, barged into Warburg's office without knocking and emptied his tools on the floor with a crash. Warburg's anger was appeased when he got a good look at the impolite workman. It was his good friend, Walter Gifford, then head of the Board of American Telephone and Telegraph Company.

At a glittering opening night on Broadway appeared a famous oil tycoon, on his arm a magnificently proportioned babe who had been dancing in a night-club chorus till a few evenings before. From the play, the tycoon took her on a dizzy round of gay spots, and finally, delighted with her understanding ways, pressed a diamond clip into her hot little palm. "You darling man," she cooed, "it's such a business doing pleasure with you!"

A stranger from the East wandered into Slip Muldoon's Crazy Gulch Saloon and tried to cash a check for a hundred dollars. Slip leaned across the bar and assured the Easterner in a stage whisper, "You look like an all-right character and your check is probably good for a hundred thousand bucks. But I don't trust them big New York banks. They'll probably gyp both of us!"

At one of those unbearably fancy new candy stores on Fifth Avenue, seemingly modeled after the boudoir of a big-time French courtesan, the wife of the editor of a Jewish newspaper wandered in to sample the wares. "I'll take five pounds of those chocolates over there," she decided. "Modom means the bon bons, no doubt," a suave clerk in a cutaway corrected gently. "I also would like five pounds of those cookies," continued the lady. "Ah," breathed the clerk, "our petits fours. Shall we deliver your purchase in our Rolls limousine now drawn up before the portals?" "Nah," said the lady. "I'll carry it home myself." This was too much for the elegant clerk. "Don't be silly," he burst out. "Why schlepp a package that big around the streets?"

A prosperous-looking gent approached the manager of one of Miami Beach's swankiest new hostelries and asked to be shown the best available room. The manager led him to the most expensive suite in the establishment, pointing out, "This overlooks the ocean." The customer said it wouldn't do. The manager took him to his second-best accommodation, saying, "This isn't on the ocean, of course, but it does overlook our steam-heated swimming pool." Again the customer demurred. When he also rejected a third suite, "overlooking the tropical garden," the manager became a trifle impatient, and asked, "Just what have you got in mind, sir?" The customer announced firmly, "What I'm looking for is a room that overlooks the rent."

There have been so many new luxury hotels erected in Miami Beach in the past twelve months that the current fashion is to accost any tourist, ask him where he's stopping, and regardless of his reply, sneer, "That's last year's hotel."

A well-lubricated drummer staggered into a hotel lobby, and picked up a pen to register. As he did so a remarkable facsimile of a bedbug crawled across the desk. The drummer recoiled and informed the reception clerk, "I've been in lots of hotels, and I've been bitten by some mighty smart bedbugs, but—hic—this is the first time one ever came down to see what room I was getting!"

"Miss Potter," reproved her landlady, "I definitely thought I saw you sneaking a young gentleman up to your room with you last night." "You're not the only one," agreed Miss Potter. "I thought so too."

The Algonquin's famous boniface, the late Frank Case, loved William Faulkner personally, but was no admirer of his tortuous prose and grim pictures of depravity in the old South. Faulkner met him in the lobby one morning and complained, "I have kind of an upset stomach today." "Ah," sympathized Case, "something you wrote, no doubt?"

"Henry darling," said the blushing bride as the honeymooners drove up to the portico of the St. Regis, "let's try to convince all

the hangers-on in the lobby that we've been married for ages."
"Okay, my love," said Henry dubiously, "but do you think you
can carry four suitcases?"

Two Catskill hotel proprietors met on a train to New York. "Nu,
Sam," said one, "how's business this summer?" "I'll tell you,
Myron," was the reply, "we've got them sleeping under the beds.
The roof leaks."

Mrs. Goldschmidt is never going to let her husband talk her
into vacationing at sumptuous Morpheus Arms in the Catskills
again. "In the first place," she explains, "all the young girls did all
day was look for husbands. And in the second place, all the husbands did was look for young girls."

The late Ernie Byfield, boniface of Chicago's Ambassador East
Hotel, had his own way of expressing himself. A friend met him,
obviously elated, on the street of a Swiss village one day. "Why so
happy?" asked the friend. Byfield explained, "I just made a sucker
out of the Alps. I climbed them in spats."

The manager of a swanky hotel at French Lick stumbled over a
porter who was crouching in the corridor shining a pair of shoes.
"Ichabod," remonstrated the manager, "haven't I told you a hundred times not to clean shoes in the corridor, but to take them
down to the basement?" "Can't do it this time, boss," said Ichabod.
"The man in this room says he's from Scotland, and he's hanging
on to the laces."

One of the great stars of Hollywood cowboy sagas wired Toots Shor, the restaurateur, "Arriving New York in time for dinner, November ninth. Reserve table for two." Shor cautiously wired back, "Are you bringing your girl or your horse?"

A merchant in Allentown comes to New York twice a month to buy goods, and his favorite place to dine on such visits is a midtown restaurant that features not only good beef but four walls full of photographs of great movie stars, jockeys, and ball players, all autographed with messages of undying affection to the proprietor, Pasquale. After a while, the merchant couldn't help noticing that none of these glamour pusses was ever seen dining at the restaurant in person. Most of the patrons, in fact, invariably looked as though they, too, had just gotten off a train from Allentown. So he called over a waiter and grumbled, "Hey, how come I never see any of the big shots whose pictures you've got coming here in person. Have you ever spotted any of them yourself?" The waiter assured the merchant gravely, "Mister, I been working here myself for eight years, *and I never even met Pasquale!*"

Robert Haas knows a man who actually saw flying saucers. He walked up behind a plump waitress in a diner with an extended fishing pole in his hand.

August Belmont, famous epicure and member of New York and Newport's old "400," was once a guest of Robert Louis Stevenson in San Francisco. Stevenson took him to a certain restaurant off Market Street, and said, "An amazing feature of this place is that no waiter is ever permitted to say that any dish whatever is lacking from the menu. Ask for a slice of the moon and the waiter will solemnly march off to the kitchen to get it for you. Then he'll come back and tell you solemnly they're just out of it."

"I'll try them out," laughed Belmont, and ordered a double order of roast behemoth, rare. The waiter jotted down the order, only to report a moment later, "I'm very sorry . . ." "Oh ho," nodded Belmont. "You have no behemoth, eh?" "We have plenty of behemoth," said the waiter sharply, "but the truth is it's all so well done I know you wouldn't like it."

At last a rich man has been discovered who has a kind word to say about the U. S. Treasury Department! His name is Bill Goetz, a famous movie tycoon, art collector, and owner of the race horse "Your Host."

You may have read how Goetz bought a hitherto uncatalogued self-portrait of Van Gogh called "Study by Candlelight" for $45,-000 in Europe, and imported it to his home in California. Then a storm broke. Many connoisseurs said it was genuine. An equal

number declared it bogus. Goetz told me how he figured a way to make the U. S. Treasury render a final verdict. Here's his story:

According to statutes on the books, art masterpieces may be imported into our country free, but on reproductions there is an impost of 10 per cent of the purchase price.

Goetz shipped his controversial Van Gogh back to Amsterdam, then reimported it, valued at $50,000. The first time it came over, customs officers had accepted it as an original without question, but now the hubbub and excitement put them in a pretty quandary.

"Why not reduce the estimated value to $500?" the Treasury men begged Goetz. "Then you pay only a nominal $50 duty, and we're off the hook." "Nothing doing," said Goetz firmly. "If it's an original—and I'm convinced that it is—I don't pay a bloody cent. If it's a copy, I pay my $5,000 duty like a good citizen."

Result: The Treasury Department had to hire the greatest art experts in the land to decide the issue. They finally rendered their verdict—the picture is genuine! Back on the wall of the Goetz study it went, now worth conservatively five times its purchase price, and the dealers who once derided Goetz as a sucker have retreated disconsolately into their galleries muttering, "If you've got to Van Gogh, you've got to Van Gogh."

In England, a famous painter of our own day, the late Sir John Lavery, stared fixedly at a lady at a party, strode to her side and confessed, "I don't recall your name, but your features are certainly familiar to me."

"They jolly well ought to be," she told him sharply. "I paid you five thousand pounds to paint them!"

The late Lord Duveen, most spectacular art dealer of our time, operated on the theory that Europe had plenty of art while America had plenty of money—and that it was his job to provide better balance. He sold one client—Mr. Jules Bache—so many expensive paintings that when Miss Green, director of the Morgan Library, first saw the Bache collection she murmured "How utterly Duveen!" S. N. Behrman, who has written Duveen's story, says that he made millionaire clients seek *him* out; he never made the first approach. Informed, for instance, that Mr. Edsel Ford had begun to acquire an expensive art collection, Duveen observed loftily, "He's not ready for me yet. Let him go on buying. Some day he'll be big enough for me!" Some of Duveen's clients —Mellon, Rockefeller, Frick, Morgan, Kress—thought nothing of paying him half a million dollars for an art masterpiece. They agreed with his oft-proclaimed theory that "You can get all the pictures you want at ten thousand dollars apiece—but to find ones worth half a million—I say, that takes doing!"

Children could resist Lord Duveen's powers of persuasion no more successfully than well-heeled adult collectors. One day at the seaside, Duveen's young daughter refused to dive into the briny; it was much too cold, she declared. Lord Duveen gravely gathered some sticks on the beach, started a bonfire, borrowed a kettle, boiled some water in it, and then poured it into the Atlantic Ocean. Completely satisfied, his daughter dove in without the slightest hesitation.

At a certain stage of life there comes to every person the irrepressible urge to collect something. Paintings, books, china, rare coins and stamps provide the usual outlet for such yearnings, but some notable individualists have gone much further afield.

The late Crosby Gaige, for instance, had a passion for models of useless inventions, such as mechanical back-scratchers. Most of them looked like the handiwork of Rube Goldberg, and they took up a whole floor of an office building by the time he died. A man in Springfield, Massachusetts, has one of the oddest collections of all. He goes in for dinosaur tracks! He sent one of his treasures, imprinted in a block of solid stone, to his son for Christmas last year. The son was not too appreciative—especially when the stone fell on his toe and laid him up for five weeks.

There are a number of allegedly living and solvent citizens (Jim Marshall does the alleging) whose names and addresses make complete sentences. Here's the evidence:

> Hans R. Dirty, Jr., Goan, Wash.
> Quoth D. Raven, Never, Mo.
> G. Thirza Mighty, Pritty, Miss.
> Ide Lamy, Down, N.D.
> Lettice Finder, Shady, Del.
> F. U. Pager, Income, Tex.
> I. M. Phelan, Slightly, Ill.
> Daniel Inner, Lyons, Tenn.
> Wish I. Newther, Reese, N.Y.
> C. U. Sunday, Early, Mass.
> Allis Frenza, Deadan, Conn.
> R. R. Crossing, Look, N.C.
> Will U. Raider, Cookie, Ga.

R is for RAILROADS

A seedy-looking gent stumbled into a parlor-car seat directly opposite a very correct Boston lady, who held on her lap an equally haughty, bespectacled little girl. The lady quite obviously found the proximity of the seedy gent objectionable. In fact, she took the extraordinary step of leaning across the aisle and whispering, "I think you should know that my little girl is just recuperating from a bad case of smallpox, which is still probably contagious." "Don't let that worry you for a moment," said the seedy one, unperturbed. "I'm going to cut my throat in the first tunnel anyhow."

There's a station on a one-track Maine branch line to which passengers descend via a rickety staircase. Alongside it is a chute used to slide down packing cases and heavy baggage.

Local tradition has it that an elderly lady once came whizzing down the chute, clutching her hat in one hand and a straw valise in the other. At the bottom she pulled herself together and exclaimed, "You'd think a big railroad company would make it a little easier for passengers to get down to their ding-busted trains!"

Two lads were sauntering along a railroad track when one suddenly stopped, picked up a girl's arm, and exclaimed, "I believe that's Gwendolyn!" "Don't be silly," chided the other. "How can you jump to the conclusion that's any particular girl just by seeing an arm?" A moment later, the first lad discovered a leg along the right of way and repeated, "I'm surer than ever that's Gwendolyn." "Nonsense," scoffed his friend. "It's not Gwendolyn at all." The same argument ensued when another arm, and then a torso turned up, but then the second lad spied a girl's head next to the track. Examining the head intently, he cried, "By George, it *is* Gwendolyn!" Then he entreated, "Gwendolyn! For Pete's sake! *Pull yourself together!*"

A little man in a Pennsylvania Railroad day-coach created quite a stir recently with his loud and repeated claims that he really was General George Washington traveling incognito. Of course, nobody believed him—till he got off at Mt. Vernon.

The president of a great Southern railroad is noted for his patience and humility. He says he got a lesson he never forgot the first day he was appointed station master in a tiny Mississippi way-stop. Two Negro farmers came along to ask some questions regarding a bill of lading, and the new official decided to put on the dog. The Negroes waited patiently while he bustled about the station doing nothing, and then one said very distinctly to the other, "Dat's life for you, brother! De littler de station, de bigger de agent." What the young official learned that moment helped make him president of the road!

When the Mobile and Southern Railroad explained to Deacon Smedley that a proposed cut-off would run right through the spot where his barn stood, and offered him ten times the worth of the property for his consent, Smedley astounded everybody, his wife in particular, by turning a deaf ear to the proposal. He defended his stand to his outraged wife by shouting, "Dang it, do ye think I'm goin' to keep running out to that barn day and night to open and shut the door every time they want to run a train through?"

A band of hoboes enjoyed an unexpected windfall when they discovered a trim forty-foot yacht tied down to a flatcar in a freight yard at Barstow, California, not long ago.

The yacht was being shipped across the country by Charles and Jessie Hilton. The hoboes moved in and lived the carefree life of the bounding main until they were discovered in Kansas. They scattered hastily, crying, "All ashore" and "Cast anchor," and lost their sea legs in the historic port of Wichita.

It seems to me that an ingenious script writer could build a hilarious motion picture around this episode. The Hiltons, meanwhile, are building a new yacht.

When the conductor on an Arkansas local came through collecting tickets, an old gentleman simply couldn't find his in any pocket. Suddenly a man across the aisle laughed and said, "Jeb, you're holding it in your teeth." The conductor punched the ticket and passed on down the aisle. "Jeb, you're sure getting absent-minded," pursued the man across the aisle. "Absent-minded nothing," whispered old Jeb angrily. "I was chewing off last year's date."

Harpo Marx came down to the Pasadena station one day to see a friend off for the East. He was engaging in some characteristic clowning on the platform when he noticed two Helen Hokinson ladies gazing with undisguised horror from the diner on the train the friend was boarding. Impulsively, Harpo hopped aboard, rushed up to the ladies' table in the diner, sprinkled salt on their menu and gulped it down.

With no change of expression, one of them summoned the steward and commanded, "Kindly give us another menu. Somebody has eaten ours."

Winston Churchill, like all men who do a dozen things at the same time, is always pressed to keep appointments and arrive at stations, piers, and airports on time. Asked why he missed so many trains and boats, Mr. Churchill explained, "I'm a sporting man, my boy. I always give them a fair chance to get away."

A returned traveler from Wales reports that whenever the through trains stop at Llanfechpwllgogerych the guards simply call out, "If anybody's getting out here, this is it."

Most people, at one time or another, have fallen asleep in a railroad car, and awakened somewhere in the yards. An unfortunate in South Africa went them one better recently, however. He curled up for a nap in an empty day coach. During the night the coach was moved to the repairs depot. When dawn broke, the sleeper yawned luxuriously, took one glance out of the window, and let out a yelp of horror. His car, suspended from a big crane, was dangling two hundred feet above the track.

Eli Bohnen, of Providence, remembers a Baptist minister in a New Mexico town who rushed down to the station every single day to watch the Sunset Limited go by. There was no chore he wouldn't interrupt to carry out this ritual. Members of his congregation deemed his eccentricity juvenile and frivolous, and asked him to give it up. "No, gentlemen," he said firmly. "I preach your sermons, teach your Sunday school, bury your dead, marry you, run your charities, chairman every drive it pleases you to conduct. I won't give up seeing that Southern Pacific train every day. I love it. It's the only thing that passes through this town that I don't have to push!"

Averell Harriman, who once ran the whole Union Pacific Railroad, was present when a young minister gave his first sermon in a Sun Valley church. It went on and on, and several members of the congregation predicted he'd never do. Harriman was more optimistic, however. "I considered it a good trial run," he said. "The young man's service will improve as soon as he gets better terminal facilities."

It was in Utah that the last spike was driven in America's first railroad to the Pacific—at Promontory on May 10, 1869—but history books have spared us some of the less glamorous details. In the first place, the Union Pacific Special from the East was held up by floods and arrived three days late. Chinese laborers on the Central Pacific and the Irishmen who had laid the tracks for the U.P. amused themselves in the interim by taking pot shots at one another. There were some forty casualties, including one innocent bystander from San Francisco. In the second place, the ceremonies dragged on too long; the crowd shivered in an icy wind, and drifted away before the climax. In the third place, Governor Leland Stanford of California, chosen to drive in the last golden spike (it was removed immediately), lifted his head on the backswing, missed the spike entirely, and fell on his face in the mud. An alert telegrapher, however, simulated the blow with his key,

and a waiting multitude on both coasts (including Wall Street)
cheered the completion of the first transcontinental railroad span.
Luckily for Governor Stanford, television was still eighty years
away.

R is for
RELIGION

Fulton J. Sheen relates that shortly after his elevation to the rank of Bishop he made the first of his many appearances on television, and stopped for a cup of coffee at the drugstore in the building where the studio was located, with his red cape already in place. The girl at the counter, obviously used to serving actors in every kind of costume, took the red cape very much in stride and asked blithely, "What's yours, Cock Robin?"

Joe Harrington, the Boston sage, tells of a Sunday-school teacher who suddenly stopped reading a passage in the Bible and asked her pupils, "Why do you believe in God?" She got a variety of answers, some full of simple faith, others obviously insincere. The one that stopped her cold came from the son of one of Boston's best-known ministers. He frowned, and answered thoughtfully, "I guess it just runs in our family."

In the Breton village of Cancale, Roger Vercel watched the traditional ceremony of the regional bishop blessing the fishermen before they set out for their annual two-month expedition on the high seas in their tiny vessels. Vercel said to the bishop, "They all revere you deeply, yet they all vote Communist. Can't you do anything about that?" "It's difficult," sighed the bishop. "They know that God controls the storms and tides, but the Communists, alas, control the price of fish."

Sister Carmelita won the big final game at a church bingo party and decided to indulge a craving she had concealed for years. She bought herself a beautiful fur coat. The day it arrived, she donned it hastily and walked proudly down Main Street, admired by all and sundry. Suddenly, however, her bishop drew alongside in his shiny new limousine and chided her for not putting her windfall to better use. "May I remind you, Sister Carmelita," he concluded,

"that no saint ever has been known to require an expensive fur coat?" "Quite true," agreed Sister Carmelita cheerfully, "but I'd also like to know of one character in the Bible who rolled around the Holy Land in an eight-cylinder limousine."

Three lads fell to boasting about the earning capacities of their respective fathers. Said the doctor's son, "My pa operated on a movie producer last month and sent him a bill for a cool five thousand." The lawyer's son spoke up, "Shucks, what's that? My old man was the mouthpiece for a big racketeer a week ago and got a fee of ten grand for one day's work—all paid in crisp new thousand-dollar bills." The minister's son said quietly, "On Sunday, my father preached a sermon in church, and it took eight men to bring in the money."

An old bishop in the nation's capital was sick to death of the socials and embassy parties he was expected to attend every other afternoon. At one of them he entered wearily, glanced sourly at the over-familiar cast of characters, and sank into the nearest chair. The hostess asked coyly, "A spot of tea, Bishop?" "No tea," he growled. "Coffee, Bishop?" "No coffee." An understanding woman, she whispered in his ear, "Scotch and water, Bishop?" Said the bishop, brightening, "No water."

A group of world leaders in the Presbyterian Church met in Scotland for a conference and, on a warm summer's afternoon, went off to explore the beautiful countryside. Coming to a temporary bridge that spanned a swift-running stream, they started confidently to cross it. When they were half way over, the bridge keeper suddenly appeared and hollered that the bridge had been declared unsafe. The spokesman for the church party didn't quite hear the keeper's admonition and called back, "It's all right, my friend. We're Presbyterians from the conference." The bridge keeper replied, "If ye dinna get off the bridge this minute ye'll all be Baptists!"

The first time four-year-old Mary was taken to church by her parents, she was absolutely fascinated by the earnest young minister, high in his pulpit, who was given to involved rhetoric and wild waving of his arms. Finally Mary whispered to her mother, "What will we do if he ever gets out?"

A distinguished Broadway star is known far and wide for the deep religious strain in her character. A few seasons ago, just before the opening of an important play, she announced to the cast, "I don't pay no mind to what any of you think. I'm going to pray for our success tonight." Thereupon she dropped to her knees on the center of the stage, cast her eyes heavenward, and implored, "Oh, Lord, help all of us give a fine performance this evening. Let me give the best that's in me. Let the rest of the company make the hits of their lives. Let the critics approve. And one thing more, oh, Lord, keep that blank-blank stage director from lousing up this play for us."

A minister in Oklahoma was preaching such a powerful sermon that an excited (and beautiful) young lady in the balcony leaned over too far and crashed through the railing. Her dress caught in a chandelier, and she was suspended in mid-air. The minister noted her undignified position and thundered to his congregation, "Any person who looks up at poor Miss Duggan will be stricken blind." A deacon in the third row whispered to his companion, "I'm going to risk one eye."

There's a venerable psychotic patient on Welfare Island who spends her entire time reading the Bible. She explains, "I'm cramming for the finals."

The parson's wife in a small Connecticut town is a wonder at making a little go a long way, and boasts that she never throws away one scrap of edible food. One of her dinners consisted entirely of leftovers. The parson viewed the food on the table with some distaste and began picking at his food in silence. "My dear," reproved his wife, "you've forgotten to ask the blessing." "If you can point out one item on the menu," he answered sharply, "that hasn't been blessed at least three times before, I'll see what a little praying can do for it."

The new minister looked at Squire Canfield coldly and said, "I'm told you went to the ball game instead of church Sunday." "That's a lie," cried Squire Canfield hotly, "and I've got the fish to prove it."

A young clergyman, about to preach his first sermon, was a bundle of nerves as he waited in the vestry. Would his voice carry? Would he hold his fashionable audience? Above all, did he look his best? "Dear me," he reflected aloud, "if only there was a glass here." A moment later the verger tapped him on the shoulder and whispered, "Here's a whole bottle. All I had to do was mention your name."

When Parson Johnson saw Mrs. Sumter, whom he roundly detested, coming up his garden path, he sought refuge upstairs in the study and remained hidden for a full hour. Finally he risked calling down to his wife, "Has that horrible bore gone yet?" His wife, equal to any occasion, answered sweetly, "Yes, dear, she went long ago. Mrs. Sumter is here now."

A young man barged into a minister's study, a lovely young lady in tow, and exclaimed, "We want to get married. I beg you to make the ceremony as brief as possible. Here are our credentials. I assure you they're in order. Those ladies knitting in the corner will do fine as witnesses." The minister, amused, performed the ritual, gratefully pocketed a fifty-dollar bill, then protested, "Remember the old adage about marrying in haste, my children. What's your hurry?" The young man, already half way to the door, explained over his shoulder, "We're double parked!"

R is for
ROMANCE

A bashful swain wrote to an advice-to-the-lovelorn column in San Francisco, "Last night I treated a young lady to dinner, theatre, a night club, and a twenty-mile ride home in a taxi. Do you think I should have kissed her good night?" "Certainly not," answered the sarcastic editor. "You did enough for her as it is!"

Hoarsely the impassioned swain begged, "Whisper those three little words that will make me walk on air." So the debutante sweetly told him, "Go hang yourself."

Rupert Hughes claims he knows the origin of kissing. "A prehistoric man," avers Hughes, "discovered one day that salt helped him survive the fierce summer heat. He also discovered he could get the salt by licking a companion's cheek. The next thing he observed was that the process became ever so much more interesting when the companion belonged to the opposite sex. First thing you know, the whole tribe had forgotten all about salt."

There was a long line waiting to use the only public telephone booth in the neighborhood, and when a young thing with blonde curls and a huge vanity bag strapped over her shoulder prepared to enter, the experienced men behind her sighed in unison and resigned themselves to the inevitable. The young thing, however, sensed what was going on in their minds. "Don't you all fret," she told them sweetly. "I'll only be a minute. I just want to hang up on him!"

Somebody has defined adolescence as the period when a girl begins to powder and a boy begins to puff. Another says a boy has reached that stage when he knows why a strapless gown must be held up, but doesn't understand how.

Roger Price is fond of extolling the virtues of his nineteen-year-old cousin Sally, who certainly sounds like an unusual lass. For instance, cites Roger, she went to one party where she had the boys neglecting every other girl in the place because she was the only one who had the sense to come naked. Another time she was approached by a virile stranger who slipped a note into her hot little palm that read, "You are the only woman I ever have loved. Come to my room, 648, at the Grand Hotel at midnight." Sally wasn't sure he was sincere, however, because the note was mimeographed.

Humphrey Jones, known as the great lover in the wholesale house where he worked, seemed so listless and depressed one morning that Coombs, at the next desk, called over, "Hey, Humphrey, I'll bet that new girl you've been raving about gave you the heave-ho." "It isn't that," said Jones glumly, "but I'm afraid she isn't quite so exclusive as she had led me to believe.

She moved into a new apartment last Tuesday, and you know what she spent all Wednesday doing? Going from one phone booth to another, changing her number on the walls!"

A winsome chick gave up her job at the Copacabana night club to marry an auto executive in Detroit. "He's the knight I always dreamed would appear out of the West to win me," she gurgled. "He's tall, dark, and has some."

Bernard Shaw's criticism of the marriage ritual: "When two people are under the influence of the most violent, most insane, most delusive and most transient of passions, they are required to solemnly swear they will remain in that excited, abnormal and exhausting condition continuously until death do them part."

"Yes, sir," said the installment furniture salesman to a prospective bridegroom, "you just furnish the bride and we'll do the rest." "If you don't mind," suggested the bridegroom, "let's change places!"

"Alone at last," sighed a bridegroom to his bride—but he was wrong, for at that precise moment, a pistol was poked into his ribs, and a gruff voice commanded, "Put 'em up." The intruder, obviously experienced, headed straight for the jewel box on the dresser, but then he got a real glimpse of the bride in her negligee. Hastily drawing a circle on the floor with his heel, he commanded the groom, "Into this circle, lug, and if you move out of it, I'll shoot you full of holes." So the poor groom stood in the circle and watched in misery while the intruder made love to his bride. When he finally made his exit—having quite forgotten the jewels, incidentally—the bride turned on the groom and cried, "How could you stand there and watch a total stranger making love to your wife? Are you a man or a mouse?"

"A man," proclaimed the bridegroom vehemently. "You didn't notice, I expect, but every time that fellow had his back turned, I stuck my foot right out of the circle."

The statistical department of Brides House, Inc., bullish by nature on everything pertaining to matrimony, announces that the average wedding presents a whopping $4820 sales opportunity to alert merchants. Furthermore, that figure includes only what's bought by the bride, groom, and members of the wedding troupe, and does not take into account the gifts. The chief items of expenditure are: household equipment, $1633; home furnishings, $1820; dresses, $360; coats and suits, $225; lingerie, $219; luggage, $180; shoes, $106; linens and bedding, $181; millinery, $96. Paste these figures in your hat, and the next time somebody groans "What price matrimony?" you'll have a pat answer ready! Brides House also predicts that 13 persons out of every 1000 in

the country will choose a mate during the coming year—and Dale Carnegie will see to it that most of them read "Ideal Marriage" before taking the vows.

Dr. Morris Fishbein, one of the medical marvels of the age that does not come in the form of pills, writes that he attended a wedding recently where he found the one male dressed in tuxedo standing mournfully in an alcove. "I take it," hazarded the good doctor, "that you are the groom." "You take it wrong," the mournful one replied. "I was eliminated in the semi-finals."

An item for the "father of the bride" department from Hasbrouck Heights, New Jersey: A delicate young bride-to-be sighed to her mother, "Oh dear, there are so many things to do before the wedding, and I don't want to overlook the most insignificant detail." "Don't you worry your pretty little head," said the mother grimly. "I'll see that he's there."

A rueful bridegroom told an inquiring reporter, "I never knew what happiness was until I got married—and then it was too late."

On the porch of Vanderschlitz Manor Mrs. Nussbaum mourned, "My boy never should have married that Davis girl. In a year she turned him into a pauper." "Really?" nodded Mrs. Gross pleasantly. "A girl or a boy?"

S is for SPORTS

Thanks to the coaxial cable, about forty million television fans can now see every play in baseball's annual classic, the World Series, with their own eyes. 'Twas not ever thus. In the old days, the nearest a real fan could get to a Series game was a seat behind a post in right field. The good seats were reserved for politicians, movie stars and Broadway big shots who might not know a squeeze play from an umpire, but thought this was the place to be when the newsreel cameras started grinding.

Miss Lily Pons, the beautiful coloratura soprano, was thus discovered in a box seat for the opening game of a recent Series. "I didn't know you were a baseball fan," commented a reporter.

"Indeed I am," enthused Miss Pons. "I wouldn't miss this game for the world. By the way, who is playing?"

Jerome Herman Dean, better known as "Dizzy" to admiring baseball fans all over the country, is even better behind the mike than he was on the mound pitching for the old St. Louis Cardinal gas-house gang in the thirties—and higher praise than that hath no diamond enthusiast.

Ted Shane has dug up a Dizzy Dean anecdote I never heard before. Seems the Diz once bet a crony two bits he could fan Joe

Di Maggio's big brother, Vince, every time he faced him one afternoon. Vince obligingly whiffed his first three times up, but on his fourth trip to the plate, lifted a harmless little pop back of the plate. Dean hollered to his catcher, "Drop it, or I'm ruint!" Then he burned over the next pitch for strike three.

Dizzy Dean thinks he knows how Red Russia could be brought into line. "I'd get me a buncha bats and balls and learn them kids behind the Iron Curtain how to play baseball instead of totin' rifles and swallerin' lies. And if Joe Stallion ever learnt how much dough there was in the concessions at a ball park, he'd quit communism and get into a honest business."

One batter, according to Arthur Daly, who never had the slightest difficulty solving the delivery of the great Dizzy Dean was Bill Terry, the famous Giant first-baseman. One afternoon Terry almost tore Dean's legs off with a wicked liner through the box. The next time up he scorched Diz's ear with a sizzler that went rocketing into center field. His third hit almost tore off Dean's glove.

Pepper Martin sauntered over from third base and suggested to the outraged Dean, "Dizzy, I don't think you're playing this bird Terry deep enough!"

Jimmy Dykes, the famous baseball player and manager, tells this story on himself.

When he first joined the A's back in 1918, he struck out four times in his first game. On his next turn Connie Mack used a pinch hitter. Jimmy sulked on the bench, but the understanding Connie soothed him. "I suppose you know why I took you out," said Mack. "You see, the American League record for striking out is five times in one game, and I didn't want you to tie it in your very first big league game."

Joe McCarthy recalls a year in the Depression when the mighty Babe Ruth was asked to submit to the first salary cut of his career. To say that he demurred is putting it mildly. He insisted on his customary eighty-thousand-dollar contract. "But, Babe," protested an official of the Yankee ball club, "these are trying times. That's more money than Hoover got last year for being President of the United States." "I know," persisted the Babe, "but I had a better year than Hoover."

Add this story to the saga of the wacky Brooklyn Dodger baseball squad that toiled without signals (because they couldn't remember any) under the indulgent management of the late Wilbert Robinson. "Uncle Robbie's" particular problem child was Babe Herman, who could whack that old apple a mile, but never learned big-league fielding or base-running finesse. Herman could always melt Uncle Robbie's wrath with a wisecrack. His little son also had a special spot in the rotund manager's heart. One day, however, when the kid climbed trustingly onto Robbie's lap, he was dumped unceremoniously to the Ebbets Field turf. The manager pointed an accusing finger at the six-year-old and barked, "Why ain't your old man hitting?"

The same Babe Herman was informed by a downtown Brooklyn bank one day that an impostor was signing his name to worthless checks and cashing them several times a week. "The next time he comes in," proposed Babe, "take him out in the back yard and knock a few flies his way. If he catches any, you'll know it isn't me."

The venerable Negro pitching star, Satchel Paige, is used mainly in relief roles these days, and accordingly gets mighty few chances to show his batting prowess. He did come to the plate in a late inning of a tie game at the St. Louis park one evening, however, and rapped a hot grounder between shortstop and third that almost any other player in the league could have beaten out with ease. "Satch" was thrown out by four steps. "Why didn't you run?" cried the Brownie manager. "Counter," said Satch. "Whaddya mean, 'counter'?" roared the manager. Satch explained, "Counter mah feet hurt."

The New York Yankees are generally regarded as aristocrats in the major-league baseball hierarchy, but their star catcher, Yogi Berra, travels around the country with a valise that looks as though it saw service in the Mexican War in the 1840s. A baseball newshawk asked Yogi, "Why don't you treat yourself to a new suitcase?" "What for?" argued Yogi. "The only time I ever use it is when I travel." Earl Wilson pointed out Yogi to a visiting Hollywood glamour girl at Nicky Blair's restaurant one evening. "That's the best catcher in the American League," said Earl. "Zat so?" gurgled the starlet. "What did he catch?"

Svenborg managed to stay on the Yale football squad all season, although he never got into a game. His only contribution consisted in acting as a tackling dummy at practice sessions, and sitting huddled up in a robe at the end of the bench during games. The Harvard fray, however, produced so many minor injuries that, near the end of the final quarter, Coach Hickman had poured every member of the squad but Svenborg into the line-up. Time was called while still another Yale stalwart was carried off the field. The coach's eyes traveled along the empty bench until they encountered Svenborg. A wild hope surged through Svenborg's veins. "Gee, coach," he marveled. "Are you gonna send me in?" "I should say not," snapped Hickman. "Just get up. I'm gonna send in the bench!"

Remember a football team that came up from the South years ago from tiny Centre College and beat the then-mighty Harvard eleven? The nickname for the valiant little Centre squad was "the praying colonels" because at crucial junctures of a contest all the boys would kneel and pray. H. Allen Smith avers that one day in the dressing room, the Centre coach suddenly cried, "Down to your knees, boys, here comes Grantland Rice!"

Kip Taylor, Oregon State mentor, has the final solution for the regulation of big-time football: one squad for offense, one for defense—and one to attend classes.

In these days when college football stadiums seat 90,000 or more spectators, it is interesting to note the comment made once by Andrew W. White, co-founder of Cornell University and its first president. Asked for permission to send the Cornell squad to Ann Arbor for a game, he replied indignantly, "I will not permit thirty men to travel four hundred miles to agitate a bag of wind."

"Pop" Gabardine, coach of a Midwestern football team, had seen his charges trampled eight Saturday afternoons in a row, the last time by a humiliating score of 55 to 0. When the squad re-gathered the following Monday, "Pop" said bitterly, "For the last game of the season, we might as well forget all the trick plays I tried to teach you dimwits. We're going back to fundamentals. Let's go! Lesson number one: this object I am holding is known as a football. Lesson number . . ." At this point, Coach Gabardine was interrupted by a worried fullback in the front row, who pleaded, "Hey, Pop, not so fast!"

California's Governor Earl Warren had to submit to quite a ribbing from Governor Adlai Stevenson of Illinois over the repeated failure of California's entries in the Rose Bowl football game to cope with elevens from the Midwest's "Big Ten." "Boast on," said Governor Warren finally, and with resignation, "but remember this: a whale never gets really harpooned until he comes up to spout."

Between halves of a tough professional football game, three stars of the winning team fell to talking about the circumstances that surrounded their leaving college to play for money. "I was a senior at Cornell," said the first, "and got grounded on calculus. I couldn't even begin to know what the prof was talking about." "It was advanced trigonometry that did me in," said the second. "In fact, it ran me right out of Kansas State in my junior year." The third player, late of U.C.L.A., sat staring moodily into space. Suddenly he spoke. "Say, did you boys ever run into a subject called long division?"

When Alfred Vanderbilt was elected President of the Thoroughbred Racing Association, he made a tour of all the leading tracks in the country to inspect the plants and racing conditions. Arriving in Lexington, Kentucky, he found a big sign strung across Main Street that read, "Welcome Vanderbilt." "Boy," he said appreciatively, "they sure take their horse racing seriously in this town." "Shucks, Al," his host informed him, "that sign isn't for you. Kentucky's football team is playing Vanderbilt University here tomorrow."

Millie Considine came back from the Kentucky Derby with a tale about an old Louisville hostelry that traditionally named one of its rooms for the winner of the big annual racing classic. There was a Zev room, a Gallant Fox room, a Whirlaway room, etc. After the 1946 Derby, however, the management was reluctantly compelled to abandon the idea. Winner that year was Assault.

Jonathan Daniels probably covered a thousand horse races—Kentucky Derbies and other classics of the track—during his newspaper career, but none of them made the impression on him occasioned by a race between five camels at a Carolina carnival early in the century. Nobody remembers who persuaded the owners of the five camels to stage the race, but the first thing anybody knew, news of the contest spread throughout the state, and people began to bet on the outcome. Perplexed bookies established initial odds of four to one against all five camels, but just before the race so many big bets were planked down on the one named Ben Ali—all of them, apparently, made by the Arab owners —that the bookies grew suspicious, and refused all further bets. Furthermore, they watched the race with eagle eyes for any sign of dirty work.

The race, to all intents and purposes, however, was fairly run. All five Arab owners pressed their mounts with equal fervor and determination, and when Ben Ali won easily, the bookies could find no excuse for withholding payment to the winners. One of them, his exchequer badly depleted, asked the Arab who had finished third, "What made all you birds bet everything on Ben Ali?"

The Arab explained, with a grin, "Mister, Ben Ali is what is known in our country as a bell camel. From the day of their birth, camels are taught to follow the bell camel!"

A huntsman in Texas had a harrowing experience one night this fall. He had killed a huge rattlesnake outside his tent before supper, and, just before going off to sleep, decided that the rattles would make a nice memento. With a practiced hand, he cut off the rattles in the dark.

The sight that greeted him the next morning stood his hair on end. The snake he had killed still had its rattles!

An intrepid bear stalker was recounting his triumphs to the boys around the cracker barrel one midwinter night. "I guess my closest shave," he recalled, "came the day I was walking unsuspectingly along a narrow mountain path when suddenly a giant grizzly crept up behind me, locked my arms in a tight embrace and then began squeezing the life out of me."

"What did you do?" obliged one of the boys with the expected show of suspense. "What the dickens could I do?" groaned the huntsman. "I had to marry his daughter."

A prominent decoration in the Gumbiner living room was a moosehead—but it was hung upside down. Mrs. Gumbiner's explanation was, "Papa shot it while it was lying on its back."

My uncle Al likes fishing in Wisconsin, and is still boasting about the prize muskegon he caught back in 1893 or 1894. "I'll tell you how big that fish was," he's fond of saying on little or no provocation. "The guide took a picture of it for me, and the picture alone weighed sixteen pounds!"

Amateur horseshoe pitchers, content to make one ringer out of ten and hopeful only of landing all their shots within a foot of the stake, wavered between incredulity and despair when they read that Ted Allen, of Boulder, Colorado, established a world's record with twenty-nine consecutive *double* ringers! Allen also killed a rabbit at forty feet by hanging a horseshoe around its neck. Hank Bradshaw testifies that any tournament topnotcher can light a match tied to the stake with one shoe and extinguish it with the next. He also says most of them will give you ten to one you can rest your chin on the top of the stake while they throw ringers under it. That's *your* chin, brother: not mine!

Reminds me of the time Squire Parsons visited the State Fair and planked down $1.40 in "slim dimes—the tenth part of a dollar" to see fourteen consecutive performances of Señor Hidalgo hurling knives into a board and making a silhouette with them around the body of his buxom blonde wife. Finally the squire shuffled off for home muttering disgustedly, "Shucks, the durn fool just misses her every time."

A polo expert (rated at nine goals by the international committee) explained the difference between polo and other sports to writer Bob Sylvester. "With athletes in other games," he noted, "the first thing that usually gives out is the legs. In polo, it's the money."

"A golf game involves all kinds of problems," Nussbaum told his wife. "Take the match I had with that Scotch fellow McGregor at the civic center course this morning. We're all square at the seventeenth hole, playing a two-dollar nassau, when McGregor loses his ball in a thick rough Naturally I go over and help him look for it, on account I don't want any monkey business from McGregor. He can't find his ball, however, and I start walking toward the green. Suddenly he yells after me, 'It's okay, Joe, here was that little ball of mine all the time.' I look back and there I see a ball right on the fairway, all beautifully teed up for a shot to the green, with McGregor happily pulling an approaching iron from his bag. And here, my dear, I am faced with a very serious problem. Just how am I going to be able to break the news to McGregor that all the time I've got his 'lost ball' in my pocket?"

The most believable golf story of the year appeared on the sports page of a Daytona Beach newspaper recently. It read, "At this point the gallery deserted the defending champion to watch Miss Blank, whose shorts were dropping on the green with astonishing regularity."

On the golf course at Echo Lake, Novelist Bud Kelland landed in a deep trap, and his three companions chuckled happily as they heard him blasting away out of sight. Back on the fairway, one asked, "How many shots did you have in that trap?" "Four," answered Bud. "We distinctly heard eight," he was told. "Remember where we are," he grumbled. "Four of them were echoes."

In the amusing *73 Years in a Sand Trap*, Fred Beck and O. K. Barnes tell of two confirmed rivals at the Lehigh Country Club in Allentown, Pa., who fought so consistently they finally agreed not to talk at all during a match.

All went smoothly and silently until the sixteenth hole, when the player identified as Doc walked ahead to a ball on the edge of the green while his opponent, Jack, climbed into a sand trap to play out. Jack took one swing, then another, and another, finally topping a shot clear across the green and into a trap on the other side. Then he whanged the ball back into trap number one.

As he wearily recrossed the green, Doc broke the long silence. "May I say one word?" he asked. "Well," snarled Jack, "what is it?" Doc replied, "You're playing with my ball."

T is for
TELEVISION
And Radio

Nine times out of ten, when you think your favorite television actor is wearing a white shirt, it's actually light blue or some other neutral color. The color white reflects a glare from the powerful overhead lights and casts an unflattering shadow over the actor's neckline.

With that thought in mind, Paul Hartman, who usually performs his burlesque dance routines in white tie and tails, ordered two stiff-bosomed evening shirts in blue. The mystified shirtmaker followed instructions—at $25 per instruction.

Hartman used the shirts with conspicuous success, and then consigned them to the laundry. But they didn't come back with either that week's wash or the next. They finally were delivered, accompanied by a note from the unhappy laundryman.

"We scrubbed and scrubbed these shirts," it read, "and finally succeeded in getting most of the blue out of them. If they are not absolutely white, please don't blame us."

In a round-up of the year's funniest radio "fluffs," Joe Bryan awards palm leaves with clusters to:

Jerry Lawrence for "When the King and Queen arrive you will hear a twenty-one sun galoot."

A commentator from Korea for "This brings back memories of the Bulgian Belch."

Mel Allen for "It's smope-piking time."

Ken Allyn for "Visit your nearest A and Poo Feed Store."

André Baruch for "Good evening, ladies and gentlemen of the audio radiance."

Fred Utal (first prize!) for "Have you tried Buppert's Reer?"

Jack Benny's debut in the theatre, according to a man named Fred Allen, who claims to be an authority, was so far back in the woods that the manager was a bear. Furthermore, says Fred, Benny's salary for the week was paid in honey. Shortly thereafter Jack took up golf, continues Mr. Allen, but by the time he could afford to lose a ball, he couldn't hit it that far. Even Fred concedes, however, that Jack has *some* virtues. (The whole feud, of course, is strictly for laughs; the two are devoted friends.) "There's a little good in everybody, in fact," he concludes. "Even a Mickey Finn has a couple of drops of good whiskey in it."

In *No People Like Show People,* Maurice Zolotow adds another item to the Jack Benny saga. Jack was once so down on his luck that when his agent heard a New Jersey pop vaudeville palladium was offering twenty-five dollars for a novelty animal act, he cried, "I'll take it." He borrowed two mangy Pekingese pups from a friend, carried them on-stage in the Jersey theatre, tied them to a piece of scenery, and proceeded to wow the audience with funny stories and wheezings on his fiddle. The manager forked over the twenty-five dollars with the reservation that this certainly was the most peculiar animal act he ever did see. "Don't those pups do any tricks at all?" he demanded. "They sure do," said Jack airily, "but not at these prices."

At the entrance of the CBS studio, Jack Benny was stopped by a moocher who claimed to be an old vaudeville pal and put the bee on Jack for a two-dollar loan. "I'll pay you back if it's the last thing I do," promised the poor fellow as he pocketed the two greenbacks. Benny forgot all about the incident until about eight months later, when, to his surprise, he received a letter from the man, postmarked Denver. "I've struck it rich in Colorado, Jack," he boasted. "Everything broke right at the same time. Happy days are here again. I've got a great job and a society girl is going to marry me. Thanks for everything." The letter had a postscript. "I am enclosing one dollar on account of my debt. I'll send the other just as soon as I can spare it!"

Goodman Ace says he's discovered how really to enjoy television. "We do it all with a six-foot screen," he explains gravely, and when his visitor invariably expresses astonishment, he adds, "Yes, it's a Japanese screen, and we place it directly in front of the television set."

The happiest man he's met in years, insists Robert Q. Lewis, is the parking-lot attendant across the way from the CBS studio. After ten years of juggling expensive convertibles and coupés, he's finally passed his driving test.

Tallulah Bankhead's triumph as a radio M.C. inspired one jealous rival to remark, "Tallu's gotten so high-hat she pronounces the second 'l' in 'Lincoln.'" Groucho Marx calls her technique "the timing of the shrew." She once barked at Bob Hope, "Get off this stage until I call for you." "Don't lower your voice to me," snapped Hope. "I knew you when you were Louis Calhern."

After listening to Tallulah struggle through a song on a "Big

Show" broadcast, Jimmy Durante confided, "I think you ought to have your tonsils out." "I've already had them out," she replied. Durante suggested, "Then put 'em back in."

A guest at La Bankhead's Connecticut retreat was astonished when a servant brought him a glass of straight gin the moment he awoke. "Better drink it, darling," called Tallu from the next room. "I warn you there won't be another round served up before breakfast."

When Gypsy Rose Lee heard Tallulah Bankhead boast, "In all the years I've been on the stage, I never once forgot my lines," she scoffed, "What's so great about that? No audience ever forgot *mine.*"

Miss Lee once asked her doctor to vaccinate her where it wouldn't show. "Okay," agreed the doctor. "Stick out your tongue." Gypsy told her radio audience she was descended from a long line her mother once listened to. "Whenever I go out with a wolf, I think of her," added Miss Lee. "On the way home I suggest, 'Let's walk. I'm much too tired to ride in a taxi with you.'"

A new comedy act recorded a half-hour show on radio recently for submission to a big sponsor. "But there's no audience in the studio," complained one of the comedians. "How are we gonna get laughs?" The agent said, "Don't worry. We'll tape in laughs from a Groucho Marx recording." "But won't Groucho get sore?" persisted the comic. "Nah," the agent assured him. "He doesn't know it, but we taped in *his* laughs from Fred Allen." It was Allen, incidentally, who swore that he saw one Western film on TV so old that the cowboy was riding a dinosaur. "This new medium," adds Allen, "isn't a country-wide mania—yet, anyhow. There are still several states where they think Television is just a city in Israel."

A young co-ed looked dreamily at the ceiling and declared, "The man I marry must be an outstanding personality, be musical, tell new jokes, sing and dance, stay home, neither drink nor smoke, and shut up when I tell him to." Her caller arose, looked for his hat, and told her, "Lady, you don't want a husband; you want a television set."

Ken Murray noticed that one of the curvaceous redheads in the chorus of his television show was disgruntled and morose. "Oh, it isn't you, Mr. Murray," she hastened to explain. "It's this lug from Omaha I been showing the town to the last coupla weeks. Before he goes home, he gives me a coupla checks. And every one of them bounced back from the bank, stamped, 'Insufficient Fun'."

My pet aversions in radio and television at the moment are those ham actors who turn up endlessly on commercials in white surgical robes to report on complicated and dreary laboratory tests for dentifrices and cigarettes. And what's so wonderful, incidentally, about every cigarette being so mild nobody can even taste it? Maybe those sponsors are miscalculating the toughness of male smokers. I have a notion that the first cigarette maker who announces a brand that's so strong, pungent, and full-bodied it will knock your teeth out will sell a billion packs in two weeks.

Broadcaster Robert Trout had occasion to visit the dog pound one afternoon in Washington and was so touched by the plight of the mangy mongrels he saw there that he interpolated a plea into his newscast that night: every listener who mailed in a five-dollar bill would not only save the life of a defenseless dog, but would receive said dog for his very own. Some days later the director of the pound told Trout, "Did you slay them with that broadcast the other night! The five-dollar bills are still pouring in. In fact, they've arrived in such quantities, we've had to put on a dozen extra dog-catchers to satisfy the demand."

A political broadcast in Prague, says *Variety*, ended in wild cheers from the studio audience, followed by puzzling cries of "goal!" Next day the station manager apologized (before being carted off by the secret police). It seems the studio engineer had planned the usual "ovation" by getting a record from the files that carried the sound of prolonged applause. Unfortunately he made a slight mistake and selected one taken from the broadcast of a soccer game between Hungary and Czechoslovakia.

Herb Shriner, the greatest thing in homespun wits since the days of Will Rogers, spends a good deal of his time discussing the town drunk back in his Indiana birthplace. The poor fellow wasn't always that way; he simply took a nip now and then to "quiet his nerves." He finally quieted them so completely he couldn't move at all. "I don't even like the taste of the stuff," he confessed to Herb. "I just drink so's I can forget—and I got the best durn memory in Indiana." Herb suggested that he try leaving town, and he headed for the big town—Indianapolis. He was back in a week, however. "That place ain't for me," he announced. "I'll take the good old U.S.A."

Shriner, enlarging on an old Hoosier custom of passing a suit of clothes from father on through a succession of sons, recalls, "Often a feller in our town would find a suit had enough wear in it for a couple more kids, so he went right ahead and had 'em. A woman sure hated to see one of those durable suits come into the family. One lady finally stopped propagating because she was running out of names—to call her husband."

The richest citizen in Herb's town made his fortune in a novel manner. He invented a dog food that tastes exactly like a letter carrier's ankle. For years, says Herb, this character's watch has lacked an hour hand. He's waiting for something else to bust on it so's he can get the whole thing fixed at once.

Iced tea may be a cooling midsummer drink to most folks, but in Shriner's part of Indiana it's served exclusively in January, February, and March. "Those are the only months," he explains, "we have any ice." One worry the townsfolk have been spared. There's no traffic problem. "Lucky thing we don't need one-way streets," admits Herb. "There's only one street in town. If we made it one way, folks would just walk out of town and never be able to get back."

The camera crew and cast of a big television show trekked over to the wide open spaces of Jersey City recently to shoot a couple of sequences for a horse oprey. The story involved the flight of an ornery cattle thief over the Mexican border. The camera crew set up shop on one of the main New Jersey highways. The director found one stretch that had no buildings in view and had his technicians post a sign reading "Last gas station before the border. Twenty miles of uninhabited desert past this sign." By the time the director had rounded up his cast, he was dumfounded to discover a string of seventeen cars with out-of-state licenses lined up in front of his prop gas station. Although the towers of Newark were clearly visible ahead, these cautious drivers were taking no chances. They wanted their tanks full before braving those "twenty miles of uninhabited desert."

Myron Cohen tells about the Brooklyn kid who watched six wild West programs on TV every day. His mother sought one evening to lure him away from the machine and in to dinner, but the kid shot his pistol into the air and said, "Thanks, pard, but I reckon I ain't got any hankerin' tonight for matzoth balls."

Abe Burrows, embroiled in one of those television panel shows, was faced with the problem of guessing the identity of a mystery name. "Is he living?" asked Burrows hopefully. "No," said the quiz master. "He's dead." Burrows scratched his bald pate nervously and ruminated, "Let's see now. Who do I know who's dead?"

On a kids' quiz show, a radio M.C. asked a pimply-faced lad to name man's best friend—for two shiny silver dollars. When the lad hesitated the M.C. added a hint: "The word, sonny, begins with a 'D'." "Oh, yea," said the lad, brightening at once. "Dames!" And on *What's My Line*, Hal Block asked Rocky Graziano, "Are you a pugilist?" Rocky was lost in thought for a moment, then decided, "Nah—I'm just a prize-fighter."

D is for

A woebegone Casper Milquetoast asked M.C. Roger Price on a recent TV program, "How can I keep my wife from hanging around a bowling alley seven nights a week?" Price advised him tartly, "Get her a different job. Don't make her work as a pin-boy."

The new Television code sternly decrees, "No emphasis on anatomical details." Ben Gross, of the New York *News,* sought out Dagmar to ask, "What do you think of this provision?" "Honey," Dagmar assured him, "I don't need any emphasis."

T is for
TEXAS—
And a Few Other States

Wall Street financier Arthur Goodman asked a Texas oil tycoon, "How's business holding up in your sector?" "Son," drawled the Texan, "in Houston we do more business by accident than you do in Wall Street on purpose." Later he admitted (in a much lower tone of voice), "If every boy in Texas, however, could read the mind of every girl in Texas, gas consumption in our state would drop off fifty per cent."

A Texas dowager presented herself at the Pearly Gates, and when Saint Peter asked for her credentials, proudly presented a membership card to the Symphony, receipted bills from Neiman-Marcus and the Shamrock Hotel, and a picture of herself shaking hands with Ted Dealey of the Dallas *News*. Saint Peter, duly impressed, remarked, "Come in, madam, by all means—but I don't think you'll like it."

Famous Dallas department store Neiman-Marcus had a visit from the wife of a multimillionaire oil tycoon. She wanted a new fur coat, and owner Stanley Marcus waited on her in person.

She inclined to a modest number that bore a price tag of exactly $32,000. Marcus told her, "We must warn everybody who picks out a coat of this particular fur that while it is very, very rare and uncommonly beautiful, it doesn't wear as well as, say, mink or sable, and may no longer look its best after two or three seasons. That being the case, I suppose you'll reconsider the purchase."

"On the contrary," said the customer promptly, "that being the case, I'd better have two of them!"

Vice-President Barkley was engaged in hot debate with one of those fabulous Texas oil millionaires over the merits of a neighboring Houstonian. "I'll bet he's as rich as you are," needled Barkley. "Don't let that fourflusher fool you," retorted the Texan angrily. "He's never had over thirty million dollars in his pocket at one time in his whole life."

A New Yorker was driving through a barren wilderness in West Texas when a fancy bird skittled past the car. "What kind of fowl do you call that?" he asked. The driver answered proudly, "That's a bird of paradise." "Hm-m-m," mused the New Yorker. "Kind of far from home, isn't he?"

Tony Martin, the man who made all America sing "Sole Mia," declares that Wichita Falls, Texas, is the only place in the world "where you can stand ankle-deep in mud and spit sand out of your mouth at the same time." He adds that they once had a dust storm so thick down there that a prairie dog was observed digging a hole fifty feet in the air.

An English visitor to Dallas, in a belittling mood, remarked, "You Texans don't do things as fast as I had been led to expect." "Zatso?" drawled Liz McMurray, the bookselling champion of the Southwest. "Just come down to Union Station with me and keep your eyes peeled." At the station, the superintendent was hurriedly drawing the redcaps into a single line. Just as the formation was completed, a streamliner whizzed by at a mile a minute. The Englishman got a fleeting glance at one passenger leaning out of a window with a notebook in his hand. "What was that chap trying to do?" demanded the Englishman. Answered Liz, "Just measuring the porters for new uniforms."

The Southern Methodist-Notre Dame football game was a sellout. Hordes of excited fans yelled their lungs out as the tide of fortune swayed now one way, now the other. And nobody yelled louder for SMU than a young priest who had a seat on the 35-yard line. During a time-out the man next to him admitted, "I can't figure, Father, why you are rooting for SMU. Surely you realize Notre Dame is a Catholic institution! How come?" The priest explained proudly, "First, suh, Ah am a Texan!"

Last year the Marine Historical Association at Mystic, Connecticut, enshrined the old ferry-boat *Brinckerhoff*—one of the last relics of the walking beam type—along the waterfront with other historic vessels like the whaleship *Charles W. Morgan* and the square-rigged *Joseph Conrad*. One canny visitor from New Hampshire stood before the ferry-boat, then shifted his gaze down-river towards the new highway bridge about half a mile away. His disparaging comment was, "Hmphh! Ferry-boat here, bridge there. The fools won't make a nickel!"

A boatman ran a ferry across a mountain stream full of whirl-pools and rapids. During a crossing in which the frail craft was tossed hither and yon by the swirling waters, a timid lady in the boat asked whether any passengers ever were lost in the river.

"Never," the boatman reassured her. "We always find them again the next day."

A Cleveland daily chronicles the visit of a Beacon Street Bos-tonite to a local belle which was marred by said belle's drawing on her gloves at the Cleveland Symphony. "In Boston," he told her severely, "men would as soon see a girl put on her girdle in public as her gloves." "In Cleveland," she informed him cheer-fully, "they'd rather."

A lady from Beacon Hill in Boston was taken to a session of the U.N. When she got home friends asked her what it was like. "Dreadful," said the lady. "It was simply crawling with foreign-ers!"

There's a neat twist in this story of Sam Levenson's. A cloak and suit manufacturer, obviously born abroad, was taunted on his Americanism by a bigoted blue-blood. "What kind of Ameri-can are you, after all?" sneered the blue-blood. "Why, my ances-tors came over on the Mayflower." The cloak and suit man, un-perturbed, replied, "Maybe it's lucky they did. By the time I arrived, the immigration laws were a lot stricter."

George Allen's Uncle John spent most of his declining days on his Mississippi plantation fighting over the battles of the Civil

War. One week-end, however, he journeyed to Washington on business, and was approached by a battered wreck of a man who begged for aid. Every scar and blemish, the panhandler declared, had been sustained while fighting bravely on the Union side. To Allen's amazement, Uncle John promptly coughed up a five-dollar bill, explaining to his nephew, "That was the first damyankee I ever saw shot up to my entire satisfaction."

In a local election in Mississippi, officials tabulating the ballots were astounded to discover a Republican vote. There being no precedent for this phenomenon, the sheriff decided, "Let's hold it out till we get a full count." Then—wonder of wonders!—another Republican vote turned up. "That settles it," roared the sheriff. "The low-down varmint voted twice, so we won't count either of them."

A Nashville lady put down her paper with a sigh and reflected, "To think a Southern boy could go so far wrong." The old girl in the adjoining rocking chair, startled by the Nashville lady's vehemence, exclaimed, "I do declare, Mary Lou! What Southern boy are you runnin' down?" "That Joe Stalin," pouted the Nashville lady. "You know, of course, he's from Georgia."

Father Edward Murphy, a wise and witty Catholic priest in New Orleans, and an implacable foe of racial intolerance, tells of an old colored man who drove his dilapidated jalopy through a red light on Canal Street. Arrested and taken before a judge, the old man explained, "Yo' honor, Ah saw all the white folks goin' through the green light, so Ah jus' went through the red." "The case was dismissed," adds Father Murphy.

Emmet Dedmon tells about a book salesman who was selling his line to a dealer in the deep, deep South. "Our next novel," said the salesman with an apologetic cough, "deals with the problem of—er, incest." "That's the trouble with you Yankees," snapped the dealer. "You make a problem out of everything."

A familiar character on Wall Street some years ago was a colorful broker named Pop Schwed. Pop loved nothing better than to reel off apocryphal tales of his youth in the wide-open town of Goldfield, Nevada, just after the turn of the century. There was one hellion there, he recalled, who went berserk every time he had six drinks inside of him, which was *usually*. An itinerant medico persuaded him that if he didn't forswear all hard liquor at once he'd be dead inside two months. One evening the reformed character was in the toughest dive in Goldfield, disconsolately sipping a beaker of ginger ale, when a prospector sashayed to the bar, pumped his faithless wife and her paramour full of lead, shot out the lights as a parting gesture, and vanished into the night. The paralyzed silence that followed was finally broken by Pop Schwed's reformed friend. "Waiter," he barked hoarsely, "for God's sake! A double order of ham and eggs!"

A couple who never before had ventured west of Hoboken were making their first transcontinental trip aboard a Canadian streamliner. At one stop far along the line they left the train for a little exercise, and inquired of a man on the platform, "What's the name of this town?" He answered, "Sascatoon, Saskatchewan." "Goodness," marveled the husband, "we've come so far the natives don't even speak English here!"

Harry Oliver, editor of *The Desert Rat* (a newspaper published four times a year) swears that an Indian strode into a white man's court and pleaded to have his name shortened legally. "What's your name now?" asked the judge. "Chief Train-whistle," said the Indian. "And what do you want to shorten it to?" pursued the judge. The Indian folded his arms majestically and grunted, "Toots."

Oliver once persuaded a honeymoon couple headed for Yellowstone Park that the whole thing was a fake. "Those geysers gave out years ago," he assured them. "The government secretly installed underground boilers with time clocks and pressure gauges. They couldn't stand the thought of losing all that tourist revenue. They even bring out those mangy bears every summer from zoos in the east." The honeymooners were so outraged they changed their plans and went to Reno instead.

In their colorful memoir, *Trail Driving Days*, Dee Brown and Martin Schmitt recall a wild night in a saloon in Mingusville, South Dakota, back in 1885. A Bad Lands drunk had just shot up the premises and sent the bartender to cover behind the counter when he spied a bespectacled tenderfoot minding his own business at a rear table. The drunk announced boldly, "Four-Eyes will now set up drinks for the house." Four-Eyes turned slowly, and after two shots from the drunk went wild, knocked him senseless with a single punch to the solar plexus. After that Tenderfoot Rancher Theodore Roosevelt was affectionately known in those parts as "Old Four-Eyes."

Those were the days, add Brown and Schmitt, when the wildest town of all was Dodge City. When a liquored-up cowhand

boarded a Santa Fe local one afternoon and demanded a ride to
hell, the conductor suggested, "Give me two dollars fare and get
off at Dodge."

If just a little of the rainfall that beats down so persistently on
the coastal region of Washington and Oregon could be transferred to the bone-dry areas of lower California and Arizona not
so many hundred miles to the south, it would be a wonderful deal
all around. One day you're listening to a Southwestern farmer
praying for any kind of shower to break a seven-month drought;
the next a University of Washington professor is saying, "That
majestic peak about sixty miles to the southeast is Mount Rainier,
of course. I use it as a weather guide every morning. If I can see
it when I awaken I know it's going to rain later in the day. If I
can't see it I know it's raining already!" When Seattle folk *can* see
Mount Rainier or when Mount Hood is visible to the citizens of
Portland, incidentally, the common phrase is "Oh, look: the mountain is out today."

The cause of all the rain is the Japan Current, which warms the
air blowing in from the Pacific. The warm air turns into rain when
it collides with the formidable Cascade Range.

"The far ends of the earth" is an empty phrase today. As Willis
Brown points out, there is no spot on the globe in 1952 that is
theoretically more than forty hours' flying time from your nearest
airport!

U is for
UNIVERSITIES

Albert Einstein, whose theories about relativity and the fourth dimension are said to be understood by only twelve people in the world besides himself, graciously allowed a film producer to take some shots for a documentary movie in his Princeton, N.J., residence not long ago.

Left alone momentarily in the library, the producer noticed a big blueprint on Dr. Einstein's desk.

Since he himself was having a new house built at the time, and had blueprints coming out of his ears, he felt an uncontrollable impulse to have a look at the Einsteinian conception.

Unable to make head or tail of it, he looked for the legend in the lower right-hand corner. Immaculately lettered, it read, "One inch equals a hundred million light years."

Money means little to Dr. Einstein. When he first joined the Princeton Institute for Advanced Study, the salary he requested was so low officials had to double it to preserve some semblance of Institute standards.

He once used a $1500 check from the Rockefeller Foundation as a bookmark, then lost the book. The Foundation's records were out of kilter for months. When they finally sent a duplicate check, Einstein wrote back, "What's this for?"

Orpah Anderson tells me this happened at a school in a northern Minnesota town. A strapping, healthy-looking girl appeared to register for a course in English. The recording clerk asked, "Have you a hobby?" The girl replied, "No, ay ban single."

Donald Clark quotes a Columbia professor's appraisal of a high-flying colleague: "Such time as he can spare from the adornment of his person, he devotes to the neglect of his profession."

The University of Michigan prides itself on the exchange students it attracts from every corner of the world. One day some delegates from the Far East arrived unexpectedly at the Ann Arbor station clad in white suits with turbans wound around their heads. The station master called up then-President Ruthven and asked, "What'll I do with them? They don't seem to understand the questions I ask them. Only one speaks any English." "Send the one who speaks English to my office and hold the others till you hear from me," instructed Dr. Ruthven. In due course the emissary who "spoke English" arrived before Dr. Ruthven, bowed low, and gravely began, "Sir or madam, whichever the case may be . . ."

Gargoyle, the humorous magazine at Michigan, is one campus publication that isn't devoting all its efforts to unsuccessful imitations of the *New Yorker*. In the issue I saw, the cartoons were raucous and uninhibited; the jokes had that well-remembered

tang of typical undergraduate wit. Examples: She: I saw a Texas
Ranger carrying two rifles. He: That's nothing. I saw a cowgirl
packing a pair of 38's. . . . Didja hear about the pregnant bedbug? It's going to have a baby in the spring. . . . Girl: I nearly
fainted when the fellow I was out with last night asked me for a
kiss. Boy: Baby, you're gonna die when you hear what I have to
say. . . . Sam: What did the usherette say when her strap broke?
Ed: I dunno. What did she say? Sam: I have two down in front.

Two collegians had celebrated their team's football triumph
too copiously, and were driving home at midnight in rather erratic
fashion. For miles, their road paralleled the tracks of the Chicago
and Northwestern Railroad. Suddenly a passenger train rumbled
by them going in the opposite direction. The driver commented,
"Didja notice that every house in that village we just passed was
still lit up?" "Not only that," added his passenger, "but the first
house was on fire."

Ohio State University once invited a distinguished old judge
to speak at a convocation. They didn't realize that the gentleman,
always eccentric, had grown worse with the years, and was somewhat senile into the bargain. He seized his typescript firmly,
plodded up to the lectern, and began reading in a high, cracked
voice. When he got to the bottom of Page One, he turned the
leaf, and continued reading. It soon became apparent to the
startled audience that the judge was rereading Page One. And if
that wasn't enough, the third page was another duplicate!

By this time, everybody realized that the typist had delivered
the judge's speech in triplicate. Seventeen pages were read three
times over by the unsuspecting old gentleman. The chairman then
rushed out for an aspirin, and the audience rushed out to have
hysterics.

The father of every candidate for admission to Vassar is required to fill out a questionnaire regarding his daughter's qualifications. One of the questions is "Would you call your daughter a leader?" A father in Red Bank, New Jersey, meticulously honest, answered, "I have never noticed my daughter assume the role of leader, but I do know she is an excellent follower." Vassar's reply, as reported by the *Journal of Education,* was, "As our freshman group next fall seems to be composed almost exclusively of several hundred leaders, we congratulate ourselves that your daughter will also be a member of the class. We shall thus be assured of one good follower, at any rate. Her application is approved with enthusiasm."

"Did your girl like the Bikini bathing suit you brought her from Paris?" asked Williams, '53. "Did she!" enthused Williams, '52. "She tried it on immediately—and you should have seen her beam."

The dean of one Midwestern seat of learning was leading the robed group of notables and faculty members across the campus to Commencement ceremonies in the quadrangle when he stole a glance at his watch, made a mental calculation, and suddenly wheeled to the left. The procession wheeled after him, and solemnly followed him en masse—to the gents' room!

Another dean suffered the misfortune of sitting down on a newly painted bench just before graduation exercises began. He turned disaster into triumph, however, by opening his remarks with, "I had hoped to bring you an unvarnished tale this morning, but fate decreed otherwise."

"Why did you assault this poor man?" a judge demanded of a college student near the tag-end of a football week-end. "Well, judge," explained the student, wriggling in the grasp of the cop who had haled him into court, "I was in a phone booth innocently conversing with my girl when this bohunk opens the door and heaves me out of the booth." "And that incensed you?" prompted the judge. "Mildly," admitted the student, "but what really made me see red was when he reached in for my girl and heaved her out, too."

Mingling with the throng that poured out of a California university stadium after a big game, a visiting Easterner enthused to his host, head of the chemistry department, "What a plant you have here! What a campus! How many students would you say you have?" The chemistry prof answered sourly, "About one in a thousand."

Two sweet co-eds at the University of Minnesota were happily carving up an ex-roommate over the telephone. "And, my dear," continued one, "who do you think she's been dating like mad the past month? Her X-ray specialist!" "Hmphh!" commented the other. "I wonder what he sees in her?"

Professor Irwin Edman, famed for his absent-mindedness, dropped in unexpectedly on his old friend, the family doctor, and chatted happily about his impending trip to France for almost three hours. Finally the doctor arose from his chair, and remarked pointedly, "Well, Irwin, I have an operation to perform at eight

in the morning. I trust everyone in your household is well."
"Good heavens," gasped Irwin, "that reminds me. I came here to
tell you my cook is having a fit."

V is for
VIPS IN WASHINGTON

Presidents come and go, but the shenanigans designed to charm the voters remain about the same. A delegation from the west, come to visit Teddy Roosevelt in Oyster Bay, for example, found him striding out of the house in a pair of levis, with a pitchfork in his hand. "You can talk to me while I work, gentlemen. I've raised some bully hay this season. James, where's that hay of mine?"

Back came the voice of James: "Sorry, Mr. President, but I just ain't had time to replace it since you forked it up for yesterday's contingent!"

Woodrow Wilson was a great reader of books, and the author he admired above all others was Mark Twain. When his presidential train passed through Hannibal, Missouri, therefore, Mr. Wilson ordered a three-hour wait-over that he might wander for a bit among the boyhood haunts of the famous humorist. Accosting a native, the President said, "I'm a stranger in these parts. Could you tell me where Tom Sawyer was supposed to live?" "Never heard of him," maintained the native. "Well, how about Huck Finn?" persisted Mr. Wilson. "Never heard of him nuther," declared the native. The President made one more try. "How about Puddinhead Wilson?" he inquired. The native's face brightened.

"I heard of him all right," he said cheerfully. "In fact, I even voted for the durn fool."

When Cal Coolidge was President, he liked to raid the icebox occasionally for a late snack, and generally took Colonel Starling, his Secret Service man, with him. Coolidge usually whipped up two sandwiches of Vermont cheese.

"That cheese," says Starling, "was as strong as a billy goat. Mr. Coolidge would turn to me and exclaim, 'I'll bet no other President of the United States ever made a cheese sandwich for you.' 'No,' I would answer. 'It's a great honor.' Coolidge would add gloomily, 'I have to furnish the cheese, too.'"

When Ex-President Herbert Hoover was an undergraduate at Stanford, he served a spell as manager of the baseball team. One day Benjamin Harrison, himself just retired from the Presidency of the United States, tried to get into a game without a ticket. He didn't get by Herbert Hoover! In fact, he ended up by buying another ticket in advance for the next week's game. "That," recalls Mr. Hoover, "was my first contact with a great public man." He acted with similar dispatch and decisiveness when he found himself shepherding hundreds of stranded Americans in London in 1914. One heedless debutante from Lansing, Michigan, went right on collecting a $5000 trousseau despite the crisis, and, since she no longer trusted any foreigners, had every parcel delivered in care of the Hoovers at the Savoy Hotel. Just as promptly as a package arrived, the hastily assembled Hoover committee turned it over to some unfortunate whose entire baggage had been lost in the confusion. The debutante's father cabled he would sue for damages. Mr. Hoover invited him by a collect return cable to come and try it.

Another casualty of those hectic August, 1914, days was a twelve-year-old American kid who was sent along to visit his grandparents in Croatia, and when war broke out was stranded, helpless, in Hamburg. By great good fortune, however, he ran into the fully accoutred members of a wild West show, and promptly attached himself to the troupe. By the time they reached London, the kid was determined that his future lay in show business. His father cabled Mr. Hoover to make sure he was in good hands and bound for home. "Stop worrying," advised Mr. Hoover. "Your boy is headed for America under the excellent charge of Chief White Feather, of Pawhuska, Oklahoma."

Ex-President Herbert Hoover vacationed recently in a small Canadian resort. The clerk examined his signature in the register, and was obviously impressed. "Any relation of G-Man Hoover?" he asked. When Mr. Hoover said no, he tried again. "How about the Hoover who makes those vacuum cleaners?" Again Ex-President Hoover said no. "Oh, well," consoled the clerk. "No harm done. We do get a kick, though, out of entertaining relatives of real celebrities!"

There is no bee with a more virulent or lasting bite than the presidential bee. Once a man gets stung by it, he's never quite the same again as long as he lives. It was Mrs. Franklin D. Roosevelt who told me that at Hyde Park, and she added with a smile, "I'm the girl who ought to know." Paul McNutt, who campaigned actively for a while for the Democratic nomination in 1940, once answered an inquiring reporter, "Would I like to be President? Lady, there have been moments when I wanted to be President so bad my teeth ached."

Just before the balloting began in the 1940 Republican Convention, recalls Stefan Lorant, the late Wendell Willkie sought to enlist the support of crusty delegate Jim Watson of Indiana. "Sorry, Wendell," snapped Watson, "but you're just not my kind of dependable, day-in-and-day-out Republican." "I am now," maintained Mr. Willkie, "though I admit I once was a Democrat." "Once was?" snorted Watson. "Well, let me tell you what I think of converts. If a fancy woman truly repented and wanted to join my church, I'd welcome her with open arms. I'd even lead her personally to the front pew. But by the eternal, I wouldn't ask her to lead the choir!"

No President was the subject of more jibes and anecdotes than Harry S. Truman. Like him or not, one had to admire the unfailing good nature with which he greeted them—at least, in public. He himself retold the one, for instance, about the three most disastrous occurrences in our history: the Galveston Flood, the San Francisco Earthquake, and the failure of a certain haberdashery in Kansas City. There was another about a Californian who remarked to a man from Houston that he heard Truman was going to raise taxes. With no further ado, the Houstonian arose, and knocked the visitor cold with an uppercut to the jaw. A friend protested, "What did you want to do that for to a man who merely said 'Truman's going to raise taxes'?" "Is *that* what he said?" mumbled the Houstonian, his face flushing with embarrassment. "I thought he said 'Truman was *raised in Texas*'!"

Then there was Walter Richards' story of the day during the 1948 Presidential campaign when Mr. Truman's train stopped on an Indian reservation and the President emerged to deliver a speech. "I am appalled," he said, "at the treatment of you noble redmen and women by administrations previous to mine, particularly the Republicans." He made a gesture as though he was chopping a Republican in the neck and continued, "As our train pulled in, I saw squaws washing clothes by the riverside, pum-

meling them on rocks, even as your ancestors did. I intend to see
a Bendix installed in every teepee!"

The Indians broke into loud cries of "Oompah-oompah!"

The President beamed broadly and continued, "And I understand you are still obliged to dry beef for jerky. Well, I intend to
see that every wigwam is equipped with a deep freeze."

Again the Indians shouted "Oompah-oompah!"

The President broke into his broadest grin and soared to a
climax. "If re-elected I intend to see that your noble chief drives
a Cadillac as big as mine, and a new Pontiac shall stand before
every teepee."

As he bowed, the Indians roared out their mightiest "Oompah"
and their handsome chief came forward and placed a war bonnet
on the President's head. Then he led the Great White Father to
the corrals for another presentation, delivering the speech in the
impeccable English of a Carlyle graduate. "The Indians of this
reservation take great pleasure in presenting as a token of our
esteem a silver-mounted saddle and our very best Indian pony."
As the President prepared to mount the handsome animal, the
Chief suddenly cried out, "Be careful, Mr. Truman. Don't step in
the oompah!"

There's a sign on the bulletin board of the Clinton, Ky., school
where Alben Barkley earned spending money in his youth as
assistant janitor. It reads, "Al Barkley swept here."

Warns an English diplomat: "If you aspire to be a statesman
today, you'd better watch your appease and accuse."

In general, United States senators try to agree and disagree
with a certain amount of moderation and decorum, but every

once in a while there have been explosions on the floor that did not stop short of fisticuffs.

After one such violent outburst, a senator from Vermont had worked himself up to such a state that occupants of the Visitors' Gallery distinctly heard him mutter to himself as he stomped off the floor:

"I'm going home to dinner. If it's ready, I won't eat it. If it isn't, I'll raise hell!"

A Texas Democrat had successfully campaigned for a seat in the House of Representatives. To show his appreciation, he promptly introduced a bill to finance the widening of Trinity River back home. A Republican congressman from up north jumped to his feet in indignation.

"What can the government do for a piddling trickle like the Trinity?" he demanded. "Why, I can spit halfway acrost it." The Speaker of the House banged with his gavel and cried, "You're out of order." "You're damn right, I'm out of order," agreed the Republican. "If I was in order, I could spit all the way acrost it."

Every politician, suggests Carl Sandburg, should have three hats handy at all times: one for throwing into the ring, another for talking through, and a third for pulling rabbits out of if elected!

A staunch Republican from Maine was being shown the wonders of the Grand Canyon. "Yes, sir," said the guide. "It took about five million years for this awe-inspiring canyon to be carved out of the rocks." "Hmm," added the man from Maine. "Government project, I presume."

A congressman's wife sought the advice of a "K" Street fortune-teller, who prophesied, "Prepare yourself for widowhood! Your husband is about to die a violent death."

The wife sighed deeply and asked, "Will I be acquitted?"

In Detroit, a seven-year-old protégé of Harvey Campbell's held up a picture of Abraham Lincoln and gravely declared, "This is the man who frayed the sleeves." "You're a bit off the beam," explained Harvey. "Mr. Lincoln is the man who freed the slaves. The President who frayed the sleeves didn't come along until many years later."

Country-wide scandals in the internal revenue department led one businessman to declare, "I'm all ready to pay the current installment on my income tax, but I don't know what jail to mail the check to." . . . Joe Eckhouse, handsome department-store executive, classifies the Eiffel Tower as "The Empire State Building after taxes." . . . A Cabinet member pleading for still higher taxes was taken apart by a syndicated gossip columnist. A reporter asked him, "How do you classify gossip columnists, sir? Would you call them newspapermen?" The Cabinet member snorted, "Would you call barnacles ships?"

It's unlikely that a certain Senator's wife will be wearing to any more public functions a medallion her husband picked up for her on an air junket to Hong Kong. She was very proud of it for quite a while—until the evening, in fact, that a Chinese Nationalist diplomat, over to address the U.N., informed her gravely that the literal translation of the Chinese characters on the medallion read, "Licensed prostitute, City of Shanghai."

Preparing to attend a banquet given by Gwendolyn Cafritz, now Washington's number-one hostess, a Senator from a Rocky Mountain state slipped on the top step of a marble staircase and landed solidly on his posterior two floors below. The next morning he called from his bed of pain to apologize to the famous hostess.

"You're forgiven," she said, "but you ruined my seating arrangement." "*Your* seating arrangement," he exclaimed. "You ought to see *mine!*"

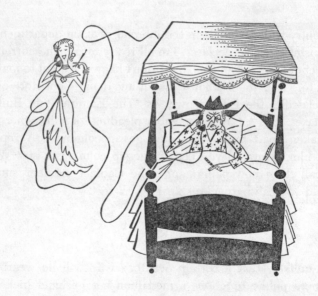

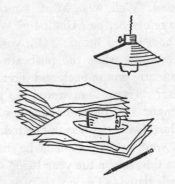

W is for WRITERS

Only one man in a million dares to make a living by draping live hooded cobras around his neck, and there was a notable sparsity of volunteers for the job of riveting that new television mast to the top of the Empire State Building.

Yet when it comes to writing a book—a job that in some ways is infinitely harder to master than that of any snake charmer or steeplejack—every man, woman, child, prison inmate, illiterate and confirmed lunatic firmly believes he possesses all the talent necessary. A typical note accompanying an unsolicited manuscript reads, "My friends have insisted that I simply *must* put my experiences into a book. Please mail contracts and advance royalties by Monday as the landlord is getting impatient." Nine hundred and ninety-nine out of every thousand manuscripts, unfortunately, are unpublishable. Nine hundred of them are unreadable.

Playwright Moss Hart discovered how the general public felt about writers when he journeyed to the lower East Side of Manhattan in search of local color for a script he is preparing. Picking his way through the maze of pushcarts and pedestrians on Hester Street, he suddenly heard his name being called.

The voice belonged to the proprietor of one of the pushcarts, who cackled, "Well, well, Moss, I recognized you immediately! Don't you remember me? Goldberg? We sat next to each other in public school in the Bronx." "Oh, yes! Goldberg . . ." repeated Hart uncertainly, while the pushcart man continued pounding him vehemently on the back and inquired, "What are you doing for a living?" "I write," answered the playwright. "Write what?" said the man. "Oh, plays and movies and things like that," explained Hart. Goldberg was fascinated.

"I don't want to get personal," he declared, "but what did you make from this, say, in the year 1950?"

Hart calculated, "I'd say it was in the neighborhood of $250,000." Goldberg shot a contemptuous look at his pushcart, clapped a hand to his forehead and exclaimed, "$250,000! From *writing?* Why couldn't I have thought of that?"

Elliot Paul, author of *Springtime in Paris*, cherishes as his favorite memory the time his then-publisher, the late Horace Liveright, mailed back the manuscript of *The Governor of Massachusetts* and told him to cut 10,000 words. Paul kept it a week, returned it without opening the package. Liveright wired, "Congratulations. Now it's perfect!"

Occasionally a writer comes along who can sit down at a typewriter and bang out a column or story at will. Most writers, however, can think of more ways to delay getting down to their work than even a temporary kitchen maid. Lee Rogow cites the case of one Hollywood scenario scripter who simply had to have a job completed by the following morning. His understanding wife disconnected the phone, inserted a fresh page in his typewriter, grabbed both kids by the hand and left him in sole possession of the premises. They rode to the end of the bus line and back, saw a double feature at the neighborhood movie, and came home at the tag end of the day to see how far Daddy had gotten. He hadn't done too badly. As they walked though the door, he was just polishing the last piece of their eighty-piece sterling-silver dinner set.

In his uninhibited and engrossing autobiography, William Carlos Williams, who is at one time a prize-winning poet and one of the busiest small-town physicians in New Jersey, gives the following report of the first time Marcel Proust met James Joyce:

Rabid partisans had placed two chairs side by side in the middle of the room. There the two heroes seated themselves, and everybody waited for the wits to sparkle and flash. Joyce said, "I have headaches every day. My eyes are terrible." Proust replied, "With me, it's my poor stomach. What am I going to do? It's killing me. In fact, I must leave at once." "I'm in the same situation," declared Joyce, rising, "if I can find someone to take me by the arm and get me out of here. Good-by." Proust's exit line was "Charmé. Oh, my stomach, my stomach!"

My own first meeting with James Joyce was on the spectacular side. I found him in Sylvia Beach's Paris bookshop with one arm in a sling, a bandaged foot propped up on a stool and a patch over one eye. Noting my dismay, Miss Beach hastened to assure me, "Don't think he always looks this way. He's been run over twice this week by taxicabs!"

Humorist Stephen Leacock had a long string of college degrees, and Canadian associates usually addressed him as "Doctor." The purser of an Atlantic liner, who had heard him thus referred to for three days, stepped up to him one evening and said, "Doctor, could I prevail upon you to examine the star of last year's Ziegfeld Follies? She slipped on the promenade deck and I'm afraid she has sprained her hip." Leacock reported ruefully later, "I rushed there like a startled gazelle, but alas! two doctors of divinity had beaten me to it."

An author preparing an article on censorship unearthed the following interesting facts: In 1885 Concord, Massachusetts, home town of Thoreau, banned *Huckleberry Finn* as "trash suitable only for the slums." In 1929 Russia blacklisted Sherlock Holmes for his "disgraceful occultism and spiritualism." In 1931 China banned *Alice in Wonderland* on the ground that "animals should not use human language" and that it was "disastrous to put animals and human beings on the same level."

During Mark Twain's reporting days in Virginia City, fame and fortune were still very much in the future. The wife of the owner of a big silver mine met him on C Street one day with a cigar box held tightly under his arm. "Mr. Twain," she reproached him, "you promised me you were going to give up smoking cigars." "Madam," replied Twain with great dignity, "this box does not contain cigars. I am moving my possessions from one abode to another."

Twain, says Vincent Starrett, once visited the celebrated Madame Tussaud's wax works in London, and was admiring a replica of Queen Victoria when he felt a sudden stab of pain in his posterior. Wheeling angrily, he found himself face to face with a flabbergasted British matron, her umbrella still pointed at him. "O lor', it's alive!" she gasped, and fled into the night.

Amy Lowell, famed American poetess, sold her first effort to a national magazine at the age of six. The editor quoted the letter she had written to accompany the poem. It concluded with the

eye-opening sentence, "I have always been a loving son to my father, Augustus Lowell." When her father inquired, "Why on earth did you refer to yourself as my 'son'?" Amy replied, "Because I couldn't spell 'daughter.'"

When Danny Kaye made a great hit in James Thurber's *Walter Mitty*, Producer Sam Goldwyn thought he'd like to have Thurber as a permanent addition to his writing stable. The catch lay in the fact that Thurber was working very happily for the late *New Yorker* Editor Harold Ross and had no desire whatever to dally further with picture-making. "I'll pay you five hundred dollars a week," wrote Goldwyn. "Sorry," answered Thurber after some delay, "but Mr. Ross has met the increase." Goldwyn thereupon raised the ante to a thousand, then fifteen hundred, and finally twenty-five hundred a week, but each time got nothing for his pains but the courteous response, "Mr. Ross has met the increase." There followed a long interim of silence. Then one day Mr. Goldwyn wrote again. This time, for some unknown reason, his offer went down to fifteen hundred. Thurber wrote back, "I'm sorry, but Mr. Ross has met the decrease."

There will never be an editor more sorely missed than the same Harold Ross, who founded the *New Yorker* in 1925, and guided it unerringly until his death in 1951. A fastidious and impeccable craftsman at all times, Ross in personal life was a cranky, untidy curmudgeon, whose wild gestures, tousled hair, and rasping voice made him stand out like a sore thumb in all literary and social conclaves. After a row with him, Dorothy Parker once exclaimed, "When the revolution comes, it will be everybody in the world against Harold Ross!" Ross himself referred to his more irascible moments as "those times I went crazy." After hiring a promising lad who sought a place on the staff, Ross assured him, "Don't be too pleased with yourself. I hire any blank blank fool who sticks his face in here." Then he added, "Don't think you're going to start as a reporter. You'll begin as managing editor just like everybody else." One of the last things Ross told his staff was, "From now on I flatly refuse to buy one more story I don't understand." With all his roaring and grumbling, however, Ross left more friends behind, more writers and artists seriously saddened by his death, than any other editor in recent years.

Appointments mean little in the life of Budd Schulberg, talented but vague author of *What Makes Sammy Run?* and *The Disenchanted.* The blare of a be-bop band or the sound of a padded glove against a punching bag will distract him from a scheduled conference, with a fifty-thousand-dollar movie contract at stake. He was leaving for a formal dinner party in New York one day when the maid at his Bucks County farm asked him to deliver a dachshund pup to a friend who ran a beauty shop in Harlem. Budd, intrigued with the mission, promptly forgot the dinner party. He also forgot his driver's license—and the address of the lady who ran the beauty shop. At two the next morning I was awakened by a phone call from the lieutenant at the Harlem police precinct. "We picked up a fellow driving aimlessly around

Harlem without a license," he told me indignantly. "Says he's an author of yours. Says, too, he's trying to deliver a dachshund. At two in the morning, mind you! I hate to bother you with a cock-and-bull story like that . . ." "Wait a minute," I interrupted, "that must be Budd Schulberg, and it's perfectly all right. He does things like that. He's also the author of *What Makes Sammy Run?*" The baffled lieutenant settled for an autographed copy.

An author offered a publisher a sensational biography of a prominent Broadway personage. "It's full of dynamite," agreed the publisher, "but I'll have to have my lawyer check it carefully for libel." "That won't be necessary," said the author. "Every story I use in the book was told to me by somebody!"

Clyde Beck, erudite Detroit editor, presided at a dinner in honor of bibliophile John Winterich recently. Mr. Beck informed a large and enthusiastic gathering, "Our guest this evening needs no introduction," which was a lucky break, all things considered, because at this point Mr. Beck lost his balance and fell off the speaker's platform. Winterich restored order by assuring his audience, "Mr. Beck is an improvement in one respect. The last fellow who introduced me at a dinner suffered a heart attack."

At the conclusion of an Authors' League meeting, a group of distinguished men of letters repaired to the coffee shop of a mid-town hotel for a late snack. One of the authors inadvertently knocked over the salt. Being superstitious, he quickly threw a handful over his left shoulder to ward off bad luck. A young waitress was bending over the table to distribute portions of scrambled eggs, and the salt went straight down the back of her dress.

She wriggled impatiently, put down the tray to scratch herself, and remarked tartly, "Nothing doing, big boy. You won't get me that way!"

One of the most improbable anecdotes about the late George Bernard Shaw concerns an evening when a lady dramatist hornswoggled him into attending the tryout of her new play. "Now, you naughty man," she chided kittenishly, "you're not to sneak out in the middle of my drama." Shaw was planked down behind her and leaned forward to get a better view of the proceedings. Halfway through the first act, the authoress felt a tickling sensation on her neck. Groping in the dark, she felt a loose strand of hair and tucked it firmly into place with a big hatpin. Suddenly Shaw, thoroughly bored by this time, decided to fall back in his seat. He cried, "Ouch!" Then he told the authoress, "Madam, if you will kindly take my beard out of your hair, I promise I won't budge out of this seat until your confounded play is over."

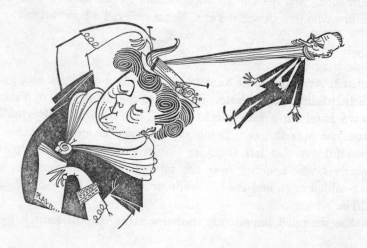

W (and X, Y, and Z) are for WOMEN

A long-time inmate of a Displaced Persons camp finally got his visa and sailed off for America, faithfully promising to send for his wife the moment he achieved a respectable bank balance. Unfortunately, he forgot all about her until he received a letter from her some six months later. Unable to read, he persuaded the neighborhood butcher to divulge the letter's contents to him. The butcher, who had a voice like a foghorn on the *Queen Elizabeth,* opened the letter and read hoarsely, "Why haven't you sent for me? I need some money right away. Minnie."

The immigrant snatched the note from the butcher's hands, stuffed it angrily into his pocket and forgot about it until a month later when he found himself dining with a gentle young rabbi. Again he asked, "Will you read my wife's letter to me, please?" This time it was the soft, modulated voice of the rabbi that echoed, "Why haven't you sent for me? I need some money right away. Minnie." The immigrant nodded with satisfaction. "Anyhow," he remarked, "I'm glad to notice that she's changed her tone!"

The advertising manager of a big Chicago daily has decided that women are like newspapers, reports *Tide,* and lists the following reasons to support his thesis: They have forms; they are made up; they have bold types; they always have the last word; they have great influence; they carry news wherever they go; they are much thinner than they used to be; and finally, every man should have one of his own and not borrow his neighbor's. The manager adds this postscript: Back numbers are not in demand.

A long-suffering husband took one look at his huge pile of unpaid bills for the month and reached for the family shotgun. "I'm going to end it all," he threatened. His wife remained totally unimpressed.

"Put down that gun before it goes off by accident," she ordered. "If you have something to say, shut up!"

Phil Silvers, in *Top Banana*, mourns, "Ever since the honeymoon, my wife has been hitting the ceiling. What a lucky thing for me she's such a rotten shot!"

Neal O'Hara visited an old pal whose equanimity was upset by his wife's dramatic announcement that she was so sick of wearing old rags she had marched into Filene's that afternoon and bought ten new dresses. "Ten!" shrieked the wounded husband. "What could any dame want with ten new dresses?" The wife answered promptly, "Ten new hats."

"I'm getting mighty exhausted contesting my wife's will," admitted Mr. Hecubar to a confidante. "I never knew she had died,"

said the shocked confidante. "That's the trouble," sighed Mr. Hecubar. "She didn't."

A woman stalked into the office of the head of a private detective agency and demanded an interview. Before the startled head of the firm could say a word, the woman launched into a tirade against her husband. Finally, when she stopped to get her breath, the detective was able to get a word in.

"Just what do you want me to do, madam?" he asked.

"I want my husband and that woman followed," snapped the visitor. "I want them followed night and day, and then I want a complete report on what she sees in him."

A fantastically henpecked husband finally did something entirely on his own initiative. He dropped dead. His nagging wife mourned his loss—and the fact that she had nobody left to badger. A visitor sympathized, "How you must miss dear Wilbur." "Yes," said the widow wistfully, "it seems but yesterday that he stood at that very door, holding it open until two flies got in."

In the powder room of a Cambridge residence, Mrs. Cabot-Lodge preened herself and said loftily, "That South African gentleman says the nicest things! He remarked particularly on my birdlike appetite." "Hmmph," commented Mrs. Lowellstall. "He runs an ostrich farm!"

Sam Himmell writes about a new millionaire in Scarsdale who was showing a friend around his modernistic "push-button" mansion. "This is the best gadget of the lot," he exulted. "After a

night out, I sometimes feel like stepping into a nice hot bath
right here without the trouble of going into the bathroom. I just
press this button——" He pressed the button and in rolled the
bathtub, full of nice hot water—and the millionaire's wife.

An upstate social leader was expecting a large group of friends
at her home one evening, and knowing her husband's propensity
for using guest towels indiscriminately when he returned from
the office, put a sign on the ones she had trotted out especially
for the occasion that read, "If you use one of these towels, I'll slay
you in cold blood." Unfortunately, she forgot to remove the note
before the guests started arriving. At the evening's end she found
the note still there—and not one towel touched.

Erskine lounged into the office an hour late for the third time
in one week and found the boss awaiting him, arms akimbo.
"What's the story this time, Erskine?" he asked sarcastically. "Let's
hear a good excuse for a change." Erskine sighed, "Everything
went wrong this morning, boss. The wife decided to drive me to
the station. She got ready in ten minutes, but then the draw-

bridge got stuck. Rather than let you down, I swam across the river (look, my suit's still damp), ran out to the airport, got a hitch in Mr. Harriman's helicopter, landed on top of Radio City Music Hall, and was carried here piggy-back by one of the Rockettes." "You'll have to do better than that, Erskine," said the boss, obviously disappointed. "No woman can get ready in ten minutes."

Mrs. George Backer boasted to her Swopian Literary Circle that her husband had given up smoking for a year. "That must have taken plenty of self-control," said Arlene Francis admiringly. "Exactly," agreed Mrs. Backer, "and that's just what I've got."

The origin of the word "incompatibility" is perfectly clear to Comedian Abe Burrows. "When a husband loses his income," points out Burrows, "you'll notice how promptly his wife loses her patibility."

John Daly says he can prove that men are warmer than women. Just consult a weather report. Doesn't it always read something like, "Max. 82; Min. 34"?

When Pat O'Leary's wife presented him with his eleventh offspring in the space of thirteen years, the office force chipped in to present him with a well-earned gift—a silver tray with what they told him was the O'Leary coat of arms emblazoned thereon. "What's the idea of putting that funny lookin' duck on me coat

of arms?" protested O'Leary. "That's no duck," explained the
office manager. "That's a stork with his legs worn off."

Mr. Honeyfuggler is looking for a new job. He lost his old one
when he thoughtlessly introduced his bird-brained bride to the
head of the firm at an office get-together. "So you're my Henry's
boss," gurgled Mrs. Honeyfuggler. "He's told me so much about
you, Mr. Legree!"

Charles Lee is showing friends a cartoon he clipped from an
English weekly. It depicts a couple of fellows playing darts in a
London saloon. One of the darts has gone out of line and clipped
a table sitter in the back of the noggin. The table sitter's girl
friend is impatiently grumbling, "Oh, you and your stabbing pains
in the head."

A publisher's wife told Irving Hoffman, "It's not true that I
married a millionaire. I made him one." "What was he before you
married him?" asked Irving. The wife answered, "A multi-millionaire."

The president of the Wallager Falls bridge club enjoys showing off her young son's store of scientific knowledge to her fellow
members. One day she urged, "Go on and tell them, Jerome, what
it means when steam comes out of the spout of the kettle." "It
means," said Jerome, "that you are about to open one of Father's
letters."

The housekeeper of a crusty old bachelor was given to writing voluminous reports when her employer was away. As he left for a vacation he told her, "I want all the news, but for the love of heaven, be brief!" Four days later he received this note from her: "There has been a flood. Where your house was, the river is. Respectfully, Bridget Schinasi."

The new maid had been functioning, in a manner of speaking, for two weeks, and since she had shown no response to instruction, threats, or cajolery, Mrs. Brown decided to try sarcasm on her. "Do you know, Maymie," she said, "that man was created from dust?" "Yas'm," said Maymie. "And that when people die they turn back into dust?" "Yas'm," said Maymie. "Well," said Mrs. Brown forcefully, "I looked under the parlor rug this morning, Maymie, and there's quite a crowd there either coming or going!"

George Heister tells of a tired businessman whose grueling day at the office was capped by his wife's announcement that the maid had walked out. "What was the trouble this time?" he inquired wearily. "*You* were!" she charged. "She said you used insulting language to her over the phone this morning." "Good grief," cried the husband. "I thought I was talking to you!"

Somerset Hemingwell sat happily typing the final pages of his new novel. In the yard, his nine-year-old son had just tripped over a tree root and broken his leg. The boxer puppy had chewed up Mrs. Hemingwell's best curtain, the twins had spilled a can of paint in the parlor and were now trying to pull each other's hair out, and the nurse had given notice. Mrs. Hemingwell paused in front of her husband's door and called out, "Lunch will be ready in a few moments. How far have you gotten with your manuscript?" Mr. H. answered, "It's going like a house-afire. The hero is just proposing to the heroine." "Give it a happy ending," begged Mrs. H. earnestly. "Have her say 'no'!"

Laughter INCORPORATED

**The cream of the recent crop of
stories and anecdotes, harvested,
assorted, and prepared for market**

BY BENNETT CERF

With illustrations by Paul Galdone

Never in history has the average American citizen found more need for a saving sense of humor. Beset by threats of destruction by atomic bombs, inflation, mounting taxes, overcrowded cities, witch hunters, propagandists, caterwauling commentators, and the incessant clamor of radio and television commercials, he must laugh occasionally to keep from blowing his top altogether. It's far too easy today to see only the shadows, and ignore the patches of sunlight that remain. This collection of stories and anecdotes is designed to guide him back, if only momentarily, to the funny side of the street.

The contents of *Laughter Incorporated,* like those of my previous volumes (*The Pocket Book of War Humor, Try and Stop Me, Laughing Stock, Anything for a Laugh,* and *Shake Well Before Using*), are in large part unoriginal. Some of the stories obviously reflect my own adventures, but the greater part of them I have heard, read, or remembered, and then rewritten in my own words. Any raconteur or columnist who claims he originates more than one out of every hundred stories he retells is obviously all bull and a mile snide. His sources are the same as mine: wits who take justifiable pleasure in recounting their bons mots, press agents whose job it is to wangle the names of their clients into print, kindly friends who write or phone to pass on the funny stories that have come to their attention. If those occasional columnists who claim so insistently that they "originated" stories whose origins often can be traced back fifty years and more would

devote the time involved to checking the accuracy of some of the
other paragraphs they perpetrate, the people who really respect
the craft of journalism would be able to sleep more soundly at
night.

Much of the material in this volume appeared first in my "Trade
Winds" column in the *Saturday Review of Literature*, and in my
syndicated box for King Features. I thank the editors thereof for
permission to reprint it here. I also am indebted for similar cour-
tesies to the editors of the *Saturday Evening Post*, *Reader's Digest*,
Good Housekeeping, *Pageant*, *True Magazine*, and *Cosmopolitan*.

There are dozens of "joke books" published every year. The
ones that stand out from the pack do so not only because of the
stories selected, but of the manner and sequence in which they
are presented. The sequence in *Laughter Incorporated* represents an attempt to employ association of ideas. Every story
vaguely suggests the one that follows it—or at least it did before
I wielded my blue pencil in the final proof revisions. Furthermore,
that "association of ideas," I must ruefully admit, may not be apparent to strangers who have no way of knowing the peculiar
way in which my mind functions. Skeptics will have to take the
will for the deed.

I do not doubt that you've heard lots of the stories in this book
before. Some of them, however, you may agree are worth recalling. And if even a quarter of them are new to you—if they provide
you with a few real laughs—you've had your money's worth.
Somerset Maugham once remarked, "It's quite unnecessary to
make new jokes. In fact, I rather despise the man who does. He
is like the miner who digs up diamonds, but I am the skillful
artist who cuts them, polishes them, and makes them delightful
to the eye." A hundred story anthologists should rise and say
"Thank you, Maugham." They should also remind their readers
that nobody yet has gotten into a serious fight while he was
laughing.

For the rest, I only hope that I've stepped on no toes, tickled
some funny bones, and helped detour Mr. Gloom from your door
and the wolf from mine.

Bennett Cerf

New York City
August, 1950

The prevalent theory that women have absolutely no sense of humor is a dastardly canard, and in making this statement I may add that I am quoting my wife verbatim. Myself, I let no question of sex—or race, creed, or color—deter me from telling a funny story. I ask only that the person be within listening distance.

I begin this collection with stories that, in the past year, I have told with the greatest success to the girls I run around with, provoking them to laughter, tinkling and spontaneous, in which I have unfailingly joined.

A prominent Wall Street banker was leaving his home in White Plains to catch the 9:15 when his wife called out, "Please take my shoes and leave them at the Grand Central repair shop on your way to the office." The banker took the shoes under his arm without bothering to wrap them, and swung aboard the train with his mind teeming with details of million-dollar deals. A fellow commuter noted the shoes and boomed enthusiastically, "That's the way to do it, Joe. Don't let her gad about." . . . .

The wild and woolly finishes of recent Major League pennant races worked up one dyed-in-the-wool fan to such a pitch he had to seek the aid of a prominent psychiatrist. "Doctor," he complained, "I've got the baseball fever so bad I can't sleep any more. The minute I close my eyes I see myself either batting against the slants of Mel Parnell or pitching to Stan Musial or trying to steal signals from Casey Stengel. You've got to help me." The analyst gently said, "One remedy has been effective for centuries. Why don't you close your eyes and imagine you have a beautiful girl in your arms?" The fan interrupted angrily, "What! And miss my turn at bat?" . . . .

A visitor to Picasso's studio found the great painter staring dejectedly at his latest creation and muttering, "It's a failure." "How can you say that?" protested the visitor. "I think it's a masterpiece." "No," said Picasso, "the nose is wrong. It throws the picture out of perspective." "Then why not fix the nose?" asked the visitor. "That's not possible," said Picasso. "I can't find it." . . . .

From art circles comes another story concerning the visitor who was brought to admire the paintings of Verbena Abernathy, the Grandma Moses of the Ozarks. "What an original talent," gushed the visitor. "How I wish I could take those glorious colors home with me." "You're going to get your wish," cackled Verbena happily. "You're sitting on my palette." . . . .

Dr. George Gallup, the unquenchable pollster, was driving casually down the right-hand lane of a Los Angeles superhighway one day in early Spring when, on a sudden impulse, he made a sharp left turn. The chauffeurs of two cars speeding in the outer lanes avoided him by a miracle, but a motorcycle cop did not. "Your license, mister," he demanded angrily. When he had examined it, he inquired, "Not *the* George Gallup?" "Yes, I am," admitted Gallup. "Too bad, Doctor," said the cop. "I am afraid you just made your *second* serious mistake." . . . .

Some ladies like puns better than others, but all of them laughed at the following examples. That is, they didn't laugh: they groaned. It's not considered good form to laugh at a pun. You express your appreciation by wailing piteously, and the harder you wail, of course, the better you like the pun.

1. There was a little girl in Barcelona, Spain, named Carmen Cohen. Her mother called her Carmen, of course, but her father, for reasons only he could explain, always hailed her by her last name, Cohen. As a result, by the time the unfortunate little girl had reached the age of twelve she didn't know whether she was Carmen or Cohen.

2. A famous race horse was enjoying a workout at the Churchill Downs track when he stopped to speak to another horse that

was tethered to a post. "I can't remember your mane," mused the thoroughbred, "but your pace is familiar."

3. Farmer Klopfer had a cow that needed analysis as badly as the baseball fan I told you about above. Seems the poor cow had a fodder complex. Furthermore, she loved to imbibe ink and always mooed indigo.

4. There was a fellow out in Battle Creek, Michigan, whose name was Joe Kissinger. He didn't like the name Kissinger so he had it changed to Mackay. Two months later he tired of Mackay and changed to Johnson. Then he decided he had made another mistake and changed to Cartmell. By this time all his friends had begun to ask, "I wonder who's Kissinger now?" . . . .

The ladies, bless their hearts, have a special weakness for bright remarks of the kiddies, although I personally have been waiting impatiently for eight years to hear my eldest say one thing worth repeating. I liked particularly the story of the youngster who had an unfortunate habit of swearing—usually at the very worst time. His parents had tried every known method of curing him, without the slightest success, but the father had one ace left in the hole. He knew that his son had always wanted to own a rabbit, and he offered one in exchange for a solemn promise that there would be absolutely no more swearing on the part of his offspring. The bargain was made, and the boy got his rabbit. For two weeks, he stuck manfully to his bargain. Then came disaster. A couple called one Sunday afternoon, and the lady said, "I hear you have a rabbit, Christopher. Wouldn't you like to show it to us?" The boy was delighted and rushed out to the garden to collect his pet. Just as he brought it into the drawing room, however, the rabbit proceeded to give birth to an enormous litter of baby rabbits. The boy watched in consternation for a moment, dropped the mother rabbit to the ground, and cried, "Holy smoke, the damn thing is falling apart." . . . .

Runner-up to the rabbit fancier was a moppet at the Bronx Park Zoo who was fascinated by the antlers on a herd of deer. When he spied a doe in the enclosure, he yanked his mother's skirt and exclaimed, "Look at that one, Mom. No fenders." There was also the eight-year-old boy whose father asked, "Why did you kick your little sister in the stomach?" "Couldn't help it," the boy said. "She turned around too quick." . . . .

This is a shaggy-dog story, and I heard it originally from Mac-Kinlay Kantor who, in the course of a tour of military flying fields (to gather material for some magazine articles he had in mind), alleges he encountered one Air Force captain who was sixty-one years old. "Yes, sir," boasted the captain, "I'm the oldest junior officer in the whole Air Corps, and if you'd like to know why, here are the unvarnished facts:

"During World War Two, when we were engaged in our island-hopping campaign in the Pacific, I was based for months on one island where the C.O. delighted in getting us out of our comfortable beds in the middle of every night for an alert. After it had happened for thirty-two nights in succession, I got a great idea. I got hold of a tame orangutan that hung outside the canteen begging for food, dressed him in an air-officer's uniform, and trained him painstakingly to run to my plane whenever the alert sounded. He'd climb in, close the plexiglass dome over his head, pull down his goggles, switch on the engine, turn over the propeller, and keep his hand on the throttle until he heard the 'all clear.'

"It worked like a charm for weeks. One night, however, the 'all-clear' never came. I rushed over to the field just in time to see my plane, with the orangutan at the stick, take off in perfect style. When the last plane zoomed off, there were only two people left on the field—me and the C.O. He gave me a withering look and strode off, without saying a word.

"Well, sir, that's why I'm the oldest captain in the Corps. And I wouldn't mind—if it weren't that the damn orangutan is now a lieutenant-colonel!" . . . .

A crack New York reporter was hired by a Hollywood producer at fifteen hundred dollars a week (exactly fifteen times the salary to which he had been accustomed) to write a series of Western scripts for a cowboy star. The very day he reported for work, the star embarked on a wild spree and disappeared from sight, and the reporter had nothing to do but sit in the sun and draw a salary. Four weeks of this unaccustomed idleness were all he could stand, and he protested to the producer, "I'm not cut out for this sort of life. I am going back to my old job in New York." "Wait," pleaded the producer, "we've practically cornered our missing hero now. Meanwhile, if you must keep busy, I've got a job for you. It's full of human interest, too. Every day a parcel of women come out here to see the studio. We've got to be nice to them because they can murder us if they've a mind to. The fellow who usually conducts these tours is sick. You'll be doing me a genuine favor if you take over for him."

"Might as well," conceded the writer. He assembled his group and began pointing out the sights. One dowager indicated a building he had neglected to mention. "What is that?" she demanded. The reporter consulted his diagram and explained, "That's just a place where we store spoiled film." "Fine thing," snorted the dowager. "The whole country suffers from a housing shortage, and these rascals use a beautiful building like that just for the storage of spoiled film!"

"You don't know the half of it," agreed the reporter. *"They're also paying me fifteen hundred dollars a week just to point it out to you."* . . . .

Stray characters who provided occasional merriment included (1) The harassed father who looked despairingly at a month's accumulation of bills and sighed, "My salary now runs into three figures: my wife and two daughters." (2) The Tin-pan Alleyite who burst into the inner sanctum of a music publisher and cried, "Boss, I got a new song that will knock your eye out." The publisher pointed glumly to a patch over his right eye and answered, "I already heard it." (3) The lady who told her new maid, "I declare, I can write my full name in the dust you've left on this piano." "Bless my soul," answered the maid with delight. "It's sure nice to be working for a lady with education!" (4) The customer who accused his tailor, "Four days ago you sold me a suit for seventy dollars, and now there's nothing left of it." The tailor answered, "What do you think is left of the seventy dollars?" (5) The scissors-grinder who announced happily, "I'm having my biggest season. I never saw things so dull." (6) The wily Londoner who opened his request for the hand of a Scotsman's beautiful daughter with "Mr. MacTavish, I think I can show you a way to save yourself some expense." (7) The crabby lady golfer who loaded down her pint-sized caddy with a huge leather bag containing twenty clubs, and then grumbled steadily at him for sixteen holes. On the seventeenth fairway, about a hundred yards from the green, she demanded, "Boy, do you think I can get home with my number seven iron?" The caddy replied fervently, "Lady, ah doan even know wheah you live!" (8) The girl who rushed into a drugstore and asked, "Have you anything for ants?" "You bet," answered the clerk. "Where you got 'em?" (9) The sailor who treated all his girls to wine because he wanted a little port in every sweetheart. (10) And, finally, the hundred-year-old farmer who gave this explanation for his happy life: "When I works, I works easy. When I sits, I sits loose. And when I worries —I sleeps." . . . .

Let's conclude this roundup and allow the ladies to go back to more serious reading by telling about the retired colonel who lived next to a lunatic asylum. One of his regular afternoon naps on the lawn was rudely interrupted when a beautiful young lady, completely without clothes, came bursting through the hedge, hotly pursued by three interns dressed in white. The old colonel was just recovering from his astonishment when a fourth intern dashed into view carrying in each hand a heavy pailful of sand. The colonel noticed that a considerable gallery was watching from the other side of the hedge, so he called out, "What's the idea of the fourth intern with the pails of sand?" "That's his handicap," was the explanation. *"He caught her the last time."*

That great editor, Maxwell Perkins, always maintained that guests at a literary cocktail party never listened to what anybody else was saying. To prove his point he shook hands with Marcia Davenport at a gathering in her house and said, "I'm sorry I'm

late, but it took me longer to strangle my aunt than I expected."
"Yes, indeed," beamed Miss Davenport. "I'm so happy you have
come."

• • •

Mrs. Russel Crouse was interviewing a new nurse, and asked
why she had left her last post. "I didn't like the setup," said the
nurse frankly. "The child was backward, and the father was
forward."

• • •

The late Frank Crowninshield, wittiest raconteur of our time,
particularly cherished the answer the Duke of Portland gave him
years ago when he asked, "What London club do you like best?"
After due consideration, the Duke rumbled, "I use a filthy thing
called the Albermarle. The food and wines are capital. I'm a great
fellow for gluing and they have glue in the library. But the principal reason I like it is I don't know any of the members."

• • •

Crowninshield was an inveterate golf player, making up in zeal
what he lacked in skill. When Frank began chopping his way
around the course, players behind him resigned themselves to the
fact that they would never get home in time for dinner. Grantland Rice called him a "floating hazard." One day in the locker
room, Crowninshield announced cheerfully, "Boys, when I die, I
want to be cremated, and then have my ashes strewn over the
links. Then when the wind blows, all of you can say, 'There's Old
Man Crowninshield holding up the course again.'"
Probably Crownie's most widely quoted line in a golf match
was pulled when he was all square with Condé Nast going down
to the green of the sixteenth hole. He tugged his caddy's sleeve
and asked loudly, "Is that my dear friend's ball in the trap or is
the son-of-a-so-and-so on the green?"

• • •

A Newark motorist, reports the Ford *Times,* headed for a vacation in the White Mountains, and tarried for lunch in Boston. After a long search for a parking space he found an opening that barely sufficed between two imposing limousines, and after a great deal of jockeying, succeeded in wedging his car therein. When he alighted, however, he found that the rear left wheel was a good two feet up on the sidewalk. Too overheated and hungry to rectify the situation, he shrugged his shoulders and let the car stay that way, hoping the Boston constabulary would note the out-of-state license plate, and overlook his sin.

His hope was not in vain. When he returned from lunch, this neatly printed note was tucked beneath his windshield wiper: "Dear New Jerseyite: In Boston one does not park upon the sidewalk. Sincerely yours, Sergeant Murphy."

• • •

Emily Kimbrough lectured recently in Pittsburgh. Half-way through her talk, she leaned her elbows on the lectern. There was a ripping, crunching sound, and the lectern disintegrated under her. Pieces of kindling wood, studded with nails, went flying into the audience, and Miss Kimbrough narrowly avoided tumbling after them herself. A janitor emerged from the wings, helped Miss Kimbrough to her feet, and glared at the shocked audience. "I told you ladies," he shouted, "to warn your speakers about that lectern. It's got worms in it!"

• • •

When Somerset Maugham, the author of *Of Human Bondage,* *The Razor's Edge,* and dozens of other famous novels, visited Bombay, he was very definitely neglected by the snobbish English colony. Finally, however, a dowager condescended to speak to him at a large reception. "Mr. Maugham," she hazarded, "could you by any chance be related to Lord Maugham, the Lord Chancellor?" "Yes," he said. "He's my brother." The dowager summoned her friends. "This Mr. Maugham," she informed them breathlessly, "is a brother of the Lord Chancellor!" Then with hardly a pause, she said to Mr. Maugham, "Will you come to lunch on Wednesday?"

• • •

According to a folk legend down Oklahoma way, one native son who had crossed the river Styx had sufficient gumption to say to the Devil, "Your memory isn't so hot. There's an old Indian on a reservation in Oklahoma who's got you skinned a mile." The Devil accepted the challenge and said he'd give the audacious spirit his soul back if he could prove he was right.

The Devil journeyed to earth and confronted the Indian. "Do you like eggs?" he asked. The Indian said, "Yes, I do." The Devil then disappeared for thirty years, after which he suddenly approached the Indian again, waved his hand in greeting, and said, "How?" The Indian answered, "Fried."

The man got his soul back. What he did with it, unfortunately, is not told in this particular story.

• • •

It was this very same Indian who was known the length and breadth of Oklahoma for his invaluable weather predictions. The old farmers in the neighborhood came to depend upon him. There came a day, however, when one farmer, demanding to know when he could expect some rain, met with a great disappointment. The majestic red man shook his head sadly and grunted, "No can tell you. Radio busted."

• • •

A butler in His Majesty's household in London was determined that his son receive a college degree. "My own history demonstrates clearly the value of an education," he pointed out. "When but a lad, I applied for the position of footman to one of the wealthiest dowagers in the realm. 'In my service,' she said, 'you must wear a uniform with breeches; it is necessary, therefore, that I see your ankles.' I lifted my trousers. She seemed favorably impressed and went on, 'The knees also appear prominently when one wears formal breeches. I had better see them too.' Once again

she approved and then is when my education stood me in good stead. 'Madam,' I intoned with the dignity and savoir faire one learns only in the best schools, 'and now may I be permitted to show my testimonials?' The job was mine—and you see where it has led me! *Now* will you go to college?"

• • •

Gus Eysell, the man in charge of the mammoth Radio City Music Hall, has conducted all kinds and nationalities through the mazes of the institution, and usually knows in advance just how they are going to react to the vast auditorium, the complex lighting system, the orchestra that comes up on a moving platform from the cellar, and the marvelously trained Rockettes. One visitor who stopped him cold, however, was a farmer who never had been to New York before, and was being shown the sights because he had won a corn-growing contest. He never batted an eye during the entire tour, and spoke for the first time when he gazed up at the balcony from the center of the stage. What he said was, "This place sure would hold a lot of hay."

• • •

Harold Ross, editor of *The Stars and Stripes*, the doughboys' newspaper in World War One, came home from Paris after the Armistice, with the basic plan for the *New Yorker* magazine churning in his not too-well-ordered but ever-active mind. Scarcely off the transport, he encountered Secretary of War Newton D. Baker at a party, and listened in grave silence while Mr. Baker outlined the strategy that had brought the Allies victory. When Mr. Baker had concluded, Ross conceded, "Well, Mr. Secretary, you've cleared up everything except how Joe Higgins was ever made corporal of my squad."

Today, all of Ross' most extravagant dreams for the *New Yorker* have come true, but far from bringing him contentment, success finds him nursing occupational ulcers, and wailing about petty details that prevent his concentrating on higher things. He claims he even has to pick out postage stamps, and blow the noses of his underlings when they come down with colds. He was enlarging on this theme to a famous author one morning when his secretary burst into the office and gasped, "Quick, Mr. Ross! A man has just tried to commit suicide in the men's room." Ross threw his hands into the air, and said to the author, "See what I mean?"

Ross has moved the desks and partitions in the *New Yorker* office so frequently that James Thurber once hung a sign in the entrance hall that read, "Alterations Going On As Usual During Business."

• • •

The law firm of Button, Button, Button, and Button recently added a new partner named Zipper. He replaced one of the buttons.

• • •

Radio circles are agog with the rumor that the manufacturers of Serutan are planning a new program to be heard every Tuesday from 9:30 to 9.

• • •

A demure miss was engaged by a manufacturer to distribute little boxes of a new kind of candy free to passers-by. At the close of her first day's work she ran into an old friend, who asked, "Is it true you're going to be married soon?" "Next month," was the answer. "That's wonderful," said the friend. "What are you doing in the meantime?" "Nothing much," admitted the miss. "Just giving away free samples."

• • •

Cyrus Ching, the government's ace labor mediator, faced one of his toughest problems when he came to grips with a stubborn Sioux Indian negotiator in a Southwestern strike recently. The Sioux, representing a thousand defiant strikers, presented his demands in writing, and wouldn't budge an inch. Furthermore, the only answer Ching could extract from him was "Ugh." For two solid days he grunted "Ugh" at the termination of every plea of Ching's, and stared stolidly into space.

Ching had one last conference with the owners and then approached the Sioux again. "I think I have good news for you," he smiled. "The owners will grant your men a two-dollar-a-day increase in pay." The Sioux again said "Ugh"—but this time he added, "Are they willing to make it retroactive?"

• • •

Joseph Henry Jackson overheard the most priceless line of the season. Two society leaders were lunching at San Francisco's "Top of the Mark," discussing Jimmy Roosevelt's burgeoning political career. "I heard him on the radio last night," sniffed one of the ladies. "He'll never go far. Sounds just like his father."

• • •

One of the news scoops of the year occurred at the Cochrane Dude Ranch in Idaho last August. A bull threw a Senator.

At Scott's, two stamp and coin collectors got together to talk about old dimes.

At Alcatraz, a convict frantically summoned a guard, pointed at the rain pouring through the roof, and snarled, "This pen leaks."

At the Ringling Circus, a girl told her escort, "What a thrill! I just met a two-headed man face-to-face-to-face."

At a big nudist camp in Jersey, a costume party was the highlight of the season. A lady with varicose veins won first prize by going as a road map.

In Philadelphia, a young gentleman checked in to a hotel with a very blonde young lady and miscellaneous baggage, flabbergasted the room clerk by registering, "Mr. Yankee Doodle and Fife."

At Milo Sutliff's estate, the Italian gardener announced that his brother had been killed by a weasel. "A weasel?" echoed Sutliff in astonishment. "How come?" The gardener explained, "He driva hotmobil. Come to crossing. No heara da weasel."

• • •

This is Sinclair Lewis' story.

A gambler at a Las Vegas roulette wheel was very partial to Number Eleven. Unfortunately the little silver ball and Number Eleven did not even strike up a speaking acquaintance during an entire evening, and 2 A.M. found the gambler all alone at the table, low in spirit and finances.

He was about to put all of his remaining chips on Number Eleven again when a flutey, unearthly voice whispered in his ear, "Put it on Sixteen." The gambler wheeled around. Aside from himself and the yawning croupier, there wasn't a soul in sight. Utterly mystified, but impressed, the gambler shifted his stake to Number Sixteen. It came up! As he was about to rake in his chips, the shrill voice counseled, "Let it ride!"

Number Sixteen came up again!

The gambler, jittering with excitement, found himself awaiting that mysterious voice once more. Nor was he disappointed. "Put the whole pile on Twenty-two," it commanded. The gambler obeyed blindly.

The wheel spun. As it slowed down, the silver ball hovered on the very edge of Number Twenty-two, then skittered out into the green Zero.

The flutey voice cried, "Damnation!"

• • •

Book business experiences a seasonal lull in May every year, and publishers promptly begin weeping into their champagne cocktails at the Waldorf. Somebody asked Publisher Cass Canfield during this period, "How's business?" "Great," answered Canfield. "Our cat caught four mice yesterday."

A bookseller near the Communist official headquarters in New York got into the spirit of the occasion and complained, "Even self-confessed Reds won't buy leftist literature any more. Radical books sell so poorly now that with every copy I have to give an extra pair of pamphlets."

A hard-pressed dealer in Worcester tried holding up deliveries until his account at the bank looked less anaemic. One aggrieved customer wrote, "Four weeks ago I sent you a check for a dictionary with no index. All I have received to date is no index."

Writers get distressed occasionally about the sad state of literature, too. George Kaufman met one young novelist who was moaning about the state of his finances, and pointed out, "You can't sell a piece until you've written it. Why is it that I've seen nothing under your name for months?" "I did have a story in the last issue of *Flair*," protested the novelist, "but it fell out."

Alexander Alekhine, the chess master, once missed a train connection in an Austrian village. To kill time he wandered into a little inn where the local doctor was crowing over his forty-eighth consecutive chess victory. "I am unbeatable," declared the doctor modestly. Alekhine decided to teach him a lesson and challenged him to a game. To the utter amazement of the world's champion, the unknown doctor trimmed him in twenty-one moves.

"You have developed an absolutely new attack," marveled Alekhine. "I wonder why, however, you never used your rooks."

"You mean those pieces on the end?" asked the local doctor. "Around here, we've never learned how they move!"

• • •

The wiles and methods of professional card sharps aboard ocean liners and trains have been advertised so widely that suckers are not so plentiful as they were in days of yore. A famous Damon Runyon quote is the advice an old farmer gave his son who was leaving to make his way in the big city: "Remember, son, if a slick gambling feller comes along and offers you even money he can make the jack of spades jump out of a deck and spit prune juice in your face, don't take him—or sure as heck, you're goin' to wake up covered with prune juice!" One sharpshooter grew so discouraged at the slim pickings, he turned honest and wrote a book exposing the methods of his crooked compatriots. It has sold over a hundred thousand copies.

Friendly games, where all the participants are simply bursting with good will, are, of course, another story. John Voelker, prosecuting attorney of Marquette County, Michigan, tells of a game in which the town's leading doctor was taking a frightful shellacking until lo! a hand of stud came along in which he finally drew aces back to back. Furthermore, everybody stayed. On the next turn of the cards, the doctor drew another ace! Unfortunately, his friend Joe, sitting at his right, chose this moment to suffer a heart attack and slumped over the table.

The players rushed him to a couch where he breathed his last. "What'll we do now?" the white-faced players implored the doctor. "Out of respect for the dead," he replied promptly, "I suggest we finish this hand standing up."

In another poker game, a henpecked husband turned out to be the only winner. He didn't like to quit when he was so far ahead, but as the hours went by, he grew visibly more apprehensive. Suddenly, at about 2:30 A.M. he had an inspiration. He called his wife on the phone and when she answered, he cried to her, "Don't pay the ransom, darling. I've escaped."

• • •

The chivalry of the ante-bellum South is not dead, according to Kay Kyser. He defines a typical old-fashioned Southern gentleman as a man who hadn't embraced his wife for six months, but shot another man who did.

• • •

Texas Guinan, whose night clubs in the twenties lured gangsters, playboys, and butter-and-eggmen alike, and whose "Give this little girl a great big hand" started more than one curvaceous chorine on the road to stardom, found herself with two young ladies of her ensemble aboard a Hollywood-bound train one summer evening. Frankly bored with one another, they conceived the notion of rounding up three unattached men in the dining car, and setting up a game of poker. Their quest brought quick results: a pair of conservatively dressed, obviously prosperous young men, and one elderly gent who seemed trustworthy, despite a very gaudy necktie.

The game proved so enjoyable that it was continued, with interruptions for eating and sleeping, clear into the Los Angeles terminal. There the two young conservatives were met by a flock of detectives and hustled off to the hoose-gow. It seems they had robbed a Chicago hotel of some fifty thousand dollars in cash. The man with the gaudy necktie was accorded quite a greeting, too. He turned out to be Thomas R. Marshall, twenty-eighth Vice-President of the United States.

• • •

A ham actor was jailed on a counterfeiting charge, and complained to the warden, "My personality is being crushed here. You have taken away my illustrious name and given me a mere number." The warden, who was in a good humor, said, "If it will make you any happier, we'll give you a new number." The ham actor, mollified, conceded, "I guess the old one will do—but could you possibly *put it in italics?*"

• • •

Joe E. Lewis, the great night club entertainer, loves gambling so dearly that it's quite possible to believe the story that when a luxury liner sank in mid-Atlantic, and Joe was faced with the prospect of countless hours aboard a leaky raft amid the turbulent ocean waves, his sole thought was, "Dammit, this had to happen the one day I bet on high field in the ship pool."

• • •

In his early barnstorming days, Lewis stopped once at a boarding house whose proprietress could make a pound of food go further than any other landlady in history. She produced a platter of cold cuts one Sunday that were actually transparent. "Did you cut these?" asked Lewis politely, indicating the slices. "I did," said the landlady. "Okay," said Lewis. "Then I'll deal."

• • •

A guest at a summer resort in the Catskills was asked to name the three things in modern life he found most delectable. After some reflection, he replied, "First, I like as much herring as it's possible to eat. Second, some creamy cheese cake. And third, a little more herring."

• • •

A group of serious-minded ladies in Providence, Rhode Island, staged a séance last month. After the medium had impressed them all no end with the usual display of table raising and floating banjos, she announced that if anybody present would like to speak to the dear departed she thought she could arrange things. Mrs. Goldberg promptly declared that she would like to exchange a few words with her Uncle Moisha who had passed away in Pinsk the previous winter. After a considerable amount of bell ringing, moaning, and off-stage humming, a voice announced distinctly, "Hello, Sadie. This is Uncle Moisha."

"Well, well," said Mrs. Goldberg. "How are things going with you, Uncle Moisha?"

"Couldn't be better," reported Uncle Moisha cheerfully. "I really have no cause whatever for complaint."

"That's fine," said Mrs. Goldberg. "But do you mind if I ask just one more question?"

"Fire away, my dear niece," said Uncle Moisha.

"All right, then," said Mrs. Goldberg. "Where the hell did you learn to speak English?"

• • •

Brian Donlevy still gets laughs with his story of the Aberdeen brothers who learned their old father was seriously ill in London, and dispatched the eldest son to look after him. "Wire us when you've seen him," said the other two, "and remember you can send ten words for a shilling." That night they received the following wire: "Arrived safely. Father dead. Funeral Tuesday. Rangers two, Celtics one."

• • •

Judge Jim Wallace, of the New York Supreme Court, remembers when two natives of County Cork occupied adjoining cells in the death house. The dread morning arrived when Paddy was scheduled to be led to the electric chair. The Governor had failed to grant a reprieve, and Paddy knew his case was hopeless. As the guards came to lead him down "the last mile," his friend Mike in the next cell strove desperately to think of something cheering to say. At the last moment, he waved his hand through the bars and called jovially, "Well, Paddy me boy, more power to ye!"

• • •

In one of Clarence Darrow's first recorded court battles, the grizzled veteran who opposed him sought repeatedly to belittle him in the eyes of the jury by referring to him as "my beardless adversary." Darrow concluded his summation by remarking, "My opponent seems to condemn me for not having a beard. Let me reply with an anecdote. The King of Spain once entrusted a youthful liege with an important message to the court of a neighboring monarch. The latter flew into a rage and cried, 'Does the King of Spain lack men, that he sends me a beardless boy?' The young ambassador answered, 'Sire, had my king but known you imputed wisdom to a beard, he would have sent you a goat.'"

Darrow won the case hands down—and was launched on one of the most brilliant careers in the history of the bar.

• • •

The seven-year-old hopeful of a fisherman accompanied his father to a stream and wandered off for a walk. A few minutes later the father heard a strange cry of anguish, and found a man hopping on one foot, caressing the other foot, and groaning with pain. "What's happened?" asked the father. "I guess it's my fault," said the seven-year-old. "This man told me he hadn't had a bite all morning—so I bit him."

The Pun-American Congress has singled out for special honor the following members in good standing:

Peter Windsor, whose Swedish friend inserted an ad in a Stockholm paper reading, "I am no longer responsible for my wife's debts. She has left my bed and smörgåsbord."

Mary Vassar and Joe Amherst. Joe asked, "May I kith you?" Mary answered, "You kin."

Mr. Cyanide in Atlanta who asked to speak to a Mr. Potassium in Waco. "And remember," he cautioned the long-distance operator. "It's a poison-to-poison call."

Paul Gibson, whose friend, a bell ringer, got tangled up in his rope and tolled himself off.

Pyke Johnson, Jr., whose prevaricating dentist made his own teeth and now has to lie in them.

Phineas Wagstaff, who swallowed four pages from the *Congressional Record* and rushed to the medicine chest for relief. "What on earth are you doing?" called Mrs. Wagstaff. Her husband explained, "Boring from within."

Bob McMillen, associate editor of *Farm Journal,* who dawdled over a second cup of coffee one Sunday morning, reading *The Canterbury Tales.* His father demanded, "What have you got there?" McMillen answered, "Just my cup and Chaucer."

And finally, Pablo Del Payo, somewhat near-sighted, who approached an effeminate Spaniard in Barcelona, and asked, "Are you Juan?" "Si, si," said the Spaniard eagerly. "Are you one too?"

* * *

One of Arthur Brisbane's best newspaper yarns concerned a cub reporter on the Providence *Journal* whose first assignment was an interview with the priest of a local Roman Catholic church. He was told that the Reverend Father was in the rear of the church receiving confessions. The young reporter hurried to the confession box and murmured apologetically, "I beg your pardon, Father, but I'd like to see you for a few moments. I'm a reporter from the Providence *Journal.*" The Reverend Father clucked his tongue sympathetically and answered, "Young man, I have listened to confessions for the past thirty years, and yours is certainly the most harrowing I've ever heard."

* * *

When the late Adolph Ochs was running the New York *Times*, one of his pressmen named Carr was the proud father of eight children. He dutifully reported every birth to Mr. Ochs personally and was rewarded each time with a bonus of $50.00. One morning he appeared before Mr. Ochs again, hat in hand, and announced cheerfully, "Well, sir, my wife has just presented me with another little Carr." Mr. Ochs produced the expected $50.00 and said drily, "Might I suggest that you make this new little Carr the caboose?"

• • •

Tell-people-the-facts technique on the front page of the Raymond (Washington) *Herald:* "When the car overturned both girls were injured, Miss Thompson about the face, and Miss Cromwell in the back seat." . . . And a column on fishing in a Portland daily contained this Freudian slip: "For sheer tricks, fight, and stamina, give us a small-mouthed lass any time!"

• • •

George Frazier tells about a newcomer on the staff of *Life* magazine who chafed because he was not given enough work to do. Finally he marched into the office of Managing Editor John Shaw Billings and complained, "I've been here at *Life* for weeks now, Mr. Billings, and no one's even spoken a word to me." Billings looked up from his galley proofs and asked sourly, "What do you expect *me* to do? Set a precedent?"

• • •

RED PASTURES

It was Rudyard Kipling who designated Russia as "the bear that walks like a man." Today, he'd probably substitute the word "scare" for "bear." The obvious aim of Soviet propaganda is to paralyze its satellites and enemies with fear and confusion. A few brave souls in the border states, however, have refused to have their wits frightened out of them. Their derisive and satirical jibes are circulated internally at the risk of the tellers' lives, and then smuggled through chinks in the iron curtain. Retold in America, they may be responsible for a certain amount of confusion. One high-school student in Chicago, for instance, still insists that Kremlin is the trade name of a widely advertised hair tonic. Upon being apprised of this fact, the local Soviet consul is said to have stamped out of his study in a rage—a radical departure if ever I heard one!

From Prague and Budapest have come these illuminating stories in the past months:

A janitor in a once-fashionable apartment house in Prague padded through the halls one night in his bedroom slippers, banging on every door, but reassuring the tenants, "It's not as bad as you think, comrades! It's just that the building is burning down."

An urchin in Slovakia was being catechized by a Soviet inspector. "Who is your father?" queried the inspector. "The incomparable Stalin," proclaimed the urchin. "And your mother?" "The incomparable Soviet Union," said the urchin in the same parrot-like tone. The inspector allowed himself the shadow of a smile, and asked, "What would you like to be when you grow up?" The urchin answered fervently, "An orphan."

A Budapest merchant, traveling through Russia and bordering states, sent his friend a series of tell-tale postcards. The first read: "Greetings from Free Moscow," the second, "Greetings from Free Warsaw," the third, "Greetings from Free Prague." Then there was a month's silence, after which a final message arrived, postmarked Paris. This one read "Greetings from Free Rabinowitz."

Three prisoners at a labor camp in Czechoslovakia engaged in surreptitious converse. Whispered the first prisoner, "I'm here because I was suspected of being in sympathy with Radak." The second reported, "I'm here because I was said to be plotting *against* Radak." The third prisoner said, "I'm Radak."

An old cohort of Benes and Masaryk in Prague, undone by the events of the past two years, decided to commit suicide. The police had confiscated his revolver and he didn't have enough ration stamps for a rope, so he walked to the city hall and screamed at the guards, "Down with Stalin! Let's drive the Russian swine out of our beloved fatherland." He figured he would be shot immediately. The guards, however, threw down their machine guns, jumped over the fence, and cried, "Hurrah! Hurrah! The Americans have arrived!"

In Hungary, everybody listens to foreign radio broadcasts, at the risk of incurring the vast displeasure of the authorities. To date, there is no law against the practice, but still nobody takes unnecessary chances. A stranger accosted a policeman in Budapest one evening and asked what time it was. The policeman didn't bother consulting his watch. He looked up at a row of flats and announced, "It's exactly eight thirty." "Remarkable," said the stranger. "How do you do it?" "Very simple," answered the policeman. "They're all closing their windows. The London program must be coming on."

The commissioner in charge of public housing in Warsaw had been ordered to economize. In his report he declared proudly, "We estimate that in the past six months we have saved twenty-three million bricks, five hundred thousand panes of glass, and thirteen million hours of labor." "Excellent," beamed the chief.

"How many houses did you build?" "None," said the commissioner. "That's how we economized."

A Stockholm explorer was scaling a Himalayan peak with a Russian companion when a miniature snowslide bowled them over and left them dangling over a precipice, clinging to a fragile rope. "We're goners," groaned the Russian. "Afraid of the precipice?" gasped the Swede. "No, the rope," said the Russian. "My factory manufactured it."

A movie producer in Prague sought official sanction for a picture based on the life of Adolf Hitler. "Are you insane?" cried a commissar. "Hitler invaded Russia without provocation, destroyed hundreds of our cities, and killed millions of our comrades. And you want to glorify him on the screen?" The producer was conciliatory. "So he did do wrong in Russia," he admitted. "Can't everybody make a little mistake now and then?"

Comrade Petrov, vice-commissar of the Bureau of Supply, explained to a group of visitors in Moscow, "When there is food in the villages and none in the cities—like today, alas—that is right deviation. Should we ever reach the point where there was food in the cities and none in the villages, that would be left deviation." Ivan, a puzzled guest from Czechoslovakia, interrupted, "What if there were food both in the cities *and* the villages?" "That, Comrade," snapped the vice-commissar, "would be capitalist propaganda."

Stories deriding the intelligence of Soviet emissaries are legion. The one I like best concerns the Russian delegate all dolled up in a frock coat (appropriated) who drove his fine horse and carriage (also appropriated) up to a Prague café, and told the proprietor, "My horse is thirsty. Give him a bucketful of your best cognac." It took fourteen bottles of cognac to fill the bucket. The horse lapped it up with obvious relish. "He's still thirsty," decided the Russian. "I think he can take about another half-bucketful." The horse consumed this too and the Russian then asked, "What do I owe you?" "Twenty-one bottles of fine cognac are not cheap," said the proprietor. "Your bill amounts to nine thousand crowns. I think a man who runs up a bill like that deserves something on the house. What will you have, sir?" "Who, me?" said the Russian in astonishment. "I can't drink, you fool. I'm driving."

Saint Peter, concerned about the state of affairs in America, sent his most dependable and conservative disciple, Saint Theresa, to look over the situation and give him a personal report. She stopped first in New York, and phoned at the end of three days to say things were even worse than they had feared. "Let me come home," she begged. "No," said Saint Peter. "Finish the job. Go on to Chicago." She called him again from Chicago with an even more dismal tale. "It's a nest of corruption," she reported sadly. "Sinners on all sides. I can't take any more of it. Allow me to return to Heaven." "Patience and fortitude," counseled Saint Peter (where had he picked up this expression, he wondered fleetingly). "They tell me Hollywood is worst of all. Have a look around out there and then you can come home."

Two weeks went by without further word from Saint Theresa. Saint Peter, beside himself with anxiety, was about to turn the case over to the celestial FBI when the phone finally rang. An operator said, "One moment puh-lease. Hollywood calling," and then a sweet voice came over the wire: "Hello, Peter darling? How divine! This is Terry."

• • •

On a sunny Shabboth (Saturday) afternoon on the Promenade in Karlsbad, two old Jewish friends met for the first time in years. After exchange of the usual amenities, Jacob's expression grew serious and he said, "Shmuel, people are telling me you don't go to the Synagogue any more. Can it be true you no longer believe in God?" Shmuel looked uncomfortable, and hurriedly changed the subject.

The next afternoon, Sunday, the old friends met again. This time Jacob was insistent. "You must tell me, Shmuel," he said. "Don't you believe in our God any more?" Shmuel replied, "Here is a straight answer to a straight question. No, I don't." Jacob asked, "Why didn't you tell me that yesterday?" Shmuel, deeply shocked, exclaimed, "God forbid—on a Shabboth?"

• • •

In Nathan Ausubel's *Treasury of Jewish Folklore* appears the story of a famous preacher of Dubno whose driver stopped en route to a lecture date and said, "Rabbi, do me a favor. For once I'd like to be the one receiving all the honors and attention, to see what it feels like. For this one engagement, exchange clothes with me. You be the driver and let me be the rabbi."

The preacher, a merry and generous soul, laughed and said, "All right—but remember, clothes don't make the rabbi. If you're asked to explain some difficult passage of the Law, see that you don't make a fool of yourself."

The exchange was effected. Arrived at their destination, the bogus rabbi was received with tumultuous enthusiasm, and obviously loved every minute of it. Finally, however, there came the dreaded moment when an extremely tricky question was put to him.

He met the test nobly. "A fine lot of scholars you are," he thundered. "Is this the most difficult problem you could ask me? Why, this is so simple even my driver could explain it to you." Then he called the Preacher of Dubno: "Driver, come here for a moment and clarify the Law for these dull-witted fellows."

• • •

Another Ausubel story concerns the merchant from Chelm who drove his horse and loaded wagon to a neighboring town and was asked by a prospective customer, "What are you selling today?" The merchant whispered in his ear, "Oats." "Why the secrecy?" demanded the customer. "S-s-sh," soothed the merchant. "Not so loud. I don't want the horse to hear."

• • •

Wallace Reyburn, author of *Some of It Was Fun,* entered Naples with the victorious troops who threw out the Nazis near the end of World War Two. A grateful native offered to introduce him to a sister at home. "Is she beautiful?" asked Reyburn. "Oh, bella! bella!" enthused the native. "Young?" "Si! Si! Si!" "And is she pure?" persisted Reyburn. The native turned from him in disgust, remarking, "These Americans and Canadians are all crazy."

• • •

The man who wrote one-page synopses of all the new novels and plays for one of Hollywood's biggest studios was two hours late for his daughter's wedding. "Where can the old boy be?" asked the bridegroom anxiously. "He's probably upstairs," said the bride's mother, "condensing the wedding ceremony."

• • •

Writer Frank Scully had an important lunch date with Louis B. Mayer, head of MGM. "How did it go?" asked Scully's wife when he returned home. "Fifty-fifty," reported Frank. "I showed up and Mayer didn't."

• • •

The late D. W. Griffith was fond of telling people that in the big Civil War battle scenes of his *The Birth of a Nation* he employed 50,000 extras. When people pointed out that this must have cost him a half million dollars a day for over a hundred days, and marveled "How did you stay solvent?" Griffith would chuckle and say, "I worked out an infallible system. Our soldiers used real bullets."

• • •

Leon Shimkin, one of the heads of the giant publishing firm of Simon and Schuster, once signed up for a course in "Cultivating Human Relationships and Developing Personality." The man who gave the course was named Dale Carnegie.

Mr. Carnegie's siren song lulled Shimkin into a state of blissful intoxication. "You ought to write a book for Simon and Schuster," he declared. "I already have written two," said Carnegie sharply, "and they turned both of them down." "You couldn't have used the material of this lecture course," averred Shimkin, undaunted. "All you have to write about is how to make friends——" "And influence people," added Carnegie. The two men fell into each other's arms and rushed out for a beaker of buttermilk. History— and Dale Carnegie—were made that night.

In its various editions the book that resulted has sold over three and a half million copies, and put Dale Carnegie into the same bracket with Andrew.

Shimkin shared the front seat of a Fifth Avenue bus recently with a fussy and aggressive matron who was determined not to ride past her destination. She pestered the driver all the way up the avenue, and, as a climax, poked him vigorously with her umbrella. "Isn't that Seventy-third Street?" she demanded. "No, madame," replied the enraged driver. "That is my behind."

• • •

Two elderly ladies checked into a sporty new hotel in Miami Beach. The first thing they noticed was a furtive little man circulating from guest to guest in the lobby, whispering, and collecting money. They were told he was a bookie—a man who took bets on the horses.

In vacation abandon, they decided impulsively to risk two dollars themselves. They lost. That night one of the ladies tossed around in her bed and sighed so lugubriously that the other counseled her, "Becky, you shouldn't cry so over spilled milk. Stop

worrying because you lost. It was only two dollars." "It ain't losing
I'm worrying about," Becky answered. "I was worrying about if
we had won. What would we have done with the horse?"

• • •

David Niven was one British star in Hollywood who rushed
back to join the colors the moment World War Two broke out.
Attired in his spic and span new uniform, he made for his London club wondering if any of the old Colonel Blimps dozing in
the lounge would recognize him.

One of them obviously did. "I say there, Niven," he har-
rumphed. "Where have you been keeping yourself?" "In Hollywood, sir." "Hollywood?" "Yes, sir. That's a rather interesting city,
sir, on the west coast of the United States." Colonel Blimp mulled
this over for a moment and closed the conversation with, "Hmpf!
Dashed if I knew we had a garrison there."

• • •

According to Niven's friend Doug Fairbanks, Jr., David had
been assigned in his youth to a remote army post in India. Female
talent was scarce, and the one really beautiful girl, unfortunately,
was the wife of the colonel.

One morning at mess, the colonel suddenly asked, "Niven, are
you in love with my wife?" Niven turned brick red and stammered, "Certainly not, sir." "Then, demme," barked the colonel,
"stop telling her you are. It makes her nervous."

• • •

A Broadway columnist, reports *Punch*, visited England, and as
is his custom, promptly claimed that all the funny stories in circulation there had been "originated" by himself. "I am always
being told one of my own stories," he brayed. *Punch* summed it
up as "a plain case of the tale dogging the wag."

• • •

Harry Hershfield acted as toastmaster for a big industrial concern's jubilee banquet. "Your president achieved success by watching the little things," Hershfield told his audience. "One day a minor employee arrived late with one eye closed, his left arm in a sling, and his clothes in tatters. "It's nine-thirty," pointed out the president, "and you were due at eight-thirty." The employee explained, "I fell out of a tenth-story window." The president snorted, "It took you a whole hour?"

The crusty president of a country bank suddenly decided to be candid on his eightieth birthday when somebody asked him, "How did you get started in the banking business anyway?"

"Wasn't nothing to it," confessed the old moneybags. "I jist hung out a sign sayin' 'Bank.' Fust thing you know, a feller comes along and deposits $100. A little later, another comes along and deposits $200. By that time I was so confident I put in ten dollars of my own money."

• • •

Here are a few stories I picked up on my recent visit to the Ozarks:

An arthritic mountaineer came into a small and totally unexpected inheritance and decided to buy a second-hand jalopy to ease the burden of his declining years. The cheapest he could find in all Missouri was $135, but the dealer reminded him, "You get five good tires thrown in free; they haven't gone more'n 30,000 miles." "Forget the tires," said the mountaineer. "I don't want any on my car. When I'm riding I want to know it." . . . .

The same character had his own system for telling the hour. A neighbor drove past the shack and called out, "Know what time it is, Jonathan?" The mountaineer studied the shadow on his porch, shifted the tobacco in his cheek, and answered, "'Bout four and one-half planks till supper time." . . . .

During quail season, Bruce Cooper met an old farmer hunting with an ancient pointer. Twice the dog pointed. Twice his master kicked at a matted growth, wheeled sharply and fired into the empty air. When Cooper saw no birds rise, he asked the farmer for an explanation. "Shucks," grinned the old man, "I knew there warn't no birds in that grass. Spot's nose ain't what it used to be. But him and me have seen some wonderful days together. He's still doing his best—and it'd be mighty little of me to call him a liar." . . . .

A lady was alone in her home in Crane knitting peacefully when a telegram arrived, telling her a distant cousin had passed away and left her a million dollars. Half the thrill of getting news like that, of course, comes from telling others about it. The little lady dropped her knitting, ran to the telephone, and cried excitedly, "Hello, operator! Get me anybody!"

● ● ●

A newspaperman was captured by a band of cannibals. "Unhand me," he demanded. "I'm in the newspaper business, and demand the immunity of the press." "Most interesting," observed the cannibal chief, who was a graduate of Oxford. "Are you an editor?" "No," said the captive, "but I'm an assistant editor." "Let me be the first to congratulate you on your impending promotion," said the chief warmly. "After dinner you'll be an editor-in-chief."

This is not the only time the chief gave his followers a cannibelly-laugh. There was the day, for instance, he broke them up by remarking, "I passed a young man in the woods this morning." And the day the witch doctor told him, "There's nothing wrong with you that couldn't be cured with a good dose of salts." "O.K.," said the chief, "catch me a couple of shipwrecked sailors."

When the chief came down one morning with a severe attack of hay fever, it was his wife's turn to get into the act. "It serves you right," she pointed out coldly, "for eating that grass widow."

• • •

John Guldahl, just back from Tokyo, tells of a Brooklyn corporal in the American Army of Occupation who learned he was going to be shipped back to America, and cried in panic, "I've got to kill me a Jap before I go home, or I'll never be able to look my Flatbush pals in the face again." "Pipe down on that nonsense," advised his buddy. "The war's over. You'll find yourself in the guard house if you don't look out."

The corporal was not to be dissuaded. He brandished a slightly rusted bayonet and charged out of the barracks. Shortly thereafter his buddy heard a great commotion down the street. He found a Jap, quite dead, in the roadway, and the corporal, seriously wounded, groaning nearby.

"Now you've done it," mourned the buddy. "Tell me what happened before the M.P.s find you."

"I saw this Jap," explained the corporal weakly, "and I says to myself, 'There's your man.' So I goes up to him and cries, 'Tojo is a low-down rat.' He answers, 'Your commanding general is ten times worse.' Then, just as we were shaking hands, a jeep musta hit us."

• • •

For a supreme example of courtesy I give you the story of a wealthy Chinese gentleman who occasionally entertained American visitors in his sumptuous Shanghai home before it was engulfed by the all-conquering Red Armies.

Before taking two important American businessmen in to dinner, he showed them his prize possession—a Ming horse, some five feet high, in exquisite detail, wrought centuries ago by a master craftsman. "There are only four of these left in all the world," he explained proudly. "Even the experts cannot gauge its present-day value. Nothing possibly could induce me to part with it."

At dinner, unfortunately, one of the Americans got exceedingly drunk, and, more unfortunate still, insisted upon mounting the Ming horse when he left the table. Before his horrified companion could stop him, he flung one leg over the priceless relic, slipped, and crashed to the floor with the porcelain splintering into a thousand pieces around him.

The Chinese gentleman merely sighed, and stooped to help the drunken American to his feet. "Do not trouble yourself about this mishap," he said gravely. "It makes the three remaining specimens that much more valuable."

• • •

Another athletic drunk appeared at a ticket window in Louisville with a companion slung over his shoulder out cold. "One seat to Cincinnati," he demanded. The ticket seller said, "How about that big lug you're carrying?" "Him," deprecated the drunk. "Thass jus' my little six-year-old boy Abner." "Six years old, eh?" said the ticket seller. "Why, he's fully six feet tall, weighs about 185, and has a beard three inches long." The drunk dumped his companion on the platform and grumbled, "Dammit, Abner! I told you to shave!"

• • •

A Southern colonel, who cherishes the prejudices of his grandfather, was horrified when his gawky and strong-willed daughter elected to attend a college in New England. The daughter was well aware of his feelings, so when she actually fell in love with a Massachusetts lad she broke the news with some trepidation. "Daddy," she hazarded, "what would you-all say if I married a damyankee one day?" "Say?" roared the colonel. "I'd say we were beginning to pay 'em back at last!"

• • •

There was quite a party staged out in San Francisco recently when the flourishing firm of Levi Strauss & Co. celebrated its hundredth anniversary. The city's finest, including the governor, the mayor, and several booksellers, turned out to honor the house

that makes "levis," one of the most popular and distinctive forms
of dress in all the United States. The first pair of levis was made
out of some canvas the founder of the company had intended for
wagon or tent covers. He changed his plans when he discovered
how desperately the gold miners needed a garment that could
withstand the rigors of their daily routine. The first miner who
bought a pair of his new overalls went up and down the state
proclaiming the wonders of "those pants of Levi's" and the name
clung. As for the copper rivets that have been a distinguishing
mark of levis to this very day, they were originally demanded by
a millionaire prospector named Alkali Ike, who complained that
the gold nuggets he invariably carried were ripping his pockets
wide open. The rivets made him a contented man—and his companions demanded counterparts. Now, of course, they're little
more than decorations.

The company says its levis are so tough one satisfied customer
used a pair to tow a truck out of a ditch in Wyoming. Another
man broke his leg but wouldn't let the intern who treated him
cut off his pants. "Pull 'em off," he commanded, "no matter how
much it hurts me. Another pair of levis would be too hard to get."
When Howard Cullman, head of the New York Port Authority, Broadway Angel Number One, and manufacturer of Parlia-

ment Cigarettes went West last winter, he ordered a pair of levis specially manufactured for himself. It was no usual request but the owners of the business hold Mr. Cullman in high esteem and decided to humor him. "Have your tailor send us your measurements," they instructed him, "and we'll do our best for you." A Fifth Avenue tailor duly noted the most minute details of the Cullman physique and air-mailed them to San Francisco. The foreman of the Levi Strauss plant studied them for a moment, then announced firmly, "There is no such person."

• • •

An ingenious merchant brought out a new line of suits made of spun glass. A bright young advertising man suggested as a theme song, "I'll be seeing you in all the old familiar places."

• • •

A gangling hayseed in an ill-fitting, mail-order suit shambled into a flashy but expensive Chicago hotel, and demanded the best room in the place. "Can you afford it?" the clerk asked suspiciously. By way of answer, the hayseed produced a roll of banknotes big enough to choke a rhinoceros. The clerk's demeanor changed abruptly. "Yes, sir," he boomed. "Welcome to our hotel! Kindly sign the register, sir." The hayseed clutched the pen as though it were a baseball bat, and laboriously made a cross in the register.

A beautiful blonde in the lobby also had gotten a look at the hayseed's bankroll. She strolled languidly to the desk, and favored him with a provocative smile and wiggle. When she trailed off, the hayseed sniffed the aura of her perfume, and said reverently, "Man, oh man!" "Want to take her to dinner?" asked the clerk. "I think I could arrange it for you."

"That would be mighty kind of you," said the hayseed. "I won't fergit it. But before you talk to her, better hand over that register again." While the puzzled clerk watched him, he drew a rough circle around the cross he had made previously. He explained craftily, "There, that fixes everything. If I'm a-going traipsing round with a gorgeous blonde, I certainly ain't going to do it under my right name!"

• • •

An irate guest at a small-town inn grabbed the telephone and hollered into it, "Are you the confounded desk clerk of this dilapidated joint?" The nettled clerk answered, "Yes, I am. What's eating you?" "That," said the guest coldly, "is what I'd like to know."

• • •

Waldorf attendants recall a bronzed, six-foot, Gary Cooperish sort of fellow who flew into a rage in the lobby one night because all the elevators were delayed for one reason or another on upper floors. Finally one descended. It was operated by a wisp of a girl. The six-footer stamped inside and bellowed, "Where the devil have you been? Do you realize I have to get packed for a mountain climbing expedition? Second floor—and make it snappy!"

• • •

A famous Washington newspaperman was dining at Galatoire's, in the old French quarter of New Orleans, and raved over the trout Marguery. He summoned the proprietor and said, "I'd like to have the recipe for this dish." The proprietor smiled, and answered suavely, "I'm sorry, sir, but we have the same policy here as you journalists. We never reveal our sauce."

• • •

Grover Whalen has revived the story of the fastidious diner who objected to the way his steak had been prepared and had it sent back to the kitchen. The waiter brought it back with a message that the chef considered the steak perfectly okay in every particular. "He does, does he?" bellowed the outraged diner. "You just march that steak back to the chef and tell him to ram it down his throat." Back came the waiter with the same old steak. "I'm very sorry, sir," he reported, "but there are two steaks and four lamb chops ahead of you."

* * *

John Mason Brown, following the lead of all good parents, utilized the Easter vacation to take his two small boys to Washington. They saw everything, with a side trip to Mount Vernon thrown in as a matter of course.

Several months later, Brown came across a picture of Mount Vernon in a magazine and decided to determine how much, if anything, his boys had learned from their trip to the capital. "Meredith," he asked the one aged eight, "do you know what place this is?" "Don't be silly, Pop," answered Meredith. "Everybody knows that. It's Howard Johnson's."

* * *

Emily Kimbrough attended a luncheon in a fashionable suburb of Philadelphia where the eight-year-old daughter of the house was permitted to sit at the table after being reminded that "little children are seen but not heard." She behaved like a little soldier all through the meal, never uttering a word. As coffee was being served, however, she felt she simply had to say something. She waited for a lull in the conversation to put in her two cents' worth: "Do you ladies know there are a kind of dog with two rows of buttons on its stummick?"

* * *

Other children who have made news recently include:

The misbehaving youngster who was asked by Francis L. Duffy, "Do you know where bad little girls go?" "Certainly," she answered. "They go almost everywhere."

The little boy and girl who sought to enter one of the town's swankiest night clubs. The doorman asked, "What made you kids think of coming here anyhow?" They produced a copy of *Cue* and showed him the listing: "El Morocco. Dinner dancing, 8 to 12."

Paul Porter's young daughter who reported on a neighbor's problem child, "Teacher says she's a jubilant delinquent."

Ten-year-old Homer Miller, who, when asked to spell weather, hazarded, "W-A-E-T-I-O-U-R." The teacher regarded him with a certain degree of wonder and said, "Homer, that is certainly the worst spell of weather we've had around here for years."

The son of the gay and popular Robert Considine, who bade his parents good night as they left for one of their innumerable parties. Mrs. C. asked, "Do you want to play with your trains tonight or just stay with Nursie?" The boy answered, "What would Daddy do?"

The little darling who countered Freddie March's playful "I'll bet you don't even know who made you" with "Do you mean originally or recently?"

The moppet who swallowed a quarter, a dime, and a penny. Asked how he was progressing, the family doctor reported, "There's no change yet."

And finally, Irita Van Doren's three-year-old grandson, who awoke in the middle of the night, complaining that he had had a horrendous dream. He wouldn't go back to sleep until he was

allowed to stow his favorite cap-pistol under his pillow. A half-hour later two shots rang out. His parents rushed in to find him twirling his gun in the approved Hopalong Cassidy manner. "That dream came back," he explained, "so I shot it. Of course, this is just a pretend gun—but luckily, the dream didn't know that!"

• • •

Joe Frisco, the stuttering comedian, is an unending source of stories for the hard-pressed columnists. One of the latest chronicles the touch he made from Charlie Farrell, the ex-movie star and present hotel magnate in Palm Springs. "It's only a hundred d-d-dollars," pleaded Frisco. "I need it for a new set of teeth the dentist is making f-f-for me." Farrell gave him the century note, but three days later Frisco was back asking for more. "What did you do with the hundred I gave you Tuesday?" asked Farrell suspiciously. "I had b-b-bad luck, Charlie," confessed Frisco. "My t-t-teeth finished seventh!"

Another Frisco story had him lost in the fog while driving his roadster from Palm Springs to San Bernardino. There was a car ahead of him picking its way through the enshrouding mist, and Frisco decided to follow closely behind it. This labor-saving device worked fine until the car that was guiding him stopped short —and Frisco's runabout smashed into its rear bumper.

The excited comedian jumped to the ground and hollered, "Why don't you s-s-stick your hand out when you c-c-come to a stop?" A voice hollered back, "Why should I—in my own garage?"

• • •

The Theatre Guild once gave a dinner whose object was to raise sufficient cash to purchase a couple of Gobelin tapestries for the new playhouse. Alexander Woollcott, the toastmaster, began his remarks with "Those Gobelins are going to get you if you don't watch out."

• • •

Another snapshot of the late A. Woollcott the Wrecker in action: A poetess perpetrated a slender volume entitled *And I Shall Make Music.* Mr. W. dismissed it in a *New Yorker* review with "Not on my carpet, Lady!"

An equally famous "capsule critique" is S. J. Perelman's dust-off of *Graustark:* "Chacun à son goo."

• • •

At Glenn McCarthy's Shamrock Hotel in Houston, crooner Tony Martin pointed out that a starring career in Hollywood was fraught with pitfalls. "One day," he argued, "you're making love to Betty Grable, Linda Darnell, or Lana Turner and the next day, poof! you're a has-been." "Ah," sighed McCarthy, "but look where you has been."

• • •

Lana Turner, as a matter of fact, appeared one evening at Romanoff's in a daring, low-cut evening gown. Attached to a fragile chain around her neck was a golden replica of an airplane—an exquisite piece of workmanship which nestled provocatively in just the proper place. "Prince Mike" Romanoff asked Charles Brackett, "What do you think of Lana's airplane?" "Lovely," breathed Brackett ecstatically, "and what a landing field!"

• • •

An imperious and aging movie star viewed the rushes of a day's work in the studio, and complained to the boss camera man, Leon Shamroy, "You are not photographing my best side." "How can I?" snapped Shamroy. "You're always sitting on it."

• • •

A guest at one of those Florida health resorts flatly refused to follow the prescribed schedule of set-up exercises and workouts. "I came here to eat and rest," he insisted. "Exercise is ridiculous."

As the guest was checking out, the proprietor pleaded: "Before you leave, just do one bit of exercise for me—to keep my record clear. Please just bend down, keep your knees stiff, and touch your valise." The man bent over and said, "Well, I'm touching

my valise. What now?" "Open it," said the proprietor, "and give
me back my towels."

• • •

The social set in Toledo, relates Cleveland Amory, decided to
stage a charity horse show. The knowing horsewoman in charge
of the proceedings, however, took sick on the eve of the affair,
and another girl, who knew nothing about horses, volunteered to
hold down the post. Her first phone call came from a man who
had several horses entered. "This is most embarrassing," he apologized, "but I'm afraid I'll have to ask you to scratch one of my
horses for me." "I'll be glad to," said the girl pleasantly. "Where?"

• • •

The maharajah of an interior Indian province decreed that no
wild animals could be killed by the populace. Soon the country
was overrun by man-eating tigers, lions, panthers, elephants, and
boars. The long-suffering people finally could stand it no longer
and gave their maharajah an unceremonious heave-ho. As the
noted Indian sportsman, Mufti Considine, points out, it was the
first instance on record where the reign was called on account
of game.

• • •

In Texas, they tell a story of the days when the redoubtable
Ma Ferguson first tossed her sombrero into the political arena.
She came back from a succession of stump-speeches all over the
state, and reported happily, "Looks like I'm going to sweep Texas."
Pa Ferguson took the pipe out of his mouth, and suggested gloom-
ily, "How about starting with this living room?"

• • •

A millionaire decided to build a luxurious bungalow on his
mountain retreat. A famous architect gave him a set of blueprints,
and he sent them on to the local handy-man to execute. When

he arrived at his place the following summer, however, he found that not a single lick of work had been done. "I wasn't gonna throw away your good money," the native explained. "A lunatic musta drawn up them blueprints for you. Why, he put in two bathrooms!"

• • •

Two men were responsible for the phenomenal rise of *The Saturday Evening Post:* Cyrus Curtis, who bought it in 1898 for $1000, and George Horace Lorimer, who became its editor on St. Patrick's Day, 1899. John Tebbel tells how Lorimer determined once and for all that his decisions on editorial content were final. "My wife didn't like that lead story in this week's *Post*," reported Owner Curtis. Editor Lorimer answered calmly, "I'm not editing *The Saturday Evening Post* for your wife." Curtis kept his own counsel thereafter.

Lorimer never permitted an off-color situation, indecent word, or suggestive paragraph to be printed in the *Post*. One lapse occurred when Katharine Brush's *Red Headed Woman* was serialized in 1931. Installment one ended with a secretary dining tête-à-tête at her boss' apartment. Installment two began with her still there for breakfast. When several strait-laced readers protested, Lorimer stuck by his author. "The *Post*," he answered firmly, "cannot be responsible for what the characters in its serials do between installments."

Mary Roberts Rinehart toured Europe during World War One for the *Post*, all expenses paid. She came home wearing a handsome fur coat. Noting Lorimer's suspicious glance, she explained hurriedly, "Europe was colder than I expected. This coat was very useful. It covered many a general's knees." "With you in it?" asked Lorimer.

• • •

Oscar Dystel tells a story about the Westbrook Pegler of bygone days, when he was a rising young sports writer, and F.D.R. had not yet come along to curdle his disposition. Pegler sold his first short story for seventy-five dollars to a magazine that is notorious for the inadequate fees it pays contributors. The story was so good that within a week of publication, other editors ordered pieces from him at prices ranging from three hundred dollars to a thousand. He just had closed the thousand-dollar deal when the editor who had bought his first story wired him, "Will take ten more from you at same price as first one." Pegler wired back, "Sorry but I've turned pro."

• • •

There is a well-known leading man on Broadway who has lost several important parts as a result of chronic inability to resist the charms of glamorous blondes. One manager in particular branded him a libertine and refused to permit him even to enter his offices.

As luck would have it, it was this very manager who got hold of a play with a role that the leading man coveted more earnestly than anything in his whole career. The actor wrote a long, self-debasing letter to the manager, freely admitting previous delinquencies, but concluding, "I am through with women forever. Give me this part, and I swear to you that during the entire run I will not so much as permit a female to address me by my first name."

The next afternoon the actor was walking down Fifty-second Street with a luscious lady he had known for all of twelve hours when he collided squarely with the manager.

The manager's face clouded with anger. The hapless actor swallowed hard, and stammered, "Don't jump to conclusions, old man. I would like you to shake hands with my wife."

"Your wife!" roared the manager. "You damn scoundrel, she's *my* wife!"

• • •

One of the beauties in the Copacabana chorus wrote a note telling off a rival in the same troupe. She was so proud of her composition that she showed it to Editor Ted Shane, who in turn showed it to me. It read as follows:

You Empty-Headed Skunk: What's the idea of stealing my man, you female rat, you? Wait till I lay my hands on you, you phony blonde, you. I'll pull every bleached hair out of your ugly head, one by one, before I scratch your eyes out. Yours truly, Helen. P.S. Please excuse the pencil.

Jimmy "Schnozzola" Durante thinks that the funniest line he ever had in a show was from a scene of "Jumbo," the Rodgers-Hart-Hecht extravaganza that Billy Rose produced in the Hippodrome in 1936. Durante appeared upon the stage with a mammoth elephant in tow, supposedly stolen from a circus owner who was holding out on Jimmy's back salary. A constable stopped him and demanded, "Where did you get that elephant?" Durante, the picture of outraged innocence, answered, "What elephant?" "That was such a wonderful line," recalls Jimmy, "that even the elephant busted out laughing a coupla times a week."

At one performance the elephant, named Tuffy, forgot that he had been house-broken. Durante sent the audience into hysterics by exclaiming, "Hey, Tuffy, no ad libbing."

• • •

Billy Rose tells of the night Houdini first introduced the trick of putting a dozen needles and a piece of thread into his mouth,

and then producing them all neatly threaded. "I want a gentleman in the audience," he announced, "to examine the needles
and thread, and then look into my mouth to make sure nothing
is concealed there." An elderly little man climbed up to the stage,
and peered intently into Houdini's bridgework. "Well," said Houdini finally, "don't just stand there. Tell the audience what you
see."

The little man said, "Pyorrhea."

• • •

A musical-comedy producer scheduled an audition for new
show girls. One girl was as pretty as a picture and sang well
enough too, but she carried herself abominably. The producer
said, "You'll do nicely if you can ever learn to watch your posture.
The way you slouched across the stage was awful. Learn to stand
upright, throw your head back, understand? Hold your breast well
out." "Yes, sir," said the girl, "which one?"

• • •

One of Ed Wynn's funniest acts found him dressed as a huntsman, rifle in hand, horn slung over his shoulder, ready to go out
and bag his prey. Just before he sallied forth, he took a look at
himself in a pocket mirror, and gasped, "Thank the Lord I'm not
in season."

In the same show he was operating a pretzel stand when a cop
informed him, "Hey, fella, you can't sell those pretzels here without a license." Wynn answered, "I knew there was some reason
I couldn't sell them, but thanks for telling me what it was."

In *Manhattan Mary*, Wynn played a waiter (Ona Munson was
Mary) and told a patron who ordered caviar, "Here's some tapioca
pudding and a pair of smoked glasses." Somebody else grumbled,
"I don't like all the flies in here." "Point out the ones you don't
like," suggested Wynn, "and I'll evict them." A third customer demanded lamb chops au gratin. Wynn shouted to the kitchen,
"Cheese it, the chops."

Resting between rehearsals of one of his top-drawer television
shows, Wynn was asked for his favorite joke of the past decade.

After a moment's thought he answered, "One of my all-time favorites was certainly a gag I whipped up for the tin salvage drive
in World War Two. I told my audiences: 'Ladies and gentlemen,
the government wants all the old tin cans from your kitchens.
The simplest method is to cut the ends out of a can, put it on
the floor, jump on it to flatten it out, and then hand it in to the
government. I tried it this morning. I cut each end out of the can.
I put it on the floor. I jumped on it hard. It flattened out *beautifully*. Of course, it took me three hours to scrape the beans off
the wall.'

"I must say," concluded Wynn, "that story always got a great
laugh. You'd be surprised to know how much tin it raised too!"

• • •

When Pat O'Brien bought a high-powered, new convertible, he
asked a priest to give it his blessing. The priest agreed, but cautioned, "Remember, Pat, that this blessing is no good above forty
miles an hour."

• • •

Eddie Cantor tells about an acrobatic team who invariably went
on last in the old two-a-day vaudeville line-ups. While the pair
huffed and puffed through their arduous routine, blasé audiences
would reach for their hats and coats and walk out on them. At
the start of their twelfth year on the Keith-Orpheum circuit their
agent said, "Boys, if you ever expect to get anywhere in this profession, you'll have to dream up a new finish for your act." "New
finish?" echoed one of the acrobats indignantly. "Nobody's seen
the old one yet."

Cantor, incidentally, is not even satisfied with packing Carnegie
Hall for a one-man show these days. He claims that on the side
he has devised a new radio quiz program. Your name is selected
at random from a local telephone directory, and if you're at home
when Cantor calls, he borrows twenty dollars.

• • •

Cantor's life-long pal, George Jessel, presiding over a banquet in his inimitable fashion, suddenly stepped off the dais, dropped to one knee, and warbled "Rock-a-bye Your Baby to a Dixie Melody" in flawless fashion. As the party was breaking up, Gene Markey said to him, "George, I never knew you could sing that well."

"I can't sing at all," protested Jessel. "I was just imitating Al Jolson."

When a ham actor told Jessel "I'm a sensation at the Roxy. Last night I had the audience glued to their seats," Jessel snapped, "Wonderful! How clever of you to think of it." "I know a girl," he says, "who is an even better after-dinner speaker than I'm supposed to be. By that I mean that every time I see her, she's after a dinner."

When Larry Adler, the harmonica specialist, returned from a war-time tour of Palestine (now Israel) he told Jessel, "I made it my business to pray at the Wailing Wall in Jerusalem." "What for?" asked Jessel knowingly. "Better billing?"

• • •

Lawrence Langner, head of the Theatre Guild, is noted for his absent-mindedness. He boarded a train at Westport one morning and found that he had forgotten his ticket. "It's all right, Mr. Langner," said the regular conductor on the run. "I'll collect it some other time." "It may be all right for you," said Langner petulantly, "but how do I know where I'm going?"

In his bedroom on Eleventh Street, Langner keeps an old cuckoo clock. One morning the clock went out of order and cuckooed twenty-seven times. Langner jumped out of bed in a panic, crying, "My God, that's the latest I've ever been."

• • •

The biology professor peered at his class and said, "The time has come for us to dissect a frog. I have one in my pocket for the experiment." He took a crumpled paper bag out of his pocket and extracted from it a very tired-looking cheese sandwich. The professor trembled visibly, and ejaculated, "Goodness me, I distinctly remember eating my lunch."

• • •

In Hoboken, a Rutgers professor qualified for the absent-minded championship by forgetting his car was aboard a Forty-second Street ferry, and trundling off in a suburban bus. Ten minutes later he frantically dashed back to find the crew towing his car off the ferry, and owners of the vehicles stalled behind it airing their vocabularies. "Hey, that's my car," cried the professor. A policeman stared at him open-mouthed, tore up a report he was compiling, and called up to the pilot house, "Stop worrying, Captain. Here's the body."

• • •

A not-too-reliable report has it that a horse was recently graduated from Harvard. At the Commencement exercises a guest speaker (a Yale man, no doubt) remarked, "This is the first time in history that Harvard has graduated an *entire* horse."

• • •

On the very day of a graduation ceremony at Radcliffe College, according to Edward Allen, all the chairs were given a fresh coat of varnish. What's more, the weather was hot and humid, and when the governor of the state tried to arise to address the respectable assemblage, he discovered that he was stuck firmly to the seat (a situation used, you may remember, in a recent motion picture called *The Bishop's Wife*). Anyhow, the governor was a gentleman with rare presence of mind, for he captivated everybody by remarking promptly, "My friends, I had expected to bring you a plain and unvarnished tale, but circumstances made it impossible."

• • •

When Herbert Wise, the chess champion, returned to the fresh-water college he had attended in his youth, the prexy suggested that he have a look at the dormitory room he had occupied as a student. The lad who was living there at the time unfortunately had chosen this evening to smuggle in a beautiful young co-ed to help him with his history—a gross infraction of rules. When he heard the president and Mr. Wise in the hall, he hid the girl hastily in the clothes closet.

Wise looked at the familiar old room, sighed, and remarked, "Same old desk, same old chairs." Then he opened the closet door, saw the flustered co-ed, and added softly, "and the same old girl!"

"It's my sister, sir," stammered the young man.

"And the same old lie!" chortled Wise.

When Alexander Meiklejohn was president of Amherst he made a speech in Kansas City enlarging upon the blessings of university training. He was not too pleased with the headline in a local paper the following morning. It read, "Meiklejohn Shows Need of College Education."

• • •

Thirty-eight years ago Philosopher George Santayana came into a sizable legacy and was able to relinquish his post on the Harvard faculty. The classroom was packed for his final appearance, and Santayana did himself proud. He was about to conclude his remarks when he caught sight of a forsythia uncurling in a patch of muddy snow outside the window. He stopped abruptly, picked up his hat, gloves, and walking stick, and made for the door. There he turned. "Gentlemen," he said softly, "I shall not be able to finish that sentence. I have just discovered that I have an appointment with April."

• • •

A young graduate of Cornell married a lovely Vassar girl, and confided to his older brother, "There's only one tiny thing marring my happiness. I simply don't know how to address Margaret's mother. You don't go around saying 'Good morning, mother-in-law' or 'pass the gravy, mother-in-law,' do you? And I can't call her 'mother,' because I feel that somehow wouldn't be fair to the memory of our own mother. How did you get around this when you married Ethel?"

"Simplest thing in the world," his older brother confided. "The first year I addressed Ethel's mother as 'hey.' After that we called her 'grandma'."

• • •

Martyn Green, brightest star of the D'Oyly Carte Gilbert-and-Sullivan troupe, recently brought over this story from England.

In the maternity ward of a big London hospital, a nurse told a nervous floor-pacer, "Congratulations, sir! You are the father of triplets—three bouncing, beautiful boys." "That's wonderful," cried the father. "Can I see them now?" "Certainly," the nurse assured him. "You can also pick out the one you wish to keep." "I don't think I understand," said the father. "Aren't all three mine?" "Of course they're yours," replied the nurse, "but two of them are for export."

• • •

Mrs. Krankheit picked three o'clock in the morning of a freezing January day to wake her long-suffering spouse and complain, "Hubert, you never make love to me the way you did when we were married thirty-five years ago." "Please, Ruby," he begged, "be a good girl and let me get a little sleep. I got a hard day at the office tomorrow." "You used to be so romantic," she persisted. "A regular wild bull! Remember, you used to bite me on the fingers, on the cheek, on the neck. . . . Why don't you do it any more?" "Ruby," he explained wearily, "such monkeyshines is for honeymooners. We're too old. Let's go back to sleep." "Just once," she continued, with the hint of tears in her voice, "you should bite me like you did thirty-five years ago."

"All right," he agreed reluctantly. "Go over to the dressing table and get me my teeth."

• • •

Quentin Reynolds calls attention to the fact that Montgomery's campaign in the Near East altered a centuries-old custom of the natives in those parts. "Since time immemorial," says Reynolds, "Arabian men rode majestically on the family donkey while their wives, laden down with all sorts of burdens, trudged patiently behind on foot. After 1942, however, all that was changed. The wife was emancipated. She now walks in front. There are many unexploded land mines. . . ."

• • •

A silver-haired old lady beamed at a young couple who were locked in a passionate embrace at the New London station. The girl was still sniffling as she climbed aboard the train; the boy stood forlorn on the platform.

When the train started, the old lady went over to pat the girl on the shoulder. "I suppose," she said, "you're crying because you have to leave your husband?" "Not at all," whimpered the girl. "I'm crying because I have to go back to him."

• • •

Timid salesmen who give up too easily may learn a valuable lesson from a little poem being circulated by Wall Street's Douglas Laird. It's called "The Secret of Closing Sales":

> He asked if she ever could love him.
> She answered him, no, on the spot.
> He asked if she ever could love him.
> She assured him again she could not.
>
> He asked if she ever could love him.
> She laughed till his blushes he hid.
> He asked if she ever could love him.
> By God, she admitted she did.

• • •

A druggist met an old customer on the street and asked, "Well, Tom, did that mudpack I suggested improve your wife's appearance?" "It did for a couple of days," replied Tom mournfully, "but then it wore off."

• • •

The evening before their marriage, an ardent suitor told his bashful bride-to-be, "You don't know how to make love, darling. Now tonight I'm going to show you first how Cousin Joe makes love, second how Uncle Louis makes love, and third, how Brother Theodore makes love."

The next morning the young man received a telegram from the girl reading, "I'm sorry I cannot marry you. Have just eloped with your Uncle Louis."

• • •

The Dallas income-tax bureau received a return from a bachelor who claimed a dependent son. A kindly inspector sent back the form with a note, "This must be a stenographic error." Back came the report with the added notation, "You're telling me!"

• • •

A newly-made oil millionaire finally persuaded his blonde secretary to swap a kiss for a diamond necklace and steak dinner at the Shamrock, but just as he was collecting his share of the deal, his wife popped in. She took one look at the proceedings and called the obituary editor of the Houston *Chronicle*. "My husband's dead. Tell your readers," she ordered grimly. "How terrible," sympathized the editor. "When did he pass away?" The wife said, "He starts tomorrow."

• • •

A song writer who prefers to remain anonymous sat down at his Remington one summer afternoon and banged out the following epic:

> My yTpust is one her vacation,
> My trpist's swau fpr a week,
> My trpudt us in her vacarion
> Wgile these damb keys pley hude and seej.
>
> CHORES:
> Bren Buck, bting bzk,
> Oy, brung bacj mub Oonnie to me, to me,
> B8&ng, b4xj, be-ng, bicz,
> Oj brong brsk m-beInio-imx.
>   Oh Helk!
> dabit dabit dabit &oe...?!!

• • •

A company that publishes one of the great encyclopedias advertised for a male stenographer who could also answer routine letters. A Chinese applicant didn't quite get the job with this letter: "Me Chinese Bing Foy drive typewriter with hell of noise and my English is it. Last job left itself from me for simple reason that big man was dead on account of not my fault. So what of it? If you same anxious like me I will arrive on day as you can guess."

• • •

Randy Williams, general manager of Macmillan, declares that selling books requires the power of suggestion rather than a ton of equipment. As an example, he tells how Macmillan sold 200,-000 copies of *The Secretary's Handbook*. "There was no such thing as a list of private secretaries," says Williams, "so we acquired the next best thing: a list of important men who certainly had one secretary, and probably more. To each of these gentlemen we addressed a letter with the slogan, 'Don't Fire Your Secretary!' emblazoned on the envelope. Of course, nine out of ten secretaries tore open the letters themselves to see what was inside. What they found was so glowing a tribute to *The Secretary's Handbook*, they insured themselves against being fired by ordering a copy immediately."

An eager student drank in Mr. Williams's words, and wrote in her notebook, "Always open the boss's mail."

• • •

Publisher Alfred Knopf tried out a new secretary the other day. She was mighty pretty too. Mr. Knopf tightened his orange cravat, flicked a grain of dust off his magenta trousers, and dictated a seven-page letter to Author Thomas Mann. When he finished an hour later, he found the big, beautiful blue eyes of the new secretary fixed on his.

"I hope you'll excuse me, Mr. Knopf," she told him, "but I didn't quite get what you said between 'My dear Thomas' and 'as ever yours'."

• • •

Mr. Knopf's son, Pat, was leaving his office at his usual quitting hour of three-thirty when he noticed a truck driver at the curb struggling unsuccessfully with a heavy case of books. "I'll give you a hand," volunteered Pat. The two seized opposite ends of the case and huffed and puffed several moments to no avail. "I'm afraid it's hopeless," gasped Pat. "We'll never get it on the truck." "ON?" screamed the driver. "I'm trying to get it OFF."

• • •

The new phone operator at a midtown publishing house was obviously a total stranger to a switchboard, but she was so pretty

and so anxious to please, nobody had the heart to fire her. One of the senior partners, seeking to talk to John Steinbeck in California, was connected in turn with a cousin of the late Gertrude Stein in St. Louis, the Martin Beck Theatre in New York, and Steinbach's Department Store in Asbury Park. He preserved his equanimity, however, until just past noon when he confronted the flustered operator and announced in a tone of icy rage, "This time you've gone too far. You now have me conversing with myself!"

• • •

An agent submitted a sheaf of essays to a publisher, and protested bitterly when they were rejected. "You are passing up a potential genius," he declared. "This man's writings will be studied in colleges one day." "Stuff and nonsense," laughed the editor. "You're just making a Montaigne out of a molehill."

• • •

A publisher's life is not even a safe one any longer! The well-known English publisher, Hamish Hamilton, discovered an error in a book he had just published about Lord Wavell, and wrote a note of apology that appeared in the London *Times*. The next day the following sinister message was slipped into his hand by a bearded stranger:

Dear Mr. Hamilton:

Having not be long to Englannd, but study Nuculea Psychics to Universsite Bangkor, to the Nord of Wale, but before Universitte Sidi-Ben-Tayonbeh, where my fater, Ibrahim Donadiych Rector of, I protesting much to atitud make Chaim Weitzmann, old enemy our famille, vis-a-vis Wawel, also old enemy our famille. Gere is old Peshian say thad where are two enemies, is bette killing both tha kill one and not killing othe, wich is nown Wistom of Suleiman. If you come Lebanon you wil also be kill, but not befor to enjoi Lebanese khospitaliti.

Wit best wishess for happi life wile this last, maibi not tou long, I is,
                                   Your brother
                                   Yakub Sidi Ben Kuweit Saadi Pasha

• • •

In another publishing office, the sales manager, Miller, was ragging the advertising director, a Beau Brummelish individual named Sussman. "I defy you," said Miller, "to show me one order that advertising ever put on our books." "I will," promised Sussman, "just as soon as you can show me a single load of hay that the sun ever put in a barn."

• • •

Two buck privates from Iowa saw the ocean for the first time from the deck of a transport bound for the coast of North Africa. "Did you ever see so much water in your life?" marveled the first one as he looked out of the porthole, the second day out. His companion observed, "You haven't seen nuthin' yet. That's just the top of it."

• • •

"Did I ever tell you," inquired the garrulous war hero, "of the time I was aboard a destroyer that was torpedoed in mid-ocean? I had to live for sixteen days on a can of sardines."

"Goodness," gasped a sweet young thing, "weren't you scared of falling off?"

• • •

D-Day on the Normandie beachhead produced many individual acts of heroism and noteworthy news items that were overlooked in the general excitement. One GI, for instance, says Allan Ullman, doubled up in pain just as his landing barge hit solid land. "It's my stomach," he groaned. "I'm dying." An alert medical officer made him strip immediately, but could find no exterior evidence of anything wrong. He thereupon put a stomach pump to work. The first results of the operation were normal in every respect, but the doctor was astonished suddenly to dredge up a tadpole, a crab, and several varieties of small fish whose habitat is the Normandie coastline. As the doctor was scratching his brow, the GI's buddy suggested, "Doc, do you think you ought to be using that pump while Joe is sitting in the water?"

• • •

A GI from Oklahoma, narrates Steve Cochran, was engaged in hand-to-hand combat with a Jap. As they threshed about in the jungle, the GI gasped, "Where you hail from, mister?" The Jap answered, "Yokohama." "Holy smoke!" said the GI. "What are we fightin' fo'? Ah'm from Tulsa."

• • •

General Stilwell, "Vinegar Joe" to his troops who worshiped him, prided himself on his ability to speak Chinese—and write it as well. When a kid from San Francisco's Chinatown asked for his autograph, the General spelled it out for him in Chinese, and watched to hear the kid's exclamation of surprise. What the kid said precisely was "Jeepers! A five-star general and he can't even write English!"

• • •

When General Stilwell was in China, legend has it that several Shanghai bankers invited him to participate in a red-hot poker game. Since the bankers could not speak a word of English, an interpreter was provided to keep the General au courant. Things proceeded on an even keel until the General was dealt a four-flush. He thought this was worth a hundred-dollar bet. The Chinese banker sitting next to him exclaimed, "Ah moy." The interpreter said, "He is raising you two hundred." The next banker exclaimed, "Ah, foy." Said the interpreter, "He's raising it five hundred more." The third Chinaman declared, "Ah, goy." The interpreter said, "Gee whiz, he's upping it another thousand." By this time the General was perspiring freely, but he decided to string along with the pot. He drew one card, but when he looked at it, his hopes were dashed. He had failed to fill the flush. "Ah, pfooy," he cried in disgust. The Chinese bankers threw in their hands. The interpreter slapped the General on the back and told him, "Your million-dollar bluff has won the pot."

• • •

An ex-GI, undergoing an examination for appointment to the New York police force, was asked, "If your beat was a lonely path in Central Park, and a beautiful young girl rushed up to you and declared that a strange man had suddenly grabbed her, and hugged and kissed her, what would you do?" The GI replied without hesitation, "I would endeavor to reconstruct the crime."

• • •

A wealthy grain merchant bought a new car and was enjoying his first ride in it no end until a motorcycle cop stopped him and suggested a visit to the local magistrate. "He was doing sixty," reported the cop. "Nonsense," declared the merchant. "I never got her up above forty." The merchant's wife put in her two cents' worth at this point. "He wasn't going faster than twenty-five," she averred. A friend who had been riding in the back seat added, "I'd say we were virtually at a standstill when this officer came along." The magistrate threw up his hands and cried, "Stop right now—before you folks back into something."

• • •

Judge Eder pointed a finger at the defendant and thundered, "You admit that you drove over the victim with a truck?" "I do, Your Honor," quavered the defendant. "What defense have you to offer?" asked the Judge. "All I can say, Your Honor," said the defendant, "is that I had no idea it was loaded."

• • •

A particularly ornery hoss thief was brought to trial in the cattle country the day after the state put its brand-new electric chair into operation. The judge, bursting with civic pride, explained to the prisoner, "This is an enlightened community and before you get the fair and square trial you are entitled to by law, I'm going to ask you one question. What current do you want—AC or DC?"

• • •

Martin Stone, who is making a fortune today with the "Author Meets the Critics" and "Howdy-Doody" television programs, began his professional career as a lawyer. "And to show you how resourceful Martin was in legal procedure," said one of his associates, "there was the time one of his clients phoned from the death house in Sing Sing and wailed, 'I'm scheduled for the electric chair in twenty minutes. You're my lawyer. Tell me what's my next move.' Quick as a flash, Martin knew the answer. His advice was, 'Don't sit down.'"

• • •

A biography of Chief Justice Salmon P. Chase, who headed the Supreme Court in the crucial years from 1864 to 1872, reveals that he was as agile-tongued and irresistible in the drawing room as he was on the bench. A few years after the Civil War ended, the Chief Justice was introduced to a flaming beauty from Alabama. "I must warn you," she told him archly, "that I am a rebel who has not been reconstructed." The gallant jurist promptly responded, "Madame, reconstruction in your case—even in the slightest degree—would be nothing short of sacrilege!"

• • •

Here's a story that sounds as though it came straight from the headquarters of the Republican National Committee:

It was a day late in 1980, when socialized medicine had become the law of the land. A man was seized with a violent cramp in his stomach and sought relief at the modern white structure erected for the purpose in his home town. Upon entering the building, he found himself in a hall with two doors. One was marked "male," the other "female." Naturally, he entered the door marked "male."

He found himself in a room with two doors. One was marked "Over 21," the other "Under 21." Since he was 52, he entered the door marked "Over 21."

He found himself in a room with two doors. One was marked "Serious illness," the other "Minor indisposition." Since he was doubled up with pain by this time, he staggered through the door marked "Serious illness."

He found himself in a room with two doors. One was marked "Democrats," the other "Republicans." Since he had voted a straight Republican ticket all his life, he entered the door marked "Republicans"—and found himself out on the street.

• • •

Another anecdote aimed at the Democratic administration is this reputed report by a Kansas farmer: "The bugs got my berries, a hail storm ruined my garden truck, and the drought spoiled my wheat, but I'm doing mighty good on the crops the government paid me not to plant."

• • •

Mrs. Pomeroy's maid took to her bed one afternoon, obviously ill, and the family physician was summoned post-haste. When Mrs. P. left him alone to examine the patient, the maid confessed, "Doctor, I'm not sick at all. I'm shamming. That skinflint owes me three months' back salary and I'm not getting out of this bed till she pays me." The doctor's face brightened. "She owes me for my past ten visits here," he declared. "Move over."

A doctor examined a very pretty new patient carefully, then beamed, "Mrs. Atherton, I've got good news for you." The patient said, "Pardon me, Doctor; it's MISS Atherton." "Oh," said the doctor. "Well, Miss Atherton, I've got bad news for you."

• • •

S. Tupper Bigelow, of Toronto, relays the tale of a young doctor who hung up his shingle in a small town and waited for his first patient. Some days later one arrived—covered from head to foot with an angry, dangerous-looking rash. The puzzled young medico hastily consulted his text books but could find no help there. Finally he said to the patient, "Did you ever have this affliction before?" "Oh, sure, Doc," the patient replied. "I've had it twice before." "Well, damnation," diagnosed the doctor, "you've got it again."

• • •

Dr. Morris Fishbein tells of one medico who wrote out a prescription in the usual legible fashion doctors use on such occasions. The patient used it for two years as a railroad pass. Twice it got him into Radio City Music Hall, and once into Ebbets Field.

It came in handy as a letter from his employer to the cashier to increase his salary. And to cap the climax, his daughter played it on the piano and won a scholarship to the Curtis Music Conservatory.

•   •   •

Fritz Kreisler was strolling down Lexington Avenue with a friend one day when he passed a fish store. A row of flounders was in the window, their cold, beady eyes staring sightlessly into space. "Heavens," cried Kreisler with a start, "that reminds me! I'm supposed to be soloist at Carnegie Hall this very minute!"

A Hollywood starlet once upset precedent by *asking* Kreisler for an autograph instead of *giving* her own to wild-eyed bobbysoxers. The starlet's disarming request read "It doesn't matter whether you write it or print it, Mr. Kreisler. I copy all my autographs over anyhow alphabetically in my scrapbook."

•   •   •

Artur Rubinstein, the great pianist, was such a social lion in Paris that he scarcely found time to practice. In desperation, he instructed his butler to tell all callers, regardless of their importance, that he was not at home. The recognized leader of boulevard society phoned one morning while Rubinstein was playing one of his most tempestuous and difficult stand-bys. "The master is not in," said the butler dutifully. "Poppycock," snapped the great lady, "I hear him playing distinctly." "Oh, no, madam," the butler assured her. "That's just me dusting the keys."

•   •   •

On a Monon streamliner out of Chicago I fell in with a trio of be-bop experts on their way to fill a night-club engagement in Louisville, and managed to understand almost a third of everything they had to say. The leader in particular reminded me of a character Garson Kanin loves to talk about. This exponent of rhythm in the super-modern idiom—let's call him Jones—kept himself hopped up continuously with marijuana, and when he was drafted in 1943, found himself unable to cope with army life when his supply suddenly was cut off. As a desperate expedient, Jones decided to plant a marijuana patch around his barracks. Day after day he watered his prospering shrubs industriously and without interference. Just before they were ripe for plucking, however, the official recognition he had been dreading materialized. A full colonel strode into the area, and Jones's company was drawn up for inspection. "Private Jones," barked the colonel, "step two

paces forward." "Here's where I get it," thought Jones. The colonel eyed him sharply, then pinned a decoration on his lapel. "This medal," he explained, "is for the only man in the outfit with sufficient pride to plant a little greenery outside his barracks and tend it in his own spare time!"

• • •

America's leading composers of popular music have one thing in common. When surrounded by convivial companions, all of them love to sit down at the piano—and play their own compositions. Truth to tell, they cannot help themselves. Should they ever protest that they are "not in the mood" they are accused of being ingrates and spoil-sports.

The composer who needed least urging was the late George

Gershwin. He frankly delighted in playing his songs on all possible occasions—and how he could play them, too! I remember one dinner party at George Kaufman's house where not only Gershwin, but Irving Berlin, Richard Rodgers, and Arthur Schwartz were present. We were having dessert in the ground-floor dining room when Kaufman rose and announced dramatically, "When I give the signal, all composers can make a break for the piano on the second floor. The one who gets there first can play his own songs for exactly one hour." Everybody laughed and settled back for more talk. When we finally did climb back to the second floor, however, there was George Gershwin seated at the piano, happily improvising the theme of "Embraceable You." "I'm a little bothered by that crack Kaufman made downstairs," he confided to me. "Do you think he was kidding?"

That reminds me of a remark of Gershwin's after he had taken out a luscious blonde from the chorus of *Of Thee I Sing*. "She looked good enough to eat," reported George. "And oh boy, *did* she."

• • •

When Mischa Elman made his triumphal debut at Carnegie Hall, the rapturous audience demanded encore after encore. Finally his father whispered to him, "Make the next one quick, Mischa. The bank closes in twenty minutes."

• • •

A current favorite of night-club comics concerns the French horn player whose toupee fell into his instrument, and who spent the rest of the evening blowing his top.

• • •

Here are a couple of musical tidbits I collected while visiting with Lily Pons and her husband, André Kostelanetz (two of the most amusing and attractive people in New York).

A pompous old bore was once forcing his attentions on Miss Mary Garden. The diva was wearing an extremely low-cut evening gown. "I can't imagine what's holding it up," said the old boy with a roll of his eyes. "Possibly," suggested Miss Garden, "it's your age."

The pianist Moritz Rosenthal suffered in silence one day while a bitter rival was receiving most of the plaudits of a group of giddy clubwomen. When one lady begged the rival for a "teentsy weentsy message" in her autograph album, however, Rosenthal could stand it no longer. "Why don't you write down your repertoire?" he suggested.

The Flonzaley Quartet had just concluded a concert at Town Hall when a lady descended upon the second violinist, and demanded a look at his instrument. She examined it minutely, and then exclaimed, "It looks exactly like a first violin!"

An American band was making a world-wide tour and played one concert at the palace of an all-powerful maharajah in deepest India. The maharajah was so delighted with the performance that he ordered the treasurer to fill the instrument of every player in the company with golden sovereigns. This pleased everybody except the flute player.

The following evening the band made the mistake of doing a repeat performance. This time the maharajah was bored—so bored, in fact, that he stopped the concert in the middle and cried, "These men are deliberately trying to break my eardrums. I order my guards to stuff their instruments down their throats." The flute player beat his head with the palm of his hand and wailed, "Out of luck again. With me they can do it."

• • •

Dorothy Berliner, the celebrated pianist, arranged a recital by her youngest students. At its conclusion, a repast of ice cream and home-made layer cake and brownies was served. One young musician had brought her little brother as a guest. When they were leaving, Miss Berliner asked, "Well, Fenimore, did you enjoy the recital?" "You bet," answered Fenimore. "That is, all but the music."

• • •

A gentleman was needled by his wife into buying a pair of seats for a benefit in Madison Square Garden at fifty dollars a throw. Every star in town was included on the program, and the cause was a worthy one, but even so, the price seemed too steep to the gentleman, and he approached the proceedings in a super-critical mood. The singers were off-key, he insisted, the dancers clumsy, and the jokesters inaudible.

Finally came the pièce de résistance. Across a thin, taut wire stretched high above the arena, a daredevil hopped on one foot. On the free foot he balanced a lighted lamp. There was no net spread under him. And while the spellbound audience, two hundred feet below, followed his every move, he played "Some Enchanted Evening" on a violin!

The gentleman's wife nudged him and said, "Isn't he wonderful? Are you still sorry you came?" The gentleman snorted and observed, "Heifetz he ain't!"

Herbert Hoover, commenting on the mistakes of New Deal economists, called to mind the small girl who said, "Mother, remember that china plate you told me had been handed down to us from generation to generation?" "Yes," said Mother. "What about it?" The small girl answered, "This generation just broke it."

• • •

A banker's young son was an inveterate liar, and the family was trying every expedient to reform him.

"Son," the banker proposed one evening, "if you can tell me a lie without a second's thought, I'll give you fifty cents."

"Fifty cents nothing," declared the boy. "You just said a dollar."

• • •

Little Linda, a darling child with golden curls and an irresistible dimple, discovered suddenly that she had a stomach-ache in the middle of the pastor's Sunday sermon. "Mummy," she whispered, "I am terrible sick." "Control yourself until the service is over," urged her mother. Linda did her best, but it was strictly no soap.

"I'm going to be sick all over the pew in a minute," she promised. Her mother, now thoroughly frightened, said, "Well, if you must, tiptoe out of church and go round to the bushes in the garden and then come back when you feel better."

Linda was back in the pew in less than a minute. Her triumphant mother whispered, "I knew it was just your imagination. You couldn't have been sick out in the garden and gotten back so quickly." "I didn't have to go to the garden, Mummy," said dear little Linda. "I found a box right in the back of the church marked 'For the sick.'"

• • •

In ad-man J. M. Kesslinger's home town, the young Chief of Police spotted a black sedan burning up the road at something like eighty miles an hour. He gave chase, and brought down his quarry about five miles down the turnpike. To his amazement the driver of the sedan turned out to be his parish priest.

"I'm dreadfully sorry," apologized the priest. "It's a brand-new car and I just didn't realize how fast I was going."

"I'll let you go this time, Father," grinned the Chief, "provided you say ten Hail Marys and fifteen Our Fathers."

• • •

The Norfolk and Western Railroad's alert publicity department broadcasts this story with a moral:

A motorist was a hundred yards from an open railway crossing tearing along at sixty miles an hour. A train, coming down the track at the same speed, was an equal distance from the intersection.

Problem: Did the motorist get across?

Solution: Yes, the motorist got a cross all right—a beautiful marble cross purchased by his widow from his insurance money.

● ● ●

On her way to a funeral, Mrs. Howard Field saw a little summer bonnet in a window that caught her fancy, and impulsively bought it for $25.00. Thinking it improper to enter the chapel with the gay little milliner's box, she asked an usher to take care of it for her. You can imagine her dismay when she saw it being placed with the flowers on top of the coffin. When the services were over, Mrs. Field went out to the burial grounds in the hope of retrieving her new bonnet. She was too embarrassed to do anything about it however, and saw her new Spring hat carefully lowered into the ground. This is said to be the only formal funeral on record where a casual acquaintance of the dear departed wept more sincerely than the immediate family.

● ● ●

The late Joshua Liebmann, author of the fabulously successful *Peace of Mind,* presided at the funeral of one of Boston's most unpopular citizens. The next day he overheard members of the congregation tearing the reputation of the deceased into shreds. He was accused variously of being a skinflint, a cheat, a four-flusher, and a tyrant. A stranger, however, disagreed violently. "You've got the poor fellow wrong," he pointed out softly. "I happen to know he was the soul of generosity, consideration, and gallantry." "Your partner, I suppose," said somebody sarcastically. "No. I never even met him," declared the stranger, "but I married the lady who divorced him some years ago."

● ● ●

Senator Bob Taft tells a story of a thrifty widow who wanted the town's leading minister to conduct memorial services for her dear departed, but was worried about the size of the tab. The minister said, "For $200 I will deliver a eulogy that will enshrine your husband in the hearts of the entire city for the next ten years." "That's too much," said the widow. "I could give a pretty good talk for $100," said the minister reluctantly. "Nothing fancy, you understand, but no one will be able to doubt the solid virtues and endearing qualities of your late spouse." "That's still too much," said the widow. "Can't you give me anything for about $15?" "I suppose I can," admitted the minister, "but I must warn you that for that price I will have to tell the truth about him."

• • •

When J. Edgar Hoover was first earning his reputation he tracked down a jewel thief who was known equally for his daring and his overwhelming conceit. Hoover engaged the unsuspecting burglar in friendly conversation and finally pointed to a big diamond ring the man was sporting. "That's a mighty handsome ring," conceded Hoover. "How would you like to sell it to me for $1000 in cash?" "Don't be silly," answered the man contemptuously. "They're offering more than that as a reward."

• • •

In Tempe, Arizona, they tell some tall tales of the early days before the railroads brought civilization—and winter dude ranches.

Once a ranch hand was up for trial for horse thieving, and they couldn't find twelve jurors willing to give him a fair shake in court. The judge roared, "There'll be no hanging in this town while I represent law and order! Round up twelve lawyers and herd 'em into the jury box." By combing the surrounding country, they managed to find twelve men with law degrees of sorts, and the long-delayed trial got under way. The townsfolk expected a quick verdict of "guilty," and so did the judge, but the twelve lawyers stayed locked in the jury room for eight solid hours. Finally the judge summoned them and demanded, "Haven't you danged fools decided on a verdict yet?" "Heck, Judge," demurred one of the jurors, "we got our verdict in three minutes. What we can't seem to agree on is a *foreman*."

• • •

Another time, a Shakespearian troupe ventured into Tempe and gave a rather startling performance of *Macbeth*. At its conclusion the audience roared so lustily for the author that the manager of the outfit decided to go out and take a bow. He hastily put on a fake beard, walked to the center of the stage—and the audience shot him.

• • •

"When we arrived in China," a lady, back from a world cruise, told her friends, "we went riding in one of those jinrickshas, and believe it or not, they have horses that look just like men!"

• • •

Irvin Cobb was aboard a river steamer that was stopped en route by an impenetrable fog. An anxious passenger inquired, "What's wrong?" "Can't see up the river," explained Cobb. "That's funny," exclaimed the passenger. "I can see the stars overhead perfectly plain." "Interesting but irrelevant," said Cobb. "Unless our boiler busts we're not going that way."

• • •

Red Smith, of American Airlines, was on his way from London to the flying field when a careless pedestrian darted in front of the taxicab. The driver swerved sharply and managed to miss him, giving the side of his cab a resounding slap with his left hand as he did so. Smith unscrambled himself in the back seat and asked, "What was the big idea of that slap?" "Simple, guv'nor," explained the cabbie, who probably studied Freud in his off-hours. "If I'd sounded my horn he'd have known I saw him and he'd ignore me and go on the same way next time. When I banged my cab, however, he thought he'd been hit—and he won't forget it in a hurry."

• • •

When Lowell Thomas commutes from Pawling to New York, he avoids the smoking car because the smoke irritates his throat and makes him sound a bit less mellifluous at the microphone later. One day, in the non-smoker, however, a gent plopped himself in the other half of Thomas's seat, and lit a giant stogie.

Unwilling to create a scene, Thomas waited for the conductor to come by and punch his commutation ticket. As he handed it over, he tapped the conductor's arm, and nodded to the gent with the stogie. The conductor nodded back, gave his ticket another punch, and moved on down the car.

Herb Shriner, a radio comic in the Will Rogers tradition, observes, "A man will soon be able to get clear around the world in two hours: one hour for flying, and the other to get out to the airport." "We didn't need a plane in Kansas one day last summer," he adds. "Wind blew so hard it got a hen turned clear around the wrong way. Before it could get straightened out and headed into the wind again, it laid the same egg six times!"

• • •

Shriner carries in his pocket a classified ad clipped from his home-town paper: "Man wanted to work in dynamite factory; must be willing to travel." That recalls the solemn warning made by Hollywood's Samuel Goldwyn some months ago: "Gentlemen, do not underestimate the danger of the atom bomb. It's dynamite!"

• • •

Glen Boles, ex-American yodeling champion, avers that a party of Londoners got lost in the Swiss mountains one week-end. For an entire day and night they kept shouting, "'Alp! 'Alp!" And that's how the Alps got their name.

• • •

A native of Rowayton, Connecticut, obviously lacking in civic pride, describes his birthplace as "The Athens of South Norwalk." An even more disrespectful neighbor says, "Rowayton is the only town where both sides of the tracks are wrong."

• • •

Senator Ed Ford describes a visit to a friend who rather fancied himself as a big-game hunter. On the floor was a fine bear rug, and when the host saw Ford looking at it, he expanded his chest and boasted, "I shot that bear myself. He came upon me unawares in the forest. The fight raged for an hour. Obviously, it was a struggle for survival—either the bear or me!"

Senator Ford nodded and said, "I think the bear makes a much better rug."

• • •

The summer home of the distinguished barrister, Randolph Guggenheimer, is named Barn Yesterday. Shortly after its completion, a pipe burst and a plumber had to be summoned late at night. Mr. Guggenheimer and his wife waited for the plumber at the entrance to the estate. "Before you begin," said Mr. Guggenheimer, "I want to acquaint you with the cause of the trouble."

The plumber bowed very low to Mrs. Guggenheimer, and said, "I am certainly pleased to meet you."

One of the most lucrative customers of the ski instructor at an Adirondack winter haven was a fat lady who took exactly forty lessons before she mustered sufficient courage actually to attempt the gentlest slide in the vicinity. She negotiated the first ten yards on her skis and the final hundred and twenty on her very ample posterior. The instructor pulled her out of a snow bank at the bottom of the hill and told her gravely, "That was splendid, just splendid. All you have to do now is eliminate the middle track."

• • •

Morey Amsterdam tells the heart-breaking story of a golf pro who lost his job, and was pacing the streets in his spiked golf

shoes, the only footwear he had left. He hadn't eaten a bite in
three days, when suddenly he looked down and saw an unused
meal ticket on the sidewalk. He stooped down to grab it, but in
his excitement, accidentally stepped on it with his spiked shoes
and punched out every meal in the ticket.

• • •

Louis J. Ansbacher, millionaire paint manufacturer of Elberon,
New Jersey, was playing golf with his daughter Marian on the
St. Andrews course in Scotland for five pounds a hole. Already
irritated because he had lost three holes in succession, Ansbacher
really blew his top when a missed putt of less than two feet cost
him still another. He looked up angrily but not a soul had said
one word, or moved an inch. The green was perfect. The wind
had subsided completely. Suddenly, however, Ansbacher spied a
tiny boat in the distance, just over the horizon. He threw his putter
angrily on the ground and grumbled, "How the heck can anybody
putt with all these ships sailing around here?"

• • •

At the edge of the water hole on the Century Golf Course, a
boy leaned over the fence bordering Anderson Road, watching
foursomes plumb their balls into the water. A baby brother, barely
old enough to toddle, stood beside him. One of the players' balls
landed only two feet from where the youngsters stood. "Young
man," he cried in agitation as he came running up, "don't you
know any better than to expose your little brother to these golf
links?" "It won't hurt him," said the boy confidently. "He's deaf."

• • •

It was at the same Century Club that a member entered the
locker room so obviously crushed in spirit that the golf pro asked,
"What ails you, lad?" "I just killed my wife," the member admitted despondently. "How?" gasped the pro. "I was standing on
the practice range," explained the member, "and didn't notice that
my wife had come up behind me. I took a full back swing, hit

her on the head, and she dropped dead." "Tough break," said the pro. "What club were you using?" "A niblick," said the member. "That's the club!" approved the pro.

• • •

The Holeproof Hosiery Company has thousands of letters from satisfied customers but one it cherishes more highly than most comes from Golfer "Chick" Evans. "A half hour after donning a pair of your socks," he testified, "I got a hole in one."

• • •

Geoffrey Parsons, of the New York *Herald Tribune,* tells of a lad in Stamford who was suffused with family pride. "My father," he announced, "is the best damn tennis player in Westchester." Noting that he had not made the desired impression he amended his statement to "My father is the best damn tennis player in the whole world." His father thought it time to tone him down a bit and said, "Tommy, better just say I'm the best tennis player in our house." "But that's not true, Daddy," said the boy. "Mommy is."

• • •

A Princeton junior appeared in the middle of a tennis tourney and asked casually, "Whose game?" A shy young thing looked up approvingly and murmured, "I am."

• • •

A lady who was worried at the failure of her twenty-eight-year-old daughter to find a husband persuaded her to insert a classified ad in the "personal" columns, reading: "Beautiful, exotic young heiress seeks correspondence with devil-may-care gentleman who wants to go places fast." Two days after the ad appeared, the mother asked anxiously, "Well? Any answers?" "Just one," sighed her daughter. "Who wrote it?" demanded Mama. "I can't tell you," said the daughter. "But this was my idea," shouted Mama, "and

I insist upon knowing." "All right," said the daughter wearily. "It was Papa."

• • •

That old cynic, Henry Mencken, claims that a woman will go to any length to attract attention to herself. He cites the case of a maiden in a sorority house who showed up at breakfast with a new engagement ring on her finger. To her disgust, none of the other girls noticed it, despite all her squirmings and gesticulatings. In desperation, she finally proclaimed, "Good grief, it's stifling in here. Guess I'll take off my ring."

• • •

Mr. Morrel was driving his wife and her girl friend from Mt. Vernon to Stamford. The girl friend asked, "Why does your husband always put his hand out when he's driving?" Mrs. Morrel answered, "I suppose it's because the worm is getting ready to turn."

• • •

Benjamin was one of the best chauffeurs in Minneapolis and was an expert mechanic in the bargain. The dignified society queen who employed him had only one complaint: he was extremely sloppy about his own appearance. One day she decided that the time had come to lecture him on his weakness. "Benjamin," she began severely, "how often would you say it is necessary to shave?" Benjamin gazed at her intently. "With a weak growth like yours, ma'am," he replied politely, "I should say that every third day would be sufficient."

• • •

A parsimonious merchant went off to Florida on a fishing trip but left his wife at home to shiver in the January blasts in Duluth. She wired him for additional funds. He sent her a picture of all the fish he had caught, and scrawled on the back, "I send you one million kisses." She wired back—collect: "Thanks for the handsome check you sent. The milkman cashed it for me this morning."

Neal O'Hara tells about a dowager's first visit to a gambling casino in Florida. Her indulgent husband gave her a hundred dollars to squander at roulette. "What number shall I pick?" she faltered. "What's the difference?" said the husband. "It's just blind luck. Try the number that corresponds with your age." The lady planked the hundred-dollar bill on 28. The little ball whirled around and landed in 35. The wife fainted.

• • •

A newly-married society girl was determined to prove to her husband what an accomplished cook she was, and on the servant's day off, set about cooking a chicken for his dinner. She plucked the fowl carefully, arranged it neatly in a pot, and put it in the oven.

Two hours later she heard a loud banging on the oven door. Investigation proved that the disturbance was being made by the chicken. "Lady," it cried piteously, "either give me back my feathers or turn on the gas. I'm freezing to death in this oven."

• • •

A friend of financier Bernard Baruch spoke so often about his love for hunting that Baruch finally invited him to his South Carolina plantation for a turkey shoot. The friend tramped the field for two days, shooting madly, but failed to hit a single turkey.

Mr. Baruch made no comment. The next morning, however, the friend was ambling along a path near the playhouse when he saw a well-fed gobbler sitting motionless in a tree. He crept up close to the turkey and fired point-blank. He was overjoyed when the turkey fell at his feet. It was only when he picked it up to stuff into his bag that he noticed a card tied around the turkey's neck. The card read, "With the compliments of Bernard Baruch."

• • •

When Frank Farrell went to hear a lot of famous industrial tycoons sound off at a convention banquet he expected the usual generalizations and high-sounding phrases—certainly nothing that would provoke a hearty guffaw. The witty president of the Reynolds Tobacco Company, however, double-crossed Farrell and delighted the rest of the audience by confiding, "I had so much fun at a party the first night of this convention that I still have no idea whether my goose was cooked or vice versa."

• • •

The Park Avenue Prevaricators' annual tournament was won this year by the brazen member who insisted he had dropped a bottle of hair tonic by accident into Lake George. Soon all the fish began to grow long beards. Anglers simply sat in their shacks, planted red and white barber poles at the edge of the water, and hollered "next."

• • •

Well, I'll be shaggy-dawgoned if that doesn't edge us into talking-animal country! For instance, there were the two flounders who met in a placid stretch of water near Sandy Hook. "What's the good word?" asked one. "Can't complain," answered the other, "I'm managing to keep my head below water."

• • •

And I'm sure you know about the termite who boasted to his fellows, "This'll bring down the house."

• • •

Papa Bear, Mama Bear, and Baby Bear, wandering through the Nevada desert, decided to take a rest. Papa Bear sat down on a piece of cactus, and jumped to his feet, hollering the equivalent of "Ouch." Mama Bear sat on another piece of cactus, and also arose screaming. Baby Bear, however, squatted on the same piece of cactus, and remained there in apparent calm and comfort. Papa Bear watched him with growing concern and said reproachfully, "Mama, don't tell me we're raising one of those Dead End kids!"

• • •

A tender, fragrant little rosebud looked around wonderingly and asked, "What brought me here?" The rose answered briskly, "The stalk, of course."

• • •

The telephone bell on a prominent economist's desk rang insistently. When he answered, a voice informed him "You're all wet about the cost of living reaching a new high! My wife and I live sumptuously—eating everything we like—on sixty-eight cents a week."

"Sixty-eight cents a week!" echoed the economist. "I can't believe it! Won't you tell me how? And to make sure I get the story straight, please speak louder."

"I can't speak louder," came the answer. "I'm a goldfish."

• • •

A hen and a pig were sauntering down the main street of an Indiana town when they passed a restaurant that advertised "Delicious ham and eggs: 75 cents." "Sounds like a bargain," approved the hen. "That owner obviously knows how to run his business." "It's all very well for you to be so pleased about the dish in question," observed the pig with some resentment. "For you it is all in the day's work. Let me point out, however, that on my part it represents a genuine sacrifice."

• • •

When Lynn Farnol was a neophyte in the advertising business, his boss tipped him off to a unique opportunity to make a little side money. A man engaged to conduct an auction at a nearby farm had taken ill, and a substitute was required post-haste. Lynn volunteered, and did nobly until he was asked to auction off a persnickety buck goat. He phoned his boss, and beseeched, "How do I describe this creature? I never saw the likes of it. It has a gray coat, a mean and nasty look, gray whiskers, and smells to high heaven." "Holy mackerel," shouted the boss. "Don't auction that. That's the farmer!"

• • •

Two tramps beseeched an Indiana farmer for a hand-out. "Fill that shed with kindling wood," proposed the farmer, "and you'll get the best meal you've et in weeks."

The tramps were hungry—and there wasn't another house in sight, so they reluctantly accepted the farmer's offer. Fifteen minutes later he went out to the shed to see how they were progressing. He found one tramp leaning on the ax-handle, watching with deep interest while the other tramp executed a series of amazing ballet steps, flip-flops, and somersaults.

"Cricky," said the farmer to the tramp on the side lines, "I didn't know your friend was an acrobat."

"Neither did I," admitted the tramp, "till I cracked him on the shin with this ax."

• • •

Ida Kay insists that this happened on a farm just outside Williamstown on Easter Sunday. A prankish youngster filled a chicken coop with eggs dyed every color of the rainbow. The rooster took one look at the dazzling display, ran straight out of the barn, and killed the peacock.

• • •

In *An All Sorts Treasury,* Columnist Joe Harrington of the Boston *Post* tells of a typical taciturn Vermont couple who sired a baby boy. The lad shot up like a bean stalk and soon was performing yeoman chores on the farm—but he never spoke a single word. His parents were mildly alarmed.

Sometime after his seventh birthday he was helping his father in the vegetable patch, which was separated from the barnyard by a wooden fence. Suddenly he observed that a prize bull had broken through the fence and was heading for his father with lowered head and nostrils distended. The boy hollered, "Look out, Pa! The bull!" Pa dove over an unbroken section of the fence and shattered all records to the family wash-and-recreation cubicle. There he reviewed the situation, and joyously exclaimed to his son, "Why, Will boy. You talked! Why ain't you ever talked before?" The boy answered, "Shucks, Pa. I never had nawthin' to say."

• • •

A New Hampshire farmer had three beautiful young daughters. The oldest found herself a husband and moved to Twin Cities, Minnesota. A year later she had twins. The second daughter then got married and established her home at Three Rivers, Ontario. Sometime later, she had triplets. Finally the youngest daughter came to the farmer and said that she too was going to become a bride. "I wish you all the luck in the world," said the father, "but take my advice and don't let that man of yours march you off to live in the Thousand Islands."

• • •

Cape Codders are a hardy lot. Old Jeb Sawyer of Eastport, for instance, was still working eight hours a day at the fishing wharf when he reached his hundredth birthday. The company thought it high time he retired on a pension, but Sawyer didn't like the idea at all. "Ding bust it," he exploded, "when I took this job in 1870, the manager gave me his solemn word that it was PERMANENT."

• • •

There's another spry old fellow in Barnstable—ninety-five if he's
a day—who runs his business in his own way. Playing checkers
in the rear of the store, his opponent said suddenly, "I think I
hear a customer up front." "Keep quiet," cautioned the local John
Wanamaker. "Maybe he'll decide nobody's here and go away."

Another time he sought a loan of a thousand dollars from the
town's leading banker, who was somewhat hard of hearing.
"Speak a bit louder," ordered the banker, "and reduce the amount
a little."

• • •

Senator Bridges of New Hampshire tells the story of one of his
neighbors who maintains his farm with the aid of a single spavined nag. The Senator spotted him in his field one morning, urging
the steed on with calls of "C'mon there, Blue Boy! Giddap, Man
o' War! Easy, Assault! Steady there, Whirlaway," and so forth.

"Why do you give him all those names?" laughed the Senator.

"Don't let him hear you say that," cautioned the farmer. "His
real name is Spot. But when I put blinders on him and call all
those different names, he imagines all the other horses are helping
him."

• • •

There is nothing more helpful than the advice of a friend—
particularly if, like Herbert Bayard Swope, you know when to
heed it.

Swope has always enjoyed wagering trifling sums on the horses,
but when he was appointed chairman of the New York State Racing Commission, he was seized with sudden doubts. Wouldn't it
look a bit odd for such a dignitary to be betting himself? Wouldn't
mean skeptics suspect that he had been given a couple of "sure
things" by unsavory characters in search of favors? Swope took his
problem to twelve good friends and true. Every one of them said,
"You're right, Herbie! Better lay off instead of on while you're the
Commissioner." Finally, however, he uncovered a thirteenth pal
who assured him that nobody would give a darn whether he bet
or not.

Vastly relieved, Mr. Swope faithfully followed the advice of Friend Number Thirteen.

• • •

A prominent jockey at Belmont wooed and won a Port Washington belle who outweighed him by a cool hundred pounds. After the wedding festivities, he begged the best man to come with the bride and himself to their newly rented bungalow. The best man demurred. "It just isn't done," he pointed out. "It's only for a minute," explained the jockey. "I just want you to help me carry her over the threshold."

Sheila Brown, best female judge of horseflesh in the publishing business, came home from Belmont one evening with self-satisfaction written all over her face. "I licked them today, boys," she exulted. "I licked them in the first race, the second race, the daily double, the third race, the fourth race, the fifth race, the sixth race, and if I'd had a nickel left, I'd have licked them in the seventh race, too."

• • •

On the morning of a Derby Day in Louisville, sportswriter Red Smith crept into the pressbox, showing every evidence of a strenuous session the evening previous. Grantland Rice whistled, and gasped, "Man, you should see your eyes." Red replied wearily, "If you think they look bad from where you sit, you should see them from this side!"

• • •

Moose McCormick, the famous old right-fielder of the New York Giants, left his present post at Lafayette College to take in a horse race. He had sworn to himself that he would do no betting that afternoon, but he'd always been tempted by long shots and when he saw one horse quoted at 100 to one, he couldn't resist putting down $5.00 on the nose. The nag gave him a wonderful run for his money and led, as a matter of fact, right down to the stretch. In the last hundred yards, however, the favorite came up fast and pulled into the lead. As the horses came down to the wire almost neck and neck, McCormick could contain himself no longer. He jumped to his feet and bellowed at the top of his lungs, "Slide, you bum, slide."

• • •

A father told his wife and children, "Pack up your duds. We're moving to Constantinople." The kids set up a terrific caterwauling, and insisted, "We dowanna live in Constantinople," but the mother silenced them in short order. "Run along and get ready," she ordered. "Daddy knows what's Bosphorus."

• • •

The man from Cook's shepherded his party into Cairo's most beautiful mosque and announced, "Here the sons of Egypt's most aristocratic families learn to worship God and His prophet Mohammed." A squeaky little voice on the edge of the crowd interrupted, "That isn't the way my father in Nanking tells it."

The guide looked pained and remarked, "There seems to be a little Confucian around here."

• • •

One of General Doolittle's intrepid flyers was ambling down a Morocco street when a veiled beauty, doused with a rare, haunting perfume and bedecked with diamonds and emeralds, fell panting into his arms. A hundred yards behind her charged a six-foot-four savage, brandishing a naked sword, and howling like a dervish.

"Queek, queek," whispered the veiled goddess, "which way is the Khan?"

"Lady," said the aviator solemnly, "I'm sorry to say I don't know. I'm a long way from home."

• • •

There is no more touching tale in all Indian folklore than the saga of good old Chief Shortcake. When he died, the whole tribe mourned and the lamentations of his faithful squaw were heard for miles around. Neighboring chiefs arrived in full pomp and ceremony and announced, "We've come to make funeral for Chief Shortcake." "Not on your life," announced his widow. (Please don't shoot any poisoned arrows at this point.) "Squaw bury Shortcake."

After the Chief had been laid to rest, incidentally, his brother sauntered into an El Paso hock shop, asked the cash value of his tepee, beads, and wampum belt, and explained tersely, "Me Pawnee."

• • •

A distinguished Chinese gentleman named Wong sent his wife from Shanghai to Manila for a holiday. She failed to return on schedule. In fact, she failed to return at all. Mr. Wong finally followed her to Manila, found that she had given birth to a lovely baby with blue eyes and blonde hair. He reminded her, "Two Wongs don't make a white." The undismayed Mrs. Wong replied, "That's quite true, my dear, but this was purely Occidental."

• • •

Frank Sinatra was invited to lunch one day with the bigshots in the MGM executive dining room. He reported later that the conversation had shifted ever so briefly from inevitable shop-talk to the subject of self-control. One producer—Sinatra disguises him under the name of Brown—asserted boldly, "I haven't touched liquor, played cards for money, or bet on a horse race in twenty years." "Gosh," interjected Sinatra, "I wish I could say that." "Why don't you?" urged L. B. Mayer. "Brown just did."

• • •

Ronald Colman told Herb Stein about a Hollywood phony who spoke with a fake Oxford accent, wore a fake purple star and Phi Beta Kappa key—and worst of all, passed a lot of fake checks. At the end of his rope, he decided to commit suicide, and went down to the Santa Fe railroad tracks. He calmly smoked several imported cigarettes while three or four heavy freights puffed by. A tramp who was watching jeered, "If you're gonna do it, why don't you do it?" "Don't be vulgar," squelched the phony. "A man like me waits for the Super Chief."

Gypsy Rose Lee, the somewhat different strip-tease artiste, made one of her early appearances with a troupe whose manager knew how to lure the yokels. His ads read, "Fifty beautiful girls; forty-five gorgeous costumes." "And it was I who persuaded 'em," adds Gypsy, "that I was the extra five girls!"

Today Gypsy says, "I know men aren't attracted to me by my

mind. They're attracted by what I don't mind." She recalls that one of her most expensive costumes was pilfered while she was playing an engagement in London. She cabled her insurance broker, "Gown lifted in Hotel Imperial." He cabled back, "Your policy does not cover that."

• • •

Clark Gable once starred in an aviation "epic" although he was openly disdainful of the quality of the scenario. The picture was being shot on "location"—at an old army flying field in Texas. Gable arrived one morning as the director was planning a scene involving a test flight by a couple of secondary actors in the story. Gable glanced at the dialogue for the scene and scoffed, "Do you mean to say you're going to send those boys up in this script?"

• • •

Honeysuckle was the kind of girl Milton Berle said he'd have liked to take home to meet his mother—if he could have trusted his father. When Honeysuckle was ensnaring her prey, her guardian called down from above, "Honeysuckle, is that young man of yours there yet?" "Not quite," she called back gaily, "but he's getting there." As she walked demurely to the altar, she whispered in her guardian's ear, "It won't be wrong now."

Honeysuckle's husband was neither better nor worse than most. He was inclined to agree with Samuel Rogers' famous observation on marriage: "It doesn't matter whom a man marries; he is sure to find, the next morning, he has married someone else." When she stayed too long at her mother's, he devised an infallible method for getting her home. He mailed her a copy of the local society page—with one item carefully scissored out.

Honeysuckle sought a doctor's advice on how to avoid having a baby until she wanted one. "Drink lots of orange juice," he counseled. "Before or after?" she queried. "Instead of," said the doctor.

The end of Honeysuckle's saga is vouchsafed for by Captain Burrell of the Thirty-second Precinct. According to Burrell, she minced into his bailiwick one night, smiled warmly at him, and murmured, "Where do I go to apologize for shooting my husband?"

• • •

Good advice is a fine thing to have, of course, but sometimes it doesn't work out just right. Herb Stein, for instance, writes of a beautiful young hopeful in Hollywood, who was assured by her agent, "The only thing you need to land a fat contract at Paramount is better posture. Learn to walk correctly and you're in." So the girl went to an expensive school and spent her days walking up and down with a book balanced on her head. And the day after she was graduated, Paramount bought the book.

• • •

Jimmy Durante's car once bumped into a stout lady who was crossing Seventh Avenue against the traffic signal. She waved an umbrella in his face and cried, "Half-wit! Moron! Imbecile!" "Madam," Durante informed her with quiet dignity, "you just passed me without knowing it."

• • •

The last time Harpo Marx visited New York, representatives of a dozen worthy charities descended upon him to request his appearance at benefits. One lady was particularly persistent and, after twelve telephone conversations in two days, Harpo finally agreed to appear for her. She called for him to escort him personally to the proper place in order to make sure that he wouldn't elude her. Just as they were closing the door of the suite, his phone began ringing. "Don't you want to go back and answer it?" she asked. Harpo sighed gently and said, "Why bother? It's undoubtedly you again."

• • •

Edward G. Robinson's pictures usually involve him in criminal proceedings—sometimes on the side of the law, more often against it. He explains how he makes up for the different parts: "If my hat brim is turned up, I'm a copper. If the brim is turned down, I'm a public enemy." Robinson recalls one occasion when he was playing a gangster, with his brim accordingly turned down. "Suddenly it snapped up," he says, "and there was only one thing left to do. I arrested myself."

• • •

Ghost writers are in great demand these days in Hollywood—but the great men who require their services are exacting taskmasters.

One producer, for instance, hired a college professor to write a learned paper for him defending the morals of the community and flaying critics who declared his pictures were a sorry sort of advertisement for the American way in foreign countries. He read a draft of the proposed article with furrowed brow, and then told the professor, "It's all right, but I want you to take out those fancy words. I want to know what I'm talking about."

Another magnate fired a new ghost writer because, he explained, "He doesn't understand my style of writing as well as the last fellow I had."

Then there was the day the old friend of a famous comedian passed away, and the comedian was asked to say a few words at the funeral. He called up his gag writer and said, "I've got to make a speech at a cemetery tomorrow. Rush me over a page of funeral jokes."

• • •

Sid Skolsky reports that a surprised Hollywood resident ran smack into a burglar piling the family plate into his burlap bag. "Well, well," exclaimed the resident, "I hope you'll stay long enough for me to fetch my wife. She's certain she's heard you in the middle of every night for the past ten years, and I know it'll be a pleasure for her to meet you."

• • •

Jack Benny has won thousands of laughs with his burlesque violin rendition of "Love in Bloom." The fact is, however, that he rather fancies himself as a violinist, and likes to be taken seriously when he renders an occasional classical air for his friends.

At a big party in Hollywood one night, Benny brought out his fiddle, and put everything he had into a piece. When he finished, and the applause had died down, Arthur Hornblow called, "Give us 'Poet and Peasant,' Jack."

"What!" exclaimed Benny, surprised and flattered. "Again?"

• • •

WHO CALLED THAT PRACTICAL
JOKER A HUMORIST?

In the good old days a fellow could win a reputation as a practical joker by simply putting a tack on the teacher's seat or pulling a chair from under a crippled grandmother of eighty just as she was sitting down to rest her weary bones. If somebody had to go to the hospital as a result of this hilarious byplay it was just an extra dividend. Now, however, your practical joker (under no circumstances to be confused with a "humorist") has graduated to more elaborate shenanigans. His hoaxes are planned with the care devoted to a major military campaign. Time is no object and neither is money—if he happens to have it. Somebody has estimated that if all the effort expended on sleazy practical jokes in the past year had been channeled into a more worthy endeavor, there might be fifty thousand fewer homeless war veterans in the country today. I take it you suspect by this time that I hold most practical jokers in extremely low esteem. You're right.

The meanest practical jokers in the world are the ones who conspire to put a blight on the wedding ceremonies of their best friends. Perhaps you read in the papers recently about the collection of goons who masqueraded as masked, bearded desperadoes, and charged into a bride's home with guns waving. The bride suffered a nervous collapse, and the memory of her wedding day has been marred forever. The goons probably are still convinced that they demonstrated their capacity for friendship and a keen sense of humor at the same time. Another bridal couple arrived at the Chicago airport with a fifteen-pound ball and chain attached to the bridegroom's right ankle. Fellow-workers in his railroad maintenance gang had shackled it to his leg just before he escorted his bride to the plane in Minnesota. The bride was still sobbing when she reached Chicago, and a motley assortment of morons stood simpering while the groom sought a hacksaw to cut himself free.

One of the dirtiest tricks ever played on a bridegroom, I think, was perpetrated at the bachelor dinner of a well-known socialite. Too much champagne had done him in completely. When he recovered consciousness, his right arm was in a sling. He had broken it, his friends told him mournfully, executing a Highland Fling on top of a table. There was not a word of truth in the story. The poor fish spent his entire honeymoon with a perfectly sound right arm bound up in a plaster-of-Paris cast.

The greatest predilection for practical jokes is displayed by a group of medical students. Maybe the very nature of their chosen profession makes these gentlemen more callous and unfeeling than the general run. Human skeletons, of course, are just everyday routine to an embryo physician, but what jolly fun it is to pop one suddenly into the face of somebody who never has seen one before in his life! A group of students who drove up one afternoon to the toll gate of the Triborough Bridge added a new touch to the old act. The officer in charge saw the usual arm extended from the car, but when he clutched for the quarter, the whole arm (stolen from a stiff in the dissecting laboratory) came off with it. The students drove away whooping with joy. The officer collapsed.

At Bellevue, there was a doctor on the staff who acquired modest proficiency as a ventriloquist on the side. Finding himself in need of an unskilled apprentice to help out in his laboratory, he devised his own peculiar method for testing the intelligence and nerve of the gangling youngsters who applied for the job. To the first applicant he handed a bowl of piping-hot gruel, and remarked casually, "There's a skeleton in the coat closet over there. Feed him!" The boy proffered the bowl with shaking hands, and when the skeleton announced "Uh, uh! That's too hot!" he dropped everything and made for the nearest exit. Two more kids fell victim to the amateur ventriloquist's grisly gag, but the fourth applicant took it in stride. When the skeleton announced, "Take it away! It's too hot," he simply jammed the bowl between its ribs and answered cheerfully, "Then blow on it, you dumb jerk." Turning to the doctor, he added, "Pardon me, Doctor, but you ain't no Edgar Bergen." He got the job.

The Hollywood chapter of the Practical Jokers' Club contented itself for years with such relatively simple hoaxes as a phony waiter who told mortified dinner guests in loud asides that they were using the wrong fork, and then poured gravy down the back of their necks. But mighty hoaxes from little acorns grow, and today's pranksters in the film capital think nothing of ripping up a victim's entire apartment or sending him on wild-goose chases clear across the continent. One film magnate built a new million-dollar sound stage of which he was inordinately proud. When Professor Uberschmaltz of Heidelberg came to test its qualities he was even prouder—for a rival producer had convinced him at dinner a few weeks previous that when it came to sound effects, Uberschmaltz was the McCoy. On the day of the test, Uberschmaltz had this very important babe in the Hollywoods whispering to him close-up on the new stage, and yelling his lungs out from a distance of two hundred yards. Finally, Uberschmaltz shook his head sadly and said, "Your new stage shtinks. I can't hear a damn thing." The next day the enraged producer learned that "Uberschmaltz" was a stooge smuggled into the studio by the rival producer.

His revenge required a much bigger build-up and a lot more of film stockholders' money. The rival producer began to hear rumblings that his public and private activities were under investigation by a certain senator in Washington, with a threatened denouement that would blow Bergman and Hayworth right off the front pages. Then it appeared that there was just a chance the inquisitive senator *might* be lured into visiting Hollywood.

The producer fell for the story hook, line, and sinker. The "senator"—an extra coached by the victim of the sound-stage fiasco, of course—was greeted at the train by the producer himself, his entire executive staff, and every pretty girl on his lot. For a full week the bogus politico was wined, dined, and photographed with his arm around various parts of the biggest stars' anatomies. A final banquet in his honor lasted for hours. The producer was so mortified when he learned the truth, he fired two secretaries.

The practical jokes that really delight me are the ones that bounce right back and smack the perpetrators in the face. Like the occasion, for instance, when a neophyte in the new issues department of J. P. Morgan and Company was informed "Mr. Morgan is very deaf, you know, and doesn't like to be reminded of it. When he asks you a question, be sure you shout the answer in his ear." The first time the young man heeded this advice, Mr. Morgan, of course, bellowed, "What the devil do you mean by shouting at me this way? Get out of here!" Thereafter, however, the victim of this trick was the one junior clerk Morgan recognized. Inside of two years he was one of the heads of his department, and had the unique pleasure of firing his tormentors personally.

Hy Gardner, the columnist and radio star, served under a colonel during the war who made his life miserable. Back in civvies, however, the colonel didn't hesitate to phone Gardner when he blew into New York that he was open for a little free loading and entertainment. "Nothing elaborate," he insisted. "Say, a good steak dinner, two down front for *South Pacific*, and a little night club where I can make with the dancing." Confronted with an opportunity he had dreamed about for years, Gardner called back to say everything had been arranged for Monday evening. First there was to be a dinner at Gallagher's Chop House (he neglected to state that Gallagher's is closed on Mondays). Next, he said, his old pal was to pick up a pair of house seats for *South Pacific*. (It was a week the show was closed to provide the cast a brief vacation.) And finally, the colonel was to drive down to a famous Long Island night spot. (It was shuttered for the season.) Well pleased with his handiwork, Gardner tuned in for the explosion. The colonel called about two the next afternoon, but what he said was, "Hy, you're the sweetest guy I ever met to go to all that trouble for me. I don't know how to tell you, but I ran into a couple of pals at cocktail time. One drink led to another, and I'm afraid I missed the steak dinner, *South Pacific,* and the night club. Give me a rain check, will you?" "Oh, well," philosophizes Gardner, "revenge is a base motive anyhow."

A noted pixie from the café society beat turned practical joker at an old Paris restaurant this spring. He isn't proud of the exploit, so I'll disguise him in this story as Mr. Twombley. The restaurant was the Tour d'Argent, on the banks of the Seine, where pressed duck and a wonderful soup are the specialités de la maison. Twombley was there with a group of American friends. When the soup was served, he emptied the pepper shaker into his portion, tasted it, coughed ostentatiously, and summoned the proprietor. "So this is your famous soup," he scoffed. "It's terrible. Taste it yourself." The proprietor sampled the soup and went into a frenzy. "The chef has gone mad," he decided. "Let me make an investigation in the kitchen." He came back a few moments later wringing his hands. "It is worse than I feared," he reported. "I have had the whole evening's supply of soup—enough for two hundred portions—poured down the drain. I have discharged the chef who has been with me for thirty years. Can Monsieur forgive us?"

Somehow the joke had lost its savour for Mr. Twombley. He fidgeted through the rest of the dinner, then squared his shoulders, and confessed to the proprietor like a little man. "I myself poured a shakerful of pepper into my soup," he admitted. "I didn't expect the consequences to be so drastic. I beg you to re-hire the chef and give him this fifty-dollar traveler's check to recompense him for his embarrassment. And I insist on paying for every portion of that soup you threw away."

The proprietor and the chef allowed themselves to be placated. Twombley paid the bill, and made for the door, considerably wiser and infinitely poorer. As he was climbing into a taxi the proprietor tugged at his sleeve, and whispered, "Monsieur Twombley, I saw you empty the pepper into that soup."

• • •

The late Hal Sims was stuck with a terrible partner in a so-called friendly bridge game in an Atlantic crossing one evening.

After butchering a hand that should have meant rubber, the bewildered tyro asked Sims, "How would *you* have played that last hand of mine?" Sims answered bitterly, "Under an assumed name."

• • •

Back from London, Columnist Irving Hoffman reports that Princess Margaret was sitting with the royal family at a box at the Palladium for the triumphant opening of Danny Kaye's new act. When the orchestra struck up "God Save the King," the Princess turned to her father, and in a loud stage whisper, remarked, "Listen, Pop, they're playing your theme song!"

After the show, the King and Queen accepted Kaye's invitation to a small party backstage. Danny produced a bottle of rare Scotch. The King downed his drink with obvious relish and remarked, "Where did you get that Scotch, Danny? I haven't tasted anything so good in years." Kaye answered, "Your Majesty, you just don't know the right people."

When Helen Hayes was appearing in the role of Queen Victoria, she received hundreds of letters from fans who claimed to have met the Queen in person. Some of their reminiscences were more fantastically unbelievable than others. One lady, for instance, claimed to have been strolling with Victoria through the gardens of Buckingham when she came upon her oldest son, aged nine, lambasting a younger playmate. "What's the big idea?" demanded Victoria—in more regal language, of course. "I just wanted to show him I'm the Prince of Wales," explained the future Edward VII. Victoria yanked him across her knees (that's the lady's story!) and gave him a fanning, pointing out grimly, "I guess I'd better show you I'm Queen of England."

* * *

In the early days of the blitz, Winston Churchill motored hurriedly to Canterbury to see that proper precautions were taken for the protection of the famous cathedral there. Later he explained to the Archbishop, "We have bolstered the edifice and approaches with sandbags to spare. Every device known to man has been applied. No matter how many close hits the Nazis may make, I feel sure the cathedral will survive." "Ah, yes, close hits," said the Archbishop gloomily, "but what if they score a direct hit upon us?" "In that event," decided Churchill, with some asperity, "you will have to regard it, my dear Archbishop, as a summons."

* * *

Addressing a group of prominent Jewish businessmen in the course of a visit to the United States, Winston Churchill brought down the house by recalling, "I advocated a free Jewish state in Palestine in years when that was a very unpopular notion in certain government circles. Be assured, gentlemen, that I shall never desert you in your hour of glory!"

Mr. Churchill said that the Israeli embassy in London was mortified to discover that all the other embassies made a point of offering a cup of tea in the afternoon to the bobbies assigned to posts in front of their buildings. The Israeli staff hastened to make amends to *their* bobby, explaining, "Forgive us if we don't know all the fine points as yet. We haven't had an embassy for two thousand years!"

* * *

Legend has it that Lord Louis Mountbatten encountered a colored sentry while he was in command of the China-Burma-India theatre. Lord Louis asked, "Are you Indo-Chinese?" The GI replied, "No suh, ah is outdo'-Mississippi."

• • •

In his *Where I Was Born and Raised,* author David L. Cohn quotes this wonderful sermon that he heard delivered from the pulpit of a tiny Negro Baptist church in the Mississippi Delta:

"Education is like a sucker on a pump. You sho' can't git no water widout it. It's like de polish on a shoe. You can git anything you wants wid education. Jes' suppose Henry Ford was settin' in his room. In come his wife. 'Henry,' she say, 'us is down to us las' slice of meat an' de meal in de bar'l is gittin' low.' Do dat worry him? Naw, dat don't concern him at all. What do he do? He reach for his checkbook, an' write out a check. Dat's what education is."

• • •

Dr. Harvey Cushing always got a laugh with his after-dinner story of the actor who turned surgeon. He took out a man's appendix in the operating theatre, and was so gratified by the applause, he took out the patient's tonsils as an encore.

• • •

A world-wise history teacher in an Oklahoma City high school ended one lecture by saying, "Will Aaron Burr win his duel with Alexander Hamilton? Will the American people go for the Monroe Doctrine? Come to class next Monday and find out."

• • •

A young relative of Professor Irwin Edman saw a big worm crawling in a garden, seized a knife from a table, and casually cut the worm in two. Irwin protested, "What made you do a thing like that?" The youngster explained, "The worm looked lonely. I thought he ought to have a friend."

• • •

Kiddie stories: A little girl who had just been promoted to the fourth grade in Town School wept on the shoulder of her teacher of the third grade. "Oh, Miss Young," she sobbed, "why aren't you smart enough to teach me again this season?" . . . . An indignant lad of ten sought out the local rent-control office and reported, "I rented a seat at the Paramount Theatre and was evicted without notice eight hours later." . . . . The Sunday-school teacher asked Willie, "If you had a large, good apple and a small, wormy one, and you were told to divide with your brother, which would you give him?" Willie answered, "Do you mean my big brother or my little one?"

• • •

Ted Brown, the Houston bookseller, tells about one nine-year-old girl who became so enamored of adventure tales and tabloids that she neglected everything to concentrate on reading. Her room became an unholy mess, and all of her mother's exhortations fell on deaf ears. One afternoon, however, the mother returned home to find her daughter's room as spic-and-span as the operating theatre of a big hospital. Not one thing was out of place. "How wonderful!" she exclaimed. "What got into you?"

"I've realized how important housework is," the daughter informed her. "I read in the paper where two ladies got a year apiece in jail—just for keeping a disorderly house."

• • •

The widow of Will Rogers notes in her memoirs that Will, Junior, never could learn to tuck in his shirttails when he was a youngster of ten. "Pleading and punishment got me nowhere," she recalls, "but I finally hit upon a scheme that cured him overnight. I sewed an edging of lace around the bottom of his shirts."

• • •

In the heart of the feudin' country in the Kentucky hills a little wooden schoolhouse was thrown open for the Fall term. The spinster who taught the entire class recognized all the pupils except two—a spindly little girl who clutched an even tinier little boy firmly by the right hand. When everybody was seated, the teacher rapped for silence and addressed the little girl. "What's your name?" she asked. "Bitchy Hatfield," was the answer. The class tittered and the teacher glared. "I don't want any of your vulgar nicknames," she said sternly. "I want to know your real name." "It's Bitchy Hatfield," the little girl insisted. The teacher stood up and said, "If you refuse to tell me your proper name, you can walk right out of this schoolhouse." The little girl stuck out her lower jaw, got up and grabbed the hand again of the little boy who sat next to her. "You might as well come along with me, Ratface," she said. "She'll never believe your name either."

• • •

A moonshiner in the Georgia hills was caught red-handed by a posse of revenue agents. The moonshiner, despite his seventy years and long gray beard, tore himself loose from the sheriff's grasp, and headed cross-country with the speed of a gazelle. The sheriff, a kindly—and lazy—soul, marveled at the old boy's agility, and said, "Let's let him go."

Five days passed, however, and the moonshiner failed to return. Just as his relatives and neighbors were concluding that his unusual exertions had been the death of him, he stumbled home in a state of complete disrepair. "Where you been, Beauregard?" asked his partner. The moonshiner answered simply, "I been comin' back."

• • •

A notably constructed young soprano from old Kaintucky, suh, once complained to Clifton Fadiman on a radio program that her conservative pappy wouldn't let her take a job in a summer stock company in sinful Hollywood. "Doesn't your pappy trust you?" inquired Fadiman, contriving to sound incredulous. "He trusts me all right," answered the soprano demurely, "but he doesn't trust anybody else."

• • •

A young lady in the Blue Ridge Mountain country gave birth to a healthy ten-pound daughter, and promptly accused a neighboring farmer of being the father. The farmer, however, produced an airtight alibi: the records showed that he had been released only three months before from a five-year stretch on the chain gang. He was dumfounded when the judge finally declared him responsible for the infant's support. The judge silenced his protest by declaring, "Jeb, I follow an ironclad rule in this here court. When the maker cannot be found, the last endorser is held responsible."

• • •

Out Minnesota way folks pay a lot of attention to their legendary hero, Paul Bunyan. As a matter of fact, prizes are given every year to the people who contribute the most ingenious new "tall tales" about his exploits. A recent winner was Mr. Harold B. Jennings of Brainard, Minnesota. Here's his story:

One day Paul Bunyan was strolling through the North Woods followed by his faithful blue ox, Babe. Paul had a wanderlust. A tourist had told him the story of how George Washington had thrown a dollar across the Potomac. Paul allowed as how he'd like to take a crack at this game himself.

Packing himself a small lunch of five roasted pigs, twenty-five ducks, and forty bushels of wild rice, Paul headed east. He wasn't sure he'd know the Potomac, but decided he'd keep his eye open for the biggest river in the East. When he finally saw a great expanse of water, he was sure it was the Potomac.

He didn't have a dollar but found a farmer's wagon and removed the four wheels. To his embarrassment, the first two wheels landed in the water, but on his last two tries, there was no splash of water, only a cloud of dust as they landed on the opposite shore.

And so, to this day, two farmers in a coastal village in France

talk about how a couple of wagon wheels suddenly descended
upon them from out of the sky. Paul Bunyan never knew that he
had mistaken the Atlantic Ocean for a river.

• • •

Brentano's book store in New York has leased a concession to
a lady who specializes in sea-shells, a collectors' fad that seems
to be enjoying a revival. The best customer to date was a lady
who ran up a bill of $90. "I'm moving to Hollywood," she ex-
plained, "and I want these shells to remind me of my old home
on the Atlantic coast." Nobody told her that every shell she bought
came straight from a beach in the South Pacific.

• • •

The librarian of Staten Island's roving bookmobile was confronted recently by an importunate youth who demanded, "that
book you talked me into borrowing three weeks ago." The gratified librarian asked, "Was it so good you want to read it over
again?" "Heck, no," said the bookworm. "I wrote my new girl's
phone number in it."

• • •

David Dempsey submits a report about a proper Bostonian who
was deeply shocked when a bookshop clerk tried to sell her *America's Cook Book* instead of the time-honored *Boston Cook Book*.
"What in the world is this?" she sniffed. The salesgirl replied,
"Why, this has recipes from all the other parts of the country."
"Young lady," retorted the customer, "there are no other parts of
the country."

• • •

When Margaret Ford, author of several outstanding books for
children, married the erudite nature-lover, John Kieran, the entire literary world shared the couple's happiness. Later Margaret
told a couple of delectable stories about their honeymoon. It seems

that a few hours after their nuptials, John heard a sound in the distance, and burst from the room. He was gone for all of a half hour. Upon returning he explained happily, "My dear, I'd have recognized that call anywhere, though I haven't heard it in years. It was a hairy woodpecker!" Margaret reported ruefully, "I'll bet I'm the only bride in America who was deserted on her wedding night for a hairy woodpecker!"

Later in the week Margaret heard a mouse scampering across the floor in the adjoining room. No mouse lover she, she screamed loudly and begged John to go and dispatch it. When he returned she looked at him suspiciously and asked, "John, did you kill that mouse?" "I simply couldn't do it, dear," he admitted. "The mouse turned out to be pregnant!"

• • •

William Faulkner, famous author of *Sanctuary* and other novels of the South, once served as postmaster at the University of Mississippi. When he decided to quit the job, he wrote a letter to the Postmaster General in Washington which is still shown there gleefully to preferred visitors. "As long as I live under the capitalist system," stated Faulkner, "I expect to have my life influenced by the demands of moneyed people. But I will be damned if I propose to be at the beck and call of every itinerant scoundrel who has two cents to invest in a postage stamp. This, sir, is my resignation."

• • •

Donald Lindsay, of Cleveland, has compiled a list of "New Editions, Musical and Literary, for an Era of Deflation": "Two Saints in One and a Half Acts"; "None but the Lonely Half a Heart"; "Three Characters in Search of Half an Author"; "The Three and a Half Who Were Hanged"; Tarkington's "Eight and a Half"; Hecht's and MacArthur's "Tenth Century"; "The One and a Half Musketeers." Lindsay adds that he is now working on stories of the profile that launched 500 ships, the 300 who rode into the jaws of coma, one soul with but half a thought, and five little Indians.

• • •

Bill Hall, tireless student of the works of A. Conan Doyle, dismisses as a foul canard the report that Sherlock Holmes once confronted Dr. Watson with the statement, "Ah, my dear Doctor, I see you have donned your long winter underwear." "Amazing," Watson is supposed to have replied. "How did you deduce that?" "Elementary," explained the peerless Holmes. "You have forgotten to put on your pants."

• • •

A well-known author was hit by a car on his way to his favorite bar, and was knocked unconscious. The proprietor of the bar sent for an ambulance, and watched first aid being administered. "He's coming out of it, boys," said the proprietor finally. "See that motion? He's trying to blow the foam off his medicine."

• • •

Lee Lyles, vice-president of the Santa Fe Railroad, was checking over the losses that resulted in a single year from horses, cattle and hogs being killed on the right of way. The owners of the slaughtered animals had very fancy ideas of the recompense they deserved. Lyles told the attorney for the road, "It strikes me that nothing improves the blood of livestock as much as crossing it with a Diesel locomotive."

* * *

A new clerk at the Twentieth Century-Fox studio in Beverly Hills was standing in front of the Administration Building when he saw a driverless Cadillac rolling down the incline to the entrance on Pico Boulevard. He raced across the lawn, jumped into the moving car, and jammed on the emergency brake.

At this point, Darryl Zanuck, king bee of the studio, appeared from behind the car. "Gee, Mr. Zanuck," boasted the clerk, "this Cadillac was running down the hill and I stopped it." "Yes, I know," said Mr. Zanuck grimly. "I was pushing it."

* * *

Have you heard the story of the rancher who had occasion to telephone the legal firm of Shapiro, Shapiro, Shapiro, and Shapiro? The conversation went as follows:

"Hello. I'd like to talk to Mr. Shapiro."

"Mr. Shapiro is in court arguing a case."

"Oh. Then I'll talk to Mr. Shapiro."

"Mr. Shapiro can't come to the phone. He's in conference with an important client."

"Oh. Then I'll talk to Mr. Shapiro."

"Mr. Shapiro isn't in today. He's playing golf at Bonnie Brae."

"Oh. In that case, can I talk to Mr. Shapiro?"

"*Speaking.*"

• • •

A farmer was making one of his infrequent visits to a moving-picture show. The slapstick comedy showed a group of shapely maidens coyly undressing beside a pond. Just as things reached an interesting point, a railroad train obscured the view. When it had passed, the girls were already splashing about in the lake.

The farmer remained rooted in his seat for four continuous showings. Finally an usher inquired, "Are you here for the winter, Pop?" The farmer answered, "I'm going to stay here till that train is a couple of minutes late!"

• • •

A California picture exhibitor installed a wishing well in the lobby to amuse children who were waiting to get in. He hastily removed it after the first day, however, when an irate adult strode out of the theatre, dropped a penny in the wishing well, and said very loudly, "I wish I hadn't seen the picture they're running here this week."

• • •

At a big party in Hollywood, all the well-known wolves concentrated their attention on a beautiful blonde whom none of them had ever seen before. The one who reached her first whispered, "May I take you home this evening? I dearly love to take experienced girls home." "I am not an experienced girl," demurred the blonde. "You're not home yet, either," the wolf reminded her.

• • •

The casting manager of a studio in financial straits reported, "That big-shot you told me to get wants a thousand bucks to play an Indian for two days." The head of the studio chewed angrily on his cigar and bellowed, "Give him five hundred and have him play a half-breed!"

• • •

An ill-starred producer conceived the notion of co-starring Mae West and the late W. C. Fields in a motion picture. The first of many pitched battles came over the question of who should get first billing. "If you weren't such a ham," stormed Miss West, "you'd admit that never in history has a gentleman been billed ahead of a lady." "Oh, yeah!" chortled Fields. "How about 'Mister and Missus'?"

• • •

A Hollywood columnist once circulated an erroneous report of Fields' death. The bulbous-nosed comedian called up the editor in a rage. "I hope you noticed," he roared, "that your foul newspaper announced my death this morning." "That I did," admitted the editor coolly. "May I ask where you're calling from?"

• • •

Longest word: "And now a word from our sponsor. . . ." Last words: "So he won't dim his lights, hey? Then I'm darned if I dim mine." Sweetest words: "Your dentist has the measles and will have to cancel your appointment today." Most frightening words: "This is the income tax department." Words of wisdom: Clemenceau's summary of the girls in the Folies Bergere: "They have such gay behinds—but such sad faces!"

• • •

Just as a lot of wisecracks she never even heard are attributed to Dorothy Parker, so baseball boners pulled by bushers all over the country are pinned to the Athletics' inimitable screwball, Rube Waddell. The following stunt, however, really was performed by Waddell. He wielded a pretty hefty bat for a pitcher, and was allowed to swing for himself one day in the eighth inning with the score 2–1 against the Athletics, two out, and the tying run on second. The catcher of the opposing nine saw a chance to pick off the runner at second and heaved the ball in that general direction. It ended in center field, and the runner hot-footed for the plate. He'd have made it, too, with plenty to spare, but as the throw came into the plate, Waddell, to the amazement of everybody in the park, swung at the ball, bashed it out over the right field fence, and was promptly declared out for interference. "Why did you do it?" wailed Manager Connie Mack. "They'd been feeding me curves all afternoon," explained the Rube sheepishly, "and this was the first straight ball I'd looked at!"

• • •

The Boston Red Sox, woefully shy on pitching strength one spring, brought up a young left-hander who had a world of stuff,

but less control than is generally expected even from southpaws. "How wild is he?" somebody asked Manager Joe McCarthy. "How wild?" echoed McCarthy. "The other evening I sent him in to pitch batting practice at Fenway Park, and he hit a man who was watching on television in a bar on Scollay Square!"

• • •

In Fred Russell's sparkling new *Funny Things About Sports* he tells of a day Connie Mack yanked Pitcher George Earnshaw from the mound because Lou Gehrig had lofted two of his offerings over the right field fence. "This fellow I've put in now knows how to pitch to Gehrig," Mack told the disgruntled Earnshaw. "Watch him." When Gehrig came up for his next lick, he teed off on the new pitcher's first delivery and sent it over the center field wall on a dead line. As Gehrig jogged around the bases, Earnshaw whispered to Mack, "I see what you mean. Make him change direction, eh?"

• • •

When Ty Cobb was in his prime, a fresh recruit pitcher popped up with the New York Yankees who claimed that he had discovered Cobb's weakness at the bat. He was given a chance to face the Detroit slugger when the Tigers came to New York. Cobb faced him four times and made four three-base hits. The rookie was just as cocky as ever when he strode into the clubhouse. "I told you I knew that guy's weakness," he announced. "He's got a weakness for three-base hits."

• • •

The Tigers came into the Yankee Stadium for a series some years later with a young pitcher just up from the Three-Eye League. He had a good fast ball and an incredible appetite. He was warming up languidly in the bull pen for the first game with the Yanks, munching contentedly on a ham sandwich, when the Detroit manager suddenly signalled for him to come in and pitch. The rookie put his sandwich carefully on the bench and asked,

"Who have I got to pitch to?" A teammate answered, "Babe Ruth. And Gehrig comes after him." "Don't nobody touch that sandwich," ordered the rookie. "I'll be right back."

• • •

Leo Durocher recalls with a nostalgic gleam in his eyes a tale about the murderous Yankees of that Ruth-Gehrig era. Mark Koenig led off one inning with a triple to left. Tony Lazzeri sent him in with a double to right. Then the Babe and Lou Gehrig followed with tremendous drives into the right field bleachers.

That brought up the Yankee third baseman, Jumping Joe Dugan. On the first pitch, he shortened his bat, laid down a perfect bunt, and beat the throw to first with plenty to spare. Manager Miller Huggins came steaming out of the dugout and bellowed, "I ought to fine you a hundred bucks for breaking up a rally."

• • •

Arthur Daley, author of the anecdote-packed *Times At Bat,* has statistics to prove how seldom ball players' spring holdouts result in better contracts from the management. One of the few times the player won out was when Hi Myers, of the old Brooklyn Dodgers, out-foxed Prexy Charles Ebbets.

The letterhead on which Myers wrote that his proffered contract was inadequate bore the flamboyant heading "Myers' Championship Stock Farm." Ebbets didn't know that the stationery had been printed specially for the occasion, and that Myers' elaborate holdings consisted of one spavined horse, one cow, and a couple of chickens. "This fellow must be independently rich," thought Ebbets. "I better go right down to his farm and placate him."

Now it was Myers' turn to grow panicky. But when Ebbets arrived he saw a fine herd of fat cattle in the north pasture, and dozens of sleek horses in another. Obviously, Myers' Stock Farm was flourishing. Ebbets gave him the raise he demanded and departed. Myers spent the next two days returning cows and horses to friendly neighbors within a radius of fifty miles who had come to his rescue when the need was greatest.

• • •

Wilbert Robinson managed the Brooklyn team in those dear old days. In fact, the club's nickname was changed temporarily from "Dodgers" to "Robins." Robinson liked players who could hit the ball out of the park. A good slugger meant more to him than all the great pitchers in the game.

One day a scout phoned him long distance all the way from Denver. "I just saw a pitcher that will set the National League on fire," he declared. "He's got a blinding fast ball, perfect control, and a dipsy-doodle drop that fades out of sight. He pitched a perfect game today: no hits, twenty-two strike-outs. Only one guy hit a foul more than fifty yards!"

"To heck with the pitcher," proclaimed Robinson. "What's the name of the guy who hit the foul?"

• • •

In a book about the Cincinnati baseball team by Lee Allen, he tells of a famous meeting between Tip O'Neill, outfielder of the Reds, and a prominent Cincinnati minister.

Tip said, "I hope you are coming out to the game with the Giants on Sunday." "Sorry," answered the minister, "but I can't go to ball games on Sunday. Sunday is my busiest day." Tip said, "I know, on account of the double-headers it is my busiest day too." "That may be," allowed the minister, "but I am in the right field." "So am I," said Tip. "Ain't that sun terrible?"

• • •

There was a bit of a mix-up at the Colony Florist Shop in Meadstown the other day: wrong cards were attached to two imposing floral wreaths. The one that went to a druggist moving to an expensive new building read: "Deepest sympathy"; the one intended for the funeral of the town's leading banker read "Good luck in your new location."

• • •

From Detroit comes a story of the day when a big ministers' convention and a powwow of automobile salesmen were held si-

multaneously in the same hotel. The salesmen were topping off a
big dinner with "spiked watermelon" for dessert, but the hard-
pressed waiters scrved it to the ministers by mistake. The maître
d'hôtel was frantic when he heard of the mix-up. "That watermelon is soaked in alcohol," he moaned. "Get it away from those
ministers before they run me out of town."

The waiters returned to say it was too late: the ministers were
busy chewing away at the prized watermelon. "What did they
say?" asked the harassed maître d'hôtel. "How do they like it?"

One waiter answered, "I don't know how they like it, boss, but
they're all putting the seeds in their pockets."

● ● ●

Before the turn of the century, when New Yorkers still went
to work in hansom cabs and horse cars, every director of the old
New York Life Insurance Company who attended the annual
meeting received an equal share of a substantial sum set aside
for this purpose in the by-laws. There were about fifty directors
and all of them were wealthy, so under ordinary circumstances
a bare quorum showed up. One meeting, however, took place the
day after the great blizzard of 1888. The directors all figured that
not many of their associates would venture out in such weather,
and that those who did manage to make it would receive a correspondingly larger share of the fee. The roll call disclosed that
for the first time in the company's history every director was
present!

To give you some idea of how high the drifts were after that
1888 blizzard, they tell of a young couple who went sleigh-riding
down Broadway when the storm abated. "Look," said the girl,
"there's a chicken sitting on the snow." "That's no chicken," said
her companion. "That's the weather vane on top of Trinity
Church."

● ● ●

Jim Hack, a top executive today for the New York Life Insurance Company, told a *Tide* reporter how he sold his first
five-figure policy years ago. The prospect was a tough, hard-to-

convince sales manager. Hack wangled an interview, and mumbled, "You don't want any life insurance, do you?" "You're darn right I don't," roared the sales manager, but as Hack started inching toward the door, he added, "Come back here, young fellow. It's my job to train salesmen at this plant and I want to tell you you're about the worst excuse for a salesman that has ever crossed my path."

Hack sat down meekly and listened to a one-hour dissertation on the art of selling. At the end of it, the manager had worked himself into such a magnanimous mood that he signed an application for a $10,000 policy. He handed it to Hack and concluded, "Now remember my advice. Learn a couple of standard, organized sales approaches." "Oh, I've done that already," said Hack happily. "I've got a standard approach for every type of prospect. What you just heard is my standard approach for tough sales managers."

• • •

The president of a Wall Street underwriting corporation called Floyd Odlum on the phone. "We're negotiating with General So-and-So for a ten-million-dollar loan for his new asphalt factory," said the president. "I recall you once had some dealings with the General, and I'd like to know what estimate you formed of his character." "He's an engaging fellow," said Odlum cagily, "but I'd hate to go to sleep some evening with my finger in his mouth."

• • •

Mr. Kidder, of Kidder Peabody, was strolling through the cashier's cage when he spied an unfamiliar character briskly counting thousand-dollar bills. "You look like a bright young fellow," commented Mr. Kidder. "Where did you receive your financial training?" "Yale," said the character. "Fine," boomed Mr. Kidder, "and what did you say was your name?" "Yohnson," was the reply.

• • •

I have a distant cousin in the insurance business who once engaged in a very hot debate with a rival agent on the merits of their respective companies. The rival declared, "There is no company like ours for prompt payment. If one of our clients dies on Monday, the heirs have our check in full by Tuesday morning."

My cousin was visibly unimpressed. "Our head office," he declared, "is located on the 45th floor of the Empire State Building. One morning last week a client jumped out of a window on the 70th floor. We handed him his check as he passed our floor."

When Harrison Smith, the erudite editor, was a lad, his millionaire uncle, Winchell Smith, was the hero of the family. One day young Hal asked his uncle, "Just how does a young man go about making his fortune these days?" "Pluck, my boy, pluck," advised Uncle Winchell. "That's understood," agreed Harrison, "but whom do you suggest I pluck first?"

• • •

A watch repairer looked at the miscellaneous collection of tiny wheels and springs a customer had deposited on the counter, and said, "Are you sure this once was a watch?"

"Oh, yes," the customer assured him. "I guess I never should have dropped it."

"Dropping it, you couldn't help," said the expert. "But tell me: why did you bother picking it up?"

• • •

An eccentric Wall Street millionaire died recently. When his will was opened, the lawyers discovered he had lived up to his reputation to the very end. This is what they read:

"To my wife, I leave her gigolo and the knowledge that I wasn't the fool she thought I was. To my son, I leave the pleasure of earning a living. For thirty years he has thought the pleasure was all mine. He was mistaken. To my daughter I leave $100,000. She'll need it. The only smart thing her husband ever did was to marry her. To my valet I leave the clothes he has been stealing from me regularly for the past ten years; also my fur coat he wore last winter while I was in Palm Beach. To my chauffeur I leave my Rolls-Royce and station wagon. He has almost ruined them, and I want him to have the satisfaction of finishing the job."

• • •

A New York landlord, impatient over restrictions imposed by the emergency rent laws, tried to evict a tenant illegally. The knowing tenant replied in writing—and it was one of the shortest notes ever penned. The exact words were: Sir, I remain. Yours truly.

• • •

When Stanton Griffis, now our ambassador to Argentina, became a trustee of Cornell University in 1930, one of his first achievements was to lure to the faculty staff a famous professor who had declined all previous overtures. He explained that he owned a house in Westchester on which the Manufacturers' Trust Company held a substantial mortgage. He didn't see how he could relieve himself of this obligation. "Leave it to me," said Griffis.

Griffis went straight to Harvey Gibson, high mogul at the Manufacturers' Trust. "You're holding a mortgage for something like forty thousand dollars on the house of a poor college professor. That's not a very good risk," he pointed out. Gibson agreed. "All right," said Griffis. "How about letting a group of the professor's friends pay it off for fifty cents on the dollar? That's probably more than you'll ever realize any other way." Gibson was favorably inclined, and said he'd think it over. The next day, however, Griffis learned the mortgage would have to be paid off in full. It appears that John D. Rockefeller, Jr., had guaranteed it when it was made. "Setbacks like that merely sharpen a fellow's mettle," philosophizes Griffis.

• • •

A little man strayed into a corner of a clubroom where a quartet of publishing tycoons were playing bridge.

"I made forty thousand in the cotton market last month," remarked Tycoon Lewis Miller idly.

"I picked up fifty thousand in a turn on Plymouth Oil," added Tycoon Nat Wartels.

"And I stashed away seventy-five thousand in a big day at the track," Tycoon Manny Siwek chimed in.

The little man interrupted the conversation by clearing his throat audibly, and commenting, "My yellows were off half a million last week, but reds soared two million and blacks were up four million more."

"What business are you in?" asked the publishing tycoon, vastly impressed.

The little man said, "Jelly beans."

• • •

The source of all wisdom—and cash loans—in the German village of Stadt Lengsfeld was paunchy Banker Henkel—stingy, cranky, and unbelievably conceited. To feed his ego, fellow townsmen came to him with their every problem, though they scarcely listened to the weighty words of wisdom he poured into their ears. Banker Henkel had a solution for everything, and so long as it cost him neither a pfennig nor the slightest personal trouble, he offered it freely and cheerfully.

One day a farmer, whose property was heavily mortgaged to Henkel's bank, marched his fourteen-year-old son into the oracle's presence. "It's time Fritz here was deciding his future," said the farmer, "and I've taken the liberty of seeking your valuable advice in the matter." "I have a little experiment that seldom fails in such situations," said Henkel, obviously pleased. Sending Fritz from the room, he placed upon his desk-top a Bible, a thousand-mark note, and a bottle of whisky. "Now," he explained, "we'll call Fritz in, and point silently to the desk. If he picks up the Bible, he'll enter the church. If he picks up the thousand-mark note, he's cut out for a business career. If he picks up the bottle of whisky—we're in trouble."

The father nodded understandingly, and Fritz was summoned. He took a hasty look at the desk-top, stuffed the Bible in one pocket, the thousand-mark note in the other, tucked the bottle of whisky under his arm—and fled precipitately from the room. The father clapped a hand to his head. "Now we're *really* in trouble," he groaned. "Fritz is going to be a banker like you!"

A flashy character barged into a Detroit saloon, demanded a double jigger of Scotch, downed it in one gulp, planked a five-dollar bill on the counter, and walked out without another word. The bartender folded the fiver carefully, pocketed it, and remarked to the bar flies, "Can you beat a phony like that? Laps up a double Scotch, leaves a five-dollar tip, and beats it without paying!"

• • •

There's a saloon in the old ghost town of Virginia City that is now just a tourist trap. Eighty years ago, however, its patrons were the toughest collection of hombres in the U.S.A. One of them returned from a visit to San Francisco and observed, "Hey, when did you start sprinkling sawdust on the floor here?" "That's not sawdust," the proprietor pointed out. "That's yesterday's furniture."

• • •

Robert Sherwood was buttonholed on the way to a rehearsal by a wavering gentleman, exuding the delicate fragrance of cheap bourbon, who demanded, "Hey, where'sh Alcoholics Anonymoush?" "You want to join?" asked Sherwood incredulously. "Heck, no," roared the other. "I want to resign."

• • •

Another tipsy gent dropped a nickel into the telephone coin box, dialed a number with great deliberation, and cried, "Hello! Hello!" A voice at the other end of the wire called back, "Hello yourself." The inebriated one banged the receiver down, and bellowed to the world at large, "This phone has an echo!"

• • •

After Monty Woolley had spent two days at a Palm Springs hotel, he ordered a bouquet to be sent to the girl who operated the switchboard. "She'll appreciate the thought, I'm sure, Mr. Woolley," purred the cashier. "Appreciate my foot," snarled Woolley. "I thought she was dead."

• • •

Two old Shakespearian troupers were boasting of their triumphs:

"When I played the death scene in *Hamlet*," said one, "the entire audience burst into tears. One lady had hysterics."

"What's that?" scoffed the other. "The night I did that scene at Daly's Theatre on Broadway, my insurance agent, who was sitting in the third row, rushed to my house and paid my wife my life insurance."

• • •

When Lew Dockstader's Minstrels were one of the biggest attractions in the country, the great Dockstader himself invariably checked with the box office before registering at his hotel, no matter how small the town he was playing happened to be. He regarded an empty seat as a personal insult. At the end of the season, he had all his treasurer's reports bound in leather, and read them over and over as a form of relaxation.

The day his troupe visited Charleston, South Carolina, he suffered a grievous shock. The rack on the local op'ry house was chock-full of unsold tickets. Dockstader collected the entire company, ordered them to get into their uniforms, and made them parade four solid miles in the midsummer sun. He led the procession himself, although he nearly collapsed from the heat.

In a state of exhaustion, he returned to the box office, and said, "If *that* didn't make them buy tickets for this evening, I'll retire from show business."

The treasurer looked puzzled. "I don't know what's biting you, Mr. Dockstader," he said. "We've been sold out for your performance for over two weeks. These tickets you see in the rack are for the show that's coming in after you!"

• • •

The knife-throwing expert and his beautiful young assistant stood in front of their tent at the State Fair while the spieler described the wonderful act that would be performed within. Mrs. Silas Hawkins was attracted by the knife thrower and Mr. Silas Hawkins detected in the assistant a few curves he had never seen before. They paid their two slim dimes—"the tenth parts of a dollar"—and entered the tent. Eventually the assistant stood against a wooden wall and doffed her spangled robe. Silas Hawkins gasped audibly. Then the knife thrower stepped upon the platform and it was Mrs. Hawkins's turn to gasp. The knife thrower pulled back his right arm and the steely blade went zinging through the air. It buried itself in the wall one-eighth of an inch from the assistant's shell-pink ear. Silas Hawkins jumped to his feet with a cry. "Doggone," he said, "he missed her."

William A. Brady, the late producer and husband of Grace George, recalled, "To keep up morale in my staff, and to fool rival producers and theatrical reporters, I always instructed managers of my road companies to add three hundred dollars to their nightly reports of box-office receipts. The system worked fine until one of them wired, "Only theatre in town burned to the ground this afternoon. No performance. Receipts $300."

• • •

When Ole Janssen secured a job as janitor in a famous night club, he was given a pass key to every room in the building including the girls' dressing rooms. Two weeks later the manager ran into him in the hall and said, "What's the matter, Ole? You haven't come round to collect any wages yet." "By golly," gasped Ole. "I get wages too?"

• • •

A rundown old Shakespearean actor was given a chance by a Hollywood director to make a few dollars as an extra, but when he learned that his part would consist of exactly three lines, he rose to his feet, thrust one hand inside his coat, and proclaimed, "That miserable role you are asking me to portray would completely destroy my reputation as an actor." The unfeeling director answered, "That's why I am offering it to you. It's your one big chance."

• • •

Radie Harris knows a sweet young thing who dreamed of seeing her name in lights on Broadway, and rashly accepted a manager's invitation to talk over possibilities at luncheon in his bachelor apartment. When she arrived, she found the bed unmade and the host very amorously inclined. She fled home to mama, and tearfully confessed her disillusionment. "It's men like him who give the theatre a bad name," snorted mama. "Imagine, one o'clock and his bed not made."

• • •

The famous vaudeville team of Smith and Dale, whose "Dr. Kronkhite" act is still convulsing the populace on television, tell about one patient of the good doctor who was advised to take up horseback riding to cut down his middle-age spread. A few weeks later Dr. Kronkhite encountered his patient aboard a venerable nag in the dead of night. "Why ride at such an hour as this?" asked the doctor. "Economics," explained the patient. "In the daytime the crook who owns this horse wants six dollars an hour for renting it to me." "And what does he charge you at night?" demanded Kronkhite. "At night," said the patient, "he isn't there."

• • •

Another popular vaudeville act in America, about 1920, was the team of Bert Savoy and Jay Brennan. Savoy impersonated a brash and uninhibited female; Brennan was the perpetually-shocked straight man. When Brennan asked, "Do your apartments overlook the river?" Savoy would answer, "No, but they overlook everything else. You *must* come up!" Later Savoy admitted that "she" had been evicted. "I gave a party for a crowd of mounted policemen," was the explanation. "Nobody minded *that,* but the other tenants objected when the boys brought their *horses* up too."

When Savoy lamented the passing of her dear husband, Brennan interrupted a chant of woe by exclaiming, "There's some terrible mistake. The body is still warm." "Oh, it is," answered Savoy angrily. "Well, hot or cold, it gets buried tomorrow."

The act of Savoy and Brennan was broken up by the untimely death of Bert Savoy, who was struck by lightning while bathing at the Long Island shore. Jay Brennan is still active in radio and motion pictures.

•　•　•

For many years the theatrical weekly, *Variety,* has been famous for its terse, jargonistic headlines. When the stock market crashed in 1929, for instance, *Variety's* front-page banner read "Wall Street Lays an Egg." When a raging blizzard cut Buffalo's theatre receipts in half one week, *Variety* summed up the situation, "BLIZ BOFFS BUFF BIZ." When small-town movie exhibitors turned thumbs-down on rural subjects, *Variety* headlined "STIX NIX HIX PIX."

It seems that the New York *News,* however, has decided to give *Variety* headline writers a run for their money. News captions have been growing friskier by the day, culminating recently when a strip-tease artist in a Fifty-second Street bistro was pinched on a morals charge. The *News* covered the trial, and reported, "Three Judges Weigh Her Fan Dance: Find It Wanton."

•　•　•

Abel Green, the editor of *Variety,* tells about a vaudevillian who boasted to an agent, "My name is Projecto, and I can fly. Just let me show you my act." The blasé agent consented to go with him

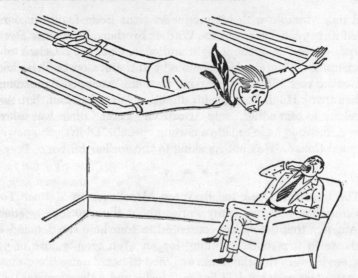

to an empty theatre nearby. True to his word, the actor promptly took off from the stage, spiraled to the ceiling, circled the auditorium a couple of times, and zoomed down in a perfect glide. The agent yawned and said, "So you can imitate boids. What else can you do?"

• • •

The late Jules Leventhal, who managed road-company productions of great Broadway hits, was famed for his honesty, his accent, and his frugality. Once he sent out a troupe to play Nugent and Thurber's *The Male Animal,* one scene of which called for a football coach to hand a professor a cigar. When Leventhal scanned the expense sheet for the first week, he rebelled at the item, "Cigars, eighty cents," and ordered, "From now on, when the coach offers that cigar, have the professor answer, 'No, thanks, I don't smoke.'"

• • •

The late Paul Armstrong, a famous playwright a generation ago by virtue of his *The Deep Purple* and *Alias Jimmy Valentine,* had more trouble with his producers than Bette Davis encountered forty years later with the Warner Brothers. When *The Deep Purple* wowed an opening-night audience, George M. Cohan told Armstrong, "It's great, kid. You ought to thank George Tyler and the entire cast." "I'm not speaking to them," snapped Armstrong. "Then thank Hugh Ford for his direction," urged Cohan. "I'm not speaking to him either," said Armstrong. Later Cohan was asked why Armstrong hadn't made a curtain speech. "Didn't you know?" grinned Cohan. "He's not speaking to the audience."

• • •

The immortal Duse, recalls Ward Morehouse in *Matinee Tomorrow*, had heard so many stories about the atrocious weather in America that before she consented to tour here she demanded a clause in her contract calling for an even temperature of 72 degrees in every dressing room assigned to her. An ingenious master carpenter exclaimed, "I fix," and fashioned a thermometer that registered exactly 72 come blizzard or heat wave. "Wonderful country," remarked a contented Duse before sailing for home. "It renn, it snow, it frizz, it blow—but de termometer, he is always 72." As an afterthought, she remarked, "Funny, I sink, how much hotter 72 ees in Chicago than it ees in New York!"

• • •

In his smash hit, *A Streetcar Named Desire*, Tennessee Williams revived the story of the colored gentleman who sat in his favorite rocker on the porch and watched a rooster pursue a hen round and round the house. A girl came out of the house and sprinkled corn on the ground in the middle of the relay race. The hen ignored it, and continued its flight. The rooster, however, gave up the chase instantly and started to peck at the corn. The Negro gentleman murmured softly, "Lord, oh Lord, ah hopes I never gits as hungry as that!"

• • •

Miriam Hopkins made her debut as one of the "Eight Little Notes" who served as the chorus of the First Music Box Revue. On the out-of-town tryouts an aging soprano was penciled in for a leading role, and sought to impress Miss Hopkins. "I'll have you know," she declared, "that I insured my voice for $50,000." "That's wonderful," said Miss Hopkins. "What did you do with the money?"

• • •

John Barrymore once found himself in a little town on the Riviera without a razor in his bag. Furthermore, it was Sunday, and both local barbershops were closed. Barrymore, headed for a rendezvous with the belle of the neighborhood, ran his hand over his two-day growth of beard, and frantically sought the hotel manager.

"Can't you find somebody in this town who will give me a shave?" he demanded.

The manager finally produced a solemn-faced fellow who said he would do the job. "I must ask you to lie flat on your back, however," he stipulated.

Barrymore figured it was a custom of the country, and did as he was told. He found his barber's touch so gentle that he dozed a bit while the job was performed. As he was paying, he remarked, "I can't understand why you made me lie on my back." "Pure habit, sir," was the reply. "This is the first time I ever shaved a live man."

• • •

One of the most successful writers of gangster scripts on the Coast learned angles in the hard school of experience. The neighborhood in which he grew up, he explains, was so tough that whenever a cat stalked down the street with ears and a tail, everybody knew it was a tourist. A hardboiled kid who lived next door to him poured a pan of water on a passerby, and shouted a number of interesting four-letter words as an accompaniment. The infuriated passerby yelled, "Come down here and I'll beat the tar out of you." "Come down?" repeated the offending brat. "You're nuts. I can't even walk yet."

• • •

Behind the necktie counter of a swank Manhattan haberdashery, presides a young man who studied originally to be a mortician, but found the work too lugubrious. "Customers sometimes balk at paying ten to fifteen bucks apiece for a fancy tie," he commented. "I usually calm them by proving statistically that no matter how high prices go, it's still infinitely cheaper to live than to die. Take shaving. Suppose it costs you a half dollar or seventy-five cents. Know what a family pays to have a dear departed shaved? Five bucks! Sometimes even ten! A woolen overcoat sells for a hundred dollars tops. A wooden overcoat sells for three hundred bottom—and you know what you can do with those silver handles. A taxi ride to the cemetery rarely exceeds two-fifty. The same trip in a hearse costs ten times as much. The clincher is this: your wife or mother-in-law will tell you all about yourself for nothing, but look what they have to pay a minister to talk about you at some dismal funeral parlor. See what I mean? How about a couple of foulards for Spring?"

• • •

An irate mother marched up to the credit department of a big toy store a few days after Christmas and complained, "This water gun you sold me is no good. Maybe it was broken in transit." She pointed the gun at the credit manager, pulled the trigger, and promptly caught him squarely in the eye with a stream of purple ink. "That's funny," she mused. "It didn't work yesterday."

A lady stuck her head into a furrier's shop on lower Fourth Avenue and announced, "I'm looking for a Russian skunk." "Stick around," counseled the clerk. "The boss is due back from lunch in ten minutes."

• • •

Robert J. Landry was overcome by the advertising magnate who told an account executive, "You're fired; turn in your ulcer."

• • •

Washington gossip has it that Mr. D. Burpee, the big seed and flower man, found himself seated next to glamorous Clare Boothe Luce at a concert. The famous gentleman held out a hand and announced, "I am Burpee." The famous lady replied, "I quite understand. I am often troubled that way myself."

• • •

The new office boy reported promptly at 9 A.M. The boss said, "I'm glad you're in early, Willie. I want the phone number of Arthur J. Zacharias right away. Look it up in the directory."

Four hours later the boss tapped the lad on the shoulder and said sarcastically, "How are you doing finding that phone number?"

"I'm doing fine," said the boy. "I'm up to the F's already."

• • •

Mrs. Washburne was sitting in her husband's sumptuous office when a beautiful, stream-lined blonde undulated in. "I'm Mr. Washburne's wife," said Mrs. W. "That's nice," said the blonde. "I'm his secretary." "Oh," said Mrs. W., "were you?"

• • •

Allen Boretz was at the bedside when the president of the Amicable Loan Company breathed his last. As the doctor drew the sheet over the face of the departed, Boretz heard him murmur, "He has gone to his co-maker."

• • •

When Forain, the French engraver, was on his death bed, his family, gathered about him, simulated confidence in his recovery. "You're looking much better," his wife assured him. "The color has come back to your cheeks," said his son. "You are breathing easier, Father," his daughter observed.

Forain nodded and smiled weakly. "Thank you all," he whispered. "I'm going to die cured."

• • •

A young doctor had just hung up his shingle on the lower East Side of Manhattan when a patient appeared suffering from a very bad cold. "Cad you cure this code?" he sniffled anxiously. The young doctor thought hard and said, "Go home, take a hot bath, and then stand naked in a draught without drying yourself." "That wid cure my code?" said the patient doubtfully. "I didn't say that," answered the doctor, "but that will give you pneumonia, and pneumonia I know how to cure."

Dr. Pullman, the socialite dentist, was happily yanking teeth in his office on the seventeenth floor of a Madison Avenue skyscraper with his comely nurse, Ruth Gordon, in attendance, when a sharp cry gave them a start. Rushing to the window, they saw a good friend who had an office some floors above them go hurtling past.

A couple of moments later, another friend burst into the office. "Did you hear about Johnny Jones?" he gasped. "He jumped or fell thirty floors. He's lying down there on Madison Avenue, and he looks terrible." "I can't understand that," said Miss Gordon. "When we saw him go by just a minute ago, he looked wonderful."

• • •

Another patient of Dr. Pullman was named Linscott. As he climbed into the chair, he reached a hand into his pocket. "You don't have to pay in advance," the doctor assured him. "I know," said Linscott. "I was just counting my money before you give me gas."

It developed, however, that Linscott didn't need gas after all. The good doctor peered into his mouth and in his most soothing manner, told him, "Not a thing to worry about, sir. You can stop trembling. I won't have to extract a single tooth." Linscott had barely sighed with relief when Dr. Pullman added, "Of course, I'll have to take out the gums."

• • •

A worried lady in Scituate entered a notions store and purchased two packages of invisible hairpins. As she paid for them, she asked, "Are you absolutely certain these hairpins are invisible?" "Lady, I'll tell you how invisible they are," the clerk assured her. "I've sold four dollars' worth of those pins this morning, and we've been out of them for three weeks."

• • •

Lucius Beebe once checked his imposing fur-lined winter overcoat at a busy, brash Broadway night club. When he sought to retrieve it, the check girl couldn't find it in her overcrowded cubicle. Lucius stood around impatiently for a half hour, and finally strode out into a snowstorm without it. The girl called after him, "Hey, you cheap skate! No tip?"

• • •

The publicity man for a big chemical manufacturer reports that his boss, a solemn gentleman, not given to idle chatter, offered him a lift home one evening in his Cadillac runabout. At a traffic stop, a gawky, badly dressed girl, wearing spectacles, crossed in front of the car, looking about as unhappy and discontented as it is possible for a human to look. To the astonishment of the publicity man, his boss suddenly leaned out of the car, and gave her a wolf whistle, beckoning her to climb in. The girl looked shocked, then ran to the sidewalk. The boss stepped on the gas as the light turned green and murmured with vast satisfaction, "That's my good deed for today."

• • •

A romantic young friend of George Allen, the White House humorist, persuaded a luscious Washington belle to go riding with him in his new convertible. After parking in a secluded dell, Romeo offered Juliet a cigarette. "I never smoke," she informed him. He then produced a silver pocket flask, but she added, "I never drink either." Desperate, Romeo suggested a stroll in the woods, and to his surprise, Juliet accepted. Two hours later they were back in the car, Juliet contentedly curled up in the shelter of his arms. "There," she told him in triumph, "see what fun you can have without all that nasty smoking and drinking?"

• • •

John Straley, the Wall Street wit, has performed a notable whitewashing job with his story of an impetuous swain who told his lady love, "Honey, I'm going to kiss you to death tonight." "I dare you," responded that timid, shy young thing. The suitor's talents, however, failed to send her into raptures. After some minutes, in fact, she pulled a feather out of a pillow and began to stroke him lightly on the forehead with it. The suitor inquired, "What's the big idea?" "Comparatively speaking," she answered crossly, "I'm beating your brains out."

• • •

Major Putney May took his daughter Patricia to the opening of a lavish Broadway musical. To the prissy Major's embarrassment, the show proved raucous and vulgar. Toward the end of act one, he confessed to his daughter, "I'm sorry I brought you, Pat. This is not a show for a young lady like you." "Don't give up so early, Pop," the unperturbed Pat assured him. "Maybe the second act will be livelier."

• • •

A little bit of a man with spectacles and an umbrella was brought before Judge Maguire in Magistrates' Court recently. Behind him towered his wife, a Junoesque creature who looked strong enough to tear telephone books in half with her bare hands. Judge Maguire was amazed to discover that the shrimp was accused of beating his wife. "Guilty or not guilty?" he barked. "Guilty," said the little man promptly. "$50.00 fine," said Judge Maguire.

After the fine had been paid and the ill-assorted couple had disappeared into the gloaming, the court clerk said to Judge Maguire, "Weren't you a little hard on that poor little fellow?" "I don't think so," answered Judge Maguire. "I punished him for bragging."

• • •

The Ford *Times* ran a cartoon recently by Cal Dunn that made hundreds of male readers weep into their hot toddies. It showed a weary husband who has just dug a fifty-yard path from his private garage to the road through a six-foot snowdrift. As he is about to open the garage door, with an evident air of triumph, his dear little wife calls out from the kitchen, "Oh, I forgot to tell you, dear. I took the car over to mother's yesterday before the storm started."

• • •

Study in mixed emotions: the man who saw his mother-in-law go over a cliff in his new Cadillac convertible.

• • •

In a cemetery in darkest Brooklyn, a grief-stricken man stood over a grave for three days running, beating his breast, and repeating in mournful cadence, "Why did he have to die? Why did he have to die?" An attendant sought to console him, and asked, "Was the deceased your father, maybe, or a brother?" "Neither," sobbed the mourner. "He was my wife's first husband."

• • •

An old roué sidled up to a beautiful blonde at the Morocco bar and hissed in her ear, "Be mine and you shall have a sable coat, a suite at the Ritz, and a Cadillac convertible." The blonde gave him a reproachful look and assured him, "I never accept presents from strangers—but haven't we met somewhere before?"

• • •

When Richard Spong, now teaching at Michigan State, was undergraduate editor of the Dartmouth newspaper, he sent a Freshman cub to cover a wedding some miles outside Hanover. The bride—a Vassar graduate—informed the young reporter loftily, "You may say that when we return from our honeymoon, we will reside at the old manse." The story the Freshman handed in to Spong read, "After their honeymoon, the young couple will dwell at the home of the bride's father."

• • •

Gene Fowler's classic account of the execution of Ruth Snyder and Judd Gray (reprinted in Ward Greene's newly published *Star Reporters*) appeared originally not only in the New York *American*, but in hundreds of other newspapers throughout the country, including a small daily in a town in west Texas which we shall call Dunnell. The managing editor of this paper spread it on the front page. His staff consisted of one cub who was so impressed by the story that he cut it out and put it in his scrapbook.

At this point, asterisks denote the passage of several years.

A murder is committed near Dunnell. The guilty man is caught and the cub is assigned to the case. In his cell he makes the acquaintance of the murderer and even wins his friendship to the extent that, at the request of the murderer himself, he is assigned to the execution which takes place several months later at a town we shall call Buntsville. That night the execution story by the cub begins coming over the wire from Buntsville and it is a honey. The managing editor, reading the first 200 words, says to himself, "This sounds familiar. Where have I read this stuff before?" Buntsville notifies him that there are 3000 more words coming and they do come, and by the time he finishes the yarn he realizes that the cub has lifted outright Fowler's story of the execution of Ruth Snyder and Judd Gray, and merely substituted the name of the Texas murderer.

Here's where we fool you. The managing editor did not kill the yarn. He decided that nobody would remember Fowler's story, and he spread it all over the paper. He was right. Nobody did remember Fowler's story, least of all the owner of the paper, who arrived at the office the next day, gave the cub a bonus, fired the managing editor and made the cub managing editor in his place!

• • •

The subject of Fowler's latest biography is Jimmy Walker, and the reason it is so successful is that he did not try to make the Broadway haunts of the popular but superficial "good times" mayor sound like the dignified court of St. James's. Jimmy was a party boy from first to last, and unfortunately for him, the party ended too soon. He died as he had begun, however, with the cheers of his friends ringing in his ears. Their dollars, however, jingled in their own pockets. The little "tin box" may have been looted by others; Jimmy's own cupboard was bare.

When Al Smith first observed Jimmy Walker's way with the public, he commented, "This boy is a greater strategist than General Sheridan, and he rides twice as fast." Jimmy, however, was two hours late to his own wedding! Years later, he needed all his strategy to win the heart of Betty Compton. The lovely actress ignored him for weeks, but finally allowed him to drive her through traffic to the stage door in his official car. Jimmy disliked fast driving but now he told his chauffeur not only to step on the gas, but to keep the siren sounding. After some blocks, Miss Compton remarked, "I'm sufficiently impressed, Jimmy. Now tell him to stop the siren." Jimmy said, "I prefer human sirens anyhow."

When Miss Compton's *Fifty Million Frenchmen* opened, Mayor Walker threatened to slap fifteen building violations on the theatre that housed it. Manager Ray Goetz saw the light and gave Miss Compton a better dressing room.

Mayor Walker once dreamed up the idea of purchasing a hundred gondolas for the lake in Central Park, and demanded a sizable appropriation therefor. An alderman from Brooklyn protested that the sum mentioned was excessive, and stopped Jimmy cold for one of the few times in his career by proposing, "Let's buy one male gondola and one female gondola, and let nature take its course!"

Judge Seabury's charges against Jimmy Walker, which resulted in his resignation, totaled over sixty thousand pages. The Mayor's final comment was "He has made a piker of Dr. Eliot and his five-foot-shelf." When he quit, a reporter consoled him, "Everyone is for you, Jim. All the world loves a lover." "You are mistaken," Walker replied. "What the world loves is a winner."

• • •

Jimmy Walker was not the only Mayor of New York to capture the imagination of the public. "Butch" La Guardia achieved a full measure of fame, and then came another outstanding personality in the figure of William O'Dwyer, who began his professional career as an ordinary cop, pounding a beat in Brooklyn. Nobody is prouder of the fact than O'Dwyer himself.

On his very first day as an official member of the force, O'Dwyer was ordered to report to the 143rd Precinct, in the darkest jungle of Dodgerville. He never had been in Brooklyn before in his life, but followed directions carefully, and succeeded in getting off at the right subway station. Once out in the street, however, he had no idea of which way to turn. Reluctantly, he buttonholed a native and made his first official inquiry in uniform. "Could you please tell me the way to the nearest police station?"

He was given the proper directions, but sheepishly admits he can still hear the derisive shout that followed him on his way: "Go back to Manhattan and the Giants, ya big bum!"

• • •

Messmore Kendall, the Broadway play backer, tells in his autobiography of his youthful experience as personal secretary to President Theodore Roosevelt. No matter how carefully he typed a letter, he was distressed to note that T. R. always made a correction or added a postscript by hand. He finally asked the President, "Are these mistakes mine, or do you just change your mind about the wording of every letter you dictate?" "Neither," Teddy Roosevelt assured him patiently. "It's just that I've discovered people treasure a letter from the President more when he has added something in his own handwriting."

• • •

One of Heywood Broun's pet hates was ghost-written political speeches—particularly when they failed utterly to reflect either the convictions or the personalities of the big shots who were delivering them. Warren G. Harding pulled one of these phony orations at a newsmen's banquet shortly after he had assumed the Presidency—a pompous, cliché-laden address that sounded more like a circus press agent than a President of the United States. There was some polite applause as Harding resumed his seat. Then Broun jumped up and cried "Author! Author!"

• • •

Calvin Coolidge story number 46,811: When Cal Coolidge was President, his wife gave him a portrait of himself as a birthday present. It had been painted by a local youth, touted by Northampton savants as "another Picasso—or anyhow, Norman Rockwell." Coolidge propped it up on the mantelpiece, where a senator, come to pay a duty call, spotted it a short time later. The senator and the President gazed at it in silence for five full minutes. Then Coolidge remarked, sourly, "You're right."

• • •

Reminiscing about his days as Governor of New York, Franklin D. Roosevelt admitted that he would sometimes pause in the anteroom on the way to his office, and purposely tell the people waiting there for him a particularly stale joke. "I didn't bother seeing the ones who laughed hardest," he recalled. "They were the ones, I knew, who wanted the biggest favors."

• • •

Ex-Governor Horner of Illinois told this story to Lloyd Lewis: "When I was a boy, my grandfather told me that if I was to be invited to nice places, I mustn't crumple crackers in my soup. So I didn't, but I never had soup without wanting to—bad.

"Then came a time when President Roosevelt had six Midwestern governors to luncheon at the White House, and there was the soup, and there were the crackers, which I ate one by one as my grandpa would have wished. Suddenly there came a sound that froze me—the sound of crumpling crackers, splashing lightly into soup. From the corner of my eye, I saw the President of the United States, scion of the bluest blood in America, crackling crackers into his soup with aristocratic assurance.

"I dropped whatever conversation I was making, seized my crackers with both hands, snowed them into my soup, and damned my dear grandfather for fifty wasted years."

• • •

A favorite yarn of President Truman—although he cannot cite his authority for the facts—concerns John Quincy Adams, sixth President of the United States. Adams, according to Truman, hated newspaper reporters in general, and lady newspaper reporters in particular. One of the latter, named Anne Royall, had been trying in vain to pin him down for an interview for weeks.

Then she made her big discovery. A kitchen maid at the then new White House tipped her off to the fact that the President liked to slip away to the Potomac River very early on summer mornings for a swim in the raw. Miss Royall sneaked up behind him one day, sat firmly on his clothes, and refused to move until he answered twenty questions. The President was outraged but too modest to defy her. Miss Royall got her interview, and a very angry, teeth-chattering Chief Executive got his bathrobe.

When Thomas Jefferson presented his credentials as U.S. minister to France, the French premier remarked, "I see that you have come to replace Benjamin Franklin." "I have come to succeed him," corrected Jefferson. "No one can replace him."

• • •

Schiller, in his biography of Frederick the Great, tells of the monarch's visit to a Potsdam prison. One prisoner after another assured him that he was innocent, and the victim of a frame-up. Finally one man, however, looked down at the floor and said, "Your Majesty, I am guilty, and richly deserving punishment." Frederick bellowed for the warden. "Free this rascal and get him out of our prison," he ordered, "before he corrupts all the noble innocent people in here."

•　•　•

Arthur Steiner, the Viennese raconteur, tells of the time his good friend, Franz Lehar, the composer of *The Merry Widow*, was down on his luck. Poor but proud, Lehar sent an underling to pawn his watch, and warned him, "Don't take less than a hundred shillings. And when you get it, fold it in an envelope and bring it to me at the Bristol bar. If I'm with somebody, just tell me, 'This comes from the British Ambassador with his compliments.'" The underling found Lehar at the Bristol some time later and reported mournfully, "The British Ambassador sends you his compliments—but says he can't give you more than fifty shillings on your watch."

•　•　•

Two farmers at a Dublin Fair were fascinated by a booth where little celluloid balls bobbed on top of water jets. Customers were offered substantial prizes if they succeeded in shooting any one of the balls off its perch. One of the Irishmen spent six shillings in a vain attempt to pick off one ball. Finally his friend pushed him aside and picked up the rifle. "Watch how I do it." He took a single shot. All six balls disappeared.

As they walked away from the booth laden with prizes, the unsuccessful one marveled, "However did you do it, Shaemas?"

"It just took knowing how," explained Shaemas. "I shot the man who was working the pump."

•　•　•

In the days of the bloomer girls, two Irishmen aboard a tandem bicycle struggled valiantly to the top of Fort George Hill. "Phew," exclaimed the one in front, "I never thought we'd make it." "Me neither," agreed the one in back, "and if I hadn't kept on the brake, I bet we'd have slid all the way back at that."

•　•　•

Mrs. Gogarty condoled with Mrs. Devlin after the demise of the latter's husband. "And what did he be dying of?" asked Mrs. Gogarty. "Gangrene," sighed Mrs. Devlin. "Well," said Mrs. Gogarty, "thank God anyhow for the color of it."

• • •

A Baptist lady went to visit her young married daughter. Her new son-in-law was an Episcopalian, and though she accompanied the couple to their church on Sunday, she resolutely refused to join in the singing of hymns. "Why didn't you sing with us?" complained the daughter later. "I know how proud you are of your voice." "I just couldn't bring myself to do it," confessed the mother, and then blurted, "I'm on another network."

• • •

An English teacher in our nation's capital asked a new student, "What do you know about Keats?" The student scratched his head and replied, "Please, teacher, I don't even know what they are."

In another part of Washington—the Department of Indian Affairs to be exact—an assistant director was showing friends a request he received from an earnest young lady in Vermont. "Please send me at once your free bulletin," she asked, "for I have long desired to have an affair with an Indian."

• • •

At a very fashionable Indian sewing bee, Mrs. Rain Cloud admitted to a group of intimates that her daughter had indulged in a bit of gambling at the State Fair some months earlier. "It looks like little Golden-Tint-of-Sunrise took a chance on a rug," she mused. "Did she get anything?" asked the squaws in concert. "But definitely," said Mrs. Rain Cloud. "She got a papoose!"

• • •

An elderly lady, obviously reluctant, was ordered to tell the court her eye-witness account of a fracas in the Blue Ridge Mountain country. "Fact is, jedge," she began resentfully, "it actually didn't amount to nothin'. Fust thing I knowed Hal Kittleson called Bill Alexander a liar and Bill knocked him down with an ax handle. One of Hal's friends got kinda riled and sliced a piece outa Ol' Bill. Then Ed Phreaner, who was a friend o' Bill's, shot Hal, and two others shot him, and three or four more began to get cut up a bit here an' there. Well, jedge, that nachelly caused a little excitement, an' they commenced fightin'."

• • •

When old Seth Abernathy celebrated his hundredth birthday, a reporter said to him, "Pop, I'll bet you've seen plenty of changes around these parts." "Yep," agreed Seth. "And I've been against every durn one of them."

• • •

Jesse Stuart's favorite hillbilly story concerns the young swain who bearded a grizzled mountaineer in his corn-likker still and stammered, "Mistah McCoy, ah reckin ah'm askin' for yar daughter's hand." McCoy reached for his shot-gun and roared, "No ya don't! Either ya takes mah whole gal, or ya gits nothin'!"

• • •

A salesman in Missouri was held up in a small town because heavy rains had caused a washout on the railroad. "This looks like the flood," he observed to a waitress in the local hotel. "The what?" she asked. "The flood," he repeated. "You know the flood, when Noah saved the animals on the ark. You must have read about that." The waitress assured him gravely, "Mister, on account of all this rain, I ain't seen a paper in four days."

• • •

A publication called the *Wolf Magazine of Letters* specializes in reproducing unusual missives of every description. The following, sent by a postmaster in a remote Kentucky hamlet to a customer of the U.S. mails in Dover, Delaware, was more unusual than most:

Dear Sir: The next time you send toads through this post office, please see that they are not only wrapped securely, but carry sufficient postage to cover possible additions to the merchandise in transit.

I don't know how many of the darned things you mailed originally, but when the package burst this morning there were fifteen. Our Mr. Denny, who spent the day catching flies for them, has developed warts.

If you ever tried to run a cancellation machine, you will realize the difficulty we had trying to stamp your toads. Every time we tried to cancel one, he jumped into the money order department. This place sounded more like a mill pond than a post office.

Please remit 28 cents postage due, and you'd better add 10 cents for a bottle of wart-remover for our Mr. Denny. I won't charge you a cent for handling because I'm going to try one of the toads for bass fishing this Saturday. Respectfully. . . .

●　●　●

When Editor Harry Maule returned from his Colorado angling expedition, he was asked, "Well, how were the fish in those parts?" Maule sighed, "I can't really say. For three weeks I dropped them a line twice a day—but I had no reply."

●　●　●

A group of fishermen in Maine broke camp and began their long hike back to the nearest railroad station. En route they stopped at a lonely farm house and asked if they could buy lunch. "O.K.," said the old lady at the door, "if you'll be satisfied with pork chops." The hungry men fell to with a will, and when they had finished, complimented the old lady on the fine quality of the meat.

"I should hope it was," she agreed heartily. "That wasn't none of your butchered stuff. That hog died a natural death."

●　●　●

A Maine lobster merchant received an urgent telephone call informing him that the body of his mother-in-law had been cast

up by the tide with a lobster firmly attached to each toe. When
the Coast Guard asked, "What'll we do with the body?" he answered, "Sell the lobsters and set her out again."

● ● ●

Zeke Poppin and his wife were the stingiest and orneriest couple in Ogunquit. Zeke died at the age of 88, and a few years later
it became apparent that his wife was about to join him somewhere
or other in the beyond. She summoned her one friend and said
weakly, "Hetty, bury me in my black taffeta dress, but afore you
do, might as well cut the back out and make yourself a Sunday-
go-to-meetin' gown out of it. It's fine material!"

"Couldn't do that," demurred the friend. "When you and Zeke
walk up them golden stairs what would them angels say if your
dress ain't got a back in it?"

"They won't be lookin' at me," said Mrs. Poppin tartly. "I buried
Zeke without his pants."

● ● ●

A crusty old Arkansas farmer was approached one day by an
eager young salesman who was peddling a set of books on scientific agriculture. The old farmer was a difficult prospect. "What
do I want them things for?" he scowled. "If you had these books,
sir," the salesman pointed out, "you could farm twice as good as
you do now." "Hell's bells, son," roared the old farmer, "I don't
farm half as good as I know how now."

● ● ●

A Scotch farmer was reading his evening paper (by the light
of the moon) when his little boy came running to tell him that
there was a strange cow in the pasture. "What'll I do with it?"
he asked. "What a silly question," said the Scotchman. "Milk 'er
and turn 'er oot."

● ● ●

Sandy McTavish, the Aber-Dean of Nickel Nursing, outsmarted himself last week. He took such long strides to preserve his four-dollar shoes that he split his seven-dollar trousers!

Sandy told his wife of a bad dream he had had. "Suddenly every animal that was in your fur piece and coats was standing at the bedside snarling at me," he wailed. "Shame on you," chided his wife. "A strapping man to be frightened by a couple of mangy alley cats!"

• • •

When a noted Scotch comedian last played the Palace Theatre in New York, an old friend he hadn't seen in thirty years gained access to his dressing room and begged for a loan. His business had failed, his wife had deserted him, his son was in jail, and his daughter had run away with a salesman. "In fact," he concluded, "if you don't help me, the only thing left is the poorhouse over the hill." The Scotch star called the doorman and said, "For heaven's sake, throw this man out. He's breaking my heart!"

• • •

Ray McLarty sent a ten-dollar bill to a young cousin who always was asking him for some gift or other. McLarty wrote, "Here is the ten-spot you said you need so desperately—but there was a spelling mistake in your request. '10' is written with one zero, not two."

• • •

The star reporter of the Belfast *News* was so impressed at the launching of His Majesty's carrier *Bulwark* that he wound up his ecstatic dispatch, "The Duchess smashed a bottle of champagne against the bow with unerring aim, and then, while the huge crowd cheered madly, she slid majestically down the greasy slipway into the sea."

• • •

A senior in the Pulitzer School of Journalism observed, "Even barbers make more money than authors do today. I don't know whether to take a job in Greco's barber shop when I graduate, or write novels." Dean Ackerman suggested, "Toss a coin, my boy. Heads or tales!"

• • •

Roy Howard, intent upon adding a Midwestern daily to the Scripps-Howard chain, encountered an owner who proved to be just as tough a trader as he. Howard went up to $640,000, which he declared was "tops." The owner held out for $650,000. Finally, Howard, always ready to take a chance, proposed to toss a coin for the odd ten thousand. The owner, against his better judgment, managed a strangled sort of "O.K." Howard took a shiny new quarter from his pocket, handed it to the owner, and said, "You flip it. 'Tails,' it's $650,000."

The coin came up tails. The owner gulped; pocketed the coin, and rushed out for a double Scotch. Howard didn't say a word for a full minute, but suddenly began to cuss. "Calm yourself, boss," said an associate. "After all, the toss was your idea." "It isn't that," spluttered Howard. "He walked off with my quarter."

(Mr. Howard himself has been known to quote James Gordon Bennett's advice to a cub reporter: "Remember, son, many a good story has been ruined by over-verification.")

• • •

Merryle Rukeyser, the financial expert, tells of one brash Wall Street banker who agreed to address a conference on a subject he knew nothing about. The day before the meeting he sent his secretary to the public library to dig up some pertinent facts and figures. The secretary returned empty-handed, saying, "There isn't a man alive who could get the information you want in less than five years."

At the conference the banker impressed everybody, particularly his secretary, with the detailed statistics that he reeled off. Here, obviously, was an expert! The audience took copious notes and applauded ecstatically.

On the way back to the office, the secretary said, "On the level, boss, how did you get all those statistics?" "I just used my common sense and some imagination," admitted the banker. "You said it would take five years to get the real facts. It will take any one of those birds just as long to prove I'm a faker."

• • •

When Thomas Edison's private desk was opened fifteen years after his death, a card bearing the following admonition was found among his papers: "When down in the mouth, remember Jonah. He came out all right!"

• • •

The crafty cashier at Zira's Gypsy Tea Room, back of the Metropolitan Opera House, amuses the stars with her old-world maxims. One of her best is this: If one man calls you a horse, pay no attention. If a second man calls you a horse, think it over. But if a third man calls you a horse, buy a saddle!

• • •

H. W. Fowler knows a little boy who accompanied his father on an expedition to buy a new cow. The father gave his prospective purchase a going-over from head to foot, poking, probing, and pinching the animal very thoroughly. "You see, son," he explained, "when you buy a cow you want to be sure it's a sound one." The boy nodded approval. A week later the boy came running breathlessly to his father in a distant corner of the farm. "Come quick, pa," he entreated. "A traveling salesman's pulled up behind the barn, and it looks like he's going to buy Sister."

• • •

A station agent at Saginaw heard a crash on the platform. He dashed out to see the tail end of a train disappearing round a bend, while a disheveled gent lay prone on the ground, surrounded by upset milk cans and the contents of his opened suitcase. An owlish youngster stared at the gent, but made no effort to assist him. "Was he trying to catch the train?" the station agent asked the youngster. "He did catch it," reported the youngster, "but it got away again."

• • •

A Bermuda school teacher has a young student who promises to give Kathleen Winsor, the *Forever Amber* authoress, a run for her money when she grows up. The teacher, in French hour, asked "What is the difference between 'madame' and 'mademoiselle'?" The hopeful student answered "monsieur."

• • •

Cecil Osborne, Jr., writes about a six-year-old girl who bearded a bank president in his den, and demanded a contribution to a fund her school was raising to send poor children to camp. The banker laid a dollar bill and a nickel on the desk and suggested, "Take your pick." The little girl picked up the nickel and said, "Mama tells me I should always take the smallest piece." Then she picked up the dollar too, and added with a grin, "but I wouldn't want to lose the nickel, so I'll take this piece of paper to wrap it up in."

• • •

Two lifelong denizens of a lunatic asylum were engaged in solemn conclave. "I have decided to conquer England," declared one. "Historians will never be able to say that Julius Caesar rested on his laurels." "England, hey?" mused the other. "Well, Julius, if I were you—and incidentally, I am. . . ."

• • •

One of Harvey Stone's neighbors has a son whose head, unfortunately, is twice the size it should be. Heartless classmates invented so many offensive nicknames for him that finally he refused to go to school. His mother sought to reassure him. "Your head's no bigger than any of the other kids," she told him. "In fact, you're the handsomest boy in the school. Now just you cheer up and go round to the grocery store and bring home five dozen bottles of ginger ale." "I got nothing to carry them in," complained the boy. "Nonsense," said the mother sharply. "Use your cap!"

• • •

Two gentlemen were introduced in the lobby of a Chicago hotel. "Pardon my not getting up," said one. "You see, I'm ailing from arthritis." "Perfectly all right," beamed the other. "I'm Goldfarb from Grand Rapids."

• • •

A guest at Grossinger's confided to his companion, "My wife had a funny dream last night. She dreamed she had married a multimillionaire." "You're lucky," sighed the companion, "my wife dreams that in the daytime."

• • •

Two Jewish refugees passed the home of John D. Rockefeller, Jr. "If I only had that man's millions," sighed one of them, "I'd be richer than he is." "That doesn't make sense," the other reminded him. "If you had Mr. Rockefeller's millions, you'd be just as rich as he—not richer." "You're wrong," the first assured him. "Don't forget that I could give Hebrew lessons on the side!"

• • •

I wonder how many remember the shenanigans of Montague Glass' greatest creations, Potash and Perlmutter? These two hot-tempered and argumentative partners called one another every name under the sun, but if an outsider attacked, they were as united and indivisible as Park and Tilford or Haig and Haig!

One of Potash's rages was provoked by a high-salaried salesman who was too lazy to cover his accounts properly. "Look at you sitting here twiddling your thumbs," screamed Potash. "Why aren't you out selling?" "Listen, Mr. Potash," the salesman assured him. "If I could sell like you think I should, I'd be in business for myself!"

There came a day when Potash and Perlmutter invested in a motion-picture company, and Perlmutter hired a slinky siren of the then-popular Theda Bara-Pola Negri type. "How much you paying her?" demanded Potash suspiciously. "Seven hundred a week," admitted Perlmutter. "Robbery," cried Potash. "You've gone crazy." "Calm yourself," said Perlmutter. "You don't seem to understand that this girl is a Kipling vampire." "For seven hundred dollars a week," decreed Potash, "she should Kipple for somebody else."

• • •

Presiding over a prosperous rental library north of Ninety-sixth Street is a wise and discerning lady who suffers untold frustration day after day because her patrons unerringly pass over the books she wants them to read and clamor for the sexy trash. Last week was particularly trying for her: nineteen customers in a row demanded the same sensational just-published tome. When the twentieth betrayed by a certain diffidence and embarrassment that she, too, was going to ask for this book, the librarian's anger overflowed. "I don't really want it for myself," was the customer's familiar gambit, "but my husband, who just wants some relaxation when he comes home from the office, made me promise I'd get it for him." The librarian slapped the book down on the counter and rasped, "You want to read dirty books? *Read* dirty books. *But don't explain.*"

• • •

In the last month of the war, Ilka Chase was invited to a cocktail party at the Pensacola naval base. Knowing that top brass would be present, she washed her hair specially for the occasion. This turned out to be a miscalculation. The water in Pensacola is very hard and Miss Chase couldn't get the soap out of her hair. In desperation she poured vinegar over her head, with the result, she says, that she entered the party "reeking like a salad bowl."

"Fliers prefer honey to vinegar, I guess," she adds, "for the officers of the U. S. Navy kept their distance. My escort introduced me to yards of glittering braid, saying pleasantly, 'This is Miss Chase. Smells, doesn't she?'"

• • •

Even when hostilities in World War Two had ceased, fresh eggs were as scarce in London as uncut emeralds. When one store received its scanty allotment from an American shipment it put up a sign reading, "These eggs are reserved exclusively for expectant mothers." A handsome young lady studied the sign gravely, then whispered to the clerk, "I'll be deeply obliged if you'll put a dozen of those eggs under the counter for me. I'll call for them in the morning."

Louis Kronenberger, drama critic of *Time*, and his wife Emmy have a nine-year-old son who has been educated in one of New York's most progressive schools. Recently Kronenberger pere and mere became involved in a domestic argument, and Kronenberger pere's voice rose steadily as his exasperation increased. Suddenly the son ended hostilities by pulling on his father's coattails, and imploring, "Father, please lower your voice. The neighbors will think you're yelling at *me!*"

. . .

A couple of *Life* reporters arrived in a remote town in Yucatan and announced that they had made the journey from Vera Cruz by jeep. "Nonsense," scoffed the native pundit. "There aren't any roads through that impenetrable jungle." "Quiet," begged the *Life* men. "Our jeep hasn't found out about roads yet and we don't aim to spoil it."

. . .

A famous lady commentator, late for a broadcast, squeezed into a crowded Fifth Avenue bus. Thrice a gallant gentleman with a Vandyke beard attempted to rise, but the lady pushed him back into his seat each time. "None of this outmoded false gallantry," she chided. "I'm a working woman and I can stand just as well as the next one."

On his fourth attempt, the gentleman thrust out his jaw (and beard) and said firmly, "This time you simply must let me get out, madam. I'm seven blocks past my stop now."

. . .

A housewife who devoted most of her life to spending twice as much as her husband earned, complained constantly about the apartment they lived in. "All our friends live ten times better than we do," was her chorus. "We simply must move into a more expensive neighborhood." One night her long-suffering spouse came home and told her, "Well, we won't have to move after all. The landlord just doubled our rent."

. . .

A chronic eavesdropper overheard this gem aboard a Fifth Avenue bus: "You know, I wouldn't say anything about Dolly unless I could say something good. And oh, brother, is this good. . . ."

. . .

Two old friends met at Seventh Avenue and Thirty-eighth Street. "Did you hear about Sam?" asked one. "He's taken a turn for the worse." "What happened?" demanded the other. The first answered, "He died."

• • •

When Harry Hershfield was a youngster, an uncle tried to lure him into his silk-jobbing concern. "But don't think you're coming in here and start at the top," warned the uncle. "You'll begin as a partner, just like all the rest of us!"

• • •

Coat-maker Friedman was haggard from persistent insomnia. "Count sheep," advised his partner. "It's the best-known cure." "What can I lose?" sighed Friedman dubiously. "I'll try tonight."

The next morning he looked more bleary-eyed than ever. "Sheep I should count," he mocked his partner. "I counted up to 50,000. Then I sheared the sheep, and made up 50,000 overcoats. Then came the problem that kept me awake all the rest of the night: *where could I get 50,000 linings?*"

• • •

For eight days and nights Mr. Berkowitz had been unable to sleep. All kinds of medicine had had no effect whatever, and in desperation, the Berkowitz family summoned a renowned hypnotist.

The hypnotist fastened a beady eye on Mr. Berkowitz and chanted, "You are asleep, Mr. Berkowitz! The shadows are closing about you. This vale of tears is becoming misty and obscured. Soft music is lulling your senses into a state of beatific relaxation. You are asleep! You are asleep!"

The anxious family looked at the ailing man—and sure enough, he was asleep! "You're a miracle worker," the grateful son told the hypnotist—and paid him a substantial bonus. The hypnotist, highly gratified, departed in triumph. As the outside door closed, Mr. Berkowitz opened one eye. "Say," he demanded, "is that lunatic gone yet?"

• • •

Jerry Lewis tells about the battered heavyweight who refused a thousand-dollar bribe to "take a dive" in the second round of a bout with a highly publicized and overrated newcomer. The battered pug's explanation was, "I never lasted till the second round yet, and I ain't gonna start now. The time I fought Joe Louis, I had him plenty worried, though," added the pug. "He thought he'd killed me!"

• • •

Lou Little, Columbia's great football coach, once kept a big lummox on the squad all season in the vain hope that he could teach him the fundamentals of blocking and tackling. His varsity line averaged 168 pounds; the lummox weighed 210. "All that beef going to waste," Little would moan. But the lummox, patient, willing, eager to please, simply couldn't learn.

In a skull practice before the season's final game with Dartmouth, Little suddenly pointed at the lummox and demanded, "You, there! What would you do if we had the ball on their five-yard line, fourth down, and thirty seconds left to play—with Columbia trailing by two points?"

The lummox pondered briefly, and then answered, "I'd move down to the end of the bench, Mr. Little, so I could see better."

• • •

A hapless football team in the Middle West had just fumbled away its eleventh consecutive game. The dejected coach was handed a penciled message reading, "Cheer up, Coach! We have no team either." It was signed "Sister Bernadette, St. Ursula's Convent."

• • •

Bob Considine was an innocent bystander at the fracas in an uptown gin mill that followed close on the heels of the 1949 football game between Notre Dame and North Carolina in New York's Yankee Stadium. A well-lubricated Southern gent kept shouting, "If Choo-Choo Justice coulda played today, our boys woulda run those Notre Dame fellahs cleah off the field." A Notre Dame alumnus finally tired of this raucous routine, poked the Southern gent in his midriff, and observed, "Mister, we could beat North Carolina with our Protestant squad!"

• • •

De Pauw University's Mickey Boeke won a local humor contest sponsored by Life Savers with the story of the botany professor who told an inquiring student, "No, son, that's not a poplar tree at all. They seem to prefer the lamp post down the street." He also told me about the waiter who brought a tray of food to twins in an Italian spaghetti emporium and demanded, "Which twin had the tortoni?" Mickey is going to end up as a columnist if he doesn't watch out.

• • •

The following six jokes appear to head the campus wit parade this semester:

1. *Wife to husband:* You swore terribly at me in your sleep last night.
   Husband: Who was asleep?
2. *Papa Robin:* How did that speckled egg get in our nest?
   Mama Robin: I did it for a lark.
3. During a grouse hunt, two sportsmen were shooting at a clump of trees near a stone wall. Suddenly a red face popped up over the top of the wall.
   "Hey, you almost hit my wife!"
   "Did I?" cried the man, aghast. "I'm very sorry. Have a shot at mine over there."
4. *Bright young thing to oarsman after his crew had lost the big race:* "Never mind, dear, you were wonderful. You rowed faster than anyone in the boat!"
5. *Senior:* Is this ice cream pure?
   Waiter: As pure as the girl of your dreams.
   Senior: Gimme a pack of cigarettes.
6. *Teacher:* What does y-e-s spell?
   Daughter of chorus queen (in school for first time): Mink.

THE SIGN OF THE BOSS

Not so many years ago, electric signs were constructed with individual bulbs that blinked on and off like an old lady trying to stay awake at a concert. The daring boss who went in for a new-fangled neon display in red or green could attract more attention than a Giant rooter at Ebbets Field.

Today, with twenty neon signs to a block in even the tiniest hamlet, it's not so easy to stand out from the pack. Rugged individualists have had to fall back on their own ingenuity to provide something unusual for the show windows. And how far back some of them have fallen! It's given cause for alarm to many observers—particularly the ones who abhor puns. They have made it plain that they do not care to converse in this new sign language.

Let us begin our exhibit with the sign in front of a lingerie shop in Hollywood: "Destiny may shape your ends, but if it doesn't, we have the best girdles in town." A competitor has christened his maternity-gown section, "The Ladies' Ready-to-Bear Department." The electric display above a barbershop at a Midwestern flying field reads, "The Hairpot." A fish store outside of New Bedford is called "The Crab Bag." In Bayshore, a haberdasher used a lot of red paint for the announcement, "Altercation sale: partners splitting up."

A dairy proprietor in Texas plasters the sides of his delivery trucks with the challenge, "You can whip our cream, but you can't beat our milk." Another dairyman boasts, "If our eggs were any fresher, they'd be insulting." A chiropodist in Little Rock begs, "Let me be the master of your feet."

In Brooklyn, an optometrist hired a sandwich man to parade Flatbush Avenue advising, "Your eyes examined while you wait!" In St. Louis, a tailor attracted even more attention with the huge announcement, "Pants half-off." Near the Polo Grounds, another tailor boasted, "We fix everything but football games." A bakery took advantage of a new fad to advertise, "Special! Canasta cake! It melds in your mouth." Right next door, a sign in a candy shop read, "By popular demand, this place is under new management."

Restaurant owners as a rule are content with hackneyed signs like "Not responsible for overcoats unless checked" or "Try our Sizzling Salisbury Steaks" (when I was a boy, they were called hamburgers), but there are some who like to experiment. Here are a few unusual displays reported from beaneries in various sections of the country: "The best dollar meal in town for three dollars"; "Eat here once and you'll never eat anywhere else again"; "Pies like mother used to make, 25¢. Pies like mother thought she made, 60¢"; "Our silverware is not medicine. Don't take it after meals." In a Chicago "el" station: "Have a frankfurter and roll downstairs." In a Richmond diner, "Yankee pot roast—Southern style." In a Provincetown pub: "Due to a shortage of beer, we are short of beer." In a Forty-fifth Street lunchroom: "Our hotcakes are selling like tickets to *South Pacific*." In a Miami Beach cocktail lounge: "Please do not stand up while the room is in motion." The latter calls to mind the famous sign that was pasted over the bar of an officers' club in Guam in 1944: "Air corps colonels under twenty-one will not be served unless accompanied by their parents."

A diaper service in Chicago advises, "Rock-a-dry Baby." A sign outside a dancing studio in Atlanta reads, "Not only do we keep you from being a wall-flower: we remove the pot." A kennel specializing in dachshunds suggests, "Git a long little doggie." Another delicately labels its rest rooms, "Pointers" and "Setters." The most sentimental—and probably most effective—kennel sign I know reads, "The only love money can buy. Pups for sale."

Sign noted in a ladies' shoe shop: "Our size four shoes are comfortable on size five feet." In a toggery featuring "kiddie klothes": "Get your cowboy outfits at Hopalong's (Formerly Nussbaum's)."

In a windowful of bathing suits: "The latest in seat covers!"
Christopher Morley suggested the slogan that adorns the window
of a Sixth Avenue antique shop: "If you don't know what you
want, we have it." Another dealer, in California, frankly pro-
claims, "We buy old furniture and books. We sell rare antiques."

A painter named Loew, in Haverhill, styles himself "Loew, the
Varnishing American"—and in letters five feet high at that. A
photographer's studio in Maine, gutted by fire and water, hastily
put up a sign, "Good night, sweet prints." A good samaritan heard
the pun drop, and supplied funds to give the spunky proprietor a
fresh start. A pixie in Dixie who sells phonograph records isn't
satisfied with *one* unusual sign; he has *two:* "Let us put some
good wax in your ears" and "The Chants of a Lifetime." A five-
and-ten in Altoona boasts, "We're giving the country what it
needs: a good five-cent bazaar."

Beauty-shop owners seem particularly susceptible to signus
trouble. Observe these bits of evidence: "Don't whistle at any girl
leaving here—it may be your grandmother"; "Let us be the masters
of your fat"; "We can take your breadth away"; "We fix flats";
"What have you got to lose? We'll show you!"; and—oh, no!—"We
can make a young colt out of an old 45."

Traffic regulators have noted that speedsters now regard old-
fashioned "Stop, Look, and Listen" signs as part of the scenery.
They are much more apt to be slowed down to a mere seventy
by such exhibits as these: "Drive carefully. Don't insist on your
rites"; "The average time it takes a train to pass this crossing is
fourteen seconds—whether your car is on it or not"; "Go slow—
this is a one-hearse town"; "167 persons died here last year from
gas. Eleven inhaled. Nine put a lighted match to it. 147 stepped
on it"; "Crossroad: better humor it." At a narrow and precipitous
pass on a road in the Rockies, Casper Milquetoasts are urged on
with a sign that points out "Sure you can! Thousands have." A
warning posted at the entrance to a bumpy, dirt backroad in a
frequently-flooded area of Missouri reads, "Take notice! When
this sign is under water, road is impassable!" At a Southern Pacific
crossing near Needles, a local junk dealer consolingly advertises,
"Go ahead and take a chance! We'll buy what's left of your car!"

When all the rooms in a California hostelry are occupied, the
reception clerk slaps this sign on the desk: "Don't go away mad;

just go away." A notice near the newsstand of an inn at Rochester, Minnesota (home of the Mayo Clinic) begs, "Please do not discuss your operation in the lobby." Elliot Paul actually purloined a sign from a small hotel in Illinois that reads, "Do not take lady friends up the back stairs. They have just been painted." Certainly the most elegant piece of sign language extant today in a hotel adorns the Rice bootblack stand in Houston: "Your pedal habiliments artistically lubricated and illuminated with ambidextrous facility for the infinitesimal remuneration of fifteen cents per operation."

Interested in keeping trespassers off your lawns and shrubbery? Try one of these gentle hints: "Don't ruin the gay young blades"; "Your feet are killing me"; "These flowers are under your personal care." Last year fire-prevention authorities in Pennsylvania achieved notable results with signs portraying a huge match labeled "This is the forest prime evil." The head of a Florida maternity hospital can't understand why so many people stop to chuckle over a sign on the front lawn stating "No children allowed here."

Some of the funniest signs I've heard about were crudely lettered, hastily contrived affairs intended for very special occasions. Like the placard posted by barrack mates over the bunk of a GI who had boasted of superhuman achievements with the fair sex on his leave in Louisville: "Temporarily out of ardor." Or the warning on an entrance gate of an Iowa farm: "Beware of shooting anything on this place that isn't moving. It's probably my hired man." Or the legend painted on the back of a two-ton truck: "This vehicle stops for red lights, railroad crossings, blondes, and brunettes. For redheads it will back up fifty feet."

Our fellow citizens obviously mean to go on expressing themselves in their own vernacular, and according to their own peculiar bents, despite carpings of purists and conformists. Should you think, perchance, that perpetrators of some of the above signs and exhortations strained too hard to be original, or failed to achieve quite the effect they desired, at least give them an "A" for effort. It was their way of building better mousetraps. They were determined, if the ghost of Robert Burns will forgive me, to forget not only auld acquaintance, but auld long signs as well.

• • •

A shopper down South dashed into a department store and demanded, "Where do you keep your mousetraps? I have to get one in a hurry, because I must catch a Baton Rouge bus." The floorwalker answered, "I'm sorry, madam, but our traps don't come that big."

The same floorwalker was on duty when a lady asked, "Where do I get some silk covering for my settee?" He answered, "I suggest the lingerie department. Two aisles down and turn to the left."

• • •

A Wall Street humorist vows that a senior partner of J. P. Morgan walked angrily to the front door of the imposing Morgan edifice on Wall Street and shooed away a female in a slantingly striped dress who was standing at the top of the steps. "Stand somewhere else, lady," he ordered. "As long as you are there, people keep coming in for haircuts."

• • •

An orthodox Jewish lady on Delancey Street was deeply distressed when her only son fell in love with a girl with red hair, a turned-up nose, and an Irish brogue. She grumbled about the situation for weeks, but one day turned up for her weekly pinochle game in high good humor. "That girl my boy is making eyes at," she announced, "is Jewish after all. I got a look at her compact last night when we all went to the movies together, and there was her name plain as day: HELENA RUBINSTEIN."

• • •

At a charity bazaar a beautiful young nurse sold kisses for five dollars each. A stout party, old enough to know a lot better, bought twenty dollars' worth, and declared, "I'll double the order if you promise to nurse me when I'm a patient in your hospital." The lass agreed, pocketed the greenbacks, and said sweetly, "By the way, my post is at the City Maternity Hospital."

• • •

In the White Plains branch of the Hall Clothing Company, a housewife was helping her husband pick out a new suit. Whenever he liked one, she cried, "Take it off. It's terrible." Finally, however, she grew tired of the argument and said, "Oh, well, suit yourself. After all, you're the one who'll have to wear it." The man corrected her quietly, "That goes for the coat and vest, anyway."

• • •

From the diary of a globe-trotting young cinema queen:

Monday: The Captain saw me on deck and was kind enough to ask me to sit at his table for the rest of the trip.

Tuesday: I spent the morning on the bridge with the Captain. He took my picture leaning against the "Passengers not allowed on this bridge" sign.

Wednesday: The Captain made proposals to me unbecoming an officer and a gentleman.

Thursday: The Captain threatened to sink the ship unless I agreed to his proposals.

Friday: I saved eight hundred lives today.

• • •

Two sallies recently made their Groucho Marx in Hollywood. "The first time my wife saw me," he told one group, "I was on the screen. Then she opened the window and let me in." A dinner guest at his house complained, "These sausages seem peculiar. They're meat at one end, but bread crumbs at the other." "Correct," said Groucho. "It's expedient. In times like these, nobody can make both ends meat."

• • •

An MGM star returned from Europe with a couple of undeclared bottles of perfume carefully hidden among her unmentionables. A customs inspector had just about finished examining her baggage, when his hand roamed to the danger zone of the valise. Her small daughter clapped hands excitedly, and burst out, "Oh, Mummy, he's getting warm, isn't he?"

• • •

According to a Hollywood journal, a cinemadorable was in the process of getting married for the fifth or sixth time. The officiating clergyman, flustered by all the publicity and glamour, lost his place in the ritual book. The star yawned and whispered, "Page 84, stupid."

• • •

A well-known picture star made a dramatic entrance into Dave Chasen's restaurant, then strode to a table as though the eyes of the entire world were upon him. Irving Lazar observed, "That fellow is such a ham, I'll bet he uses a clove for a collarbutton."

• • •

The vigilant manager of a Brown Derby restaurant observed a tourist carefully wash a spoon in his finger bowl, then repeat the process with the spoons of his wife and two children. "Why are you washing those spoons?" he asked suspiciously. "This is a new suit," explained the tourist. "Do you think I want to get pistachio ice cream all over the pockets?"

• • •

Hollywood's most distinguished language-assassin was asked to a dinner recently. "I can't make it," he announced regretfully, "but I hope you'll give me a raincoat." He turned down an invitation to the Mardi Gras in New Orleans, too, saying, "Even if they had it in the streets, I wouldn't go."

• • •

A man known as a heavy drinker looked up from his paper and said to his wife, "My dear, every time I breathe, three Chinamen die." His wife, knitting placidly, replied, "I'm not surprised."

In his cups the next evening, he and a companion boarded a Wilshire bus, and handed a quarter to the first man in uniform he saw. The man, definitely not amused, thundered, "Don't give this to me. I'm an admiral." "Let's get out of this thing quick," the drinker urged his friend. "I don't know how it happened, but we've gotten on a battleship."

• • •

A traffic officer stopped an out-of-state motorist and said, "I'm going to give you a ticket for driving without a tail light." The motorist got out to investigate, and set up a wail of dismay. "Come now," said the officer, "it's not as serious as all that." The motorist explained, "It's not the tail light I'm worried about. What's become of my trailer?"

• • •

Rastus Jones explained to the deacon his emphatic statement that if he ever were forced to make a choice, he'd prefer involvement in a collision to an explosion: "If you is in a collision, Deacon, there you is, but if you is in an explosion, where is you?"

• • •

Judging by the speed with which new models of jet-propelled airplanes supersede one another, a single hour should soon suffice to transport a passenger from Thirty-eighth Street and Broadway to the Thirty Eighth Parallel in Korea. Somebody at Elgin Air Base recently asked the Commanding Officer, "How can a layman possibly tell these models apart?" The C.O. explained tersely, "If you can see them, they're obsolete."

• • •

"Since my wife's friends at the Century Club assured her she's a poet," complained a Westchester barrister, "she's awakened me every day this summer at 7 A.M. chanting, 'Lo, the morn.'" "That's better than my wife," grumbled his neighbor, a book publisher. "Mine wakes me at the same time saying 'Mow the lawn!'"

• • •

Sylvestro Watkins, in *The Pleasures of Smoking,* recalls the declaration of Mark Twain: "Giving up smoking is the easiest thing in the world. I've done it a hundred times." And when Clergyman Charles Spurgeon was asked how a man of the cloth could justify his habit of smoking cigars and a pipe, he replied calmly, "I cultivate my flowers and burn my weeds."

Dr. William King observes that a gossip is one who talks to you about other people, a bore is one who talks to you about himself, and a brilliant conversationalist is one who talks to you about yourself.

George Heister points out that architects cover their mistakes with ivy, doctors with sod, and brides with mayonnaise.

A house-to-house salesman claims that five words are the secret to his success. When a woman opens the door, he inquires softly, "Miss, is your mother home?"

Sterling North points out that a bustle is like a historical romance: both are fictitious tales based on stern reality.

Colonel Francis Duffy estimates that it costs about six cents a mile to run the average American automobile today. "Of course," he adds, "running it some places, such as past a red light, the rate is slightly higher."

A General Motors publicist explains that it takes a woman longer to dress than a man because she has to slow down for the curves. And Jane Pickens defines a motorist as a man who, after seeing a serious wreck, drives carefully for several blocks.

Edward Laycock, literary editor of the Boston *Globe*, claims he knows a wonderful way to improve the flavor of salt. "All you have to do," says Laycock, "is take a pinch in your hand, and spread it over a fat, juicy sirloin steak."

Ed Diamond offers this distinction between a careful woman and a careless one: The careful woman only loses one glove.

George Meredith believes "Women will be the last thing civilized by man." Noel Coward thinks they "should be beaten once a day like a gong." The Countess de Poitiers assures us that "The years a woman subtracts from her age are not lost; they are added to the ages of other women." Dumas complains that "Women inspire us with all the great things they prevent us from accomplishing." And John Barrymore wraps up the subject by warning, "The only way to fight a woman is with your hat. Grab it and run!"

• • •

Harry Hansen and Charlie MacArthur, bound for a luncheon in the Wedgwood Room of the Waldorf, entered the revolving door on the heels of an imposing figure in uniform. He wore gold epaulets, a plumed hat, three rows of medals on his chest, and carried a huge sword at his side. "Who can he be?" wondered Hansen. MacArthur answered in a confidential whisper, "Argentinian Secret Service."

• • •

The untimely death of Ernie Byfield, world-famous boniface of the Ambassador Hotel, robbed Chicago of one of its most engaging personalities. Byfield built up the attractive Pump Room to a point where no outstanding star of society, stage, screen, or literary world would dream of passing through town without putting in an appearance there.

Byfield borrowed for his Pump Room the old Muscovite custom of serving victuals on a flaming sword. "It didn't spoil the food much," he explained in one of his more candid moments, "and the customers seemed to like it." An inebriated journalist once threw the staff into an uproar by collaring a beplumed majordomo and bellowing, "I want an order of scrambled eggs—and dawgone it, I want 'em served on a sword!"

Other widely circulated Byfieldisms (by repeating his stories to anyone who would listen, Ernie cleverly enabled as many as six columnists at a time to claim they had "originated" the same gag) were his remarks when a Girl of the Year inadvertently wore the same chinchilla three nights running ("She marched out of here like a woman unpossessed"); his admonition when Admiral Byrd escorted Mrs. Byfield to dinner ("Remember now, Admiral: no exploring!"); and the explanation of how he had entered hotel business in the first place ("My father owned the Hotel Sherman. He bumped into me in the lobby there one morning—and took a liking to me.").

Byfield admitted that he sometimes carried a memo in his pocket of all the "ad libs" he proposed to use at a party. He'd consult this card from time to time under pretext of looking at his watch. One day while driving to a party his wife saw him searching frantically and in vain for his card of "ad libs." "What's the matter, darling?" she asked sweetly. "Did you forget your personality?"

• • •

Rita Hayworth, describing the innate courtesy and tact of the French mayor who performed the wedding ceremony for her and Ali Khan, told of the day he had to make out a passport for a wealthy but slightly disfigured old crone who had rented a chateau on the Mediterranean shore. He knew how vain the old girl was, so in the space reserved for personal description he noted "Eyes glowing, beautiful, compelling, tender, and passionate, but unfortunately one of them is missing."

• • •

An out-of-towner, impressed with one of those signs that read "Climb One Flight and Save Forty Dollars on a New Suit," was shown a number of shoddy garments by an eager clerk, but refused to bite. Aware that the boss was watching him, the clerk made a special effort with the next number, whirling the customer around and around before the mirror, and crying, "It fits like a glove! Menjou will be jealous of you."

When the customer again said "no," the boss took over, produced one blue serge suit, and made his sale in two minutes flat. As the customer exited, the boss said, "You see how easy it is when you know how. He went for the first suit I showed him." "Yah," agreed the clerk, "but who made him dizzy?"

• • •

I know that everybody who reads this book has had his full share of embarrassing moments, but I wonder if any of you found yourselves in a spot to compare to a friend of mine who met a lady at a concert recently and, between numbers, tapped her on the shoulder and murmured, "Beg pardon, but your stockings appear to be badly wrinkled." The lady shot him a look of unadulterated hatred and answered, "I'm not wearing stockings this evening."

• • •

Speaking of hosiery, a retailer who was rather proud of the selection he carried (yes, he had been stocking up) found himself with one demand he could not satisfy offhand. A damsel had noticed a sign on the rear end of a truck that warned, "If you can read this you're too darn close," and thought it would be rather cute to sport nylons with the same message embroidered around the tops. "It's an irregular request," said the retailer dubiously, "but I suppose we can do it for you. Would you like block letters or script?" "Neither," answered the damsel firmly. "BRAILLE."

HOW NOT TO TELL A STORY
A Few Elementary Pointers

The one thing that every introvert, extrovert, megalomaniac, Casper Milquetoast, octogenarian, and infant prodigy in America is convinced he can do superlatively well is tell a funny story. Since this state of mind—or great delusion, if you will—obviously is permanent, and since, to make matters worse, the tempo of modern life has developed in people's voices a penetrating, raspish quality that makes you hear what they are saying whether you want to or not, it seems fitting to conclude this compendium with a list of elementary rules that may at least prevent our determined raconteurs from making *all* the possible mistakes every time they swing into action.

I feel qualified to draw up such a list on two counts. First, since editing my college funny paper almost thirty years ago, I have been guilty of every one of the common errors myself. Second, since my various collections of humorous anecdotes achieved a modest success, every man, woman, and child I meet seems to think that the thing in the world I desire most is to hear more witticisms of uncertain vintage along the same general lines. I very soon discovered that the most irritating thing I could do was admit that I had heard the story being unfolded about forty times before. I learned to mask my emotions under a frozen, desperate smile, ready to burst into hollow laughter at the appropriate moment and cry, "Yes, sir, you really have given me a new one there. Use it? You bet I will!" At the same time, I began to study the things people do when they are launched upon a joke or anecdote, and the following compilation of "Don'ts" is based largely upon my bitter and highly involuntary experiences.

1. *Don't make a story too long.* The commonest and most fatal mistake of the amateur story teller is to stretch his yarn beyond all reasonable limits. The audience, usually waiting only for an opportunity to get the floor itself, loses all interest. The punch line is buried in a morass of unnecessary verbiage. I have seen so magnificent a raconteur as Herbert Bayard Swope bogged down by the introduction of too many extraneous details. Mr. Swope has a trick of weaving the names of his listeners into a tale he is spinning to insure their absorbed interest. His heroine is "a beautiful girl like little Ginny here at my right." His locale is a town where "I remember seeing you doing something you shouldn't have, Marie." His time is set by a "That must have been about twenty years before young Bennett here was born"—and so on until everybody at the table has been included. It is a device that delights a spectator who appreciates a true artist at work, but even Mr. Swope sometimes carries it too far. They had a saying at the offices of the old morning *World:* "If Swope can't get away with it—don't you try!" Great professional comics like Lou Holtz or Joe Laurie, Jr., can stretch out a story for ten minutes, and actually milk it for additional laughs en route. Ordinary folk cannot.

2. *Don't forget your point in the middle of a story.* The most pathetic spectacle in Raconteurritory is the man who suddenly slows down in the course of his narrative, scratches his head, and announces sheepishly, "Good Lord, I've forgotten how it ends." He leaves his listeners with the same sense of utter frustration as an inept local columnist who provoked George S. Kaufman into declaring, in the days of rationing, "They're after So-and-so to find out what he's done with all the points he's dropped from his stories." If you haven't got your punch line absolutely straight in your mind, *don't start.*

3. *Don't laugh too much yourself.* A character to be avoided at all costs is the man who breaks himself up in the course of a story, shaking so with imbecilic laughter that you understand little

of what he's trying to tell you, and care less. A hearty laugh at the *end* of the story, constituting yourself a sort of cheer leader, is not only permissible, but, if not carried to excess, sound strategy. While the story is in progress, however, let your audience do the laughing—if any!

4. *Don't lay hands on your audience.* Particularly repulsive is the bruiser who accompanies his stories with a series of pokes, jabs, and punches in the tenderest parts of his victims' anatomies. I remember seeing Alfred Knopf, the publisher, cornered one day at a literary "tea" by one of his heftiest, and most important authors. Said author had him backed into a cul-de-sac of the cocktail bar, holding him firmly with his left arm, while he punched home the point of his story with the right. Mr. Knopf was laughing bravely, but the look in his eye suggested a Hatfield watching a McCoy being chosen as the bravest man in town.

5. *Don't tell your story more than once to the same audience.* I have seen more than one narrator so intoxicated by the laughter that greeted his rendition of a story that he promptly repeated either the whole of it, or at least the tag, usually raising his voice

the second time to insure further response from his audience. Almost as disastrous is the plight of the man who allows himself to be persuaded to retell the same story more than twice in the same room. The wise artist limits his encores. It's bad enough to subject your wife to hearing your gems over and over again. She is used to it (or is she?). Your friends won't be so docile. If possible, try to remember the people to whom you have told a certain story; highly though they may cherish you, you will go down in their esteem if you carol "Here's a new one I just heard today," and then launch into the same tale you told at the previous Monday's poker session! Lowell Thomas once made the mistake of telling the same story at successive Dutch Treat Club dinners. A friend could not resist saying, "That story wasn't quite as good tonight as it was a year ago." Thomas, no mean hand at repartee, turned the tables with a quick "Neither are you, my friend."

6. *Don't give the point of the story before you begin.* Many a hapless amateur has killed a good anecdote by introducing it in some such fashion as "Did you fellows ever hear the story of the soft-hearted Ku Klux big-shot whose friends call him Kleagle Tender?" Or, "Did I tell you about the wife who directed a man inquiring for her husband to a fishing camp, suggesting that he look for a pole with a worm at each end?" If his audience says "no," he begins his story without realizing he has no ammunition left. A good detective-story writer saves his solution for the last chapter!

7. *Don't insist on telling a story after your victim informs you he has heard it.* A dreary type indeed is the determined monologist who swings into action with something like "Have you heard the one about the downhearted octopus?" and although everybody in the room immediately choruses "yes," proceeds to tell it anyhow. This is one way of insuring yourself a Micky Finnish. Oscar Wilde's comment on a bore of this ilk was "He's been invited to all the best homes in London—*once!*"

8. *Don't oversell your story in advance.* The man who prefaces a recital with "This is the funniest story you ever heard in your

life" is apt to find the burden of proof sitting too heavily on his shoulders.

9. *Don't tell your stories at the wrong places.* A quip that convulsed the boys in the club car can fall awfully flat at Mrs. Waxelbaum's tea for the bishop. And a tidbit that had the English professors at the Faculty Club in stitches for an hour may be just beyond the comprehension of the babe you met at Leon and Eddie's. Probably you have heard of the gentleman who told an unknown dinner partner a joke that made a monkey of the guest of honor. When he had finished she remarked coldly, "Do you know who I am? I am the guest of honor's wife!" "Do you know who I am?" groaned the narrator, and when the answer was "no," cried "Thank God!"—and fled the room. *You* may not be so fortunate!

10. *Don't tell your stories at the wrong time.* The best story in the world will fall flat if it is told at an inappropriate moment. A gathering engaged in serious discussion often will resent the introduction of unseemly levity. The man who can toss off a funny story in the right spot is a wit; the oaf who is telling them *all* the time is a nitwit.

11. *Don't always "know another version."* A man who can get himself disliked very thoroughly is one who is not content to let somebody else win an uninterrupted laugh, but must always top the other's story with "Oh, I know another version of that same joke—very ancient, too." If he tells his story (and to borrow from myself, try and stop him!) the result, if the similarity actually exists, is anticlimactic and painfully unproductive of merriment; if, as is more often the case, there is no similarity at all, he is shown up as a fool, and a jealous one at that.

12. *Don't tell stories that depend for their humor on events or personalities never heard of by your audience.* Many stories, hilarious if you know the people involved, or the circumstances that provoked the original situation, are unbelievably dull to a stranger. It is stories of this type that can win you a speedy reputation as a "name dropper"—or a plain, unmitigated bore. In some parts of the country you must be more careful of personality angles

than in others. New Englanders in particular are suspicious of strangers and don't like liberties to be taken with their landmarks or prominent citizens. Remember the story of the man of ninety-three who died last summer at Nantucket. The local paper's obituary concluded "Although not a native, Mr. Blank came to this island at the age of two."

13. *Avoid dialect stories as much as possible.* Dialect stories are the hardest to tell properly. The endeavor of amateurs to impersonate Scotchmen, Negroes, or Hebrews is often too horrible even to think about. If you must tell stories of this type (and be sure that no supersensitive member of your audience is going to be offended), take the dialect part as much for granted as possible, and concentrate on putting over the punch line. Personally, I find it difficult even to enjoy dialect on the printed page, and have deliberately avoided many recognized classics on that account. When I hear some noisy limelight hogger begin, "This feller Pat says to Mike, 'Begorrah, me fine buck, oi——'," I make a dive for the radio and find actual relief in a long-winded commercial.

This list of don'ts has grown more formidable than I intended, and will probably make me self-conscious in my own joke telling for months to come (Loud cries of Hear! Hear!). Further, I notice that my injunctions number thirteen. Reminds me of the man who spluttered indignantly, "Me superstitious? I should say not! I'm afraid it would bring me bad luck!"

Shake Well Before Using

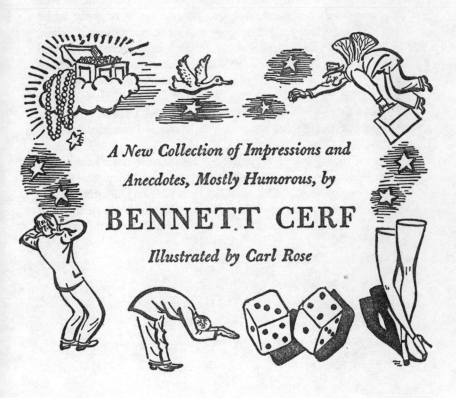

A New Collection of Impressions and
Anecdotes, Mostly Humorous, by

BENNETT CERF

Illustrated by Carl Rose

Contents

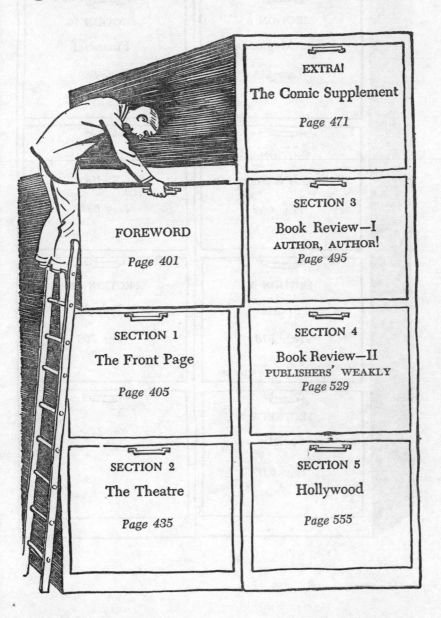

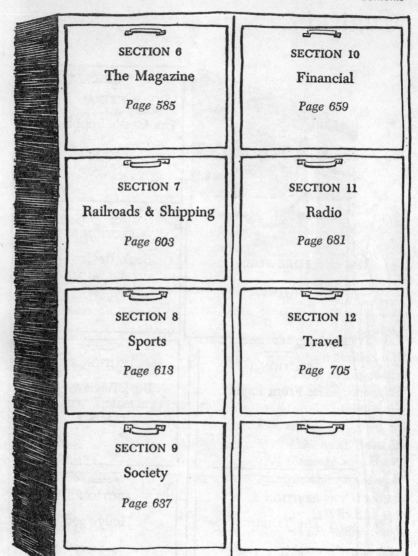

Foreword

Like Try and Stop Me, *its predecessor*, Shake Well Before Using *is a collection of stories that are, for the most part, not original, although I have edited and rewritten all of them in my own words. Wherever possible, I have indicated their source, or at least the place where I heard or found them. Tracking some of them down to their real origin would require a combination of J. Edgar Hoover, Lord Peter Wimsey, Sigmund Spaeth, and the entire Northwest Mounted Police. What difference if some of them predate the decline of Rome? I repeat that any story you never heard before is new to you.*

I said all this very clearly in the foreword of Try and Stop Me, *but a few of the boys were so busy "originating" the stories from precisely the same wits and press agents who told them to me, or from the same compendiums and radio programs, that they didn't seem to hear me. Reading their strident claims, I recalled a line of Richard Brinsley Sheridan's: "What a memory for jokes—and what an imagination for facts."*

I have attempted to divide the contents of this volume in the

*manner of a metropolitan Sunday newspaper, with the hope that
there will be at least one section to appeal to everybody's taste.
Only a "Help Wanted" section is missing, and that may become
necessary after the reviews appear.*

For permission to reprint pieces of my own in Shake Well Before Using, *I am indebted to the* Saturday Review of Literature,
Omnibook, Good Housekeeping, Reader's Digest, Town and
Country, Holiday, Reader's Scope, True, Variety, *and* Coronet. *I
also wish to express my gratitude for the collaboration of Carl
Rose, whose masterly illustrations for* Try and Stop Me *were responsible in no small measure for its success. When I began this
sequel, I counted upon his further participation as a matter of
course.*

*For twenty years I have been a publisher myself at Random
House and the Modern Library. Publishing, in fact, is my true
love, and I would drop this collecting of anecdotes and jokes like
a red-hot poker if it interfered for a moment. Under the circumstances, many people have asked me, "Why did you take* Try and
Stop Me *to another publisher? Why didn't you do it yourself?"
In the first place, Simon and Schuster substantiated my belief
that they could do more with this kind of book than any other
publisher in the country. In the second place, I was far too modest
to say things about the book myself that I could demand from
others. Their advertisements were perfect, and I learned every
last superlative by heart.*

*A country's humor, like any other fashion, changes with the
times. In recent years, the school of the wise-crack, the bitter insult, the rapid-fire repartee has held sway. Columnists and radio
scripters rush for their typewriters to chronicle the latest insults
bandied by the accepted masters of the art. The "oyez" of the
town crier became the "Oh, yeah" of the present-day wise-cracker.
But just as the reader of today finds scant amusement in the chronicles of Bill Nye, Artemus Ward, and other celebrated wits of yesteryear, the humor of the moment probably will horrify rather
than titillate our children and grandchildren.*

I believe that our favorite humor in the decade ahead will have

*a more gentle and nostalgic quality, and be based more on charac-
ter and situation than on rapier thrusts by ruthless operators who
don't care how many people they hurt, so long as they get their
laughs. The change will come slowly, and at the moment it is no
more than a ripple on the surface, but the trend is clear. I hope
readers will find some indication of it in the pages that follow.*

BENNETT CERF

New York

The Front Page

In 1748, Voltaire defined an optimist as "a madman who maintains that everything is right when it is wrong."

In 1858, Artemus Ward corrected Voltaire. "An optimist," he thought, "is anybody who doesn't give a darn what happens as long as it happens to somebody else."

In 1900, "Mr. Dooley" (Finley Peter Dunne) gave *his* notion of an optimist: "A man of eighty-five who gets married and starts looking for a new home nearer a schoolhouse."

This year, on West Forty-fifth Street, a precocious youngster named Harold Ross disdained the foregoing, and demanded, "Pop, what is an optimist today?" His guardian, a fellow named Raoul Fleischman, answered sagely, "An optimist today, my boy, is somebody who cannot possibly have read the front page of any newspaper for the past three years."

This is an age where everybody knows the troubles we got, but nobody knows what to do about them. "A little laughter," suggested an American reporter to a Russian delegate to the United Nations, "might clear the air a bit around here." "Clearer air," replied the dour Russian, "would enable us only to see our difficulties more distinctly."

I persist, nevertheless, in my belief that a dash of good humor, a little wit, and an ounce or two of nonsense, shaken well before using, will provide a remedy for premature despair and departed spirit, and shut out the voice of gloom for a little while at least.

❋   ❋   ❋

One person who was perturbed most deeply about the state of the world today was an officer of the Cleveland Trust Company. He visited his reference library and, at the next meeting of the board, had the following quotations jotted down for the edification of the directors:

1. "There is scarcely anything around us but ruin and despair."
2. "Everything is tending toward a convulsion."
3. "Thank God, I shall be spared from seeing the consummation of ruin that is gathering about us."
4. "In industry, commerce, and agriculture, there is no hope whatever."
5. "Nothing can save the British Empire from shipwreck."

The directors felt better, however, when they heard who had expressed these lugubrious sentiments—and when: 1—William Pitt, in the 1790s; 2—Earl Grey in 1819; 3—The Duke of Wellington, on his deathbed in 1851; 4—Disraeli in 1849; 5—Lord Shaftesbury in 1868.

* * *

The world could use more tough old birds like the retired British colonel who was seated in his usual chair at a London club, listening with growing irritation to the boastful reminiscences of a group of RAF pilots. "It's all very well for you whippersnappers to talk," he rumbled finally, "but your show was child's play compared to the Boer War. The hot sun beating at your brain; the sand burning up your feet; the Fuzzy-Wuzzies attacking you night and day. Why, in one day alone, I had a hand-to-hand encounter with ten of the blighters. Killed eight of them. The other two impaled me with a spear through my chest to a rubber tree. Hung there for three days."

One of the pilots said politely, "Gad, sir, that must have been painful."

"Not particularly," answered the colonel. "Only when I laughed."

* * *

The world also could use more indomitable souls like the Frenchman who came here on a vital loan mission at a moment when affairs in his native land had reached their lowest ebb. His own spirits remained unflagging, however, and he set out with Mayor O'Dwyer for a tour of New York as though he didn't have a thing to worry about.

They arrived in front of the Empire State Building. "Tallest in the world," boasted the mayor. "What do you think of it?" The Frenchman gazed at it admiringly and commented, "It reminds me of sex."

Mayor O'Dwyer, a bit puzzled, said, "I've seen lots of reactions to the Empire State Building in my time, but this certainly is a new one. May I ask just why it reminds you of sex?"

The Frenchman explained simply, "Everything does."

❋　❋　❋

The world could use, as a matter of fact, a few witty, down-to-earth commentators on its follies like the one and only Will Rogers, the man who made his country laugh.

PHILOSOPHER WITH A ROPE

Some Stories About Will Rogers

On the evening of August 15, 1935, a shiny, red seaplane swooped down on a shallow river in Alaska, some three hundred miles inside the Arctic Circle. A handful of curious Eskimos ran to the riverbank. "We're lost," the pilot called to them, "which way is Point Barrow?" One of the Eskimos shouted, "Northeast—only fifteen miles away."

The seaplane took off, wavered uncertainly in the air for a few moments, and then plunged nose-first into the earth with a sickening thud. The two occupants, crushed to death in a flight that would have taken ten minutes, had covered, between them, over a million air miles in the preceding three years. The pilot was Wiley Post, holder of the round-the-world record. His passenger was Will Rogers, America's ambassador of good-will to all the nations on earth.

Will Rogers' portfolio consisted of his homespun wit and sound common sense. He put into pithy phrases the inchoate thoughts of his fellow-men. He never looked up to the mighty—or spoke down to the masses. "He called a spade a spade—and made the spade like it." He brought a troubled world a little peace of mind with a piece of rope. How desperately we need another Will Rogers today!

All of his life, he signed hotel registers, "Will Rogers, Claremore, Oklahoma," but he really was born at Oologah, a few miles north. "You might say," he explained, "that Oologah was a suburb of Claremore. When I was born in 1879 it had about ten houses to Claremore's fifteen." When his future wife, Betty, visited Oologah she was bound to notice him, because he was the only boy in town. He came calling with a banjo, and warbled, "Hello My Baby, Hello My Honey, Hello My Ragtime Girl"—not good, but loud.

Will's father was one-eighth Cherokee, his mother one-quarter. He was deeply proud of his Indian blood. "My forefathers didn't come over on the *Mayflower*," he boasted, "but they met the boat." Rogers, Senior, was affectionately known as "Uncle Clem" throughout the Indian Territory; when Oklahoma applied for statehood in 1906, he was the oldest member of the Constitutional Assembly ("Alfalfa Bill" Murray was the youngest). On his son Will he lavished wealth and affection, and planned a fine education for him. But the boy had different ideas. "In school," he wrote, "I got to know more about McGuffey's Fourth Reader than Mr. McGuffey." He preferred horses to books, and confined his studies to branding irons and lassos. Disapproving neighbors never did get over clucking tongues at his delinquencies. One of them watched his featured turn in the Ziegfeld *Follies* and reported, "He's still acting the fool like he used to do at home." The shy, modest Will, himself, often signed his love letters to Betty, "Your ignorant Indian Cowboy."

Will Rogers reached Broadway via the unlikely route of Argentina and South Africa. He sailed to Buenos Aires under the mistaken idea that what the natives there craved most was American cowboys. When his stake ran out, he joined a troupe called "Texas

Jack's Wild West Circus," and toured South Africa and Australia
under the billing of "The Cherokee Kid—The Man Who Can
Lasso the Tail Off a Blowfly." By the time he was finished, he
could, too!

Rogers made his New York debut at the old Madison Square
Garden in April, 1905. He participated in the "Wild West Exhibition" in the National Horse Show. On the opening night, a
steer broke loose and headed straight for the big-wigs in the arena
boxes. Will roped it in the nick of time. Those of the big-wigs
who hadn't fainted cheered wildly. On the strength of the front-

page stories, Will rode his favorite pony, Comanche, into the number-one vaudeville house of the day—Hammerstein's Victoria Roof.

His act was approved, and he never lacked engagements thereafter, but he really didn't become a headliner until he started talking—and that was an accident, too. He got his ropes tangled up one day, and while he was straightening them out, he explained his difficulties to the audience. His Oklahoma drawl made people laugh, and Will looked up angrily. Then he realized they were laughing with him. He kept on talking—and he never stopped.

In 1912, Rogers deserted vaudeville to appear with Blanche Ring in *The Wall Street Girl.* The opening-night audience in New York seemed to like his specialty, but in the middle of it there were excited murmurings, and people began slipping out of the theatre. Will's dismay vanished when he learned that the news of the sinking of the *Titanic* had just come through. It was a dramatic moment. The authors of a recent garbled screen "biography" of a popular composer must have thought so too—because they "borrowed" it for the big scene of their rather astonishing script.

By the time I matriculated in the Columbia School of Journalism in 1917, Will Rogers was a shining star of the Ziegfeld *Follies,* and the student body was delirious when he agreed to come up and talk to us. It had been my idea to ask him, so mine was the privilege of escorting him to the campus. Coming up on the subway, he noticed an "ad" for some hair-saving concoction and commented, "Shucks, the only thing that can stop falling hair is a floor." I laughed and said, "Why don't you use that?" "I have," said Rogers.

"What you budding journalists need," he told us at Columbia, "is more suckers like me. I'm a hopeless addict of the newspaper drug. I read about eight papers a day. When I'm in a town with only one paper, I read it eight times." Throughout his life, he insisted, "All I know is what I read in the papers." When his column, "Will Rogers Says," was being syndicated to over 500 journals, it got so that all many Americans knew was what they read in Will Rogers.

His stories about the Ziegfeld beauties were unending. "It's tough on Mr. Ziegfeld when we start touring," he declared. "In

every town some millionaire comes along and marries one of those
wonderful chorus girls Mr. Ziegfeld worked so hard to find. Some
of them don't come back to the show for three or four weeks!" He
helped the girl who played "The Spirit of Tulip Land" to make
out her income tax, but she rebelled at listing all of her alimony
payments. "The government'll catch up with you," warned Rogers.
"How can they?" asked the winsome lady. "I can't even keep
track of myself." "The girls are so beautiful," sighed Rogers. "It's
sad to think that twenty years from now, they'll all be five years
older!"

Will Rogers' wit was pointed and timely—but it was never malicious. He went straight to the heart of a subject. Politicians and
diplomats might becloud an issue with a ten-page speech of double talk; Rogers would clear it up with a one-sentence quip. His
field for the most intensive comment was the American scene,
and in that panorama the target most often hit was Congress.
Once asked, "Is the field of humor crowded?" he replied, "Only
when Congress is in session." Then he added, "There isn't much
credit to being a comedian when you got the whole government
working for you. All you have to do is report the facts, and I don't
even have to exaggerate."

People in high places began to seek his company, and invited
him to speak at countless banquets and dinners. Even Chauncey
Depew, after-dinner champion of his era, was forced to admit,
"He's asked to more dinners than I am," but he added, "Of course,
I don't have to bring a rope." Rogers would appear at a benefit
performance in Texas, hop to England for a party at Buckingham
Palace, and be back for a game of polo in Long Island in the
course of a typical fortnight. Wherever he was, he typed out his
daily paragraph of comment on some highlight in the news. He
was the guest of five Presidents at the White House, beginning
with Wilson and ending with Roosevelt.

President Harding once hurt Rogers' pride unintentionally.
After telling Rogers he wouldn't be able to come and see the *Follies* in Washington, he was taken by his hosts to a Marx Brothers
musical in another theatre. When Rogers read about it the next
day, he wired Harding, "I will never forget." He didn't either.
Harding, deeply distressed, made many efforts to placate him,
but even Ziegfeld could not effect a reconciliation. "I know how

he feels," Harding told Albert Lasker, the advertising magnate.
"It's his pride. You know, I'm part Indian too." Incidentally, when
President Coolidge posed later in the regalia of a heap-big chief,
Rogers wired him, "Politics makes strange redfellows."

Another politician who offended Rogers was a lieutenant-
governor of California, who substituted for the ailing governor at
a banquet, and made the fatal error of trying to stop "The Cherokee Kid" by introducing him as follows: "No use of my making
any jokes because the next speaker is the biggest joke in the state.
Like all conceited actors, he's talking to himself over in the corner
this very minute instead of listening to me and trying to learn
something." Rogers shambled to the platform and drawled, "I'm
afraid I *was* whispering to the lady next to me. I was asking her,
'Who is that fellow shooting off his mouth?' Nobody around us
had the faintest idea, but finally a man near the door said, 'Maybe
it's the lieutenant-governor.' 'What does he do?' I asked. 'Nothing,'
said the man. 'Don't he even get up in the morning?' I asked.
'I guess he does that,' he said, 'just to ask if the governor's any
worse.'" It was the last time that particular lieutenant-governor
ever monkeyed with a buzz saw. It was the last time, in fact,
he ever was lieutenant-governor.

At one dinner given in Will Rogers' honor at the Hotel Savoy
in London, the guests included Bernard Shaw, J. M. Barrie, Harry
Lauder, and G. K. Chesterton. He advised them to give the Irish
home rule—and reserve the motion-picture rights. At another affair, he shared speaking honors with Justice Hughes. They were
billed, "Charles Evans Hughes, Humorist, and Will Rogers, Diplomat." "I can't understand all these formal shindigs," he admitted. "I think it would be better if more people worked for their
dinners, and fewer dressed for them."

City traffic bothered and confused him. "One way to stop these
traffic jams," he suggested, "would be to allow on the streets only
the automobiles that had been paid for." For his vacations, he
liked to slip off to a secluded ranch, and play at being a cowboy
again. He was branding calves one sweltering afternoon, soaked
with perspiration, when he overheard a caustic, "Some folks sure
got a hell of a idea of a vacation." Another summer, he traveled
several thousand miles to witness a total eclipse of the sun. When

it was over, somebody asked him, "What did you think of the eclipse?" Rogers answered, "Which one?"

Lady Astor, born Nancy Langhorne in Greenwood, Virginia, U. S. A., once invited Rogers to her luxurious English country estate. He looked over the establishment, and commented, "Nancy, you certainly have out-married yourself." From the home of the American ambassador to France, he sent his niece a picture-postal of the Venus de Milo, and wrote on the back, "See what'll happen to you if you don't stop biting your finger-nails." One reason he was liked, he believed, was that when people came to him for advice, he found out the advice they wanted and gave it to them. "This made them think they were happy, and I was smart. It was as easy as that. I learned it from old Josh Billings. There was a *real* humorist." He told the members of the New York Stock Exchange, "Country folks would appreciate you fellows more if you just sold them stocks that were going to go up. If they're not going up, don't let people buy them."

Radio had not yet blossomed into full flower in Will Rogers' time. Disk jockeys were unknown, and so were stars who drew ten thousand dollars a week. Nevertheless, Will did all right for himself on the air, although he never quite got used to a microphone. He cleaned up in Hollywood, too. The talkies came and Rogers got them. His biggest hits included *They Had to See Paris, State Fair, A Connecticut Yankee in King Arthur's Court,* and his last film, *Steamboat Round the Bend,* in which he co-starred with his old friend Irvin S. Cobb. He took Hollywood in stride. "It's a comfortable kind of show business," he admitted. "Not much night work, and the only place you can act and at the same time sit down in front and clap for yourself." His favorite greeting for screen writers was, "Hi, brother! Whatcha spoiling today?" He told an interviewer, "Shucks, I can't act. I just talk natural. And I'm sure different from the other movie stars: I still got the wife I started out with."

When the already undemanding California marriage laws were amended to permit even quicker marriages, Rogers wrote: "When you got married in this state, you used to have to give three days' notice. That was longer than most marriages in California was lasting. So they did away with that. Now you don't have to file nothing at all. In fact, you don't have to give your right name, according to this new law. You just pay a small amusement tax, that's all."

Political parties were fair game for Will Rogers, and he delighted, during election campaigns and national conventions, to take them to task. In 1932 he established the "Bunkless Party," with himself as presidential nominee. His party platform was brief: "I want it understood first that my platform is made out of the planks carried in by the voters. And anybody with ten votes can have a plank. We are leaving room between the planks for any wisecracks we think we should insert. We will not only give the farmer relief—we'll cure him of being a farmer."

Doctors were not Will Rogers' favorite characters. When sickness prevented his reporting at the studio one morning, alarmed executives sent a titled specialist, who had just arrived in town amidst appropriate fanfare, to examine him. The specialist looked him over carefully and said, "You've been working too hard. What you need is relaxation and a good laugh or two. Take a few days off and go to see Will Rogers. He'll put you back in shape." "I hope you won't forget that," said Rogers sourly, "when you're figuring out your bill." Mrs. Rogers relates that Will never wore

glasses until Thomas Meighan observed him reading a newspaper
at full arm's length. "You'll ruin your eyes that way," warned
Meighan. "Here, try my glasses." Rogers did, and found them
so satisfactory that he took them home with him. For the rest of
his life, his glasses were ground to Meighan's prescription. He
never consulted an oculist.

A few years before his death, Will Rogers wrote, "When I die,
my epitaph, or whatever you call those signs on gravestones, is
going to read, 'I joked about every prominent man of my time,
but I hardly ever met a man I didn't like.' I am proud of that. I
can hardly wait to die so it can be carved. And when you come
around to my grave you'll probably find me sitting there proudly
reading it." Will Rogers got the epitaph he wanted. He also got
the enduring love of his fellow citizens. Hotels and theatres are
still being named after him. Of the two Oklahomans who are honored with statues in the Capitol at Washington, one is Sequoya,
who made his whole Cherokee tribe literate, and the other is Will
Rogers, the philosopher with a rope, who made his whole country
laugh. It was a healthy laughter, and it cleared the fog beshroud-
ing many serious controversies of the day. Humor like that, spontaneous, unforced, is rare and enduring. It becomes part of the
folklore of a nation. Rogers must have suspected this himself. In
the last months of his career, he was told by some wiseacre that
his material was getting "corny." "I guess you mean," he said
amiably, "they still laugh at my jokes."

*   *   *

One career diplomat who shared Will Rogers' happy knack for
saying just the right thing at just the right time was Maurice Francis Egan, who served valiantly under several administrations, beginning with President Cleveland. That was before men like
Goebbels and Ciano had reduced diplomacy to hysterical bluster
and brute force.

One of Egan's typical stories concerns a great banquet at the
White House when a callow young attaché from an important foreign embassy cut into his heart of lettuce and found a live worm
crawling inside it. He was about to thrust the plate away when
he noticed that Mrs. Cleveland's eyes were upon him. He stiff-

ened in his chair, and promptly ate the lettuce, worm and all. "That was unnecessary, but spectacular," applauded Mrs. Cleveland. "I think you will go far, young man!" Fifteen years later the young man was back in the United States—as Ambassador.

* * *

During Mr. Coolidge's tenure of the White House, there was a similar display of diplomatic nicety. The ambassador from Great Britain was breakfasting with the President, discussing an important trade agreement. He was somewhat taken aback when Mr. Coolidge carefully poured his cup of milk into a saucer, but, gentleman to the last, did precisely the same with *his* milk. The President smiled slightly, but said nothing as he stooped down and gave his saucer to a gray cat waiting patiently at his feet.

* * *

Up Newport way, they tell a story of how the late Admiral Sims first attracted the attention of President Theodore Roosevelt. Sims, then a lieutenant j.g., sent a letter direct to the President in which he stated bluntly, "The trouble with our Navy is that it simply does not know how to shoot." The startled President sent for Sims forthwith. The lieutenant did not retract. Instead, he proposed that a floating target be built, and that the entire Eastern flotilla steam by and fire at it. "Did the President order the target built?" asked the man to whom Admiral Sims was telling the story years later. "He did," said the Admiral. "And did the Navy know how to shoot?" persisted the questioner. "Hell," said Sims, "they haven't hit that target yet!"

* * *

David C. Mearns, of the Library of Congress, recalls that when President and Mrs. Coolidge left Washington for one of their summer vacations, the White House was renovated from top to bottom. A wire from Vermont revealed the fact that they were coming back the next day—a full week ahead of schedule—and a hurried caretaker beseeched Mr. Mearns for help. "The President's books are scattered all over the floor," he said. "*Please* come over and arrange them properly on the shelves before he returns."

The next day was a sweltering one, but Mr. Mearns toiled manfully. His temper was not improved when the President's big white dog, very friendly but very clumsy, padded into the room about sundown, and began knocking over piles of books and raising hell in general. Mr. Mearns couldn't get rid of him, so he did the next best thing. He knocked off work for a while and went out for a few cooling potions.

When he returned two hours later, the library appeared empty, but just as he settled down to complete his task, the white dog bounded out from behind the window curtain, and made for him, barking joyfully. "Damn," muttered Mr. Mearns, and shied a book at the dog. It missed. The horrified Mr. Mearns next heard a distant cry of "Ouch," and President Coolidge stepped out from behind the curtain, rubbing the back of his head. The two men stared at each other for a moment, and then Mr. Coolidge broke the silence.

"Warm, isn't it?" he said.

* * *

A gentleman with an unwieldy box of flowers under his arm was about to board a Madison Avenue bus recently when Mignon Eberhart, the well-known mystery writer, hailed him. She was sure she recognized him, but for the life of her couldn't recall his name. He looked equally puzzled, but let the bus go by, and shook her hand warmly. There followed one of those animated, super-cordial exchanges of amenities that always feature the meeting of two people who aren't sure of each other's identity. Finally, the gentleman said, "It's been fine seeing you again, but I really must run." Just as he stepped on the bus, Miss Eberhart remembered, in a frightening flash, one, why his face was familiar, and two, that she never had met him in her life.

It was ex-President Herbert Hoover.

* * *

Sir Sidney Clift reports that he was standing with his friend, Winston Churchill, in a passage leading into the House of Commons recently, when Sir Stafford Cripps, no favorite of Mr. Churchill, brushed by. Churchill grimaced, and remarked, "There, but for the grace of God, goes God."

* * *

Dale Harrison relays the story of a young private secretary who was called on the phone one morning by a lady whose voice was unfamiliar. "I saw your husband in Germany," said the stranger. "Perhaps you will have a bite with me tomorrow so I can tell you all about him." They arranged to meet in a hotel lobby. When the secretary asked, "How will I recognize you?" the stranger told her, "Just look for a tall, gray-haired lady. I'll be waiting for you." That is how she came to have lunch the next day with Mrs. Franklin D. Roosevelt.

* * *

A battleship anchored in New York Harbor, and an ensign seized the opportunity to bring his best girl aboard for a tour of inspection. On the bridge, he pointed down to a big bronze plaque and explained, "This marks the spot where our brave captain fell." "I can see why," said the bright-eyed damsel. "I darn near slipped on it myself."

* * *

One of those new-fangled jet planes was delivered to a Texas air base. The Commanding Officer examined it gingerly, called on his most experienced pilot to test it. "Remember, Captain," he cautioned, "nobody knows how fast this fool thing can go. Besides, all the instruments aren't in it yet. So take it easy, boy!"

The Captain promised and took the plane aloft. It was easy for him to manage and he couldn't resist letting it out. As he roared through space, he contacted the ground and asked, "How fast am I going?" Someone responded, in German, "Twelve hundred miles an hour." The pilot gasped and said, "Are you certain?" The reply, "Of course, we're certain," was in Russian! The pilot said, "Good Lord!" A voice nearby answered, "Yes, my son . . . ?"

* * *

Ted Lawson, co-author of *Thirty Seconds Over Tokyo,* told me a fine story about Alex de Seversky, who, like Lawson, lost a leg as a flier in wartime. Seversky one day was trying to cheer a disconsolate aviator in a similar predicament. "The loss of a leg," he said with conviction, "is really not so great a calamity. Look at me. I dance, I fly, I drive a car, I go everywhere. Women were more interested in me the moment they discovered I had one artificial limb. And another thing: if you get hit on a wooden leg, it doesn't hurt a bit! Here, try it!" The soldier took his cane and cracked it across Seversky's leg with terrific force. "You see," laughed Seversky. "If you hit an ordinary man like that, he'd be in bed for five days! Cheer up, old man," he waved airily, and left the ward. In the corridor, he collapsed. The wounded aviator, of course, had hit him on his real leg.

* * *

SEEING RED

More revealing than a thousand editorials and sober analyses by "experts" are the stories sweeping America today about Soviet Russia and its leaders. Obviously, Russia is the enemy. Stalin and his henchmen are depicted as pirates, egomaniacs, and hypocrites. Reports from Moscow indicate that the same kind of stories are in circulation there, with America on the receiving end of the jibes and insults. Subtlety and caution have been abandoned.

If the stories referred to represent "humor," it is the humor of complete disillusion—deadly poison coated with laughing gas. "Funny stories" provide the surest and quickest vehicle for propaganda and campaigns of hate. Herr Goebbels knew what he was doing when he clapped into jail every comedian who told a joke that reflected in any way on the Nazi regime.

Analyze the following stories, and draw your own conclusions.

1. At the Yalta conference, F. D. R., Churchill, and Stalin all sported new cigarette cases. F. D. R. proudly showed the inscription in his case: "To our far-seeing president from a grateful people." Churchill then produced his: "For Winnie, who is leading us through blood, sweat and tears to victory. From the citizens of Britain." Stalin made no move until the others urged him. Then he reluctantly threw *his* new case on the table. It was studded with diamonds and emeralds, and the inscription read: "To Prince Serge Waderewski, with the esteem and devotion of the Warsaw Polo Club."

2. A Russian soldier, idling along a road in Germany, saw a peasant pitching hay, and demanded, "What time is it?" The peasant plunged the prongs of his pitchfork into the ground, and stepped back to measure the shadow. Then he announced, "It's exactly 3:34 P.M." The Russian soldier checked with a watch on his right wrist, and cried in astonishment, "You're absolutely right! Give me that pitchfork!"

3. Stalin lost a pair of cherished gold cuff-links, and sounded an alarm throughout the land. Thirty-seven suspects were rounded up, and sentenced to be shot. The night before the executions, Stalin found the cuff-links under his bureau, and wired police

headquarters. "Cuff-links recovered. Release suspects." Back came
the answer, "Executions must proceed as scheduled. Have full
confessions from all thirty-seven prisoners."

4. At the conclusion of a particularly hectic session of the
United Nations, one of the heads of the Russian delegation was
seized with pangs of hunger, and barged into the first restaurant
he passed. "A ham sandwich, and make it snappy," he told the
waiter in his best U.N. vernacular. The waiter smiled and said,

"I guess you didn't notice the sign on this restaurant. We don't serve any meat. This place is one hundred per cent vegetarian." The Russian was amazed. "This room is packed," he pointed out. "Do you mean to tell me all these people are actually vegetarians?" The waiter leaned over and whispered, "Keep this under your hat, but only ten per cent are real vegetarians. The rest are merely sympathizers."

5. Moscow's city fathers decided to erect a beautiful new statue in honor of the revered Russian poet, Alexander Pushkin, and inaugurated a nation-wide competition to secure the best possible design. The prize was so big that literally thousands of sketches were submitted. They showed Pushkin standing, sitting, riding horseback, composing *Boris Godunov,* fighting his fatal duel with Baron d'Anthes. The committee, swamped, argued pros and cons for weeks, finally announced the winning design. It was a statue of Josef Stalin, reading a poem by Pushkin.

6. Oriana Atkinson, clever wife of Critic Brooks Atkinson, accompanied her husband to the Soviet Union and returned with a rather jaundiced view of the situation. She tells of meeting one Russian girl who seemed very nervous and distraught. "I'm overtired," admitted the girl. "I've gone without sleep for two whole nights rehearsing for a spontaneous demonstration tomorrow."

7. Stalin was reviewing a crack regiment in Red Square when someone in the ranks sneezed. Stalin stopped in his tracks and demanded, "Who sneezed?" Nobody answered. "Shoot down the front rank," ordered Stalin. When the order had been executed, Stalin again asked, "Who sneezed?" Again there was silence. The Premier, apoplectic, roared, "Shoot down the second rank." This done, he put his hands on his hips and demanded, "Now maybe the man who sneezed will speak up."

From the very rear row came a terrorized voice, "It was I, Comrade Stalin, who sneezed!"

"Aha," said Stalin. "*Gesundheit!*"

8. A schoolteacher in Moscow distributed new photographs of Stalin and suggested that her charges pin them up on their walls that evening. The next day everyone but Ivan reported that instructions had been carried out faithfully. "Don't you love our leader?" the teacher asked Ivan. "Oh, yes," he answered, "but I

couldn't hang my picture on the wall because we have no wall. Our family lives in the center of the room."

9. A new jet plane transported a citizen of Pinsk to Minsk in four minutes and thirty-two seconds. The citizen was overwhelmed. He rushed to the home of a friend in Minsk and cried, "What a nation we have! Not only the greatest constitution, the greatest leaders, and the greatest army, but now we have a wonderful plane that brought me here from Pinsk in less than five minutes!"

The friend refused to be impressed. "So you got here from Pinsk in less than five minutes," he agreed. "What good does that do you?"

"What good?" echoed the traveler. "It enables me to be first on line to buy a pack of matches!"

10. An American general was asked, "How many atom bombs do you think it would take to destroy Switzerland?" "That's very hard to say," he admitted. "It's a small country. I'd think four or five might do the trick, but of course, that's just a wild guess." "How about France?" was the next question. "A bigger target," said the general, "is that much harder to estimate. Maybe a couple of dozen bombs would suffice. Maybe it would require fifty. Maybe a hundred. How can anyone possibly know?" "Well," persisted the interrogator, "how many bombs would it take to wipe out Russia?" "Eleven hundred and sixty-two," snapped the general.

* * *

When he died, Arthur Brisbane was one of the richest editors in the history of American journalism. There were two reasons for this: he was a genius in his line—and he had a constitutional aversion to incurring unnecessary expenses. A biographer summed him up as "a man who never took his eye off the main chance, and never cringed once from either adulation or money." Upon being introduced to an English diplomat one evening, Brisbane remarked pleasantly, "I'm delighted to meet you, sir. Did you know that my income was over two hundred and sixty thousand dollars last year?"

In the midst of the depression of 1933, Brisbane wrote a ringing editorial to the effect that businessmen could not expect to enforce the terms of contracts entered into in the boom years of 1928 and 1929. "Be fair about this," he counseled. "Scale down the terms to bring them in line with current values." One of the tenants in a Brisbane office building, who had signed a ten-year lease in May, 1929, for a whopping big sum, sent a copy of the editorial to Brisbane with a note attached thereto reading, "If you practice what you preach, you'll scale down my rent by ten per cent." To the tenant's amazement he received a letter in longhand from the chief by return mail which read, "O.K. Consider it done." There was a postscript, however. It said, "In the future, don't bother to read my columns so carefully."

Arthur Brisbane's most unfortunate prediction was printed in the Chicago *Record-Herald* in 1913. "Motion pictures," he declared, "are just a passing fancy and aren't worth comment in this newspaper."

* * *

A fair young graduate of the School of Journalism got a job as cub reporter on a Long Island daily. Her first story won the editor's approval, but he pointed out a few minor inaccuracies. "Remember," he said, "it was Joseph Pulitzer, founder of the School of Journalism, who declared that accuracy is to a newspaper what virtue is to a woman." "That in itself is not entirely accurate," said the girl triumphantly. "A newspaper can always print a retraction!"

* * *

In Gene Fowler's early days as a reporter he was writing a story in a hotel lobby when the desk clerk called to him that there had just been a shooting in a room on the sixth floor. Fowler rushed up to the room, picked up the dead man's telephone, and called his editor. "Have you seen the body?" the editor asked. "Have I seen the body?" answered Fowler. "I'm *sitting* on it."

Fowler claims he interviewed another killer named Jock McAllister a few hours before he was scheduled to be hanged. "Your only chance," Fowler assured him, "is to get a last-minute reprieve from the governor. He's at home in Albany. Better wire him immediately."

Fowler says sadly, "The hanging took place that midnight, however—right on schedule. When the guards came to get Jock McAllister, they found him frowning over a telegram blank, still trying to boil his pleas to the governor down to ten words."

* * *

Gene Fowler is now collecting material for a biography of the late Jimmy Walker, and already has enough colorful stories to fill a thousand-page book.

Walker's popularity survived a political scandal that would have destroyed most men. He was the all-time master of the ready quip. I remember the evening he attended a banquet honoring Heavyweight Champion Joe Louis, when the Brown Bomber was released from the Army after valiant and untiring service. The scheduled speakers had delivered carloads of platitudes, and everyone was squirming with boredom when the toastmaster suddenly spied Jimmy Walker in the audience, and called on him.

Walker spoke a single sentence that brought the crowd to its feet cheering. "Joe," he said simply, "you have planted a rose on the grave of Abraham Lincoln."

A few days before he died, Jimmy Walker, dapper and irresistible as in his heyday, visited Random House. He was toying with the notion of bidding on the Ogden Reid residence and transforming it into headquarters for his flourishing radio and recording business—and he wanted to see what we had done in the Fahnestock wing across the courtyard. In the course of his tour, Jimmy told two more stories that Gene Fowler might be able to fit in somewhere.

The first concerned a day early in 1943 when a newly camouflaged destroyer darted out of a British port to escort an American battleship into Plymouth Harbour. The destroyer zigzagged back and forth in the path of the battleship and then signaled by blinker, "What do you think of our camouflage?" The exasperated captain of the battleship signaled back, "It's magnificent. Where the hell are you?"

The other was about a church father who was inveigled into a round of golf and enjoyed it so thoroughly that he became a fanatic on the subject. Finally the archbishop had to send for him. "My son," said the archbishop, "I have always encouraged healthful exercise, and I consider golf both an excellent diversion and a means of communing with mother nature. But if one plays golf too much, one is apt to neglect his real duties."

The father was crushed. "May I ask why you seem to think I am overdoing it?" he asked humbly.

"I noticed," said the archbishop gently, "that when you approached the altar this morning you were holding your psalm book with an interlocking grip."

* * *

Stanley Frank and Paul Sann tell a classic story about a cub reporter in Johnstown, Pa., at the time of the disastrous flood in 1889. The first flash reached the nearest big-time newspaper office late at night when only this newest addition to the staff—a droopy youth just out of school—was on tap. The editor hustled him to the scene of the catastrophe, and spent the next hour in a frenzied effort to get his veteran reporters on the job. By then it was too late, however. All wires were down, and the valley was isolated. For twenty-four hours the only reporter in the devastated area was one green beginner!

The press of America waited feverishly for his first report. Finally it began to trickle in over the telegraph. "God sits upon a lonely mountaintop tonight and gazes down upon a desolate Johnstown. The roar of swirling waters echoes through . . ." The editor tore his hair and rushed a wire back to his poet laureate: "Okay. Forget flood. Interview God. Rush pictures."

PORT OF NEW YORK AUTHORITY

The port of New York Authority is one of the crowning achievements of the late Governor Alfred E. Smith. Under his prodding, and with the co-operation of Governor Edge of New Jersey, President Harding approved the Authority in 1921 to end for all time the interstate bickerings over pier privileges, transportation, car floats, and lighterage that were retarding further development of the nation's busiest harbor. To keep the new setup out of the hands of political hacks and plunderers, it was ordained wisely that no members of the Authority were to receive one penny of pay. Today such men as Chairman Howard Cullman, S. Sloan Colt (President of the Bankers Trust Company), Bayard F. Pope (Vice Chairman of Marine Midland Trust), and Donald Lowe (President of the Lowe Paper Company) are giving their time and energies gratis to the constant improvement of the port district. They offer an object lesson in how two neighboring states can pool resources to the benefit not only of themselves, but the entire country.

The Holland Tunnel, begun before the Authority came into existence, was the first major enterprise entrusted to its care. On its own, the Authority built the George Washington Bridge across the Hudson, and the Bayonne, Outerbridge, and Goethals Bridges down the bay. Then came the Lincoln Tunnel. Last year, more than forty-one million vehicles used the various facilities of the Authority. In 1932, the Port Authority Building, occupying the entire square block between Fifteenth and Sixteenth Streets and Eighth and Ninth Avenues, was completed. Now under construc-

tion are the two biggest truck depots in the world, and a Union Bus Terminal. When these structures are completed, some of New York's most pressing traffic problems will have been solved.

With the acquisition of New York's airports—La Guardia, Idlewild, Floyd Bennett, and Newark—the Port Authority's importance to the community has increased a hundredfold. The Idlewild project is so enormous that it staggers the imagination. It will give employment to over 60,000 people. Only thirty per cent of its income is expected to come from the airlines in landing and hangar fees; the balance will come from the concessions—hotels, restaurants, theatres, and the like. It will be, in effect, a permanent World's Fair.

The Port Authority has had its embarrassing moments, caused principally by the efforts of an expert and high-powered publicity corps. There was the occasion, for instance, when, several years

back, reporters and newsreel men were summoned to the Jersey
City end of the Holland Tunnel to see a demonstration of a new
machine guaranteed to extinguish fires in the tunnel in thirty seconds flat. An old jalopy was soaked with kerosene, and Chairman
Cullman, resplendent in frock coat and wing collar, stood ready
with a hose in one hand and a six-page speech in the other. The
blaze was ignited. "Action!" cried the cameramen. Cullman
turned on the hose.

Unfortunately, the Jersey City water department had chosen
this exact moment to turn off the pressure to repair a leak. While
the cameramen clicked blissfully, the jalopy burned to a cinder,
and the apoplectic Cullman, still clutching the nozzle of his hose,
turned to Mayor Hague and bellowed, "What is the meaning of
this outrage?" The Mayor was about to offer a rebuttal, when the
water suddenly was turned on, catching the good Mayor squarely

in the kisser. The newsreel men reluctantly surrendered the nega-
tives after considerable persuasion.

A comparable crisis occurred on Navy Day, when an elaborate
ceremony was arranged to take place on the George Washington
Bridge, just as President Truman's yacht steamed underneath. For

the occasion, Annin and Company produced the biggest American flag of all time. It stretched clear across the roadway of the bridge, and was guaranteed to withstand a "sixty-mile gale." Somebody miscalculated sadly, however, because, an hour or so before the ceremony, a gentle zephyr blew upstream, and, with a ripping sound, the flag took off from its moorings and disappeared in the general direction of Wappingers Falls. Lawrence Tibbett sang "The Star-Spangled Banner" anyhow, Ray Massey hastily substituted an editorial from the New York *Times* for the speech he had prepared on Old Glory, and Chairman Cullman eased the tension to a certain degree by assuring everybody that the flag had been fully insured.

Another time, the Authority's undaunted publicity staff decided to lavish its attention on the driver of the hundred-millionth car to trundle up to the toll gate of the Holland Tunnel. The awards included photographs, front-page stories, and enough assorted baubles to furnish a four-room apartment. With the Authority's customary hard luck, however, the hundred-millionth driver turned out to be a peroxide blonde who was planning a clandestine visit to the wicked city and who blanched with terror at the prospect of all the publicity. "My husband'll murder me," she moaned, and then added hopefully, "He'll murder you, too." The committee hastily decided it had miscounted, and bestowed its largess on the driver of a five-ton truck, who took it in stride.

When I sent this piece to Mrs. Lee K. Jaffe, director of public relations of the Port of New York Authority, to see if I had gotten my principal facts straight, she pointed out, "You forgot to mention the Gowanus Grain Terminal, which the State of New York transferred to us in 1945." "What's a grain terminal got to do with the Port Authority?" I scoffed. "What's a piece on the Port Authority got to do with *Shake Well Before Using?*" she countered.

She had me there.

* * *

Dean Alfange tells a story about a candidate for mayor who made forty campaign speeches in a single day, and staggered home in a state of complete exhaustion. On his doorstep he found a blue fairy who told him, "As a reward for your fine work, any wish you care to make will come true. But remember that whatever you ask, the man running against you will get just twice as much." "That's an interesting proposition," admitted the candidate. "I'm half dead tonight. I think I'll ask to stay just that way."

*   *   *

After a round-table radio broadcast, Philosopher Irwin Edman and a star reporter on the New York *Herald Tribune,* a dyed-in-the-wool Republican newspaper, joined a heated discussion in the next room. "I must admit," said the reporter, "that in 1932 I voted for Roosevelt. Gosh, I hope we're off the air!" Edman told him, "You're not only off the air. You're off the *Tribune.*"

*   *   *

In London, shortly before the war began, the literary set turned out *en masse* for a banquet in honor of a distinguished American publisher, just then winding up his twenty-fifth annual visit to the shores of Albion.

Numerous British luminaries felt that the occasion demanded elaborate expressions of esteem for the guest of honor, but, while they went on and on orating, the subject of their encomiums unfortunately went on and on imbibing whiskies and soda. When he finally was called upon to speak himself, only a herculean effort enabled him to get to his feet. He swayed dizzily, blinked at his audience, and suddenly remarked very clearly, "Gentlemen, as I was saying——" With this he sat down and promptly fell asleep.

*   *   *

In Chicago, a proposal was made that the new Municipal Airport be named after Secretary of State George Marshall. Colonel McCormick is said to have planned an enthusiastic front-page endorsement of the idea when a white-faced underling burst into his office and cried, "Colonel, if this thing goes through, do you realize what the name of that airport will be? *Marshall Field!*"

*   *   *

Here are a few tidbits that were ignored by the front pages—
for reasons that may not be too obscure:

—At a recent bankers' convention a speaker asked, "Can you
name a single commodity that has not gone up since 1940?" Washington Dodge, Wall Street broker, snapped, "Money."

—Charles Allen Smart, author of *R.F.D.* and *Sassafras Hill,*
rushed breathlessly into his publisher's office, and apologized,
"Forgive me for being late, but I just met my recent commanding officer, and he let me off at the wrong floor."

—A Park Avenue doctor's overdue bills now bear a sticker reading, "Long time no fee."

—A man whose children had attended a progressive school and
followed a schedule he strongly disapproved told his wife coldly,
"Madam, your two sons do not know their R's from a hole in the
ground."

—Dwight Hutchinson reports that his young daughter, just going in for culture, came to him in some distress. "It says in the
paper," she announced, "that Tommy Manville is going to get
married for the ninth time. Now how can a man who wrote *The
Magic Mountain* behave in such a fashion?"

* * *

Arthur Mayer, recently back from the Far East, swears to the
truth of this story:

He reached Shanghai late one night and hurried to his hotel.
He was still in the process of unpacking when the Chinese equivalent of a house dick knocked on the door. China being at the opposite side of the world from the U. S., its mores and manners
are frequently the complete reverse of ours. The dick did not look
under the bed but asked in his best pidgin English, "Want gur?"
"Want what?" asked Mayer. "Gur," answered the hospitable hotel
representative. He then proceeded with appropriate gestures to
indicate clearly what a "gur" was and what a "gur" could do. His
pantomime was so perfect that Mayer had little trouble grasping
the thought, but he was tired and anxious only for a bath and
bed. He pointed to his gray hair and to his eyeglasses as a reasonable excuse for his strange lack of interest in the suggestion.
As a pantomime artist, however, he was apparently not the equal

of the Chinese. Half an hour later, when he emerged from his tub, there was again a knock on his door. The house dick had returned, this time accompanied by a charming if somewhat mature Russian lady, her blond hair streaked with gray and a pince-nez on her nose.

*   *   *

A very dignified lady entered Ray Washburne's bookshop in Williamstown and announced that she was looking for something "new and good" to read. Washburne suggested Pat Frank's *Mr. Adam*. "What's it about?" she asked. "Well," said Washburne, "an atomic bomb suddenly renders every male in the world completely sterile—everyone but a single fortunate chap, that is, who was working deep in a mine shaft at the time of the explosion, and emerges with his powers unimpaired. You can imagine the spot in which he finds himself then!" "It sounds very interesting," agreed the dignified lady. "Tell me, *is it fiction or non-fiction?*"

SECTION 2

The Theatre

While book publishers like to regard themselves as reckless gamblers, risking fortunes on the public reception of the masterpieces they sponsor, the fact remains that, compared to show producers, they are very small potatoes indeed. The most incautious plunger in the book business would be hard put to lose more than ten thousand dollars on any one publication, no matter how scandalously he misjudged and overadvertised it. Compare that with the three hundred thousand dollars apiece lost on no fewer than four ill-starred musical productions in the past two seasons!

Of course, it might be pointed out that the Broadway producers stand to win correspondingly greater sums when they actually hit the jackpot, and that, when they do lose, the money frequently is not their own. Anonymous angels always seem available, panting to sink hard-earned shekels in a business they know nothing about for the privilege of being kicked out of rehearsals and getting opening-night tickets in the ninth row in the balcony. This bolstering, however, only softens the blow when the ax falls. Usually some of the money comes out of the producer's pocket anyhow, not to mention the months he may have devoted to casting and rehearsals, and the loss of prestige involved in more spectacular Broadway debacles. Considering the stakes, the play impresarios take their lickings and confess their blunders with a grace and show of sportsmanship that book publishers might do well to emulate. A few classic examples will illustrate my point.

Some years ago Mr. and Mrs. Fredric March gave up lucrative picture offers to star in a legitimate drama that struck their fancy. The critics disagreed violently, and to a man. In one evening the hopes and plans of a year were washed down the drain. The play closed, but the Marches won the cheers of Broadway by running in all the papers an ad that reproduced a *New Yorker* cartoon of a trapeze artist missing his partner completely in mid-air, and murmuring simply, "Oops—sorry." The only other line that appeared in the copy was the signature of the Marches.

Norman Bel Geddes once produced a play called *Siege* and was so optimistic about its chances that he spent a fortune for a massive set that showed four stories of an old Spanish fortress (this was the set that led George Jean Nathan to remark that Geddes had an edifice complex). When the critics completed their massacre of *Siege*, however, some of the pieces of the set had been blasted as far as Stamford. Undaunted, Geddes appeared at a masquerade party the very next night, dressed as an undertaker, with every one of the critics' requiems pinned to his right lapel.

One of the most spectacular successes of all time in the theatre today is Oscar Hammerstein. Co-author of *Allegro, Oklahoma!, Carousel,* and *Carmen Jones,* and co-producer of *I Remember Mama* and *Happy Birthday,* his income for the year before taxes may reach the million mark. But when Hammerstein took a quarter-page ad in the Christmas issue of *Variety,* did he so much as mention his triumphs? Not Oscar! He delighted his confreres by listing six successive failures that had marred his record before

the click of *Oklahoma!* and cheerfully concluded, "I've done it before and I can do it again."

* * *

Oscar Hammerstein's very first writing chore for the stage gave scarcely a hint of the triumphs that lay in store for him. He was the head of my college fraternity in those days, and when his first play opened in New Haven, we dug up just enough cash to send one loyal frater to cover the event. We chose lots to determine who would make the journey, and the winner was pledged to wire a concise report as soon as the final curtain descended.

Oscar's play was called *The Light*. Shortly after midnight, the

expected telegram reached us. It read, *"The Light* will never il-
luminate Broadway." Our scout's prediction was all too accurate.
Oscar himself recalls ruefully that the New Haven audience's one
solid laugh was the result of an accident. In the second act, the

distrait heroine had a line that read, "Everything seems to be falling down around me." Just as she delivered it on the opening
night, her panties slipped, and fell to the stage.

*   *   *

There is an iron-clad rule in the theatre that enables a producer
to fire an actor without salary at any time within a two-week rehearsal period. If the actor survives the fortnight's ordeal, he is on
the pay-roll for good.

One actor had had an extraordinary run of bad luck. In six successive try-outs he had been notified by wire on the thirteenth day of rehearsal that he had failed to make the grade. Now he had been playing a part for the same period of time in a seventh play. If no wire arrived by midnight, he was in! He needed the money badly, for he and his wife were down to their last fifty dollars.

Anxiously, they watched the clock. At 11:50 P.M. they were just preparing to celebrate when the blow fell. A Western Union boy handed them a telegram.

The heartbroken actor opened the wire with trembling hands, but suddenly he gave a wild cry of relief. "Darling," he shouted to his wife, "your mother dropped dead!"

* * *

A great star, now a grandmother but still beautiful, dropped in to Sardi's for a bite with a lovely young thing who had just been graduated from Vassar. The star's manager, at another table, took one look at the youngster and sent over a note which read, "Who is that ravishing kid?" The star answered, "Me."

* * *

Harry Lauder's American secretary had a young daughter. After ignoring a number of pointed hints, the Scotch comedian finally gave her a pass for one of his matinees. "Orchestra seats," exclaimed the secretary. "How wonderful!" Then she added sadly, "But my little girl hasn't got a dress that's pretty enough for the orchestra." "We'll soon remedy that," said Sir Harry. He tore up the pass for orchestra seats and made out a new one for two in the second balcony.

* * *

Margaret Case Harriman, after slaving for months to complete a revealing profile of Helen Hayes, met a dowager at a dinner party who told her, "That series of yours on Helen Hayes was a masterpiece, the most informative piece the *New Yorker* ever ran." Then the dowager lowered her voice and added, "Now tell us, my dear, what she's *really* like!"

* * *

Billy Rose, assembling a night club show that featured a lot of favorites of twenty and thirty years ago, recalled a juggler who hadn't appeared in New York since the Palace gave up vaudeville. He tracked the juggler down, and wired him, "Name the lowest figure you'll take to appear in the new show at my trap on Forty-fifth Street." The juggler wired back, "Leaving at once."

Rose's greatest achievement to date, probably, was his famous Aquacade at the New York World's Fair. When the curtain fell on the opening night performance, the press agent is said to have clapped a hand to his forehead and moaned, "I'm ruined! It's ten times better than I said it was!"

* * *

A television salesman tried to sell one of his elaborate models to Ed Wynn. "Just think," he said, "you can sit comfortably in your hotel room, press a button on your television set, and a beautiful, scantily clad girl is suddenly standing before you." "In hotels I go to," Wynn said, "you can get the same thing without television."

Wynn introduced one young lady at The Carnival Night Club as "Miss Soft Drink," explaining, "she'll go out with anybody from 7 up."

* * *

Bobby Clark, one of the greatest comedians of our time, would like to revive the lion act he did in burlesque with his old partner McCullough. It is a project that should be encouraged, if necessary, by a special grant from Congress.

The manager of a side-show offered Clark a dollar to wrestle with a lion. When Clark demurred, the manager assured him, "Our real lion has escaped. This fellow (McCullough) will wear a lion skin and the suckers will never know the difference." Clark, of course, perked up at once when he heard this. And the real lion, of course, walked into the cage behind his back while he told the audience what he was going to do to the "king of beasts."

The next ten minutes provided more belly laughs than any other act I can remember. Clark whacked the lion with his cane, kicked it in the rump, played leap frog with it, and waved a flashlight in its eyes. When the lion roared, he would cry, "That's great! You sure are fooling the audience." Occasionally he'd sniff and declare, "What a performance! You even *smell* like a lion."

For the pay-off, the lion would start chasing Clark around the cage. The manager yelled, "Hey, I've been trying to tell you! That's the *real lion* in there with you!" Clark's final speech was, "This is a hell of a time to tell me!"

* * *

THE VERY LAST WORD

The dubious but widely quoted pronouncement of Rudyard Kipling that a woman is only a woman is proof in itself that Mr. Kipling never had the opportunity or desire to study any of the great actresses of the world at close range. Only women? These ladies are sirens, enchantresses, tacticians, financiers, and, when other great actresses of the world are within earshot, vitriolic wits with all the destructive power of an atomic bomb.

Legendary, for example, are the exploits and bon mots of Mrs. Patrick Campbell, queen of the English stage, who created the title role of *The Second Mrs. Tanqueray,* and in her declining years conquered Hollywood with her acting and her tongue. In the course of a violent argument with that noted vegetarian, George Bernard Shaw, Mrs. Campbell rasped, "Some day, Shaw, you will eat a pork chop, and then God help womankind!" His play, incidentally, required a large cast, but was not a conspicuous success. Mrs. Campbell was appraising the house from a peephole in the curtain on the third night when Shaw inquired, "How are we doing?" "Better than last night," she answered, "but we are still in the majority." After a very dull week-end, she took pen in hand and wrote in the hostess' elaborate guest book, "Quoth the raven." To the producer husband of a famous motion-picture star, Mrs. Campbell cooed, "What an attractive wife you have! She has such tiny little eyes!"

A taxicab driver once demurred at transporting her and a dis-

G.B.SHAW

agreeable pooch (named "Moonbeam"), but she swept into the vehicle and commanded, "The Empire Theatre, my man, and no nonsense." The dog, never housebroken, misbehaved en route, and the driver gave Mrs. Campbell a furious "I-told-you-so" look as she descended. "Don't blame Moonbeam," she informed him loftily. "*I* did it."

Minnie Maddern Fiske, the American star whose mere name was enough to bring tears of adoration into the eyes of the late Mr. Woollcott, did not take the success of younger rivals too gracefully. Standing in the wings one day with her young niece, Emily Stevens, while Blanche Yurka rehearsed an emotional scene, Mrs. Fiske remarked in a most audible stage whisper, "My dear, I hope you will let this be a lesson to you. Act if you must, but never Yurk!" An impetuous playwright once burst into Mrs. Fiske's home, and accused her of mislaying the script of a priceless play he had submitted to her. "I never mislay plays," she told him. Then she rang for the butler and said, "James, it's cold in here. Put three more manuscripts on the fire."

An actress noted for her risqué lines opened in a new theatre. "They'll never hear her in that barn," said a critic. "The acoustics are terrible." "How nice," commented Ethel Barrymore. "Now she can be obscene but not heard." Later Miss Barrymore was told that the actress had acquired a new husband, and had made a full confession of her past life to him. "What honesty! What courage!" marveled the critic. "What a memory!" added Miss Barrymore.

Constance Bennett is generally considered the shrewdest business woman who ever starred on the screen. She has made almost

as much in outside ventures as she did when she was one of the highest-salaried actresses in Hollywood. "I don't know why Connie works so hard," said a friend. "After all, she can't take it with her." "If Connie can't take it with her," replied one of Miss Bennett's sisters grimly, "she won't go."

On a cool autumn evening in 1924, an English producer named Charlot presented a musical revue that had won enthusiastic approval in London. Blasé Broadway theatre-goers attended in a skeptical mood: they had seen English successes fall flat on their faces in New York many times before, and, besides, the names of the principal performers were unknown to them. A few hours later, however, they were throwing their hats in the air over two new stars, and indeed they never have stopped, for the stars were Beatrice Lillie and Gertrude Lawrence. As these two great performers moved on from one triumph to another that first season it was only natural that a certain tension and asperity should develop between them, and since both ladies had sharp tongues and ready wit, their little jibes began to be collectors' items in all the favorite haunts of café society. At one party Miss Lillie slipped on the highly polished marble floor, and sat down unexpectedly on a broken bottle. While more considerate guests rushed for iodine and adhesive tape, Miss Lawrence murmured, "At any costs, Bea always cuts a figure!" Later, when refreshments were passed, Miss Lillie retaliated by reminding the hostess, "Nothing for Miss Lawrence. You know she *nevah* eats this time of year." And when somebody estimated that Miss Lawrence's gown must have cost six hundred dollars, the future Lady Peel whispered, "That may be, but you can see for yourself that her heart isn't in it!"

A dull and conceited man-about-town accosted Miss Lillie at Condé Nast's house one evening and said loudly, "I believe you invited me to a party at your hotel last Wednesday." "That's quite possible," admitted Miss Lillie cheerfully. "Tell me: did you come?" Jules Glaenzer, head of Cartier's, boasted of the business his firm was doing. "That's nothing," Miss Lillie assured him. "You ought to see the business Gertie does behind me while I'm singing a number!"

Years later, Gertrude Lawrence scored her greatest triumph in *Lady in the Dark* but still had time to see that a brand-new star, Danny Kaye, did not get too much of the applause. While Kaye was taking a bow before the ecstatic first-night audience, Miss Lawrence muttered to the producer, Max Gordon, "You keep this theatre so hot, it has taken the polish off my nails." Her feud with Kaye ripened with the passing months. After one matinee, Moss Hart, the author of *Lady in the Dark,* rushed into her dressing room and cried, "Danny Kaye just told me that Rudolf Hess has landed in England!" "Oh," said Miss Lawrence coldly, "so you're still talking to Danny Kaye!"

Miriam Hopkins had an after-theatre date with Nancy Carroll a few years ago, and arrived almost an hour late. After a series of greetings and passionate embraces such as only two mutually suspicious stars can accomplish, Miss Hopkins gushed, "I'd have been here on time if I hadn't been waylaid in the lobby by about three hundred of those silly little autograph hunters. They're such a bother. *Do you remember, Nancy?"* In the last year of the war, Leonora Corbett eyed the expensive made-to-order Red Cross uniform of a lady who had recently co-starred with her and gasped, "Nobody told me this party was to be fancy dress." Joe Lewis' ex-wife, Martha Stewart, boasted that a gentleman friend had arms like piston rods, shoulders like freight cars, and the strength of a Diesel locomotive. "How interesting," Lewis heard another Copacabana queen murmur. "What track does he leave on?"

Inevitably, a discussion of this sort is bound to catch up with the one and only Tallulah Bankhead. It is this distinguished daughter of the South who inspired Publicist Richard Maney to remark, "The screen had just started to talk when Miss Bankhead interrupted in 1930." She is invariably polite, and seldom fails to ask visitors questions about their own pursuits. Unfortunately, however, she never gives them time to answer. Meeting a fellow Thespian who had been desperately ill for months, she commanded, "Tell me *all* about your sickness." "It really was pretty rugged," began the actor. "I was on the operating table for seven hours. . . ." "Stop being such a blasted hypochondriac," interrupted Tallulah. "I want to tell you about my new play." Eddie Foy, Jr., confided to Tallulah that he always had longed to be a cover boy. "Magazine or manhole?" she asked. After the first act of an important opening, the author, sensing failure, held his head in the wings. "Cheer up," roared Tallulah, clapping him resound-

ingly on the back. "After all, your four other recent plays were
flops too."

They say that Miss Bankhead once was lured to a sneak preview of a motion picture and told in advance that it had been
made by an independent producer. When the picture was over,
she is quoted as saying, "The one thing I can't understand is what
that producer had to be independent about." I have heard the
same sally credited to the comic Violinsky—but Miss Bankhead
is prettier. A friend left her at the Stork Club one evening for a
conference with a theatrical manager who had incurred her wrath
a few months earlier. Tallulah called after her, "If your teeth are
missing when you come out of that so-and-so's office, you'll know
who has them!"

I have saved for last the story of the luncheon conversation between Lynn Fontanne and her long-time friend and co-worker,
Estelle Winwood. The ladies had sheathed their daggers in deference to the absent Alfred Lunt. "Dear Alfred," mused Miss Fon-

tanne tenderly. "What he has meant to me through the years! I wonder what I would be doing today without him." "I'll tell you exactly, my pet," said Miss Winwood with sudden asperity. "You would be playing your mother, just as I am doing."

* * *

When an author has determined to be dissatisfied and depressed, there is nothing in the world that can make him change his mind. Take the case of the late George M. Cohan as an example. The last years of his life were embittered by the thought that the parade had passed him by, and that lines and devices for which people had cheered him in happier days were now regarded as "corny" and obvious. A succession of failures sharpened his resentment. Then came *Ah, Wilderness!* and a chance to star in a sure-fire hit. Cohan appeared in another author's play for the first time in years. The first-night audience gave him an ovation, and the critics sang his praises to the sky.

Was Cohan happy? He was not! When a friend said, "Well, George, this is something like again, isn't it?" Cohan shook his head dejectedly and grumbled, "Imagine my reciting lines by Eugene O'Neill! Why, he ought to be on the stage reciting lines by *me!*"

Irving Berlin made another classic remark—but he was only kidding. He had been turning out a string of smash hits, besides coining a fortune from the revival of his old stand-bys in pictures. Congratulated on his great run of luck, Berlin thought for a moment and then said, "Oh, I don't know, I've only sold 'Mandy' once this year!"

At one of the first performances of *Annie Get Your Gun*, Dick Rodgers, the producer, stood in the lobby during the intermission with Berlin, composer of the hit-studded score. Berlin moved away, and a stout lady standing nearby obviously recognized him. She nudged her husband, and Dick heard her say wonderingly, "Sam, to look at him who would think?"

* * *

Howard Cullman, the play backer, hired a new butler recently, named Jenkins, whose deportment on his first morning proclaimed him a gem. Cullman's clothes were laid out beautifully, breakfast was served in the best manner, and as he was leaving, Jenkins handed him his hat and neatly folded newspaper. There was a short flight of stairs to descend, and unfortunately, Cullman tripped over something on the top step. When he tripped again the following morning at the same spot, he became suspicious. The third morning he caught Jenkins red-handed, or red-footed, slyly preparing to trip him deliberately again.

Cullman figured that the butler needed a psychiatrist more than an employer, so he fired him. A week later, Dick Rodgers got Cullman on the telephone. "I've been interviewing a butler named Jenkins," he said. "He's given you as a reference." "He's a fine butler," Cullman answered him, "but I warn you: he'll trip you up. I think he's nuts." Rodgers laughed indulgently and hung up.

A few days later Rodgers met Cullman at the Ritz Grill. The composer had a black eye and a bruised lip. "You guessed it, Howard," he told Cullman. "I hired your butler."

*   *   *

A heart-warming chapter in the history of show business was written at the Bijou Theatre when the curtain rose for performance number 3,183 of *Life with Father*. In the audience sat most of the plutocrats who had had the foresight and good fortune to invest in this gold mine when it was "established in 1939" at a summer theatre in Maine. On the stage, Dorothy Stickney and Howard Lindsay returned in triumph to re-create their original roles. For this was the performance that shattered the all-time long-run record of Broadway.

Left in the shade were the previous record-holder, *Tobacco Road* (3,182) and the runners-up, *Abie's Irish Rose* (2,237), *Oklahoma!* (2,205) and *The Voice of the Turtle* (1,557). Left in the shade, too, were the experts of "Information Please," whose failure to reel off this list in its proper order enabled the gentleman who suggested the question to walk off with a $500 savings bond and all the trimmings.

There had been some hope of persuading co-author Russel Crouse to repeat for the great occasion an earlier triumph in the

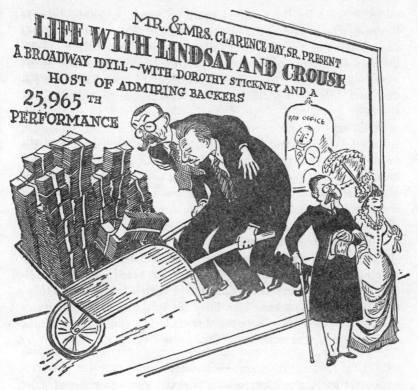

LIFE WITH LINDSAY AND CROUSE

MR. & MRS. CLARENCE DAY, SR., PRESENT

A BROADWAY IDYLL ~ WITH DOROTHY STICKNEY AND A

HOST OF ADMIRING BACKERS

25,965 TH
PERFORMANCE

BOX OFFICE

exacting role of Dr. Somers (it consists of the single line, "How do you do?") but he did not feel equal to it. "I played it once on the road," he explained, "just to see if there was a doctor in the Crouse."

Undone by the excitement of it all, Crouse took his bride to a Carolina luxury resort for a breather. When he announced that he was returning ten days later, Lindsay wired, "Why not remain for a few days more of well-earned rest?" Crouse answered, "I can't rest at fifty-eight dollars a day."

* * *

Broadway producers complain that it's futile for them to discover promising new talent; the moment a newcomer makes a hit, he (or she) is seduced by the siren song of a Hollywood scout

and vamooses for the Coast without so much as a thank-you to
the man who provided the opening chance. "To rub it in," added
one showman, "the film companies who steal our talent usually
demand four pairs of free seats for the openings so they won't
overlook any bets." Oscar Serlin, producer of both *Life with Father* and *Life with Mother,* had an experience that emphasizes
the point.

Serlin was casting a new play and wanted a fresh, unknown
beauty for the leading ingénue part. He was impressed with the
reading of a youngster whose only previous professional experience was a couple of walk-on extra roles in pictures a year before.
She hadn't had a job in months and was tearfully grateful when
she heard that Serlin would seriously consider her for a big part
on Broadway. "Come back tomorrow," he suggested. "Oh, I will,
I will," she promised happily.

The next morning he offered her a run-of-the-play contract. Her
reaction was not exactly what he had expected, however. Evidently she had been talking things over with a friend from Hollywood. "I don't think I can sign this," she told Serlin. "For heaven's
sake, why?" he asked. "Suppose this show is a smash hit and runs
for two years," she explained. *"I'd be stuck in it!"*

*   *   *

"THE GREATEST SHOW ON EARTH"

The annual tour of the mammoth Ringling Brothers and Barnum
and Bailey circus lasts forty weeks, and by the time the props
and the pachyderms are back in their winter quarters in Sarasota,
it has covered the entire country. The itinerary varies from year
to year, but the first month of the show is always spent at Madison
Square Garden. The circus is the one professional entertainment
unit that regards New York City as a try-out town. If its performance is running smoothly by the time it is under the big canvas
top, everybody is highly satisfied.

That the circus today is the most dazzling and original in its
history, and really lives up to its traditional modest billing as "the
greatest show on earth," is due to the uncanny showmanship of
one man: its producer and part owner, John Ringling North. John
knew that the lush days when *anything* was good enough had

gone out with the OPA. "If I'd continued to give them the same
tired acts we featured during the war years," he told me, "I'd
probably be selling apples in the lobby this minute." Instead, he
sailed for Europe, combed the Continent for novelty acts, and
came home with forty that truthfully could be labeled "First Time
in America." At least four of them practically stop the current
show and the beating of your own heart at the same time. I suggested that he get hold of one pair of acrobats who were about
to be deported, just so he could bill them as "The *Last* Time in
America." John thought I should stick to book publishing.

North joined the circus in 1916, when he was thirteen, and,
barring time off for Yale, military service, and an unexplained detour into Wall Street, he's been there ever since. His first job was
in the ticket seller's cage. Frugal farmers' wives would somehow

contrive to gather strapping sons up into their arms and brazenly
attempt to get them in for half price. It was John's job to bellow,
"Come, come, ladies! Let your menfolk walk!" The first time he
ever saw the circus from a plushy ringside box at the Garden was
the night he acted as host for three other future greats: Robert
Benchley, Charles MacArthur, and Ginger Rogers. They had
dined and wined copiously before their arrival, and the performance was in full swing when they were seated. Directly in front
of them a juggler was balancing flaming torches on his forehead,
nose, and chin, and manipulating a couple of Indian clubs at the
same time. One false move and he would have been enveloped
in flames. Benchley watched him in awe for a moment, then whispered, "And I can't even get a cup of coffee to my lips!"

Benchley also informed intimates (who didn't believe him, of
course) that a clown had confided to him, "Wait till Mr. North
hears about the act my brother Al developed! He got himself shot
out of a cannon." "How did he stand the shock?" asked Benchley.
"That's hard to say," admitted the clown. "We never found him."

For many years the head publicity man for the Ringling Brothers was Dexter Fellowes, who could toss off flowered phrases with
less effort than John L. Lewis. The young North accompanied
Fellowes one morning to the city desk of a St. Louis newspaper.
"Hulloo and happy tidings," cried Fellowes. "The circus is in
town!" The editor scowled and said, "What circus?" Fellowes
threw his hands in the air and demanded, "When they say the
band is playing 'God Save the King,' do you ask *what king?*"

For generations, one of the standard products offered for sale
by circus hawkers has been "pink lemonade." The origin of this
peculiar potion, according to North, goes back to the days when
one Peter Conklin was handling the refreshment concession for
Mabie's Mighty Circus in the South. One afternoon was such a
scorcher that lemonade sales reached unprecedented heights, and
Pete Conklin ran out of his principal ingredient: water. He rushed
into the dressing room of Fannie Jamieson, the lady trapeze
artiste, and, heedless of her protests, seized a tub of water in
which she had been soaking her bespangled red tights. "Aniline
dye never hurt anybody," pronounced Pete. To the reddened water he added a spot of tartaric acid and sugar, and promptly began shouting, "This way for the only lemonade in the world

guaranteed *pink*." The customers were intrigued, and, when nobody came down with even a mild convulsion, pink lemonade
became standard equipment in the refreshment tent.

Relegated to the sideshow in the circus today are the two goril-
las who once were the greatest attraction: Gargantua and Toto.
They are billed as "Mr. and Mrs. Gargantua," although keyhole
gossips swear that the widely advertised romance never got to
first base. One malicious report has it that Toto, like Gargantua,

turned out to be male; the other that Gargantua simply doesn't
give a damn. North admits that, in his effort to further the cause
of true love, he once ventured a step too close to Gargantua's cage
in Sarasota. The gorilla took a single swipe and came up with a
sizable section of Mr. North's shirt and necktie. He carefully
folded up the piece of shirt and guarded it fiercely; the necktie
he threw to Toto. North regards this as a distinct reflection on
the taste of himself and the Countess Mara.

A forty-week guarantee and the Ringling scale of salaries are
unheard of in the European circus world. So is the Ringling practice of paying all but the incidental expenses of the performers,
once New York is left behind. (On tour, the circus feeds over

1,400 people—more than two full-strength infantry battalions—
three times a day.) Foreign acts accordingly regard a Ringling
engagement as a fruition of their wildest dreams. One Belgian
artist, however, was compelled to tear up a contract after it had
been signed, to the mutual consternation of John Ringling North
and the Belgian. His act was a distinct novelty: it featured two
enormous pigs—one black, one white—which had been trained to
do a number of astounding tricks. For a finale, they played cornets
with their snouts, the tune being, appropriately enough, "Who's
Afraid of the Big Bad Wolf?" North felt that the act would give
his circus the one new comedy act he was seeking, but the U. S.
Government made the best laid plans of pigs and men gang very
aft a-gley. "There's hoof-and-mouth disease reported in Belgium,"
declared the authorities. "Don't put those pigs on a ship if you
want to preserve them. They will be slaughtered under the law
before the vessel touches American soil."

John North tried every known device to land his two talented
porkers in Florida, but the authorities were adamant. Finally he
wrote the Belgian trainer that the deal was canceled, but he was
so anxious to get him here that he offered to pay his passage and
full salary for a solid year if he would come and train a couple of
American pigs. "You can have the same act ready for the next
season," he pointed out. The Belgian replied in due course: he
would consider the offer, but he was not at all sure he'd accept it.
Somebody had warned him, it appears, that American pigs are
very stupid!

I told the pig story to Russel Crouse as a typical example of
what promoters of international amity and understanding are up
against. Russel was promptly reminded of a couple of pig stories
of his own. One of them concerned a pig owned by Bob Burns
who swallowed a stick of dynamite, rubbed against a building,
and caused an explosion that razed four city blocks. "It sure was
upsetting," mourned Burns. "For a couple of days we had a mighty
sick pig on our hands."

The other story involved Arthur Hornblow, the MGM producer.
A cozy farm idyl he was supervising called for the services of a
little black pig, and he found just what he was looking for in
Oswald, whose owner rented him to MGM for $35 a week. Half-
way through the picture, Oswald failed to appear for work. Horn-

blow phoned the pig's owner, who reported sorrowfully, "Oswald is a very unhappy pig. I don't think he'll work any longer for $35 a week." It developed that only a boost to $200 a week would salve Oswald's injured feelings. "Blast Oswald," shouted the enraged Mr. Hornblow. "We'll find another black pig."

This proved more difficult than anyone had anticipated. The studio finally impressed a snow-white pig into service, and carefully painted it black. By the end of the day, four stars, thirty-one extras, and Mr. Hornblow were smeared with black paint. The pig itself looked like the latest thing in polka dots.

Faced with open mutiny, and the loss of fourteen days' shooting on the script, Mr. Hornblow acted with the promptness and decision that have made his name a by-word in Culver City. He bought Oswald for $2,000 in cash.

* * *

One of the greatest "riots" ever staged in a theatre was a thoroughly rehearsed affair. *The Playboy of the Western World* was the show, and the sponsors wanted the première in Philadelphia to duplicate the furore that attended its unveiling in Dublin. Sure enough, the performers were greeted by a shower of reasonably decayed vegetables, duly reported by the press. Months later, it developed that the "incensed playgoers" were a band of well-trained supers from the cast of *Everywoman,* playing in the theatre next door.

They say that the plot was betrayed by an aggrieved Irish patriot named Schultz who insisted he should have been paid a bonus. He threw twice as many tomatoes as anybody else!

* * *

Marc Connelly, a slow and meticulous worker, had promised a producer a new play, but when a full year went by without further word, the producer waxed impatient and called Connelly on the telephone. "Where's that play?" he demanded, "I want to get my cast assembled." "It's coming along," Connelly assured him vaguely. "Just how much have you written?" demanded the producer. "Well," said Connelly, "you know it's to be in three acts and two intermissions. I've just finished the intermissions."

* * *

The day of the old vaudeville monologist has passed, probably forever, but the jokes that I heard at the Alhambra Theatre when I was a kid have the strangest habit of popping up on current radio programs.

Only the other evening, for instance, I heard the venerable gag of the New England grocery lad who visited New York for the first time and came back with a magnificent diamond ring on his finger. His employer examined it suspiciously and asked if it was a real diamond. "If it ain't," the clerk answered, "I sure been skunked out of six bits."

* * *

Another headliner told the familiar story of the village cop who came home very late and tried to slide into bed without waking his wife. She sat up, however, and said, "Dooley, would ye be runnin' to the drugstore and buyin' me an aspirin? Me head is splittin'." The cop got dressed in the dark and stumbled into the drugstore. While the druggist was wrapping up his purchase he said, "Say, aren't you Constable Dooley?" "That I am," said Dooley. "Sure now," said the clerk, "and what are you doing in that fireman's uniform?"

Finally, one of the biggest stars of all won a great laugh with that old, old classic of the henpecked husband who finally stood up to his wife while he was visiting Central Park Zoo. The amazed wife raised her umbrella with murder in her eye and the husband, reverting to type, broke into a wild run for safety. The keeper had just opened the door of the lion's cage and the poor husband jumped in, slammed the door shut, and took refuge behind one of the Kings of the Jungle. His wife waved her umbrella with futile rage on the outside of the cage and cried, "Come on out of there, you dirty coward."

* * *

The Magazine of Sigma Chi's memorial issue to George Ade included articles by some of America's greatest writers and became a collectors' item overnight.

By common consent, Ade's most memorable lines (in fact, they became shopworn clichés) were: "The cold gray dawn of the morning after," "He made me feel like thirty cents," and "Early to bed, early to rise, and you will meet very few prominent people." Ade also named the famous product "Cascarets" and coined the slogan, "They Work While You Sleep." Purdue's most loyal alumnus, he lost no opportunity to sing its praises. At one banquet he found himself surrounded by graduates of the Big Three. "Purdue?" frowned one paunchy son of Eli. "I don't believe I ever heard of that school." "Maybe you haven't," snapped Ade, "but I've got a lot of Yale men working for me."

Ade's most successful play was The College Widow. His mother came to see it and said, "George, do you really get more than five hundred dollars a week for doing that?" "Yes, Mother," answered Ade. "George," she said earnestly, "you keep right on fooling them."

THE REAL O'NEILL

Eugene O'Neill is not only generally recognized as the greatest playwright in America, but is certainly the only man of letters who is responsible for the success of a national chain of roadside restaurants. Those familiar, orange-roofed hostelries of Howard Johnson, whose twenty-nine flavors of ice cream tickle the palates of gourmets in thirty-nine states, owe their existence to Eugene O'Neill, and his play *Strange Interlude*.

Perhaps it would be more precise to say that Mr. Johnson's real angel was the capricious censor who suddenly declared that *Strange Interlude* could not be performed in Boston. The Theatre Guild promptly opened the play in nearby Quincy, and all of Boston trooped out to see it. Before or after the play, or both, the playgoers, with morals and appetites apparently unimpaired, tried to squeeze into what was then Howard Johnson's only res-

taurant, and came away to spread the fame of his chicken pies and banana splits.

Regular meals and schooling were no part of Eugene O'Neill's boyhood. His father was the matinee idol, James O'Neill, who spent most of his life acting in *The Count of Monte Cristo*. Gene was born in the old Cadillac Hotel, on Forty-third Street and Broadway, and spent his early years in theatre wings and theatrical boardinghouses instead of nurseries and kindergartens. In his one year at Princeton, the legend of his drinking prowess was born, although his exploits in that direction were dwarfed later by the F. Scott Fitzgerald set and relegated, in the words of Croswell Bowen, to "run of the ginmill." Gene insured his precipitate departure from Princeton by hurling a beer bottle through a window of the home of the division superintendent of the Pennsylvania Railroad. "They claim now it was Woodrow Wilson's window I broke," he says with some indignation. "That's not true. I had great respect for Mr. Wilson. In fact, he's the last politician I did have respect for."

Convinced that he was not cut out to be a scholar, O'Neill sailed for Spanish Honduras on a gold-mining expedition. He came home with no gold, but a fine case of tropical malarial fever. For recuperation he chose the unlikely haven of a waterfront saloon called Jimmy the Priest's. Years later it served as the setting for Act One of *Anna Christie*. His rent was three dollars a month. In 1911, he took to the sea again, in a Norwegian barque bound for Buenos Aires. An Argentine meat-packing plant, where he worked briefly, burned down a few days after he quit. "I didn't do it," says O'Neill, "but it was a good idea."

Eventually Gene sailed back to New Orleans, where he had an unexpected reunion with his father. The elder O'Neill, as usual, was starring in *Monte Cristo*—in an abbreviated version for the Orpheum vaudeville circuit—and with some misgivings added Gene to the company. Gene played a jailer. After his debut, he was informed by his father, "Sir, I am not satisfied with your performance." Gene answered, "Sir, I am not satisfied with your play."

Before he had written his first play, O'Neill had crammed enough hard living into twenty-five years to provide him with limitless themes and characters. A year in Professor Baker's famous playwriting class at Harvard helped him master technique, and a long association with the then lusty and precedent-defying Provincetown group served as his post-graduate course. His self-confidence was finally established by the unqualified endorsement of Henry Mencken and George Jean Nathan, whose *Smart Set* magazine at that time carried the combined prestige of the *New Yorker,* the *Atlantic Monthly,* and *Harper's Bazaar.* It was Nathan, too, who first brought *Beyond the Horizon* to the attention of a Broadway producer. O'Neill has never forgotten his debt of gratitude to Nathan, and listens respectfully to his advice to this very day. Some of it is good.

Beyond the Horizon, of course, won the Pulitzer Prize in 1920 (O'Neill won it again in 1922 with *Anna Christie* and in 1928 with *Strange Interlude*), but before it was produced, several managers shied away from it. One, George Tyler, wouldn't even read it. "Plays by actors' sons never are any good," he told O'Neill. After the opening performance, James O'Neill asked his son, "Are you trying to send the audience home to commit suicide?" Once its success had been established, however, Eugene O'Neill's position was secure. Every producer courted him, and his father asserted proudly, "I always knew he had it in him."

Basically, Eugene O'Neill is the serious and brooding genius reflected in his writings, but when he smiles the entire room is illuminated. His humor often leans distinctly to Minsky, and he can chant a scandalous sea ballad with the best of them.

O'Neill's primary interest in the theatre is neither money, fame, nor the approval of Broadway critics and playgoers. He writes plays because he cannot help it. They burn in his mind, and he pours them out on paper, regardless of their commercial appeal or their length. He never has written a play with any particular star in mind—in fact, he prefers to work with co-operatively obscure players. "They try to play the characters I have created," he says, "not to make my characters fit their own personalities." He refuses flatly to make cuts in his scripts unless he himself thinks they are indicated. When a player in *The Iceman Cometh* complained that one of his speeches was too long, and threatened to cut it on the opening night, O'Neill warned him grimly, "Leave out one line, and the curtain will never go up for a second performance."

At the tryout of *Ah, Wilderness!* the curtain fell so late that the stagehands demanded overtime. George M. Cohan, the star, furthermore, was introducing new business and mannerisms to prolong matters further at every performance. Everybody connected with the Theatre Guild endeavored in vain to persuade O'Neill to wield his blue pencil. Finally, Russel Crouse, publicity representative at the time, volunteered to try. O'Neill liked Crouse and let him make his plea without interruption. "I'll think about what you've said," he promised. The next morning he phoned Crouse and said, "You'll be happy to learn I've cut out fifteen minutes." Crouse scarcely could believe his ears. "When? How?" he sputtered. "I'll be right over to get the changes!" "There aren't any changes in the *text*," O'Neill assured him, "but you know, we've been playing this thing in four acts. I've decided to cut out the third intermission."

O'Neill, like all other successful playwrights, has been plagued by occasional and utterly unwarranted plagiarism suits. In one of them the decisive factor was the uncut (or "unopened," to use the term experts insist is correct) pages of a novel. When *Strange Interlude* was the reigning success of the Broadway season, the inevitable crackpot appeared to charge it was stolen from her privately printed masterpiece. O'Neill protested bitterly that he never had heard of either the lady or her novel, but she produced a statement in court which showed she had mailed a copy to Producer Lawrence Langner, of the Theatre Guild.

Langner, on the witness stand, had a sudden inspiration. "Limited editions usually are numbered," he said. "What was the number of the copy you sent me?" "Number fifteen," proclaimed the lady triumphantly, "and I have the record here to prove it." Langner asked for a recess, rushed down to his house, and returned with Copy Number Fifteen of the book—with all the pages uncut. The judge threw the case out of court.

Eugene O'Neill recalls one critic whose suggestion he followed without question. The day after *The Hairy Ape* opened in New York, an old sailor friend from the days when he roistered on the waterfront wrote him, "I liked the show a lot, but for God's sake tell that Number Four stoker to stop leaning his prat against that red-hot furnace."

Someday the world will know more about the inner thoughts of its greatest living playwright. O'Neill has written the story of himself and his heritage in a play called *The Long Day's Voyage into the Night*. It is completed, but locked away in a safe, where it will remain, unopened, until twenty-five years after his death.

*   *   *

To Jed Harris, unpredictable, headstrong producer of such theatrical landmarks as *Broadway, The Front Page,* and more recently, *Our Town* and *The Heiress,* befell an experience recently that might be credited, with no tax on the imagination, to a score of other luminaries of the stage, screen, or literary world.

Harris became convinced that his hearing was defective, hied himself to the country's foremost ear specialist, and demanded an immediate examination.

The specialist sat him down in an office chair, hauled an ornate gold timepiece out of his pocket, and held it against Harris's ear. "Can you hear this ticking, my boy?" he asked. "Of course," said Harris impatiently.

The specialist walked to the doorway of his sanctum and held up the watch again.

"Can you hear the ticking now?" he demanded.

Harris concentrated a moment, and answered, "Yes. Very clearly."

The specialist now walked into the next room, and fully twenty

paces from his patient, asked for the third time, "Can you hear my watch now?" Harris knitted his brow, closed his eyes, and was silent for a moment. Then he said, "Yes, Doctor, I hear the ticking plainly."

The ear specialist put the watch back in his pocket, nodded cheerfully, and held out a hand to his patient. "Mr. Harris," he said, "there is absolutely nothing the matter with your hearing. You just don't listen."

* * *

Louis Sobol is authority for the story that Miss Beatrice Lillie toyed with the notion of vacationing in Bermuda after her last play ended its run. She contacted the owner of an estate there and asked for particulars by mail. The owner answered, "My place is on a small island, so you will need my boatman to ferry you to Hamilton and back. The estate rents for $25,000, but with the boatman's services included, the price will be $30,000." Miss Lillie cabled, "Kindly rush photograph of the boatman."

* * *

From Moss Hart's croquet court, where there is no rest for the wicket, there is a panoramic view of the beautiful farmland of Bucks County, Pennsylvania, still verdant in the afternoon sun, but tilled no longer, alas, by the farmers who were born there. Nationally famous writers and antique dealers have bought out the sons of the soil with beads (from Cartier's) and wampum (certified).

Within a few miles of the Fields of Moss are the rustic retreats of Squires Oscar Hammerstein, George S. Kaufman, Howard Lindsay, Jo Davidson, Kenyon Nicholson, Budd Schulberg, Glenway Wescott, and Richard Pratt. They are the new middlemen of the region; producers and publishers send them royalties which they promptly turn over to the antique dealers.

One of these dealers, however, has just announced his intention of backing an elaborate musical comedy next season. Dispossessed farmers, biding their time in temporary lodgings in nearby Doylestown and Flemington, profess to see in this a definite turn

in the tide. From here in, they feel, it is only a matter of time before the great write fathers go back where they came from, and allow the natives to return. They admit it will be fun to regain their ancestral seats—even if they no longer can recognize them. As one of them (who reads old joke books in his spare time) put it, "Gimme a couple weeks to put the outhouse back out, and the dining room table back in, and the place'll be as good as it ever was."

Moss usually makes the trip from New York in something less than two hours, winging through the traffic snarls of Route 29 with the aplomb and unconcern of an experienced chauffeur. In his early days at the wheel, he admits, he was somewhat less sure of himself and, in fact, had to post a ten-dollar reward for anybody who would ride with him.

George Kaufman, against his better judgment, once consented to climb into the front seat with him for a drive to the home of the late Alexander Woollcott in Katonah. Moss swung the car boldly out of the garage, catching a vegetable truck in dead center. For a moment George thought it was raining oranges and rhubarb. He was gentle and understanding about it, and even the Italian driver didn't send a bill for damages until the following morning. Silently, the fruit was piled back into the truck, and Moss started the car again, proceeding without incident until he smacked the traffic island at the next corner. They reached their destination two hours late with a "no parking here" sign cleverly caught in the right rear fender.

When it came time to drive home, Mr. Kaufman thoughtfully decided to take the train, and Robert Sherwood assumed the role of sacrificial goat. This time the playful Moss drove head-on into two mildly astonished motorcycle cops who were passing the time of day in the middle of the empty road. Moss was cannily proceeding at the rate of eight miles an hour, so the only injury the cops suffered was to their dignity. One of them approached Moss with ominous restraint and asked, "Would you mind telling me your name?" "Moss Hart." "And your occupation?" "I am a writer." "And the gentleman with you?" "That is Robert Sherwood." "And his occupation?" "He's a writer, too."

The cop turned triumphantly to his sidekick. "I told you," he said, "they were a couple of nuts!" Then he added wearily to Hart, "Drive on, young fellow—but try to remember that motorcycle cops aren't in season this month."

*   *   *

When it comes to worrying about the gravity of temporary aches and bruises, Playwright George Kaufman takes a back seat for nobody. Wielding a croquet mallet with his customary deadly accuracy one Sunday, he suddenly suffered a spell of dizziness, and could scarcely wait for his doctor's office to open at nine o'clock the next morning, that he might be tapped and examined from head to toe.

The doctor took him over to the cardiograph machine, and George did a bit of major-league pacing while the results were being studied. Finally the doctor reappeared from his sanctum and spread the charts on the desk before him. He cleared his throat nervously and said, "George, there is something I might as well tell you. You'll find it out sooner or later anyhow."

Kaufman clutched the corner of the desk until his knuckles were

white and told himself, "This is it. Be brave! Take it like a man."
"The fact is," continued the doctor, "I'm going to be married."

❋ ❋ ❋

Herbert Bayard Swope, who dines at hours that seem very peculiar to his more rational friends, called George Kaufman one
evening at 9:30 and inquired, "What are you doing for dinner
tonight?" Kaufman told him, "I'm digesting it." A self-made millionaire boasted, "I was born into the world without a single
penny." Kaufman spoiled the effect to a considerable extent by
murmuring, "When I was born, I owed twelve dollars." Referring
to a belligerent writer, given to speeches on the plight of the
world, Kaufman remarked, "He's in the chips now—but most of
them seem to have stayed on his shoulders."

You don't hear much these days about the Lucy Stone League, but there was a time when the papers were full of its activities. Lucy Stone was a determined young lady who thought it was degrading for a woman to take the name of her husband when she was married, so she formed a league of women who agreed with her and insisted on keeping their maiden names although they sometimes had six or seven children, and even grandchildren. It was George Kaufman who supplied them with the motto: "A Lucy Stone gathers no boss." When Moss Hart announced proudly, "My son Christopher is three weeks old today," George said, "Now you're sure of your cut in the picture rights."

Finally, Max Gordon visited the Kaufman estate and noted some new wrought-iron furniture set under the trees. "Aren't those pieces new?" asked Gordon. "Yes, indeed," Kaufman assured him. "We picked them up from the Torquemada Estate."

❊ ❊ ❊

Mr. Kaufman would make the ideal hero for a little story I'd like to write one day. The role calls for just such a wit, who is discovered walking innocently down Fifty-second Street, where he suddenly comes upon two famous columnists rolling in the gutter, locked in mortal combat. "For goodness' sake," he says to one of the enchanted bystanders, "why are these two great men beating each other's brains out?" "You ought to know," answers the bystander. "They are fighting over which one of them originated a story they heard you tell at dinner last night."

❊ ❊ ❊

When that great comedian, W. C. Fields, died, everybody began digging up stories about him. By common consent, one of the funniest concerned the time he was acting as host to a dinner party of a score of the most distinguished ladies and gentlemen in Hollywood. In the middle of the dinner his secretary burst in upon him and said, "I hate to bother you, Mr. Fields, but the head of your studio is on the phone for the eighth time in the past three hours and now says he simply must talk to you immediately about a matter of the very greatest importance." Fields'

reply will go down in history. "Give him an evasive answer," he
thundered. "Tell him to — himself."

This secretary was one of a long series, both male and female,
who tried to satisfy their employer's exacting and capricious demands. After firing one young gentleman Fields explained, "That
fellow is so dumb he can't find his backside with both hands."
About another one he declared, "Talk about nitwits. When I said
hello to this idiot, he couldn't even think of anything to answer."

Fields, fiercely proud of his ability to hold his liquor, rashly challenged Mark Hellinger to a brandy-drinking bout. "I got Mark so
plastered," he boasted forty-eight hours later, "it took three bell-
hops to put me to bed."

Just a few days before he died, Fields reminded his doctor, "If
they insist upon having an epitaph for me, don't forget the one I
made up several years ago: 'On the whole, I'd rather be in
Philadelphia.'"

* * *

Billy Rose remembers one time when W. C. Fields' nose was
put slightly out of joint. The man who did it was the inimitable Joe
Frisco. The night the Ziegfeld *Follies* of 1927 opened in New York,
Frisco did his own number and then was supposed to introduce
Fields. The latter waited in the wings ready to make his entrance
on a burst of applause. Instead of introducing Fields, however,
Frisco pulled a piece of paper out of his pocket and said in an
excited voice, "I have just learned that Charles Lindbergh is in
the audience." This was just after Lindbergh had flown the Atlantic and the crowd went wild. After several minutes of pandemonium, Frisco held up his hand for quiet and said, "I guess I
made a mistake. It must be somebody who looked like him. Anyhow, the next act will be W. C. Fields."

* * *

Joe Frisco has had his ups and downs in the theatre. He remembers one period when he was so far down that he had to eat a
performing parrot. "What did it taste like?" asked his friend
George Jessel. Frisco answered, "A little like t-t-t-turkey, g-g-g-

goose, d-d-d-duck. . . . You know, that p-p-p-parrot could imitate anything."

When Frisco *is* in the big money, he shows a positive genius for spending it twice as fast as he makes it. "Use your bean," counseled his agent. "Put away ten thousand dollars a year for the next ten years, and you'll have a hundred thousand in the bank. When the next depression hits us, you'll be sitting pretty." "Not me," scoffed Frisco. "With m-m-m-my luck, we wouldn't have any next depression, and there I'd be s-s-stuck with a hundred thousand bucks."

✻   ✻   ✻

The Comic Supplement

PRACTICAL JOKERS

Banana peels in the path of fat pedestrians and thumb tacks on the chairs of pompous teachers are the most elementary forms of the practical joke—and the harder the unfortunate pedestrian falls, or the higher the teacher bounces, the more uncontrolled is the resultant hilarity. The lengths to which some of the most famous people in the world have gone to develop practical jokes are inexplicable.

The late President Roosevelt got a laugh out of pulling a chair from under a member of his cabinet at a crucial moment in the country's history. King Edward VII, mistaken for a simple farmer by a Dutch peasant, kept an important conclave at The Hague waiting five hours while he played out the role to his heart's content in the peasant's cottage. One of the most important and highest-paid executives in Hollywood suspended all activities at his studio for four days in order to introduce a well-coached extra to one of his hated rivals as a famous senator bent on exposing the film world, and watch the rival make a blithering fool of himself in a series of elaborate receptions, sight-seeing tours, and banquets. Colonel Lindbergh endangered the lives of scores of correspondents by landing his plane in such a way as to splatter the lot of them with mud.

For sheer originality in practical jokes, a zany named Hugh Troy takes the cake. Troy's career began innocently enough when he bought a bench identical with the ones that have adorned the paths in Central Park, New York, for generations, and sneaked it into the park when no cop was looking. When he attempted to carry it out with him, he was arrested for stealing city property, but confounded the cop and the police lieutenant by producing a bill of sale that proved the bench was actually his. Troy made the mistake of trying the same trick in Prospect Park the next night. The police were laying for him this time and gave him three days in the hoosegow for "disturbing the peace."

Troy next bought twenty dollars' worth of fake jewelry at neighborhood five-and-tens and spent hours taking out the vari-colored bits of glass that passed for diamonds, rubies, and emeralds. He gathered all of them into a small valise, and sauntered up Fifth Avenue. Directly in front of the old Tiffany's he released the catch on the valise. A cascade of "precious stones" spilled out on the pavement, and it took police reserves a full half hour to quell the resultant stampede.

Troy's third exploit was to dress up a squad of accomplices as workmen and dig a two-foot-wide trench across Thirty-fourth Street. The police obligingly helped him hang red lanterns at the edge of the ditch, and diverted traffic for two days before they

discovered the whole thing was a hoax. Oxford students dupli-
cated this project with signal success at the busiest crossing in
Regent Street, London, the following season.

Troy's farewell Manhattan appearance was made in the Wall
Street district. He parked an ancient model-T jalopy in front of
the Sub-Treasury Building and surreptitiously approached a score

of idle taxicab drivers, one by one. To all of them he gave identical
instructions: "When you see me start that old Ford over there, just
follow me." The result was a strange procession, led by Troy, with
twenty cursing cab drivers trying to jockey their way into line
directly behind him. A half mile up Broadway, just below City
Hall, a traffic cop stepped into the picture and halted the parade.
At this point, Troy deemed it wise from a standpoint of health to
transfer his interesting activities to other climes, and I lost track of
him. The Oxford students that he launched on a bright career,
incidentally, were heard from once more after their Regent Street
coup. The late Lloyd George addressed a university assemblage
from the rear platform of a special train in the Oxford station. At
a given signal, he closed in a rare burst of eloquence and ap-

preciative farewells, and the train pulled out. The jolly students, however, had uncoupled the last car, and as the train tooted away, Mr. George was left bowing repeatedly at the station, and wondering what had gone wrong.

Ben Hecht once found several hundred copies of a technical book on a remainder counter. The book was over a thousand pages long, hopelessly dull, and carried no index. Hecht mailed copies anonymously to his most egotistical friends, with a typed note inside that read, "You will be amused, although possibly slightly offended, by the references to you in this volume." The hunt, they say, went on for days.

Ted Geisel, whose inspired drawings bear the pseudonym of "Dr. Seuss," had a classmate at Dartmouth whose consuming fault was an insistence on being "up" on the very latest things in music, literature, and art. One day Geisel burst in on him and shouted, "Who do you think is in town? It's Wimperdinck, the great Belgian surrealist! Surely you know his work!" "Of course I know his work," said the friend impatiently. That was exactly what Geisel was waiting for. He planned a big meeting at Wimperdinck's studio. En route, he remarked, "By the way, Wimperdinck has an advanced case of leprosy, but you're in no danger if you don't let him touch you. I've had a line painted down the middle of the studio, and Wimperdinck has strict instructions to stay on his side." The man who portrayed the role of Wimperdinck had been decorated in hues that were wondrous to behold. His face had been painted a bilious green, with huge red splotches at regular intervals. The friend blanched when he saw him, and screamed bloody murder when Wimperdinck, crying, "My benefactor! My discoverer!" hurdled the white line and enfolded him in a bearlike embrace. "It was a lesson that made a better man of him," says Geisel, the philosopher.

A shoddy trick was played on a prospective benedict in Chicago recently. He passed out cold at his bachelor party. When he came to, his right arm was in a cast. He had broken it, they told him, in a battle royal. The poor victim spent his entire honeymoon with a perfectly good arm in a tight cast.

Joe Cook's Lake Hopatcong home was a whole nest of practical jokes, which had the added virtue of hurting nobody. Guests were greeted at the door by a dignified butler in full livery, who took their hats and coats and promptly threw them out the window (into a hidden room beyond). There was a beautiful fish mounted on a wall in the living room. The engraved plaque read: "This fish was purchased at the Washington Market on July 8, 1934." The first hole of the private golf course was so arranged that no matter how a ball was hit, the player made the hole in one. The balls themselves were plucked from a "golf tree" that stood next to the first tee. After the game, Cook took his guests to "Schultz's," in the cellar, for a drink. "Schultz has a rival named Pestramo," Cook would whisper. "For God's sake, don't mention Pestramo in Schultz's presence, or I won't answer for the consequences." After a round at Schultz's, Cook would say, "It's only fair that we give Pestramo a little patronage." When the guests filed into Pestramo's across the road, it didn't take them long to discover that "Schultz" and "Pestramo" were one and the same man in different make-ups. The entire estate was peopled with old vaudeville pals of Cook's who were temporarily down on their luck.

A quiet block in Greenwich Village will never be the same since one determined jokester invaded it last summer. He appeared first with two accomplices at Number Nine and said, "We've come for that parlor sofa." While the servant watched in silence, the sofa was carried from Number Nine and taken to Number Thirty-four. "We're delivering that parlor sofa," he explained—and left it standing in the hallway. By noon, a considerable amount of heavy furniture had been shifted hither and yon, and a great deal of explaining was necessary before order was restored. The same genius once upset a dinner party by sliding an imitation pearl into an oyster on his plate. "What luck," he cried. "A pearl! And it's a whopper too!" The excited hostess pointed out that it was her house and her oyster, and that the pearl, therefore, belonged to her. The guest said nothing doing. The jest ended in a general free-for-all, with the hostess in hysterics on the chaise-longue.

I particularly like a story that Earl Wilson and Morton Downey tell about their pal Ted Husing. They passed him in a radio broadcasting booth one evening, where he was giving a long script his customary impassioned interpretation. Realizing that he couldn't interrupt his broadcast, they sneaked up behind him, took off his shirt, pants, shoes, and socks, and left him there in his underwear. "Be sure to drop in at Studio C," they told a group

of sightseers on the way out. "Husing is giving one of his most
unusual performances."

There have been occasions where practical jokes backfired on
their perpetrators. When John Galsworthy was visiting California,
some imbeciles faked a dinner invitation to him from Governor
Hiram Johnson. Galsworthy arrived at the appointed hour. The
resourceful Governor, sensing the situation, whipped up a half
dozen other important guests in jigtime, and the unsuspecting
Galsworthy reported later that this was one of the most rewarding
evenings of his whole stay in America. Another group invited Elsa
Maxwell to a banquet, but didn't tell her she was the only female
in the party. A hundred men, dressed in tails and white ties, were
ready to chortle at Miss Maxwell's discomfiture, but she had gotten wind of the plan, and turned the tables completely by appearing herself in masculine full dress. One Park Avenue hoax
ended in unexpected tragedy. Invitations to a swanky cocktail
soirée were mailed to a hundred guests by a group who counter-

feited the signature of a wealthy but tight-fisted socialite. When the guests arrived, they had some trouble getting into the apartment. The involuntary hostess, utterly unaware of the trick being played upon her, had died peacefully in her sleep a few hours before. The ringleaders of that escapade had some tall explaining to do to the authorities.

The average, garden variety of practical joker is an easy enough fellow to understand and tolerate. The ones who baffle you are the pranksters who go in for more elaborate game, who seem to figure that no amount of personal inconvenience, time, or expense is too great for the sake of one little laugh. A study of their antics may convince you that the decline of Western civilization hasn't very much further to go. Take the case of the late Al Boasberg, for instance.

Boasberg drew down a huge salary as a motion-picture and radio writer. Some of the funniest Marx Brothers gags were created by him. His happiness, however, depended upon the number of hoaxes he could put over on his long-suffering associates. One day he stepped outside his circle with painful results.

There was a massive and ungainly portico on his Hollywood house and he engaged a workman to remove it. When he arrived home two days later, most of the portico had already disappeared.

"Hello, there," called Boasberg cheerfully. "When are you going to start on *my* portico?" The workman paled slightly and said, "What do you mean? This *is* your portico. I'm almost finished with it." "There's some mistake, I'm sure," protested Boasberg gravely. "I distinctly told you Number 2412 Cambridge Drive. This is Number 2312. I don't think the owner of this house is going to like your chopping it up a bit."

The poor carpenter was appalled. "This is terrible," he muttered. "I coulda sworn you said 2312." He dropped his tools and went galloping into the house to make his peace with the unknown owner. Boasberg's joy was short-lived. The proletarian's sense of humor was unfortunately unequal to the occasion, and when he discovered the truth, he promptly gave Boasberg two beautiful black eyes.

Boasberg's father was a lovable soul whose passion was auction sales. The junk he brought home defies description. One of his purchases was a hideous Victorian wall mirror that he picked up

"practically for nothing—only seventy dollars." Two nights later Boasberg brought a stranger to the house for dinner. When his eyes fell on the mirror he let out a cry of surprise. "It's a Salzburg mirror! Where on earth did you get it, Al?" "It's mine," declared the father excitedly. "Salzburg you say? What's it worth?" "That's hard to say," declared the stranger. "They're so scarce nowadays. However, I'd be happy to give you twelve hundred dollars for it right now." The exultant father was about to close the deal when Al crushed him with a firm "I should say not. Only twelve hundred dollars for a genuine Salzburg mirror! Preposterous!"

A week went by. The Boasbergs' next guest was a distinguished-looking woman who didn't notice the Salzburg mirror until she was leaving the house. *Her* offer was five thousand dollars, and when Al turned that down too the father was beside himself. Both of these visitors, of course, were studio extras who had been coached very carefully by Boasberg. For the *pièce de résistance* he introduced a gray-haired gentleman with a Vandyke beard, dressed in frock coat and striped pants. It developed that the one thing in the world he was seeking for the London Museum was a Salzburg mirror. "Only two known specimens in the world, you know. I'd give fifteen thousand dollars for one this minute." "I got one, I got one," shrieked the father, and dragged out his monstrosity with trembling hands. "It's genuine, all right," decided the expert. "My offer stands!" At this point, Boasberg said "no" once too often, for his poor father suffered a heart stroke and was in the hospital for three months.

An equally famous Hollywood practical joker is Gene Fowler. The owner of the old *Morning Telegraph* made the mistake of appointing him editor one day, and before nightfall Fowler had added two dozen faithful cronies to the staff, each at five hundred dollars a week. The enraged proprietor naturally threw them all out—Fowler the farthest. Gene went up to the old New York Athletic Club, then located on Fifty-ninth Street and Sixth Avenue, to drown his sorrows with Sports Editor Bill McGeehan. Their tenth-story room fronted on Central Park; across the way, a flock of tame ducks paddled and quacked happily in the Park pond. After the ninth or tenth round of highballs it seemed the most natural thing in the world to Gene and Bill to stage an impromptu duck shoot, and soon terrified pedestrians on Fifty-ninth Street heard a rapid volley of shots over their heads. The hunters didn't bring down a single duck, but they did manage to wing a Mr. Alonzo Swiggle, of Freeport, Long Island. They also found themselves in earnest conversation with the forces of law and order.

Fowler once served a spell as press agent for Promoter Tex Rickard. When it came to staging championship boxing bouts, Rickard had few superiors, but he was a pigeon for any crazy

inventor who managed to corner him. Fowler was in the office
the day a long-haired individual came up to demonstrate a brand-
new fire extinguisher. All he needed was fifty thousand dollars to
put every other extinguisher out of business. While he was out-
lining his financial setup to Rickard, enthralled as usual, Fowler
sneaked outside, emptied the extinguisher, and filled it with gasoline. Then the party repaired to the Madison Square arena for a
demonstration. Fowler persuaded Rickard to watch with him
from the balcony. A small blaze was started, and the confident
inventor turned his extinguisher on it. They had to sound two
alarms before the fire was put under control, but Fowler is still
convinced that he saved Rickard fifty thousand dollars by his
master-minding.

Practical jokers almost ruined a nobby testimonial dinner in
honor of Elsie Janis and her proud mother, Mrs. Bierbower. They
rang in a phony waiter named Vince Barnett, who carried out his
assignment so successfully that he actually continued with the
same sort of thing as a profession. The first time Barnett passed
Mrs. Bierbower, he spilled a plate of soup over her, and further
enraged her by whispering in her ear, "Serves you right, you old
battle-ax." They barely had succeeded in calming her down
when Barnett came along again. This time he whispered, "You're
using the wrong fork, you goon. Your manners are positively worse
than your daughter's." Mrs. Bierbower called for her wraps, and
was halfway down the stairs before they succeeded in convincing
her that it was a put-up job. She showed she was a good sport
by shaking hands with Barnett, and engaging him later to practice similar foolery at her own residence.

The same pair that launched Barnett on his unique career ex-
ercised their wits to better advantage many years later. Adolf
Hitler had initiated his terror inside Germany, and decent people
all over the world were registering their protest. One well-known
writer, however, always prompt to voice his love for democracy
when it didn't inconvenience him, picked this moment to book
passage on the Nazi steamship *Europa*. Waiting for another boat,
he explained lamely, would hold him up three full days. "We give
you our word," his two erstwhile friends told him, "that if you sail
on the *Europa*, we'll wait until you're in mid-ocean and send you
a wireless reading 'Never mind Göring and Goebbels. It's H. we're

after!'" The writer knew they weren't fooling this time. He changed his booking to the *Aquitania*.

In Chicago there lived a man who raved so continuously about his wonderful dog "Inky" that his friends determined to silence him at any cost. One of his boasts was that he never had to go home to take his dog for an airing. "I just call my number on the phone," he explained. "When Inky hears the ring, he knows what it means. He nudges the door open, and goes out by himself." After several demonstrations, one of the man's associates sneaked up to his house, and, the next time the phone rang, picked up the receiver and yelled, "Woof, woof, woof!" Then he wired: "That blasted dog of yours is even smarter than you said he was." That did it!

One of the most successful literary hoaxes of the year was pulled by two G.I.s with time on their hands in Australia, with the editor of a typical hoity-toity poetry magazine as the victim. He printed a sheaf of free-verse by a new genius with a long dissertation on its nuances and hidden meanings. Then the news came out that the "free-verse" was a word-for-word transcript of a particularly dull pamphlet from the Department of Agriculture on the development of the soy-bean industry. Another tempest in the literary teapot was caused by Jack Baragwanath, mining engineer, bon vivant, and husband of Neysa McMein, when he wrote up his adventures under the title of *Pay Streak*. Baragwanath had a separate dedication page printed up for every one of his friends, and tipped into the volume he sent them. Results were varied. Edna Ferber, for instance, was deeply flattered to know that she was the inspiration of the entire volume—until she discovered the identical dedicatory message addressed to George Kaufman in *his* copy. One famous newspaper magnate was horrified to discover that *Pay Streak* was dedicated to him—"the most colossal jackass in New York." He threatened to sue, but Nelson Doubleday, the publisher, in on the joke, reminded him that the resultant publicity, even if he won his case, might not be altogether desirable. His next thought was to buy up the entire edition. Doubleday thought that was possible. "How many copies did you print?" he demanded. "A hundred and fifty thousand," said Doubleday blandly. They told him it all was a joke just in time to prevent his suffering a stroke of apoplexy.

The two literary lights who love a practical joke above all others probably are Henry Mencken and George Jean Nathan. One day when they were editing the *American Mercury,* they heard Alfred Knopf invite Joseph Hergesheimer over to New York for a gala party to celebrate the publication of his novel, *Balisand.* The night before the party they entertained him at his hotel, the Algonquin. At dinner they regaled him with tales of a terrific new cocktail they had invented. "One of them," said Mencken, "sends an ordinary man straight under the table." "The only man who tried two," added Nathan, "was unconscious for days." They were aware of Hergesheimer's pride in his drinking capacity, and were not at all surprised when he demanded a sample of this incredible new concoction. Only Hergesheimer wouldn't stop at two. *He* drank three. The drinks were absolutely harmless, but Mencken and Nathan actually convinced Hergesheimer that he was dead drunk. They convoyed him to his room, undressed him, put him to bed, and made him promise not to stir until morning. After he

had gone to sleep, they sneaked back into his room and upset it completely. As a crowning touch, they festooned his pants around the chandelier. Then they woke him up. "Joe," they chorused reproachfully, "you promised you wouldn't stir. Now look what you've done."

Hergesheimer gazed in wonder at the wreckage around him. "Honest, fellows, I didn't know——" he began. "That's not the worst of it," said Mencken. "What do you mean by insulting the phone operator of a respectable hotel? She's practically hysterical. There are two cops downstairs waiting to drag you to the station house. Fine publicity for a man in your position!"

"Oh, Lord," groaned Hergesheimer. "What will Knopf say! And my book coming out tomorrow too."

"Luckily for you," broke in George Nathan, "we are your friends. We can get you out by the fire-escape and aboard the four A.M. train for Philadelphia before the police get wise to you."

That explains why, on the eve of publication of one of his most successful books, Joseph Hergesheimer, after thanking his friends profusely, dressed in the dark, climbed down twelve flights of the Algonquin fire-escape, and sneaked home to Philadelphia aboard the milk train at 4 A.M. That explains why, also, the first time that he heard George Gershwin's song, "I Got Plenty of Nothin'," he is reported to have said with great feeling, "Humph! What he *should* have written was 'I Got Plenty of Nathan!'"

* * *

On from Grand Rapids for his semi-annual fling in New York, the general manager of one of the country's biggest manufacturers of dining-room sets registered at the Waldorf and sallied forth in search of adventure. He found it right in the lobby in the form of a stunning and exotic young lady.

He smiled at her. She smiled back. When it developed that she was a foreigner who obviously couldn't even understand a word of English, let alone speak it, our hero took a piece of notepaper and rapidly drew upon it a sketch of a taxicab. The lady nodded. A few minutes later they were seated at a table in the Stork Club. On another piece of paper he drew a picture of a couple dancing. She nodded again. She was a wonderful dancer too! For what happened next we quote a paragraph from a letter he sent to his brother the next day. "When we got back to our table, I sure was feeling fine. Suddenly this beauty grabbed my pad from me and did a little drawing herself. It was a picture of a beautiful Louis XIV bed. Now what I'd like you to explain, Walter, is this. How on earth do you think that dame knew I was in the furniture business?"

* * *

A lady turned up at a Grand Central Station ticket window with a boy in tow and demanded a ticket and a half for Boston. The agent leaned out of his booth and studied the boy for a moment. "You can't get by with a half-ticket for that boy," he proclaimed. "He's wearing long pants!" "Well, if that's your criterion," said the lady coldly, "*I* ought to ride for nothing!"

* * *

A long-time inmate of an insane asylum was pronounced cured by the examining board and came to bid the director good-bye before faring into the outside world. "What are your plans?" asked the director. "I haven't quite made up my mind," confided the ex-patient. "I may resume my medical practice. I've also been thinking about becoming a newspaper reporter. Then, on the other hand, I may be a tea-kettle."

* * *

Three good newspaper stories are going the rounds. Joe Williams recalls the dodge of a lazy columnist on the old *Telegraph* who took a long editorial of Arthur Brisbane's and reprinted it word for word in his own column, contributing one original sentence at the end. It read, "What on earth does Brisbane mean by all this?"

Cosmopolitan's promotion shark, M. I. Pitkin, tells about a circus advanceman named Flanagan who dropped in to a small-town newspaper office and asked the cost of a full-page ad. "One hundred bucks," said the editor. "And a half-page?" "One hundred bucks." "And a quarter-page?" "One hundred bucks." "Your rates aren't very elastic," commented the exasperated circus man. "How do you calculate them?" "That's easy," the editor assured him.

"Your show is due here on July 12th, I've got the only paper in town, and on the 13th I've got a note due for exactly one hundred bucks."

During Mark Twain's early days in the newspaper business in Missouri, relates Irving Hoffman, he received a letter from a subscriber stating that he had found a spider in his paper, and asking if this was an omen of good or bad luck. Twain replied, "Finding a spider in your paper is neither good luck nor bad. The spider was merely looking over our paper to see which merchant was not advertising so that he could go to that store, spin his web across the door and lead a life of undisturbed peace ever afterward."

*   *   *

The *Wall Street Journal,* gently ribbing local columnists who triumphantly credit themselves with "exclusives" on inconsequential drivel, recalled the Southwestern editor who would kill front-page stories of world-wide importance in order to scoop other papers in the region on local or sectional items. One day he accomplished the minor triumph of being the first and only editor to report a disaster in a nearby town. The following week he scored another distinct beat with this announcement: "We were the first to announce the news of the destruction of Jenkins paint store last week. We are now the first to announce that the report was absolutely without foundation."

*   *   *

Little Wendy set out for Sunday services in her best bib and tucker, equipped with two shiny nickels—one for the collection plate and one for an ice-cream cone on the way home. She scarcely had left the house when one of the coins slipped out of her fingers and rolled into a drain. "Gosh darn," said Wendy. "There goes the Lord's nickel."

*   *   *

Aaron Sussman, who has created more than one best-seller by his inspired advertising campaigns, is a rabid amateur photographer, not exactly averse to displaying specimens of his handiwork.

He and his wife returned from a late-autumn vacation to find four of his best friends waiting at his house as he drove up. "Golly, it's nice of you to come over so soon," said Sussman. "You must have missed me." "It isn't that," one of the friends explained cheerfully. "We've learned that it's best to visit you before you've had a chance to develop your photographs."

SHAGGY DOGGEREL

For the benefit of those who came in terribly late, shaggy dog stories are those frequently baffling anecdotes in which animals have voices, people have aberrations, and literal-minded auditors have conniption fits. A perfect example is the story of the mink-coated matron who ankled into an exclusive Beacon Hill psychiatrist's office leading a duck by a gold chain. "What can I do for you?" asked the psychiatrist. "You can't do anything for me," answered the matron. "It's my poor husband. He seems to think he's a duck." And the mink herself who woke up one morning, stretched luxuriantly, and informed her mate, "What a wonderful dream I just had! I dreamed somebody had given me a coat made out of chorus girls' skins."

Everything clear?

1. An eccentric gentleman made a pet of an electric eel. When the eel went into a long spell of despondency, his owner diagnosed the trouble as loneliness, and decided to find his pet a mate. After some search, he located a female electric eel, and threw it into the tank. For a moment the male eel was so excited that electricity crackled in the room like a bolt of lightning. But then he flipped the female eel into a corner of the tank, and growled angrily to his owner, "You blundering fool. You know I'm A.C.! *This dame is D.C.!*"

2. One of the visiting nurses from the Henry Street Settlement asked a young mother, "Why do you put your baby in such a high crib?" "We're usually in another room," explained the mother, "and we want to be able to hear him when he falls out." . . . Possibly she is the same character who rushed off to Madison Square Garden because her uncle was riding in a six-day bicycle race. "Ridiculous," said her companion. "That race has been over for two months." "I know," was the answer. "That's what I've got to tell my uncle."

3. An elderly widower loved his cat so dearly he tried to teach it to talk. "If I can get Tabby to converse with me," he reasoned, "I won't have to bother with ornery humans at all." First he tried a diet of canned salmon, then one of canaries. Tabby obviously approved of both—but he didn't learn to talk. Then one day the widower had two extremely loquacious parrots cooked in butter and served to Tabby with asparagus and French fried potatoes. Tabby licked the plate clean, and then—wonder of wonders—suddenly turned to her master and shouted, "Look out!"

Possibly the widower didn't hear, because he never moved a muscle. The next moment the ceiling caved in and buried him under a mass of debris. The cat shook its head and said in disgust, "Eight years he spends getting me to talk, and then the sap doesn't listen."

4. A lady went running to a doctor with a badly spoiled stomach. "What did you eat for dinner last night?" asked the doctor. "Oysters," she said. "Fresh oysters?" asked the doctor. "How

should I know?" said the lady. "Well," asked the doctor, "couldn't you tell when you took off the shells?" "My God," gasped the lady. "Are you supposed to take off the shells?"

5. A lady in Barker, Maine, called up a relative in Miami to report a whopping blizzard in progress. "I'll mail you some snow in a letter," she proposed. "It will be gone long before it gets to Florida," the relative pointed out. "Don't be silly," said the lady. "Who'd be mean enough to steal a little snow out of an envelope?"

6. A worm attended a picnic in a cornfield. It went in one ear and out the other. . . . A log in the Maine woods boasted, "Oh, boy, I slept like a human being last night." . . . Veronica, the wisest cow in a prize herd, glared apprehensively when an inexperienced hand appeared with a pail in his hand. "Uh uh," she warned the cow in the adjoining stanchion, "here comes Icy Fingers." . . . And a lonesome calf in the same herd walked up to a silo and asked piteously, "Is my fodder in there?" . . . And have *you* had enough yet?

7. "See what my friend sent me," boasted a beautiful receptionist. "An alligator purse, an alligator belt, and this lovely pair of alligator shoes." "Your friend must be a philanthropist," said her sidekick. "Not at all," replied the receptionist. "He's an alligator."

8. There are any number of stories about dogs who learned how to play card games and chess. Here's one with a new twist. A wire-haired terrier mastered poker and was a consistent winner for a long time. Suddenly, however, he began to lose his shirt, not to mention his diamond-studded leash. His mortified owner had to forbid him to play any more—because the dog's secret was out. Whenever he picked up a good hand, he simply couldn't help wagging his tail.

Out in Hollywood, incidentally, the city fathers decreed that henceforth the trees along the boulevards were reserved strictly for human beings. The next morning a picket line of canines marched up and down Vine Street. Their signs read, "This shouldn't happen to a dog!"

9. Have you heard about the penguin who suddenly disappeared from her usual haunts? Friends began wondering, and one asked her mother, "What has happened to Gwendolyn?" "Oh, didn't you know?" asked the mother penguin. "She's with Byrd."

. . . Then there was the bald eagle who strutted about all day spreading its wings, expanding its chest, and looking too noble for words. Its mate pooh-poohed, "Oh, you and your eternal 'E pluribus unums'!"

10. At the Copacabana one night Jimmy Durante suddenly announced that he once won a tango contest. "Here's a picture of the girl, me, and the silver cup to prove it," he said. The pianist looked at the picture and said, "That's not a girl, Jimmy. That's a kangaroo." Durante clapped his hands to his sides. "That explains everything," he said. "I thought we was jumpin' pretty high a couple of times." . . . A theatrical agent at the same night spot was overheard trying to sell a trained-seal act to the booker for Radio City Music Hall. "This phenomenal creature," he declared, "not only can play 'Home Sweet Home' on a saxophone and balance a whole set of dining-room furniture on his nose, but he rides on and off the stage on roller skates." "Does he do anything else?" asked the bored booker. "He certainly does," said the agent. "He pays me ten per cent commission."

11. John Ringling North was dining peacefully in Sarasota one evening when a new circus employee burst into the room and cried, "One of the leopards has escaped. What'll we do?" "Find him, and if you can't corner him, shoot him on the spot," ordered North. An hour later the man returned and said, "I forgot to ask you: which spot?" . . . The late Frank Case once told a guest of the Algonquin Hotel, "There goes John Mulholland. He's a wonderful magician and that's his mother walking out with him." "Really," commented the guest. "What was she when he brought her in?"

12. A cockroach met an acquaintance and launched into a dissertation on a new kitchen he had inspected. "It was immaculate, germ-proof, and wonderful," he reported. "Everything was gleaming white and chromium. The dishes and pans were beautiful. I crawled into the new Frigidaire. Every scrap of food was wrapped in crisp cellophane." "Stop! Have a heart!" groaned the other cockroach. "Can't you see I'm eating my dinner?"

13. An undersized but cocky woodpecker circled over the giant redwood grove in California and selected as his field of operation the most enormous tree in the area. He had just made his first tentative peck when a bolt of lightning struck the redwood. It

fell to the earth with a deafening crash. The little woodpecker
blinked the dust from his eyes and murmured, amazed, "I guess
I don't know my own strength!"

14. Two fleas met on Robinson Crusoe one afternoon and indulged in a bit of innocent chit-chat. Finally one said, "I've got
to be getting along, I guess—but I'll see you on Friday."

15. Two society leaders in Africa's nobbiest cannibal tribe were
discussing their marital troubles in the banquet room one afternoon. "I don't know what to make of my husband these days,"
confessed the first. "Don't let that bother you," the second reassured her. "I'll send over my new book of recipes." . . . Above,
a couple of flies were ambling peacefully across the ceiling. "I
will never understand human beings," remarked one fly. "Take
this room, for example. They spend a fortune putting up this beautiful ceiling—and then they walk on the floor!"

16. The first noon a new paper-hanger was on the job he
opened his lunch-box eagerly, unwrapped a sandwich, and lifted
one piece of bread a fraction of an inch. His face fell. "Cream
cheese," he announced dolefully. The second day he repeated the
process, and again reported, "Pfui! Cream cheese again." When
he sadly discovered cream cheese for the third day straight, a fellow workman remarked, "If you dislike cream cheese so much,
why don't you ask your wife to fix you another kind of sandwich?"

"Who's married?" said the paper-hanger indignantly. "I make these sandwiches myself."

17. Even a shaggy dog has an end, so I will conclude this dissertation with a story about a man with a gun on his shoulder who was leading an actual shaggy dog down the street one afternoon. The pooch broke away from his grasp and was promptly run over by an automobile. The driver, noticing the gun on the man's shoulder, was in no mood for an argument. He produced a fifty-dollar bill and said, "I hope this will recompense you for the loss of your dog."

"It sure will," said the man heartily. "I was taking him out to shoot him anyhow."

* * *

Van Cartmell, the Garden City anthologist, tells of an old colored preacher who was warning his parishioners about sin. "Sin," he said, "is like a big dog. There's the big dog of pride, and the big dog of envy, and the big dog of gluttony, and, finally, brothers, there's the big dog of sex. Now folks you gotta kill those big dogs before you're ever gonna get to heaven. It can be done—I know— 'cause I've done it. I killed the big dog of envy and the big dog of pride, and the big dog of gluttony—and yes, brethren, I killed the big dog of sex!" A small voice rose from the rear of the church: "Brother, are you sure that last dog didn't die a nat'chel death?"

* * *

Percival Wilde, the novelist and playwright, confided to his friends that he had acquired a hundred hens and wanted names for them. The following promptly were suggested: "Macduff; Chickov; Eggetha Christie; Shelley; Gregory Peck; Gizzard of Oz; Himalaya; Pullett Goddard; Fryer Tuck; Ku Klux; Turhen Bey; Hatcher Hughes; Peck and Peck; The Brooders Karamazov;—and Casanova.

* * *

After many months of delicate negotiations, the legal department of Marshall Field's in Chicago finally cleared up all litigation connected with the Case of the Perplexed Pachyderm, and hinted to Book Buyer Rose Oller Harbaugh that she be a bit more particular in the future as to the character and disposition of the feature attractions she lines up for her department.

The trouble began when Mrs. Harbaugh discovered that personal appearances of such lush, glamorous lady scriveners as Kathleen Winsor, Clare Jaynes, and Kenneth Horan brought Chicago citizens out in droves—checkbooks in hand. Drunk with success, Rose figured she'd do even better by booking an attraction that weighed as much as her eleven previous ones put together, and signed up a baby elephant to stand by one Saturday afternoon when the holiday crowds were just beginning to assemble. The baby elephant turned out to be a ton or two heavier than expected, but finally was transported safely to the third floor of Marshall Field's via one of the freight elevators. He blinked benevolently and scarcely stirred when the crowd "oohed" and "aahed" and bought every book in sight that vaguely had to do with elephants—including *Saratoga Trunk* and *A Handful of Tusk*. The trouble started only when they tried to coax him back onto

the freight elevator. He wasn't having any of it. And when one perspiring porter accidentally backed him into the sharp-edged handle of the elevator-starting device, the elephant trumpeted angrily, and charged out into the main aisle of the store.

Customers scurried in all directions. Rose Oller Harbaugh swooned. The frightened animal picked up speed and was doing about forty by the time he reached the rug department. One customer, pricing carpets for her new living room, looked up to see the cause of the commotion, screamed, and dove clear over a mahogany counter into the arms of Fred Babcock, literary editor of the *Tribune*, who was valiantly trying to head off the elephant by crying "Whoa, bossie!"

The animal finally was cornered on his third lap around the track, just about the time several surprised but ever-alert lawyers were filing their first suits for damages. The elephant, obviously an omnivorous reader, refused to budge from the book department again until they built a wooden ramp over the marble staircase to the second and main floors.

In the ten hours required to complete this operation, Mrs. Harbaugh did a lot of thinking. The result was unveiled the following Christmas season: a rollicking juvenile by Rose Oller Harbaugh, called *Eddie Elephant Has a Party,* with just-right illustrations by Suba.

*   *   *

An Indian fire writer was transmitting a message to his tribe in New Mexico when a terrific explosion not only interrupted him, but sent him flying into a ditch twenty yards away. It was the atomic bomb experiment, and the Indian pulled himself together in time to see a tower of smoke billow out into the sky. He watched in awe-stricken silence for a moment, then clucked his tongue, and murmured, "I wish I'd said that!"

SECTION 3

𝕭𝖔𝖔𝖐 𝕽𝖊𝖛𝖎𝖊𝖜—𝕴
AUTHOR, AUTHOR!

One of the penalties a man pays for building himself the reputation of a whimsical and unpredictable "character" and wit is the ever-increasing amount of time and ingenuity he must devote to keeping the tradition alive. "Characters" go out of date faster than Wall Street stock quotations. Either the columnists get fresh copy about their old favorites, or they set about creating new ones.

Literary "characters" go through certain well-defined stages.

First, they attract attention legitimately by their talents and a certain freshness and unconventionality of behavior and approach. Second, their publishers' publicity chiefs, who recognize good copy when they see it, begin to exaggerate their exploits and manufacture new ones out of whole cloth to keep the plot boiling. Third, they come to believe the cock-and-bull stories themselves and incorporate them into their autobiographies. And fourth, they begin to devote their major efforts to dreaming up new actions and utterances designed solely to fulfill the expectations of their public. There comes a time when a handful of them —the top-of-the-heap—can depend serenely on the inventions of others. Many of the best stories attributed to Woollcott, Dorothy Parker, Ben Hecht, Charlie MacArthur, and Bill Saroyan, for instance, were brand new to the principals the first time they read them in the papers. When I mailed Irwin Edman a copy of the piece I wrote about him for this book, he noted at the bottom of the sheet, "I deeply enjoyed the stories about myself—particularly the ones I had never heard before."

CASTING A SMALL PAUL

The author of today who offers the really inexhaustible fund of stories about himself is Elliot Paul, author of *The Last Time I Saw Paris*, *A Ghost Town on the Yellowstone*, and a dozen other bestsellers. Paul protests, "There's nothing unusual about me at all. Just because I refuse to be fenced in and made to live the life of a colorless drone, you fellows make up all sorts of ridiculous stories about me." His indignation, however, is short-lived. The next moment he is launched on some new fantastic reminiscence, with a twinkle in his eye, fully aware that his enraptured audience is thinking, "Boy, oh boy, what a liar!"

Paul's first literary endeavors were performed for a Boston newspaper, where he was perfectly happy until he discovered one day that the owners were paying more per week for a syndicated feature called "The Adventures of Peter Rabbit" than they were for his exclusive services. His pride stung, Paul wired the editor—collect—"You are robbing Paul to pay Peter. Demand ten dollar increase." The editor wired back, "Your resignation reluctantly accepted," and Elliot enlisted in the Signal Corps.

When World War I ended, Paul returned to Boston, where he found an empty house on the edge of the Beacon Hill section. He promptly moved in and lived there undisturbed and happy, without paying one penny of rent, while he wrote his first two novels, *Indelible* and *Impromptu*. John Farrar, then editor of the *Bookman* magazine, admired his work and asked if he might come up for an interview. Paul's best friend, Robert Linscott, at the time a junior editor at Houghton Mifflin, told him, "I understand that Farrar thinks you are a rollicking and irresponsible Bohemian. Let's give him a run for his money." Paul thought it was an excellent idea—and a Great Tradition came into being. The two conspirators sprinkled ashes on the floor of Paul's room, piled up a slew of dirty dishes in the sink, deliberately sawed one leg off the pot bellied stove and propped it up with a pile of racy French novels, and planted a large easel in one corner. Linscott picked up Farrar at South Station and told him, "Paul's a painter as well as a novelist. In fact, he's the only man I ever heard of who paints

with two hands at the same time." When they entered the studio, Paul was daubing paint furiously on a canvas with both his left hand and his right, a half-dozen brushes clutched tightly in his mouth. "Good Lord," murmured Farrar, vastly impressed, "he looks like a porcupine."

Elliot moved out of his scantily furnished domicile when a wealthy Back Bay engineer offered him free board and lodging in a fine old house in exchange for his keeping an eye on valuable equipment and instruments while the engineer was making a survey in Brazil. Elliot wasn't used to such lush surroundings, but the adjustment proved painless.

A week or so after his installation he was toying with an elaborate slide-rule when the old Negro caretaker hobbled by. Elliot had one of his sudden brainstorms. "This is a wonderful contrivance," he said pleasantly, "and after endless experimentation, I have learned how to use it. Leroy, if you will give me your physical measurements, I will tell you exactly how many more times you will fall in love in your lifetime."

Leroy regarded him with acute suspicion, but was reassured by Elliot's blandest and most innocent look. In a fever of anticipation, he produced a ruler, stripped, and measured himself from head to foot. Paul gravely made note of the statistics and, while Leroy regarded him anxiously, made a series of mysterious calculations on the slide-rule. Then he closed his eyes, rubbed his forehead with the tips of his fingers, and pronounced solemnly, "Leroy, you are going to be in love 313 more times before you die." Leroy, sixty if he was a day, was understandably delighted. Elliot envisaged a bonanza.

"It was a pleasure to compile these statistics for you as a friend, Leroy," he said, "but obviously the strain is too great on me to continue doing them for others for nothing. If you have any very close friends, however, who would appreciate learning similar facts about themselves, I will conduct the necessary research for five dollars a head."

Leroy thought the proposition was reasonable and so did his friends. Elliot was always generous in his estimates, and thoroughly satisfied customers began spreading his fame throughout Boston. There is no telling what a fortune he might have piled up had not the engineer come home suddenly to find him in the middle of computing one naked patron's potentialities on the slide-rule, with four others waiting impatiently in the drawing-room. "That man had absolutely no imagination," says Elliot. "He threw me out!"

His reputation firmly established by the success of *Indelible* and *Impromptu,* Paul proceeded to promote for himself a well-paid job with the Commonwealth of Massachusetts. His nebulous title was "Director of Activities of Returned Veterans." He hired a stenographer—at the State's expense—instructed her, "If any-body calls, tell him Mr. Paul has stepped down the hall for a mo-ment," and departed for a happy vacation of three months. When he returned, the stenographer reported tearfully, "Not one person has called. I'm going crazy doing nothing. You've simply got to find something to keep me occupied." Paul obligingly hauled over a list of the names and addresses of 250,000 veterans that was gathering dust in the State House archives and suggested, "Type me four complete copies of this list." That kept her busy for an-other three months. When she finished, it was August—and talk of the coming elections was in the air.

No man to waste an opportunity, Paul sold one of the lists to Republican headquarters for three hundred and fifty dollars and, impressed with their eagerness, allowed the Democrats to buy a duplicate for five hundred. It was only fair, he decided, to give the other two lists to the state, and he had them delivered by truck. "I guess they're still available," he reflected recently. "I won-der if one of the book clubs would be interested. . . ."

Elliot Paul feels the time has come to commit his autobiography to paper. "How many volumes do you figure it will comprise?" asked his publisher. Mr. Paul's unhesitating reply was, "Thirty-five."

*   *   *

An over-publicized author submitted to a mass interview re-cently. When it was over, one critic said, "He isn't quite as con-ceited as I'd been led to expect." "Ah, yes," added another, "but he has so much to be modest about."

*   *   *

Lunching at New York's Harvard Club, John Meeker recalled proudly, "I was sitting at this very spot when the late Edmund Pearson, author of *Studies in Murder,* came up one day and asked to be introduced. Naturally I was flattered, but said, 'Are you sure you are not mistaking me for somebody else?' 'Not at all,' answered Pearson. 'You're the fellow I want all right. For the last three afternoons in succession I've seen you sound asleep in that chair with a copy of my book open on your lap. What's it worth to you, young man, to switch to something else?'"

❉   ❉   ❉

Ring Lardner visited Paducah one day to interview Irvin Cobb. "Mr. Cobb took me into his library," reported Lardner, "and showed me his books, of which he has a complete set."

Asked by *Vogue* to supply a brief autobiographical sketch, Frank Sullivan, in the very top bracket of American humorists, supplied a few painfully inaccurate details, as follows:

Francis John Sullivan is that rara avis, a native of Saratoga Springs, where he was born in 1892, the son of Lotta Crabtree and Harold W. Ross. He made his first appearance on the stage two months later playing Fleance to Mme. Modjeska's Lady Macbeth. A promising stage career was terminated soon afterward when during a performance at Harmanus Bleecker Hall in Albany, Mrs. Modjeska dropped the budding Fleance on his head. The next day Sullivan became a humorist and startled the literary world with his brilliant novel of a man's love for the woman he loves, *What Makes Martin Chuzzlewit Run?* ("Could

not put it down."—Hamilton Wright Mabie. "Held me from start to finish."—Brander Matthews. "Perfectly corking but lacks an index."—James Gibbons Huneker.)

Frank is five feet six inches high and about the same across and sleeps in the raw. His pupils dilate normally but his mainspring needs tightening. He spent the summer of 1910 pasting labels on bottles of Saratoga water. We shall see later how this affected the campaign of 1912.

Old friends of Francis J. remember the good old prohibition days when his undeviating route led from Saratoga to Moriarty's speakeasy and back. Detained unduly on one occasion at his northern terminus, he explained all in a postcard: "I will be here a few more days taking care of my kidneys, or, as I like to think of them, Moriarty's Annex."

*   *   *

In 1906, Theodore Dreiser was appointed managing editor of the *Delineator*, celebrated his first day at the post by gravely rejecting two of his own stories.

In 1916, Ring Lardner wrote his fabulously funny diary of Jack Keefe, the bush-league ball player. He called it, *You Know Me, Al.* So many readers asked him to name the man on whom his caricature was based that he added this footnote to subsequent

editions: "The original of Jack Keefe is not a ball player at all, but Jane Addams of Hull House, a former Follies girl."

In 1924, F. Scott Fitzgerald suddenly lost confidence in himself, despite the emphatic success of his first two novels, *This Side of Paradise* and *The Beautiful and Damned*. In a despondent note to Scribner's, his publishers, Fitzgerald concluded, "I have decided to quit writing and become an ashman." A few months later, however, he finished *The Great Gatsby*, and was sufficiently restored in spirit to scribble on the top of the manuscript, "I think this is about the best American novel ever written!" Roger Burlingame relates that Fitzgerald's first notion for a title for *The Great Gatsby* was *Trimalchio in West Egg*, and when that was frowned upon by his publishers, he suggested *The High-Bouncing Lover!* At the very last moment, he cabled "Crazy about title *Under the Red, White and Blue!* What would delay be?" His publishers' one-word reply was "Fatal."

In 1929, Herbert Bayard Swope, of the New York *World*, conceived the notion of importing a famous Irish author to serve a spell as drama critic. It sounded fine on paper, but didn't work out. Among other things, the dramatist was a howling wolf. The prettiest and most brilliant girl on the staff tore into Swope's office one day and declared angrily, "You'll have to do something about that decrepit Lothario out there. I can write good copy and I can fight for my honor, but I'm damned if I can do both at the same time."

In 1930, Kay Brush wrote *Young Man of Manhattan*. Its hero was a dashing, debonair, and gregarious young newspaperman. Years later Miss Brush went on record to the effect that this character was modeled on the noted apostle of sweetness and light, Westbrook Pegler.

* * *

When George R. Stewart received his advance royalty check for *Names on the Land*, he told Joe Jackson, of the San Francisco *Chronicle*, "I'm tired of depositing little pieces of paper in a bank and seeing a single entry in a little, black book as the only reward for my writing efforts. That happened with my last book, *Storm*, but it's not going to with this new one." True to his word, he lugged a bagful of shiny, new silver dollars from the bank, and when his wife came home she found him running his hands through a great pile of them on the dining-room table. "Remind you a bit of Mr. Morgenthau?" asked Stewart. "Morgenthau nothing," said his wife. "Silas Marner!"

After *Life* ran a digest of *Names on the Land,* the author was bombarded by correspondents who deplored the omission of Bug Scuffle, Oh-Be-Joyful, Intercourse, Smitchawitchie, Peekaboo Gulch, Herculaneum, and countless other weirdly named hamlets and creeks in this great country of ours. One learned soul offered this explanation of the origin of "Spuyten Duyvil": an old Dutchman who lived nearby scoffed at the stream's formidable currents and vowed that he would swim it "in spite of the devil." By a miscalculation he succeeded only in getting drowned, but the name stuck. The spot has long since been dredged and widened for navigation, and today the only excitement at Spuyten Duyvil comes when Columbia's football warriors are in action.

When Stewart decided to write *Fire,* the story of a great forest conflagration, he studied his subject with characteristic thoroughness. He enrolled in the California Fire Training School, spent a week as a lonely lookout, and helped fight some real fires. One of them was started by a horsefly. The fly bit a horse. The horse switched his tail. The tail hit an electric-power transmission line which was sagging too low. The resultant sparks killed the horse and started a fire that burned out sixty acres before it was brought under control.

When George Stewart isn't off in some remote corner of the country digging up background material for his books, he is a professor of English at the University of California. His wife, "Ted," is the daughter of Michigan's famous Prexy Burton. The Stewarts have a daughter and son, and a beagle which did not take kindly to house-breaking. An hour after it arrived, it swallowed a needle. The Stewarts phoned for a vet and christened the pup "Haystack."

*   *   *

John Mason Brown is one of the country's most discerning and influential drama critics. He also is undoubtedly its most popular

women's club lecturer. He comes from a family of facile and continuous conversationalists. When an aunt heard how much he earned each year on the podium, she exclaimed in wonderment, "You don't mean to say that a Brown is being paid for talking!"

"When Brown presided at the dinner in honor of George Bernard Shaw's ninetieth birthday," relates Allen Churchill, "one of the speakers was Howard Lewis, president of Dodd, Mead, Shaw's American publishers. 'Mr. Lewis,' explained Brown, 'is here by the grace of Dodd.' Lewis cited the dates and current prices of a long list of Shaw first editions. As he finished, Brown rose slowly and said, 'Now that we have heard the commercial . . .'"

If Brown ever writes his autobiography, he threatens to call it *John Brown's Body.*

* * *

The celebration of G. B. Shaw's ninetieth birthday sent Statistician M. Pitkin scurrying to the files to see if any writing man of the first order could challenge his record for longevity. Here are some figures he unearthed, arranged in ascending scale. Chatterton died (by his own hand) at eighteen; Keats at twenty-six; Marlowe (in a tavern brawl) at twenty-nine; Shelley at thirty; Byron at thirty-six; Burns at thirty-seven; Poe at forty; Jane Austen at forty-two; De Maupassant at forty-three; Virgil, Molière, and Balzac at fifty-one; Shakespeare and Thackeray at fifty-two; Dante and Pope at fifty-six; Dickens at fifty-eight; Chaucer, Racine, and Hawthorne at sixty; Aristotle, Coleridge, and Zola at sixty-two; Milton at sixty-six; Conrad at sixty-seven; Cervantes at sixty-nine; Defoe at seventy; Melville at seventy-two; Sam Johnson at seventy-five; Washington Irving at seventy-six; Browning at seventy-seven; Ibsen at seventy-eight; Emerson at seventy-nine; Plato and Wordsworth at eighty; Meredith at eighty-one; Tolstoy at eighty-

two; Goethe and Tennyson at eighty-three; Voltaire and Benjamin Franklin at eighty-four; Carlyle at eighty-six; and Hardy at eighty-eight.

"There were many grizzled stalwarts there," comments Mr. Pitkin, "but in the words of Percy Atkinson, 'There is no second money in the hall of fame.' Take the case of Methuselah's grandpap, Jared. He lived to be 962 years old—only seven years less than his illustrious grandson. That wasn't good enough; he remains to this day unknown, unhonored, and unsung."

* * *

An engaging young British journalist was sent down to Shaw's country home in Ayot St. Lawrence to wheedle him into writing a piece called "How to Grow Old Gracefully." Shaw's answer was justifiably unfit for publication, but then he took pity on the journalist, and said, "I know you are trying only to carry out a ludicrous assignment. To keep you from going away empty-handed, I'll tell you how I happened to settle in this little town. I was here on a visit, and in the course of one of my long walks alone, happily, I came upon a graveyard. One of the tombstones bore an inscription that ran something like this:

> MARY ANN SOUTHWORTH
> BORN 1815—DIED 1895
> MAY HER SOUL REST IN PEACE
> HER TIME WAS TOO SHORT

"That settled it! I decided that if eighty years was the villagers' idea of a short life, Ayot St. Lawrence was the place for me!"

* * *

A budding anthologist sought to include a Shaw piece in a new collection. "I hope you understand," he wrote Shaw, "that I cannot afford to pay your usual fee as I am a very young man." Shaw replied, "I'll wait for you to grow up."

* * *

A glamorous young lady hit the jackpot with her very first novel. With part of the proceeds, she indulged a childhood fancy, and had her new boudoir done in bright yellow—yellow drapes, yellow spreads, even yellow silk sheets and pillow cases. To make the picture complete, she was laid low shortly thereafter with a sharp attack of yellow jaundice.

A famous doctor was summoned immediately, but when he entered the lady's boudoir he ran into an unforeseen difficulty.

He couldn't find her.

* * *

Many a literary great of the future, destined to have his name in lights on Broadway and to win prizes from Pulitzer, Nobel, and Louis B. Mayer, may be washing dishes in some fraternity house today to finance his college education or jerking sodas in a crossroads pharmacy. Tales of early tribulations of authors who already have hit the jackpot are varied and fascinating, and should stiffen the backbones of young writers who think their troubles are unique.

John Steinbeck, for instance, carried bricks for the new Madison Square Garden building. (The last time he was seen at the Garden he was occupying a $50 ringside seat for a prize-fight.) Later he took a winter job as watchman for an estate seven thousand feet high in the Sierras. There he finished his first novel, *The Cup of Gold*, just about the time a giant pine cracked through the roof of the main house. "The living room was wrecked," admits Steinbeck, "but my manuscript was undamaged."

Pietro di Donato also began his career as a brick-layer. In his spare time he wrote a short story that was bought by *Esquire*. An alert editor persuaded him to expand it into a novel. The result, *Christ in Concrete*, was a Book-of-the-Month Club selection. Pietro immediately tried to buy the building he had worked on last. The owners, however, preferred to keep it for their own use. The building was Tiffany's, at Fifth Avenue and Fifty-seventh Street.

Frank Yerby, whose *Foxes of Harrow* was on the best-seller lists for a solid year, wrote most of it while serving as a porter in an aircraft factory. "To put it bluntly," he says, "I got many of my best ideas in the washroom."

William Faulkner wrote *Sanctuary* while serving as clerk in the Oxford, Mississippi, post office.

Peter B. Kyne had been writing stories for peanuts when Hearst discovered his work and offered him a contract. The first figure Hearst mentioned was $500 a story. Kyne was so dazed he couldn't talk. Hearst misunderstood his silence and doubled the offer. Kyne turned white, but still no words would come. "All right," thundered Hearst. "$1500! Now, damn you, sign this contract!" Kyne signed.

Do you remember a cheap, kitchen-gossipish book about a President's reputed daughter? It was ghosted, for an outright payment of $500, by a needy young authoress who today is recognized as one of the best short-story writers in America.

Joel Sayre, author of *Rackety Rax* and *Persian Gulf Command*, did his first writing while a member of the Canadian Expeditionary Forces in Siberia in 1919. He faced a court martial there. The charge: reading, while on duty, a book by George Jean Nathan.

Similar stories could be unearthed about almost all the headliners of today. The first rungs on the ladder are the slipperiest, but the memory of them gives really great writers necessary perspective and humility after "success, that rare paint, has hidden all the ugliness."

In a progressive Cincinnati school, a stiff test for would-be writers concludes with this perplexing question: "Coleridge was a drug addict. Poe was an alcoholic. Marlowe was killed by a man whom he was treacherously attempting to stab. Pope took money to keep a woman's name out of a satire, then wrote the piece so she could be recognized anyhow. Chatterton killed himself. Byron was accused of incest. *Do you still want to be a writer—and if so, why?*"

* * *

The dreary similarity of a number of recent "sexy" historical novels brings to mind a remark made by Heywood Broun: "Obscenity is such a tiny kingdom that a single tour covers it completely."

* * *

Just before S. J. Perelman sailed from San Francisco for a round-the-world trip, he baffled a girl reporter by informing her, "I have Bright's disease—and he has mine."

Producer Harry Kurnitz's last-minute warning to Perelman was, "If you expect to have anything to do with those beauties in the South Pacific, Sid, be sure to boil them first."

* * *

Before Dashiell Hammett discovered how much more profitable it was to write about private detectives than to be one himself, Ben Hecht applied for a job in the Hammett agency. "I'm looking for experience and a couple of real thrills," he explained. Hammett scoffed, "Suppose you were in a car all by yourself, and a gang of desperadoes in a black limousine came bearing down on you at seventy miles an hour. What would you do?" Hecht replied promptly, "Eighty."

* * *

The fastest writer on record was the late Edgar Wallace, who kept two competent stenographers busy at the same time. He would dictate all morning to one of them, and after lunch, while she went scurrying off to type the material, he would proceed full-steam on an entirely different book with his other secretary. "Every time I talk to a taxi driver," he said once, "I come home with the idea for at least one new book." When a lady friend called once to invite him to dinner, his butler is reputed to have answered, "Mr. Wallace has just begun a new mystery story. Won't you hold on until he has finished it?"

On his way to Hollywood, Wallace paused once in Chicago just long enough to change trains and lunch with a newspaperman. It was the era when the Cicero gangsters were in their heyday, and Wallace had exactly two hours to hear about their most lurid exploits. Aboard "The Chief" he hauled out his typewriter, and by the time he reached Los Angeles he had completed the script of a three-act play called *On the Spot* that was based on the stories the newsman had told him. It ran a solid year in London and made stars of Charles Laughton and Anna May Wong.

* * *

If Wallace was the fastest writer of our time, Alexandre Dumas undoubtedly was the most prolific. He wrote and published, according to his own testimony, 1200 volumes. He once turned out sixty full-length novels in a single year. He said, "It should be as easy for a novelist to make novels as for an apple tree to make apples," and he proceeded to prove his point by writing nearly 70,000 pages of fiction in addition to sixty-four plays and innumerable volumes of travel and essays. He was the first and, so far as I know, only famous author to hire a corps of ghost writers and put the production of books on an assembly-line basis. One day he met his son (the author of *Camille*) and asked, "Have you read my new novel yet?" "No," said the son. "Have you?"

Dumas owned a theatre, a newspaper, and a magazine, slept only four hours out of twenty-four, and was involved in over a hundred lawsuits. For pets he had twelve dogs, three apes, two

parrots, two peacocks, a vulture, a pheasant, and a cat. He entertained so lavishly that, when he rented a château in the country,
the railroad's receipts for the local station increased 20,000 francs
the first summer. He lived like a prince of the *Arabian Nights*—
and died a pauper.

Dumas was born in 1802, the son of a famous general of the
French Revolution and the grandson of a Negress of Santo Do-

mingo. In one year (1844) he produced two of the most popular
novels ever written: *The Three Musketeers* and *The Count of
Monte Cristo*. He dissipated a huge fortune by unbridled extrava-
gance; on his deathbed (in 1870) he wryly remarked, "I came to

Paris with twenty francs. That is exactly the sum with which I die."

* * *

Franklin P. Adams reports a fabulous conversation with his local garageman. He quoted Byron and Bryant while his car was being serviced. "Who are they?" asked the garageman. "Poets," said Adams. "I see," said the garageman. "So there's two of them!" "There are five or six poets," said Adams coldly. "Well, I'll be durned," said the garageman.

Mr. Adams' interest in poetry began at an early age. At seven he could recite all the verses of "The Star-Spangled Banner"—a performance he probably could not duplicate today. For some

time he firmly believed that the first line of our national anthem was "Osage Kansas City."

Adams, who professes to be a garden lover, reported to the singularly uninterested members of the Thanatopsis Poker Club that his peonies required special care. Bernie Hart, a conversation lover, asked, "How about your dahlias?" "They're thriving," enthused Adams. "It proves that if you take care of your peonies, the dahlias will take care of themselves." Shortly thereafter the club was raided.

✿ ✿ ✿

In the Colony Restaurant, Michael Arlen told Dorothy Kilgallen why he hadn't written a novel for a long time: "You know those charming people I used to write about? I can't stand them any more!"

In Paris, Jean-Paul Sartre sent out invitations to the swanky première of his dual bill, *The Tombless Dead* and *The Respectful Prostitute*, forgot to hold one for himself, and was refused admission at the gate.

In Central Park, a flock of pigeons settled around Donald Ogden Stewart, who promptly inquired, "Have you any messages for me?"

In Vienna, a tourist accosted the author of *The World's Illusion* to ask, "Are you Dr. Wassermann?" "I am," said the novelist. The tourist's next question was, "Are you positive?"

At the Manhattan Club, a literary critic met the national chess champion and opened the conversation with, "Led any good rooks lately?"

In Budapest in 1921, Ferenc Molnar took his young bride to the première of *Liliom*. She wept so bitterly that she implored him never to write anything like it again. Today Molnar confesses ruefully, "I'm afraid I never did."

H. G. Wells spoke in Boston one evening and later attended a reception at the home of the mayor. When he left, he took the mayor's hat by mistake, and didn't discover his error until he reached Buffalo. He toyed with the idea of returning the hat, but after admiring himself in the mirror, decided to send the following note:

"Dear Mr. Mayor:

I'm afraid I've got your hat. I like it so much that I propose to keep it. I shall long remember you, your madeira, and your fine, hospitable city.

I take off your hat to you, sir.

Sincerely,
H. G. Wells."

FOREVER OSCAR

Several years ago, Paramount startled a great many people, including its own executive board, by making a motion-picture version of William Faulkner's perennial shocker, *Sanctuary*. Later MGM went Paramount one better by immortalizing on the screen a novel that seemed even less adaptable for that medium: Oscar Wilde's *The Picture of Dorian Gray*. The result was what might have been expected, but box-office receipts were sufficient to insure screening of two other Wilde properties: *Lady Windermere's Fan* and *The Importance of Being Earnest*. What Wilde himself would have said about all this—what, indeed, he would have thought about motion pictures in general—is something to titillate the imagination.

Even without Hollywood protocol to goad him, Oscar Wilde reserved his most scornful shafts for American cousins, who failed to treat him with the deference he felt to be his due when he condescended to visit this country and lecture on literature and art in 1882. His lecture manager, incidentally, was D'Oyly Carte.

Wilde's famous remark to the customs officer when he debarked—"I have nothing to declare except my genius"—started him on the wrong foot in this country, and his get-up, including flowing locks, knee breeches and silk stockings, with a big cornflower or gilded lily ostentatiously tucked into his coat lapel, attracted derisive hoots wherever he appeared. Indeed, Mr. D'Oyly Carte had counted on this precise reaction, it developed later, and was using Wilde as a sort of animated "trailer" for his forthcoming production of Gilbert and Sullivan's *Patience* in America. The central figure of that operetta, you may recall, is the super-aesthetic poet Bunthorne, whose antics and masquerades drove London Wilde.

New York found the original Oscar's posturings as ridiculous as those of Bunthorne. In Boston, the Harvard student body came to his lecture en masse in exaggerated versions of his customary dress. At a party later the nettled Mr. Wilde observed, "You Americans are Philistines who have invaded the sacred temple of art." "And you," answered the host, "are trying to drive us forth

with the jawbone of an ass." A rather silly lady sat next to Wilde
and confided that she never traveled without her diary. "Quite
the thing to do," Wilde assured her. "It's always good to have
something sensational to read on the train." No one to waste choice
lines, he later incorporated this dialogue into *The Importance of
Being Earnest*.

When he returned to London, Wilde insisted, "America really
was discovered by a dozen people before Columbus, but it always
was successfully hushed up." He added, "Democracy means sim-

ply the bludgeoning of the people by the people for the people,"
and topped his remarks with another sally that he used later in
a play: "When good Americans die they go to Paris; when bad
Americans die they go to America." His book *Intentions* was published by the English firm of Osgood, McIlvane and Company,
who advertised its "simultaneous appearance in London and New
York." Osgood died shortly thereafter. Wilde, encountered in Pic-

cadilly, remarked sadly, "Poor Osgood is a great loss to us. However, I suppose they will bury him simultaneously in London and New York."

As an example of American "justice," Wilde cited the trial of an alleged hoss-thief in a Western frontier town. The jury deliberated for an hour and returned a verdict of "guilty." "Keerect but tardy," announced the judge. "What took you boys so long? We strung up the prisoner twenty minutes ago."

Wilde's celebrated feud with Whistler was somewhat synthetic, in the manner of the Fred Allen-Jack Benny radio war of the present day. Between rounds the boys were frequent companions; their blasts were sounded with one eye on the publicity. Most often quoted is Wilde's approving "I wish I had said that" to a sally of Whistler's, and the latter's reply, "You will, Oscar, you will." Another time Wilde wrote, "Whistler is indeed one of the greatest masters of painting, in my opinion. And I may add that in this opinion Mr. Whistler himself entirely concurs." Whistler retorted, "Amiable, irresponsible Oscar has no more sense of a picture than the fit of a coat, but he has the courage of the opinions —of others. He has been invited to all the best homes of England —once."

The recent flood of diaries and autobiographies of military bigwigs calls to mind Wilde's postscript to the report of an inefficient British general in the Boer War. "We returned without wasting a single gun or soldier," boasted the general. "Or a minute," added Wilde. Another evening, a fellow-writer excused a hack job he had turned out by sighing, "After all, a man must live." "In your case," snapped Wilde, "I fail to see the necessity."

Wilde's career was shattered in 1895, when the Marquis of Queensberry charged him with improper relations with his son, Lord Alfred Douglas. Wilde recklessly sued Queensberry for criminal libel, but the charges were substantiated, and Wilde was sentenced to two years' imprisonment in Reading Gaol. Broken in spirit and health by his incarceration, he went to France upon his release, and spent his last years in Paris, poverty-stricken, and abandoned by erstwhile sycophants—including Douglas. "My great tragedy," he mourned, "is that I put my genius into my life —and only my talent into my works."

His Parisian landlord pitied him and allowed him to stay on

rent-free. When Wilde lay dying, however, evidently in a coma, the landlord expressed concern to the one old friend who appeared at the bedside. "Who on earth is going to put up the money for the poor devil's funeral?" he queried. The friend could offer no suggestions. Wilde's eyes flickered, and he said feebly, "I'm afraid, gentlemen, I am dying beyond my means."

* * *

Thomas Macaulay, famous British historian, distinguished himself at the age of four, according to Biographer Wanda Orton, when a lady asked him, "Did oo hurt oo's itty bitty finger?" He replied, "Madam, the agony has slightly abated."

* * *

When Thomas Mann, one of the greatest of living novelists, fell ill, many of his admirers expressed resentment at the grudging information given out on the nature of his malady and the progress of his cure. The silence, however, was the result of orders issued by Mann himself. "This concerns only my immediate family and myself," he said. "Only last week, I read what Tolstoy told his physician when *he* was stricken: 'I wish you would stop publishing bulletins about my sickness. What good do they do? My friends will be saddened, my enemies delighted.'"

* * *

Louise Baker, one-legged humorist who wrote the rollicking *Out on a Limb*, shared a cabin in one Atlantic crossing with a lady who thought she needed special mothering. Miss Baker had a fine time on board, and invariably retired very late. The lady demanded, "Will you tell me what a young lady on crutches does on shipboard until one o'clock in the morning?" "What do you think young ladies without crutches do?" asked Miss Baker. "Mercy goodness," gasped the lady, "you don't do that, do you?"

* * *

The editor of every anthology of American short stories includes O. Henry as a matter of course, but, unfortunately, he usually picks one of a dozen standbys that have become shopworn and over-familiar by repetition—"A Municipal Report," for instance, or "The Gift of the Magi." Hidden away in the bulk of the six hundred stories O. Henry left behind when he died in 1910 are countless others that have a habit of popping up in magazines and columns, only slightly altered—and under other by-lines.

There is one story that I told for years before I discovered it was an O. Henry original—a few paragraphs from "The Venturers," in the volume called *Strictly Business*. It concerns two rather handsome, gray-haired men, neatly but unostentatiously garbed, who found themselves occupying the same park bench one summer midday. In front of them towered one of New York's most famous hostelries. The man on the left smiled wistfully. "Beautiful hotel, isn't it?" he asked. "You know, I'd rather like eating a good lunch in its roof garden today. There's a slight drawback, however. I haven't a single penny in my pocket!"

"That's odd," said the other. "Neither have I." A moment later he added, "Let me offer a suggestion. Both of us make a decent enough appearance. Let's go up to that roof garden and order the fanciest food and wines on the menu. Just before the check comes, we'll borrow a coin from the waiter, and toss to see who walks out a free man, and who stays to face the music." "Done and done," declared the first man promptly.

The luncheon was an unqualified success. The food was delicious, the conversation sparkling. The demi-tasses were already on the table when one man, after considerable hemming and hawing, said, "Look here, old man. I'm afraid I'm guilty of a bit of deception. When I told you over in the park that I didn't have a cent with me it was God's honest truth. But please stop worrying about this lunch check. I'm worth a mint. I simply forgot to transfer my belongings when I put on my new suit this morning. Fact is, if I must confess, I occupy the most expensive suite in the place."

"I guess that makes us even," laughed the other. "I should have recognized you. I own the hotel."

*　*　*

O. Henry was the past master of the story with a surprise or "twist" ending. He was also the prose laureate of Manhattan Island. Today the "four million" of his "Bagdad on the Subway" have become nine million, the slang that high-lights his dialogue has been superseded by other passing catch-phrases, and restaurants and hotels that served as his locale were razed a generation ago, but his tales of New York remain the standard by which all other literature on the subject is judged. Only a few months ago the editor of a great metropolitan newspaper wrote a book about Manhattan. The review he cherished most, and carried in his wallet, was one that referred to him as a "latter-day O. Henry."

At the height of his career, O. Henry boasted that he could turn out one complete story—and down one complete bottle of whiskey—a day. He was always far behind in his commitments. "If only magazine editors wouldn't eat in the same restaurants I do," he said petulantly. "I find it impossible to resist them—especially when I owe them stories they've paid me for six months ago!" He lunched one day with Charles Hanson Towne, then editor of *Smart Set*, and Robert Davis, of *Munsey's*, and admitted that he owed stories to nine magazine editors. In the middle of the meal, he excused himself and moved to another table where he held a whispered consultation with Richard Duffy, of *Ainslee's*. When he returned he remarked gaily, "Change that figure from nine to ten."

O. Henry's great ambition, according to Vincent Starrett, was to write a full-length novel, and many of his stories were begun with that purpose in mind. Inevitably, however, he had to tack a hurried ending to them in order to fulfill some particularly pressing obligation. One editor lost his temper completely and sent a message reading, "If your copy is not delivered today, I promise to arrive in person and kick you downstairs. P.S. I always keep *my* promises." O. Henry replied, "If I worked with my *feet*, I would keep mine, too."

Although O. Henry was born in Greensboro, North Carolina (the leading hotel there—not to mention a popular candy bar—now bears his name), he probably was as typical and devoted a New Yorker as ever lived. "No country life for me," he declared. "Just give me a steam-heated flat with no ventilation or exercise."

His last words were, "Pull up the shades so I can see New York. I'm afraid to go home in the dark."

* * *

In the true O. Henry tradition is another story going the rounds in literary circles this year. I thought it might have been lifted from the writings of F. Scott Fitzgerald, but his daughter Frances, who ought to know, says it must have originated elsewhere.

The characters certainly resemble the kind Fitzgerald drew so faithfully—a young married couple, handsome, gay, rich as Croesus, who between them had never done an honest day's work in their lives. They lived and played on inherited millions, and the French Riviera seemed the perfect background for their will-o'-the-wisp activities. Unfortunately, another couple turned up at the resort where they were staying and trailed them so persistently that their days were ruined completely. This other couple was noisy, shallow, and ostentatious. "The very sight of that pair," they told friends, "casts a pall over whatever we are doing. They are such utter fools and wasters! Their imbecilic laughter is as empty as a cathedral on a Monday morning."

Eventually the intruders became so intolerable that the young pair moved to a resort a dozen miles down the coast, but the other two promptly followed them. From Cannes to Nice, to Mentone, to Rapallo they fled, increasingly desperate, but never for a single day could they seem to keep the objectionable pair from dogging their footsteps.

Then one day, the boy and the girl made a startling discovery. The other couple was themselves!

❀   ❀   ❀

In *Go* magazine, an enthralled correspondent described a dinner party that included Somerset Maugham. The Chinese butler remarked pleasantly, "Good evening, Mr. Maugham. I think it only fair to tell you I didn't care much for your last book." An hour later Mr. Maugham was missed by the assembled guests. A scouting party discovered him in the kitchen, hotly defending his literary style to the butler.

Mr. Maugham, in reminiscent mood, told of his elation when Sir Edmund Gosse, dean of English critics, wrote an enthusiastic review of Maugham's first novel, *Liza of Lambeth,* in 1897. Until he died in 1928, however, Sir Edmund never saw Maugham without patting him on the shoulder and murmuring, "Capital piece of work, that *Liza of Lambeth.* How smart you were never to write anything else!"

In the South last winter, Maugham stopped at a country inn where the proprietor rushed to greet him. "We've been waiting for you, Mr. Maugham," he cried. "Everybody here knows you! And to make you feel perfectly at home, all the young girls are wearing green hats!"

❀   ❀   ❀

One of William Faulkner's harmless idiosyncrasies involves removing his shoes on every possible occasion. The first time he visited New York, he took them off on a crowded subway express and couldn't find either of them when he arrived at his destination. Faulkner raised such a holler that they held the train until he crawled the length of the car on his hands and knees, and located the missing number nines at the other end.

* * *

Holbrook Jackson, in *Bookman's Pleasure,* quotes ever-modest Bernard Shaw as follows: "Whenever I have been left alone in a room with a female, she has invariably thrown her arms around me and declared she adored me. It is fate." His hostess for a week-end, however, once complained caustically to Frank Harris:

You invite Shaw down to your place because you think he will entertain your friends with brilliant conversation. But before you know where you are he has chosen a school for your son, made your will for you, regulated your diet, and assumed all the privileges of your family solicitor, your housekeeper, your clergyman, your doctor, and your dressmaker. When he has finished with everybody else, he incites the children to rebellion. And when he can find nothing more to do, he goes away and promptly forgets all about you.

* * *

Mark Van Doren once played host to a party of convivial literary folk who were having a wide and handsome time until a monumental bore—uninvited, incidentally—lumbered in and depressed the entire assemblage. After the bore had departed, he was discussed at some length. "Wouldn't you think," suggested someone, "that it would break the heart of a person like that to see how the face of everybody he addressed simply froze into an expression of acute distaste and vacuity?" "You forget," said Van Doren, "that a person like that has never known any other kind of expression!"

* * *

George Papashvily, who wrote the gay and rollicking *Anything Can Happen,* arrived at Ellis Island on a Greek boat without a penny. He sold his fine fur cap for a dollar to a chiseler who assured him he couldn't wear anything like that in America. With

the dollar he rented a fat roll of greenbacks with which he dazzled the customs inspector, returning them to the proper owner
when he stepped ashore on Manhattan. In Detroit, he prospered
as a mechanic in an auto plant, but threw away his savings for a
piece of inundated real estate. His friends went in a body to make
the salesman return the money, but this gentleman had such a
persuasive line of palaver that they ended by buying lots next
to George's.

Papashvily, like Stalin and the Mdivanis, is a Georgian. "Remember," he counsels, "that for Georgians, only too much is ever
enough." His wife Helen, who actually wrote the book, is the
owner and operator of the Moby Dick Bookshop in Allentown,
Pennsylvania. His Uncle Vanno, at the age of eighty-five, bought
a solid gross of red satin garters, with little silver bells on them.
"Ladies gonna ting-aling-aling when they walking," he explained.
"Be something different." When George expressed doubt as to
what disposal an octogenarian expected to make of 144 pairs of
garters, Uncle Vanno said cheerfully, "I don't know quite so many
ladies yet, but I'm certainly gonna make more acquaintance all
time."

Anything Can Happen is a fresh reminder that immigrants
often love and appreciate these United States ten times better
than the people who were born here.

THE TWAIN LEGEND

"When your audience is restless," a lecture manager advised a
new client, "it's always a good idea to tell a story about Mark
Twain." Fresh ones keep popping up in magazines and radio programs, old ones are refurbished and given new tag-lines, and since
the great humorist is in no position to repudiate them, the legend
will continue to grow.

At a banquet in New York, Twain was seated next to the guest
of honor, who decided to test a few of the stories he intended
to use in his speech. "I hope you haven't heard this one," he would
begin, and then barge on without waiting for Twain's courteous
but increasingly faint "No, I don't think I have." As the fifth story
began, Twain lost his temper. "Sir," he declared, "your previous

stories were old and very badly told, but at this one I positively
draw the line. Not only have I heard it fourteen times, but I invented it!" The guest of honor, crushed, declared, "I was afraid
of addressing this hyper-critical audience even before I came.
Now you have destroyed the last vestige of my self-confidence."
"Cheer up," counseled Twain. "Remember they expect very little
of you."

A hypocritical business pirate once told Twain, "Before I die
I mean to make a pilgrimage to the Holy Land. I will climb to
the top of Mount Sinai and read the Ten Commandments aloud."

"I have a better idea," said Twain. "Why don't you stay right at
home in Boston and keep them?" In Richmond one day, Twain
complained of an acute pain in his head. "It can't be the air or
the food you ate in Richmond," said a native son confidently.
"There's no healthier city than Richmond. Our death rate is down
to one person a day." "Run down to the newspaper office," begged
Twain, "and find out if today's victim has died yet."

There was another side to Mark Twain's nature. He was often irritable, unreasonable, and demanding, and it was his publisher and partner, Charles Webster, who bore the brunt of his displeasure. Webster's son, Samuel, tells the story of his father's tribulations in his fine book, *Mark Twain, Business Man*. "About once a week," he reports, "Mr. Clemens wanted a lawsuit started against somebody, or an advertisement prepared that would have started several against him." Webster thinks that if cooler heads had not intervened, Twain would have been one more name on the list of authors who wrote their greatest books in jail.

Actually, Mark Twain wrote *Tom Sawyer* in the comfort and seclusion of his Hartford, Connecticut, home, in the fall and winter of 1875-76. He was disturbed so seldom, reported his wife, that he scarcely lost his temper "more than four or five times a day." The one great crisis occurred when a twenty-year-old neighbor decided to teach a young friend just half his age how to handle a shot-gun outside Twain's window. Twain leaned out and cried, "Tarnation! March that boy off somewhere and show him how to shoot ducks." The neighbor took him at his word. Unfortunately, the duck they shot turned out to be the prized property of Mr. Twain. The younger of the culprits, whose name was William Lyon Phelps, was still telling a half century later about the tanning Twain gave him—and about the trusted older friend who had involved him in the scrape. That friend was William Gillette, whose brilliant stage career was destined to be launched a short time later in a dramatization of one of Twain's books, *The Gilded Age*.

Another neighbor of the Twains in Hartford was Harriet Beecher Stowe. Old and failing mentally, she used to wander into the Twain greenhouse and pluck his favorite flowers. Twain fussed and grumbled, and wrote his brother, Orion, "She seems to think my place is *Uncle Tom's Cabin*"—but he never stopped her.

By the time *Huckleberry Finn* was ready for the presses (in 1884), Charles Webster, besides being Twain's publisher, had become a combination whipping boy, purchasing agent, social secretary, and handy man around the house. A month before the book appeared, Twain wrote, "I can see nothing that will avert another defeat," and called Webster an incurable optimist for disagreeing with him. When the book became his biggest seller, however, Twain wrote, "My publisher discouraged me by discounting my prophecies about *Huckleberry Finn's* high commercial value."

Twain's method for disposing of suppliants who bothered him, of course, was to refer them to Webster. One man appeared before Webster with a sealed personal note of introduction, which read: "Dear Charley: Give this man what he wants, or kill him. I don't care which. Yours truly, S. L. Clemens." Samuel Webster's footnote is: "My father killed him."

A reporter visiting Mark Twain's haunts in Hannibal, Missouri, some years ago, found one old crony who discounted the glory and fame of his erstwhile school chum. "Shucks," he said, "I knew as many stories as Sam Clemens. He jist writ them down."

*   *   *

It was the day before Christmas, and all through a certain publishing house not a creature was stirring anything but a bowl of very potent eggnog. The bosses, the bookkeepers, and the shipping clerks gathered happily around the festive board. Even the editors unbent for the occasion and spoke in words of less than three syllables.

Into this happy group a stranger entered suddenly. It was an author—a lady who wrote detective stories. "I came to tell you all the plot of my new murder novel," she said sweetly, "but don't let me disturb you all on Christmas Eve. My plot will wait—five minutes anyhow." The purposeful glance she threw in the direction of Doubleday's, down the block, was not lost on the president and chairman of the board, who hurried her to a private sanctum and chorused, "Tell us at once! We know it will be wonderful."

"Well," said the authoress with a sigh of contentment, "it starts with the murder of a husband by his jealous wife. She lures him to the bridge that spans a mighty river nearby, stabs him with a hatpin, and watches his body disappear beneath the swirling waters with a satisfying plop. Then she seeks sanctuary with her old mammy twenty miles away. She has left no clue whatever. She thinks she is absolutely safe.

"She has not reckoned, however, with Mother Nature. That very evening there is a terrible flood, and the river overflows its banks."

The authoress stopped talking, and waited for applause. The president, unfortunately, looked even blanker than usual. "What's the point?" he asked finally.

"Don't you see, you silly oaf?" cried the authoress. "This is the first time in all the annals of detective fiction where the scene of the crime returns to the murderer."

* * *

'TWAS EVER THUS!

The book business has been having its full share of difficulties in the past few months, and I take it for granted that you have been hearing about them, because an unhappy publisher can holler considerably louder than Caspar Hookenlauffer, the All-American hog-calling sensation of the year. What matter if the

volume of book sales is still a full fifty per cent higher than any
peacetime year of the century? A perfectly normal recession from
the wartime peak, and a rebirth of some sense of discrimination
in public taste, is sufficient reason for many publishers to weep
disconsolately into their champagne cocktails at the Ritz Bar.
George B. Twickenham, of the Twickenham Press, is even threat-
ening to lay up his second yacht.

Flying by instrument alone through the Stygian gloom of a recent conclave of publishing contemporaries, I jotted down the
principal causes of their dismay. Costs were getting out of hand,
I learned. Book clubs and Hollywood presented grave problems
as well as revenues. Labor demanded more and accomplished
less. Authors heaped abuse not only upon their publishers, but,
to confuse the situation further, upon each other. Booksellers were
returning their overstock without authorization. The ominous war
cry of book censors and smut-hounds sounded through the land.
Advertisers were raising their rates and reviewers were lowering
their standards.

Were publishers ever before in history stymied by such formidable obstacles? Diligent research provided illuminating facts.

Item: When Rome was in its glory, manuscripts were copied
on parchment and papyrus by slaves. One year there was such
a shortage of parchment that a senator in the Forum charged it
was being diverted deliberately to prevent the circulation of odes
and essays enlarging upon the corruption of the current emperor.

Another year, a slave popped up who copied manuscripts twice as fast as any of his fellows. Said fellows promptly threw him into the Tiber.

Item: Manuscripts that went begging in Rome were bundled off to the provinces, where they were sold at the best prices obtainable. Some ended ingloriously as wrapping paper for fish dealers. Today's overstock is peddled for a fraction of its original price in bargain basements and drugstores. The principle is the same. As early as 1472, two German printers complained to the Pope that they were stuck with 12,000 copies of an ecclesiastical tome, and that they faced bankruptcy if immediate help was not forthcoming. The Pope's reactions are not recorded.

Item: Censorship had become such a menacing problem in England in the seventeenth century that John Milton was moved to write his famous plea for liberty of the press, "Areopagitica." "As good almost kill a man as kill a good book," was his cry, which has echoed through the centuries.

Item: About 1750, John Newberry began the juvenile business by publishing cheap editions of *Mother Goose* and *Goody Two Shoes*. By 1760 he admitted that his juveniles were selling faster in his store than his previous leader, Dr. James's Infallible Fever Powder. By 1770, however, he was complaining that competitors

were publishing deliberate imitations of his texts in inferior editions and at lower prices.

Item: When Sir Walter Raleigh heard that the first volume of his history of the world had sold only 1500 copies, he threw the manuscript of volume two into his publisher's fire. Izaak Walton felt that his dignity was lowered by the fact that *his* publisher was stooping to *paid advertising* for *The Compleat Angler*. The advertisement read, "An interesting discourse on fish and fishing, not unworthy the perusal of most anglers."

Item: Two hundred years ago, the poet Peter Pindar accused publishers of "drinking wine out of their authors' skulls." In 1697, John Dryden acknowledged the receipt of "an inadequate payment" from his publisher, Jacob Tonson, and added, "All of your trade are sharks, but since you are no worse than the others, I probably shall not leave you." All the way back in 100 A.D., the epigrammatist Martial complained, "My words are read in every corner of the world, yet what do I gain by it? My purse knows nought of my fame." He added that rich Romans should buy more manuscripts, and borrow less.

In other words, the problems of the publishing world today have existed, in much the same form, since time immemorial. The fact of the matter is that despite all the wailing, not one book publisher has voluntarily abandoned his pursuit in all the years I have been in the business. All of them know that there is no more fascinating or rewarding profession in all the world, and that despite temporary obstacles, American publishing, surely and majestically, is embarking upon its Golden Age.

* * *

Kurt Wolff, on his way to becoming as distinguished a publisher in America as he was in Europe before Hitler, was a friend of Paul Valéry. He once asked Valéry, "Whom do you consider the greatest French writer of the nineteenth century?" Valéry looked glum and answered, "Victor Hugo—alas!"

Valéry also declared that evening, "A true writer never really finishes a book. He abandons it."

* * *

The late Arthur Bostwick tells a story at the expense of Harper's in his *A Life with Men and Books*. A popular medium announced solemnly that she was going to publish a novel that had been "dictated to her by the spirit of Mark Twain." Harper's legal department hastily sought an injunction "on the ground that they were entitled to all his work, on whichever side of the grave it might be produced."

* * *

William Dana Orcutt came home one evening from a conference with George Hecht, manager of the Doubleday retail shops. "Hecht told me," he reported to his wife with evident relish, "that in their Wall Street shop, patronized almost exclusively by men, solid, serious books outsell frothy fiction almost ten to one. In uptown branches, however, where the customers usually are women, it's the inconsequential love stories and murder tales that get the big play. Interesting commentary on the sexes, isn't it?" "Quite right," snapped Mrs. Orcutt. "You are aware, of course, that the men are buying the good books to take home to their wives, and the ladies, wise to the ways of keeping peace in the family, are acquiring the trash to give their husbands."

* * *

A dreamy-eyed individual, obviously a poet, drifted off the elevator into the editorial department of the Viking Press and asked if he could use a typewriter for a few minutes. He sat down at the machine indicated, inserted a sheet of blank paper, and explained, "I have to add six very important asterisks to my manuscript." He did so, thanked everybody politely, took his script and asterisks, and left.

* * *

Dale Warren, the spiritual guide of Boston, reminds readers that "a book is only one-half of an equation; the other half is the individual who is reading it." He quotes Fannie Hurst as saying, "I'm not happy when I'm writing, but I'm more unhappy when I'm not"; Voltaire as confessing, "If I had a son who wanted to

write, I should wring his neck—out of sheer paternal affection";
and Burton Rascoe lamenting, "What no wife of a writer can ever
understand, no matter if she lives with him for twenty years, is
that a writer is working when he's staring out the window."

* * *

Novels that sell ten thousand copies a day are rarer than a
laudatory motion-picture review in the *New Yorker*—yet in the
space of a single decade, the dignified house of Macmillan has
published two of them: *Gone with the Wind* and *Forever Amber*.

The creator of Amber St. Clare, Miss Kathleen Winsor, has been
endowed by nature with many of the charms that made her
heroine so irresistible. The eyes of Macmillan editors bulged when
she delivered her manuscript. They bulged even further after the
manuscript had been digested. "If Amber is picked up by half as
many housewives as she was by courtiers of Charles II," said Macmillan's Jim Putnam, "we won't be able to keep the book in stock."

Forever Amber was launched on the wings of a hectic literary

tea in what some wit described as the Macmillan Bawd Room.
For once the literati not only condescended to meet the guest of
honor; they insisted on it. Harold Williams, of the American News
Company, snipped a lock of the lady's hair to paste in his memory
book. "What a profile," sighed David Appel, of the Philadelphia
Inquirer, "and it goes all the way down." A noted tea drinker from
the New York *Herald Tribune* gulped a whole flagon of straight
bourbon. Clearly the frail bark of literature was setting sail on an
uncharted sea, and everybody was a little aphrodizzy from it all.

In less time than it takes to tell, thousands of eager students of
English history of the seventeenth century were immersed in Miss
Winsor's little idyl. A radio comedian was cut off the air for suggesting that the title be changed to *Forever Under.* Lillian Friedman, St. Louis' Dorothy Parker, thought *Stop and Try Me* would
be even better. Harry Hansen wrote, "How easy it will be to do
this in pictures. All the action will have to take place off stage!"
A student of psychiatry explained, "It is not true that Amber had
a sick mind. She merely was suffering from a strip-de-carcass in-
fection." A bookseller with an eye on the cash register suggested
that Miss Winsor and Margaret Mitchell collaborate on a sequel,
featuring Amber and Rhett Butler, laid in Atlanta.

Two full years after *Forever Amber* had been published, the
State of Massachusetts suddenly decided to brand the book obscene, and vendors of same liable to criminal action. Happily, the
attempt proved futile, but it did boost the sale to two million, and
provided Attorney General George Rowell, spearheading the
prosecution, with the opportunity to present this absorbing statistical analysis of the book:

- 70 references to sexual intercourse
- 39 illegitimate pregnancies
- 7 abortions
- 10 descriptions of women dressing, undressing, or bathing in the presence of men
- 5 references to incest, 10 to the badger game
- 13 ridiculing marriage
- 49 "miscellaneous objectionable passages"

Mr. Rowell concluded his indictment by declaring, "The references to women's bosoms and other parts of their anatomy were
so numerous I did not even attempt to count them."

In short, the prosecution provided a perfect capsule formula for a foolproof best-seller.

* * *

Back in 1827, a slender volume of poetry was published in Boston. It was anonymous; the author chose to identify himself only as a "Bostonian." Strictly speaking, this was true. He had been born there, but the day he found his not-too-enthusiastic publisher, he was revisiting his native city for the first time. He was literally starving, and his clothes were threadbare and tattered; perhaps he thought that a graceful nod to his birthplace might spur the sale of his sheaf of poems.

Today, 120 years later, only six copies of the first edition of that little volume are known to exist. One of them was sold recently at auction for $10,000. The title: *Tamerlane, and Other Poems;* the author: Edgar Allan Poe.

* * *

In Chicago, a determined old dowager sailed into the Carson, Pirie, and Scott book department and demanded a complete set of Dickens and a complete set of Scott. "I don't care about the bindings and I don't care about the price; just find me the cheapest sets you can," she told the astonished clerk. "You see, I have to have them. I've left them to my grandchild in my will."

* * *

Doctoring and styling manuscripts is only part of a conscientious editor's job; a great deal of his time must be spent in wet-nursing his authors in sickness and in health, listening to their intimate secrets and boastings, preventing them and their wives, often with extreme reluctance, from bashing each other's heads in with fire tongs.

One editor I know was deeply relieved to hear that a troublesome but famous author finally had decided to sue his wife for divorce, after a series of endless and sensational battles. The terms of the settlement were arrived at after negotiations that dragged on longer than the hockey play-offs—and all through them the principals glared at each other with maniacal hatred.

The wife had already signed the papers and the husband was flourishing his pen when, to the editor's consternation, he stopped short and declared, "There's one thing more I must have—or it's no deal. My wife has a stickpin I gave her; I insist upon having it."

The wife said no. The judge ascertained that the pin was worth less than twenty dollars. "My dear friend," begged the editor, "do not sabotage this whole settlement, and find yourself still tied to a woman you loathe, for a measly, inexpensive stickpin! Why do you want it, anyhow?"

"You won't understand," brooded the author. "It's for sentimental reasons."

* * *

A literary agent whose proudest boast is that he knows George Bernard Shaw personally, and who therefore feels called upon to champion Shaw's plays vociferously at all times, has been carrying on a long-time controversy with a cantankerous client who cherishes an equal passion for the works of John Galsworthy. The agent and his client met last in the Cub Room of the Stork Club, and, although they lost no time in getting down to their favorite subject, the flow of the argument was impeded somewhat by the fact that the client had contracted a violent case of laryngitis and couldn't utter a single word. His comments had to be written down on paper, and since his adversary holds all known records for perpetual long-distance talking, he was at an even greater disadvantage than usual.

The uneven argument reached its climax when the agent maintained stoutly, "Long after John Galsworthy is completely forgotten, the name of Bernard Shaw will burn in letters of flame twenty feet high!" The client clapped a hand to his brow, seized his pad and printed "NO!!!" on it in block letters the full size of the page.

"Okay, okay," soothed the agent, *"you don't have to shout at me."*

* * *

There was another client on this agent's list for whom he made
the most extravagant claims, but for one reason or another the
young man never seemed to click. One day a secretary rushed
in and cried, "Have you heard about our white-haired boy? The
Book-of-the-Month Club has just chosen his new novel!" The
agent was silent for a fraction of a second. Then he whispered
reverently, "I always said that boy was a genius. Now I believe
it."

* * *

A Philadelphia publisher cherishes an order received for a single copy of a current favorite. "I can't remember the name of the
book," confessed the customer, "but it was about a French count
who hates a wench in the beginning, discovers she's wonderful
in the middle, and makes her his in the end."

* * *

The eye-opening statistics in Kinsey's *Sexual Behavior in the Human Male* and the avidity with which the public memorized same sent the humorists of America scurrying for their thesauruses and gag-files. Our men, they proclaimed, could count up to sex, anyhow. Our morality laws were honored chiefly in the breeches. One reader was so enthralled by the report he couldn't put his wife down till he finished it.

Professor Kinsey, announced his publisher, was now compiling data on the sex behavior of the human female. Suggested title: *The Next of Kinsey.* "I hear the report will show," whispered a gossip, "that a woman is most receptive from forty-eight to fifty-two." Playwright Robert Sherwood pricked up his ears. "1948 to 1952?" he mused. "The next four years ought to be mighty interesting!"

When a potential customer at the Whitman Bookshop in Camden heard that the price of the current Kinsey book was $6.50, he dropped it on the counter and exclaimed, "Heck, that's too much. I'll wait for the movie."

Ad-man Alan Green has the title (but no plot yet) for a novel that should sweep the country: *The Man Who Startled Kinsey.*

❊ ❊ ❊

The widow of a confirmed bibliophile, friend of H. C. L. Jackson, slowly read a letter left for her by her husband. "My dearest," he had written, "it has been a sorrow to me that you never shared my interest in rare books; but then, you have been patient. Not too often did you refer to the money I spent on this hobby of mine.

"This note will come to you after I have gone. The mere fact that you are reading it will prove that once at least you have opened one of my favorite books."

The note had been tucked in her husband's best loved volume. It was sent to her, without comment, by the dealer to whom she had sold her husband's entire library three days after his death.

❊ ❊ ❊

The annual advent of warm weather puts a temporary stop to one of the queerest customs in the publishing business—the literary cocktail party. The basic idea of these primitive functions is to parade the authors of new books before the town's leading critics, columnists, and booksellers. Unfortunately, the leading critics, columnists, and booksellers seldom show up, and a couple of hundred totally unknown gatecrashers do. The guest of honor is pinned down in a corner by some unutterable bore, the host tries vainly to signal the waiters to close down the bar, and a good time is had by none.

At one swanky function, Munro Leaf, creator of the famed Ferdinand the Bull, found himself seated last. "I guess," he said ruefully, "I'm low man on the protocol." A portly authoress boasted to Leaf that her husband always took care of her at literary jamborees. "How do you keep him glued to your side?" asked Leaf. "Witches' brew and mysterious potions," she explained coyly. It was at this point somebody noticed that her husband had disappeared completely. Three days later the authoress was still looking for him.

Another jolly *Kaffeeklatsch* almost ended in a free-for-all when a lady author with communist leanings (and two sable coats) upbraided a publisher for bidding a million dollars for Mr. Churchill's memoirs. "Churchill is a typical, obsolete, old Tory," shrilled the lady, her cheeks turning an appropriate pink. "His thoughts aren't really his own." "That's all right," the publisher assured her. "The million isn't *my* own either." The climax of the argument came when he fixed the lady with an accusing finger and demanded, "Where were you when Stalin signed the pact with Hitler?" "Where were *you*," she countered, "when Washington crossed the Delaware?" At this point the host put an abrupt end to the brilliant repartee by passing out in the coat room.

The late Arnold Bennett had a disconcerting habit at literary gatherings. He would select a chair in the middle of the festivities, settle himself comfortably, and promptly fall asleep. He had been dozing happily one evening all through a bitter argument on current trends when a particularly vehement declaration woke him up with a start. "Isn't it time for us to be going?" asked his wife in some embarrassment. "Not at all," said Mr. Bennett. "It would be extremely rude to leave so early"—and went back to sleep.

*   *   *

Most of you probably have heard what Oliver Herford said when he was asked to evaluate the work of Arnold Bennett: "I'm afraid that something I once wrote about Mr. Bennett in a critical way so prejudiced me against him that I never read another word he wrote."

*   *   *

One of the famous scenes in Bennett's *The Old Wives' Tale* describes a public execution. In his review of the novel, Frank Harris said it was clear that the author never had witnessed such a ceremony, and was the victim of a distorted imagination. Harris then proceeded to tell what an execution *really* was like, and his account was so terrifying and explicit that Bennett wrote him, "If your description only had appeared before mine, I assuredly would have utilized it. Of course, you have discovered my secret. I never *have* witnessed an execution." Harris replied, "Neither have I."

*   *   *

THE PRIVATE PAPERS OF
JOHN BEECROFT

The three flourishing book clubs sponsored by Doubleday and Company—the Literary Guild, the Dollar Book Club, and the Book League of America—boast today an enrollment of two and a half million members, some seventy-five per cent of whom happily accept and pay for the books selected for them in any particular month. It would be fair to assume that a large board of distinguished connoisseurs ponder gravely over available literary

gems before the three monthly choices are made, but the truth
of the matter is that one solitary gent picks them all. His name
is John Beecroft, and the power he wields obviously makes him
one of the most important figures in the entire book world today.

The fact that he is not better known to the general public, that
he has not yet been profiled in the *New Yorker* or glamorized in
Life is due solely to his own reticence and positive passion for
anonymity. He prefers to labor undisturbed in his office or his
Long Island sanctuary, inscrutable, efficient, and calm—as long as
he gets his own way. When he is crossed, the mild and scholarly
Beecroft charges upon his foe with the fury of a hurricane, and
leans backward so far when he considers a product from the home
office that one disgusted Doubleday editor calls him "The Hori-
zontal Man."

By the time John Beecroft entered Columbia in 1921, he had
read most of the classics, and developed a dislike for crowds. Fellow students mistook his shyness for arrogance. His eyes are steel
blue, and staring into the mirror he convinced even himself that
he was something of a cold fish, not to be stirred by ordinary
emotions. He operates under this illusion even now. In reality, he
is a bowl of mush, a pushover for a cagey moocher or a stray
alley cat. Because he was short, he had a chance to become
coxswain of the varsity crew, but to the disgust of the head coach
he quit the squad just when the berth seemed his. He explained
that it made him sick to see other people ride backwards.

When he was graduated from Columbia in 1924, Nick Mc-
Knight, now dean, found him a job with the Crowell Publishing
Company, where he wrote a reading guide to Dr. Eliot's Five-
Foot Shelf. It is being used to this very day. In 1926 he decided
that he needed more education, quit his job, and sailed for Europe. The Sorbonne in Paris was out, of course, because everybody talked French (he still cites this fact with considerable
resentment), but he did manage to get along in Italy, where he
studied architecture and life until 1928. "Suddenly I discovered
that everything new in Europe was coming straight from America,
so I decided to go home," says Beecroft. "Besides, my money had
given out." On the way home, he read one of the first advertisements of the Literary Guild—something about breaking down the
barrier between the author and the reader—and applied for a job

there the day after he landed back in New York. The official who interviewed him was a newcomer on the Guild staff himself. His name was Milo Sutliff. Until recently Sutliff was the grand nabob of the entire Doubleday Book Club operation.

Beecroft and Sutliff studied each other closely and immediately conceived the deep mutual respect and personal misunderstanding that was the basis of their entire relationship. The result was that John became editor of the Guild magazine and house organ, *Wings*—a job to which he still clings.

When Carl Van Doren resigned as editor of the Guild, Beecroft nominated himself to pinch hit. Within a few months he was entrenched so solidly that dynamite—plus a few jealous Doubleday hatchet-men—couldn't budge him.

Beecroft thinks that his biggest thrill as editor of the Guild came in December, 1937, when he made his first outright guarantee for 50,000 copies of a book. It was Eve Curie's *Madame Curie*, and his confidence, of course, was more than justified. Five novels by hitherto obscure writers that he picked subsequently were *Rebecca, Tree of Liberty, A Tree Grows in Brooklyn, Earth and High Heaven,* and *Green Dolphin Street.* The ultimate success of these books makes Beecroft's job look easy. Remember, however, that he makes his selections from novels submitted months before publication, and that dozens of publishers besiege him constantly with new discoveries on which they swear "to shoot the works." Ziegfeld never picked a chorus more unerringly.

To hold his job, Beecroft must do a prodigious amount of reading. He goes through twelve books a week thoroughly, skims over twenty or twenty-five more. All of them are in manuscript or galleys. The only bound book he has touched in the last three months was a volume of Shakespeare. He consulted it to settle a bet— which he lost. Assisting him are three full-time readers and two part-time readers. John considers their opinions gravely and then chooses what he wanted in the first place.

*   *   *

From Eastport, Maine, to Sappho, Washington, stretches the northern boundary of the United States, some two thousand miles of rugged and ever-changing country, but all of it is the back yard of one of America's most picturesque authors, Stewart Holbrook. Within the past year, Holbrook has been in Bad Axe, Michigan, to check details on a story about the Frank Merriwell books; Bemiji, Minn., on an article about the wild-rice industry; Bangor, Maine, for a story ordered by the New York *Herald Tribune;* and Seaside, Oregon, to investigate the hemlock looper, which, I am sure you know, is a species of worm that is intent upon eating up our Northwestern forests.

Holbrook was born in Vermont, but his professional career began in northern Minnesota. He was an actor in the Harry St. Clair Stock Company. Mr. St. Clair himself, a ripe sixty-nine, played the leads; his wife Jennie, just turned sixty-five, essayed the ingénue roles; and Stewart, all of seventeen, invariably was cast as an old man, wearing a moth-eaten set of whiskers that generally fell off before the second-act curtain. On the side, he yodeled and took tickets. The musical accompaniment was furnished by a single man, but St. Clair felt justified in billing him as a "full orchestra" because he invariably was one. One night he passed out cold at the piano during the first act of *Uncle Tom's Cabin.* Holbrook had to play the music and howl like a pack of bloodhounds at the same time while Eva crossed the ice. One lady in the first row was so entranced that she followed the company for two weeks.

The villain of the troupe was a young chap named William Pratt who tired of one-night stands and decided to try his luck in Hollywood. He didn't do badly there either—particularly when he changed his name to Boris Karloff.

One of the towns on the St. Clair itinerary was Sauk Center, and a Dr. Emmet J. Lewis and his wife, prominent citizens of the community, went to see a performance of *East Lynne* in December, 1884. Harry St. Clair told the story at least once a day. "That doctor hated actors as a general rule," he would boast, "but when he saw me do *East Lynne* he got so excited that he persuaded his wife to name her forthcoming baby after me. It was born February 7, 1885—a boy—and sure enough, she drove over to St. Cloud, the county seat, to name it Harry St. Clair Lewis. Unfortunately, the registrar was hard-of-hearing, and he entered the name as 'Harry Sinclair Lewis.' It was a tragic error for the poor baby, but nothing could be done about it. I understand that boy has become a writer or something. If he ever writes a play, the St. Clair Stock Company will be proud to produce it—if there's a good part in it for me."

❊   ❊   ❊

Sinclair Lewis began his literary career in the publicity department of Frederick L. Stokes and Company, book publishers. At the end of his second year he was making $23 a week and had the temerity to demand a two-dollar raise. Old Mr. Stokes gave it to him, with the comment, "You're a bright young fellow, Lewis,

but you want raises too often. This is the top salary for the job you're doing. I'll never pay you any more." Less than fifteen years later, the same gentleman offered Lewis a $75,000 advance on a new novel, sight unseen!

❊   ❊   ❊

John Chamberlain taught Sinclair Lewis the cliché game, in which one contestant poses a stereotyped question, and another has to give the appropriate stereotyped answer. Lewis loved it— played until three in the morning. A few days later he called Chamberlain in a rage. "You subverter of American literature," he cried. "You and that darn game! All day yesterday, I tried to write, and every line came out as a cliché!"

* * *

Many a tremendous best-seller literally has gone begging before some lucky publisher decided to take a chance. Vina Delmar's *Bad Girl* was turned down by eleven houses before Harcourt, Brace picked it up. Blasco-Ibáñez's *The Four Horsemen of the Apocalypse* and Emil Ludwig's *Napoleon* were refused by so many editors that the dejected authors sold all American rights for a few hundred dollars apiece.

The distinguished English publisher, Geoffrey Faber, ruefully confesses to one of the worst pieces of guessing on record. "An agent offered me *The Good Earth* and I turned it down," he admitted, "but you haven't heard the worst. When I sent the book back, it was rejected in turn by a dozen of my competitors. The agent still had faith in it, and begged me to consider it again. And I turned it down a second time!"

Bad timing has killed more than one book that might have been a rousing success with more adroit handling. One of the first victims of a publisher's failure to consider current public interest was Henry David Thoreau.

In his journal, Thoreau laments that his *A Week on the Concord and Merrimack Rivers* (now generally accepted as an American classic) was published in 1849, when the entire country could think of nothing but the gold rush in California. Who wanted a book about familiar New England at a time like that? "The edition was limited to one thousand copies," writes Thoreau, "and eventually I had to buy most of them myself. . . . I have now a library of nearly nine hundred volumes, over seven hundred of which I wrote myself!"

* * *

Somebody once defined "honorarium" as a "twenty-dollar word designed to dress up a ten-dollar editorial fee."

*   *   *

Myrtle Cherryman says she keeps her loose dollars in a copy of Dante's *Inferno*, thereby always being in a position to answer her own querulous "Now where in hell did I put that money?"

*   *   *

The head of the publicity department of a big publishing house recently got so tired of trying to please a stable of particularly temperamental authors that she set out to compile a list of the ten types that were doing the most to turn her job into a case of all irk and no play.

Number one, she decided, was the bird who never could locate his beloved opus at Macy's or Brentano's and accused his publisher of deliberate sabotage. Number two wanted to rewrite all the advertising, and couldn't understand why the firm balked at a two-page color spread in *Life*. Number three wanted the publisher to get every critic fired who had dared to suggest that his novel wasn't a cinch for the Pulitzer Prize. Number four blamed her for not getting him on "Information Please" or the Fred Allen program.

Number five always popped up at lunchtime on a busy day, and wanted a special key to the liquor cabinet. The only check he ever reached for was the payment of his advance royalties. Number six thought his publishers were there for the sole purpose of getting him hotel and plane accommodations, tickets for *Mister Roberts*, and a blonde like Betty Grable. Number seven had special ideas about type, binding, and jacket designs, and caused the entire manufacturing department to resign en masse every time he visited the office. His oration invariably began: "Of course, I don't know anything about the mechanics of publishing, BUT——"

Number eight always agreed to appear at radio dates and book-and-author luncheons, but also forgot to show up at them. This won the hearts of booksellers and radio executives and made it a cinch to line up dates for other authors on the list. Number nine compared everything that was done with the job his previous publishers had performed. Why this type always had changed publishers at least five times before was something he never bothered to explain. Number ten, the publicity head declared wearily, was a gent who combined all the bad features of the other nine, and was the most common specimen of the lot.

I daresay the publicity girl was off her feed when she compiled that list, and needed a vacation. There are plenty of notable exceptions to the above catalogue. But there also are a couple of other categories that she forgot to explore entirely. The most nauseating of the lot at the moment is the returned prodigal from Hollywood who has decided to do his publisher and his public the incalculable favor of leaving his lucrative film work long enough to make an immortal contribution to literature.

You must know the type. He arrives at the Waldorf in a blaze of luggage and publicity and summons the press to hear about his touching sacrifice. "It's costing me five hundred thousand dollars to write this novel," he declares modestly. Or "I had to turn down three pictures at a hundred thousand apiece because this great play was simply crying to be written, and I had to get it out of my system." The fifty-dollar-a-week reporters who have to take down this bilge and the busy publishers who have to listen for hours while these slaves to their art catalogue the terrific sacrifice they are making may be excused a vague sense of satisfaction when, nine times out of ten, the great masterpieces turn out to be a soggy mess of platitudinous bologna, with corny plots that went out of fashion both on Broadway and in publishing circles a dozen years before.

The publishers have learned that really good books and plays are never written by characters who reckon how much more they could have been making in the same time in a film studio.

* * *

When Henry Hoyns, chairman of the board of Harper and Brothers, died at the age of seventy-six, there died with him the last and, in many ways, the finest example of a publishing era whose like will never be seen again. To the end he was a man who believed in old-fashioned dignity, precision, integrity, and attention to detail. Not for him the flamboyant publicity tricks of the forties or the dangerous philosophy of "What's the difference how much it costs? The government is paying most of it anyhow!" One morning he okayed, in twenty minutes, a publishing venture for Harper's that involved a quarter of a million dollars, and immediately thereafter disappeared into his private office with a Midwestern salesman to check over an expense account. The salesman swears that Henry told him, "No luncheon in Des Moines could possibly have cost you three seventy unless you had two portions of dessert!"

Hoyns had had to watch pennies when he was a boy, and he could never forget his early training. As a matter of fact, it stood the house of Harper in good stead during the early days of the century, when the going was difficult. The firm's impregnable position today is due in no small part to his guardianship of the exchequer. Henry handled the reprint department and considered a day wasted when he couldn't up a reprint publisher's guarantee to a point just a wee bit higher than circumstances warranted. One of them offered him a twenty-five-hundred-dollar advance one day for a current novel. Henry leafed through his records and said, "It's far too early for a reprint. That book is still selling eight hundred copies a week in the original edition." The reprint publisher recognized this as the accepted Hoyns opening move in such negotiations, and upped his bid to four thousand. Henry allowed himself to be persuaded—against his better judgment, he explained—and went out to get a contract form. He was somewhat abashed when he returned and suggested the expunging of the entire affair from the records. The book in question, it turned out, was a Scribner publication.

* * *

On the Bowery, Joe Gould, bewhiskered eccentric, put the final flourish on his newest book, *Why Princeton Should Be Abolished.* "I may have trouble placing it," he admitted. "Most publishers today are not only illiterate but they graduated from Princeton." Lippincott of Penn, Greenslet of Wesleyan, Canfield of Harvard, and Haas of Yale smiled tolerantly. The Scribner family reserved comment.

* * *

The third Charles Scribner to occupy the presidency of his firm (the fourth is working his way up) has held the post since 1932. He is rarely perturbed by the perplexing problems of the book business although the death of his great editor, Max Perkins, put an additional burden on his shoulders. When the time approaches for his daily dash for the train home to Far Hills, however, his subordinates notice a growing look of concern on his face. His object, and that of a few other commuters and friends, is to get settled in the club car and launched on a rubber of bridge before an elderly acquaintance, who plays abominably, manages to horn in on the game. The plan has never succeeded to date, but they all keep trying. Their present theory is that the unwelcome contestant hides in the washroom of the car all day while it stands in the yards, for he is on hand to greet them no matter how early they arrive at the station.

Charles Scribner drew him as a partner one day recently, nearly fainted when he heard him bid six no-trump, but felt reassured when he saw the lay of the cards. "Even *he* can't miss this one," whispered Scribner to an onlooker—but he was wrong. His partner revoked. Scribner swears that another day the fellow absent-mindedly picked up two hands by mistake, carefully arranged the twenty-six cards, and bid, "One spade."

* * *

Frank Luther Mott's *Golden Multitudes,* the story of best-sellers in the United States, has provided the basis of a new parlor game that is intriguing the literati. Dr. Mott lists twenty-one books that have sold more than two million copies each in this country. The game consists in seeing how many of the twenty-one can be identified by individual participants. Ten or twelve titles are easy, but it is a knowing soul indeed who can dream up the remainder.

In case you haven't Dr. Mott's book at hand (The Macmillan Company rather hopes you have), here are the twenty-one books, listed alphabetically and with their authors:

Alice in Wonderland (Carroll)
Ben Hur (Wallace)
A Christmas Carol (Dickens)
Gone with the Wind (Mitchell)
How to Win Friends and Influence People (Carnegie)
In His Steps (Sheldon)
Ishmael and its sequel, *Self-Raised* (Southworth)
Ivanhoe (Scott)
The Last of the Mohicans (Cooper)
Little Women (Alcott)
Mother Goose
One World (Willkie)
The Plays of Shakespeare
The Robe (Douglas)
Robinson Crusoe (Defoe)
See Here, Private Hargrove! (Hargrove)
The Story of the Bible (Hurlbut)
Tom Sawyer (Twain)
Treasure Island (Stevenson)
A Tree Grows in Brooklyn (Smith)
Uncle Tom's Cabin (Stowe)

* * *

James Ullman's excellent novel about mountain scaling, *The White Tower*, filled his publishers, Lippincott's, with a passionate desire to do a little climbing on their own account. Ullman, an expert woodsman, volunteered to lead a group of them up a trail in the Ramapos. Near the starting point, they came to a turbulent stream. "Don't let this one frighten you, boys," called Ullman cheerfully. "We'll have to cross worse ones before we reach the summit. Just follow me." Mr. Ullman thereupon fell in up to his neck.

* * *

Will Cuppy reports the receipt of a letter from a faithful fan that reads, "Please send me the name of some good book on personal hygiene. I think I've got it."

* * *

Wendell Casey, manager of the Doubleday shop in Detroit, had a Christmas-holiday encounter which promises to become one of the classic tales of Publishers' Row. One of those beminked, pickle-faced dowagers elbowed her way through the crowd and demanded to see an assortment of fifty-cent juveniles. Despite the turmoil, Casey actually showed her more than twenty different volumes, all of which she examined leisurely through her lorgnette, and rejected as "unsuitable for my grandson." In desperation, Casey produced a dog-eared "pop-up" book, remnant of a five-year-old fad that unaccountably had been overlooked in the shuffle. "You just open one of these books," said Casey, "and you never know what will pop out." The lady looked dubiously at the faded volume, and opened it. What popped out was a two-inch cockroach—a very active one, too. The lady screamed, but Casey was equal to the occasion.

"Usually, madam," he said in a disappointed tone, "we have them carrying the American flag."

SECTION 5

Hollywood

To a man who hasn't been there in several years, the Los Angeles of today is a revelation. A beautiful new terminal has replaced the old ramshackle depot. The wide open spaces that once separated downtown L.A., Hollywood, Beverly Hills, Brentwood, and Santa Monica have disappeared. Now it is one continuous metropolis, glittering and new, all the way to the sea. The crazy signs and "nutburgers" built in the form of oranges, derbies, castles, and papier-mâché Mary Pickfords have vanished. In their place are modernistic store-fronts of glass and chromium, suggesting a magnified version of the 1939 World's Fair. And the people are dressed differently. I remember the old gag about the picture director who was roused from his sleep by a cry of fire and dressed in such a panic that, when he reached the sidewalk, his coat and pants matched. That joke is sadly out of date today, because on the city streets, at least, the outlandish sports coats and garish mufflers (instead of ties) have given way to business suits Brooks Brothers would not hesitate to display in their windows. Los Angeles, in a word, has grown up.

They say it is possible to start from one point in this fabulous place, travel eighty-five miles in a straight line, and still be within the city limits. The boulevards are crowded with shiny new cars, but judging by the manner in which they zigzag wildly from one lane to another, most of them won't stay that way long. Beautiful roads cut suddenly into the hills, where elaborate mansions are perched at angles that seem to defy the laws of gravity. To make everything more improbable, the ones at the very top are most apt to be equipped with tennis courts and swimming pools.

Friends live at incredible distances from one another, although most of them seem to derive a mysterious satisfaction from minimizing the time required to reach their lairs. "Everything in this confounded place," grumbled Harold Ross, "always seems to be just twenty minutes away!" It *is* possible to go from the jumble of traffic at Hollywood and Vine to a lonely, wooded mountainside in a quarter of an hour; I discovered that when I visited Ted Geisel. Ted's neighborhood is such a wilderness that they chose it as the setting for a film called *Objective Burma*. Ted is still looking for the dastardly Jap general who conked him squarely on the bean with an empty Pepsi-Cola bottle. The general's troops were crawling through this impenetrable jungle at 4 P.M., and taking off their make-up in the Warner Brothers studio at 4:15!

One of the most obsolete objects in modern Los Angeles is the telephone directory, now used exclusively as a door-stop in the best homes. List your name in those bourgeois columns today, and tomorrow you wake up on the wrong side of the cracks. Remember Gisela Werbisek-Piffl? This determined and accomplished young actress not only refused to change a syllable of her name, but inserted it boldly in the phone directory—and it's still

there, because I checked. As a reward, an average of two scintil-
lating wits ring her number each week in order to gurgle, "Oh,
I'm so sorry! I must have the wrong Gisela Werbisek-Piffl," and
hang up amidst hysterical laughter (their own). By the time a
visitor manages to track down a more conventional star's number,
his quarry usually has moved to the other end of town.

* * *

Harry Brand, super-publicist of Twentieth Century-Fox, collected a black eye recently. He says he ran into an open door. At
any rate, he had himself photographed with the black eye showing prominently, and sent a copy to his friend Sid Skolsky with
this inscription: "Nobody can talk that way about you when I'm
around!"

* * *

Gene Fowler sends along a story about a Hollywood mogul who
met a young eyeful on Wilshire Boulevard and gushed, "Golly,
it's good to see you again. It so happens there's going to be a
marvelous party tonight, and I want you to come to it. I won't
take no for an answer." "Where's it to be?" asked the girl. "At
my house, darling. And I think it will be an all-time high for fun.
Lots of liquor, music, sex, and nobody knows when it ever will
break up." "Sounds great," said the girl eagerly. "Who's going to
be there?" "Oh," replied the prospective host, "just you and me."

* * *

A member of the staff of a famous Hollywood producer did an
unprecedented thing a few weeks ago. The producer had just outlined his idea for a new picture. The staff man coughed nervously,
looked around for the nearest exit, and piped up, "Boss, I think
your idea is terrible." There was a stunned silence in the room for
a moment; then the producer said quietly, "Joe, please do me a
favor. When you talk to me hereafter, keep quiet."

* * *

It's probably just an idle rumor, but they do say that last St. Patrick's Day, a green-bordered envelope reached the Hollywood Post Office, addressed to David O'Selznick.

* * *

A producer of one of the Lassie pictures at MGM swears to the truth of this story. Lassie had evidently been off her feed for three or four days and her trainer decided that what she needed was a dose of castor oil. Unfortunately, no way could be found to make Lassie take it. The trainer and three assistants spent a full hour devising tricks to lure Lassie into swallowing the medicine, but she was much too smart to fall for them, and it was finally de-

cided that some other remedy would have to be sought. Just then the bottle of castor oil slipped out of the grasp of the man who was holding it and crashed on the floor. The trainer was just about to upbraid him for his clumsiness when Lassie calmly strolled over to the spot and licked up the entire contents of the bottle.

Incidentally, another rumor about Lassie has been in circulation lately. They say the president of the studio came to watch a scene being filmed one day and that Lassie was suspended for two weeks for barking in his face.

* * *

When Olsen and Johnson went to Hollywood to do the film version of *Hellzapoppin'*, a zealous studio press agent arranged for them to throw custard pies at each other for the benefit of the newsreels and the local press. Olsen and Johnson okayed the plan but changed the scenario a bit at the last moment. When the press agent signaled "Go," the two of them seized their pies and smacked them right into the astonished face of the press agent himself. One of the newspapers printed a picture of the gory scene with the caption, "Custard's Last Stand."

* * *

An unobservant literary agent (one of the best in the country) has had his burdens eased for years by a faithful and all-knowing secretary. Her marriage last fall inconvenienced him for only a few days, but recently she had to tell him, "I'm afraid I'll have to leave on Friday. After all, my baby is due in August." The agent registered panic and incredulity. "Not *this* August!" he gasped.

THE END OF THE GRAVY TRAIN

As far as the average writer is concerned, that wonderful old Gravy Train for Hollywood has been stricken from the schedule. Approximately 1,100 writers are already on the scene—fighting for about 275 jobs available at all studios combined, under present production schedules. Two hundred fortunate members of this understandably desperate band are the recognized headliners, working under long-term contracts or, by their own choice, on a free-lance basis. They can get jobs on virtually their own terms at any major lot by picking up a telephone. That leaves about seventy-five jobs for the other 900 writers in Hollywood—and every day fresh recruits arrive to make the odds even more frightening.

These figures may be challenged, but they were given to me by one of the shrewdest and most successful executives in Hollywood. Take my word that he knows what he's talking about.

"You people back east," he said, "hear too much about the big-shots. It warps your point of view. How many Hechts, Bracketts,

Wilders, Fowlers, Riskins, and Krasnas do you think we have out here anyhow? Yes, it's true Ben Hecht got a thousand dollars a day on one assignment last year, and whimsically demanded his payment in cash at the end of each session. What of it? Hecht probably saved the studio five times what he got by making rewrites and retakes unnecessary. You get fellows like that working on your script, and you cut weeks in your shooting schedule. Did I say there were 200 writers like that in the whole industry? Maybe I put the figure a little too high. Anyhow, there are that many making $1500 a week or more. But, brother, what a drop it is to the bracket just below!"

Why don't the harassed writers outside the charmed circle come back home? The typical case history of a character we shall call Jonathan Jones should give you a rough idea.

Jones was spotted first by an alert scout for a book-publishing house, by virtue of a short short story in an obscure magazine. After two years of careful nursing and editorial assistance, he produced a novel that sold 12,000 copies and won a respectful notice on page six of the *Times Book Review*. One afternoon he brought his wife joyful tidings. He had an offer from Hollywood: ten weeks at $750 a week! "I know I'll hate it out there," he predicted, "but I'll be home before you know it, and I'm a son-of-a-gun if I don't save four thousand bucks out of that loot." The writer soon learned, however, that he wasn't going to make that Western trek without friend wife—not to mention his two sons. ("Just think what a couple of weeks of California sunshine will do for those boys!")

So Jonathan Jones, his wife, and sons arrived in Hollywood. After a day in an expensive hotel suite, Mrs. Jones located a wonderful house in Beverly Hills—with a play yard and swimming pool. ("Of course, its ridiculously beyond our means, but after all, it's just for two months.") Then a kind friend got the youngsters admitted to a fine private school. ("You should just *read* the roll there! Selznick, Wanger, Crosby, Boyer, Vidor, Heyward . . . Each of those children comes from a famous family!")

Their third night in Hollywood, Jonathan Jones took his wife to Chasen's for dinner. She looked around carefully and told her husband, "If you think I'm going round to places like this in these clothes . . ." The next day she opened accounts at Bullock's and Magnin's. And another kind friend took her to a preview at Adrian's where she found the most divine afternoon gown for only $400. Of course, she couldn't be seen after that in a battered old Chevrolet. The Lincoln distributor had just one new convertible left on the floor. . . .

When Jonathan Jones's ten-week option expired, it was, alas, not renewed. Jones, furthermore, was several hundred dollars in the hole. Did he say, "I always knew this place was not for me! It's been a great experience. Let's go home and live like normal human beings again"? Of course, he didn't. Prodded by his wife and his ecstatic progeny, he rushed frantically to his agent, crying, "You've simply got to get me another assignment out here. The longer the better. I don't care what studio or what script. Take $500 if that's the best you can get. I'll lick this racket yet." . . . Jonathan was one more permanent addition to the gallant 900,

riding into the jaws of Death, into the mouth of Hell, for one of
those seventy-five open writing jobs in Hollywood.

*   *   *

A correspondent who swears he heard it with his own ears reports a story conference at a big West Coast studio in the middle
of a torrential rainstorm. The producer, irked because his new suit
and hat had been soaked, was in a particularly bad humor. He
listened in grumpy silence while a new plot was outlined and then
jettisoned it with a blunt "Absolutely no." When an assistant
dared question his decision, the producer condescended to explain. "It's too blood and thirsty."

When the conference was over, the producer's secretary remarked, "Terrible out today, isn't it?" He nodded and said, "What
can you expect in weather like this?"

*   *   *

The malapropisms of Hollywood big-shots are becoming a
pretty threadbare subject, particularly since the public became
aware that most of them originate in the minds of columnists and
press agents.

Here are three, however, which I believe to be authentic.

1. When *The Best Years of Our Lives* was previewed, the producer assured an interviewer, "I don't care if this picture doesn't
make a nickel, just so long as the whole United States sees it."

2. A Vine Street Voltaire observed, "Any man who gets himself
psychoanalyzed ought to have his head examined."

3. One producer borrowed a troupe of Indians from another,
but when they reported for work he didn't think they looked
fierce enough. He called his friend to protest. "I don't know what
you are talking about," proclaimed the latter. "Those Indians come
straight from the reservoir."

*   *   *

Evelyn Waugh's recent visit to Hollywood was unique in many
respects. His expenses were paid in full as a pure gamble by

MGM, who wanted to film his *Brideshead Revisited*, but felt that basic changes in the story were essential. Waugh listened stolidly to their pleas, flatly refused to allow the changes, and the whole project went up in smoke. A critic called him "the most self-assured and unmovable Briton who ever visited California." Waugh himself relates, however, that one man succeeded in destroying his self-assurance entirely—and he was Benito Mussolini.

Homeward bound from reporting the invasion of Ethiopia (for details see his novel *Scoop*), Waugh paused in Rome in hope of securing an audience with the Pope. "Only Mussolini can get you one at a time like this," he was told. The British Embassy persuaded Mussolini to receive him, and Waugh rehearsed in advance the precise speech he proposed to make, but the long walk to the dictator's desk, with his footsteps re-echoing on the marble floor, did him in. Mussolini, furthermore, gave him the "can't-you-see-I'm-signing-important-documents?" pantomime, before throwing down his quill and barking, "Well?" Waugh forgot every word he meant to say, and heard a voice that he recognized with some surprise as his own declare, "Sire, Ethiopia will never be conquered!" That concluded the interview. Waugh left for London the same evening.

MGM executives, apparently, used the wrong technique.

* * *

A Hollywood starlet upset precedent by *asking* for an autograph instead of *giving* one. The autograph sought was Edna Ferber's, and the starlet's disarming request read, "It doesn't matter whether you write it or print it. I copy all my autographs over anyhow alphabetically in my scrap book."

* * *

A young writer with a considerable reputation on Broadway was given a contract by a powerful motion-picture studio. When he turned in his first scenario, the head of the studio called for an aspirin and the writer's agent. "Get rid of this fellow quick," he bellowed. "He's such a highbrow I bet he writes failures on purpose!"

* * *

A Hollywood communiqué heralds a third—or is it fourth?—remake of *Little Women.* Considering the fortunes that have been made on this beloved American classic, and the fame it has brought to players on the stage and screen, it is interesting to note that the author herself, Louisa May Alcott, thought very little of its chances when she finished it in 1867. In fact, she offered to sell it for one thousand dollars outright in lieu of royalties. Her publisher considered her doubts well founded, but he took the manuscript (written in laborious longhand) home for further consideration. That night he called several times to his usually attentive niece, but got no answers. He found her so engrossed in the Alcott story that she was oblivious to the outside world. The next morning he made out a contract. Approximate sale of *Little Women* to date: three million copies.

You may recall a story that went the rounds the last time *Little Women* played at Radio City Music Hall. A drugstore nearby featured a full window display of the Little, Brown and Grosset editions of the novel. A lady pointed it out to her companion, and exclaimed, "Look at that! The picture only opened yesterday, and two publishers have put it out in book form already!"

❋   ❋   ❋

OH, KAYE

Sooner or later, the great stars of the stage and screen decide to
write the stories of their lives. This usually entails dragging ghosts
out of closets and sitting them down at typewriters with a coat of
whitewash at their sides, and strict instructions to keep out the
really salty details people would love to know. Once in a while,
however, a performer comes along who has sufficient skill, wit,
and good taste to do the job in person. Perversely, they are precisely the ones who resist the blandishments of check-waving publishers most stubbornly. Fred Allen, for instance, has turned down
countless offers for his autobiography. And Danny Kaye howls
with anguish at the very idea of putting his life story on paper.
Either of them could do a job that would make a lot of the pro-

fessional humorists of the day (Who? *Me??*) seek refuge in the grim mortuary that practically scares prospective customers to death with its sinister advertisement, "Do you want to be buried in a grave that isn't properly *drained?*"

Kaye is one of the great clowns of our time—mobile, ingenious, lovable. He can hold huge audiences spellbound for an hour at a time with his antics, often spontaneous, and the tip-off to his versatility is that octogenarians like him just as much as bobby-soxers; the gifts showered upon him after every stage appearance come from both men and women. The most hilarious chapter of his early career covers a tour of the Far East that he made in 1934 with a troupe of sixty vaudevillians, promoted by an explosive impresario named Marcus.

Mr. Marcus was a first-class tailor in Boston who suddenly turned theatrical producer when a burlesque operator went bankrupt and failed to claim a whole set of costumes he had left for dry-cleaning. The wandering minstrels picked up by Mr. Marcus to fill those costumes were, in the main, things of shreds and patches, but young Danny Kaye saw in the troupe the beckoning finger of opportunity. From Boston to Japan, the company wended its erratic course, overcoming one minor crisis after another. It was in Tokyo that Mr. Marcus' real grief began, and Danny Kaye came into his own.

The Japs simply could not make head or tail of Mr. Marcus' vocabulary. His voice became shriller, his dialect more confused. The Jap officials shook their heads, and murmured, "So sorry." "I guess," said Mr. Marcus sadly, "they don't understand my Yankee accent." Kaye's double-talk, however, sent them into gales of laughter, and won favors and concessions an Ambassador Grew never could have finagled. Several impromptu routines became a standard part of his act for years. Mr. Marcus was amazed but gratified, and, in one great burst of generosity, raised Danny's pay from thirty-five dollars a week to forty.

The troupe boasted one aged-in-the-wood soprano who tipped the scales at three hundred pounds, and high-hatted her associates. She was in the middle of an aria one evening when Kaye crawled out from under the backdrop and bit her in the left ankle. The audience screamed even louder than the soprano. Mr. Marcus summoned the whole company backstage to expose the culprit.

He looked helplessly at one face after another until he came to Kaye, who was gazing innocently into space. Mr. Marcus stared at him intently, and announced, "I don't say yes and I don't say no, but now I know eighty per cent who did it."

One of the numbers in which Kaye appeared was a comedy quartet. After performing the same routine about five hundred times, he grew restive and one evening introduced some ad-lib clowning. Hearing unexpected howls of delight from the audience, Mr. Marcus rushed backstage and shook Kaye violently by the shoulders. "What are you trying to do?" he cried. "Be funny in my comedy quartet?"

In every city and town in Japan, admiring throngs trailed Kaye and the other members of the company at a respectful distance. The people of that benighted land always have admired Americans, and even the recent war seemed to leave them basically unchanged. Just a few days before Pearl Harbor, for instance, when Carl Randau and his wife, Leane Zugsmith, authors of *The Setting Sun of Japan,* were fleeing to safety, the Nipponese customs guards pushed German travelers (nominally their allies) roughly aside, and escorted the American couple aboard their ship without bothering to examine their luggage.

The occupation troops report the same homage and admiration, especially from the Japanese children. Fortunately, no one ever has taught them the tricks of those odious autograph hounds who literally tear the clothes of idols from their backs. The Japs just follow quietly, and beam approval.

*   *   *

The film version of *The Secret Life of Walter Mitty* was a landmark in Kaye's screen career, but aged several other interested parties anywhere from ten to fifty years.

The ending was rewritten about ten times, and even the one finally shot left Mr. Goldwyn nursing considerable doubts. "I'm going to call Thurber himself and see what he thinks of it," decided Mr. G. Thurber was located in the *New Yorker* office and listened patiently while Goldwyn, in Hollywood, described the new ending in vivid detail. "Look, Mr. Goldwyn," said Thurber finally, "I don't know anything about moving pictures. I don't know what you've done with the rest of my story and I don't particularly care. I sold you the story and that's that. How can I say whether or not your new ending is right?" Mr. Goldwyn thought this over for a moment, and then cried approvingly, "Thank you, my boy. *Why* can't I get criticism like that in my own studio?"

At the preview, when Mr. Thurber saw how little was left of his original story, he discovered that he did care after all. "Anybody catch the name of this picture?" he asked sarcastically, and went home to unburden his soul in an article for *Life*. The Ancient Order of Mitty Worshippers (Frank Sullivan, President) threatened to blow out the brains of either themselves or the pro-

ducer. The general public, a surprising part of which had never heard of the secret lives of Mr. Mitty, or Mr. Thurber, or Mr. Goldwyn, for that matter, enjoyed itself very much.

* * *

According to *Variety*, Thurber signed with Mr. Goldwyn to do a screen treatment of *The Catsbirdseat* as well as *Mr. Mitty*, but when he turned in a script, Mr. Goldwyn told him to revise it. Mr. Thurber told Mr. Goldwyn to go climb a tree. What's more, he returned every penny of the $28,000 he had received in advance, and even made his agent throw in his ten-per-cent commission.

Thurber says the story is exaggerated, particularly the part about the $28,000. Anyhow, other Hollywood writers, not to mention Mr. Goldwyn, are aghast.

* * *

Thurber tells about a fellow writer whose services were enlisted by Lester Cowan, owner of the screen rights to F. Scott Fitzgerald's *Babylon Revisited*. "Fitzgerald did a script for this story," Cowan told the writer. "Since then, at least a dozen top men have tinkered with it, but still I'm not satisfied. I want you to tackle it." The writer read Fitzgerald's original script, and came back to declare emphatically, "This is the most perfect motion-picture scenario I ever read. I don't see why you want to revise it." Cowan reflected a moment, and agreed, "You're absolutely right. I'll pay you two thousand dollars a week to stay out here and keep me from changing one word of it."

* * *

For some weeks Alexander Woollcott had boasted to his friends of an unusual conquest. One of Boston's toniest society leaders had become enamored of his mellifluous radio voice and wanted to call at his East Fifty-second Street apartment the next time she came down to New York.

The lady arrived, unfortunately, a few days after Woollcott had taken off for Hollywood, but she was informed by the switchboard operator that his butler awaited her with a message from the master. Vastly impressed, she rang the buzzer of the Woollcott apartment, but fled in horror when she beheld a flunky in a coat several sizes too large for him—and no pants at all. She did not know, of course, that the coat was part of Woollcott's very best full-dress suit, nor that the flunky was his great good friend, Noel Coward.

Coward phoned Woollcott in Hollywood that evening to tell him the story, embellished with many gruesome details. Woollcott indulgently forgave him after an initial burst of wrath, and then continued gossiping for a full half hour. Finally he reminded Coward happily, "I take it you have forgotten that it was you who called me. The bill must be over a hundred dollars by this time." "Probably," agreed Coward. "I guess I also forgot to tell you that I was calling you from your apartment."

* * *

There is a subtle bit in Noel Coward's superb motion picture, *Brief Encounter*, that is flashed on the screen too quickly for many spectators to catch. The hero and heroine are visiting a local cinema to see something called *Flames of Passion*. In tiny letters under the title appears the legend "From *Gentle Summer* by Alice Stoughey."

That reminds me of the producer who hired a top writer to make a scenario of a Broadway hit the studio had bought for a modest half million or so. The producer didn't like the scenario at all. "What did I need him for?" he complained. "It's just like the play!"

* * *

A chronic prankster, freshly embarked on a career in pictures, blew in his first month's pay on a second-hand motorcycle. He started the motor in front of his house and went inside to phone his best girl, who lived six or seven blocks away. It was his plan to say, "Hello, darling. Hold the wire a moment," and then dash over to her home on his cycle, walking in on her while she still waited at the telephone. On the way to her house, however, he had a head-on collision with a truck, and spent the next four weeks in the hospital. Another evening he stretched himself full length on Ben Hecht's private roadway, hoping that Hecht would have the scare of a lifetime when his headlights picked out a prostrate body. Again fate stepped in. He fell sound asleep. Hecht put out his headlights as he entered the driveway, didn't see him at all,

and drove smack over his outstretched hand. Attendants at the
Cedars of Lebanon Hospital wearily led him back to his old bed.
One nurse suggested, "How about renting it by the year?"

* * *

The press agent for a famous male motion-picture star, whose
job depends on his getting his client's name into the Broadway
columns, no matter how, vowed last week that said client was
dozing peacefully in a barber chair when a burning hot towel was
dropped on his face. The star let out a howl of anguish. The barber apologized. "Excuse me, please, mister, but the towel was so
hot I couldn't hold it in my hand a second longer."

That's a pretty funny story. It also was funny when Lew Fields
used it in a musical comedy called *The Henpecks* at the old
Broadway Theatre in 1912. There are mighty few really new jokes
in the world, son! Incidentally, the man in the chair when Mr.
Fields did his act turned out to be a very fair dancer a year or
two later. His name was Vernon Castle.

* * *

The story of how the role of Scarlett O'Hara was finally filled
in the screen version of *Gone with the Wind* is not generally
known, and will bear retelling.

You may recall the reams of publicity that accompanied the
casting of this picture, with contests sponsored all over the country to single out an unknown beauty for the leading part. Folks
in the know in Hollywood regarded all this as the usual malarky,
and it was generally expected that either Joan Bennett or Paulette
Goddard would win the coveted contract. David Selznick called
a press conference for a Friday morning to announce the full cast
of the picture; the preceding week-end, Miss Bennett and Miss
Goddard both were guests of the Selznicks, and, coy but confident, assured each other a dozen times, "I just know it's going
to be you, my dear!"

On Wednesday, there appeared at the busy agency of David
Selznick's brother Myron a young English actor named Laurence
Olivier, who signed a contract appointing the Selznick office his

legal representative. "There's going to be quite a show at David's studio tomorrow night," Myron mentioned casually. "They're planning to burn down the Atlanta sets for the Margaret Mitchell picture. Want to come with me?" "Sure," said Olivier. "Can I bring a girl with me?" "Why not?" said Myron.

The next night, Olivier appeared on the set with Miss Vivien Leigh. She had played a small part in *A Yank at Oxford*, but was lost and unnoticed among the galaxy of stars that had turned out for the show.

A torch was applied to the massive sets, and a red glow lit the evening sky. Miss Leigh watched entranced, her profile etched sharply against the dancing flames. Myron noticed her, gulped, and tugged brother David by the arm. "Come with me," he commanded, "and see Scarlett O'Hara watching the burning of Atlanta."

That was Thursday night. The next morning, while reporters were gathering in the outer office, Selznick made a silent, photographic test of Vivien Leigh, and stood in the darkroom while it was developed. A few minutes later he made the public announcement. An unheralded English girl, who had never so much as laid eyes on the script of *Gone with the Wind*, was to play one of the most publicized roles in the history of motion pictures.

*   *   *

In Hollywood, Charles Coburn delivered a lecture to the local B'nai B'rith chapter, and then arrived an hour late for his weekly poker game. "What kept you?" he was asked. "I was making a speech," he explained. "Who to?" persisted the host. "I'm not sure I got the name just right," admitted Coburn, "but I think it was the Bonnie Briar Club."

*   *   *

The greatest excitement in Pasadena's Huntington Hotel since the dedication ceremonies of the Mt. Wilson Observatory came when a famous movie star sought to smuggle a young lady upstairs without registering. When the room clerk insisted he check in properly, he bowed low, flourished his pen, and signed, "Sir Thomas Lipton and Yacht."

* * *

When Sinclair Lewis finished *Kingsblood Royal*, he flew to Hollywood and, by way of relaxation, put in several weeks on a screen adaptation of *Adam and Eve* for Producer Leo McCarey. Word of the intriguing venture got around, and one morning a famous star of the twenties, still dressing like an ingénue although she showed signs of cracking around the edges, applied for the role of Eve. McCarey eyed her sourly and commented, "It's true I'm going to do a new version of *Adam and Eve*—but not with the original cast."

* * *

A grave crisis developed recently at the Twentieth Century-Fox studio. Just before a picture went into production, Darryl Zanuck decreed that the script needed bolstering. He furthermore decreed that only one man on earth could do the job properly:

Ben Hecht. "Get him," ordered Mr. Z., who has never had a single wish denied him since the day he blew into Hollywood from Wahoo, Nebraska. This time, however, Mr. Hecht proved elusive. "He's bound for New York in two days," reported Zanuck's emissary, "but if you want, he'll work on your script all the way from Pasadena to Grand Central Station." Zanuck had had much previous commerce with Ben Hecht, so he quickly asked, "And what does he want for this labor of love?" "Mr. Hecht says he has a fondness for full, round sums," was the answer. "The price he asks is one hundred thousand dollars."

Mr. Zanuck staggered, but rallied quickly. "Call him again," he ordered, "and ask him how much he'll take to work on the script as far as Kansas City."

* * *

The *Saturday Review of Literature* recently conducted a questionnaire to determine how many readers notice publishers' names on current best-sellers. The most shattering reply was mailed in by Novelist Edwin Corle. His child's nurse, a provocative blonde of twenty-four, had told him, "Shucks, everybody knows who brought out those books," and compiled her list in jig-time. MGM won with nine, Twentieth Century-Fox was second with five, and RKO, Columbia, and Universal got two apiece.

* * *

Paramount sent out telegrams inviting the town's elite to a cocktail party in honor of their visiting executive, D. A. Doran. "Phone your acceptances to Room Such-and-such," concluded the wires. Doran himself happened to be the only one in that room one lunch hour, so he answered the phone when it rang. "I'm coming to your party all right," said a voice over the phone, "but who the hell is D. A. Doran?"

* * *

Larry Marks, in the *Authors' League Bulletin,* cites the sad case of an agent who worried himself into such a state that he suf-

fered an almost complete retrogression to his former occupation
(tailor). He began to describe his writers as "Swatches," and, referring to literary material, would say, "The story has too much
padding in the shoulders," or, "Make the ending half an inch
shorter and not so baggy." The climax came when, in trying to
sell a manuscript to a cautious publisher, he shouted, "All I want
you to do is *feel* his material!"

* * *

In Hollywood they have dug up a script writer who maintains
a unique filing system. Rent bills are put away in a copy of
Dickens's *Bleak House;* life insurance policies in *All This and
Heaven Too;* auto licenses in *The Covered Wagon;* mining shares
in *Great Expectations;* doctors' bills in *The Way of All Flesh;* gas
and electricity receipts in *The Light That Failed.* For a bill for
his bride's new mink coat he rushed out to buy a copy of *The
Man Who Married a Dumb Wife.*

* * *

A new whodunit specialist aiming for the Hammett-Chandler
groove is Michael Morgan. In *Nine More Lives,* the bloody saga
of a Hollywood stunt man, he tells how one prankster had a re-
movable steering wheel put on his car, and fixed it so he could
steer with his knees. He'd take a girl out for a ride, speed up to
seventy, then suddenly detach the wheel and hand it to the terrified victim, saying calmly, "Here, *you* hold this for a few minutes."

* * *

David Selznick explained to a reporter that he accomplishes
more than most men by occasionally working around the clock.
"Take last Tuesday for instance," he is quoted as saying. "I worked
twenty-four hours straight—right through the night." At the close
of the interview a secretary (no longer there) is supposed to have
told the reporter, "Mr. Selznick neglected to add that he stayed
in bed all day Wednesday and Thursday."

* * *

An unhappy producer recently berated Bookseller Bob Campbell for recommending a novel whose central character was an atheist. "On your say-so I bought the picture rights," he wailed, "and now I find the Hays office objects to the atheist, even though we make him repent in the last reel." "Why don't you remind them of the text in the Bible itself?" suggested Bob. " 'There is more joy in heaven over one sinner that repenteth than over ninety and nine just persons.' " "Say, that's wonderful," agreed the producer. "Who said it?" "The Lead," answered Campbell.

* * *

All the way from Norway comes the story of a famous novelist who was invited to the preview of a new three-million-dollar motion picture. "I liked it," he said at the conclusion of the showing. "Who wrote it?" "You did," said the producer. "It's based on your last book!" "I never would have known it," admitted the writer. "I think it has the makings of a fine novel. May I use it?" "I guess so," said the producer, "but you'll have to give us an option on the film rights!"

* * *

There are so many ghost writers in California these days that they've formed a protective organization! *Tide* reports that the officers include a Chief Specter, a Keeper of the Ectoplasm, and an Invisible Ink.

* * *

Nunnally Johnson describes a literary party where the guests, amply lubricated, indulged in a game of musical chairs that lasted for a solid hour. The host realized at an early stage that there were just as many chairs as there were players, but since everybody apparently was having a fine time, he did nothing to disturb the proceedings.

Late in the night, a top writer, who makes no secret of his leftist sympathies, moaned bitterly to Nunnally about his battles with Tallulah Bankhead. Nunnally chuckled sympathetically for ten

full minutes, then interrupted, "Oh, come now. You know you
wouldn't say half these things about Tallulah if she was a
Russian!"

Nunnally had occasion last year to delve into all available lore
on the intriguing subject of mermaids. "In all the stories," he reported breathlessly, "they were pictured alike: The top halves are
beautiful girls, the bottom halves fish. If somebody will commission it, I have a different tale to tell. *My* mermaid's *upper* half
will be the fish, her lower half the girl."

Johnson adds that he knows just the star to play the title role
in pictures, but prefers that somebody else offer her the part.

*   *   *

People of the theatrical and literary worlds place the usual premium on success, but they still have time to show compassion and
understanding for those who no longer can make the grade. In
Hollywood, however, the competition is so fierce and the sense of
insecurity so pervading that nobody has any time for fallen big-
shots of yesterday. A star who has managed to hold his place
through the years unconsciously summed up the Hollywood attitude at a dinner party recently.

"The time to salt your money away is when you're rolling along
on top," he announced. "You never know when you're going to
hit the skids. For example, take the picture I'm doing. It calls for
a flock of extras. I was looking them over at the studio this morning—a motley crew—and you'd be amazed to know how many of
them *were once my friends!*"

*   *   *

Michael Gross, who makes ninety-eight per cent of the special
posters and advertising displays used by the book-publishing industry, was a guest at the Paramount Studio in Hollywood recently and at lunch time was taken to a table where the leading
gag writers are wont to congregate. After he was seated, one of
the writers yelled "sixty," and everybody snickered. The second
cried "forty-two," and another polite ripple of laughter ran
around the room. A third shouted "sixteen" and everybody smiled

politely—everybody but Gross, that is, who, by this time was completely mystified. The climax came when a fourth writer cried "ninety-four"—and a stout party in the corner laughed so hard he practically went into convulsions. Gross turned to his host and said, "I don't like to play the part of a complete hick, but what on earth is all this business about laughing at numbers?"

"You're with professional jokesters," explained the host, "and they know every gag in the world. To save time, they have given a number to each joke. When anybody calls out the number of a gag, they all laugh just as hard as if he had told the actual story."

"A time-saving device," admitted Gross, "but what about that fat lad who is still choking with laughter because somebody yelled 'ninety-four'?"

"Oh, him," came the answer, "I guess he never heard that gag before."

*   *   *

The irascible screen star, Monty Woolley, sometimes known as "The Beard," breezed through Oklahoma City recently, and did not exactly endear himself to the press when he rasped, "All I ask is that you let me alone. If the Secretary of War came to town you wouldn't pay any attention—you wouldn't even ask the President for his autograph. But let some lousy movie actor like me come along and you won't let me rest."

To imploring photographers, he added, "Nothing doing. Just use anybody with a beard. Charles Evans Hughes ought to do. He was nobody—just Chief Justice of the Supreme Court."

*   *   *

FOLLOW THE LEDERER

Since Charlie Lederer has become one of the most successful writers in Hollywood, producers find it advisable to laugh fondly over what they now call his "pixie humor." When he first bobbed up they were not so tolerant. As an apprentice at MGM, for example, he enraged Eddie Mannix to a point where Mannix banished him permanently from the lot. Lederer got in the next day, however, by hiding in the rumble seat of Mannix's own car. This time he was bounced out by force. He flew to New York and sent Mannix a wire that read, "Arrived safely."

In World War II, Lederer was a captain in the China-Burma-India Theatre, assigned to make a film called *Why We're Here* (a lot of G.I.s wanted to know). Captain Lederer's script called for considerable dialogue by General Sultan, who had replaced General Stilwell in the CBI sector. Sultan grumbled about memorizing so many lines, but agreed to go through with the job. That evening, however, he picked up a copy of Gene Fowler's *Good Night, Sweet Prince*, and discovered that John Barrymore had never bothered to memorize lines at all, but had read them from a big slate suspended behind the camera. The General threw his script across the room and said, "If Barrymore could do it that way, so can I."

This put Lederer in something of a predicament because there wasn't a slate in all India. He finally secured a supply of beaver board. General Sultan entered with his whole staff and ordered, "Write something on one of those boards to see if I can read it all right." Lederer obeyed. What he wrote was "Promote Lederer!"

General Sultan was a good sport about it, and the next day Lederer was made a major.

A fellow officer assured Lederer, "The natives here worship the

ground I walk on." "Admitted," said Lederer, "but what do they think about *you?*"

One evening in Delhi, he was taken to the home of a British colonial who proved to be a rabid and noisy anti-Semite. American officers had been briefed to avoid political arguments with the British "at all costs," so Lederer held his peace. His chance came when the lady handed him the key to a liquor cabinet set in the bottom of a credenza. The door stuck. When he applied pressure, the china on the shelves above rattled. "Be careful," she warned, "that china is priceless."

"Tell me, Mrs. Arbuthnot," said Lederer suddenly, "why don't you like the Jews?"

She looked at him in surprise and said vaguely, "Oh, I don't know. No reason, I guess."

Lederer yanked on the cabinet door. Most of the china flew across the room. "Now you've got a reason," he told her—and left.

* * *

In the early 1930's, when the heads of Paramount changed as frequently as a Park Avenue traffic light, Mr. B. P. Schulberg was replaced suddenly by a man whose ability was unquestioned but whose physical stature was not exactly herculean. In fact, he would have come about shoulder-high to the late Fiorello La Guardia, and never had to pay a dime to ride in the subway. He just walked under the turnstile.

Mr. Schulberg's wife was an important agent, representing some of the biggest stars on the Paramount lot, and in that capacity she was compelled, very much against her will, to visit the office that once had been her husband's. She was duly announced by an embarrassed secretary, and entered the sacred chamber, getting angrier with each of the three steps she had to descend in the process. "Well," she declared to the man who awaited her, "when my husband occupied this office, he at least had the courtesy to stand up when a lady entered."

The new executive stepped out from behind his desk. "Damn it," he said, "I *am* standing!"

* * *

A film mahatma invited Jerry Chodorov to a dinner party at his home. "I'm sorry but I can't make it," said Chodorov. "I'm dining that evening with Louis Blank." "Blank?" echoed the mahatma in amazement. "He's a *luncheon* date!"

* * *

A big investment trust, toying with the notion of acquiring a block of stock in a certain studio, dispatched a corps of efficiency experts not so long ago to check on conditions there. The late Bert Kalmar spotted one of them pouncing on a workman at the end of a particularly hot and irritating day. "What's your job around here?" snapped the expert. "Electrician," answered the workman. "What's an ohm?" "How's that?" asked the workman. "An ohm, an ohm," the expert repeated. "Oh, that," said the workman. "It's an Englishman's castle, you buzzard: you don't catch me that way!"

* * *

In *You Bet Your Life,* Leo Guild, ace publicist for Warner Brothers, tells about the day a Warner Bros. writer studied the rushes of some scenes he had written. They were terrible. When the lights went on in the projection room, Jack Warner asked the writer to see him in his inner sanctum. A violent electric storm was raging outside. The writer, dejected, walked down the hall with two friends. Suddenly all the lights flickered and faded. "What's that?" asked one of them. "That's Warner testing the chair," said the writer grimly.

* * *

To show that actual figures occasionally *can* be misleading, Guild cites the following motion-picture statistics: Benito Mussolini drew two dollars a day in Rome for playing an extra in Samuel Goldwyn's *The Eternal City;* Leon Trotsky made three dollars a day (in 1915) when he appeared in *Rasputin* at Fort Lee, New Jersey; and the Duchess of Windsor, then known as Wallis Simpson, was paid five dollars a day for brief appearances in a number of Hollywood productions. It's a good story, anyhow.

* * *

Harry Kurnitz advised the producers of the screen version of *Mourning Becomes Electra* that they'd probably insure bigger grosses by renaming it *Oh Boy, Do I Remember Mama!*

*   *   *

Sidney Skolsky tells the story about a Los Angeles businessman whose four-year-old son got a miniature motion-picture machine for Christmas. He had never been taken to a real movie but he loved the animated cartoons that were shown on his new machine. One day his father said, "Johnny, I've got a real thrill in store for you tonight. Cary Grant is coming over for dinner. He is a great movie actor." The little boy was very much impressed. "What is he, Pop?" he asked. "A cat or a mouse?"

*   *   *

When Emerich Kalman, Hungarian composer of "Sari," "Miss Springtime," and other successes, visited Hollywood, a big dance was given in his honor. Kalman himself selected the musical program. The guests danced to lilting waltzes, but failed to recognize any of them. Finally one guest told the leader, "Play something of Kalman's we all know. Play 'Sari.'" When the orchestra struck up the familiar strain, Kalman paled, and rushed over to the leader. "Don't play that, you fool," he whispered. "I've already sold them that piece!"

When Kalman reported to his studio, the head man told him, "We have lots of famous writers from Budapest in Hollywood. You can have your choice of collaborators. You know Ernst Vajda, of course?" "Ah, Vajda," exclaimed Kalman. "One of my dearest friends. What a play his *Fata Morgana* was!" "Then there's Bush-Fekete. How about him?" "A great writer," enthused Kalman. "A really great writer. I love him as a brother." "Walter Reisch is also available." Kalman was stumped. "I never heard of him," he confessed. "Well," said the head man, "take your pick." "I think," said Kalman, "I will work with Walter Reisch."

*   *   *

A favorite picture star who married well—and often—found it expedient to get a divorce in a hurry a few months ago. Her lawyer suggested Mexico. "But I don't speak Spanish," she protested. "That's all right," said the lawyer. "Whenever there's a pause, all you have to do is say 'si, si.'"

The star created a great sensation in the little Mexican village, and when she appeared in court, the whole town turned out to witness the event. There was a great deal of emoting and bowing, and the star said "si, si" very firmly on numerous occasions. Suddenly the crowd gave a great cheer. "Well, I guess I'm divorced," she said complacently. "Divorced, my eye," cried her perspiring attorney. "You've married the mayor!"

* * *

SECTION 6

The Magazine

The magazine section of a metropolitan newspaper is the last refuge for journalists who like to use their imagination and resent being pinned down too closely to prosaic facts. Here highly improbable tales are embellished with lurid illustrations and reproductions of art masterpieces—usually in color—and readers are not even expected to take them without several grains of salt.

Whether or not the stories in this chapter have any basis in fact, or were invented from whole cloth, no longer matters. They have been told and retold so often that they now are regarded as "folklore." I have given some of them a twist of my own, and tried to bring them up to date, but inveterate story collectors probably will recognize all of them.

*　*　*

In a drab suburb of London there lives a dignified lady whose social status is high but whose bank balance is dangerously low. I will call her Mrs. Stockwell.

Because of her impeccable family connections, Mrs. Stockwell received an invitation to the wedding of Princess Elizabeth and Philip Mountbatten at Westminster Abbey and immediately was confronted with the problem of what gift to send. Rummaging desperately through the stocks of the curiosity shops and pawnbrokers in her neighborhood, she came upon three isolated pieces of an old chess set that caught her fancy. They obviously had been carved by a master—and the price, fifteen shillings, was right. Mrs. Stockwell bought them, wrote out her card, and resolutely ordered the proprietor to send them to the Princess at Buckingham Palace. Amidst the splendor of all the other gifts, Mrs. Stockwell rather hoped her own paltry offering would be overlooked completely.

When the presents of the royal couple were put on exhibition for relatives and friends, Mrs. Stockwell peered anxiously at the glittering array. There was no sign of her chessmen. Some understanding secretary evidently had hidden them away. She turned in relief to leave the room—and then she saw her chessmen, alone in a glass display case, with a dozen people gazing at them in admiration.

Explained the placard: "These priceless pieces have been missing for a century. Three generations of the royal family have commissioned experts to search for them. Mrs. Henry Stockwell found them. Her invaluable gift completes one of the finest and most precious chess sets in the world."

Mrs. Stockwell drew her moth-eaten fur boa a little tighter about her neck and walked proudly out into the cold sunlight of the November morning.

*　*　*

A multi-millionaire in the Southwest, piratical in his younger days, but anxious to recapture the esteem of fellow-citizens in his dotage, overwhelmed the dean of the local college with a very generous donation. The wise old dean decided that the first thing to do with the unexpected funds was to hire a competent new head for the English department. The salary offered was generous, and so many applicants turned up for the job that they had to double up in the rooms of the only hotel in town.

The field narrowed down to two: one, Mr. Whitmore, a rather wistful, graying, and unquestionably erudite man of fifty; the other, Mr. Collins, a loquacious, bouncy chap at least twenty years younger, who looked more like a football coach and unquestionably had a way with him as far as the students were concerned. As luck would have it, the two men shared the same room.

The dean and his advisers found it so hard to make a final choice that they decided to leave it all to a public address in the college chapel on the subject of Elizabethan literature. Whitmore spent three agonizing days writing his speech and memorizing it; his younger rival seemingly did no preparatory work at all, and continued making time with the local belles. Just before the contestants walked over to the chapel, however, Whitmore made a disquieting discovery. The typewritten copy of his speech had disappeared.

The gathering was called to order, and Collins, the younger contestant, given priority. While his rival watched with helpless despair, he calmly pulled the purloined speech out of his pocket and read it so eloquently that the audience rewarded him with a burst of cheers.

Now it was Whitmore's turn. The speech he had written contained everything he had to say. He was too shattered by the turn of events to improvise or try a new tack. With his face burning with embarrassment, and the surprised audience wriggling in its seats, he could only repeat the speech, word for word, that Collins had delivered so eloquently before him. As he bumbled on, however, the wise old dean's eyes never left his face.

The trustees retired to reach what appeared to be a foregone conclusion. Collins was so sure of his victory that he patted his silent rival on the back and said in a patronizing tone, "Don't take it too hard, pop. After all, only one of us could win." Then the dean came back and announced his decision.

Mr. Whitmore had been chosen for the post!

"You are entitled to know how we made our choice," the dean told the surprised audience. "All of us, of course, were surprised by the eloquence and erudition of Mr. Collins. I, for one, didn't know he had it in him. But you will remember that Mr. Collins read his speech to us. When Mr. Whitmore came before us, he repeated from memory every word of that same speech, although it is inconceivable that he ever heard a line of it before in his life. What a memory, gentlemen! And since a fine memory is an invaluable asset for a teacher of Elizabethan literature, we decided that Mr. Whitmore was the man we had been praying for."

As Whitmore, dazed but happy, was leaving the campus, the old dean came up and whispered in his ear, "When you're on our faculty, my boy, if I were you, I wouldn't leave my valuable papers lying about too carelessly."

*   *   *

From Delos Avery comes a story of the legendary tyrant Ying-Nu, who was withal a man of some compassion, also endurance, for he was husband to a hundred surpassingly beautiful wives. "One of you incredibly lovely ladies," he announced to them sadly from his golden throne, "apparently has been betraying my secrets to my enemies. It would break my heart to discover which one it is. I must let the somewhat harsh law take its course. Let each tenth one of you come forth, for ten must die." But when Ying-Nu beheld the tears of the ten and observed their reluctance to have their heads chopped off, his stern features relaxed. "No, no," he cried. "It shall not be! Am I not known as a man of some compassion? There shall be instead a feast with wine and music. Come!" And Ying-Nu gently led the ten away, whispering softly to the headsman as he passed, "Off with the heads of the other ninety!"

* * *

Recommended to blabber-mouths is Henry Commager's version of Jonah and the whale. Jonah was so nervous in the whale's belly, it appears, that he paced up and down ceaselessly. The whale finally grew annoyed and called down, "Can't you cut out that continuous bouncing about, Jonah? You are ruining my digestion." "You're a fine one to talk," answered Jonah. "If you only had kept that big mouth of yours shut, neither of us would be in this fix now."

* * *

This is an era of violent change, of insecurity and crass materialism, but an old fable that I found in a volume of folklore of the Near East emphasized the fact that there are two things that remain about the same in every century and every clime: the heart and mother love.

This fable tells of a spoiled, willful son in ancient Judea who came to his mother and declared, "I have fallen in love with a maid of surpassing beauty, but she trusts not my protestations. 'And you really love me,' says she, 'you will cut out your mother's heart and place it before me on a golden tray.'" The mother gazed deep into the eyes of her son, then unhesitatingly bared her breast. And the son cut out her heart.

In mad haste, he dashed with it toward the home of his beloved. When he stumbled over the root of a tree, the heart, bleeding, called out softly, "Be careful, son of mine. If you run so fast,
you may fall and hurt yourself."

*   *   *

In a "top-secret" Nazi espionage school, where the cream of the
German secret-service operatives received final instructions, the
faculty included a Herr Linz. His particular job consisted of
teaching the little niceties of behavior that would enable his pro-
tégés to mingle freely in English society, pass as one-hundred-
per-cent Britishers, and send back vital information to Berlin. One
of his last-minute tips always was this: "Open an account at a
well-known bank, and 'accidentally' drop the book before acquaintances. This will reassure them as to both your social status
and your financial responsibility."

A great many of Herr Linz's pupils succeeded in reaching London, but every one of them was apprehended before sending a
single vital message home. The dropping of a bank book was a
little signal arranged between the British secret service and its
highly regarded agent, instructor Linz.

*   *   *

In a wrecked Italian cathedral, bewildered American officers
discovered an old wooden sword carefully preserved in a glass
case near the altar. This is how it got there.

A pompous viceroy of the province back in the eighteenth century decreed one day that no one of his courtiers was to appear in
public without his sword. Death was the penalty for disregard
of the order. A few mornings later he personally caught sight of
one of his officers without his sword. He dismounted hurriedly,
collared the mortified offender, and ordered him hanged from the
nearest post. The noble was an eloquent fellow, and on bended
knee beseeched, "If you must kill me, let it at least be a death
consonant with my rank. Have the next courtier that comes this
way run me through with his sword." "So be it," said the viceroy.

They waited quite a while for a courtier. The one who finally hove into view had just lost most of his worldly possessions, including the blade of his sword, in a gambling den. Mindful of the law, he had taken the precaution of fitting a wooden stick to the hilt and scabbard.

Abruptly ordered by his viceroy to stab one of his companions to death, this hapless knight tried first to beg off on the grounds of court etiquette, and when that got him nowhere at all, he turned his gaze heavenward, solemnly prayed, "Mercy! Mercy! To spare this man and me, turn my sword to wood!"

He drew his sword and brandished it. "A miracle! A miracle!" cried everyone. The viceroy carried the wooden sword himself to the cathedral, where it became the chief attraction for tourists until the Nazis destroyed the town.

* * *

Dean Carl Ackerman, of the Columbia School of Journalism, punched home the advantages of a clever sales approach with this story: Two beggars were soliciting alms on the same street. One of them was getting five out of every six donations. Investigation disclosed a printed sign on the successful beggar's cup that read, "It is a beautiful day in May—and I am blind."

* * *

Peggy Wood, the operetta star, watched the rain pouring down one night from the haven of a warm, friendly drawing room, and remembered this story she had heard years ago in England.

A country doctor, cursing the luck that called him out on the worst night of the year, was splashing his way homeward on his motorcycle, on an old road full of bumps and holes. Suddenly he heard a cry for help. A luckless motorist had skidded off the road, and his car was up to the hubs in mud in a ditch.

"Obviously I cannot pull you out with this motorcycle," said the doctor, "but if you'll hitch on behind me, I'll ride you into town. It's only three or four miles, and we'll find someone there to drive you back and get your car on the road again."

Before the grateful motorist climbed aboard the cycle, he was advised by the doctor to reverse his rain-coat, back to front, to protect him a little better from the driving rain. Then they set out on the rocky road to town. The doctor said nothing until he saw the first lights of the main street flickering through the storm. "Here we are," he pointed out then. "We'll soon have help for you." When there was no reply, the doctor looked behind him. He was alone on the motorcycle.

"Good heavens," he thought, "the poor fellow must have fallen off!" He turned the cycle about and began retracing the ground. A mile back he came upon his erstwhile passenger, lying motionless on the road, surrounded by a small group of wet and bedraggled cottagers.

"Is he badly hurt?" cried the doctor.

"I'm afraid so," answered one of the cottagers. "We were in our house yonder when we heard his moans above the wind and the storm. When we found him he was in terrible shape, sir. His head had been twisted clear around! My son and I twisted it back just as fast as we could, but ever since, he hasn't moved or made a single sound!"

* * *

A motorist of a different sort was Robert Considine, columnist and co-author of *Thirty Seconds Over Tokyo*. Considine was cruising in a friend's brand-new convertible one morning about ten when he discovered that it was equipped with a telephone. He couldn't resist calling his wife, Mildred. That good lady was awakened from a sound sleep to hear an operator drone, "There is a mobile call for you." "I don't know anybody in Mobile," said Mrs. C. firmly, and hung up. The operator rang her again, however, and she heard her husband say, "What hath God wrought?" "Come home," answered Mrs. Considine. "You're drunk."

* * *

There was a bit of mystery in Cambridge, Massachusetts, some years ago, and Charles Morton, of the *Atlantic Monthly*, tells how it was solved.

One of the town's leading churches boasted a clock with a fine set of chimes that rang out perfectly every hour on the hour. Perfectly, that is, twenty-three hours out of twenty-four. Every midnight, folks began noticing that the chimes were ringing thirteen times!

The mechanism was checked and rechecked to no avail. Then one canny inspector noted that the church adjoined one of the dormitories of fair Harvard. He established an outpost in the belfry and trained his binoculars on the dormitory windows. Sure enough, as the first chime of midnight rang out, a light went on in one of the windows, and disclosed a whimsical undergraduate, equipped with a .22 rifle and a homemade silencer. As the twelfth chime of the clock sounded automatically, the undergraduate took careful aim and added the thirteenth for luck.

The story has a happy ending, swears Mr. Morton. A few years after he was graduated, the intrepid young marksman designed what many military authorities regard as the best automatic rifle ever made.

* * *

In a tiny Vermont hamlet, many miles from any railroad or public highway, there lived a frugal widow who toiled hard and faithfully to support herself and her young son. It became apparent that he possessed talent as a writer, and the local schoolmaster backed his plea that he be allowed to travel to the city to seek his fame and fortune.

The widow agreed at last, and was quite reconciled to the idea until she found herself at the nearest railroad station and saw the train puffing in. Truth to tell, it was the first time either she or her son ever had seen a train. The engine seemed to her to be a great monster, belching flame, come to carry her boy away, and she drew back in terror as it thundered past her. An hour after it had gone, she still stood on the platform, trembling and in tears.

The boy was a great success as a writer, and in due course followed the way of all flesh to Hollywood. There he became so famous that even Mike Romanoff called him by his first name. The checks he sent to his beloved mother grew larger and larger, and finally she agreed to come to the Coast to see him. She arrived by plane—six years to the day from the time she had seen him off in Vermont.

He wasn't quite prepared for the beautifully clad vision that stepped off the plane. Her complexion, however, was a pale shade of green, and she reeled slightly as she hurried to enfold him in her arms. "What a flight," she complained. "Storms all the way. I really was uncomfortable."

"But why did you have to fly, Mother?" he asked. "You have all the time in the world. Why didn't you take the Century and the Superchief?"

"What?" she exclaimed in horror. "Spend three whole days on a stuffy, old-fashioned train?"

* * *

Driving to Princeton one afternoon with the late Professor Duane Stuart, head of Princeton's classics department for many years, we were halted temporarily by a flat tire, and, realizing our own shortcomings on mechanics, clanked down the side of the turnpike until we came to a garage, where the tire was changed for us by somebody who knew how. Meanwhile, Professor Stuart recalled the story of another Princeton faculty member who had found himself in a similar predicament—only he was driving alone, in full dress, and in the small hours of the dawn. He stood helplessly beside his car, cursing the banquet that had lured him to New York.

At long last another car came along. Its driver proved to be a good Samaritan indeed. He took off his coat, changed the tire single-handed, and got himself well smeared with mud in the process. The Princeton man was deeply grateful—until he discovered, just before they parted company, that his gold watch was missing. In a sudden rage, he clipped the unprepared stranger on the chin, cried, "Only a scoundrel would do a trick like this," seized the watch from the other's pocket and jammed it into his own, and drove off before the stranger could regain his feet.

He was still fuming with anger as he put his car in his garage. Then he strode into his house and up to his bedroom.

There, on the bureau, was the watch he had forgotten to wear to the banquet.

* * *

I heard another story at Princeton that day that may be familiar.

The fly-leaf of every Gideon Bible bears the legend, "If you are lonesome and restless, read Psalms 23 and 27, Old Testament."

Written in ink in the margin of one precious copy, rescued from a room in a Trenton hotel, was this addition: "If you're still lonesome when you've read the psalm, phone Homestead 8211 and ask for Gwendolyn."

* * *

The soft lights of the Champagne Room in El Morocco, the low hum of conversation, and the insinuating music of the gypsy violinist warmed the heart of Mrs. Farraday, and made her home and husband in Wisconsin seem very far away. Her companion, whom she had met so casually at a cocktail party that very afternoon, regarded her with a proprietary air that frightened and thrilled her. "I haven't felt this way in twenty years," she murmured. "Nor I," he added.

The enchantment lasted for an entire week. What's more, her companion's casual statement that he had more millions than he knew what to do with proved no idle boast. The day she left for home, Mrs. Farraday found herself the possessor of some roseate memories—and a beautiful platinum mink coat. It had been delivered just before she checked out of her hotel. The card read simply, "Thank you, my dear."

All the way to Chicago, Mrs. Farraday fingered her new coat, and wondered what to do. Before she climbed aboard the local for her home town, she had hit upon a solution that seemed foolproof. She pawned the coat at a shop near the Union Station.

"John," she told her husband after she had unpacked, "I found a pawn ticket in the station at Chicago. You might try redeeming it when you go down on Friday. Who knows? It just might be something we can use."

John took the ticket without saying a word. He just looked at Mrs. Farraday rather intently. He had been looking at her that way, as a matter of fact, ever since he had called for her at the depot.

When he returned from Chicago on Friday evening, Mrs. Farraday waited until they had finished dinner, and then asked, ever so casually, "I wonder if you remembered to redeem that silly little pawn ticket I found."

"Yes, I did," said John. "Funny things people pawn nowadays!" He went out into the hall and brought back a book which he handed her with elaborate politeness. Mrs. Farraday must have looked surprised, for he laughed dryly and assured her, "Yes, dear, the ticket was for a book."

The book was Kinsey's *Sexual Behavior in the Human Male*.

*   *   *

In some variations of the above tale, an extra fillip is added for a tag-line. The wife drops in to her husband's office a few days later, and meets his comely secretary in the lobby. The secretary is wearing the platinum mink coat.

There is also a popular version in which the husband is a plodding clerk in a wholesale house, the wife faithful and evidently happy with her modest flat, despite her striking beauty of face and figure. Every month, however, she leaves for a week-end with a mysterious "aunt," and brings back some little bauble—a piece of imitation jewelry, a glass diamond, a string of fake pearls— which she tosses carelessly in a basket, with a deprecating, "The junk my old aunt has around her flat! She really thinks I get pleasure from these ridiculous gifts."

One week-end she does not come home. She has been killed in an automobile accident—run down, evidently, by a hit-and-run driver. The despondent husband cannot bear anything about the house that reminds him of his departed love, and is about to throw away the collection of trinkets when a thrifty brother offers to try to sell it for a few sorely needed dollars.

He comes back goggle-eyed. The jeweler at the corner has examined the trinkets and told him angrily, "You're not going to get me mixed up in this business. That stuff is worth two hundred thousand dollars at the very least!"

*   *   *

In an exclusive dress shop in Beverly Hills, a regular patroness saw a new creation she fancied, and asked the price. "A thousand dollars," said the proprietor without batting an eyelash. The lady recoiled and exclaimed, "This time you've really gone too far. New look or not, you're never going to get a thousand dollars for that dress. In fact, I'll bet a hundred dollars you don't." "It's a bet," he replied, "and furthermore, when I do, I'll even tell you who bought it."

As luck would have it, the proprietor did sell the dress for a thousand dollars just a few days later, but he never figured a way to break the news to the lady with whom he bet. The purchaser, it seems, was the lady's husband, making a little gift to his private secretary.

* * *

When Thomas Mann first visited Southern California, Mrs. Bruno Frank invited the most important people in Hollywood to a party to meet him. It was a function that would have gladdened the heart of any Sunday magazine editor. For once the brilliant guests lived up to their reputations. The conversation scintillated. Everything clicked. At the height of the festivities, the late Carl Laemmle, powerful head of the Universal Studio, tapped the hostess on the shoulder. "It is a wonderful party," he told her. "Tomorrow morning, if you don't mind, my secretary will phone to get Mr. Mann's address and a complete list of your guests. I want to have exactly the same party at *my* house next week."

* * *

In the dear dead days of long ago when Prohibition was in its glory, one of its chief beneficiaries, a gentleman named Al Capone, gave a dinner dance attended by the crême-de-la-crême of Cicero. One extremely pretty girl, making her debut in this select society, was the cynosure of all eyes, as she fully expected to be, but as the evening wore on, she grew more and more restive. The host, Mr. Capone himself, had not asked her to dance with him.

"He's danced four times with that frump with all the peroxide curls and purple beads," she complained to her escort. "He hasn't even looked at me. You're a big-shot—or so you tell me. Do something about it!"

Her hard-pressed escort had a sudden inspiration. "If you knew what it meant, Capone dancing with that jane so often," he told

her, "you wouldn't talk like that. He's putting the finger on her!
She must know too much. Capone's signaling the boys to give her
a ride. She's as good as gone right now!" The girl paled, shud-
dered with excitement, and whispered, "Gee, honey, how was I
to know?"

The young Machiavelli was so pleased with his stratagem, he
couldn't resist telling it to Al Capone, who promptly decided the
joke was too good to cut short. He walked over to the girl, calmly
took her away from the man to whom she was talking, and said
loudly, "This dance is with me."

For four dances in succession, he whirled her around the floor,
at the end of which time the young lady was so frightened, she
was uttering incoherent sounds and her eyes were popping from
her head. Capone appeared more and more interested.

On the way home, much, much later, the girl's escort let her
in on his whimsical little joke.

If you're looking for a story with a happy ending, this one has
it, I suppose. The girl achieved some small measure of revenge
within twenty-four hours. Her boy friend was found dead in an
alley, his body sprayed with a dozen machine-gun slugs. She was

looking sadly at his picture, and wondering what to wear to the funeral, when a messenger arrived with four dozen long-stemmed American Beauties. The enclosed card read, "Mr. Capone expects you to have dinner with him this evening."

LITTLE MEN

A dinner party at the home of novelist Edna Ferber always gives you something to remember her by. A charming and provocative personality in her own right, Miss Ferber has the further Elsa Maxwellian ability to whip up a guest list that jells. The talk is witty and unflagging, and sometimes initiates a bitter feud that titillates the literary world for months. It is not exactly a coincidence that the hostess herself is often a key figure in these epic misunderstandings. As a special added attraction, the sporting Miss Ferber usually provides a beautiful actress or two to keep the male guests on their toes between rounds.

That we all got off on the subject of midgets the last time I visited Miss Ferber was probably due to the presence of a guest whose ancestors were famous circus stars, and who began the discussion by remarking amiably that side-show freaks were often more normal in their general behavior than a lot of authors he knew. Midgets interested him most of all.

It appeared that everybody in the room had his own midget story to contribute. There was the old one about Heywood Broun, for instance, who appeared red-eyed at a Chicago convention, and explained, "I came out in a lower from New York and couldn't sleep a wink: a dwarf in the upper above me kept pacing up and down all night." And the equally venerable fable of Sophie Tucker, who followed Singer's Midgets on a memorable all-star vaudeville bill. As she was proceeding on-stage, something went wrong with the electric lights, and the house was plunged into total darkness. Above the resultant confusion, Miss Tucker's strident voice rang out, "For the love of Pete," she cried, "get on those lights! I'm up to my who's-this in midgets!"

Of course, somebody recalled Marc Connelly's "Coroner's Inquest," one of the classic tales on the subject. It reappears about twice a year in anthologies, and even oftener in digest magazines.

It concerns two midgets who made a good living in show business until one hit a streak of bad luck and was reduced to living on the largess of the other. Like so many other humans, big and small, he ended by resenting, then hating his benefactor. Noting that the latter always sported a slender cane, he sequestered a butcher's knife and, by surreptitiously cutting the cane down a fraction of an inch every night, persuaded the friend he suddenly was growing to normal height, and would soon be unable to make a living on the stage as a midget. The friend brooded over this until one day he found the butcher's knife—and examined his cane. Some hours later, the police found the bodies of two midgets.

In a roomful of literary folk it was only a question of time until someone brought up the masterful story by Aldous Huxley from *Crome Yellow*, one of his first—and one of his greatest—books. His hero was named Hercules, and he was very rich, but alas! despite "a meat diet, constant exercise, and a little rack, modelled on those employed by the Holy Inquisition, on which young Hercules was stretched, with excruciating torments, for a half hour every morning and evening," he remained a pigmy of three feet and four inches. When he came into his estate, Hercules found a solution to his problem. First, he had his house and everything in it cut down in proportion to his own dimensions. Then he found a beautiful bride, Filomena, as tiny as himself. Their servants were dwarfs, their dogs tiny spaniels, their stable tenanted only by Shetland ponies. Everything was in perfect scale, and their happiness was complete. The birth of a son seemed the final blessing. Then the blow fell. Hercules and his bride pretended not to notice at first, but when the son had reached the age of three and was already taller than his mother, there was no longer any use dodging the issue. The son was destined to become a man of normal dimensions!

He was packed off to school, but Hercules and Filomena realized that they were only postponing the inevitable. One day the son, now a giant in a brown traveling suit, brought two friends and a retinue of servants to the house. They roared with laughter at the tiny servants and household pets, crushed the miniature furniture by simply stamping through the room. Hercules bade them good night, quietly ascended the stairs, gave his wife a fatal overdose of sleeping tablets, and then severed the artery of his left wrist. "Soon," says Aldous Huxley, "he was sound asleep. There was not much blood in his small body." . . .

There wasn't much to say after that story had been retold. When the party broke up and we walked across the Plaza, the most beautiful square in all New York, the Sherry-Netherland and Pierre Hotels somehow seemed taller than ever, the glittering stars colder and more remote in the sky.

* * *

Here's a story that pops up as regularly as clock work. The last time it came from Hollywood, and was pinned to the lovely Joan Caulfield.

There were to be ten at her house for luncheon, and the individual portions of cold cuts and salad had been neatly set out, but the cocker spaniel got into the kitchen and gobbled up one of them. Miss Caulfield banished the pup to the garden and hastily redivided the remaining nine portions into ten.

The unwitting guests arrived, ate, and made merry—until Miss Caulfield looked out of the window and saw her cocker spaniel lying dead on the terrace. "He's been poisoned," she cried in horror, and then told her guests what had happened before they came.

There followed a mad rush to the hospital, with ten beautiful but panic-stricken ladies screaming for stomach pumps at the same time. When the ordeal was over, and it became apparent they were going to survive, they headed weakly for their homes and sleeping pills. Miss Caulfield found her neighbor waiting for her.

"Wasn't it awful about your poor doggy?" she gushed. "I saw the truck run over him, but you were having such fun with your guests, I didn't want to disturb you."

* * *

An aviator, relates Roy Huggins, was sent on a mission to a distant part of the globe. When he returned to his base, he noticed it was strangely quiet. Everything was in perfect order, but there wasn't a sign of life in the place. He wandered through town in growing astonishment. Human beings and animals simply had vanished from the scene.

He tore back to the airport, filled his plane with high octane gas, and flew, terrified, to New York, London, Moscow, Shanghai. While he had been on his mission, every living creature apparently had disappeared. He was the only man alive in the world! He weighed the situation carefully and found it intolerable. Suicide seemed the only solution. He swallowed a vial of deadly poison and calmly waited for it to take effect. Just as the drug reached his brain, and the room started swimming before his eyes, he heard a familiar sound.

It was the telephone ringing.

SECTION 7

Railroads & Shipping

The publicity department of the New York Central Railroad likes to bandy the names of famous industrialists, statesmen, and picture stars who scurry back and forth between New York and Chicago aboard the once-plushy but now ultra-modern Twentieth Century Limited. One of its most prized commuters was the founder of a more famous collection of packers than Green Bay— J. Ogden Armour, Esq.

Mr. Armour, they say, was breakfasting aboard the Century one morning when he imperiously summoned the dining car steward and demanded, "Is this some of my own ham I'm eating?" The steward assured him that it was. "Humph," commented Mr. Armour, "it's damn bad ham!"

* * *

From the Chesapeake & Ohio Railroad (now more or less linked
to the New York Central through the manipulations of the dynamic Robert R. Young) comes a story of a millionaire who
bought a large estate near a tiny whistle-stop station on a neglected branch line. From Sears Roebuck he ordered a prefabricated chicken coop and, when he received word that it had
arrived, set out in a truck with his butler to bring it home. No
one was about when he spied the coop along the right of way, and
he soon had it loaded on the truck. Half a mile up the road they
passed a little man in blue who had "Station Master" written on
his cap. He took one look and shouted, "Stop that car. What do
you think you got on that truck?" "My new chicken coop," explained the millionaire. "Chicken coop, my eye," cried the station
master, "that's Grigsby Junction!"

*　*　*

Stewart Holbrook declares that it was the railroads which established the four "standard" times—Eastern, Central, Mountain,
and Western—in the United States. The agitation for such a move
was started, surprisingly, by the principal of a school for girls. The
railroads put it into practice on October 18, 1883, amidst wide-
spread prophecies of confusion and accidents, none of which were
borne out. Two adamant holdouts were a Tennessee preacher
named Watson, who pounded his watch into a pulp with a claw
hammer in his pulpit, explaining that the four time belts made
timepieces worthless, and the Federal Government, which officially ignored the system for the next thirty-five years.

*　*　*

"One of the most memorable experiences of my career," a famous war correspondent told his friend, "took place on my way
to fill a lecture date in Buffalo. I met a beautiful girl in the diner.
One thing led to another and it wasn't long before I was being
entertained in her compartment. Suddenly she burst into tears.
'My husband is the most wonderful man in the world,' she sobbed,
'and look at me here kissing an absolute stranger.' She painted this
husband in such glowing colors that first thing you know, I was
crying too!"

"A dolorous picture," remarked the friend. "What happened next?"

"Nothing new," said the correspondent. "We just kissed and cried all the way to Buffalo."

＊ ＊ ＊

Editor John Woodburn poses this problem: A single railroad track, upon which two trains are approaching each other hopelessly, relentlessly, each maintaining a constant speed of 100 m.p.h. At the throttle of Train A is a drunk. At the throttle of Train B is a Norwegian. All evidence notwithstanding, the trains do not collide. Why? Because Norse is Norse, and Souse is Souse, and never the twains shall meet.

＊ ＊ ＊

Ilka Chase tells of the day she was taken to Long Island by Mrs. Theodore Roosevelt, wife of the late General. The General had been briefed to meet the ladies at the Syosset station, but just before they reached it, they discovered the train was not scheduled to stop there. They proved equal to the emergency. As the train tootled by the station, they tossed a hastily scribbled note to the startled General. He ran out on the track to retrieve it. It was most helpful. It read, "This train does not stop at Syosset."

＊ ＊ ＊

The president of a little jerkwater railroad in the South made out a lifelong pass for the family of the president of the Atchison, Topeka, and Santa Fe and sent it to him with a note reading, "I would appreciate the return courtesy of a lifelong pass to *your* railroad for *my* family." In due course his own pass was returned with a curt note that pointed out, "Your road is exactly eleven miles long. Mine is over a thousand. Your proposal does not make much sense." The Southerner replied, "It is quite true that your road is longer—but you'll have to admit mine is just as wide."

＊ ＊ ＊

Here's another railroad story from the *Santa Fe* magazine:

A young man once found a five-dollar bill between the ties. From that time on, he never lifted his eyes from the ground while walking. In the course of thirty years he accumulated 25,916 buttons, 52,172 pins, seven pennies, a bent back, and a sour, miserly disposition. He lost the glories of the light, the smiles of his friends, the songs of the birds, the beauties of nature, and opportunity to serve his fellow-man and spread happiness.

*   *   *

Now that they have installed continuous telephone service on some of the crack transcontinental trains, a reporter who had been AWOL from his newspaper for a fortnight was enabled to call up his editor and announce, "I am speaking to you from a train that is speeding westward through Montana at eighty-five miles an hour." The editor replied, "I am not interested in your velocity and after Friday's payroll is made out will not be interested in your direction."

*   *   *

There is one comforting thought about rolling west from Dallas on the Texas and Pacific Railroad: You can ride all night and all the next day, past miles of flat land, tinny, dust-covered hamlets, occasional oil wells, and abandoned Army flying fields, without worrying about what state you're in. It's Texas, son, and when the conductor reminds you of that fact, he squares his shoulders and his eyes light up.

The president of the Texas and Pacific had his private car tacked on to a local on one occasion, and asked for a copy of the crew's train orders. They specified that over a stretch of newly laid, curving track, the maximum speed was to be forty-five miles an hour. When the train pulled into El Paso, the president buttonholed the engineer.

"What speed were you supposed to maintain on that stretch near Pecos?" he demanded. "Forty-five," said the engineer. "Exactly," said the president. "And how fast did you actually go?" "Forty-five, and not one bit faster," insisted the engineer.

The president was unimpressed. "That's most remarkable," he

declared. "*I* was in the last car in this train, and *I* have a speed-ometer there too, and *I* was going *sixty-two* miles an hour." "Well, I'll be dingbusted," said the engineer. "I never did see you go past us."

* * *

California's two biggest cities (and bitter rivals), Los Angeles and San Francisco, are only a couple of hours apart by air, but many commuters prefer the overnight ride on the Lark, which approaches perfection in railroading. The two-car dining room (the kitchen is in a third car) has a divided circular bar at the pivot, and looks like an exclusive night club.

The night I rode on the Lark, a noisy drunk was making a nui-sance of himself. "Why don't you pitch him off at Santa Barbara?" somebody asked. "Him? We get that character every night," was the surprising reply. "You mean he just rides back and forth?" I asked. "No," said the steward. "It's always the same character—but a different face."

* * *

Alfred Knopf is very particular about the cigars he smokes. His favorite brand is a pure Havana manufactured by H. Upmann,

packaged individually in a metal container that looks like a miniature torpedo. On his way back from the Coast recently, Mr. Knopf
fell into conversation with a bearded stranger in the club car of
the Chief, and automatically reached for one of his precious sto-
gies. Then, with understandable reluctance, he offered another
(his last) to the bearded stranger.

After the two men had puffed in silence for a spell, Mr. Knopf
could not resist asking, "What do you think of that cigar?" The
stranger shrugged his shoulders and said, "Not bad." "Not bad!"
echoed Knopf. "I'll have you know that's an Upmann Special."
"No, it isn't," said the other. "You see, I'm Upmann, and only
Upmann smokes Upmann Specials."

*   *   *

Over in England, two cockneys were riding up to London on
the morning train when they spied a dignified old party on the
bench opposite immersed in his morning *Times*. "Bli' me," said
one in awe, "it's the Archbishop of York." "Ye're cuckoo," scoffed
the other. After heated discussion, they bet a quid on it. "Only
one way to find out," said the first. "I'll ask 'im!"

He poked the old party vigorously in the back and said, "Beg
pardon, mate, but, to settle a bet, are you not the Archbishop of
York?" The old man put down his paper angrily and said very
distinctly, "What the blank blank do you mean by bothering me
this way? Buzz off, you blank blank blank, before I pull the bell-
cord."

The cockney resumed his seat with a puzzled air and admitted,
"I still dunno whether it's the archbishop or not. 'E wouldn't
tell me!"

ATLANTIC CROSSING

One of the thrills of a trip to Europe aboard a luxury liner in the
lush, carefree days before the war was the first eager perusal of
the passenger list to see what famous people were aboard with
you. On the *Normandie* or *Majestic,* for instance, the roll call often
sounded like a combination of Who's Who, Academy Award win-

ners, a column by Cholly Knickerbocker, and the Internal Revenue Department's list of the year's ten biggest income-tax payers. Although it usually developed that the nearest you ever got actually to meeting any of these great celebrities was a Mrs. Horace Hornfugger of Kansas City, who occupied the adjoining deck chair and insisted on telling you about her grandchildren when you were trying to concentrate on a good detective story, it was always rewarding to drop an "Oh, yes, I crossed with Garbo this summer" into your conversation when you returned home.

The return to passenger service of such vessels as the *Queen Mary, Queen Elizabeth,* and *America* has restored some of the hoop-la that once attended the sailings of the luxury ships, but the hectic farewell parties at the piers seem over for good. At least the police on the water-front beat hope so. Too often the parties wound up in free-for-alls, with occasional overstimulated visitors curled up unconscious under a berth when the ship got under way. If they were discovered in time, they were dumped into the pilot's launch without further adieu. Others, however, made a round trip to Europe on a borrowed tooth brush and a pajama top.

When the *Queen Mary* docked in New York recently, the captain submitted to a press interview, although his heart—and mind —weren't in it. When a reporter asked where he had been born, the captain replied, "I'm half Scotch and half soda—I mean English."

One of the most profitable Atlantic crossings on record was made by a notorious poet whose books usually are written in Chicago and banned in Boston. Having borrowed money from everybody possible in America, he set sail for London, getting free passage for his wife and himself in exchange for some publicity he never delivered. He then postponed his trip until his wife was obviously on the eve of childbirth. This not only insured delivery of the infant by the ship's doctor at the line's expense but permitted one of the passengers (later identified as the poet) to raise a purse of three hundred dollars in honor of the event.

On one particularly happy 1927 crossing aboard the *Ile de France,* Chaliapin, Jimmy Durante, Adolph Ochs, and Leslie Howard were a few of my fellow-passengers. What a parlay that was! The French Line disdained passengers who insisted upon debarking at Plymouth, and usually managed to anchor there at about three in the morning. I remember how cold it was as the lot of us climbed into the waiting tender. Leslie Howard, behind me, scanned the barely discernible shoreline with affection and murmured, "Good God, they found the right harbor the very first time!" His contempt (completely unjustified) for French seamanship stemmed from an incident that he described on our way to the Plymouth docks.

The mighty *Majestic,* it seems, stopped on a westward voyage to take passengers aboard at Cherbourg. The ship had been held up at Southampton, and the captain was particularly anxious to get under way. He made no effort, therefore, to conceal his annoyance when the tug bearing passengers from Cherbourg, attempting to come alongside in a choppy sea, missed completely and had to make a wide circle for a second try. Again the tug overshot its mark and went floundering off in a shower of spray. The English captain was furious. He seized his megaphone and bellowed to the mortified Frenchman at the wheel of the tender, "Anchor your tug, dammit! I'll bring the *Majestic* alongside!"

* * *

Billie Burke was in the dining salon of the *Uruguay* when she noticed that a gentleman at the next table was sneezing and sniffing dreadfully. "Bad cold, eh?" she asked sympathetically. The man nodded.

"I'll tell you just what to do for it," said Miss Burke. "Go back to your stateroom, have your steward get you lots of orange juice, drink it all, take four aspirin tablets, and then cover yourself with all the blankets you can stand. Sweat the cold out. I know what I'm talking about. I'm Billie Burke of Hollywood."

The man smiled warmly and said, "Thanks, I'm Dr. Mayo of the Mayo Clinic in Rochester."

* * *

Despite all the warning signs in the smoking room, a passenger aboard the *Nieuw Amsterdam,* who fancied himself as a bridge player, became involved in a game with three soft-spoken but beady-eyed strangers. A few hours later he came out on deck, where his wife greeted him by remarking, "Those three gentlemen you were playing with looked like very clever hands at cards." "They certainly were," he answered ruefully. "They struck up an acquaintance by telling my fortune. Now they're counting it."

* * *

Just after the *President Cleveland* sailed one blowy afternoon, she ran into a full gale. The dozen Very Important Persons who had been assigned to the captain's table appeared for dinner amidst definite signs of distress. The captain cleared his throat and spoke as follows:

"I hope the twelve of you will enjoy your trip. It is a pleasure to look into your eleven faces and realize that the eight of us will be dining together for the next few evenings. If any of the four of you would like a rubber of bridge, I'll be glad to see you both in my cabin. Waiter, I dislike dining alone, so I will dispense with the rest of my dinner."

* * *

When the storm had blown over, the brave captain of a small schooner emerged from his cabin, took a quick survey, and bawled to a new hand, "Ahoy, mate, where's the mizzen mast?" The new hand (like the captain, a member of the New York

Stock Exchange) answered cheerfully, "Lord knows, Cap'n. How long has it been mizzen?"

*   *   *

The refitted *Queen Elizabeth* is so colossal and luxurious that one passenger on the maiden voyage summoned a steward and said, "Would you please direct me to the Atlantic Ocean?"

*   *   *

In the smoking lounge of a transatlantic luxury liner, ex-Ambassador Joseph Kennedy made the mistake of engaging Lily Pons in a friendly gin-rummy game, and lost a goodly section of his protocol, not to mention his shirt, in the process. "I haven't got enough with me this evening to pay you, you professional shark," he admitted at the end of the game. "Think I'm good for it?" Miss Pons, of course, laughed, but Kennedy insisted on giving her a token of the debt. On the back of the wine card he wrote, "John Keats $82." "What does this mean?" asked Miss Pons. Kennedy bowed gallantly and explained, "Owed to a nightingale."

*   *   *

𝖲𝗉𝗈𝗋𝗍𝗌

"Believe It or Not" Bob Ripley estimates that Frank G. Menke's revised *Encyclopedia of Sports* can answer four million questions on 118 different games played in America. Who will dispute him? Winston Churchill, asked for embarrassing statistics in the House of Commons one afternoon, declared, "I will have an answer ready for tomorrow's session." The next day, true to his word, he rattled off figures for the better part of an hour. Later his secretary, amazed, asked, "How could you compile those statistics in a single day? It would have taken me and my staff six months to get them for you." "Right," agreed the complacent Mr. Churchill, "and by the same token, it will take the Opposition six months to prove I am in error."

At any rate, here are a few facts that I gleaned from a hasty thumbing through the pages of Mr. Menke's roundup of the sports world:

America spends over four billion dollars a year on sports, fully a quarter of which goes for angling. Firearms, motor boating, and golf come next, with over half a billion apiece. . . . Softball games attract the biggest number of spectators. . . . The earliest method of catching fish was "tickling." The angler slipped his hand under the belly of the fish and proceeded to tickle it. While the fish was chuckling, presumably, he was yanked out of the water. Today there are over eight million licensed anglers in the United States. Many of the ones I know are tickled if they even get a fish to nibble on their bait. . . .

Birling is the art of navigating or rolling on logs. It was first practiced along the Pacific slope but has been perfected in Washington and the Hotel Algonquin. The name of the sport sounds like the inspiration of a Brooklynite. . . . On a four-man bob-sled team, the two center men are merely ballast, and the fatter they are, the better. The original rules specified that these two passengers were to be ladies, but they ran out of available ladies very quickly, and eliminated that provision. . . .

Even Ripley must have been astonished to learn that the man who established nine pins as official equipment for bowling was Martin Luther! The game had become so popular and betting on same so prevalent in America in the 1840's that legislation was passed prohibiting it in several states. The modern game of ten-pins was promptly devised to circumvent the legislation. . . . Do you remember Thurber's wonderful cartoon of a determined wife about to pitch a bowling ball overhand? Her resigned husband groans, "All right, go ahead and try it that way!" . . .

Menke says that the longest prize fight with gloves went 110 rounds, fought by Bowen and Burke in New Orleans in 1893; the shortest was in 1902, when Battling Nelson kayoed an opponent with one punch in two seconds flat. . . . The basic blows in boxing are a left jab, a straight right hand, a left hook, and an uppercut with either hand. The Marquis of Queensberry rules specify, "No wrestling or hugging allowed." . . . Cock-fighting is illegal, in the opinion of one advocate, because it "cannot be fixed in advance." The S.P.C.A. has other reasons. Occasionally, a fighting cock quits under the gaffs, and makes the fact known by lifting his hackle—a long narrow feather on the neck. The under rim of the hackle is edged with white feathers; hence the expression, "showing the white feather." . . .

Man O'War was beaten just once in his entire racing career. The horse that accomplished the feat bore the appropriate name of "Upset." . . . The spots on dominoes are called "pips," a word I haven't heard since I was a sophomore at Townsend Harris High School. . . .

The first college football game took place in New Brunswick, New Jersey, in 1869, with Rutgers beating Princeton, 6 goals to 4. Rutgers didn't repeat the victory until November 5, 1938! . . . Some of the Princeton spectators tried to intimidate the sons of Rutgers with a blood-curdling yell that they had used themselves as a battle cry in the Civil War. Thus was born the college cheer. . . . Golf didn't really take hold in America until 1913, when a former caddy, Francis Ouimet, defeated England's best, Harry Vardon and Ed Ray, in the finals of the U. S. A. open. There are now 4817 golf courses in the United States, as compared to 2500 in all the rest of the world. . . . The greatest golf shot I ever saw was made by Publisher Alfred Knopf at the Hollywood course in Deal. Knopf's ball was buried in the side of a ditch near the fourteenth green. He elected to play it. The mud fell in all directions, the ball fell in the cup, and Mr. Knopf fell in the ditch. . . .

Hunters in a single year accounted for 656,993 deer, 9422 black bear, 80 mountain goat—and 116 other hunters. . . . Skeet is an old Scandinavian form of the work "shoot." . . . Page Cooper tells the story of a champion shot named Ambrosio, who noticed an infinitesimal speck high in the sky one morning and, seizing his ever-ready rifle, banged away at it. He was incredulous when it appeared that he had missed his target. All was well, however, when a note, written on beautiful parchment, dropped at his feet the next morning. It read, "Please don't shoot my angels," and was signed, "God." . . .

There are now over two million registered skiers in America, of

whom almost one per cent actually knows how to ski. They spend
about two hundred million dollars annually for lessons and equipment. . . . I myself made one spectacular ski run in the winter
of 1939. The scene was Saks Fifth Avenue, and the run ended in
the middle of the haberdashery department. . . . Mr. Menke
winds up on a nice expensive note with "yachting." . . . Dick

Tregaskis was aboard a converted racing yacht when he interviewed a cannibal chief in the South Pacific. "You mean to tell
me that although you attended Oxford for six years," said Dick,
"you still eat human flesh?" "I do," replied the chief loftily, "but,
of course, I now use a knife and fork."

   The Encyclopedia of Sports is an A. S. Barnes publication. The
items selected here do not begin to reveal how all-embracing and
thorough are its contents.

                              *   *   *

   Many fans think Babe Ruth's most spectacular home run came
in a World's Series game in Chicago, where, after taking a ride
from the partisan spectators all afternoon, Ruth pointed to a spot
in the centerfield bleachers, and then lambasted the next pitch
within ten feet of the mark. Ruth's own favorite homer, however,
was one he made in an unimportant weekday game at the Yankee

Stadium. He had been in a fearful slump for days, and wanted
a long hit very badly. In the third inning he caught hold of one
and bounced it off the steel girder in the upper grandstand on
which the rightfield foul line was painted. The crowd roared, and
the Babe started jogging happily around the bases—but Umpire
Billy Evans called him back. "It's a foul," he declared. "It hit just
an inch or two too far to the right of the line."

Manager Miller Huggins and Ruth's teammates rushed from the
dugout to protest, but the mighty Babe waved them away. "I'll
show the blank blank blank," he declared grimly. The next pitch
he hit on a dead line. The ball was still rising when it hit the very
same girder in rightfield—but this time it was in fair territory by
inches.

Umpire Evans doffed his cap to Ruth as he crossed home plate.

* * *

In the early days of Ruth's stardom with the Yankees, he gave
Huggins many a headache with his antics off the field. You could
chastise an ordinary player for breaking training rules, but what
could you do about the greatest star in baseball—the man thousands of fans came every day to cheer? One day, relates Robert
Smith, Huggins really lost his temper. He told a reporter, "I'm
going to speak to Ruth this time! You just wait and see!" At this
precise moment the Babe swaggered into the hotel lobby. "There's
your man," needled the reporter. "Are you really going to speak
to him?" "I certainly am," insisted Huggins. "Hello, Babe!"

* * *

When the New York Yankees visited Puerto Rico in the course
of spring "training," the Don Q Rum Company staged a great
banquet for the ball players, newspaper correspondents, and local
bigwigs. With every toast, the party grew more convivial. The remarks of Red Smith, *Tribune* sports writer, were broadcast. He
did nobly, but kept referring to his hosts as the "makers of that
wonderful Bacardi Rum." Every time he said "Bacardi," a mortified Don Q official would jump up and correct him with, "Don Q,

señor, Don Q." And every time Red Smith would answer graciously, "You're welcome."

* * *

Harry Ruby, the baseball fanatic, was lunching in his Hollywood villa when a close friend called to tell him excitedly, "Who do you think came to see me this morning? Tom Dewey!" "That's great," agreed Ruby. *"Did you have a catch?"*

Ruby's most famous response came when somebody asked him, "If a cabin containing your wife and Joe DiMaggio started toppling over a ten-thousand-foot precipice, and you had the chance of saving just one of them, which would you choose?" Ruby regarded his interrogator with something akin to pity and reminded him, "My wife couldn't hit the side of a barn door!"

* * *

One of the biggest stars in baseball today can drive the old apple to every corner of the park, but is not particularly noted for his brain. In fact, he is generally rated about one degree dumber than the famous busher Ring Lardner used to write about. On one hop of his team to the West, the star is reputed to have sent out for a bottle of Scotch while the train was held up temporarily at a wayside station because of a derailment ahead. One of the lads who had come to watch the repair work recognized the famous athlete and was delighted to perform the errand for him. He came back with a bottle of Scotch that bore an unfamiliar label but listed thereon six old Kings of England who had declared this to be their favorite brand. The ball star examined the strange bottle for a moment with unusual concentration and then handed it back angrily to the messenger. "Don't try to palm any of this poison off on me," he bellowed. "Every one of these guys who recommended it is dead."

* * *

Hans Wagner, all-time star shortstop of the Pittsburgh Pirates, says he once made an inside-the-park home run in the following remarkable manner. He sent a screaming liner out toward the centerfield fence. The guardian of that territory attempted to make a leaping catch, but unfortunately, his belt got caught in a nail in the fence. While he hung suspended in mid-air, his feet dangling helplessly, the great Hans Wagner circled the bases to the wild plaudits of the multitude.

Wagner has become something of a philosopher in his declining years. He confessed to a scribe, "As you get older, you really start to think a little bit, and then, the first thing you know, you're asleep!"

* * *

Joe Page, the Yankee relief ace, says he dreamed one night that he was in heaven, and was assigned the task of forming a baseball team of all the great stars available there. "But who'll we play against?" he asked. Just then the Devil telephoned and challenged him to a series. "Four games out of seven," suggested the Devil, "and no miracles on either side." "What chance have you got?" scoffed Page. "Every great ball player goes to heaven when he dies!" "I'm not worrying," the Devil told him. "I've got all the umpires."

* * *

"Bugs" Baer, one of the really great humorists in journalism today, tells the story of a .420 hitter, habitual leader of his league, who experienced a sudden slump, and struck out four times in a single game. When he came home, his wife rushed out to greet him, threw her arms around his neck, and inquired, "How many hits did you make today?" The batsman thrust his wife aside and grumbled, "You just do the cooking around here, understand? I'll do the hitting!"

Baer's famous description of a homely columnist: "The last time I saw him, he was the top of a totem pole in Seattle."

* * *

THE ARTFUL DODGERS

All Brooklyn was divided into three parts: Williamsburg, Flatbush, and Bushwick, but that was before the Dodgers came, saw, and

conquered. This baseball team, admitted without fanfare to the
National League in 1890, was destined to weld every last babbling
Brooklynite into a fellowship of fanatical loyalty, and make the
name "Dodgers" as sacred in the Borough as motherhood.

The exploits of Dodger players—good, bad, and incredible—
and the even more astonishing behavior of their partisans, have
become not only part of our American folklore, but common
knowledge in world outposts thousands of miles from the nearest baseball diamond. Students of primitive savage rites have
watched a ball game at Ebbets Field and hurried home to add a
hair-raising new chapter to their textbooks. A Nazi spy, trained
for a lifetime to impersonate an American, was exposed when he
failed to name the current shortstop of the Dodgers. A crackpot
Hollywood director who dared to produce a war picture without
a Brooklyn sergeant who wondered how "dem Bums was makin'
out against de Giants" was crated off to New Mexico to be used
as a fuse for the atom bomb experiment.

Ebbets Field itself is one of the smallest parks in the major
leagues. Its absolute capacity is under 35,000—less than half that
of the Yankee Stadium. The fact that one Brooklyn fan can make
more noise than six fans anywhere else convinced many radio

addicts that the figures were the other way round. When 150,000 determined citizens try to get into 30,000-odd seats, tempers flare high and so do prices. The management now designates as "box seats" locations directly behind the center fielder that went begging at a quarter a throw when I was a boy. Dodger fans do not protest. They even endure a character named Cowbell Hilda, who would have been murdered long ago in a less tolerant community. Hilda has supplemented her original cowbell with a variety of other eardrum-shattering devices, and nobody would be particularly surprised if one day she turned up with a steam calliope. Near her sits another inveterate fan who spends most of his time inflating colored balloons and releasing same at the most inopportune moments. Another group has organized itself into a jazz band, and marches hither and yon in the stands playing something that resembles music. If they get any better, owner Branch Rickey may let them into the park for half-price—but on the other hand, Petrillo may decide they are musicians and make them join the union. It's a dilemma, any way you look at it.

As a matter of fact, when Ebbets Field was completed, in time for the 1913 campaign, it seemed plenty big enough for any contingency. Charlie Ebbets, owner of the club, had had a tough time making ends meet. Even Brooklyn fans had tired of supporting chronic tail-enders. Their nickname was based on the popular idea that everybody in Brooklyn spends his time dodging trolley cars. Ebbets, however, was dodging the sheriff. When he announced his intention of building a new ball park in a section of Flatbush decorated principally at the moment by unpainted shacks, pig sties, and flop-houses, his friends hooted and his bankers fled. But Mr. Ebbets had a way with him (he had been a publisher of sorts in his youth), and the new home of the Brooklyn ball team gradually arose on the site of an inelegant garbage dump. To this day disgruntled fans can be found to point out that the transformation was never quite completed.

The modern era of the Dodgers really began in 1914, when Ebbets installed as manager the rotund and genial Wilbert Robinson, erstwhile catcher on the famous Baltimore Oriole squad, which also included John McGraw, Hughie Jennings, and Wee Willie Keeler. In the years following his active playing days, Robinson ran a meat market, which lent authority to his later and frequently repeated statements that many calves had better brains than his Dodger base-runners. The fans cottoned to Robinson's personality immediately. The fond nickname of "Uncle Robbie" was conferred upon him, and the team itself became known as the Robins. Only when Robbie quit sixteen years later was the name "Dodgers" restored—officially, that is. By that time, Brooklyn ball players were "The Bums" to real fans, "beloved Bums" when they won, plain, unadulterated Bums when they frittered games away.

Robbie was neither a stern task-master nor too astute a technician. Gradually his teams acquired a reputation for all-around wackiness that enraged supporters at first, but actually became a drawing card as the tradition mellowed. Every busher with the naturally screwy instincts of a bird-dog drifted into the Dodger fold as surely as a salmon fights its way upstream to spawn. Undisputed kingpin of the era was the fabulous outfielder Floyd "Babe" Herman, but the stage was all set long before his advent in 1926. For instance:

The Dodgers had men on first and second one day, when the man on first suddenly lit out for the keystone sack, forcing the runner ahead of him. "Yeah, I knew he was there," admitted the offender to the outraged Robbie, "but I had such a big lead, I couldn't resist." Another time, with men on first and second and none out, the batter hit a towering fly to right center. The runners hovered close to their bases for fear that the ball would be caught, but the batter lowered his head and went charging around the sacks like a stampeding bull. While the crowd howled, and Robbie tore his hair, the batter galloped past both runners in high gear. The ball fell safe, and all three Dodgers arrived at third in a neck-and-neck finish, the batter first. In the confusion, all three runners stepped uncertainly off the bag, and the rival third baseman had only to tag them to complete a triple play that certainly could never have happened outside of Brooklyn. Robbie consoled himself by reminding the three runners, "That's the first time you guys have gotten together all season."

A rookie was on the mound for the Dodgers one day when Rogers Hornsby, a murderous hitter, came to bat for the Cardinals. The rookie asked Jack Fournier, Dodger first baseman, "How should I pitch to this guy?" "Inside pitches only," advised

Fournier. Hornsby promptly drilled one down the leftfield line that almost tore off the third baseman's glove. "I thought you said inside pitches were Hornsby's weakness," complained the rookie in the dugout later. "I didn't say that at all," corrected Fournier. "I've got a wife and family to support. I didn't want you pitching on the outside so he'd be lining those drives at me." Robbie added, "There's only one way to pitch to Hornsby: low—and behind him."

Another Brooklyn first baseman earned the jeers of the bleacherites by being picked off base, after singling, on a variation of the hoary hidden-ball trick. The rival first-sacker tucked the ball under a corner of the bag, and simulated a return throw to the pitcher. When the runner took his lead, the fielder reached down, pulled out the ball, and plastered it on him. The runner thought enough of this trick to try it himself when another team —the Boston Braves—visited Ebbets Field. After a Boston player singled, our hero hid the ball under the first bag, and essayed an attitude of unconcern that would have put a Barrymore to shame. Sure enough, the Boston runner strayed off base, and the triumphant mastermind reached down for the ball. Unfortunately, however, he had tucked it so far under the base that by the time he managed to pry it loose, the runner was perching contentedly on third. On his way back to the bench, he was called names by grandstand critics that even Dodger players never had heard before. About that time, wives were forbidden to travel with the club on the road. A pitcher protested, "My wife can play first base better than that clunk out there. If he can make trips with us, why can't she?"

The only time Uncle Robbie really blew his top was during a training season in Florida, when he rashly informed the reporters with the team that he could catch a ball thrown from an airplane two thousand feet in the air. He was given an opportunity to substantiate this claim, and a big crowd gathered to watch developments. Robbie did his part nobly, but some dastardly pranksters had substituted an over-ripe grapefruit for the baseball, and when it plummeted into his mitt, the juice blinded him momentarily. "Help!" he hollered, "I'm bleeding to death." He never identified the culprits, which was just as well, because he might have murdered them. On that same trip, a rookie discovered four ducks paddling contentedly in his bathtub. Team members opined that the ducks must have flown in through the tenth-story window. "I guess that's right," said the rookie, "but how did they turn the water on?"

The arrival of Babe Herman reduced all previous exploits of the Dodgers' Daffiness Demons to child's play. Herman was a wonderful batter (he averaged .381 in 1929 and .393 in 1930), but his fielding lapses were spectacular, and when he got on the base paths, nobody, including himself, had the faintest idea what was going to happen next. He would have had to play in five thousand games, however, to perpetrate all the boners that have been attributed to him since his heyday. Other players' mental lapses are pinned on Herman in the same manner that other wits' wisecracks are credited to Dorothy Parker and Alexander Woollcott. That's the penalty for becoming a legend.

Herman indignantly denies, for example, the story that a fly ball hit him on the head one day and bounced into the grandstand for an automatic home run. "If I ever let a fly hit me on the head," he insists, "I'd have walked off the field and quit the game for good." "How about the shoulder, Babe?" asked sports-writer Tom Meany. "Oh, no," said Herman, "the shoulder don't count." Another episode generally attributed to Herman casts him in the role of pinch-hitter, with the Dodgers two runs down in the ninth inning, and men on second and third. An inside pitch caught the handle of his bat and trickled into the dirt around home plate. "Fair ball," decreed the umpire. "Foul ball," decreed Herman. The opposing catcher whipped off his mask and threw the pellet neatly into right field. The right fielder fell on his ear. The two runners scored the tying runs. Babe Herman, however, refused to enter into the spirit of the occasion. "I say it's a foul ball, you blank blank robber," he insisted, poking the umpire in the ribs. The ball was relayed finally into the plate, the catcher tagged Herman, and the umpire remarked quietly, "You're out!" The runs, of course, didn't count, and the Dodgers had dropped another contest.

Casey Stengel was congratulated one night for hitting two home runs in a single game. "Why don't you talk about the real miracle of the day?" he inquired. "Babe Herman threw a ball to the right base!" Another time Stengel sought to loosen up a young recruit. "You're too tense," said Stengel, "you take life too seriously. It's affecting your play. Why don't you be like Babe Herman—relaxed, carefree, happy?" The recruit retorted contemptuously, "That bum Herman isn't really happy. He only thinks he is!"

In the clubhouse one day, Herman pulled a cigar out of his pocket and asked for a match. Before anybody could oblige him, he took a couple of puffs on the cigar. A flame glowed on the end, and a thin line of blue smoke rose in the air. "Never mind the match," said the Babe with no apparent surprise. "I guess it was lit already."

In due course, Herman disappeared from the Dodger dugout, and so did Manager Robinson, to be followed in turn by Max Carey and Casey Stengel. Stengel made his debut as pilot in 1934, the year when Bill Terry, leader of the Giants, made a crack in spring training that bounced back to hit him between the eyes. Somebody asked him, "How do you think Brooklyn will make out this season?" "Brooklyn," laughed Terry. "Is Brooklyn still in the league?" The Dodgers didn't forget. They licked the Giants in the last two games of the season, and cost them the league champion-

ship. The Dodger fans didn't forget either. To this day, Bill Terry
is Brooklyn's Public Enemy Number One, although Noel Coward
has been crowding him a bit recently.

The Flatbush Follies continued to pack them in during the
regime of Stengel and his merry men. One day an umpire ordered
Stengel from the field. Stengel doffed his cap in mock deference,
and a sparrow flew out. Another time the team traveled to the
wrong town for an exhibition game. The Dodgers were the visiting team on an occasion when a local hero was being given a
"day." He received an automobile, a set of dishes, a traveling bag,
and various other gifts from grateful local fans—and then proceeded to strike out four times in the game that followed. "The
only time I ever got a 'day'," commented the Dodger pitcher
thoughtfully, "was when the sheriff gave me a day to get out of
town."

Stengel was coaching at third one afternoon in a ding-dong
contest at the Polo Grounds when a Dodger batter named Cuccinello hammered a hit to the bull pen in right field. Ott fielded the
ball brilliantly, and threw to third base. "Slide! Slide!" screamed
Stengel, but Cuccinello came in standing up, and was tagged
out. "I told you to slide," roared Stengel. "You'd have been safe
a mile! Why didn't you do what I told you?" "Slide?" repeated
Cuccinello with some dignity, "and bust my cigars?"

Casey Stengel gave way to Burleigh Grimes as manager, and
then came the golden era of Larry MacPhail and Leo Durocher,
with Burt Shotton on deck. Frank Graham gives the details in
his sparkling *Informal History of the Brooklyn Dodgers*. Pennants
were won, the crowds grew ever larger, the days of the Daffiness
Boys became a nostalgic memory. No longer could anybody refer
to the Dodgers as "The Marx Brothers with bleachers." But even
with the ascendancy of so sober and canny a president as Branch
Rickey, an indefinable quality keeps Dodger players and supporters in a world somewhat apart.

Only a Brooklyn pitcher could have reacted as Kirby Higbe
did when Ted Williams pickled one of his curves for a terrific
home run in an All-Star game. "A windblown pop," snorted
Higbe. "I thought the first baseman was going to grab it. Then
the wind caught hold of the darn blooper and hoisted it over the
top of the right field bleachers!" And only a Brooklyn crowd

could have achieved the ecstasy that attended the Dodgers' winning of the 1947 pennant. Arch Murray, in the New York *Post*, described the scene perfectly when he reported, "There's no use going across the East River today to look for Brooklyn. It isn't there. It's floating dreamily on a fluffy, pink cloud, somewhere just this side of Paradise. Flatbush is reeling in mass delirium. Canarsie is acting like an opium jag. The Gowanus is flowing with milk and honey. Because 'Next Year' finally came. Our Bums are in! Pinch me, Moitle, and hold me tight. We're living with the Champions of the National League. . . ."

What if the Yankees won the seventh, and deciding, game of the World's Series? What if there were moments (in the second game, for instance) when Dodger outfielders of 1947 seemed bent on eclipsing the antics of Babe Herman himself? The artful Dodgers were aristocrats of the diamond—and, what's more, gave every promise of continuing so for many years to come. The Dodger jazz band (swollen to record size) tooted proudly while the inevitable Lucy Munroe warbled "The Star-Spangled Banner." For above Lucy's sweet notes sounded the protests of Hilda Chester, so outraged by her failure to receive a complimentary strip of series' tickets that she threatened to bring only three cowbells to home games the next season. High up in the press box, a reporter draped his coat carelessly on the outside rail. In the middle of the game, the coat slipped off and descended upon the head of a gent in the grandstand below. It takes more than that to startle a typical Dodger rooter. He looked up at the press box and inquired mildly, "Where's de pants?"

* * *

On the subject of the increasing amount of professionalism in college football, Herman Hickman, head coach at Yale, tells the story of an assistant coach at a big college who tried to get a raise for himself after his team had gone through a whole season without a defeat. His annual salary had been $4000, and the assistant thought he was entitled to a twenty-five per cent boost. "You want $5000?" the head coach said to him in an astonished voice. "Don't be silly, Bill. I could get a good quarterback for that."

* * *

Franklin P. Adams figured that as long as everybody else was choosing All-American football teams, he might as well pitch in with one himself. Here were his nominations:

Cedars of Lebanon; Diet of Rice; Crossing of Delaware; Bells of St. Mary's; Dissolution of Union; Quality of Mercer; Heart of Maryland; District of Columbia; Pillars of Temple; Grist of Mills; and Destruction of Carthage.

Substitutes: Hard, Knox; Dead, Centre; Gimme, De Pauw.

         ✻   ✻   ✻

In 1939, the Alabama football team came to Pasadena for the Rose Bowl game, and Warner Brothers gave a dinner in honor of the squad. Humphrey Bogart, seated next to a distinguished but unidentified gentleman, started the conversational ball rolling by remarking pleasantly, "I know the name of every player on the Alabama team, and the names of the coaches too, but I certainly couldn't tell you who's president of the University."

"His name is Foster," volunteered his companion, "but I'm afraid the only reason I know is because I'm he."

         ✻   ✻   ✻

Bill Stern, the famous radio sports commentator, told me just about the best football story I ever heard.

Before Lou Little became head coach at Columbia, he occupied a similar post at Georgetown. One year there was a youngster on the squad who was no great shakes as a football player, but whose personality served as a morale booster for the whole team. Little was deeply fond of the boy. He liked the proud way he walked arm in arm with his father on the campus from time to time. If the team was far enough ahead, he even let him get into a game occasionally for the last few minutes of play.

One day, about a week before the big finale with Fordham, the boy's mother called Little on the phone. "My husband died this morning of a heart attack," she said. "Will you break the news to my boy? He'll take it better if it comes from you." Little did what was necessary, and the boy went home sorrowfully.

He was back three days later, and came straight to Lou Little.

"Coach," he begged, "I want to ask something of you that means an awful lot to me. I want to start in that game against Fordham. I think it's what my father would have liked most."

Little hesitated, and then agreed. "O.K., son, you'll start, but you'll only be in there for a play or two. You aren't quite good enough, and you know it." True to his word, Little started the boy—but never took him out. For sixty full, jarring minutes he played inspired football, running, blocking, and passing like an All-American, and sparking the team to victory.

Back in the clubhouse, Little threw his arm around the boy's shoulder and said, "Son, you were terrific today. You stayed in because you belonged there. You never played that kind of football before. What got into you?"

The boy answered, "Remember how my father and I used to go about arm in arm? There was something about him very few people knew. My father was totally blind. This afternoon was the first time he ever saw me play."

* * *

Anybody who has heard John Kieran confounding the experts on "Information, Please" knows that he is a wizard in Latin. To the headmaster of a certain snobbish preparatory school, however, he was only a sports writer, invited to address the Latin class as a favor to the football coach. So when the headmaster introduced him to the class, he threw in a Latin phrase, for the boys' amusement, that meant in English, "Let's make the best of this ordeal."

Kieran rose to his feet, bowed stiffly to the headmaster, and said, "Gentlemen, the only thing that outraged me more than the boorishness of the man who introduced me was his inexcusable use of the present participle instead of the past pluperfect in the quotation." He then delivered his entire speech in Latin and stalked out of the classroom.

* * *

Art Cohn, reporting the various and highly profitable American tours of the great Finnish runner, Paavo Nurmi, points out that he was as fast in a financial deal as he was on the cinder paths, and needed no agent to get all that was coming to him.

The promoters of one outdoor meet agreed to pay Nurmi a

thousand dollars to participate, but when he showed up handed him a check for $750, explaining that they had miscalculated expenses, and couldn't afford another cent. Nurmi took the check without comment.

The race was a mile long—four full laps on that particular track. Nurmi ran the first three laps in sensational style, and led the field by a wide margin. When he completed the third lap, however,

he calmly walked off the track, and made for his dressing room. "They pay me three-quarters," he explained calmly to reporters, "so I run three-quarters of a mile."

* * *

Two enterprising publishers formed a partnership and over a period of years built up a profitable line of low-priced juveniles. One spring day the elder of the two actually was lured away from work to join a golf foursome. At lunch time, however, he made a bee-line for the telephone in the locker room and called his office. "Anything happen this morning?" he asked anxiously.

"Anything happen!" echoed his partner excitedly. "We got the biggest order in our history by wire from Marshall Field, that's all." "Have Miss Jones read it to me right away," cried the senior member of the firm.

Miss Jones came to the phone and said brightly, "Here it is,

Mr. Stern. 'Ship immediately forty dozen *Pinocchio*. Stop. Eighty dozen *Black Beauty*. Stop. Seventy-three dozen *Mother Goose*. Stop. . . .'" The angry voice of Mr. Stern interrupted her recital. "Listen," he screamed to his partner, "would you be kind enough to leave that girl alone till she finishes reading the telegram?"

* * *

A Viennese publisher, visiting America for the first time, confessed that he never had seen a game of golf. The late Frank Crowninshield took him to his Long Island club, where they followed a crack foursome. One of the players landed in a deep trap just short of the first green. "He'll have to blast out of that one," said Crowninshield. "It must be impossible," added the Viennese. The player, however, executed a perfect explosion shot. The ball landed on the green, and trickled into the cup for a birdie three. The Viennese clucked sympathetically and said (this is Crowninshield's story), "Ach, what a time he'll have getting out of *that* one!"

Mr. Crowninshield, on the links one morning, incidentally, defined a Platonic lover as "a man who holds the eggshells while somebody else eats the omelette."

* * *

The chief surgeon of one of New York's biggest hospitals has an inexplicable aversion to being called "Doctor" when engaged in his favorite diversion, a game of golf. Plain "Mister" is all he wants to be, or, to his intimates, "Mac." He was beating his way through the rough at Siwanoy one Sunday when an acquaintance in the next fairway shouted cheerily, "Good morning there, Doctor." The surgeon shouted back gruffly, "Good morning to you, manufacturer of shirts, underwear, and fancy pajamas."

* * *

Colston Leigh came home from a round of golf and threw his bag in a corner. "How did it go?" asked a friend. "Well, I broke

ninety," reported Leigh, "and you know I can't afford to break
ninety clubs at the price they bring these days."

✻ ✻ ✻

Jim Russell, table tennis champion of Kentfield, California, has
poignant memories of his homecoming from the war. "I had been
in the Pacific for two years," he recalls, "and never saw a white
girl the entire time. The minute our transport landed in San Francisco, I rushed to my girl's house. I could hardly wait to get her
alone in the ping-pong room.

"She beat me, too—21–14."

✻ ✻ ✻

The major sports event of Barnard College is an annual hocus-
pocus called "The Greek Games," wherein comely and thinly clad
Barnard freshmen and sophomores cavort as charioteers, gladi-
ators, Arabian steeds, and goddesses, and in general make fools
of themselves for the edification of mystified parents and instruc-
tresses.

The "games" once precipitated a crisis in my own life. Years
ago, when I was an editor of the Columbia Spectator, Barnard
Dean Virginia Gildersleeve posted a stern edict that while Greek
met Greek, no Columbia vulgarian was to be allowed on the premises. Through the friendly offices of a lovely maid named Marie,
however, I was smuggled into one of the frolics, watched appreciatively while she pranced about in a flimsy and revealing wisp
of purple gauze (she was playing the part of the ancient watch-
man of the sacred temple), and rushed back to the Spectator office to bang out a blow-by-blow discription of the goings-on for
the next morning's edition.

I thought my piece was reasonably funny. Dean Gildersleeve,
unfortunately, did not. She came charging over to the Spectator
office and delivered an address that shook the residence of Prexy
Nicholas Murray Butler several blocks away. For a brief spell, my
college career trembled in the balance. I was saved by the late
Dean Hawkes, who persuaded Miss Gildersleeve that nobody
read Spectator anyhow.

My next meeting with Dean Gildersleeve was purely accidental. I was ushered to a seat in a theatre, and found myself directly beside her. I must have trembled slightly and turned green, because she suddenly declared, "Relax! I'm not going to eat you! As a matter of fact, I sent a copy of your ridiculous piece to a friend in Chicago."

The following Monday, *Spectator* began a thrilling series entitled "Great Women of Barnard." The first piece was about Dean Virginia Gildersleeve.

* * *

"I ain't impressed," announced guide Bill Howie, "with any of them stories about people hittin' things from a triflin' 300 or 400 yards. Lemme tell you about the day I was moochin' along a mountain trail when these here telescope eyes of mine spotted a buck. I rammed a charge down the barrel of my gun, then some wadding and a couple of ounces of salt. I shoved a bullet in on top of that. Then I let go. Bang, and the buck dropped in his tracks." One of Bill Howie's cronies asked, "What in tarnation was the idea of putting salt in your gun?" "Shucks," answered Bill Howie, "that deer was so far off I had to do something to keep the meat from spoilin' until I could git thar."

* * *

Clem McCarthy, who has broadcast the details of practically every important horse race in the past decade, can make the dullest event in the world sound exciting by his rapid-fire, staccato delivery. You can imagine the pitch to which he worked himself when four horses came into the stretch of one big race absolutely neck and neck. A rank outsider won by a nose, and when it was led into the winner's circle, McCarthy, limp with excitement, croaked into the microphone, "What a day! What a day! The only one who hasn't gone absolutely nuts is the horse."

At that moment, radio listeners heard a resounding crash. An unknown humorist grabbed the mike and hollered, "Hey, folks, the horse just kicked McCarthy!"

* * *

Soon after Dan Parker won a by-line for himself on the sports page of a big New York paper, he set about exposing the racket of a notorious race-track tout who brazenly insisted he could fix any claiming race at the Saratoga meeting then in progress and offered to do so upon receipt of the modest sum of one dollar in cash. Parker's column bristled with indignation and scorn. Within the following week, however, he received over a hundred letters enclosing currency. Would Mr. Parker forward same to the lovely gentleman who could fix races?

Parker told his story to Arthur Brisbane, who didn't believe it. When Parker produced the actual letters, Brisbane sighed, and remarked, "I was wrong all the time." "You mean about my fabricating the story of the letters?" asked Dan. "No," said Brisbane. "In my estimate of the mental age of newspaper readers. I always put it at twelve. I guess it's nearer eight."

Incidentally, Parker's book, *The ABC of Horse Racing*, was designed to prove that betting on the nags has never paid. A coupon ad headed "You can't win on horse races" pulled seventeen orders. An ad of exactly the same size and in the same newspaper headed "If you *must* bet on horse races . . ." pulled two hundred and forty.

✦   ✦   ✦

Primo Carnera's reputation as a heavyweight boxer is slightly tarnished, but he's making a big comeback as a wrestler—and he is still a source of joy to visiting reporters. When he arrived on the Coast recently, for example, a scribe asked him, "How do you like Los Angeles?" Primo flexed his muscles and answered confidently, "I pin him to the mat in two minutes."

Primo participated in the Mark Hellinger-W. C. Fields drinking bout mentioned on page 468 of this book. He held his own for a dozen straight brandies, then suddenly clutched his midriff and headed for fresh air. "Damn bananas," he explained later, "make me too sick to keep drinking."

✦   ✦   ✦

The Cincinnati sports pages, recalls Jimmy Powers, were once enriched by the spicy, rollicking reports of a writer named Bill

Phelon. Bill had a big heart, and he loved many people and things, but best of all, he loved Havana, Cuba. Someday, he promised, he would move there for good, live on frozen daiquiris from the Florida Bar, and, when he died, be buried in the shadow of the famous Morro Castle that guarded the harbor.

Phelon knew how his friends in Havana craved American cigarettes, but were discouraged from buying many by the excessive import duty. It was his amiable custom, therefore, to send them numerous cartons concealed in packages of books, magazines, and newspapers. Suddenly, the packages stopped coming. Phelon, fatally stricken, was wasting away in a Cincinnati hospital. His Havana cronies thought he had forgotten them.

One day, however, another package from Bill Phelon did arrive in Havana. "Bill has remembered," cried his friends, "there will be cigarettes for all!" This time, however, the package was a wooden box, filled with ashes. The attached note read, "Hello, boys, this is me. Bill."

His sorrowing friends sprinkled the ashes over the harbor he loved so deeply.

* * *

I suppose it's stretching the point to include them in the sports section, but I always have laughed at (1) the man who heard a square-jawed female announce: "I'm a little stiff from lacrosse," and answered understandingly, "Ah, Wisconsin," and (2) the son of a prominent New York editor who was asked by his teacher to name two ancient sports, and came up with "Anthony and Cleopatra."

* * *

And only because West Point in these so-called peaceful days reminds me of football, I conclude this section with a story told by James R. Aswell in his *Native American Humor*. It concerns the great Indian chief, Sitting Bull, who was finally captured after three decades of outmaneuvering the best that the U. S. Army could send into the field. His captors treated him with the greatest respect, and one asked if he had any special grievances to air.

Sitting Bull nodded gravely, and protested, "One white man has printed terrible lies about me for all world to read." "What

did he say?" asked the reporter. Chief Sitting Bull gave vent to
an impressive collection of bi-lingual cuss-words, and concluded,
"If Indian ever find him, he sure scalp s.o.b. say Sitting Bull graduated at West Point!"

*　*　*

Society

A wealthy and popular figure in Manhattan's literary world lives in a perfectly appointed penthouse atop a midtown skyscraper that he owns. He sublet the penthouse for the summer to a lady whose references were impeccable, but who promptly turned his premises into a house of shame. Her business, furthermore, was absolute capacity from the first night on, and her silvery laughter tinkled into the soft night air when he turned up and implored her to pack up her duds and her dolls and go play somewhere else. The poor man was distraught. Police proceedings would endanger the value of the whole property and involve him in questionable front-page publicity. His wife and High Church friends, however, demanded action. A sudden inspiration solved everything. The magnate had an accountant who was a dead ringer for the detective in every stage play. He equipped this accountant with a derby and a little black notebook, and stationed him in the only elevator that serviced the penthouse from dusk to dawn. As every man entered this elevator, the accountant would eye him closely, then pull out his little book and make notes furiously therein. The objects of his scrutiny cringed visibly. Business began falling off incredibly at the penthouse, and two weeks later the baffled madam paid a five-hundred-dollar premium to get out of the balance of her lease.

*   *   *

A writer who lives above Radio Star Morey Amsterdam's apartment called up late one night to register a complaint. "You people are making such a racket," he said, "I can't even hear myself typewrite." "That's easy to remedy," answered Amsterdam cheerfully. "Typewrite louder."

*   *   *

In New York for a visit, Miss Rebecca West was confronted by a well-known boulevardier and his young friend. Although they are several inches apart in height, these two Beau Brummels affect identical suits, shirts, cravats, and haircuts. "My God," commented Miss West, "they look like a nest of tables!"

*   *   *

Linda Young, three-year-old daughter of one of the town's leading printers, has a new English governess who is teaching her perfect manners. Her parents wonder if they are not a shade too perfect. The other morning, she followed her father to the wardrobe and asked sweetly, "Daddy, may I borrow a clothes hanger for a moment, please?" When he gave her the hanger, she curtsied prettily, took careful aim, and conked her mother squarely on the head with it. Then she returned it to her father, saying, "Thank you ever so much."

* * *

Myra Thompson tells the story of the secretary of the president of a famous university in Ohio. She took a long-distance call for him one morning when he was not in his office, and thinking that only the university operator was on the line, reported cheerfully, "I think he's gone to the john." Unfortunately, the line was open and every operator between the Ohio university and Pasadena, California, heard her, not to mention the trustee who had initiated the call. Solicitous operators all over the country spent the rest of the day calling the university and inquiring sweetly, "Has the president returned to his office yet?"

* * *

In the Columbia Faculty Club, Carlton J. H. Hayes made this deathless observation: "The artichoke is the only vegetable you have more of when you finish eating it than you had when you started."

* * *

A youngster from upstate New York asked novelist Sam Adams to help get him admitted to Groton. "You haven't a chance," Adams told him, "unless your father, and your grandfather too, were Groton boys in their day." The youngster reflected briefly, then asked, "Say, how did they get the darn place started?"

* * *

Adams, always willing to try anything once, accepted an invitation to a nudist party on a Fourth-of-July week-end a few years ago. Describing the experience to his friends in Auburn the next day, he said, "They certainly didn't do things by halves. Even the butler who opened the door for me was completely nude." "How did you know it was the butler?" asked Mr. Adams's literal-minded publisher. "Well," said Mr. Adams, "it certainly wasn't the maid."

❋   ❋   ❋

At a rehearsal in Philadelphia, Leopold Stokowski seized an offending musician by the coat collar and exclaimed, "My man, you do not know the difference between your brass and your oboe."

❋   ❋   ❋

ETIQUETTE PAYS DIVIDENDS!

Nelson Doubleday's entry into his father's publishing house in the early 1920's did not follow the customary pattern of a rich man's son "beginning at the bottom and learning the business." He had insisted on trying out his wings first, and succeeded so well that his father had to buy out his mail-order firm of "Nelson Doubleday, Inc., Oyster Bay" at a very fancy figure in order to secure his services.

One of the books that showed up best in Nelson's first mail-order tests was the Holt *Book of Etiquette*. The ads for it had been written by Lillian Eichler, then a copywriter for the advertising agency of Ruthrauff and Ryan. "This looks easy," Doubleday told her. "Why not write an etiquette book yourself?" Miss Eichler agreed. She declared later, "Nelson Doubleday could have persuaded me to compile a Greek dictionary if he'd had a mind to."

The Eichler *Book of Etiquette* was published on September 21, 1921, and, by means of a spectacular advertising campaign, sold over a million copies in its first year. You may remember some of the layouts. They involved "narrative copy" and photographs of distressed damsels impaled upon the horns of social dilemmas. One was headed "Why I cried after the ceremony," and told the heartbreaking tale of the bride who gummed up the works by standing on the wrong side of the groom, plus other *faux pas* that she never would have committed if she had read the Eichler book. A second ad posed the question, "May she invite him in?" A third challenged, "Can you tell what's wrong with this picture?" Most famous of all, and most effective in raking in orders, was the story of the girl who didn't know what to do when her beau invited her out to dinner. "Again she ordered chicken salad!" read the doleful advertisement. The Doubleday organization figures that this copy alone sold a half million books and cut the consumption of chicken salad seventy per cent.

Nelson Doubleday brought the Eichler book with him when he joined his father, "Effendi." It is still selling more than 25,000 copies a year. Miss Eichler's greatest triumph came the day Emily Post remarked to a hostess that her table was not set properly. "Oh, yes, it is," said the hostess—and produced the Eichler book to prove her point.

* * *

Elsa Maxwell credits three simple words for making guests at her parties feel welcome and at home. "When they arrive," says Miss Maxwell, "I murmur, 'at last,' and when they arise to depart I protest, 'already?'"

* * *

Abel Green's suggested slogan for "21": "All You Can Eat and Drink for $200 Per Person."

* * *

Notes Lucius Beebe: "Even when a Harvard man flunks out he becomes a Bum of Distinction."

* * *

Joseph Asher, of Rich's in Atlanta, is compiling a list of gin players he can live without. Here are a few of them. The How Is Type: Goes gin on the second card and asks if it's good. The Helping Type: Goes out fast in order to help his partner. The If Type: If he hadn't taken the nine of spades? The Look Through Type: Always looks through discards. The Talkative Type: Talks entire time game is in progress. Very quiet on other occasions. The Can't Deal Type: Always has nine cards when his opponent goes gin. The Gambling Type: Never satisfied with table stakes. Always makes side bets with all players and guests. The Roaming Type: Roams around room while not playing, upsetting highballs and disconnecting lamps. Any further nominations?

* * *

To show what family life in Washington is like these days, Kay Halle tells of the seven-year-old daughter of a correspondent who was shown a reproduction of Leonardo da Vinci's famous "Virgin and the Christ Child." "That is Jesus when He was a baby," explained the mother. "Who's that holding Him?" asked the youngster. "A sitter?"

* * *

A diplomatic publisher complimented a socialite from Richmond on her splendid appearance and added, "Do you feel as well as you look?" She answered, "There are only two things the matter with me: Dandruff and a badly spoiled stomach." "Aren't you lucky," commented the publisher, "that only one shows?"

The lady reported the conversation faithfully to her husband a moment later. He nodded slowly and asked, "Honey, did you have your hat on at the time?"

* * *

In *Try and Stop Me* I told of the late E. Phillips Oppenheim's sure-fire formula for coping with dinner hosts who broke their promises and called on him for a speech. He would clear his throat with a series of garrumphs, and declare severely, "As King Solomon remarked to the Queen of Sheba, 'Madame, I did not come here to speak.'" J. B. Birmingham, of Nutley, now writes that he can improve on this story, and I think he proves his point. In *his* version, Cleopatra pouts to an over-loquacious Anthony, "Sire, I am not prone to argue."

* * *

Field's in Chicago staged an impressive shindig to commemorate the publication of Marshall Field's *Freedom Is More Than a Word*. Annabelle Scoon noted one bobby-soxer in the audience who examined Mr. Field's autograph and exclaimed, "Isn't he cute! He's named himself after the store!"

At a banquet in Washington, incidentally, Mr. Field was introduced as "the second most famous haberdasher in America."

* * *

Arthur Kober's five-year-old daughter, Cathy, attended a birthday party where the food had been seasoned too strongly for her liking. Quite naturally she remarked to the hostess, "This is awful!" "Oh, no," corrected her nurse. "It's very good. It's just a little different. You'll get to like it." "No," said Cathy, "I won't like it. It's just awful."

On the way home, the nurse explained, "When you're eating out, dear, it's all right to say the food is good if you like it, but if you don't, just leave it on your plate and don't say anything."

The next Saturday, Cathy went visiting again. For lunch, she was served creamed chicken, which she loves, and peas, which she always has hated. She finished the chicken, tasted the peas, then looked at the nurse, and in her best Emily Post voice remarked, "These peas are delicious—but awful."

* * *

The socialite wife of a famous author was guilty of a Freudian *faux pas* at a literary reception recently. She attended very much against her will, but promised her anxious husband that she would be her most charming self. She was, too—until the very moment of departure, when she seized the hand of her hostess, and assured her warmly, "It was *so* nice of us to come!"

Another patroness of the arts found occasion to telephone a famous detective-story writer. He picked up the receiver and said, "Da*shiell* Hammett speaking." She corrected him sharply, "You mean *Dash*iell Hammett, don't you?"

* * *

A spy at Little, Brown, the Boston publishers, reports that one of their hoity-toitiest English authoresses had just swept out onto Beacon Street when a bemused pedestrian bumped into her squarely amidships. He apologized profusely, but she froze him with a look and muttered, "How gauche!"

"Simply fine, lady," answered the pedestrian. "How gauche it with you?"

* * *

PHILOSOPHER'S HOLIDAYS

Here are some new stories concerning Columbia's brilliant philosopher, man-about-town, and wit, Irwin Edman, collected at incalculable risk and expense by sitting at the sage's feet at a dinner party one evening.

Irwin and an English colleague were traveling from London to Oxford when a man in the same compartment suddenly interrupted them by observing, "Odd to hear an American voice again. I was out there for a whole year once, y'know." "I hope you found it interesting," said Irwin politely. "Not interesting," was the answer. "I should say rahther amusing." Irwin informed him gravely, "Yes, we are a nation of 145 million people systematically organized to amuse visiting Englishmen." Edman's companion chuckled softly and said, "Well played."

Irwin's colleague, later in the journey, recalled that his most important London lecture date had coincided with a devastating air raid by Nazi bombers. He bravely continued his speech while missiles fell closer and closer. Chunks of plaster fell from the ceiling and the entire building rocked on its foundations. A member of the audience finally jumped to his feet and pointed out, "It is increasingly evident, Professor, that your conclusions are not supported by your premises."

Globe-trotter Edman also visited Rio de Janeiro, and found himself engaged in conversation with a fascinating Brazilian society queen. She asked him what he did in New York. "I am a professor of philosophy," he informed her. "How interesting!" she replied. "Down here there is only one American philosopher we really know about." "What's his name?" inquired Irwin. The lady answered, "Lin Yutang."

It was Edman who first discovered Herman Wouk's Book-of-the-Month Club novel, *Aurora Dawn,* and aroused the interest of Messrs. Simon and Schuster. "In fact," said Max Schuster, "Irwin was the catalytic agent." "Exactly what is a catalytic agent?" asked an editor of the Columbia University Press. Schuster pondered a moment and explained, "A catalytic agent is one who doesn't receive ten per cent."

One summer the notoriously absent-minded Edman rented a Vermont cottage a few miles from the home of Dorothy Canfield Fisher. After a happy month there, he gave a dinner party for some of his new neighbors. An argument arose. Irwin said, "I didn't bring my encyclopedia up with me, but I'll phone Dorothy." "You can't do that," said Merle Haas. "Why?" said Irwin. "Hasn't Dorothy got an encyclopedia?" "Yes," reminded Merle, "but you haven't got a telephone."

On sunny mornings, Irwin would wander down the road to the Haas manse, and a welcome guest he was, despite a distressing habit of climbing out of the swimming pool, picking up a stray volume of Plato, and plopping himself, soaking wet, in Mrs. Haas's best chair. Mrs. Haas was busy at the time trying to house-break a new puppy. When she saw a pool of water on her library floor one day, she wailed to the French maid, *"C'est encore le chien."* The maid answered, *"Ah, non, madame, c'est encore le professeur!"*

* * *

One of our leading publishers, disdaining the theory that fifty-five is no age to start skiing, broke his leg in three places. The sight of him reminded a Park Avenue host of a similar misfortune—but his, however, was not the result of skiing. "No," explained the host. "My trouble dates back to an evening five years ago. I was staying at the Crillon in Paris, and the chambermaid came into my room with fresh towels. She was a gorgeous thing —blond curls, blue eyes, shape that reminded me of a Hershey bar—you know, all the almonds in the right places. After she gave me the towels, she said softly, 'Is there anything else, sir?' 'Not a thing,' I assured her cheerfully. 'You are absolutely sure there is nothing I can do for you?' she persisted. 'Absolutely,' I said—so she left.

"Well, sir, last night I was standing on a ladder hanging a picture, when suddenly I realized what that girl was driving at five years ago. So I fell off the ladder and broke my leg."

* * *

Press agents for road shows and carnivals will stop at nothing to grab a little free publicity and provide grist for their quills. One even staged a mock marriage between two elephants, with a third pachyderm acting as minister. A Los Angeles paper obligingly printed a photograph of the weird elephantasy on the front page. Dorothy Parker's comment was, "I give it six months!"

Miss Parker was asked another time to express an opinion of an overpraised novelist. She remarked, "He's a writer for the ages —for the ages of four to eight."

At a dinner party, Miss Parker was irked by the antics of one of those ladies of fifty who dresses like a debutante, drooling over an embarrassed colonel. Vaguely aware of a threat of mayhem in the air, she giggled self-consciously and explained, "It's his uni-

form. I just love soldiers." "Yes," agreed Miss Parker, "you have
in every war."

* * *

In Montgomery, Alabama, a wealthy general strode confidently
into his bank and sought to cash his check for a hundred dollars.
An efficiency expert had revolutionized the bank's system, however, and the paying teller declared, "I'll have to ask for your
identification, please." "Dammit," roared the general, "I've been
a depositor here for years and you know me perfectly well."
"Kindly see the second vice-president," said the teller.

The second vice-president took the general to the first vice-
president and the first vice-president took him to the president.
The president okayed the check just in time to keep the general
from having an apoplectic stroke.

As he raked in his hundred dollars, the general suddenly demanded, "What's my balance here now?" The teller investigated
and reported rather sheepishly, "$234,405.47, sir." The general
made out a new check for $234,405.47, and said, "Now, dammit,
get the president to okay this one. I want it in cash." The frightened president came pattering over on the double and protested,
"General, you're withdrawing your entire balance with us!"

"I certainly am," said the general. "I figure I better grab it while
there's still one idiot in this bank who seems to recognize me."

* * *

Salvador Dali, that somewhat different artist, has been doing
quite a bit of book illustrating lately, leaping nimbly from Billy
Rose's *Wine, Women and Words* to Cervantes' *Don Quixote*. Negotiations for the latter project were particularly delicate, and
hung by a thread at the last moment. The over-all price had been
settled, but the publisher suddenly asked, "How many full-page
color illustrations do you intend to supply?" Señor Dali, who
speaks no English—at least not during business hours—held up five
fingers. The publisher picked up his hat and coat and said, "Anyhow, it's been a lot of fun." Mrs. Dali, who acts as her husband's
agent, saved the day by hurriedly explaining, "When Dali says
'five' he means 'ten.'"

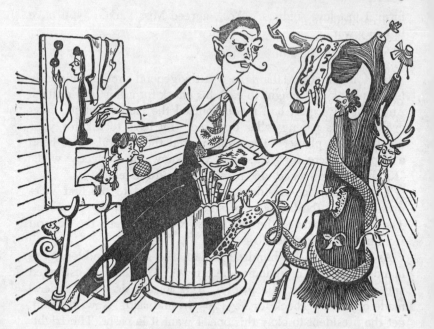

Naïve souls who think the publishers are allowed to keep Dali's
originals may be interested to know that he sold the *Don Quixote*
set to a private collector for about ten times the fee he received
for their use in book form. Possibly encouraged by this transaction,
Dali has promised to talk English more frequently hereafter. "I
really understand very well now," he admitted. "It remains only
for my friends to speak a little better." His philosophy is summed
up in a foreword he wrote for his own novel, *Hidden Faces.*
"Sooner or later," he confided there, "everyone is bound to come
to me. Some, untouched by my painting, concede that I draw
like Leonardo. Others have discovered in me literary gifts supe-
rior to the skill which I reveal in my pictures. Others proclaim that
I have a unique gift for the theatre. It is difficult to avoid coming
under my sway in one way or another."

Critics, disregarding Dali's personal eccentricities, agree that
from a technical standpoint he is one of the greatest artists of all
time. The master himself sees to it that he is publicized properly.
He delivered one lecture about his art in a diver's helmet. He
designed a window display for a Fifth Avenue department store,

and, carefully biding his time until the police, press, and a camera crew hove into view, smashed the plate-glass window in a frenzy of what might be called spontaneous combustion. For the 1939 World's Fair he cooked up a side show of diving mermaids in suggestive costumes that brought the censorship squad on the double. They were told this was Dali's "surrealist art," and were so mystified they allowed the exhibition to continue. One of them was heard to mutter, "Dali, hey? Wonder what his sisters Yanczi and Rozika, would say about this!"

The Woodward and Lothrop Book Department in Washington is still buzzing delightedly over the customer who demanded *The Autobiography of Stevedore Dali.*

❀   ❀   ❀

John Powers, head of the famous models' agency, seemed unduly agitated when a 1938 *World Almanac* disappeared from his desk. "So what?" I asked. "It's out of date anyhow. This is 1948."

"You don't understand," said John. "That 1938 edition is just the proper weight for the girls in our posture class to balance on their heads."

* * *

In the Cub Room of the Stork Club, recently, an uninhibited writer observed a diamond-laden, chinchilly female who swept past a dozen people waiting for tables, and loudly demanded immediate attention. The writer tapped her on the arm and said, "Pardon me, madam—but are you anybody in particular?"

* * *

"What a pity times are not what they used to be! Children no longer obey their parents and everyone wants to write a book." This plaint was voiced neither by a victim of the Inquiring Photographer nor a harassed publisher at the Ritz. It is a literal translation, vows E. Stanley Jones, in *The Christ of Every Road*, of the message inscribed on the oldest piece of papyrus preserved by the State Museum in Istanbul.

* * *

Frank Crowninshield cherished the answer the Duke of Portland gave him years ago when he asked, "What London club do you like best?" After due consideration, the Duke rumbled, "I use a filthy thing called 'The Albemarle.' The food and wines are capital. I'm a great fellow for gluing and they have glue in the library. But the principal reason I like it is I don't know any of the members."

* * *

Edmund Gwenn tells the story of the day John Drew entertained a group of writers and critics at the Lambs Club. He ordered kidneys for luncheon, then repaired to the bar to supervise the dispensation of liquid refreshments. A half hour later a waiter whispered, "I don't want to disturb you, sir, but your kidneys are spoiling." Drew answered, "I suspected that for years, but I didn't realize it was visible to the naked eye."

S. Jay Kaufman remembers another tense moment at the same club when an old member clapped Joe Laurie, Jr., on the back and bellowed, "Bless my soul, it's Holbrook Blinn. I haven't seen you in ages." "No wonder," said Laurie coldly. "I've been dead since 1928."

* * *

Kaufman—a columnist, author, and publicist for over thirty years—has befriended in his time scores of penniless youngsters who later became gods of Hollywood and Publishers' Row. He likes to quote an injunction from the Talmud: "When you do a kindness to a man, ask him not to do you any harm in return." A friend once told him that a novelist was going around town saying nasty things about him. Kaufman consulted a little notebook and frowned. "That's very strange," was his comment. "He doesn't owe me a cent!"

Kaufman says the hang-the-expense attitude of present-day hosts reminds him of the motion-picture magnate who found a money clip containing three crisp thousand-dollar bills at Palm Springs one day. The magnate threw the bills into the gutter, but pocketed the clip with a joyful chuckle, explaining, "I've been looking for one of these things for months."

Kaufman's best-known one-act play is called *Pea Soup* and its basic idea is lifted at regular intervals by others. The central character is an executive who must go from the Savoy Hotel in London to an all-important meeting some miles away. One of those impenetrable fogs has descended upon the city, however, and traffic is at a standstill.

The executive, completely baffled, stands helplessly in the doorway of the hotel when a stranger materializes suddenly out of the fog and says, "Can I help you?" The executive tells the address he's bound for, and the stranger volunteers to guide him there.

They make the trip on foot—through devious turnings and silent, empty streets, with the fog swirling thicker and thicker about them. Unerringly, the stranger leads the way to the designated address.

"Wonderful! I don't know how you managed to find your way in this pea soup," marvels the executive.

"It's no trouble at all for me," explains the stranger. "I'm blind."

* * *

Vincent Starrett reports that the staid members of London's Athenaeum Club were outraged by receipt of the following admonition in the mails, signed by one Stanley French:

1. Bishops who remove their gaiters
   Must not throw them at the waiters.
2. The right to dine without their collars
   Is still confined to bearded scholars.
3. Members, note: Till stock increases
   Toilet rolls are not for theses.

*   *   *

A corporal of the A.E.F. was entertained by a Duchess at one of the stately homes of England. Upon his return to barracks, everybody was agog for details. "Well," he drawled, "if the water had been as cold as the soup, and if the soup had been as warm as the wine, and if the wine had been as old as the chicken, and if the chicken had been as young as the maid, and if the maid had been as willing as the Duchess—I probably never would have come home at all."

George Clay writes that erudite members of his set have revived that plaguish old pastime, "Knock, knock," but in a French version. Example one: "Toc, toc." "Qui frappe la porte?" "Henri." "Henri qui?" "Henri soit qui mal y pense." Example two: "Toc, toc." "Qui frappe la porte?" "Racine." "Racine qui?" "Fools Racine where angels fear to tread." ("Pretty Corneille, hey?" adds Clay.)

*   *   *

BRAHMIN'S MUSEUM

Cleveland Amory's *The Proper Bostonians*, the first volume in Dutton's promising Society in America series, is not only informative and highly amusing, but actually endows the little band of relics who, I suppose, must be called its heroes and heroines, with a quality that vaguely resembles humanity. The strength and indestructibility of the Boston Brahmin lie in the fact that he prides himself on the very qualities that impress outsiders as most obnoxious and ridiculous.

Amory recalls one Beacon Hill lady who was asked by a New

Yorker where Boston women got their hats. "Our hats?" she exclaimed. "Why, we *have* our hats."

A member of Harvard's ultra-ultra Porcellian Club resented the imputation that he was undemocratic. "When I was stroke on the crew," he maintained, "I knew all but the three up front."

The defunct Boston *Transcript* had a standing injunction against any reference to human anatomy in its columns. One article went to press containing the word "navel." The horrified managing editor heard about it in the nick of time, and had the offending word cast out. He did not bother to read the full context. That evening the *Transcript's* musical critique contained the provocative statement, "Monsieur Blank was in a state of repose as complete as that of a Buddhist regarding his   ."

The story of Amory's that delighted me most concerned a breakfast at the home of Judge John Lowell. The Judge's face was hidden behind his morning paper when a frightened maid tiptoed into the room and whispered something in Mrs. Lowell's ear. Mrs. Lowell squared her shoulders resolutely and said, "John, the cook has burned the oatmeal, and there is no more in the house. I am afraid that this morning, for the first time in seventeen years, you will have to go without your oatmeal." The Judge, without putting down his paper, answered, "It's all right, my dear. Frankly, I never cared for it anyhow."

In *The Lowells and Their Seven Worlds,* Ferris Greenslet recounts dozens of other delectable stories about the inimitable Lowell clan. One day, Amy Lowell's venerable runabout broke down, and a village mechanic demanded that she identify herself before he undertook repairs. "I'm a sister of the President of Harvard," she assured him. "Call him up and he'll tell you I'm good for the bill." The garage man called the President, who inquired, "What's she doing now?" "Sitting on a wall," was the answer, "smoking a big cigar." "That's my sister, all right," said President Lowell.

*   *   *

At the National Dog Show, a dowager inquired of an attendant, "Do you know the way to the Labradors?" "Yas'm," he answered. "The gents' is in the basement; the ladies' down the hall on your right."

*   *   *

A visit to William Randolph Hearst's fabulous ranch at San Simeon, California, usually provides the dazzled guests with dinner-table conversation for weeks. One important novelist tarried there recently and, searching for some writing paper, came across a document in Mr. Hearst's own handwriting that evidently had been left in the desk by mistake. It was headed "Shopping List" and the items on it ran as follows:

> 1 pair shoe laces
> 1 croup kettle
> 2 hippopotami

FARMERS' MARKET

TODAY'S SPECIAL
HIPPOPOTAMUSES
$1493.95
TWO FOR $2987.75

The North Shore of Long Island was the scene of a gay Christmas-week party whose guest list was studded with the names of prominent authors, publishers, and journalists. It was a masquerade, and an editor of *Cosmopolitan* conceived the notion of going as a motorcycle cop. He managed to finagle equipment and a cycle, and set out in style for the party. Unfortunately, he got lost on the way. The roads in that section are quite empty after dark at that time of year, but at long last a Rolls-Royce glided by, and it was obvious from the dress of the occupants that they, too, were bound for the masquerade. The editor tagged behind.

Suddenly the driver of the Rolls became aware of the motorcycle in back of him, and he stepped sharply on the accelerator. The chase was hectic for a while, but the editor hung doggedly onto the trail, and finally the driver of the car slowed down and stopped. "Here at last," thought the editor happily, and pulled up at the side of the Rolls, just in time to have a fifty-dollar bill thrust into his hand by an expressionless chauffeur. He pocketed the bill, parked his motorcycle, and had a fine time at the party.

The next day the Red Cross received an anonymous donation of fifty dollars.

❈   ❈   ❈

When the masquerade party ended, an important Brazilian diplomat stayed the night with Van and Emmy Cartmell. Before retiring at 4 A.M., the diplomat suggested that if it wasn't too much trouble, he would like a couple of cups of hot coffee. He downed three cups—without sugar or cream—with evident satisfaction. "How many cups of coffee do you generally take in the course of a day?" asked Emmy Cartmell. "Twenty-five to thirty," said the diplomat. "Doesn't all that coffee keep you awake?" Cartmell asked. The diplomat thought for a moment. "Not always," he answered slowly, "but it helps."

❈   ❈   ❈

In a trim, inviting bungalow just outside Manhattan there lived a rising young novelist and his wife, presided over by a Scandinavian servant whom everyone described as a gem and who reminded the men at least of Ingrid Bergman. It was this paragon who disrupted the peace of the ménage by approaching her mistress in tears and announcing, "I must leave on the first of the month."

"But why?" demanded the shocked housewife. "I thought you were perfectly happy here." It wasn't that, sobbed the maid; she had met a handsome soldier a few months before, and now . . . "Don't do anything," the wife said as soon as she comprehended. "Let me consult my husband." She was back from his study in a trice. "We have decided, Hilda, that you must stay," she announced. "My husband says the patter of a child's feet will help his writing. We will adopt the baby."

In due course, a son appeared upon the scene, the author adopted him legally, and all was serene for another year, when the maid again announced she was leaving. This time she had met a sailor . . . The novelist and his wife went into another huddle, and the maid was told, "It is unfair to bring up a child alone. We will adopt your second baby, to make sure he has company."

The second baby was a darling little girl, and the bungalow resounded with happy songs and laughter, with the novelist clicking merrily on his typewriter keys.

Then the blow fell. The maid resigned again. "Don't tell me," gasped the wife, "that this time you met a marine."

"It's not that at all, ma'am," said the servant with dignity. "I'm resigning because I simply cannot work for such a big family."

* * *

SECTION 10

Financial

A man who had been very poor all his life made a fortune almost overnight and began to splurge in almost every direction at the same time. One of his greatest joys consisted in inviting old cronies up to see his sumptuous new estate. "Come and see the grounds," he boasted to one of them. "I will show you my three swimming pools."

"Three swimming pools," echoed the friend. "Isn't that a bit excessive?"

"Not at all," the host assured him. "One has cold water, one has hot water, and one has no water at all."

"One with cold water I can understand," conceded the guest. "I can even see a reason for one with hot water. But what's the idea of a swimming pool with no water at all?"

The host shook his head sadly. "You'd be surprised, Joe," he confided, "how many of my old friends can't swim."

*   *   *

One of the most successful businessmen of our time made his first big killing in the glove business. In those days, the most expensive gloves were imported from Europe, and the duty was as high as the total cost of manufacture. As I heard the story, he imported a quarter of a million dollars' worth of gloves at one time—but gave peculiar shipping instructions. All the *left* gloves were consigned to Boston; all the *right* ones to New Orleans. When the shipments arrived, nobody claimed them, and in due course, they were auctioned off by the customs authorities with other unclaimed articles. Who on earth wanted a shipment of *left* gloves? Our hero picked them up in Boston for a fraction of what the duty would have cost. Then his agent did the same with the *right* gloves in New Orleans. And thus another great American fortune was founded.

*   *   *

A few years ago, the late Tom Lamont, a senior partner in J. P. Morgan and Co., dropped into the little church where he had worshiped as a boy and listened unnoticed while the preacher solicited funds to patch the leaking roof. "O Lord, send us succor," was his plea. When the plate was passed, Mr. Lamont dropped a hundred-dollar bill into it. When the preacher saw it, he sighed happily, and announced, "The sucker has been provided."

*   *   *

Lincoln was once asked by a New York firm for information on the financial condition of one of his neighbors. He obliged with the following: "Yours of 10th instant received. I am well acquainted with Mr. ——, and know his circumstances. First of all, he has a wife and baby; together, they ought to be worth $50,000 to any man. Secondly, he has an office in which there is a table worth $1.50, and three chairs, worth $1.00. Last of all, there is in one corner a large rat-hole which will bear looking into. Respectfully yours, A. Lincoln."

* * *

Lawyer Morris Ernst was defending, in a New York court, Schnitzler's comparatively innocuous *Casanova's Homecoming*. Ernst offered to present signed affidavits by various literary luminaries. The judge said he'd be glad to see letters from Sinclair Lewis, Theodore Dreiser, H. L. Mencken, and Heywood Broun. After Ernst had won the case, the judge told him, "I really didn't need those letters to reach a decision, but my son collects autographs."

* * *

Louis Kronenberger, of *Time*, visited the home of a brand-new, black-market millionaire. The furnishings were ornate and expensive; the only thing missing was pictures on the walls. "I suppose," hazarded Kronenberger, "that you're going to acquire some old masters." "I should say not," said the hostess. "If we've got to spend all that money for pictures, we're going to get *ourselves* painted."

* * *

A shirtmaker sought to borrow a hundred thousand dollars from the bank. "That's a lot of money," said the bank president. "Can you give me a statement?" "Yes," said the shirtmaker. "I'm optimistic."

* * *

THE LAMBS GAMBLE

A suspicion is growing in publishing circles that the anthology racket is being overplayed. In the past year alone there have been over fifty new collections of one sort or another—featuring dogs, cats, doctors, dreamers, fishermen, murderers, nymphomaniacs, wits, nitwits, and what have you—and signs are not lacking that a once-avid public is beginning to cry "Uncle." The situation has not been helped by the number of amiable hacks who have been content merely to anthologize other anthologies. Ernest Hemingway's *The Killers,* James Thurber's *The Secret Life of Walter Mitty,* and Stephen Vincent Benét's *The Devil and Daniel Webster,* for example, fine stories all, have appeared in so many collections that readers who go in for these things must be able to recite them by heart by this time. A recent cartoon depicted a little vandal diligently ripping pages out of all the fine volumes in his father's library. His mother, proud rather than angry, watched him complacently and concluded, "He'll probably be a successful anthologist when he grows up!"

One of the few really original notions for an anthology is the brain child of Iles Brody: a selection of great gambling stories by famous authors of the past century. The choice is limitless, for it seems that almost every writer of note has written at least one tale concerning a desperate gamble of some description. In the words of an old grass-roots philosopher, "When a man's et, he wants to pet, and if he can't pet, he'll bet!"

A canny life-insurance agent once sold a policy to a prospect exhausted competitors had dismissed as "untouchable" by reducing his proposition to wagering terms. "I've got one million dollars to your twenty thousand—50 to 1—that says you'll drop dead within the next twelve months," he challenged. "Why, you ——," exploded the prospect, and before he recovered his equilibrium, he had signed for a whopping policy.

Beatrice Lillie once won a fortune at the Monte Carlo Casino by having a coughing spell at the right time. She was at the chemin-de-fer table and when one pot consisted of a modest five hundred francs, she called "banquo." Possibly the excitement of winning was the cause of her coughing fit, but at any rate the croupier mistook her garrumphs and noises eight successive deals for "banquo," and by the time she stopped coughing, the pot had risen to two hundred and fifty-six thousand francs! Miss Lillie cashed in her chips, walked calmly to the ladies' room, and fainted.

The late Ben Bernie was a great favorite in vaudeville and on the radio, but he was always unsure of himself as a drawing card in motion pictures. His friends, aware of his doubts, needled him unmercifully—particularly Lou Holtz, whose barbs never failed to upset Bernie for days. After Bernie had completed one picture, the producers, highly satisfied, called him in and took up his option, adding a healthy bonus. He had the new contract, signed and witnessed, in his inside pocket when he ran into Holtz. "I just saw a preview of your new picture," jeered Holtz, "and boy, is that a turkey! I'll bet you a thousand bucks they don't renew your option." "Take him up," whispered Bernie's agent. "Then show him the signed contract. It will teach him a lesson." "I haven't got the nerve," mourned Bernie. "You know I can't ever win a bet from Holtz!"

An oft-repeated tale concerns the corporal who reported to a new regiment with a letter from his old captain saying, "This man is a great soldier, and he'll be even better if you can cure him of his constant gambling." The new C.O. looked at him sternly and said, "I hear you're an inveterate gambler. I don't approve. It's bad for discipline. What kind of thing do you bet on?" "Practically anything, sir," said the corporal. "If you'd like, I'll bet you my next month's pay that you've got a strawberry birth-mark under your right arm." The C.O. snapped, "Put down your money." He stripped to the waist, proved conclusively he had no birth-mark, and pocketed the bills on the table. He couldn't wait to phone the captain and exult, "That corporal of yours won't be in such a hurry to make a bet after what I just did to him." "Don't be too sure," said the captain mournfully. "The so-and-so wagered me twenty to two hundred he'd get you to take your shirt off five minutes after he reported."

The wiles and methods of professional card sharps aboard ocean liners and trains have been advertised so widely that suckers are not so plentiful as they were in days of yore. A famous Damon

Runyon quote is the advice an old farmer gave his son who was
leaving to make his way in the big city: "Remember, son, if a
slick gambling feller comes along and offers you even money he
can make the jack of spades jump out of a deck and spit prune
juice in your face, don't take him—or sure as heck, you're goin'
to wake up covered with prune juice!" One card player grew so
discouraged at the slim pickings, he wrote a book exposing the
methods of his crooked compatriots. It has sold over a hundred
thousand copies.

Another form of gambling that should be avoided at all costs is
games involving married couples. Wars are tough enough on
battlefields without shifting them to your own drawing room! My
friend Bill Walling and I once played bridge against a beautiful
girl and a young man who were, we thought, mere acquaintances.
They fought from the first hand, criticized each other's play
throughout the evening, paid their losses grimly, and left without
even saying good night to us. Bill's only comment was. "My, my!
I never dreamed those two were living together!" He was right
too! A few days later we read they had been married secretly in
Connecticut the previous winter.

* * *

The collection department of a Detroit firm tried a new approach on a recalcitrant account in a small village in the corn
belt. "Dear Mr. Caldwell," their letter began. "What would all
your neighbors think if we came to your town and repossessed
your car?" In due course their letter came back, with this message
scrawled across the bottom, "Gents: I have taken up this matter
with my neighbors and they think it would be a lousy trick."

* * *

Frank Scully recalls the case of a young man who left a night
club with his girl and fell into an open manhole. His back was
permanently injured. Friends assured him, "This is an open-and-
shut case of neglect. You'll be awarded $50,000 at least in
damages."

Lawyers were preparing the suit when the news of Pearl Harbor came over the radio. The suit was dropped. The young man's companion was his sole witness. She was Japanese.

* * *

A case that actually reached the courts, and will cause many a headache before it is settled, concerns a man who had decided not to pay any more premiums on his hundred-thousand-dollar life-insurance policy. It was due to lapse at midnight of a certain day. Four hours before the moment of expiration, the man boarded a train for Boston, and retired to his drawing room. The next morning the porter found him dead in his berth.

Did he die before midnight? If so, his estate could collect a hundred thousand dollars from the insurance company. If he died after one second past midnight, however, his policy was worthless. Both sides lined up doctors willing to testify in their favor. None of them could be certain, of course, of the exact moment of the man's death.

Possibly a professional detective story writer—or the reader of these lines—could offer a satisfactory solution!

* * *

A high-powered insurance agent talked an aging and overworked book manufacturer into taking out a new policy. The manufacturer submitted to a physical examination and then waited in vain for a call from the agent. Finally, he called the agent and asked the reason for his silence. In an embarrassed tone, the agent explained, "You may have noticed that our company doctor makes out a chart and punches a hole in it wherever he finds something that isn't just right with the applicant."

"I noticed, all right," said the manufacturer. "What did he do with my chart?"

"I am sorry to inform you," said the agent, "that the doctor took your chart home with him and tried it on his player piano. The tune it played was 'Nearer, My God, to Thee.'"

* * *

Another insurance man, who seems to have time on his hands, has compiled the following statistics: If you have reached the age of seventy, and pursued an average American's existence, you have consumed during your lifetime a total of 150 head of cattle,

26 sheep, 310 swine, 225 lambs, 2400 chickens, 26 acres of grain, and 50 acres of fruits and vegetables. Hungry?

*　*　*

Herbert Wise defines an economist as a man who has a Phi Beta Kappa key on one end of his chain and no watch on the other.

And Irving Hoffman knows a tree surgeon who fell out of his patient.

*　*　*

John D. Rockefeller, Jr., conducts his affairs in a very comfortable but modest office. A visitor, disappointed, asked, "How can you hope to impress anybody in an office like this?" Mr. Rockefeller answered, "Whom do I have to impress?"

*　*　*

"... ON A MAGAZINE COVER"

Have you ever entertained the notion that editing a magazine would be just your dish? If so, this little piece is intended to give you pause. No job in the world offers a surer and quicker promise of a first-class case of stomach ulcers, and if you don't believe me, you have only to take a canvass of all the dyspeptic specimens now extant.

Finding new writers and artists, and then holding on to them, avoiding libel and plagiarism suits, fighting the inroads of eager beavers in the advertising department, and getting copy to the printer on time for every issue are only part of their problem. They must also live under the perpetual fear that something is going to happen while a number is on press or about to hit the stands that will make one of their leading articles—perhaps the one featured on the cover—look ridiculous.

Especially vulnerable, of course, are the news magazines—not to mention the motion-picture "fan" periodicals, which often come out with rapturous descriptions of the idyllic home life of two famous Hollywood love-birds a day or so after said love-birds have hit the front page with a super-colossal free-for-all in a night club, and marched off to the divorce courts.

The day after the Jap raid on Pearl Harbor, one of our best-known magazines appeared with a lead article designed to prove that Hawaii never could be attacked successfully. And just when our unprepared and pitifully inadequate forces were being knocked silly by Japanese aviators, another periodical was featuring a piece by an "expert" who proved conclusively that the Japs were worthless as air fighters because their planes were antiquated puddle-jumpers, their pilots were cockeyed, and their bombs were duds.

Some years ago, an enterprising editor bagged a piece by a noted octogenarian which gave in detail his secrets of longevity. Unfortunately, the day before the article appeared, the octogenarian dropped dead. Another editor lined up eight pages of colored photographs of the accession to the throne of King Edward VIII, and a description of same by the highest-paid journalist in

Britain. The editor was correcting proofs when his wife called out, "Hurry up if you want to hear Edward abdicating over the radio."

In August, 1914, a magazine featured an article about the Kaiser, calling it "The World's Greatest Peace Advocate." When it appeared, German soldiers were already tramping through the towns of Belgium. In October, 1929, a big financial digest devoted most of an issue to a wildly bullish interpretation of the market. It reached the stands during the greatest Wall Street crash in history. In April, 1947, another periodical printed Leo Durocher's picture on its cover, and hailed him as one of baseball's indispensables. Manager Durocher, unfortunately, had just been suspended from his job as manager of the Brooklyn Dodgers for the entire season. These were in no sense "boners" on the part of the editors involved; they simply were tough breaks, and there are dozens more like them on the records.

The great newspaper cartoonist, Jay Darling ("Ding"), had a comparable experience in 1935. He made a drawing labeled "The Fates Are Funny That Way," depicting a whole series of national calamities: earthquakes, floods, and train wrecks—but in the concluding panel he showed Mr. Public complaining to his wife, "Yet nothing ever seems to happen to Huey Long!" Three days later, Long was assassinated. One Western paper, in fact, received Ding's cartoon a bit late, and ran it and the story of Long's death in adjoining columns.

During the war, edition after edition of the big news weeklies had to be ripped apart at the last moment because of some sudden and spectacular happening. Even now, the editors of these weeklies spend the twenty-four hours before press time praying that nothing will occur to necessitate a complete reshuffling of an issue's contents. Their wives see them, if at all, by television. One of them hasn't spent a week-end away from his office since he came down with pneumonia trying to catch pictures of a fight between a flounder and a soft-shell crab.

Do you still yearn to be a magazine editor? Or maybe you'd like to try your hand as a circulation manager! Listen to the sad tale of one of the best of them.

At enormous expense, he installed a complicated machine that isolated all the index plates of patrons whose subscriptions were

going to run out in five or six weeks. It automatically printed their names and addresses at the tops of one of those irresistible form letters that begin, "Surely you are not going to allow yourself to miss a single issue, etc., etc.," sealed and stamped the envelopes, and dropped them in a chute without human hands even so much as touching them. The circulation manager was so proud of this machine that he wrote a long article extolling its virtue, and hailing the company that built it as a benefactor of humanity.

Unfortunately, the machine went out of kilter one sticky summer day, and before the slip-up was discovered, a baffled rancher in Montana received 11,834 letters telling him his subscription was about to expire. The local postmaster had to hire a special truck to deliver them all. After the rancher had read about two hundred of the letters, he got the idea, and mailed the magazine a check for six dollars, with a note saying, "I give up."

With or without their editors, the magazines march on!

In the late Russell Maloney's delectable pot-pourri, *It's Still Maloney,* he analyzed the quirk that permits laymen who would never dream of showing vulgar curiosity over the earnings of a banker or butcher to ask a writer blandly, "How much did you get for that last piece in the *New Yorker?*" or "How much will you make out of your new book?" Maloney said that Alva Johnston worked out an answer that for some reason is an infallible stopper: "I get twenty-six dollars a column, but I have to pay my own expenses."

One of the best of Maloney's back-stage reminiscences of *New Yorker* days concerns the time a regular poetry contributor won the Pulitzer Prize. An editor wrote him a warm letter of congratulation, and tacked on a P.S. that read, "We are returning herewith your last batch of poems, because none of them seems quite right for our present needs."

* * *

Editor Harold ("Sunshine") Ross admits that life at the *New Yorker* is not the same since the redoubtable Alexander Woollcott vanished from the scene. Ross used to goad Woollcott deliberately into writing him insulting letters. Woollcott mailed them in a fine white heat of anger, exulting, "When Ross reads what I called him, he won't dare show his face in public for a week." Ross, however, happily had the letters mimeographed, and dispatched copies to all their mutual friends. Woollcott once completed some intricate transaction whereby he came into possession of two hundred brand-new Sulka neckties, and, in a moment of unaccountable graciousness, told Ross, "Pick one out for yourself." Ross not only picked one for himself, but pilfered forty extra in the process. The next time Mr. W. paid a scheduled visit to the *New Yorker* offices, everybody in the place, including the elevator man and the young lady at the switchboard, was draped in a Sulka cravat. "Ross," snarled Woollcott, "you are the kind of poltroon I find it hard to deal with," and flounced off to air his grievance to Lynn Fontanne and Alfred Lunt. He even persuaded them to cancel their subscription to the *New Yorker*. The following summer, they discovered the latest issue on Woollcott's own table at Beomoseen. "I've forgiven Ross," he explained airily. "I'm writing a piece for him now."

* * *

One of my favorite magazine features is a lively weekly page in *Tide* called, reasonably enough, "Tidings." Recently it described Aviatrix Jacqueline Cochran's cocktail party in honor of her husband, multi-millionaire Floyd Odlum. He was lamentably late for his own party, but finally entered amidst the reverential hush that befits a director of a dozen great corporations. "Darling," was his method of making amends to his wife. "Surprise! I bought you a new airplane today." Everybody thought that he was pretty wonderful except one unappreciative drunk whose comment was heard distinctly by the entire assemblage: "Humph! All the flower shops must have been closed!"

* * *

In New York, *Tide* also reports, the promotion department of *McCall's* waxed irate at the poor reproduction which one of the magazine's four-color ads got in *Newsweek,* and planned an epic squawk. In the nick of time somebody remembered that *Newsweek* is printed in Dayton by the McCall Corporation! That recalls the story of a famous editor who chided his son for skipping English classes. "What will you do," he asked, "if you succeed me as editor, and the magazine starts coming out full of errors?" "The same as you," answered the son promptly. "I'll blame the printers."

* * *

The sales manager of one of the country's biggest paper mills played host recently to a group of book designers and manufacturing men from a dozen publishing houses. The food was excellent, the wine flowed freely, and when the sales manager arose to speak he was greeted with a salvo of applause.

"Fellows," he said with a catch in his voice, "just fifteen years ago today our mill received its very first paper order from a book publisher."

Somebody in the rear of the room caused a near-riot by shouting, "When are you going to fill it?"

* * *

Fred Melcher, head of *Publishers' Weekly,* and the only man in the United States who considers copyright bills hammock reading, cleared his throat nervously. Everybody sensed that an important pronouncement was forthcoming. Then Fred Melcher spoke. "1949," he said in slow, measured tones, "is the eightieth anniversary of the banana!"

For a moment nobody uttered a syllable. Then pandemonium

(Amy Loveman's cocker spaniel) broke loose, and in the excitement I rushed to the encyclopedia to do some checking.

Mr. Melcher, of course, was referring to the banana—or gigantic herbaceous plant belonging to the family Musaceae, as I like to think of it—in the United States. In 1870, Captain Lorenzo Dow Baker sailed his schooner out of Wellfleet, Mass., with a cargo of mining machinery destined for Venezuela. On the way home he put in at Jamaica, ate his first banana, yelled "Eureka!" and put a dozen clusters of the succulent fruit aboard for his wife and kiddies. By the time he reached Wellfleet the bananas had rotted, but Captain Baker was a persistent character. On his next voyage, he had the good sense to put green bananas in the hold and let them ripen on the way back. Mr. Baker thereupon organized the Boston Fruit Company, which became the owner of just about everything in Jamaica and adjacent territory. Before the war disrupted transportation, the banana industry reached an annual gross of over fifty million dollars and provided Sigmund Spaeth with a lifetime income from demonstrating how "Yes, We Have No Bananas!" was lifted from Handel's *Messiah*. Today it's bigger than ever.

* * *

James J. Leff recalls the story of the late Wilson Mizner's early fling in the art business. He was selling reproductions of old masters and was getting a hundred dollars for Da Vinci's "Last Supper." Competition forced him to cut the price to $65 and when he couldn't get customers at that figure he quit. His reason: "That dinner's worth five dollars a plate and I won't take a cent less!"

* * *

One of Editor Clip Boutell's best yarns concerns the time John Woodburn dined copiously at a nobby restaurant in Rockefeller Center, and then found he had left his wallet at home. The manager let him sign a chit for the amount, and a few mornings later a little man arrived at John's publishing office to present it for collection. "The man said who he was but I just couldn't believe it," the receptionist told Woodburn. "Finally I made him write it down. Look!" Woodburn looked. The slip read in a wavering scrawl, "Louis XIV."

* * *

In Cleveland, Burrows Brothers' Charlie Jackson, the only case of one-hundred-per-cent Scotch left in Ohio, is reputed to have been a principal in a minor motor accident. The other driver was Irish. Charlie offered him a drink, which was accepted. "Beautiful liquor," pronounced the appeased Hibernian. "But aren't you having a snort yourself?" "Aye," said Charlie, "but noo until the cops've coom."

* * *

A vice-president of the Chase National Bank swears to the authenticity of this incident. He gave a brand-new secretary a one-hundred-dollar bill and asked her to go outside and get it changed. She didn't come back for a full hour, and then she still clutched the bill in her hand. "I've been to every store on the block," she reported. "Nobody would change it for me!"

* * *

For three full months recently the New York *Herald Tribune* had a messenger "boy" who was over seventy years old, but few of the people who gave him fleeting or pitying glances as he shuffled by knew that in a happier day he had been the managing editor of one of pre-Hitler Germany's greatest newspapers. Idleness had driven him close to distraction in America, and finally, like an old fire-horse, he had come back to the business he had known and loved.

What place was there, however, for a wistful, apologetic refugee of seventy? When he heard that the *Tribune* urgently needed messengers, he surprised the staff by applying for one of the vacant jobs.

His love of books is what undid him. He took longer and longer to complete his errands, and when finally he was discovered poring over some old volumes in a second-hand bookstore, he admitted that that was how he had been spending many of his working hours. He took his dismissal philosophically. "I guess it's just as well," he told the foreman. "I was spending too much on taxicabs anyhow."

*　*　*

Victor Borge, the clever Danish raconteur, told a banker, "A man you really should finance is my uncle, who was determined to invent a new soft drink. He worked on a formula for a whole year, and came up with something he called '4 Up.' It was a failure, but my uncle was not discouraged. He worked another year, and produced a new concoction which he named '5 Up.' Again it failed to sell, but my uncle persevered. He took all the rest of his money, secluded himself for two years this time, and turned up with still another soft drink that he called '6 Up.' Alas, it failed like the others, and my uncle, discouraged at last, gave up in disgust."

"The point of your story eludes me," said the banker. "Why do you tell me all this?"

"I just wanted you to know," said Borge, "how close my uncle came to inventing '7 Up'!"

*　*　*

MEDICAL MIDAS

The accentuated roar of the presses at Doubleday's Garden City plant means only one thing to initiates: a new tome by the irrepressible Dr. Morris Fishbein is in the works. Newest of his products is an exhaustive manual called *Successful Marriage,* and the knowing publisher, Milo Sutliff, predicted it would outsell even the Fishbein *Modern Medical Adviser.* So did the doctor's perspicacious younger daughter, and at this sort of prognostication, the miss is as good as the Milo. *The Medical Adviser,* incidentally, crossed the one million, three hundred thousand mark in November, 1947. His other books—nineteen in all—have sold another two million copies. You can understand why Dr. Fishbein's enemies call him a "medical Midas" and a "drugstore Dumas." A few enemies more or less mean nothing in the doctor's busy life. "I've been sued for thirty-five million dollars in libel suits," is his boast, "and I have never lost a cent."

Dr. Fishbein has been editor of the official *Journal of the American Medical Association* for twenty-three years. Of the 190,000

doctors in America, 130,000 are members of the A.M.A., so the impact of the Fishbein point of view scarcely can be exaggerated. When he charges furiously against medical quacks of every description, or plumps unceasingly for better and more thorough medical research, that point of view cannot be challenged. When he fights with equal abandon, however, against any kind of socialized medicine, there are many who howl loudly—and thus far in vain—for a purge of "the medical trust's lobby horse." The unperturbed doctor marches on. When Britain's Labor Government framed its National Health Service Bill, calling for free hospitalization and operations when necessary, he cried, "A nation which fought successfully against totalitarianism now proposes to enslave its medical profession, and convert its physicians into clock-watching civil servants." The Labor Party evidently didn't hear him.

Dr. Fishbein began his literary career as a ghost writer for many

famous physicians who wielded a scalpel better than a fountain
pen. Then he began to write reviews under his own by-line. Gentle was not the word for Morris. Of one little number called
"Laugh and Grow Fat," he wrote, "There is too much laughing.
Already the number of grinning simpletons is appalling." Today,
however, he knows more jokes than I do, and tells them oftener.
At the end of World War I, he became a member of a distinguished group that whiled away Saturday afternoons in poker
games in the back of Pat Covici's bookstore on Wabash Avenue,
Chicago, and that included also Clarence Darrow, Ben Hecht,
Keith Preston, and Henry Justin Smith. There the alert Horace
Liveright encountered him, and persuaded him to write a book
called *The Medical Follies*. From that day on, at least one Fishbein title has been a continuous feature of all best-seller lists.

Time calls Dr. Fishbein "the nation's most ubiquitous, most
widely maligned, and perhaps most influential medico." To this
description I would like to add "most entertaining." What his
partner in a recent bridge game added when he made an original
bid of "seven clubs," vulnerable, and went down one, had best
be left to the reader's imagination.

❄   ❄   ❄

In the secret annals of one of Chicago's robber bands is the
story of a young gangster, quick on the trigger but slow in his
mental processes, who was sent to look over a palatial home
marked for a future looting job. He crept silently through the
shrubbery, looked into a drawing-room window, and saw a young
lady and young gentleman, both in evening clothes, earnestly
playing a piano duet.

"Better cross that lay-out off your list," he advised the leader
of the gang when he returned. "They can't have much dough.
I seen two people in there playing on one piano!"

❄   ❄   ❄

In the vestry of the Janesville, Wisconsin, Congregational
Church, I heard the story of a married couple who supposedly
bearded Hughston McBain, head of Marshall Field, in his private

office one morning and demanded, "What do you want for the entire outfit?" Mr. McBain, equal to any occasion, snapped, "Ninety million dollars cash." "You wouldn't take eighty-nine?" suggested the wife. "No, ma'am," McBain told her. "Ninety is the price; take it or leave it." "In that case," she said, "my husband and I will have to go into a huddle. He'll give you our decision in fifteen minutes." Mr. McBain murmured, "Now I've heard everything," and turned back to his correspondence. To his surprise, however, the man returned promptly in a quarter of an hour, and reported, "I'm sorry, but we have decided to turn down your proposition." "The price was too stiff, I suppose," chuckled McBain. "It wasn't that," the man assured him gravely, "but when we examined the situation, we found out there's no place to live in the back of the store!"

* * *

In Sholom Aleichem's *The Old Country* appears the original version of the meeting between a poor old man from a Russian ghetto and Baron Rothschild in Paris. The Baron's butler, seeing the old man's tattered raiment, doesn't want to let him in, but is brushed aside with a scornful "Fool! If I had good clothes, would I have bothered coming to Paris?" Then the Baron is intrigued by the promise of eternal life. The price of the secret is three hundred rubles. The old man pockets his gold—the most he has ever seen—and tells the Baron, "It's simple enough. Just move to our ghetto. No rich man ever has died there in our history."

Sholom Aleichem is credited, too, with that solid piece of advice to a lovesick Lothario: "Remember, my boy, you can marry more money in five minutes than you can make in a lifetime."

* * *

I remember an old story they tell about the richest of the Rothschilds. "How did all the members of your family amass such vast fortunes?" he was asked. The old Baron smiled faintly and answered, "By always selling too soon."

* * *

New stories of the 1929 stock market debacle still are coming to light. One concerns the Wall Street tycoon who gave his university a couple of million dollars to build a new library. By the time it was finished, the tycoon was wiped out, and the university heads offered him the job of chief librarian in his own building. He not only accepted, but has presided there very happily ever since.

Then there was the family of four brothers. Three were spectacularly successful Wall Street operators, the fourth was an amiable schlemiel who had just about enough sense to sit down when he was tired. The three shining lights took care of their less gifted brother. Every time one of them bought ten thousand shares of a stock, he'd add a couple of hundred in the name of the lame duck. In July, 1929, the fourth brother fell ill and was told by the doctor that he was the victim of an incurable disease, and couldn't live another ten months. He sold every share of stock he owned for about a million in cash, put his affairs in order, and prepared to have as much fun as possible in the little time he had left. Of course, the three geniuses were wiped out completely in October. And the lame duck's disease wasn't incurable after all. He's living on top of the world today, and the three brothers are working for him.

* * *

Up in Rochester, there lived a family who had had the same cook for twenty years (those were the days!). While she was off on a holiday, her employers decided to give her a pleasant surprise. They had her room completely refurnished and redecorated. The cook was surprised, all right. It developed that her life savings—twelve thousand dollars in cash—had been hidden in her old mattress.

By great good fortune, the mattress was recovered, and her nest egg found intact. Her employers upbraided her for her medieval habits, and persuaded her with the greatest difficulty to deposit her twelve thousand dollars in a local bank. Then, bingo! The market collapsed, the bank closed, and the family was left without a penny. "What can I say?" the white-faced husband told the cook. "This is all our fault, and if it's the last thing I do, I'm going to make good on that twelve thousand I lost for you."

"Don't give it another thought," said the cook. "I just deposited that money in the bank to make you happy. I drew it out again fifteen minutes later."

I wish I could tell that the cook loaned her employer the money, and that with that fresh start he rose to be a vice-president of the Eastman Kodak Company. That would be a neat ending, but it wouldn't be true. For that matter, I wouldn't vouch for the whole story. The man who told it to me—a Mr. Bernard Baruch —has a vivid imagination.

* * *

Bernard Baruch made his first fortune in 1902, through a series of brilliant speculative coups in the stock market, and a fight for control of the Louisville and Nashville Railroad with no less formidable an adversary than J. P. Morgan, the elder. Mr. Morgan got the railroad, but Mr. Baruch netted a profit of a million and a half on the deal.

Officials of the National City Bank have good cause to remem-

ber this auspicious moment in Baruch's career. He strolled into
the main office to open an account. The head cashier had never
heard of him, and asked, "Can you give us any references?" Mr.
Baruch calmly produced a certified check from the house of Morgan for one million dollars. He still speaks admiringly of the savoir
faire of the cashier, who, after an involuntary start of surprise,
said in a very matter-of-fact voice, "The National City Bank wel-
comes you as a depositor."

Igor Cassini, who writes the "Cholly Knickerbocker" society column for the New York *Journal-American,* asked Mr. Baruch how
he arranged the seatings for all the notables who attend his various dinner parties. "I never bother about that," Baruch assured
him. "Those who matter don't mind, and those who mind don't
matter." Baruch himself was guest of honor at a Thanksgiving-
night banquet, at which the late Jimmie Walker was toastmaster.
Introducing Baruch, Walker remarked, "You have been giving
your attention to turkey stuffed with sage. I now present to you
a sage stuffed with turkey."

* * *

SECTION 11

Radio

According to most recent estimates of the census authorities, there
are about 160,000,000 people in the United States today. By no
coincidence whatever, that is exactly the number who have con-
stituted themselves official critics of the nation's radio and television programs. The infinitesimal minority who have columns in
which to make their disapproval official have made the top comedians of the air waves their particular target this year, and, truth
to tell, said comedians are as vulnerable as a rheumatic cow at
twenty yards. Anybody who has listened to these talented and

expensive comedians stick to their same tired routines week after week must have been seized more than once with a desire to take every radio set within hearing distance and dump it into the nearest garbage can.

Two things must be remembered, however, before our headline radio wags are read out of the human race. One, the task of grinding out a "new" show week after week is maddening, if not impossible. In the old days of vaudeville, a comedian could polish his act over a period of months, and once it was set to the satisfaction of himself and his audiences, could—and did—play it over and over again for years on end. The famous routines of Weber and Fields, the Avon Comedy Four, Mr. and Mrs. Jimmie Barry, Charles Withers, and other greats of yesteryear, were not the result of a few days of hectic improvisation and tinkering, but the final product of endless smoothing and perfecting. One does not compare a glass of homemade wine with a fine vintage champagne. A top radio comic no sooner finishes one week's show than he, and his staff of harried writers, must begin worrying about next week's. "The only difference between us and white mice on a wheel," mourned Radio Scriptor Hal Block one day, "is that we have ulcers."

Two, star radio performers today are laced tightly in a straitjacket that bears the label "Hooperating." This system provides an approximation of the number of people who listen to a particular program at a particular time. The sponsors who pay radio's bills watch these Hooperatings with passionate intensity. The few stars who have latched on to a formula that landed them in the top twenty of Mr. C. E. Hooper's hierarchy are understandably reluctant to tamper with a good thing. A variation in the routine would take time to catch popular fancy. Their Hooperatings would go down and their salaries would follow. Indeed, they might be banished from the air waves entirely!

And so our greatest radio talents, the Allens, and the Hopes, and the Bennys, and the Bergens, and the Crosbys, stay carefully within their familiar grooves. They've found a bonanza—and they're stuck with it. Since the gentlemen mentioned are genuine artists—the best of the lot—they themselves throw caution to the winds from time to time, and beg for an opportunity to experiment in new pastures, regardless of consequences. Their sponsors, however, will not hear of it. The same sponsors frequently withdraw support from promising new personalities before they have had a full chance to capture the public they deserve. It takes time for a country as big as ours to appreciate fully the gifts of a comparative newcomer like Henry Morgan or Jack Paar.

If our top performers had two months instead of five days to prepare new programs, if they were allowed to experiment freely with new formulas and techniques, and if they were permitted to repeat particularly successful efforts from time to time, radio humor would soon show startling improvement. Until that unlikely day, the poor boys will have to go on struggling with their audiences of thirty million, and their five to ten thousand dollars a week.

* * *

The Mr. Hooper whose bi-weekly standing of the dubs—and champions—exerts such unholy influence on the world of radio is himself a retiring Ohioan who admits, rather wistfully, that his

first job was selling horseradish to housewives after school hours. It was rather a good thing, too, but once he had acquired a degree at Harvard, any further dalliance with horseradish was, of course, unthinkable, and Mr. Hooper drifted into the field of research. Just how far he has drifted is evidenced by the fact that he now has almost two thousand sub-researchers, deployed in the thirty-six cities where all four national networks have stations. Most of the sub-researchers spend the entire day phoning people to find out what radio program, if any, is engaging their attention. Responses are startlingly similar in all corners of the country and form an incontestable basis for the comprehensive tabulations evolved by Master-Mind Hooper.

The highest Hooper rating on record, 79, was achieved by President Roosevelt when he delivered his war proclamation after the fateful bombing of Pearl Harbor. The lowest, shared by more than one doomed aspirant, is a flat and unequivocal zero. Thirty is just about tops for a regular weekly show. Hooper himself, appearing on a "We the People" program in December, 1947, achieved the very respectable showing of 13. He had one embarrassing moment in the course of the proceedings, however, when he called a number at random, and asked, "What program are you listening to?" The answer, loud and clear, was "Amos 'n Andy."

The official name of Mr. Hooper's enterprise is "Broadcast Audience Measurement"; squirming victims refer to it in more picturesque vernacular. The imperturbable Goodman Ace explained his low rating glibly, "The folks who listen to me are so engrossed they won't miss a line to get up and answer the telephone." Joe E. Lewis says Hooper once rated *his* program and found that even fifty per cent of the *studio* audience wasn't listening to him.

Max Gordon once asked Groucho Marx why he liked doing radio shows. Groucho pointed to his latest Hooperating and explained, "Well, in the first place, nobody hears you. . . ."

*   *   *

Red Skelton has discovered the longest word in the English language. It's the one that follows the announcement, "And now a word from our sponsor." . . . Robert Kintner adds that announcers themselves always have small hands: wee paws for station identification. . . . A comedian's agent once warned him, "The next time you ad lib, Milt, don't rattle the paper so much." . . . During the warm-up period of an "Information, Please" program, Guest-Star George Kaufman unaccountably failed to answer a single question. Just before the show went on the air, Clifton Fadiman asked kiddingly, "May I ask what you have been doing for the past fifteen minutes, Mr. K.?" "You may," answered Mr. K. "I've been listening to 'Information, Please.'"

* * *

"Information, Please," incidentally, its redoubtable owner, Dan Golenpaul, and Clifton Fadiman all were named as defendants in an unusual lawsuit not long ago. Fadiman told the panel of the evening, "I want you all to close your eyes and tell me what color neckties you are wearing." Unfortunately, a lonely motorist driving down the Albany Post Road closed *his* eyes too and wrapped his jalopy around a telegraph pole. The next day his lawyer entered suit. At last reports the case was pending.

* * *

On one of those quiz shows where they give dollar bills for guessing George Washington's first name, a plump housewife walked off with the five-hundred-dollar jackpot. "What's the first thing you're going to do with this money?" gurgled the delirious M.C. "Count it," said the housewife simply.

Another show specialized in wrapping objects in deceiving and inappropriate packages, and presenting them to the first member of the *studio* audience who could identify same. The announcer stepped into a soundproof booth on-stage to let the *radio* audience in on the secret.

Edwin O'Connor was present one day when the announcer stepped out of the booth and held up to view a package big enough to contain a set of the *Encyclopedia Britannica*. "What have we here?" he asked playfully. "A set of dishes? An elephant?" "You have there," said a lady in the audience, "a small diamond ring."

"Wonderful," said the announcer, hauling the lucky lady on to the stage. "Have you X-ray eyes? Or could you hear what I was saying in that soundproof booth?" "Not exactly," said the lady. "I'm a lip reader."

* * *

When Groucho Marx was guest-star on the Bing Crosby show, he recalled, "A year ago, I had enough money to choke a horse." "What happened?" prompted Crosby. "I made a slight error," Groucho admitted. "I bet on him instead of choking him." . . . Eddie Cantor has devised a new quiz program. Your name is selected at random from a local telephone directory, and if you're at home when Cantor calls, he borrows twenty dollars. . . . Betty Grable and the great baseball pitcher, Dizzy Dean, once co-starred on a broadcast from a Veterans' Hospital. "Say something cute to Miss Grable," urged the announcer. Dean fingered his collar and proposed, "I'll show you my curves, Miss Grable, if you'll show me yours."

* * *

A new high in mortification was scored at a local radio station by a young couple who were breaking in a new song-and-patter program. It was on a sustaining basis and there was no money for expensive guest stars, but the couple persuaded their good friends, the Andrews Sisters, to appear gratis one evening to help hypo the rating.

The Andrews Sisters were in the studio waiting to do one of their most popular specialties when a new efficiency expert of the station bustled in, took one look at the girls, and barked, "No guests are allowed in the broadcasting studio. You'll have to leave at once." The host explained desperately, "You don't understand, Mr. So-and-so. These are the *Andrews* Sisters!" "I don't care whose sisters they are," declared the expert. "Get 'em out of here." As an afterthought he called over his shoulder, "And fire Andrews, too."

* * *

HERE COMES McBRIDE

About twenty minutes before one o'clock, Eastern Standard Time, every weekday, a bevy of eager-eyed, chattering ladies troop into Studio 3E of the National Broadcasting Corporation to watch their radio idol, Mary Margaret McBride, go through her paces. They are but the visible fragment of a devoted and attentive audience of six million housewives who take Mary Margaret's words for gospel and rush out to buy the products that she endorses so casually but effectively.

At ten minutes before broadcasting time, Vincent Connolly, Princeton '33, who introduces Mary Margaret, and struggles valiantly to keep her on the beam, takes his place, followed, usually, by the guest-star of the day, clutching his or her notes nervously,

and ignored politely by the audience who want nobody but Mary Margaret. In the nick of time she appears, unhurried, serene, her whole attitude implying clearly, "Goodness, have all you people turned out just to hear little old me?" The ladies settle back in their seats with delighted sighs. The guest of the day relaxes instinctively. Mary Margaret fusses with a sheaf of notes. The gong sounds and she begins. And very soon the reason for her tremendous success becomes apparent. Miss McBride really knows about the person she is interviewing—and about the work that has made that person worth having on the program. The products of the sponsors creep unobtrusively into the conversation. Mary Margaret's thoughts, it develops, are about as scattered as a Times Square crowd on New Year's Eve, her approach as vague as a pay-off punch by a heavyweight champion.

Mary Margaret McBride was born in 1899 in Paris, Missouri, about halfway between Hannibal and Fulton, where she was sent to school. The schoolhouse had been endowed by Mary Margaret's great-aunt, who told her that the post of "lady principal" was waiting for her some fine day. Mary Margaret, however, had different ambitions, and when her horrified aunt heard that they included writing, she not only withdrew all financial support but hid the family silver. Mary Margaret enrolled at the University of Missouri, financed herself happily by writing a chatter column for a local daily at ten dollars a week. Three days after she got her diploma in 1919, and headed for Washington, the daily suspended publication. Possibly this was a coincidence.

In Washington, she landed a job in the Senate building, quit when Missouri Senator Reid said her middy blouses were "too undignified." "Dignity," says Mary Margaret, "is something you are born with or without. Too many people confuse dignity with pomposity and pretense." Her college chum, Pauline Pfeiffer (later the second Mrs. Ernest Hemingway) helped her secure a place on the staff of the Cleveland *Press*. Her first big assignment was to cover a local religious convention. The meeting ended in a near-riot when the delegates disagreed on a labor platform. Mary Margaret left this out of her story. "What on earth was the matter with you?" railed her editor the next day. "Were you drunk?" "I was not," said Mary Margaret indignantly. "I just didn't think labor questions belonged in a religious story. But I was cold sober." "Maybe it would have been better if you'd been drunk," grumbled the unfeeling editor. The publicity director of the convention, however, looked with greater favor upon her reportorial restraint, and whisked her off to New York as his assistant. The name of this perspicacious gentleman was Tyler Dennett, who later became the president of Williams College. Mary Margaret found herself at a desk next to Estella Karn, destined to be her lifelong friend and devoted personal manager. But she longed to get back to newspaper work, and when the New York *Mail* advertised for a crack reporter at the then princely stipend of $40 a week, Mary Margaret was first in line.

The editor and owner of the *Mail*, Henry Luther Stoddard, interviewed her himself. "Where are you from?" he asked. "Paris," she answered. "Paris, eh?" said Stoddard, visibly impressed. "You don't look French." "I mean Paris, Missouri," explained Mary Margaret. "Where in God's name is that?" he grumbled. "Ever cover a big fire?" "Just give me the chance," she begged. Three days later there was a whopping three-alarm blaze in the Bronx, and the story on the front page of the *Mail*, pulling out all the stops, was by-lined by Mary Margaret McBride. "It was the big thrill of my life," she says today. "I felt that I had arrived."

Prodded by Estella Karn, Mary Margaret now began to write feature articles for the magazines. Her four-part story about, and in collaboration with, Paul Whiteman, called "Jazz," appeared first in the *Saturday Evening Post*, and then was published in book form by Sears. Her standard price for articles rose to one thousand dollars, then two. She began dabbling successfully in the stock market. And then, suddenly, came the 1929 crash, which wiped out her savings, and the ensuing depression, which crippled the market for her writings. Mary Margaret found herself back where she started—plus a lot of expensive habits she had picked up en route. At the nadir of her fortunes, on a cold, dismal day in that cold, dismal winter of 1933-34, a chance knock on her door by Opportunity changed everything. Opportunity in this instance bore the attractive guise of Carol Hill. Radio Station WOR, she explained, was looking for a woman's program. Would Mary Margaret like to audition for it? She would and did—and got the job. She explains modestly, "I was the only one of fifty applicants who made no salary demands. I meant to but I just forgot. I think that's why they gave me the nod."

The very first McBride broadcasts established the pattern that ultimately made her a national celebrity—a friendly, homey, casual discussion of anything that seemed to enter her head. She called herself "Martha Deane" in the beginning, and established the name so securely that WOR retained it when she moved to another chain, and continues to use it to this day. Sponsors, reluctant at first, were soon tumbling over one another's heels to sign on the dotted line. Today, on NBC, she has thirteen, with a long waiting list champing at the bit. As soon as it became apparent that her program was definitely "big time," she persuaded Estella Karn to abandon everything else and become her personal manager. It was Estella who introduced the notion of occasional guest-stars—now a basic feature of her programs. It was Estella, too, who helped keep her always three jumps ahead of the shrill imitators who popped up inevitably on other networks. A guest of Mary Margaret McBride does not appear on these other programs if he knows what's good for him.

Three-quarters of an hour a day, five times a week, over Station WNBC, is quite a formidable assignment but Mary Margaret thrives on it. "I seem to have that 45-minute tempo," she explains. (By the time this volume appears, her show will be expanded to a full hour, to say nothing of a television stint on the side.) Roughly two-thirds of the time is devoted to the visiting firemen, the rest to a seemingly haphazard celebration of the virtues of the sponsors. "Did I forget anyone today?" Mary Margaret will ask. "Well," the imperturbable and irreplaceable Vincent will answer, "you forgot to tell about the special sale of Baldwin apples at all the Bohack stores this week." An hour later there isn't an apple left in a Bohack branch. Often the guest-stars become so enthused by the McBride endorsements that they sail right into the commercials with her.

The list of McBride guests includes authors, actors, politicians, Swiss bell ringers, screwball inventors, trapeze artists, hog callers, and flagpole sitters. Since the products she boosts range from shoe polish to noodle soup, and dog biscuits to grated coconut, the net effect of any broadcast, obviously, would be sheer pandemonium without the soothing touch of a master-mind to make it jell. For my money, Mary Margaret is the greatest impresario radio ever has developed. Her fans accept her recipes and suggestions as gospel. Her native state of Missouri has designated November 22 as "Mary Margaret McBride Day," with appropriate annual ceremonies led by the Governor. One devoted fan named a rose after her; nobody was surprised when it won the grand prize the first time it was exhibited. General Omar Bradley chose her program in preference to a score of others for his first interview after his triumphal return from Europe. "Maybe my wife will appreciate me at last," he said happily. Her assistant, Janice Devine, assured me of the truth of the legend that a Hollywood star listened breathlessly to a McBride endorsement of Sweetheart Soap, then rushed out to wash her face for the first time in fifteen years.

She frankly prefers authors as her guest-stars—and what a job she does with them! They are so at ease they frequently forget they're broadcasting. One day Jesse Stuart told her several wonderful, racy stories about his grandpaw in the Kentucky hills, then drawled, "We goin' on the air soon?" When he heard they actually had been on an open microphone for thirty-five minutes, he took a deep, audible breath and exclaimed, "Hell, ma'am, I never would have talked like that about old Grandpaw. I was so comfortable, I thought we were rehearsin'!" An all-out McBride recommendation is reflected immediately in the sale of a novel or autobiography. The book business hasn't had so potent a booster in radio since the death of Alexander Woollcott.

For Mary Margaret's tenth anniversary on the air, NBC executives decided upon a public reception. So many admirers clamored for tickets, it had to be transferred to Madison Square Garden. Mrs. Franklin D. Roosevelt flew up from Washington to be the star guest. "How fitting!" exulted the delirious press department of NBC. "The First Lady of the Land pays tribute to Lady Number One of the Radio."

As a matter of fact, it was the same Mrs. F. D. R. who once was the innocent cause of Mary Margaret's only failure to be at the mike on time. The two were to discuss Mrs. Roosevelt's *If You Ask Me,* and Mary Margaret went down to Washington Square to escort her distinguished guest to the studio in person. Their taxicab, unfortunately, was caught in a traffic jam, and at one minute to one, they were still four blocks from the studio.

"Let's get out and run for it," proposed Mrs. F. D. R. For once
Mary Margaret was not quite equal to the occasion. "I don't think
we could make it," she sighed—thereby depriving Fifth Avenue
strollers of what certainly would have been one of the great sights
of the century.

Vincent Connolly carried on until the two ladies puffed into
their places. "Getting around town these days is a caution," Mary
Margaret declared, and six million anxious listeners settled back
in relief that nothing more serious had befallen her. "You know
what we really need, Vincent?" she continued in her girlish,
dreamer-like fashion. "It's a pitcher of that delicious, economical,
iced Ehler's Tea!"

*   *   *

Mary Margaret McBride lost one devoted listener in the person
of Scenario Scripter George Oppenheimer's mother. Delayed one
noon hour at her modiste's, she missed the introductory patter of
Mary Margaret's program, and tuned in just in time to hear a
dulcet-voiced visitor confide, "The naked one on the bear rug is
George Oppenheimer." "Hollywood has been too much for my
poor, poor boy," she cried, but in the nick of time discovered that
the speaker was Dorothy Stickney, innocently showing Miss Mc-
Bride her album of baby pictures of intimate friends, a hobby she
has pursued for years.

*   *   *

Fanny Brice (Baby Snooks to you) displayed her perspicacity
at a tender age when she was helping out in her aunt's candy
store. Her aunt had stocked up heavily on peppermint sticks, but
though the price seemed right (a penny a stick) the neighborhood kids weren't having any. The ten-year-old Fanny borrowed
a hammer, broke the sticks in twelve pieces each, and put a hand-
made sign in the window: "Big bargain today only! A dozen pieces
of peppermint for a cent." The entire stock was cleaned out in
three hours.

Miss Brice's advice to young ladies: "Never marry a man for
his money. The thing to look for in a husband is a gentle, even

disposition. Of course, a man without a big bank account is always grouchy and bad-tempered. Remember, girls, every household gets the same amount of ice—but the rich get it in August and the poor get it in January."

"I owe my own success," confided Miss Brice, "to the peaceful home life I enjoyed as a child. Anything my mother wanted to do, Pop let her, saying that she had a perfect right." Miss Brice thought for a moment and added, "She had a pretty good left too."

*　*　*

The Columbia Broadcasting Company rounded up a group of amateurs for auditions one morning and Andrew Hecht came along to report developments.

One applicant draped a cowbell around his neck and began rendering "Chloe" in a series of plaintive "moos" in an old gallon-jug. By wagging his head energetically he got a series of accompanying "clunks" from the cowbell.

When he concluded he looked up happily and demanded, "How did I do?" "You're great so far," Hecht assured him. "Now let's see you give milk!"

*　*　*

NOTHING BUT ACE'S

One of the best-known and most original wits in radio is Goodman Ace. For years he not only wrote but produced and acted with his wife in a popular program called "Easy Aces." He quit voluntarily at the top to become a vice-president and director of comedy programs at CBS. The titles were imposing, but the restless Mr. Ace gave up that job too, explaining that he didn't feel comfortable as a "desk jockey." His final bit of advice concerned a comedy program that he rated "hopeless." "Let it pursue its dreary way until you can find a substitute," he counseled. "In the meanwhile, close the show with the announcement 'This is NBC.'" At the moment, he's back on the air himself. His new act is called "mr. ace and JANE."

Despite his vast earning power, Ace would not be in his present state of affluence and independence had he continued plunging on horseraces. At the height of his fever, he installed a Teleflash machine in his living room, and received descriptions and results of races the country over. This service, with Ace's spontaneous wit and delicatessen as added attractions, filled his apartment from morning to night with enthusiastic fans, many of whom he knew personally. They would listen to the odds, rush to the phone, ask for long distance, plank down bets in Maryland, Kentucky,

and California, and return via the icebox, grumbling, "Hmphh! No more smoked salmon!"

Once, during a January cold spell, a guest bemoaned the fact that he was missing the season in Florida. Ace did what he could to remedy the situation. He had the living room covered with white beach sand. His wife Jane finally rebelled: "Either you get rid of that Teleflash and stop betting on the races, or we move to Madison Square Garden." Ace capitulated, remarking sadly, "Just when I had the horses right where they wanted me." When anyone asks how his wife Jane is faring, his usual reply is, "She's all right, if you like Jane."

Goodman Ace graduated to radio by way of the drama desk of the *Journal-Post* in Kansas City. His reviews were of the hatchet, or Irving Hoffman, variety. Covering a headline act on a local vaudeville bill—a comedian with a low voice—Ace commented, "You can't hear him beyond the first three rows, so be sure to sit back of the third row." A rival critic once begged by note for a thousand-dollar loan, adding, "If you don't give it to me, I swear I'll jump off the twenty-second story of the Kansas City Athletic Club." Ace replied, "Here's five hundred. Jump from the eleventh."

* * *

The legion of loyal friends of Abe Burrows was gratified but not surprised when he achieved a radio program of his own. For years he fretted in anonymity as the author of the Duffy's Tavern scripts, and helped create that wondrous character, "Two-Headed Gruskin." On the side he convulsed the cognoscenti of Hollywood and Broadway with songs like "The Girl with the Three Blue Eyes (What Makes Her Different?)," "Have You Seen Levine in His Flying Machine (My God, What a Horrible Sight)," and "She Sang Him the Indian Love Call, But He Looked at Her and Said 'Ugh.'" Burrows bills himself as "The Velvet Foghorn," and explains, "My songs are peculiar; they aren't written in any key." His notion of a rousing campaign song was "My Father Wants a Third Party; He's Been Thrown Out of Two Tonight." His "documentary" on Boulder Dam made Henry Kaiser cry with laughter. His take-off on a Norman Corwin radio show is so devastating that Corwin admits it haunted his creative hours for weeks. "Norman was a wonderful sport about it," enthuses Burrows. "Of course, he isn't talking to me, but . . ."

Burrows served a brief spell as producer at Paramount. "I prefer not to stub my toes at the outset on a new picture," he told the Board of Directors. "Won't you let me get into my stride by doing a good remake first?" "That's very modest of you and very wise," said the Chairman. "What picture would you like to remake?" "*Going My Way*," said Burrows.

Back in radio, Burrows declares, "All I need now is sex appeal.
Mine is the only show women turn off to listen to hockey games."

*   *   *

The country-wide success of Abe Burrows on the radio is proof
anew that many citizens in "the sticks" have just as ready an appreciation of subtle humor and satire as smart-alecks on Fifty-
second Street or Sunset Boulevard. Program directors who insist
on "writing down to their audiences" to a point where their routines must seem inane to a normal child of eight are invited to
take notice.

They might consider also an experience that proved to be a
turning point in the career of Joe E. Lewis. He was making his
first appearance at a big Hollywood café—the Trocadero—and
Louis B. Mayer was among the notables in the audience. Lewis
particularly desired the approval of Mayer, since he was considering a whirl in pictures, and he sang until he was hoarse. The
audience clamored for more. "I had given them all my sophisticated songs," says Lewis, "and the only thing I had left was a
thing called 'Sam, You Made the Pants Too Long.' It had gone
fine in Dubuque, but I figured it was much too corny for these
hep characters. Well, I did it. I was so apprehensive, I rammed
my hands in my pockets, and without knowing it, I was making
my own pants too long. It turned out to be the biggest hit of the
evening, and has been a mainstay of my act ever since.

"You see, what I had forgotten was that Louis B. Mayer and
most of those other sophisticated big-shots out there, originally
came from places like Dubuque themselves!"

*   *   *

One of the most dramatic broadcasts of the year developed
from a routine interview of a man in Spokane who was describing
his new fire-resistant paint for Christmas trees. The broadcast
emanated from his own plant. Just as he was waxing most eloquent, somebody hollered, "Fire!" The announcer took over and

described with gusto the burning down of the works, including the complete stock of fire-resistant paint.

* * *

If some alert publisher would compile a book of radio fluffs—the inadvertent mistakes of rattled performers and announcers—it might achieve as big a sale as Juliet Lowell's *Dear Sir or Madam,* or Viking's book of famous boners. In a single week, one bemused master of ceremonies declared, "And now we bring you the only living ex-President of the United States, Mr. Hoovie Heber—I mean Mr. Heevie Hoober—oh heck, you know who I mean," and another, extolling the virtues of a huge corporation, labeled it "the largest producers in America of magnoosium, aleeminum, and stool!"

The Prince of Pilsen once was announced as *The Pill of Princeton.* A local toastmaster, overwhelmed by having Walter Pidgeon as a guest, assured him over a national hook-up, "Mr. Privilege, this is indeed a pigeon." A routine commercial began one morning, "Does your husband wake up dill and lustless?" The reddest face ever seen in a studio was the result of one announcer who concluded his spiel by advising his audience, "If you want that exhilarating new thrill, try Buppert's Rear."

The whole radio world knows the legend of the favorite teller of tales for boys and girls who concluded one of his regular sessions of treacle and sunshine and, mistakenly believing he was off the air, added a heartfelt, "That ought to hold the little bastards." The kiddies' hour never has been quite the same.

* * *

Fred Allen is not only one of the most brilliant stars in radio, but is unique in that he writes most of his material himself. "I guess I'm the only man in radio," says Allen, "who has written more than he can lift. Ah, radio! This drudgery, this sham, this gold mine!" His ad libs are really authentic and the laughs frequently delay the show to such an extent that his time runs out before the program is concluded. This amiable practice, plus his steadfast refusal to submit to censorship, probably has caused the death of half a dozen stuffy vice-presidents. All things considered, that may not be such a bad thing.

Allen points out that if anybody wants incontrovertible proof of the theory that the male is hardier than the female, he need only consult the New York telephone directory. It lists over three hundred "John Smiths"; not a single "Pocahontas"!

Pursuing a time-honored mock feud with his old pal Jack Benny, Allen declares that he saw Benny walk into the lobby of the Palmer House with a new set of false teeth. "They were so loose," says Allen, "that every time he took a step they clicked. When he called 'Hello, Fred,' three elevators started upstairs."

As though Fred Allen didn't cause him enough trouble, Jack Benny has to contend with the dusky Rochester (real name: Eddie Anderson) on his own program. Rochester often tops him in belly-laughs. The fact that Benny lets him get away with it is one reason why the name "Jack Benny" is always close to the top of Mr. Hooper's ratings. When a Benny motion picture is shown in Harlem, Rochester's name is featured above the star's. "I never minded his stealing my pictures," says Benny, "until I heard that my next one might be *The Life of Booker T. Washington.*"

*   *   *

George Lawton, author of *Aging Successfully,* made his very first appearance on the radio when he participated in the "Town Hall Meeting of the Air" program in Asheville, N.C. There were over five thousand people in the audience and Mr. Lawton, who opened the debate, was nervous to begin with. Then, in rapid succession, the electric lighting system went out of commission, he lost a page of his manuscript, and a lady in the front row had an epileptic fit. By the time his remarks were concluded, Mr. Lawton figured that he had aged successfully about fifteen years.

*   *   *

A member of the staff of the Phoenix *Flame* attended a garden party at the home of one of Radio's Very Greatest Comedians. "How was it?" asked Editor Higdon later. "Wonderful," enthused the staffer. "He's certainly one of the great wits of the age! What repartee, what satire, what awareness of world problems! And he's so modest with it all. He appeared actually surprised when everybody laughed. What I can't understand is how such an at-

tractive personality can put up with that colorless, dull little goof
who seems to cling to him like a shadow." "Don't tell anyone,"
whispered Higdon, "but that's the fellow who writes every line
of the Great Comedian's material."

* * *

As irritating to the more conservative executives of radio as unsold time, static, and the frank airing of all sides of controversial
problems, is the easily recognized voice of Henry Morgan, the
gadfly of the air waves. Morgan insists on playing the game by
his own rules, most iconoclastic of which is that sponsors were
born to be kidded, not worshiped. Several of his temporary
sponsors are suspected of signing him just to prove they are understanding good fellows with a sense of humor sufficiently developed to appreciate a laugh at their own expense. Usually they
have stopped laughing long before Morgan's contract comes up
for renewal.

Here are a few of the things the growing Association of Ex-
Sponsors of Henry Morgan hold against him:

He complained that a maker of peppermint drops was gulling
the public by putting a hole in the middle.

He auctioned off the entire executive board of the Mutual
Broadcasting Company, fetching $83 for the lot, including plant
and good will.

He announced with proper enthusiasm that a popular candy-
and-nut bar was a meal in itself, but added that, after three meals
of them, "your teeth fall out."

He broadcast a list of missing persons in Philadelphia and threw
in the name of the chief of police and the manager of the local
radio station.

Extolling the virtues of a brand of iodine, he suggested, "Try
drinking a bottle for a broken arm."

His idea of a boost for a popular make of automobile was, "Our
cars are now rolling off the assembly line; as soon as we keep them
on the assembly line, we'll start delivering them."

After conducting a shaving test on stage to demonstrate the
virtues of a certain razor, he announced blandly, "We'll continue
as soon as we mop up the blood." (His sponsor that evening
groaned, "He's slashing my throat with my own razor!")

Asked to deliver a routine weather report, he predicted, "High winds, followed by high skirts, followed by me," and added, "Looks like it's going to be Muggy, with Tuegy, Weggy, and Thurgy coming up."

In private life, Henry Morgan is often as unpredictable as he is before a microphone. He cut one week-end visit short because, he said, the ten-year-old son of his host persisted in going around all day emptying ash trays. "What's wrong with that?" asked a friend. "I guess you don't understand," sighed Morgan. "He was emptying them into his mouth."

* * *

Milton Berle was introduced one evening as "that man with the pointed head." He admitted the charge and added, "It has its advantages. When I was an infant, my mother didn't have to tuck me away in a crib; she just threw me into a dart board." Berle in turn introduced the "Father of the Year"—a gentleman who actually had sired twenty-seven children. The father promptly stole the show by confessing, "I'm pretty tired. I'm usually in bed by this time every night."

* * *

Forthright editorials in countless newspapers have removed at least one taboo from radio's list of "don'ts" but there was a period when "March of Time" was not allowed to mention the name of a certain disease on the air. They gave the program as best they could and, as he was signing off, the announcer managed to make his point by saying, "This terrible disease which we must all fight is said to get its name from that famous Greek poet, Syphilis."

* * *

A prominent radio announcer took his young daughter to a church dinner. The parson invited the youngster to say grace. She bowed her head and said, "These victuals, good friends, are coming to you through the courtesy of Almighty God."

* * *

A bright young star of the Theatre Guild was scheduled to do a radio show one Sunday evening in Los Angeles. Lawrence Langner, High Nabob of the Guild, made a note to phone her from Westport, Conn., and congratulate her. By some miracle, he actually remembered it and when the call came through assured her, "My dear, you were absolutely superb."

"It's very nice of you to tell me that, Mr. Langner," she said coldly, "but I must point out that I won't begin the broadcast yet for fifteen minutes."

Mr. Langner was taken aback—but not for long. "Don't forget, my dear," he reminded her smoothly, "that it is three hours earlier here."

* * *

It was five minutes before the end of a tense Army-Navy football game. The score was 28–28; Army had worked the ball to the Navy three-yard line. The stands were in an uproar.

Suddenly a man who had been following the fray on his television set snapped off the current.

"What's the idea?" cried his outraged guests. "We'll miss the most exciting part."

"I know," admitted the host, "but do you think I'm going to get caught in that mob?"

* * *

SECTION 12

Travel

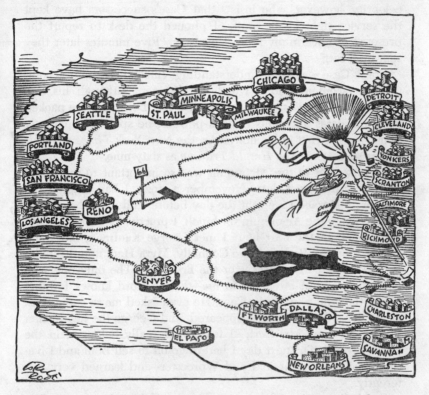

The Algonquin Hotel continues to attract the front-page figures of the literary and theatrical worlds, but it doesn't seem the same without Frank Case. Case *was* the Algonquin. He was the manager when it opened its doors in 1902 (even persuaded the owner to abandon the contemplated name of "The Puritan") and never strayed far from it until the day of his death, June 7, 1946. His wife had died just a few months before. Woollcott, Broun, Benchley, O. O. McIntyre were gone. George, the headwaiter who treated literary folk like Argentine millionaires and rich bankers like tatterdemalions, had moved on to other fields years earlier. Now, a nostalgic story was ended for good. The magically contrived air of a hospitable, friendly country inn in the heart of New York was dissipated, and the halls suddenly appeared in their true light—slightly musty, old-fashioned, more like an Aline Bernstein stage set than a present-day hostelry. Dorothy Parker is one celebrity, however, who insists that Case's successors have kept the service right up to snuff. "I phoned the desk to report the presence of mice in my room," she says. "Five minutes later they sent up a cat!"

Frank Case was kind, understanding, efficient, both an accomplished raconteur and a wonderful listener. Although his two books, *Tales of a Wayward Inn* and *Do Not Disturb,* were packed with anecdotes about his famous patrons, he spoke so sparingly about himself that in his obituaries the New York *Times* gave his age as seventy-six, the *Herald Tribune* as sixty-nine.

My first visit to the Algonquin was so important to me that I remember the exact date—November 2, 1923. I had entered the employ of Horace Liveright the day before, and when he offered to take me to the Algonquin for lunch, I practically swooned with excitement. In the next hour I met George Kaufman, Heywood Broun, Dorothy Parker, Marc Connelly, Myra Hampton, Franklin P. Adams, and Frank Case for the first time. The only one who paid the slightest attention to me—though Lord knows I didn't blame the others—was Mr. Case. He even asked me to come back at five for a drink. When I appeared, and George the headwaiter said, "This way, Mr. Cerf," I felt that I really belonged in the literary world. The next day I had to go off to sell Boni and Liveright books in Springfield and Worcester—and learned very differently.

Frank Case became the owner of the Algonquin in 1927. Nobody will ever know how many patrons he permitted to remain during the depression years "on the cuff." When he suddenly closed the Algonquin bar long before Prohibition came in, he explained that he "didn't want to get rich from doling out liquor." The immediate reason, I believe, was that one of his most celebrated tenants, in his debt for hundreds of dollars, squandered a sizable advance royalty check on a disorderly and interminable brawl, in which, to make matters worse, valuable furniture and glassware were demolished. At about the same time, too, a world-famous novelist, in his cups, backed naked into a hot-water pipe and just missed scalding himself to death. Case sat up with him all night.

Frank Case set out one time to attract some additional patronage from the South, and sent his advertising agent a rough draft of the copy he proposed to run. The agent thought Case's suggestion was the finished article, and the advertisement that appeared in the *Saturday Review of Literature* read precisely as follows: "A gentleman of the South, his wife and family, will find all the hooey and whatzis of a refined home at the Algonquin." The ad pulled so well that Case repeated it unchanged for weeks.

One of the many literary celebrities who make the Algonquin their New York home is William Faulkner, who, for all his tales of violence in the South, is himself an extraordinarily gentle and polite fellow. Faulkner looked decidedly below par when he checked in one evening, and Case asked what was wrong. "My stomach is bothering me," said Faulkner. Case nodded, and remarked, "Something you wrote, no doubt."

The day I saw Frank Case laugh hardest was when I brought the literary editor of the *New Masses* to the Algonquin to interview Gertrude Stein. The setup was so promising that Case persuaded me to take him along to Miss Stein's suite. Alice Toklas, he, and I sat breathless while Gertrude pinned the editor in a chair and told him, "As far as the general public is concerned, you foolish Communists—and all other people who waste their time with politics—are like janitors. When my flat is warm and clean, and the elevator is running regularly, and the garbage is collected twice a day, I never give a thought to the janitor in the cellar. But—let the hot water fail to run, or the mail be undelivered, and I begin to think, 'That darn janitor doesn't know his job.' If things continue to go wrong, I see that the old janitor is fired and a new one gets the job. It's the same way in government. Let my own life go on undisturbed, and my private affairs prosper—and I don't give a continental whether the government is being run by a Communist, or a Seventh-Day Adventist, or a Hottentot. When they start interfering with my own business, however—by heaven, I, and all the other people in the country,

suddenly become aware of the men who are mismanaging it. We
just go out and get ourselves a new janitor."

By this time, the *New Masses* editor was apoplectic with rage.
"Miss Stein," he sputtered, "I came here to discuss your books
and your views on literature, not to be called a janitor."

"Nevertheless," said Miss Stein cheerfully, "that's what you are
—a janitor. Now run along and get yourself a worthwhile job and
stop filling your head with a lot of nonsense."

The editor strode forth to demolish Miss Stein in print, and
Mr. Case and I rushed off to tell the story. Both of us dined on it
for weeks.

*   *   *

Big-shots of the sports, theatrical, political, and financial worlds
patronize the chophouse of Toots Shor to be insulted by the boss
and, incidentally, eat some of the best food in town. Favorite customers rate the ripest insults. A candidate for President blocked
the entrance one evening, shaking hands with friends. "Hey, you,"
boomed Toots, "how about spending a little money at my bar
while you're campaigning in here?" To placate his host, the candidate said, "Your roast beef is wonderful." Toots answered, "Remember that the next time you're on the radio!"

A Hollywood tycoon, dining at Shor's for the first time, said to
his companion, "I hope the food here is up to my standard." Toots
overheard and reminded him, "I've seen some of your pictures."

A four-star general complained one evening that the cheese
cake was spoiled. Toots strolled over to learn the cause of the
commotion. The waiter explained, "The general wants you to
taste it yourself." "I should say not," exclaimed Toots. "Let *him*
get sick."

"I don't want to be a millionaire," philosophizes Toots Shor. "I
just want to live like one."

*   *   *

At another midtown restaurant, popular with stage folk and
columnists, the menu is the attraction, and not the service. Publisher Max Schuster asked one idle waiter, "Can you give me the
time?" The waiter answered, "Sorry, that ain't my table." Schuster

asked another servitor, "Which way is the washroom?" The reply
was, "Mister, I only got two hands."

* * *

EVEN FURTHER INSIDE U.S.A.

A matter of three or four hours by motor from New York, over
perfect roads, lie the tranquil and beautiful hills known as the
Berkshires. Facing the tallest of them, Greylock, from the porch
of Sinclair Lewis's new estate in Williamstown, on the first evening of a vacation, I wondered why anybody was fool enough to
spend his life in a clamorous, dirty city. I had left behind worries
of inflation and "corrective depression," people screaming "fas-
cist" and "communist" at one another, pathetically inefficient politicians, and a gang of "diplomats" who made the plumbers of
Versailles look like wonder boys. An overpowering sense of fore-
boding had hung over everything, blotting out sunshine and hope.
Here, in the cool, crystalline twilight, the vague dread disappeared. All the fools in the world could not spoil the panorama
spread out before me, nor the fresh, clean tang in the air.

Literary history had been made in these hills. On Greylock, or
Saddleback, as it is sometimes called, Thoreau had spent a chilly
night in 1853, and complained later that mice had made a fine
meal of his shoes while he unsuspectingly was studying old documents he had found in the shack on the summit. In Lenox, a few
miles south, was the hill down which Edith Wharton's Ethan
Frome had coasted to tragedy. In Stockbridge was the old summer home of the Longfellows, called "The Oxbow." Nearby
Oliver Wendell Holmes and James Russell Lowell did their best
work. And here, in the year 1851, Herman Melville finished *Moby
Dick* at almost the same time that his neighbor, Nathaniel Hawthorne, wrote the last pages of his *House of the Seven Gables*.

Of the tortured friendship of Hawthorne and Melville, many
tales are told. Periods of mutual confidence and esteem would be
followed by months when the two scarcely spoke to each other.
The moody Hawthorne usually was responsible for the quarrels;
he depressed Melville one night to a point where he almost threw
the priceless manuscript of *Moby Dick* into the fireplace. Haw-

thorne's son, Julian, wrote in his memoirs, "The two people who visited our house most often when we were children were Mr. Melville and the milkman, Luther Butler. We liked the milkman better. We drank his milk—and he never read Father's books!" Melville's final break with Hawthorne was a crushing blow, and the comparative failure of *Moby Dick* completed his disillusionment. The reviewers of his day failed utterly to realize the true worth of the book; his publisher lamented the fact that the $700 advance he had paid on it probably would never be earned back!

* * *

A flutist at the Berkshire Music Festival figured in a famous Toscanini episode. The maestro interrupted a rehearsal to upbraid the unfortunate fellow and ended by firing him on the spot. The departing flutist muttered, "You blank-blank egomaniac. I'd like to . . ." Toscanini cut in angrily, "No, no! None of your apologies!"

* * * *

In Williamstown I met a newspaperman who had toured with Mr. Landon during the election campaign of 1936, and still spoke feelingly about it. "If Landon had made just one more speech," he concluded, "I'm convinced that F. D. R. would have carried Canada."

* * *

On a crisp and clear summer night in Maine, there was an amazing display of the Northern Lights, and a grizzled old guide named Leo had a chance to square accounts with a lady who had offended his dignity by showing greater interest in the where-abouts of Louise Dickinson Rich (author of *We Took to the Woods*) than in his tales of fabulous salmon runs or nights under the stars. When Leo spotted the Northern Lights he ran to the tent of his party to advise them to hurry out and see the brilliant illumination. To the lady he added, "Don't forget your pocket flashlight."

"Why?" she asked. "Help you see the Lights," he assured her.

While the others exclaimed with proper awe at the spectacle, the lady concentrated on pointing her Eveready in the proper direction. Then she tried it *without* the flashlight.

"Leo," she said, "you won't believe it, but I can see those Lights every bit as well with this thing turned off!"

* * *

This is illustration Number 968 of why I think the publishing business is the most glamorous and exciting in the world. In 1942, Random House published Cecil Brown's *Suez to Singapore*, which I still consider one of the best of all the war books. Cecil Brown devoted one section of it to the exploits of a great sub-marine lieutenant named "Moon" Chapple. When "Moon," 230 pounds of superb efficiency, good humor, and better looks, re-turned (now a captain) to America, I had the privilege of meet-ing him, and, better still, he invited me to climb aboard one of his subs for a trial spin.

I met Captain Chapple at the New London base, where, through the courtesy of Admiral John Wilkes and Captain Chapple, I went out with him on the 313-foot super-submarine *Sirago*, and ex-perienced the thrill of four dives in Long Island Sound. The sub was handled so perfectly by Commander Fritz Harlflinger and his crew of eighty that had my attention not been riveted on the periscope and instruments, I could scarcely have told when we were submerging or coming to the surface. Aside from a slight tilt, there was no sensation whatever. The excitement came in watching the operation through the periscope.

A long course of indoctrination via the movies proved utterly futile: no beautiful Madge Evans was stowed away in an ensign's duffle bag, nor was a cook's apprentice called upon to perform an emergency operation for acute appendicitis.

After the last dive, the crew was ordered to rush on deck and man the guns for immediate action. Unfortunately, I was designated as a lookout and ordered to follow the skipper up the hatch. It took me only slightly longer to negotiate this maneuver than the eighty members of the crew combined. When the operation was completed, "Moon" lauded my magnificent dexterity, but could not resist adding, "Of course, by the time you managed to climb out, we could have been sunk by a rowboat."

A few moments later, while we were proceeding at full speed, the cry "Man overboard!" rang out. "Good God!" exclaimed my host. "It's Cerf." It developed, however, that this was merely another drill. The "man" was a yellow balloon, and the crew retrieved it in a choppy sea in less than four minutes.

Men in the submarine service receive fifty per cent more pay than in the regular Navy, and they are worth it. They are wonderful boys. The censors did all they could to keep the public from realizing the full scope of the submarine force's contribution to the winning of the war, but the true story slowly is becoming available. If you have a copy of *Suez to Singapore* handy, check up on Captain "Moon" Chapple (pages 462 to 471).

*   *   *

In Montreal, Louis Untermeyer, reading aloud a saccharine and corny poem, suddenly stopped and asked his audience, "What do you think of this poem?" Wilfred Werry, secretary of the Canadian Authors' Association, answered, "I should say it was still in the process of Eddie Gestation."

*   *   *

In Miami Beach Moss Hart concluded a happy fortnight at the Lord Tarleton Hotel, and asked for his bill. He took one look at the total, paled and murmured softly, "The Lord giveth and the Lord Tarleton taketh away."

＊　＊　＊

The old French quarter of New Orleans—where the iron balconies still abound, though artists and writers are being crowded out by fashionable antique shops—is dominated by the Cathedral. It was built in 1795 by Don Almonaster, and faces Jackson Square. Hard by is the hall where the orgiastic Quadroon Balls sent gales of scandal through the city every Saturday night. On either side are two red-brick apartment houses—the first in the United States —built in the 1840s by Don Almonaster's daughter, the Baroness Pontalba.

Legend has it that the original tenant in one of the Pontalba apartments was a lady of great beauty but questionable virtue who had more money and wielded greater influence than any half-dozen of the society leaders who snubbed her. When Andrew Jackson, now President, returned in triumph to New Orleans, this lady invited him to dinner, but, prompted by his advisers, he did not even bother to answer her invitation. The lady fumed—and bided her time. Some years later a project was formulated to beautify Jackson Square, and erect a statue of the President in the center. The model selected showed Jackson on horseback, hat in hand. Public subscriptions were lagging until the lady made a proposition: if the statue was placed facing her apartment, she would make up the entire deficit. The committee agreed, and so, for the balance of her life, the lady who had been ignored by Andrew Jackson in the flesh had the supreme satisfaction, every time she looked out of her window, of seeing his statue looking straight at her and doffing his hat.

＊　＊　＊

Devout citizens in New Orleans have their favorite saints, and frequently take classified ads in the newspapers to thank them for services rendered. The fashion in saints seems to change from year to year. Lyle Saxon tells of the time Saint Rita was getting more thanks than all the other saints combined. In a store that specialized in religious articles, he asked the proprietress, "Do you sell many statues of Saint Rita?" "By the dozen," she replied, "and it makes me sick and tired. Last year everybody wanted Saint Raymond. I couldn't get enough statues of that saint. All of a sudden, they stopped buying him. So here I am stuck with fifty statues of Saint Raymond!" Another customer suggested, "If I were you, I'd pray to Saint Rita to help you sell them!"

*   *   *

During an unseasonable cold spell in Natchez, Mississippi, an old Negro, inadequately clothed, stood shivering in front of the Eola Hotel, his collar turned up, and his face the picture of woe. "Oh, wind," he muttered, "where was you last August?"

*   *   *

The Chicago Loop parking ban led to a famous practical joke whose aftermath was by far the funniest part of the story. A veteran bookman was tendered a dinner to celebrate his twenty-fifth anniversary with one firm. At the climax of the evening, he was presented with a special pass, signed by Chicago's mayor, giving him the unique privilege of parking his car as long as he liked anywhere in the Loop. Tears of gratitude came into the bookman's eyes. He had no idea that the pass was a complete fake. His "pals" sat back to await the hullabaloo when he tried to use it for the first time.

Then came the pay-off. The Chicago police, it developed, were just as convinced by the pass as the man who flashed it! He used it blissfully for at least three solid years, and, for all I know, it is still seeing service. Not one copper ever questioned its validity. The bookman took special pleasure in demonstrating its magic powers whenever one of his would-be tormentors was riding with him in the car.

*   *   *

An architect suggested Gothic style for a new building on the University of Chicago campus. "Let's write and ask the people at Oxford what they have to say on the subject," suggested a member of the committee. Back came a letter from an Oxford don: "I'm sorry to inform you we have not used Gothic at this university for the past six hundred years!"

*   *   *

Ernie Byfield, whose Pump Room is the place where stage and literary celebrities *must* be seen when they are in Chicago, played host recently to Jinx Falkenberg and Larry Adler. Both Jinx and Larry can do wonderful things, the only difference being that Larry needs a harmonica. At any rate, they asked Byfield how he happened to go into the hotel business. "It was one of those quirks of fate," answered Byfield. "My father owned the Hotel Sherman. He bumped into me in the lobby there one morning—and took a liking to me!"

That reminds me of a remark Samuel Goldwyn made at his
studio once, apropos of nothing: "I ran into Moss Hart last night.
He was at my house for dinner!"

Byfield once entertained Admiral Byrd at dinner in the Pump
Room. The Admiral rose to dance with Byfield's lovely wife,
Adele, and the host brought down the house by warning him
loudly, "Remember now, Admiral: no exploring!"

A Chicago couple once decked their eleven-year-old daughter
in her prettiest party dress and took her to dinner at the Pump
Room as a birthday gift. The father had promised to dance with
her to her favorite tune, Jerome Kern's "Won't You Make Believe?" When he led her onto the floor, however, a headwaiter
pointed out that children were not permitted to dance at the
Pump Room—something or other to do with a city ordinance. The
little girl was disconsolate. Byfield, closely surveying his empire
as usual, noticed how near to tears she was, and made it his business to learn the cause. A few minutes later he bustled up to her
table and said obsequiously, "My dear miss, when the headwaiter
told you that children were not allowed to dance here, he did not
realize, of course, that now you are a young lady of eleven! Please
forgive us all—and I hope your father will ask you to dance again."
The music struck up—by a curious coincidence it was "Won't You
Make Believe?"—and a proud and happy little girl whirled off in
a birthday dance in her father's arms.

The late Ben Bernie always stayed at Byfield's hostelry when
he played Chicago, and indulged his consuming weakness for
bean soup with slices of frankfurter floating on top. One evening
he ordered three portions. "Ben," remarked Byfield, "is observing
lentil again."

Bernie created a minor sensation when he checked out. He
called the porter on the phone and commanded, "Send up a bag
for the boys."

*   *   *

Citizens of Galesburg, Illinois, are raising a fund to purchase
the house in which Carl Sandburg was born. They plan to turn
it into a public shrine, and fill it with books, pictures, and manu-

scripts connected with Sandburg and Lincoln. Hazel Duncan relates that Sandburg once drove with a Tennessee hillbilly over a narrow, hazardous mountain road. "Hilly, isn't it?" said Sandburg. "It ain't the hills," replied the native. "It's the hollows."

* * *

One short paragraph from Carl Sandburg's *Abraham Lincoln: The War Years* is destined to become a full-length motion picture at RKO. It will be the story of nine-year-old Grace Bedell, who lived in the village of Westfield, New York, in 1860. The first time she saw a photograph of the newly elected President of the United States, she thought he would be better-looking if he grew whiskers, and what is more, she sat down and wrote him so. Mr. Lincoln gravely replied that it might look like a piece of silly affectation for him to begin raising a beard at this stage of his career. No, answered Grace, it was the right thing for him to do, for he looked much too solemn, and she believed other little girls, like herself, would be scared of him without whiskers.

When Mr. Lincoln's special train carried him to New York, and the inauguration at Washington, he ordered a stop at Westfield and, from the rear platform, announced, "I have a correspondent in this place named Grace Bedell, and if she is present I would like to see her." Grace stepped forward, and Mr. Lincoln told her, "You see, I let these whiskers grow for you, Grace. I hope you think I'm better-looking now." Then he kissed her, and Grace cried with joy, and the train moved on, and maybe one or two spectators realized that they had witnessed a wonderful example of American democracy in its truest sense.

* * *

Minneapolis and St. Paul, separated only by the Mississippi River, have a little private war of their own, not unlike Dallas and Fort Worth. Neven Stevenson, of Dodd, Mead, recalls that when his firm published H. V. Morton's best-seller, *In the Steps of Saint Paul*, two Minneapolis stores refused to stock it.

❉   ❉   ❉

The bustling state of Oklahoma has provided a happy hunting ground for oil prospectors, wheat farmers, cattle men, and the directors of the Theatre Guild. Textbooks omit the most colorful details of its turbulent early history; it will remain for someone like Stanley Vestal, sage of the University of Oklahoma, to tell the real story. Many of the leading families today are descended from the "Boomers" who staked out claims in the first official "run" to the territory in 1889—or the "Sooners," who beat the gun and had already moved in when settlement was legalized.

The spacious state capitol is the only one in the world where the lawns are decorated with oil wells. Some of them are still producing. It is also minus a dome. Ample funds have been voted several times for its construction, but they always disappear before the contracts are parceled out. One local bookseller figures that that nonexistent dome has made almost as many men rich as the natural gas and zinc ore.

The biggest event in Oklahoma's recent history was the local unveiling of the musical comedy smash hit that bears its name. It played eight performances in the 6,000-seat Municipal Auditorium, and of the 48,000 natives who succeeded in snagging tickets it is estimated that at least one-twentieth actually heard the words being spoken on the vast stage. Another 48,000 tried to get in, but their checks had to be returned. Governor Kerr had assembled a parade featuring over fifty bands, thirty-five floats, 2,000 horses, and a vast array of stage-coaches, chuck wagons, and prairie schooners, but, alas, when the big day dawned (November 25, 1946) a combination hail-and-wind storm whipped through the streets and the parade was canceled. Ray Parr described the welcoming committee as a "worry with a fringe of icicles on top." "What really broke our hearts," said Governor Kerr, "was the fact that the weather had been perfect for five weeks before—and it was perfect again for five weeks thereafter. Just that one day was terrible!"

The visiting dignitaries were soothed with potent "hors d'oeuvres," and initiation into the tribe of Kiowa Indians. Lawrence Langner was named "Some-Kei-Tigh-Keah" ("Master of Entertainment"), and obliged with the most bloodcurdling war-whoop since the initiation of the 1943 hog-calling champion. His wife,

Armina, who actually was born in the Cherokee Strip, was dubbed "Pah-Gah-Kee-Ah-Mah" ("Daughter of the Prairie"). Dick Rodgers, Oscar Hammerstein, and Lynn Riggs received elaborate tom-toms, which they dutifully sounded over a coast-to-coast hookup. Agnes de Mille was so excited that she left her ceremonial robe in a hotel room, but they drove her back in a fire engine to retrieve it. Oklahoma won't forget that week's parties and festivities for a long time to come!

* * *

Ramon Adams's *Dictionary of Western Words* (University of Oklahoma Press) inspired Charles Lee to plague his readers with this: "Anybody who ever hobnobbed with a bronc-snapping, bush-

whacking, line-riding, leather-pounding, range-bumming wind-
mill monkey (cowboy to you) ought to know what is meant by
(1) a shakedown, (2) a muley, (3) a juniper, (4) a puncture
lady, (5) a zorilla." Puzzled? One is a bed; two is a harmless cow;
three is the Westerner's equivalent of a hayseed; four is a woman
who sits and gossips at a dance, putting a knife into someone's
reputation; five is a type of black cattle of the early longhorn
breed.

* * *

The citizens of the gay and booming metropolis of Dallas buy
more books and accord more hospitality to visiting literati than
any other place on earth. This is due partly to the fact that, in
Elizabeth Ann McMurray, John McGinnis, Jimmie Albright, and
Lon Tinkle, it harbors four of the outstanding personalities in the
American book world. It is also due to the Dallasites' insatiable
craving for culture. Good books, good paintings, good music not
only stimulate their souls, but engender an intoxicating feeling of
superiority over their hated neighbors in Fort Worth, thirty miles
to the west. Their guide, cheerfully acknowledged by everyone,
including himself, is John Rosenfeld, the Woollcott of the Southwest. John traces the dotted line; the populace signs. Dallas was
vaguely pleased when a local wit dubbed it "The Athens of the
Alfalfa Fields."

In 1936, Texas staged a mammoth centennial celebration. Dallas wanted it very much; so did Fort Worth. Dallas won, and laid
out a series of exhibits that plumbed deep in the arts of Texas.
Fort Worth countered with a garden of beautiful girls, planted by
an inspired horticulturist named Billy Rose, and broadcast its
defy, "Dallas for education; Fort Worth for entertainment." That
left everybody happy, particularly Billy Rose, who got a thousand
dollars a day for his efforts, and was worth it. The only time they
had to call out the Texas Rangers was when one incredulous patron hit the jackpot on a slot machine. The fair grounds were
preserved in Dallas, and one of the country's best and fastest-
growing art collections is now housed there, directed by Jerry
Bywaters. Rosenfeld has a hand in it, of course. He also is the
moving spirit in the flourishing Dallas Symphony. On his last

birthday, the eighty members of the orchestra sent him individual wires of congratulation. After seventy-seven had been delivered, John opened one that read, "Thank God this will soon be over. (Signed) Western Union."

Probably the most colorful figure in all Dallas is Everette Lee De Golyer, pre-eminent geophysicist, key man in oil administration in Washington during the Second World War, and owner of a fabulous library of works on the Southwest. Before his senior year in college, De Golyer crossed the border for the Mexican Eagle Oil Company and promptly brought in the well that has produced more oil than any other in the world—130,000,000 barrels! At thirty-three, he organized with Viscount Cowdray the Amerada Petroleum Corporation. From that point on, the figures are too big for me to comprehend.

The De Golyers' six-year-old granddaughter is a chip off the old block. Mrs. De Golyer told her one day about her great-grandmother, something of a family legend. The little girl asked to see her. "You can't," said Mrs. De Golyer, "she's dead." The granddaughter asked, "Who shot her?"

One of the most highly prized items in the De Golyer library is a thin volume by Ward Dorrance entitled *We're from Missouri*. Mr. De Golyer reads the following excerpt aloud with obvious relish:

An old gentleman, of this village, senator and patriarch, has for years made no secret of his labors upon a manuscript: "Pre-eminent Sons of Bitches of Boone County, Missouri." From season to season, publication is deferred because, at the moment when the author has wiped his pen, he invariably encounters a person whom he has not treated, whose exclusion would leave an edition less than definitive.

The Dallas institution that every woman visits first is the fabulous Neiman-Marcus store. It is really a collection of superb specialty shops under one roof, featuring merchandise that could be obtained only, if at all, by visits to a score of different establishments on Fifth Avenue, Michigan Boulevard, or Wilshire. Mr. De Golyer once asked Neiman-Marcus to send some costume jewelry over to his office; he wanted to make a modest anniversary gift to his wife. A suave salesman arrived with several pieces, priced from forty to sixty dollars each. He saved until last an emerald ring. Mr. De Golyer has always had a weakness for emeralds. "I think I like this best," he said. "How much is it?" The salesman coughed discreetly and murmured, "$55,000." De Golyer challenged Stanley Marcus another time to find him one item in the store that sold for a dollar. Stanley searched for some time, and finally came up with a pocket handkerchief.

The public-relations genius of Neiman-Marcus is Marihelen Mc-Duff. She arranged the first party the store ever gave exclusively for members of the press. While it was at its height, the Jap surrender came through. Stanley Marcus called for silence and announced the end of the war. One reporter remarked, "Wouldn't you know it!"

In her spare time, Miss McDuff has organized a potentially powerful new organization named "Neurotics National," designed principally for advertising magnates, editors, publicists, and people in general who have been rejected by Alcoholics Anonymous. The club's official organ will be named *The Daily Dilemma*. "If we can just get the country's neurotics into one organization," muses Miss McDuff, "we'll be a bigger force than the CIO or the Southern Democrats."

*   *   *

To Americans in general, San Francisco means the days of '49, and clipper ships, and the Barbary Coast, and the Golden Gate, and hills that are steeper than in any other metropolis in the world. It is the city whose heart was destroyed by earthquake and fire in 1906, that rose again in new beauty and with all the old spirit.

To book-lovers, San Francisco is the city that inspired Bret Harte, Ambrose Bierce, Frank Norris, and Jack London, and, in later years, so many disciples that today there are more books in print about San Francisco than even London or New York.

To the denizens of Publishers' Row, San Francisco means Joseph Henry Jackson, dean of West Coast critics and commentators, and the Grabhorns, greatest American printers of our day, and booksellers who have spent their lives in the trade and regard books as literature—not merchandise.

The old ferries have been replaced by two giant bridges—al-

ready inadequate to handle the rush-hour traffic. Even the cable cars, cherished relics of a city that was, are threatened with extinction—if the present unsentimental and economy-minded mayor has his way. When I was there, it appeared, however, that the cars would stay, and the mayor would just about escape with his life. The view from the cocktail lounge atop the Mark Hopkins nobody can destroy; it is the most exciting in the country. Trader Vic continues to perform miracles with spareribs in Oakland across the bay. (Could it have been sheer forgetfulness that prompted the omission of this one recipe from the cookbook he whipped up for Doubleday?) The Palace and St. Francis cling to the outmoded belief that hotel food can be properly cooked. The DiMaggio family serve delectable crabs on Fisherman's Wharf. The buildings where the concept of the United Nations was formulated look deserted and forlorn. On the wall of one a cynic has chalked, "Geneva papers, please copy." . . .

One day shortly after the turn of the century, a Boston publisher whose warehouse was cluttered with several hundred sets of a fair-to-middling encyclopedia ran into a real estate promoter who also was suffering from enlargement of the inventory. The latter

had sunk his fortune in a California subdivision named Huntington Beach. There were sidewalks and lampposts and sand and
the Pacific—but no houses.

The publisher bought the land tract for a song, and the following week his canvassers offered frugal New England farmers an
irresistible bargain: a set of the encyclopedia at the original published price, plus a choice lot in sunny California as an outright
gift. The scheme worked like a charm, and the relieved publisher
sold his entire stock. The buyers tucked their deeds, unread, in
trunks in the attic, and their encyclopedias, also unread, in glass-
enclosed parlor bookcases.

Years later oil was discovered in Huntington Beach—and the
very heart of the deposit was the tract that had been given away
with the encyclopedias! Some of the farmers who had bought the
sets had vanished completely; the children of others were persuaded to sell what they thought were worthless deeds for a few
hundred dollars. A few, however, anxious to see for themselves
why slick attorneys suddenly were camping on their doorsteps,
bought railroad tickets for California. The trip proved worth
while. Some of the wells brought in on the Huntington tract are
still producing. "Encyclopedia Number Four" was one of the richest in all California.

A few miles from the Stanford campus in Palo Alto there is a
beautiful estate whose present owner neither toils nor spins. He
owes his life of gilded ease to the fact that his father, who owned
a scrabbly potato patch in Maine, was one of a handful of lucky
and tenacious folk who fell for the blandishments of a book can-
vasser, and bought an encyclopedia on the installment plan. . . .

Near the attractive Middleton-Harper Bookshop is a candy
store that bears the intriguing sign, "Awful Fresh MacFarlane, the
Scotch Candy Maker. Twenty Degrees Sweeter Inside." . . .

Stuart Cunningham, of Lieberman's Book Shop on Market
Street, had a legal tangle with William Randolph Hearst over
Edmund Wilson's *Memoirs of Hecate County*. The winnah and
undefeated champeen: Stuart Cunningham. One of the jurors
was a tough and dour-faced longshoreman, who scowled grimly
throughout the trial, and obviously was regarded as an ace in the
hole by the prosecution. After Cunningham had been acquitted,
the longshoreman told him, "When I first read *Hecate* I couldn't

reconcile it with Wilson's critical essays, but then I went back and read his early novels, and detected the similarities!" . . .

The last time I visited San Francisco, Joe and Charlotte Jackson gave a glittering party at their home in Berkeley. C. S. Forester was there, and Eudora Welty, Milla Logan, Mark Schorer, George Stewart, Jim Hart, John Bruce, Al Doering, most of the English department of the University of California, and a lot of other attractive people I never got around to meet. The space above the fireplace, however, was bare. A framed Chinese embroidery, highly prized by the Jacksons, had hung there for years. Its disappearance was a result of a visit by Irita Van Doren, editor of the *Herald Tribune Books*, on her way to Japan.

Half of the town turned out to meet her, and Joe thought the occasion called for a roaring fire in the living room. Unfortunately, he forgot to open the damper. The wood in the fireplace was very dry, and the room was soon filled with suffocating smoke. "Water! Water!" cried the guests. Joe took an elaborate wind-up and caught the guest of honor head-on as she descended a staircase from her dressing room. Another volunteer pitched too high and drenched the Chinese embroidery. By the time the fire, not to mention the thirsts of the excited guests, had been quenched, several copies of Joe's latest anthology, *Continent's End*, had floated into the kitchen on the crest of the tide.

Gump's, San Francisco's famed headquarters for oriental wares, undertook to restore the damaged treasure. "Be careful of it," begged Joe. "It's priceless." Gump's promised. I was back in New York when the burden of Gump's report reached me via sources I believe to be reliable. "In the first place," said Gump's to the Jacksons, "your priceless embroidery is worth about twelve dollars and fifty cents. In the second place, we regret to inform you that for the past fifteen years you have hung it upside down."

* * *

AROUND THE WORLD
IN FIVE PAGES

When Irita Van Doren landed in Japan, she found U. S. Occupation officers principally occupied with trying to keep warm. A

few days after her arrival, the Japanese servant in the house where she was staying came into the breakfast room, his teeth chattering, and announced, "I know this is Christmas Day, and that on such a day you do not wish to hear bad news. So I will not tell you until tomorrow that we have no more coal!"

* * *

Bill Hall, Ambassador at Large to the American book trade, says he learned the importance of detail on his first trip to China. A Peking book dealer treated him to a sumptuous dinner of over a dozen courses. Hall was worried at the amount of food that was carried uneaten from the table. "It will not be wasted," he was assured. "It goes to a restaurant down the street not so high-grade as this." Hall asked, "What happens to their leftovers?" The answer was, "It keeps traveling until it's all gone." Hall had a sudden disquieting thought. "How do I know," he asked, "that what *we* are having doesn't come from an even better place *up* the street?" "No," said the Chinese merchant, "everything starts here."

* * *

When Anne Baxter visited the Cachipay Hotel, in Bogotá, she picked up its prospectus, every precious word of which is reprinted here verbatim:

CACHIPAY HOTEL

First class hotel confortly stating with all the modern elements for stablishment of its class; is situated in one of the stations more beautifull of the Girardot railway, ideal clime or its temperature that is only 20° besides for the landscape that surrounds it and the wonderful flora that adorn and enrich. During many years is the part there elegant families and foreign put interviews that they wish to rejoice of a clime absolute spring. For the passangers that wish to do station for no to ascende to Bogotá neither descende to Girardot in the same day is indispensable, specially for the persons that ascend to the wish to elude the molestation of the belvet exchange.

The best part of summering and the more near to Bogotá, potable water, splendid bath, swimming tunk, bar, sport yard, gardens, movies, European kitchen, and executed services of all class.

1,620 metres on the level of the sea.

The environs are full of enchant an the tours that can do every day are many always variegates and always full of emotions. The turist also can leave the train of the morning and regress in the train of the evening.

PRECIOS:

The price of one day for person with all services of rigour in these cases is $4.00.

REMARK: The other expenses are separate count.

I hope this solves your vacation problems. Hail Colombia!

* * *

Miguel Covarrubias, the author of *Mexico South* was describing the rugged, impassable terrain of eighty per cent of that country. "I was driving on a dirt road on the hills about fifty miles from Mexico City one day," he said, "when I lost my way. Eventually, I passed a farmer and asked him, 'How can I get from here to the city?' He looked at me quite calmly and said, 'You can't.'"

When Samuel Grafton was in Mexico, he met one local official who had spent a few seemingly unproductive months in New York and Massachusetts. "In the cities no bull fights," he complained. "In the country no Indians! What kind of place do you call that?"

* * *

An American tourist wandering through a remote section of Mexico stopped in at a lonely little ranch house to ask directions, and was surprised to come face to face with what was obviously a one-hundred-per-cent American cowboy. He was seated on a magnificent coal-black stallion with the brand "Bar-H" burned into its skin. After a certain amount of small-talk, the visitor remarked, "That's a mighty fine horse you've got there. If you could rub out that brand mark I'd give you $1500 for him." "Brother," the cowboy assured him, "if I ever coulda rubbed out that mark I'd still be living in Amarillo, Texas."

* * *

Warner Olivier tells a story of the days when a high-pressure mail-order expert was hired to boom sales of the *Encyclopaedia Britannica*. The name of an untutored planter deep in the native bush of Australia turned up unaccountably on one of the mailing lists, and in due course he received a series of the mail-order demon's dynamic bulletins. The last of them warned him sternly that his set in Sydney would be reserved for him only two days more. After that, as far as the *Encyclopaedia Britannica* was concerned, he was strictly a dead duck. The planter, seized with panic, drove forty-eight hours without rest to get his prize before it was too late. "Where is it?" he demanded hoarsely of the agent in Sydney. When the agent pointed to the set on the table, the planter stared incredulously, and then groaned in dismay, "My God! They're *books!*"

* * *

All the way back from Jerusalem to Cairo, a British desert corps slogged through the sand, living exclusively on dehydrated meat and dehydrated vegetables.

The day they reached Cairo, the footsore warriors were detailed to stand guard at the Royal Museum. One private looked
down at the mummy of an ancient Egyptian queen, dead some
three thousand years, and cried out in horror, "They've gone one
step too far. Now they're dehydrating women!"

* * *

One of India's richest maharajas engaged a crack American engineer to construct a dam some miles above his capital. The engineer's job, completed in record time, was obviously perfect, and
the delighted maharaja, besides paying the substantial fee agreed
upon in advance, tried to present the engineer with a basketful
of gleaming rubies as a token of his appreciation. The engineer
would have none of them, however.

"I'm glad you like the job I did," he said simply, "but I can't take
your rubies. We don't do things that way in America. The fee I
set was more than adequate, and I want no more." The maharaja
then offered him a diamond that dwarfed the Hope stone, and
other priceless gifts, but the American kept refusing them. Finally
the potentate said, "You simply must accept some gift from me,
my friend, or it will be my turn to be offended." "Okay," agreed
the engineer, "but let's make it a token gift—something simple.
For instance, golf clubs are rather scarce at home now. Golf is my
favorite recreation. Give me a couple of good golf clubs and we'll
all be happy."

The maharaja agreed to this, and the engineer returned to
America, where he promptly forgot about the entire conversation.
Some three months later, however, he received a cable from his
friend, the maharaja.

"My agents have combed the United States," it read, "and selected three golf clubs, which I have bought for you. I am sorry
to say, however, that only two of them have swimming pools."

* * *

To end this book with a story that may contain a hint for maintaining sanity, and even good humor, in a crisis-weary world, I
whirl you back to New York, where two eminently successful

psychoanalysts occupied offices in the same building. One was forty years old, the other over seventy. They rode down on the elevator together at the end of an unbearably hot, sticky day. The younger man was completely done in, and he noted with some resentment that his senior was fresh as a daisy. "I don't understand," he marveled, "how you can listen to drooling patients from morning till night on a day like this and still look so spry and unbothered when it's over."

The older analyst said simply, *"Who listens?"*